# THE
# GUARDIAN OMNIBUS
## 1821–1971

# THE GUARDIAN OMNIBUS
## 1821·1971

AN ANTHOLOGY OF
150 YEARS OF GUARDIAN WRITING
CHOSEN AND EDITED BY

## David Ayerst

COLLINS
ST JAMES'S PLACE
1973

William Collins Sons & Co Ltd
London · Glasgow · Sydney · Auckland
Toronto · Johannesburg

First published 1973
© 1973 Guardian Newspapers Ltd

ISBN 0 00 211292 2

Set in Monotype Garamond
Made and printed in Great Britain by
William Collins Sons & Co Ltd Glasgow

# Epigraph

\*

## The Paper and its Writers

'I have been asked why I have given myself so whole-heartedly to the service of one particular paper. Nature implanted in me an independent spirit. Like Mr. Gladstone, I regard my mental freedom as my most precious possession; and nowhere, as far as I know, can a contributor find as much scope for his individuality as in the 'Manchester Guardian.' Of course my convictions accord in the main with the great principles on which the paper has been built up. Otherwise so close a relation would have been impossible; but now and then the right of private judgment will assert itself. Perhaps I may have been at one time too little of a Home Ruler; at another, too much of a Disestablisher. Here, the cloven foot of Socialism may peep out from under the decorous garments of official Liberalism; there, my love of the Church to which I belong may obtrude itself unduly on the notice of those who worship at different altars. Yet none of these self-assertions have ever caused estrangement between the rulers of this paper and their unruly scribe. But, putting all personal considerations on one side, I am proud to serve the 'Manchester Guardian,' because I esteem it the most high-minded, and the least self-seeking, of all English newspapers. To be disinterested seems to me the highest virtue of journalism; and the episode of the South African War, even if it stood alone, would show that there is at any rate one paper in the country which, when a moral cause is at stake, dares to jeopardize popularity and profit.'

*G. W. E. Russell* on the twenty-fifth anniversary
of his first contribution, July 6, 1912

# Contents

*

## CONTENTS

*Note: Dates centred in headings are
the dates of publication.*

# Illustrations

\*

# Preface

*

MUCH of the pleasure in producing a book lies in the friendships it brings. No one has been more fortunate than I in this respect. The help which I have received from my colleagues on the *Guardian* staff both in London and Manchester, and from the staff at William Collins, has been immeasurable. It has also been essential. No one, I am confident, who knows anything about the work that has gone into this book will be astonished that I acknowledge a special debt to Ken Murphy and Frank Singleton, the *Guardian* librarians in London and Manchester, and their colleagues; to Tom Kirkham, the head reader in Manchester; to Richard Ollard at Collins; and to my secretary, Mrs. Crang. They are the same team who collaborated with me in *Guardian: Biography of a Newspaper*. We have worked together now for eight years, and, however they may feel about it, I at least have enjoyed every day of this long time – thanks to them.

Since the paper's 150th anniversary its archives have been deposited in the University of Manchester Library. This has enlarged the circle of people for whose ready help I have much reason to be thankful. But indeed the list could be extended almost indefinitely. I am not less grateful to those whom I set off on a wild goose chase in my search for the writers of unsigned articles than to those who ran my quarry successfully to earth.

A whole bookshelf would not contain all the books in which the writers have gratefully acknowledged their thanks to the *Guardian* where their work first appeared. Now the *Guardian* can return the compliment by expressing its thanks to all the writers and artists whose work appears in this book. A list of all those who are known appears in the biographical index of contributors.

*Burford, May 1973*

# A Journey through Time

*

THIS is not another book about the *Guardian*. It is a book by the *Guardian* about its own times. It is not a book of reminiscences, though it will provoke them in readers. It is just what a newspaper is, a record of instantaneous observation, of how things seemed at the moment they were happening. Its comments are not an historian's balanced judgment of the past, but a contemporary's 'off the cuff' opinion. That is their value.

A similar collection from almost any other long-established newspaper would show abrupt political changes, often the result of a change of ownership. The unity would be only that imposed by the paper's title. The unity of this collection from the *Guardian* is organic. For four generations – two of Taylors and two of Scotts – the owners of the paper shared a common outlook. Sons and nephews[1] were not rebellious – partly perhaps because their elders grew strangely younger in outlook as they grew older in years. When the fourth generation decided for safety's sake to put the ownership of the paper in the hands of trustees, the only direction they were given was to see that it was carried on 'in the same spirit as heretofore,' a phrase as vague as the British Constitution, but one which nobody had any difficulty in understanding.

Of course there have been changes. If a present-day leader-writer, for instance, discussing the death penalty, had looked far enough back he would have seen that he was making the paper eat its own words.[2] But the *Guardian* has changed its mind more because times have changed – and sometimes the *Guardian* has helped to change them – than through instability of character. The paper's views have developed in a fairly straight line. Admittedly they have sometimes wobbled, but not often.

Just because the *Guardian* runs true to form this is a one-sided book. It has a built-in bias – the outlook of a succession of intelligent, liberal-minded, middle class Englishmen, to varying degrees Left of Centre in politics. This consistent bias, which must be allowed for, is part of

1. In fact J. E. Taylor was Scott's first cousin but the difference in age was so great that he may rank as an honorary uncle.
2. See p. 81

the value of these extracts. But there are, of course, as the *Guardian* knows only too well from experience, plenty of other Englishmen. What the paper wrote in 1901 or in 1956, for instance, cost it dear at the time.[1]

This is a long book, but it contains fewer words than do two typical issues of the paper. And the *Guardian* of May 5, 1971, the paper's 150th anniversary, was No. 38,811. Clearly no one person has ever read all the words the *Guardian* has printed, and nobody ever will. And yet, the *Guardian* has long been a writer's paper. Its back numbers still have power to make the past present. A journey through time in its company, noting how the landscape changed as generation succeeded generation, promised good exploring. But could it be done in one volume? Seven years' work on the companion book, *Guardian: Biography of a Newspaper*, had given me a reasonable working knowledge of what the paper had done and said. I remembered how a mid-Victorian leader-writer – Acton, perhaps, or Jeremiah Garnett – had written that Thackeray 'does with morals what Cuvier did with physiology, and reconstructs an extinct species from examination of a single bone.'[2] The 'single bone' used in this book has turned out to be nearly 300 extracts. The discarded ones would fill a king's charnel house.

Those who like 'arithmetical calculations of a repulsive aspect', as the *Guardian* once described an important blue book,[3] may care to know that the number of words quoted from the paper's first fifty years averages round about a thousand a year (the *Guardian* only became a daily half way through this period); from the second fifty years, about 2,300; and from the last, about 2,600. Compare this with the *Bedside Guardian*'s 80,000 words a year.[4] The odds against any particular news story or leader being included in this book must be more daunting than the odds against a big win on the pools. A newspaper tries to cover the whole of life, and so this book includes racegoers, musicians, actors and audiences, parsons and fishermen as well as trade unionists, politicians, suffragettes, Nazis and Communists. Nothing, I hope, has been included which is not a characteristic *Guardian* piece, a test as ill-defined yet definite as 'the same spirit as heretofore.' All, I hope, are characteristic also of the time when they were written so that they may serve the purpose of Cuvier's bone.

At first the world portrayed is confined largely to the busy, aggress-

1. e.g. p. 225 or p. 671

2. *Guardian:* October 16, 1852.

3. The Select Committee on Education in Manchester and Salford (*Guardian*: November 13, 1852).

4. Incidentally only two of the pieces in this Omnibus had appeared in a *Bedside Guardian*.

ive, new world of industrial Lancashire which Southerners like
Disraeli visited as if it were a strange and savage country. This is not
because the *Guardian*'s interest was confined to a 50-mile radius, but
because its own direct observation was. What it quoted from other
papers, and later the stories it took from news agencies, are outside the
scope of this book. Some stories which a reader might expect to find
are conspicuous by their absence. There are various reasons. Perhaps
the *Guardian* was not there – there is nothing, alas, about the American
Civil War. And, since no British paper reported as it happened all that
led up to Edward VIII's abdication, the story would be better told in
an American newspaper anthology than here. I have left it out.

Perhaps a story, though part of our folk memory, stands by itself,
something which could have happened anywhere at any time, throwing little light on anything else. There was not room for both Sidney
Street and Tonypandy so Sidney Street had to go.

There are certain kinds of newspaper work which are much under-
represented in terms of their importance to a paper. Thus there is only
one bit of straight economic reporting from a City Editor. There are
fewer hard news stories than might be expected. The fact that a story is
'exclusive' matters greatly at the time both to the paper and its readers,
but it is not a durable quality. Its effect is lost if, reprinted later, it has
to be labelled 'nobody else had this story till next day.' And in fact,
when the final uncovering and disentangling is done, the story is
perhaps best left to be retold with an historian's hindsight – one hopes
with due acknowledgment to the original source.

This journey through time leads from the carefully guarded anonymity of the older journalism to the lavishly personalised papers of the
present day. But the change is more one of presentation than of substance, at least where the *Guardian* is concerned. It has always been a
paper for which men with literary tastes were glad to work because it
would 'print what you wrote' and allow you to write about things as
they happened to strike you. Orator Hunt's visit to Manchester on the
eve of the Great Reform Bill election deserved and got a straight report,
but a reader who turns to page 56 will notice the strong individual
character of the reporter's work. A hundred years later *Guardian* reporters were still nameless men but often identifiable by how they
wrote. There can be no harm now in giving them, when it can be discovered, the recognition that they would have got to-day as a matter
of course. So John Harland in 1831 and Howard Spring in 1925
appear among the contributors.

If the old anonymity had produced a different kind of journalism
there would have been a case for leaving its writers to the obscurity

to which they were inured. But a comparison of the writing in chapter 4, for instance, and in chapter 13 seems to me to show no such distinction. A good deal of work has gone into finding out who wrote what. Often the identification is certain; sometimes no more than probable; occasionally, I fear, it may be wrong. The fact that the search has seemed to me worth while even at its most exasperating moments is perhaps some indication that readers will be glad to find many of these pages from back numbers carrying almost as many 'by-lines' as the *Guardian* on their breakfast table.

Leading articles are perhaps a different matter if only because in England they are still anonymous. In Europe they are not. As long ago as 1893 Zola attacked the English system because it left the reader no more certain that the leader writer believed in his argument than that a barrister necessarily believed in the innocence of his client. The *Guardian* argued the point with him in a leader[1] which was probably by W. T. Arnold. It pointed to the editorial resignations on grounds of principle which twice in recent years had occurred in the *Pall Mall Gazette* after political take-overs and added, 'the extent to which a writer can and does legitimately assert his individuality under the anonymous system is a subtle and curious question of which M. Zola knows nothing.' I have respected the anonymity of *Guardian* leaders as far as the present is concerned, that is to say since Suez. The case for the anonymous leader was, and is, that it alone commits the paper itself to a particular view, that the paper itself is more important than any individual member of its staff, and that an unsigned leading article carries a more responsible judgment to its readers than a signed column would do. A leader writer thinks twice before committing his paper to a view which he might lightly venture in a signed article. That at least is the theory, and it is not far from the practice. Perhaps inconsistently I have named where I can the writers of earlier leaders, but this provides some indication of 'the extent to which a writer can and does legitimately assert his individuality under the anonymous system.' It must be recognised that leaders, unless by the Editor himself, are more subject to editorial revision than any other part of the paper because they carry collective responsibility.

For other reasons as well as for the breach of anonymity C. P. Scott would have been astonished and perhaps perturbed at what has happened to *Guardian* leaders in this book. There are relatively few at anything like full length; often they have been cut to a few lines. But the reason is simple and, I hope, sufficient. Leaders are usually comments on something well known at the time, but unknown or half-forgotten

1. September 23, 1893

now. The context must be provided before the comment can make sense. Often when this has been done, the comment is found to be implicit (or sometimes explicit) in the way the news story was handled. When Scott distinguished the sacredness of fact and the freedom of comment he did not build a Chinese Wall between the news and leader columns.

Roughly, and with many exceptions, I have tried to stick to a rule of 'one of a kind at a particular time.' The *Guardian*'s investigations of working class life a hundred years ago would make a book on its own, but here there is only room for a token. The same is true of its Irish reporting and of its coverage of Germany between the wars, to name only a few examples.

One would like to linger, but this journey through time has to be by forced marches.

The point at which personal recollection gives place either to ignorance or a half-memory of history lessons must vary with age. On the far side of the line, wherever it falls, a reader may well be glad of the help of short, elementary footnotes. Anyone born after 1929, for instance, might well miss part of the point of Leo Amery's furious denunciation of Neville Chamberlain ('In the Name of God, Go') if a footnote on page 551 did not tell him that Amery was a former Conservative Cabinet Minister. The footnotes are there to make this book as self-contained as possible.

Some of the extracts are part of a longer article; others have undergone internal pruning. In order to make easy reading these cuts have not been indicated in the text. There has been no re-writing, nor have words been added except for continuity and within square brackets. What has been removed is either detail which time has made irrelevant or what might be called a sub-plot for which there is no room. Any reader who wishes to go further into a particular incident and consults the files of the paper will find everything that the *Guardian* printed. This, however, as every journalist knows, is not always everything that the writer wrote. For many years the *Guardian* gave no title at all to its leaders, and often little more clue to the contents of a news story – when Orsini tried to kill Napoleon III the story had the truthful but inadequate headline, 'France.' I had to supply titles for these early extracts, and have carried on the practice because what is suitable for newspaper make-up would look out of place in a book. I have introduced paragraphs to relieve the often unbroken columns of the early years, but I have preserved the original punctuation. I have also kept old spellings such as Ashton-Underlyne and 'develope,' and various *Guardian* idiosyncrasies of spelling such as the refusal for many years to allow morale its customary final 'e,' or Shakespeare to have his second 'a.'

Some readers may like to know more about the newspaper and about the writers of many of these passages. A good deal of this information is to be found in *Guardian: Biography of a Newspaper*. The index of contributors show the relation between the two books.

# CHAPTER ONE

# The Last of Old England

*

The *Guardian* was born in 1821 when Old Sarum had two members of Parliament but no inhabitants, while Manchester had over 150,000 inhabitants but no M.P.s. Roman Catholics were voteless. The memory of Peterloo, when a Reform demonstration was broken up by regular troops and yeomanry with heavy casualties, was only two years old. The criminal law was fierce. The processions in Manchester to celebrate George IV's coronation that summer were made up largely of handcraft workers and of Sunday School children who learnt to read and write on Sundays because on weekdays they were at work. Men travelled by stage coach or canal because there were no railways.

But times were changing. A railway was built from Liverpool to Manchester though there was still none in London. Roman Catholics gained equal rights. Fewer crimes carried the death penalty. By the end of 1831 the Reform Bill was about to become law. Manchester would get its M.P.s; Old Sarum would disappear. The middle class would get the vote; the working class would not. The split between moderate and radical reformers was growing wider. The *Guardian* was moderate.

This is the England pictured here by three young men. John Edward Taylor was 29 when he started a weekly newspaper called *The Manchester Guardian*. His assistant, Jeremiah Garnett, was 27. They were joined towards the end of 1830 by 24-year-old John Harland. What the paper thought comes out not only in Taylor's leading articles but in the asides introduced into the news columns by Garnett and Harland.

# George IV is Crowned; Caroline is not

The Prince of Wales had married Princess Caroline in 1795, but deserted her next year. She was as popular with the radicals as George was unpopular. A bill to divorce her had to be abandoned in 1820 for fear of revolution. She was forcibly kept out of the Abbey at the coronation.

## THE CORONATION DAY

### IN MANCHESTER
### July 21, 1821

On Monday the oxen and sheep designed for distribution amongst the populace, having been decorated with ribbons, were paraded through the principal streets of the town. They appeared to be very fine cattle; but this exhibition of them seemed to be regarded with considerable distaste. It was not possible to avoid thinking how soon the poor animals were to be slaughtered; and the seeing of them decorated for death like the victims of old for the altar, presented to many minds the carnivorous propensities of our race, under circumstances of more than ordinary repulsiveness.

### THE SUNDAY SCHOOLS

It was at midnight, for the clock had just struck twelve, when the celebration of the day commenced by the firing of cannon (we believe at the Old Quay); and the cheers of some nocturnal revellers were echoed far amid the silence of the hour. The bells presently struck up a merry peal, and, with the cannon, which were continually discharged, served as larums to rouse our immense population to prepare for the enjoyments of the day. At a very few minutes past six, the children of the different charity schools, attended by their teachers and friends of the Institution, and those of the Established Church by a number of clergy, began to assemble in St. Ann's Square. Precisely at half past seven they set out for Ardwick.

There followed a full descriptive account of the procession, of which the following extracts are typical:

The children of the various Schools belonging to the Established Church (7,430), preceded by a number of friends with flags, one handsomely decorated with the King's Arms. The girls were principally dressed in white, with white caps in lieu of bonnets, many of them wore purple silk sashes, having their medals suspended and their caps ornamented by ribbons of the same colour. The very striking neatness of the dress of these females, and their healthy appearance, was particularly agreeable, and afforded a practical reply to those puling philosophers who so loudly declaim on the degeneracy of a manufacturing population. The children least distinguished by their neatness or their good looks, were those of Blakeley, the only country school which attended in the procession.

The scholars educated in the Catholic Sunday Schools (1,500), preceded by the friends and supporters of the institutions, and displaying a very neat white flag with the Cross (the peculiar ensign of their religion), represented on it in gold. The girls were dressed mostly in white, with a neatness even surpassing that displayed by the scholars of any of the other schools. They wore muslin caps and bows of purple ribbon.

We have seldom witnessed a scene which gave us as much pleasure, as that which we have now been faintly attempting to describe. The immense number of the more humble class of our fellow subjects in this vicinity, who are receiving from the care and charity of their wealthy and benevolent neighbours, a valuable and well-grounded education – the important moral advantages which this education involves – the cleanly appearance of the children who were assembled – the neatness of the dress, both of boys and girls, but particularly of the latter – and their quiet and orderly demeanour – all these together gave birth to a train of reflections, and hopes of a most gratifying and animating character. He, indeed, who could look upon such a scene without emotion, must have been more or less than man.

## THE GRAND PROCESSION

About half-past ten o'clock the gentlemen of Manchester and Salford began to assemble in St. Ann's Square. They went in procession, six abreast, to the Crescent, Salford, where the military and the representatives of the various trades were already assembled. Three guns were fired as a signal exactly at twelve o'clock, and the procession almost immediately began to move in the following order:

the firemen, the troops – the 16th Lancers, the 29th Infantry and the Manchester Yeomanry (of Peterloo fame), – six mail coaches, the sixty watchmen 'with lanterns, sticks and rattles,' and the ringers with handbells. Then came the trades:
300 tailors, 1,400 dyers, besides barbers, saddlers, joiners, wool-combers and many other trades. Near the rear were

MR. ORMROD'S BRASS & IRON FOUNDERS
A man bearing a flag the number of station in the
procession.

A man carrying an elegant brass staff 7 feet long. | A beautiful brass crown carried by a worker in brass | A man carrying an elegant brass staff 7 feet long.

The principal on horseback.
Head engineer and confidential clerk.
Two clerks.
Band of music.

Supported on each side with three men workers in brass with brass swords, the men wearing blue sashes. | Elegant flag | On one side bearing the King's arms, on the reverse side, a steam engine, & hydraulic press, with the motto St. Geo's Foundry, Minshull-street, London-Road.

A Smith bearing an anvil with hammer and tongs.
The smiths three abreast with white leather aprons.
The turners three abreast.
The fitters up three abreast.
The filers three abreast.
A steam engine of one horse power working.
The engineers three abreast.
A millwright carrying a model of a wheel.
The millwrights three abreast.
The pattern makers three abreast.
The moulders three abreast.
A boiler maker carrying a steam boiler.
The boiler makers three abreast, carrying their
rivetting hammers.
The Boroughreeves of Manchester and Salford.

Steward of the Manor | Sir Oswald Mosley, Bart.<br>Lord of the Manor. | Steward of the Manor

The Stewards of the Ball.
The Secretary to the Committee, carrying a red
morocco Port Feuille.
The Committee.
The Surveyors of the Highways.
Gentlemen of the Towns six abreast.
A Rear Guard of Lancers.

The time occupied by the procession in passing Ardwick, we found to be one hour and thirty-six minutes.

Many of the trades, however, walked very open; and a calculation has been furnished to us by a friend, according to which it would appear that the number of persons belonging to the various trades was 7,018, and the total of those in the procession, exclusive of the military, about 10,050 – that there were in it 101 flags and banners, 22 bands of music, 5 men in armour, and 20 carriages of various descriptions.

## THOSE WHO STAYED AWAY

At several places in the line of progress, particularly in Salford, at Bank-top, at the entrance of Ardwick Green, and in Great Ancoats-street, the Manchester yeomanry were very discourteously greeted by the populace. With this exception, the most perfect good humour prevailed. There was, however, no manifestation of popular enthusiasm. The people seemed to enjoy the display they were making – they were satisfied with themselves, and with those around them, but there was no ardent or general cheering, even at those times when such cheering was expected and indeed called for. Much to the credit of the town's officers, and of those by whom the procession and the various devices of the trades were arranged, there was no display whatever of party insignia; – nothing which could give pain to persons of the most opposite political opinions.

It is evident, however, that, amongst many of the most important trades of Manchester, there was a strong disinclination to unite in the observances of the day, from an idea that for them to assist in the celebration of a coronation from which the Queen was excluded, would seem to imply an approbation on their parts of the proceedings against her Majesty. Amongst these trades we may name the general body of the spinners, the weavers, the calico printers, the fustian cutters, &c. Had the coronation of the Queen taken place with that of his Majesty, we conceive that the procession of the trades would have been, beyond comparison, more numerous than, in point of fact, it was, and that there might then have been expected, and would have been displayed, an animating exhibition of general hilarity and joy. As it was, the show was splendidly got up, and the whole went off very well, but as we have already said, we observed no symptoms whatever of enthusiastic feeling. We were pleased beyond our expectation, for we fairly admit that we looked with little interest either to the coronation itself, or to the proceedings here adopted for the celebration of it. We hope, however, that we shall never be so fastidious as to suffer our

personal feeling or opinions to render us insensible to the not ir-
rational enjoyments of others even though they should be such as we
feel no inclination to partake.

### A DISGUSTING EXHIBITION

The only part of the procession which we saw any occasion to
censure was the disgusting exhibition of the tailors, in imitation of
Adam and Eve. Covered from head to foot with tight flesh-coloured
dresses, and wearing aprons of fig leaves, there was something excessively abhorrent to propriety, in allowing the persons representing
these characters (both of whom were men) to form part of a procession
into which, assuredly, nothing should have been admitted that could
give pain to persons of the utmost delicacy and refinement.

Here we should have been glad to close our account of the proceedings of the day, but we have a further duty to discharge, unpleasant,
and perhaps invidious. About five o'clock, commenced the distribution
of Meat and Beer to the populace. Scenes were exhibited which even
the pencil of a Hogarth would fail adequately to portray. At the New
Market, Shudehill, the meat and loaves were thrown out high from the
doors and windows of the warehouse where they had been stored; the
populace scrambling for them as they could. It resembled the throwing
of goods out of the windows of a warehouse on fire rather than anything else that we can compare it to. There was shameful and general
confusion. At an early hour, the stage erected for the applicants to
stand upon gave way, and one person was killed, and several dangerously wounded by the fall. When the liquor was distributing we saw
whole pitchers thrown indiscriminately among the crowd; men holding up their hats to receive drink, – people quarrelling and fighting for
the possession of a jug, – the strong taking liquor from the weak, – boys
and girls, men and women, in a condition of beastly drunkenness,
staggering before the depository of ale, or lying prostrate on the
ground, under every variety of circumstance, and in every degree of
exposure; swearing, groaning, vomiting, but calling for more liquor
when they could not stand, or even sit, to drink it. Every kind of excess,
indeed, which the most fertile imagination can conceive, or the most
graphic pen describe, was there witnessed in numerous and loathsome
extravagance. Never did we see, and we hope to God, never again
shall we see, human nature so degraded.

There are two or three lives lost, and fourteen patients in the Infirmary, several of them dangerously injured, from the events of the
day.

SAMUEL BLACKSHAW, well known in Manchester, as a Spoon Seller, a Deliverer of Bills, &c. taken from the Original in the shop window of the Artists, 261, Deansgate, who *positively must very shortly*

## Crime and Punishment

### A POACHER TRANSPORTED?

August 3, 1822

At the quarter sessions for the county of Stafford, held on the 18th of July, a person named Thomas Lee, a farmer of considerable property, was tried for stealing a casting-net, under the following circumstances: – The servant of a Mr. Jaggard had been using the net, and had left it lying in a field *which did not belong to his master.* On his return some time afterwards, the net was missing, and it was found three months afterwards, in the house of Lee, who, before it was found, denied having it, but afterwards said he had bought it from a man named Jones. Jones was first tried for stealing the net, and Lee was the principal witness against him. Jones made no defence, but the presiding magistrate directed the jury to acquit him, and *desired* the prosecutor to prefer a bill against the witness Lee. The bill was found; and he was tried on the 19th; the only evidence against him being, that the net was found in his possession, and that he had previously denied all knowledge of it. He was convicted, and the chairman sentenced him to *seven years' transportation.* – The severity of the sentence in this case may probably excite a feeling of surprise; but that feeling will be a good deal diminished, on learning that Lee was suspected by the magistrates of *poaching*; and the chairman actually assigned as a reason for so heavy a punishment, 'that the prisoner opened his house as a *rendezvous for poachers.*'

## THREE HANGINGS

### December 1, 1821

Before day-light on Tuesday morning, a considerable concourse of people were assembled to witness the dreadful scene of the execution of three of our fellow creatures, viz.: – Ann Norris, for a robbery in a dwelling-house: Samuel Hayward, for a burglary at Somerstown, and Joseph South, for uttering a forged ten pound note. The Rev. Mr. Cotton was in early attendance to administer all the consolation in his power to them. About half-past seven o'clock the Sheriffs arrived, and shortly after proceeded to the room where the irons of the culprits are usually knocked off. All was silence, when the clanking of the irons announced the approach of Joseph South, a youth apparently about 17. – To describe the scene is impossible; – there appeared in him a perfect resignation to his fate, which will be best appreciated by his own words – 'I am going to die, but I am not sorry for it – I am going out of a troublesome world.' This is all that was said audibly by him. The second prisoner, Samuel Hayward, soon after appeared, a young man in the flower of youth and of prepossessing appearance; he approached with a firmness quite remarkable. He held a conversation with the Sheriffs and with the Rev. Mr. Cotton, but in a tone inaudible to the bystanders – he appeared perfectly resigned to his fate – he once, in a low tone of voice, ejaculated 'O God!'.

The usual preparations being made, precisely at eight o'clock, the bell tolled, and the solemn procession proceeded toward the fatal spot. On their way the female culprit joined them, and the whole moved slowly on to the lobby. The boy first ascended the scaffold, without any apparent change in his resignation; and, during the time, the young man, Hayward, seated himself and appeared perfectly lost to all earthly objects; he was shortly summoned to the fatal tree, and, with a firmness that did not forsake him to the last, approached his fate. The woman was (as usual) last: she seemed deeply affected.

Everything being adjusted, the Rev. Mr. Cotton commenced reading part of the funeral service; and at fourteen minutes past eight the drop fell, and they closed their earthly career. When will some mode of punishment be found to save these sacrifices of life?

## A SOLDIER FLOGGED TO DEATH

### August 3, 1822

John Furnel was tried by a court-martial, for having in his possession a silver spoon, which had been stolen from the mess. He was sentenced to receive 300 lashes, which punishment was inflicted. After lingering in great torture until Friday the 19th July he expired.

The first witness examined at the inquest was the adjutant of the regiment, who stated that the man was tried by a court-martial for the offence we have mentioned, and was sentenced to receive *three hundred lashes*, which were inflicted upon him on the 23rd of June; that no more lashes were given than the number ordered by the court (quite enough, we should think). The next witness was the surgeon, who stated, that, after the flogging the man was sent to the hospital at Hull, where he remained until the regiment marched for York, when he was put upon one of the baggage carts. Witness examined his back at the conclusion of the first day's march, and found it going on well; but during the second day the man complained very much, and witness examined him on the arrival of the baggage at Market Weighton, when he found that a mortification had commenced, and that the man was in a high fever. He examined him again on the third night, when he found that the fever had subsided, but the mortification had increased. As witness did not know of *any proper medical man* under whose care he could leave him, he was taken on to York (another day's march!) where he was sent to the hospital, where witness left him, and where he died. The weather was excessively hot during the march. This terminated the evidence; and the jury, after due deliberation, brought in a verdict

'That the deceased received 300 lashes, and that he died of the same, and of the fever, mortification, and debility arising therefrom.'

One of the jury who went to view the body, said that *the bones of the back were as bare of flesh as if they had been scraped with a knife.* – Whether any or what steps will be taken to investigate this shocking business we know not; but the public will agree with us that some inquiry is imperiously demanded. Here is a man tried for being privy to the stealing of a silver spoon belonging to the mess; and tried by whom? By *the mess*, by the officers, by the *prosecutors in the case*! One would think, *a priori*, that a jury of prosecutors was not the most likely to temper justice with mercy, and the 'mess' certainly do not appear to have erred, in this instance, on the side of lenity. Then to think of carrying a man, jolting on a baggage cart, under a burning sun, for *two days* at least *after mortification had taken place in his back*, because, forsooth, the surgeon did not know of any *'proper medical man'* with whom to leave him! Why he had better have left him with any old woman in any village through which he passed. But Market Weighton, where he first discovered that mortification had taken place, is (as the name imports) a *market town*, and there surely he might have discovered some *'proper medical man,'* under whose care the poor fellow could have had a better chance for recovery, than a two days' march to York was likely to give him.

# PIRACY

A pirate schooner in the Gulf of Florida captured the *Industry* (Capt. Cook) and the *Vittoria* (Capt. Hearn). Their crews were taken on board the pirate. When Capt. Hearn reached Liverpool he wrote:

## October 12, 1822

A boat-load of the most desperate robbers human nature can furnish, headed by an Englishman, who, it appears, had formerly been mate of a West Indiaman, came on board armed with muskets, pistols, and cutlasses. He ordered me, together with my chief-mate, second, and three of the crew, to go into the boat. I did so, and was taken on board the schooner, which had still American colours flying. We were then strictly searched, and every thing taken from us.

The chief of the robbers then came to me, and told me he knew I had money stowed away. I made answer I had not – what I had he had already taken away; he then said he would more than probably find it out, for he would do to me what he had done to a master of some vessel he had previously taken, which was, that he had put him into a large fire on shore, and then he confessed where he had stowed the money; for which, however, he still burnt him alive.

About five p.m. the chief robber took Captain Cook, together with his crew, on board the *Industry*, put them all below, excepting Captain Cook, whom he tied to the windlass, and made four of his men fresh load their guns and fire at him; but they, having a little more of the human being left than their master, fired at random, which was the preservation of Captain Cook's life. The chief robber again came to me with his knife in one hand and a cutlass in the other, and declared he would cut my throat. I asked him what would that profit him, since he had taken my ship and my all from me? His reply to me was, that if any English ship of war got hold of him, he would be hung. I answered, more than probable. Night coming on, and the vessels still running down the land, we were put below, and two sentinels placed over us, and at ten at night they came to anchor in four fathoms. The head robber then went on board the *Vittoria* in his boat; and, according to the statement of my carpenter, G. Lewis, who had never been taken out of the *Vittoria*, made him take down all the lining of the cabin and break open my trunks, &c.; he there found a few dollars, and after drinking some time, he left the *Vittoria* and came on board his own schooner. About midnight he called for one of the prisoners; my second mate was going on deck, when he was stopped by the sentinel, and ordered to keep below. At this time we heard a great noise upon deck for a few moments, but in a short time all was again silent.

When the morning came they agreed to give us the *Industry*, but not a single thing, only as we stood; so you may suppose in what a deplorable state I am at present. I can only add by thanking the Almighty that I am spared with my life; for if the chief robber had not been killed (which was the noise I have already alluded to) that night, which we did not know of until we were all on board the *Industry*, he had made a vow when he left the *Vittoria* that the moment he got on board the schooner he would have my life, and was only stopped by one of his own people murdering him; and he was thrown overboard very quietly for fear we should know of it.

## CAMP FOLLOWERS

### August 10, 1822

Forty-five of the miserable women who infest the streets, and who had all been taken into custody on the preceding night, were brought up and charged under the new vagrant-act with being idle and disorderly persons. Mr. Lavender stated that these women had lately become a great nuisance and were so repeatedly complained of, that he was under the necessity of taking a number of them into custody. The prisoners had all been apprehended after half-past twelve o'clock, and none were taken but such as were in the habit of frequenting the streets. It did not appear that any of them were riotous or disorderly.

Mr. Norris explained to the prisoners the provisions of the vagrant-act by which he was empowered to commit to prison for a month all persons in their situation. He could inform them that there was already a treadmill[1] in that gaol, and another would shortly be erected; and he would assure them that if they were brought before him for being disorderly, he would certainly commit them. In that case they would be set to work at that mill an employment which they would find exceedingly irksome and laborious. As they were probably ignorant of the act he would discharge them all for this time; but he advised them to take care that they were not brought before him again. They were then all discharged.

This lenity is all very well in the first instance; but it is highly necessary for the future that the law shall be strictly administered; for the number of abandoned women, of the lowest class, has been so great ever since we had such a quantity of soldiers in town, and their manners are so audacious, as to constitute them a very notorious evil.

## Arts

## THEATRE ROYAL: A POLITICAL PERFORMANCE

### October 26, 1822

On Saturday evening last, Mr. Braham and Mrs. Bunn appeared here in the musical play of *Guy Mannering*, which attracted the most numerous and respectable audience we have seen here for some years. The house was absolutely crammed in every part where a peep of the stage could be obtained. Even the doors of the boxes were blocked up by

1. The treadmill had been invented by Sir William Cubitt in 1818.

spectators, and benches were placed in the lobbies to enable those behind to see over the heads of those in front. All this, no doubt, was very flattering to Mr. Braham and very profitable to the managers; but, unfortunately, it has incapacitated us from giving any thing like a *critique* on the performance. It was our fate to be in the rear, and therefore almost unable to obtain even a sight of the *dramatis personae*. Of Mrs. Bunn we heard almost as little as we saw. It was only occasionally that we could hear even Mr. Braham's songs; but when they were audible, we observed the same beauties and the same faults by which his singing has always been marked; the same power and compass, the same sweetness and flexibility of voice and the same profusion of unnecessary and injurious ornament.[1]

One of his songs was *Scots wha hae wi' Wallace bled*; which he judiciously gave in a more chaste and simple style, and the superiority of this over the others was very striking. His clear and fine volume of voice gave full effect to every word, and the indignant tone with which he demanded 'wha sae base as be a slave?' with the descending in semitones to the contemptuous 'let him turn an' flee,' was the finest thing we ever heard. The song was rapturously encored, and given a second time with increased feeling, spirit, and effect. The last line was not finished when loud and general encores rung through the house; and Braham at once complied with what seemed the unanimous wish.

At the moment he commenced the song for the third time, an individual who sat at the back part of one of the centre boxes in the lower tier, and whose name we understand is Landor, immediately commenced vociferating 'off, off,' and 'God save the King,' in the most vehement manner. In his attempt to annoy the audience, and create a tumult in the house, which we suppose he regards as an exploit not unbecoming a person having the *appearance* of a gentleman, he was but too successful. Loud shouts of 'turn him out' were mingled with cries of 'go on – go on,' which, together with the continued noise of the original disturber, rendered it impossible to hear a single word of the song. The uproar continuing, the performers came forward and sang 'God save the King'; at least we *guessed* they did so, for the words were wholly inaudible from the whistling, groaning and hissing that prevailed. We observed a number of respectable individuals in the pit who joined in opposition to the song, vexed no doubt at the interruption occasioned by the ultra-loyalist, who had been shocked at the very

1. John Braham (*c*.1774–1856), a short, stout tenor whose voice had a compass of nineteen notes. 'The volume of sound he could produce was prodigious,' according to the *Dictionary of National Biography*, 'and his declamation was magnificent. His great fault seems to have been that though he could sing with the utmost perfection he generally preferred to astonish the groundlings by vulgar and tricky displays.'

name of liberty, and appeared to have paid his party the bad compliment of supposing that the epithets of tyrants and slaves were meant to apply to them.

We have no hesitation in saying, that much as we admire both the words and music of *Scots wha hae wi' Wallace bled*, we could not but consider it being called a third time as, at least, supererogatory. If, however, Mr. Braham's encores were to blame, what are we to think of a person who could conduct himself as did the individual we have had occasion to mention? We have no objection to *God save the King*. But when it is called for, as in this instance, evidently with a view to incite tumult, we think neither managers nor performers should suffer the disturbers of the audience to derive from success an encouragement to future efforts. Any person who, under whatever pretext, becomes turbulent and noisy in the theatre, is unfit for decent society, and ought promptly to be turned into the street.

## THE FIRST MANCHESTER MUSIC FESTIVAL

### October 4, 1828

When we consider the great wealth and the immense population of Manchester and the surrounding district, it certainly does appear a little extraordinary that this should be one of the last places in which an attempt has been made to establish those periodical meetings, which, under the name of musical festivals, have afforded so much pleasure and satisfaction to the inhabitants of Birmingham, York, Derby, Chester, Liverpool, and, indeed, almost every town of importance in the kingdom; and which, in addition to the refined and intellectual pleasure they have afforded, have generally left a considerable surplus towards the support of the public charities of the towns or the counties in which they have been held. The surprise in this is a good deal increased by the reflexion that in no town in England, except the metropolis, is music so enthusiastically admired, or so liberally patronised, as in Manchester; and in no district in England is there so great a number of excellent vocal and instrumental performers, as in the country in the immediate neighbourhood of Manchester.

The avidity with which [tickets] were purchased was an excellent omen for the success of the festival. On Monday the choice of seats in the patrons' gallery and body of the church, and in the pit and boxes of the theatre, took place in the public room of the Town-hall. The gentlemen who had purchased tickets attended in the order of the numbers which they had drawn; and chose their seats from an inspection of plans which were laid before them. The process was rather tedious, and occupied nearly the whole day; but it was conducted throughout with the greatest regularity and precision.

After a very wet and tempestuous night, the sun broke out on Tuesday morning with great brilliancy, and smiled upon the commencement of the festival. From a comparatively early hour the streets in the neighbourhood of the Collegiate Church[1] were crowded with persons, who were anxious to obtain a sight of the company proceeding to attend the cathedral service, with which the festival was opened. At half-past nine o'clock the doors of the church were opened; and great numbers, both in carriages and on foot, hastened thither to secure the most favourable seats. Before the commencement of the service, at eleven o'clock, every seat in the church was occupied, and considerable numbers of persons were standing in the aisles.

Purcell's 'Te deum' followed; the opening chorus of which was admirably sung by the full orchestra. The succeeding quartet was, on this occasion, sung as a trio. We thought at first that Mr. Knyvett, in undertaking the alto part, had ventured beyond the compass of his voice, but he got very cleverly through; and his peculiar and remarkable tone, though not always perfectly agreeable to the ear by itself, sounded admirably in conjunction with the fine tenor of Vaughan, and the rich, deep, soft bass of Phillips. The succeeding chorus, 'The holy church,' though well sung, presented nothing deserving of particular notice. It was in the chorus, 'Day by Day we magnify thee,' that the full power of the numerous and excellent bass and tenor voices in the orchestra was first called into action; and we never heard any chorus more correctly sung. It was a complete *chef d'œuvre*. The air, 'Vouchsafe, O Lord,' was most admirably sung, and gave very evident satisfaction to the audience. The chorus, 'O Lord in thee have I trusted,' was very good; but the 'Amen' chorus, at the end of Dr. Croft's 'Jubilate,' was, perhaps, the best of the whole performance.

In addition to the admirable singing of the vocal performers, Mr. Greatorex produced an effect with the organ which was truly extraordinary. The whole instrument appeared to be sounding at once, and harmonised delightfully with the various parts of the vocal music. With regard to the instrument itself, we may take this opportunity of remarking, that it appears to have been prodigiously improved by the alterations which have been made for the festival. That it was previously good, we were well aware; but we were not prepared for the mellow and powerful tones which, under the hands of the distinguished musician who presided, it emitted on this occasion. There are not, at

1. Now Manchester Cathedral

this moment, many better instruments of the kind in this country.

Before the sermon '*Martin Luther's Hymn*' was sung by Madame Catalani.[1] There has been of late so much difference of opinion relative to the present state of this lady's voice, and we have heard so many conflicting statements as to her performance of this particular hymn, that we feel great diffidence in offering any observations upon it. In the first place, however, we may safely remark, that we have certainly heard her sing it better but, after making all possible deductions, the performance was still an extraordinary one. The sublime simplicity of the air (which strikes us as being almost the perfection of devotional music) was admirably preserved in the execution; and the whole produced an effect which no other performer could have equalled. The trumpet accompaniment by Harper was exceedingly fine, and has been greatly and generally admired. Indeed we never, on any occasion, heard tones of such exquisite softness produced from that instrument. But we have some doubt whether it was such an accompaniment as the composer intended; or such as best accords with the character of the words and the music of the hymn. It struck us that Mr. Harper would have displayed more taste if he had employed less skill. Instead of the thrilling and piercing tones of the dread trumpet announcing the dissolution of the universe, he gave us sounds which imitated rather the breathings of the flute, and died away in the most exquisite and melodious sweetness. To our humble thinking we have heard a more effective, and striking, and *appropriate* accompaniment in a country church from a performer who could hardly sound three notes upon the instrument. We are aware that this opinion will be accounted somewhat heretical by musicians, but we cannot help avowing it.

The sermon, which of course inculcated the duty of charity, was extremely liberal and unobjectionable, but did not present much novelty of thought or expression. It lasted 47 minutes.

## TUESDAY'S CONCERT

The band, which was composed chiefly of picked performers from the Philharmonic Concerts and the King's Theatre, with the addition of a number of the most eminent of the professors resident amongst ourselves, may be almost said to have been perfect; we believe, at least there can be no exaggeration in affirming, that it was superior to any band that is to be found at any single institution, even in London, and perhaps, at no festival even, has the selection of the most eminent

1. Italian operatic soprano 1780–1849; the organist, the trumpet player and the three men soloists mentioned are all included in the *Dictionary of National Biography*.

artists on the various instruments, been conducted with more judgment, discrimination and taste.

The beautiful symphony of Beethoven, with which the performances began, was well calculated to display the power of the band, and the superior abilities of the gentlemen who composed it. Yet in the first chords there was a little wavering, a circumstance not to be wondered at, when it is considered that the symphony had never been rehearsed, and that some of the performers, placed at a great distance from their leader, required a little time to get acquainted with the effect of the respective situations. In a moment, however, every thing was right, and the remainder of the piece was played with almost unequalled beauty and precision.

## PAGANINI

In 1832 Nicolo Paganini (1782–1840) appeared in Manchester. The orchestra comprised 10 violins, 2 flutes, 2 oboes, 2 clarinets, 2 horns, 1 trumpet, 2 bassoons, 2 tenors (violas), 2 'cellos, 2 double bass, 1 trombone, 1 drums.

### January 14, 1832

We have heard him; we have listened to him; but we feel so incompetent to convey to our readers any adequate idea of him, that we are tempted to abandon the task altogether. Something, however, will be expected from us; something, therefore, we must say; and we will begin with his first appearance on the stage, which is not the least extraordinary of the wonderful points about him. Reader, you have seen some of the portraits of Paganini; some, probably, which were avowedly meant for caricatures of his person and his countenance: you have probably thought that, even for caricatures, his peculiarities were grossly exaggerated. Reader, you were under a mistake. So far are they from being exaggerated caricatures, that what appears to be the most extravagant of them, fails by falling short of the extent of those peculiarities. It rather seems as though Paganini has been made for a caricature of the portraits, than the portraits drawn as caricatures of Paganini. His smile on receiving the applause of the audience is the most extraordinary, the most unearthly expression that ever marked the countenance of a human being; but to form the most remote conception of it, he must be seen. We shall certainly not attempt to describe it.

Then his performance! It is almost as little amenable to the powers of description as his countenance. At all events we feel quite incapable of giving an adequate account of it. Those of our readers who feel an interest in these matters, will, no doubt, have read in the musical publications of the day, a very full description of his extraordinary powers; his amazing power and compass on the instrument; his *pizzicato* accompaniments; his playing two parts at the same time; his sonatas on one string; and a great variety of other musical miracles which he works.

But these, astonishing as they undoubtedly are, must not be compared with his genuine performances on the instrument, unaided by trick of any description. Of this kind of music he unfortunately gives far too little; there was little or none in the first evening's performance; but last night he gave a piece entitled, if we recollect aright, for we have not the bill before us, '*Théma sulla preghiera di Pietro l'Eremita*,' which, in our humble judgment, was worth all the rest of his evening's performance. It is an adagio, full of soul and expression; and gave full scope to his powers. In playing this piece his tones were the most extraordinary, that we ever heard from any musical instrument. They seemed to be susceptible of all the varied intonation of the human voice; to be capable of expressing all the varieties of human passions; in short, they wanted nothing but articulation to form a complete language.

Eight years later Harland[1] published in the *Guardian* a number of ballads, some of them topical, sung in the pubs of Manchester. One of these, by Alexander Wilson, referred to this visit.

### January 21, 1840

PAGANINI, OR MANCHESTER FIDDLING MAD

*Tune: 'King of the Cannibal Islands.'*

There's none more fond of music's cheer
Than I myself, as you may hear;
Ten shillings an *ingo*'s[2] rather queer,
I'm not inclined to pay so dear.
With fiddle and bow in hand he came,
Newspaper puff and *foreign* fame,
High-sounding and *jaw-breaking* name,
Then gulls us prettily to our shame,
Italian, Pagan, Jew, or Turk,
From Charley Wetherell down to Burke,
I wish every man to be *paid* for his work
But not like Paganini.

1. John Harland
2. 'Ingo' is a term known amongst sporting men, chiefly in reference to the cock-pit grand-stand, &c; and it is here used, as there, for the admission or going in; 10/– being, the price charged at some of Paganini's concerts. (*Harland's note.*)

(Chorus)
With leeddle tweeddle deeddle dee,
Poor John Bull, how he wheedles thee;
Too old to learn and too blind to see,
Thou'rt gammon'd by Paganini.

Then native genius patronise,
And don't be gulled by *sound* and lies,
By fiddles and brooms, and mice and noise,
And squalling, grinding, trulls and boys.
If genuine talent you'd maintain,
Be pleased to send to Ancoats Lane,
Blind Tom[1] shall eclipse the Farm Yard strain,
And fiddle a week for a guinea.
A manly grace poor Tom can boast,
His form well fed on English roast,
A different thing to the fiddling ghost,
Who gammons and puffs the ninny.
(Chorus)

## Reporting a Prize Fight

Tom Oliver, 'the Chelsea gardener,' was near the end of his career; 'Gas' Hickman, so-called from his work, was much younger. Garnett, a keen sportsman, pretty certainly wrote the introductory sentence to this report from a Warwickshire paper:

July 23, 1821

(The following detailed account of the business is so spirited, and withal such an admirable specimen of that dialect of the English language which is usually termed 'flash,' that we cannot resist the temptation of laying it before our readers.)

Everything being in readiness, the appetites of the spectators being sharp set for the 'turn to', the heroes of the day made their appearance. At one o'clock they 'shewed' at opposite sides of the ring, and tossing

---

1. A young man, born blind, a native of Manchester, of great natural genius and skill as a musician; and it is said that, after hearing Paganini produce on his instrument the various discordant sounds of a farm yard, he immediately afterwards produced on his own violin a very striking imitation of the freak of Paganini. 'Tom' is now and has been for some years the landlord of a public-house in Great Ancoats-street, at which he has appropriately enough hoisted the sign of 'The Paganini'; and there he is said to delight his guests by the skill with which he still handles the fiddle. (*Harland's note.*)

up their *casters*, entered the ropes. They greeted each other in a friendly manner, and passed the usual compliments, to shew that they were 'only in fun.' Having 'doffed their toggery,' or, in the vulgar tongue, having stripped for action, they proceeded to the 'scratch.' The men were both in excellent condition, and Oliver had the advantage in size. Gas however exhibited not alone a Herculaean frame, but a decided character of activity: he was all well braced and elastic muscle. Every eye was intensely directed to catch the first onset; and even the *prigs*, so eager were they in sport, forgot, for a while, to dip their hands into their neighbour's pockets.

### THE FIGHT

Round 1. Both men approached with caution, and eyed each other with mutual confidence in their own superiority. Gas made a little play, but Oliver drew off, as if he were not inclined, by too much eagerness, to place the issue in doubt. Gas seemed anxious to begin, and hit short on Oliver's arm. Oliver smiled in defiance. Oliver had now re-treated to the corner of the ropes, where some trifling civilities were exchanged. Gas closed on his man, but Oliver broke away. They again faced each other, when Gas suddenly opened his *retort*, and let fly right and left on Oliver's *mug*, and then closed. Gas now continued to *pepper* his man in the most terrific manner; and after *waltzing* like two enraged bears for a few seconds round the ring, they both went down. Oliver was immediately handed, with great politeness, to his second's knee; but he seemed deaf to his civilities, and looked round with all the simplicity of a man who did not exactly know where he was. To speak classically, he was in a condition of 'doldrum.' (The cry among the Fancy was, 'It's all up with him.' 'Gas has blown up his pipes,' and some thought he could not come again.)

4. Gas attempted to deliver another of his terrific right-handed 'toddlers' on Oliver's face, but Tom had the good fortune to give him the 'go-bye,' and Gas went down with the force of his own exertion. Oliver, in essaying to make a return, fell over his antagonist.

5. Gas now showed some marks of violence on his left eye, which began to puff; but he came to the scratch like a man who knew that his task was easy, and that it would soon be done. Oliver put in several hits, but they were mere pattings with a pillow, when compared with the 'scrunching' deliveries of Gas, who went in upon him and battered his carcase like a kettledrum. It was in fact like the bonassus[1] to an ear-wig. Oliver at length went down quite exhausted. Compassion for

1. Bison

Oliver, who still shewed true game, now begot him some cheers; but the performance had evidently arrived at the last act, and very nearly at the last scene.

Oliver was knocked out in the 9th round.

## The Railway Age: A Tragic Beginning

The *Guardian* took part of its report of the opening of the Liverpool and Manchester Railway from *Gore's Liverpool Advertiser* which was greatly impressed by 'the gorgeous car' prepared for the Duke of Wellington. 'This carriage was truly magnificent, the sides being beautifully ornamented; superb Grecian scrolls and balustrades, richly gilt, supporting a massy handrail all round the carriage, along the whole centre of which was an ottomon seat for the company. A grand canopy, 24 feet long, was placed aloft upon gilded pillars, so contrived as to be lowered when passing through the tunnel. The drapery was of rich crimson cloth, and the whole surmounted by the ducal coronet.' The Duke's carriage, pulled by the *Northumbrian*, ran on the southern track; on the northern there was a procession of six trains. Garnett was in the third, pulled by the *Rocket*. He takes up the story:

September 18, 1830

### THE FATAL ACCIDENT TO MR. HUSKISSON[1]

We shall now endeavour to supply some further particulars of the dreadful accident to Mr. Huskisson, and of its lamented and fatal termination. Having been, to a certain extent, eye-witnesses of it, we have no doubt that our account will be found more accurate and more circumstantial than any which has hitherto been published.

The carriages conveying the Duke of Wellington and other distinguished visitors had stopped at the watering-station at Parkfield, for the purpose of taking in water, and, at the same time, allowing the various carriages forming the procession, on the northern line of road to pass by, in order that all might have a view of the duke and his distinguished associates. It happened that the place where the grand carriages were thus kept standing, was most unfortunately chosen,

1. William Huskisson (1770–1830), President of the Board of Trade 1823–1827, removed many protective duties, favoured Catholic Emancipation and parliamentary representation for Manchester.

for on each side of the rail-road was a deep pool of water, approaching within about three feet of the rails; so that any person who descended from the carriages was compelled to descend *between the two lines*. The directors had, indeed, in their placards, particularly requested that no person would descend from the carriages when they stopped for the purpose of taking water, but this caution was very generally disregarded. After the two leading engines in the procession, the *Phoenix* and the *North Star*, had passed the grand carriage, an interval of several minutes took place before the arrival of the *Rocket*, which was the next in order; and a number of gentlemen descended from the carriage, and walked to and fro upon the road. Amongst them was Mr. Huskisson; but he, we believe, had a cogent reason for alighting, arising out of the peculiar state of his health.

He was standing near the grand carriage along with several other gentlemen, and was, we believe, engaged in conversation with a lady in the carriage; when some alarm was created by the rather rapid approach of the *Rocket* engine with its train of carriages. If all the gentlemen had stood still in the middle of the space between the two lines (which are four feet eight inches asunder) *no harm could possibly have happened to them*; but, probably not being aware of that fact, all the gentlemen endeavoured to get out of the way with great precipitation. Not being able to retreat to the north side of the railroad, on account of the pool of water, they all endeavoured to return to the carriage from which they had descended, and Mr. Huskisson who was last, had his hand upon the door, waiting until the person who preceded him had gone up the steps. The door was so large as to extend, when standing open, across the whole of the space between the lines, and Mr. Huskisson, having his hand upon it of course stood very near the line on which the *Rocket* was approaching.

At this moment the engineer of the *Rocket* called to him to get out of the way, and a similar call was made to him from some person in the grand carriage. These calls, and the near approach of the engine, appear to have bewildered him, and prevented him from adopting the only course by which he could escape, namely, that of standing close to the carriage into which he had been endeavouring to enter. This, however, he did not do, but remained standing at the extremity of the open door, against which some part of the approaching engine struck, and forced it back with some violence against the side of the carriage, and Mr. Huskisson, at the same moment, fell upon the ground between the two lines of rails. Whether he was struck by the door, or caught by the wheel or some part of the *Rocket*, or whether (as stated by one person, who saw him) he threw himself upon the ground, from an idea of avoiding the danger in that manner, are points which, perhaps will never be determined. It has, indeed, been stated in more than one newspaper, that Mr. Huskisson fell across the line on which the *Rocket* was travelling, and that his head and body lay beneath the carriage by which the injury was inflicted. That, however, was certainly not the fact; for, being in one of those carriages, we had a distinct view of his head and body at the time of passing him, which, of course, would not have been the case if he had lain beneath them. Indeed, from the position in which he lay, we, and we believe every person who saw him from those carriages, believed that he was out of the way of the wheels, and that he would sustain no serious injury. There is some reason to think that, in the first instance, no part of his person lay upon the rails, and that the engine and perhaps the first carriage passed him without inflicting injury upon him; but in struggling to get out, or to escape the danger, his left knee was thrown across the rail in a bent position, so as to bring both the thigh and the leg beneath the wheels of the succeeding carriages which passed over them in a slanting direction.

Though we distinctly heard Mr. Huskisson shriek as the carriage passed, we had no idea that any serious mischief had happened, and that was the general impression of all who were near us. The dreadful truth, however, soon became known, and a scene of distress and consternation ensued, which it would be impossible adequately to describe. Several of the directors and of the distinguished visitors from the Duke of Wellington's carriage immediately crowded around to offer their services; and Lord Wilton, with great presence of mind, immediately put a handkerchief round the mangled limb, and twisted it with a stick, to form a *tourniquet* for the purpose of stopping the effusion of blood, which, however, was not very extensive. Whilst this operation was performing, Mr. Huskisson said, 'Where is Mrs. Huskisson? I have met my death. God forgive me.' Shortly afterwards he again inquired for Mrs. Huskisson, and she came, or rather was brought to him, when a scene ensued which may be conceived, but which we shall not attempt to describe.

The *Northumbrian* engine, and the carriage which had contained the band, were detached from the state carriage; and Mr. Huskisson having been carefully placed upon a board, was carried upon men's shoulders, and deposited in the carriage of the band, and Mr. Stephenson taking charge of the engine, set out towards Manchester at a most terrific rate, travelling from the place where the accident happened to Eccles Bridge at the rate of 34 miles an hour.

On the arrival at Eccles of the carriage in which Mr. Huskisson had been placed, the unfortunate gentleman was removed as soon as possible into the vicarage; whilst the Earl of Wilton, with Mr. Stephenson, the engine having been detached from the car, proceeded rapidly to the station in Manchester, to procure surgical assistance.

Mr. Ransome immediately proceeded in a carriage to his house, to fetch the instruments necessary for an amputation, and on his return, he with Mr. Whatton, Mr. Garside and Mr. White also surgeons of Manchester, took their stations on the *Northumbrian*, and dashed off with almost frightful rapidity to Eccles. When they arrived at the Vicarage they found him in a state of great weakness and exhaustion; the pulse was imperceptible at the wrist, and only a faint sort of flickering could be distinguished higher up in the arm. The surgeons were convinced that if amputation was resorted to, the patient would expire under the knife, and therefore it was not attempted. Large quantities of laudanum, we believe, in the course of the afternoon, not less than 240 drops, were administered as a sedative; but it was evident, by the convulsive twitchings of the lacerated muscles, that Mr. Huskisson still suffered the most acute and agonizing pain.

About four o'clock Mr. Whatton happened to be left for a short time with Mr. Huskisson, who took his hand and said, 'I wish you to tell me candidly what you think of my case.' Mr. Whatton replied, 'It is a very bad one, and I fear, sir, you cannot survive.' Mr. Huskisson rejoined, 'No, that I have fully made up my mind to, from the first; but how long do you think I have to live?' The answer was, 'It is impossible to say exactly; but probably not more than four, five, or at most six hours.' 'Thank you,' said Mr. Huskisson, and terminated the conversation. In the course of the afternoon Lord Wilton suggested the propriety, if he had any worldly affairs to arrange, of his doing so without delay; and a sort of republication of a previous will, with some additions, was drawn up by Mr. Wainwright, his secretary. It is an extraordinary fact, and evinces the uncommon firmness and self-possession of the right hon. gentleman under such awful circumstances, that after he had signed the paper he turned back, as it were, to place a dot over the i, and another between the W. and the H.

In the course of the afternoon, a wish was expressed that he should take the sacrament, but his breathing having become considerably affected, the surgeons asked him whether he would be able to swallow the elements. He said he thought he should, and expressed a wish, at any rate, to try. Accordingly the solemn rite was performed by the Rev. Thomas Blackburne, the vicar of Eccles, who first took the sacrament himself and afterwards administered it to Mr. and Mrs. Huskisson. Shortly after this Mr. Huskisson observed to Mr. Ransome 'I hope I have lived the life of a Christian.' His breathing then became sensibly more difficult; he, however, warmly thanked Mr. Ransome and Mr. Whatton for their attentions to him, took an affectionate leave of the sorrowing friends who surrounded his bedside, and a most tender 'farewell' of his devoted wife, and precisely at nine o'clock, expired.

## COMMENT

Never have we witnessed an instance in which the decease of any individual whatever, has excited so deep and general a sensation of regret, as has been created by that of Mr. Huskisson. Such is the value which every body considered his life to be to his country, that it seemed from their looks and expressions, as though each felt that he had lost some private relative or benefactor.

Few men have been more the subjects of calumny than Mr. Huskisson. Few public measures have been so virulently and so unjustly attacked as those relaxations of our commercial code, with which his name is associated. But the time was just at hand when he might fearlessly have appealed to 'experience and the evidence of facts' – to the increasingly prosperous state of every interest which it has been alleged that he had ruined – to testify the soundness of his views, and to confute the prognostications of his enemies.

## Peel Loses the Home of Lost Causes

In 1827 Sir Robert Peel had resigned from the government because he opposed giving Roman Catholics the vote. He was now back in office and had changed his mind. In February the King's Speech announced that a bill to remove Roman Catholic disabilities would be introduced. Peel resigned his seat for Oxford University to give his constituents the opportunity to vote on his new policy. The *Guardian*, which strongly supported emancipation, sent Garnett to cover the by-election. Peel lost to Sir Robert Inglis, but remained in Parliament as the member for Westbury. Peel did not succeed to the baronetcy until 1830.

### March 7, 1829

The excitement produced by this contest was quite unexampled in the annals of the University. Electors were summoned by the friends of the parties from the most distant parts of the kingdom. Every horse and post-chaise that could be procured on the roads to Oxford was put in requisition by one or other of the parties, and at the inns it was with difficulty any but a person in the interest of one or other of the candidates could procure a bed. At an early hour on Thursday morning numerous stage-coaches, post-chaises and private carriages filled with voters, were seen crowding into Oxford in all directions; and notwithstanding the very unfavourable state of the weather, the square in front of the Hall of Convocation was crowded with electors and friends of the parties, who, for the sake of securing early access to the hall, on the opening of the door, bore the pelting of the rain for a long time with exemplary patience and equanimity. – As the hour fixed for the election (namely, 12 o'clock) drew near, however, the assembly began to exhibit signs of impatience, and at length became as turbulent as the free and independent burgesses of any potwalloping borough in the united kingdom. They battered at the door with their hands, feet and umbrellas; and, in order to induce the opening of the door, they had recourse to a ruse by calling out 'Doctors, doctors,' as if some person of that venerable order had been waiting for admittance. In this, however, they were disappointed; for the door-keepers, knowing full well that the 'doctors' were all admitted by another door, refused to open until the appointed time. At length, a few minutes after twelve, the door was opened; and a most terrific rush was made into the hall of convocation, which, being of very moderate dimensions already occupied by those who enjoyed the privilege of a separate entrance, it was filled in a trice; and a great number of persons were wholly unable to make their way into it.

After some degree of order was obtained, the vice-chancellor declared the object of the meeting in a few Latin sentences in the usual manner. He also read the writ, commanding the election of a representative, in the room of the right hon. Robert Peel, and announced that the convocation was ready to receive the nomination of candidates and votes in their support. Dr. Marsham, Master of Merton College, proposed Mr. Peel as a fit and proper person to represent the University in parliament. For himself, he (Dr. Marsham) did not hesitate to say, that he had always been, and still continued a decided opponent to all further concessions to the Roman catholics, no matter what might be the nature or extent of the securities which they had to offer. – (Loud applause, mixed with cries of 'Why, then, support Peel!'). But it was his decided conviction that his majesty's ministers had never taken such a step as that now proposed to be introduced, without a conscientious feeling that they had just grounds to go upon. Believing that to be the case, he considered Mr. Peel to be still upon his trial; and if he saw that he did not fully redeem the pledge he had given, by making out a sufficient case to prove the pressing necessity of his change of conduct – and if he did not further prove his sincerity by providing ample security for the safety of existing establishments in church and state – then he would take the first opportunity of opposing his election on a future occasion. But at present, he could not withdraw his confidence from the gentleman, who had so long been their tried supporter, in favour of a gentleman who was, at all events, untried in their service.

During the whole of his speech, Dr. Marsham was continually interrupted in the rudest manner, by hisses, cries of 'Poll, poll,' – 'No speeches; we came here to vote,' – and a variety of other exclamations of the same kind. Towards the conclusion of the doctor's address, indeed, the signs of impatience became almost alarming. The hall being rather hot, from the number of persons who had crowded into it, a cry of 'Break the windows,' was raised in various parts of it; and one 'master,' who had probably a pretty fresh recollection of his collegiate pranks, began to poke his umbrella through the glass with great assiduity and effect, – a proceeding which was regarded with the most laudable composure by the assembly.

Amidst the uproar which succeeded, a Mr. Girdlestone, a scholar of Balliol College, repeatedly endeavoured to obtain a hearing, for the purpose, so far as we could understand him, of stating why he could not vote for Mr. Peel. He said he trusted the convocation would allow the same latitude of discussion which prevailed at county elections; but the mention of the word 'discussion' produced a perfect tempest of uproar; and, after many ineffectual attempts to proceed, the speaker was compelled to desist, amidst the greatest tumult, which was at length stilled by the voice of the vice-chancellor, who announced that the poll had commenced, but that the noise was so great that he was unable to hear the votes.

During the confusion which prevailed, some London masters, not of arts, but of the art of transferring the property of others into their own pockets, were very busy at work; and, we believe, reaped a very plentiful harvest. Amongst the sufferers was a son of Mr. Justice Parke, who lost a very valuable gold watch; and several other gentlemen lost purses and pocket-books, some of them containing, we understood, considerable sums.

### THIRD DAY

The concourse of members at the Convocation Hall, was visibly less this morning than on either of the preceding. The friends of Sir

Robert Inglis appeared quite confident of success, and those of Mr. Peel resigned to defeat. 'It's all up,' was the common salutation amongst them on meeting. The general observation now was, 'Why does not Mr. Peel resign? It's useless to prolong the contest now that there is no earthly chance of success.' At twelve o'clock Mr. Short, on behalf of Mr. Peel's friends, stated that they had no longer any wish to delay the termination of the election, as they felt they could not materially alter the state of the poll – (cheers). The vice-chancellor declared that after this statement he should keep the poll open till two o'clock and then certainly close it. At a quarter past one, an officer called out, 'Magistri ad suffragandum prima vice.' It is usual to make this call three times, at certain intervals, before the poll closes. Dr. Ratcliffe, vice-principal of St. Mary Hall, was soon after brought into the hall in a chair, being too ill to walk, and gave his vote to Sir Robert Inglis. The vice-chancellor declared, 'The poll is now closed' and said, the total numbers polled during the election were: –

| | |
|---|---|
| For Sir Robert H. Inglis | 755 |
| For Mr. Peel | 609 |
| Majority in favour of Sir R. H. Inglis | 146 |

This announcement was received with loud acclamations which lasted several minutes, intermixed with cries of 'Bravo! bravo!' The vice-chancellor then pronounced in Latin, that Sir Robert Harry Inglis was regularly and properly elected one of the burgesses to represent that most learned University in parliament. The acclamations were renewed with deafening effect. The vice-chancellor then caused the sheriff's precept to be read, and inquired in Latin, whether the doctors, masters, and scholars were agreed in the return of Sir Robert Harry Inglis; which was answered with cries of 'all,' and continued cheering. The vice-chancellor then sealed the return, and said, 'We now dissolve this convocation.' He immediately left the throne and one of the doctors exclaimed with enthusiasm – Three cheers for the vice-chancellor, which were instantly given. Three cheers for Lord Eldon; and three cheers more for the return of Sir R. H. Inglis, followed. Three cheers for the king were proposed, but hisses burst forth, and were mixed with cheers of nearly equal proportion. Three cheers for Mr. Peel were then proposed; but the proportion of hisses was still greater than in his majesty's cheers. One cheer more for Sir R. H. Inglis was then called, and in the midst of the general cheering the assembly retired from the hall.

# The Great Reform Bill Struggle

## ORATOR HUNT AND THE ELECTION CAMPAIGN

In November, 1830 Lord Grey introduced the Great Reform
Bill. It was thrown out at the committee stage in March, 1831.
'Orator' Hunt, the radical leader, visited Manchester during the
election campaign. John Harland had just become the *Guardian*'s
chief, and, as he said, at first sole, reporter. He set a new standard
of verbatim reporting.

*April 9, 1831*

On Wednesday last, the town was placarded with announcements that
the member for Preston would again visit Peterloo, and address the
populace. In order to receive him with due honours, a barouche and
chaise were put in requisition, which, with seven musicians, a volunteer
fifer, and seven flags, collected from various quarters, formed the head
of the procession, the tail (like the comet's) being by much the greater
bulk of the whole, and composed, as we need hardly say, almost entirely of idlers, operatives (who on this triumphal occasion chose to
lose half a day's work that they might feast their eyes and ears with
their idol) and women. Mr. Hunt got into the barouche, and was
drawn to Peterloo, where he harangued the concourse, which was
stated to be more numerous than on any occasion since the year 1819.

### REFORM BILL A CUCKOO'S NEST

To be sure (he said) public meetings had been held in Manchester,
and Bolton, and Blackburn, aye, and even at Preston too, and other
places; and all the country was running wild for the reform bill. But
when people chose to run wild after any thing, they should take care
and keep their eyes open or they might run into a quagmire. The
ministry proposed by this measure, and it had been openly said in the
house of commons that it was their intention, to extend the representation in parliament to what they called the middle classes, that they
might join with the higher orders, to keep the lower class down; and
he was afraid, if the people of England did not keep open their eyes
and look after their rights, that this measure would succeed. He did
not mean to say, that he did not wish the bill to pass, – in God's name
let it pass – but when it came he thought that like cuckoos' or mares'
nests, there would be but few good eggs in it. He had asked the
question night after night in the house of commons. 'Do you propose

to benefit the people of England by this measure?' And what was the case? Why, when Sir Robert Peel charged them with going to make a democratical house of commons, and going, by this measure, to give power into the hands of the people, they said 'No, we are going to keep the power out of the hands of the rabble; we are going to give representation to the £10 houses, in order to prevent the people from getting what they have so long demanded.' Yes, their policy, a policy which they had openly avowed, was, to get one million of the middle classes, the little shopkeepers and those people, to join the higher classes, in order to raise yeomanry corps, and keep up standing armies, and thus unite together to keep their hands still in the pockets of the seven millions, and take from them enough to keep a host of lazy, idle drones, who don't work at all.

He had been asked, supposing the reform bill should pass, who were the people of Manchester to send? (A voice from the crowd 'Hugh Birley,' accompanied by groans and cries of no, no). He had been told of him before, but on his expressing a desire to know who he was, 'Don't you know' said someone, 'that's Cap. Birley, who came up to the hustings in Aug. 1819.' 'What!' exclaimed Mr. Hunt, will the people of Manchester send a master butcher of Peterloo to represent them in parliament? (No, never.) Was there no better man in this country to recommend than such a fellow as that? (Shouts of 'Potter').

## HOW TO WIN VOTES

Mr. Potter, he understood, was a very good man, but he was engaged to Wigan. The first day of the Wigan election, let every man in Manchester, between the ages of 15 and 45, march over to Wigan, to accompany Mr. Potter, to the number of 20 or 30,000 men, and he would have them go and exercise what he called a constitutional influence over the election of Wigan. 'If you meet a voter,' said Mr. Hunt, 'say to some ten or twelve of you, take care of him, and see if you can't persuade him to vote for Potter. Use kind entreaties; and if these fail, I would advise them to take him by the arm, and give him a gentle squeeze, and let one take hold bold of his other arm (and I know you Lancashire men give something like a feeling squeeze when you like): and if he still refuses, *I would not say I would pull his arms off, but I would very near do it.* That is what you are called upon to do, and my opinion is that if you don't do it, you will never get this reform or any other.'

He next addressed the mob, whom he appeared to identify with the people of England, on the advantage of unity. The whigs, he said, were strong, because they were united; but the people were *a rope of sand*. If they would but stick together, they possessed ten times more power than all their oppressors put together. 'Don't quarrel among yourselves,' said the peace-making orator, when he was interrupted by a fight or two in the crowd, and considerable consequent uproar. When some degree of order had been restored, he exclaimed, 'Of what use is my addressing you; the moment I speak of being peaceable, there is a battle amongst you? I want you to think of what I say to you, and if what I have said upon reflection appears right, act accordingly; but if there is any thing you cannot make up your minds upon, wait a bit – don't decide till you can make up your minds. All I want of you is to be human beings; to see you exercise your own discretion and judgment. If you do this, I hope to see the day when the people of England will be better fed, better clothed, when they will have less labour and get more pay for it.' – After announcing that he would take a cheerful glass of wine with his friends in the evening, the orator bowed and sat down; and the multitude gradually withdrew from the field.

In the evening, those of Mr. Hunt's friends who chose to pay half-a-crown for the privilege, were admitted into his presence, at the White Lion Inn, Hanging Ditch, and were entitled to listen to sundry speeches of a similar nature with that recorded above, (for which reason we think it unnecessary to trouble our readers with any report of them) and to a pint of wine. A hundred tickets had been issued; but these were found too few, and we believe that about 130 were disposed of. Mr. Hunt withdrew a little after eleven o'clock, but the wine-bibbing was protracted, we understand, to a late hour.


## THE DUTY OF THE PEOPLE[1]

The General Election gave Lord Grey a majority. The Reform Bill was now safe in the Commons. Its fate in the Lords was doubtful.

### September 17, 1831

Whilst there has never, in modern times, been a crisis more important to the cause of order, liberty, and good government in this kingdom than the present, so, fortunately, there has been none at which the duty of the people at large was more clear and definite.

It becomes, therefore, now a question of immediate and almost

1. From a leader by John Edward Taylor.

thrilling interest, how, on this most vital measure of political regenera-
tion being ushered into the house of peers, that dignified assembly of
hereditary legislators will receive and deal with it. We believe it is at
least doubtful whether even ministers themselves have, as yet, any
distinct foreknowledge. In other words we are of opinion that it
mainly depends upon the conduct of the people of England themselves
at this juncture, whether the peers give their sanction to the reform
bill, or venture to incur the awful responsibility which will assuredly
follow its rejection.

Again and again has it been declared in parliament, not only by the
tories; but by their foolish and unprincipled fellow-labourer Mr.
HENRY HUNT, that to *that* bill the people of England have become
indifferent; that the public appetite for it has palled; and that destruction by the peers may take place without any hazard of formidable
ulterior consequences. These assertions are false; they are not merely
beside, they are in direct contradiction to, the truth. It is for *the people*,
– for those, we mean, who are interested in the security of property
and the preservation of public order – for those whose prosperity and
even means of existence are bound up with the maintenance of peace
and the support of good government, to come promptly forward, and
by their acts to give to these calumnies of the avowed enemies, and the
false friends of reform, an indignant and decisive refutation. 'Now is
the appointed time,' *now* is the season at which the whole nation in
one loud acclaim should declare its attachment to the reform bill, and
call on the peers to establish an irrevocable title to the public confidence
and gratitude by speedily passing it into a law.

To avert this danger [of mutilation by the Lords] what is the duty
of the people? It is to meet – to meet in their counties, cities, towns,
and villages, and to petition – decently and respectfully, but firmly and
strongly, to petition – that the house of peers will pass the bill. There is
a large majority of the peers who have no borough interest; and consequently who are free from the corrupt inducement which the possession of such property too often supplies to desire the continuance
of the present system. These at least, it may reasonably be hoped, will
not be insensible to the propriety of deferring to a strong manifestation
of public opinion. That opinion is well known to be in favour of
reform, and needs, we feel certain, but to make itself adequately appreciated, in order to *command* success. Public meetings, properly conducted, held in all parts of the kingdom, and praying for the passing
of the bill, may win over the hesitating, confirm the timid, restrain the
factious, and even act upon the *fears* of those who are inaccessible to
the operation of higher and better motives.

## THE BILL OR REVOLUTION

The Lords rejected the Bill. The moderate reformers in Manchester called a protest meeting. The radical reformers decided to
muscle in. The situation was threatening. When the *Guardian*'s
leading article was written on the night of October 14 the news
of that day's revolutionary riots in Bristol had not reached
Manchester. The leader is probably Taylor's.

October 15, 1831

### 'COME AND BRING ARMS'

It appears, that, from the very first intimation of an intention to
convene a meeting in this town, a plan was formed by a set of persons
calling themselves the political union of the working classes, for
turning that meeting to their own purposes. Delegates were sent by
the political union to the various towns and villages in the vicinity, for
the purpose of urging the inhabitants of these towns to attend the
meeting, although, by the terms of the requisition, it was confined to
the inhabitants of Manchester. What were the precise instructions given
to the persons employed on this service, we are, of course, unable to
say; but if the nature of their commission may be judged of from the
manner in which they executed it, there can be little doubt of the
existence of a deliberate design to instigate a very extensive armed
insurrection, – a design which was only defeated by the good sense of
the people, who were to have been made instruments in the hands of
a few wicked and desperate men. One of these emissaries repaired to
Middleton, where he urged the people to come to the meeting on
Wednesday; and to come prepared to defend themselves. He desired
those who had arms to bring them, and promised that those who had
none, should have arms put into their hands at Manchester. He openly
showed that their object was not reform but revolution. Other delegates went on the same or the following day, to Rochdale, Oldham,
Stockport, Ashton, Eccles, Barton, Swinton, and indeed, we believe
to almost every town and village within a dozen miles of Manchester,
and in each place, we believe, the same solicitations were used, and the
same efforts made, to induce the people to come armed to the meeting.
   Although the plans proposed by these delegates were countenanced
in each of the places they visited, by a few violent or thoughtless
individuals, we are happy to state that the bulk of the labouring
classes, who were intended to be ensnared, positively refused to have

anything to do with such desperate schemes, and declined the invitation held out to them. A man, whom we believe to have been one of the prime movers in the plot, boasted that he and his associates could assemble nearly two hundred thousand armed men at Manchester; but if they ever entertained any such expectations, they were greatly deceived; for the number of persons who came from the country, probably did not exceed a thousand. What proportion of these adopted the suggestions of the delegates, by coming armed, it is, of course, impossible to say; but we have no doubt there was a number of armed men at the meeting; and after it had terminated, pistols were discharged in various places by individuals who were evidently returning from it.

## ONE DAY STRIKES

Another plan was also adopted by the parties to whom we have alluded, with the view of swelling the number of the working classes at the meeting, namely, sending bodies of men to most of the factories in the town, on Wednesday morning, and insisting on the hands being turned out,[1] in order that they might attend the meeting. Nearly every factory in the town was visited in this manner; and wherever there was the slightest delay in complying with the mandate, a shower of stones was poured through the windows of the factory and, in some cases, where some of the work-people showed a disinclination to leave their employment, they were severely beaten for their want of zeal.

## HOW THE MEETING WAS RIGGED

The people who came from the country, and a considerable body of persons, chiefly Irish weavers, who appeared to act under the directions of the political union, assembled in a deep mass near the lower end of the field; whilst the requisitors and the more respectable part of the meeting stationed themselves at the upper end, near the church, where a sort of hustings, composed of two or three carts, was speedily erected. Before the proceedings commenced, however, the unionists, finding that this arrangement would not answer their purpose, sent a body of men to remove the carts to the part of the field where they had stationed themselves; and when the proceedings commenced, they formed a close and compact mass in front of the carts, occupying nearly the whole of the ground from which the speeches could be heard, or even a view obtained of the faces of the speakers. The result of this manœuvre was, that the more respectable part of the meeting,

1. A 'turn-out' was the contemporary term for a strike.

finding that they could neither see nor hear, left the field in very great numbers. At a quarter past-twelve o'clock, when the proceedings commenced, there were certainly upwards of 20,000 – probably at least 25,000, people in the field; but before half-past one the number had diminished to about ten thousand; and, from the cause we have already mentioned, the greater portion even of the respectable working men had quitted the place. By half-past two o'clock, the number was still further diminished; and, before the close of the proceedings, was reduced to about six thousand, – the great majority of whom consisted of the people from the country, and of Irish weavers interspersed with no inconsiderable number of thieves and pick-pockets, – some of whose exploits are alluded to in our report of the proceedings. Under these circumstances it was not at all surprising that the amendment of the political union should have been carried.

## THE THREAT OF REVOLUTION

From the very inconvenient situation in which our reporter was placed, some very inflammatory language addressed to the meeting by Brooks [one of the members of the union] escaped him. One of the observations of this man clearly implied a knowledge that some of his auditors were armed. He said 'He had no doubt they would be ready to march wherever their services might be required. *He would not then say "Shoulder arms," for that might lead to a very awkward discovery!*'

From a review of the whole circumstances attending this meeting, we are quite satisfied that the explosion of a most dangerous conspiracy was prevented solely by the disinclination of the sound and industrious part of the working classes to engage in any scenes of violence and blood. Whether they would have displayed the same good conduct, if the ministers had resigned, and their places had been supplied by a cabinet of anti-reformers under the auspices of the Duke of Wellington, we shall not even attempt to conjecture: but we cannot help thinking that under such circumstances the peace of this town would have been imminently endangered.

We want, therefore, a full and efficient reform; a reform according to 'the bill'; we want it and must have it; we must have it quickly, in order (to say nothing of other reasons) that incendiary revolutionists and agitators may no longer be enabled, by artful pretexts and misrepresentations, by erecting a superstructure of lies upon a basis of fact, to impose on the weak and ignorant and hurry them, along with the radically wicked, into outrage or insurrection.

These are not mere vague generalities; there are, in this town, known apostles of tumult, daily proceeding in a manner, which no government that is fit to be supported can long tolerate. There is a society here, some of the members of which boast of great organisation, which hardly seeks concealment, and which is understood to be affiliated with other societies in different parts of the kingdom, the undeniable, indeed, we may say, the avowed object of the leaders of which, contemptible as both by their characters, talents and stations, these men are, is nothing less than to instigate to rebellion. A variety of facts are detailed in other parts of our paper, amply illustrative of the truth of this assertion.

The sting must be extracted from these reptiles. Measures of precaution or coercion may in the meantime be necessary; but the only certain mode of depriving such persons of the power to do mischief, is to apply both to them and to the friends of that rank corruption which has generated them, the medicament of a parliamentary reform.

> The Bill became law in June, 1832 after the King had promised to create as many peers as might be needed to give the government a majority.

### LETTER TO THE EDITOR

Sir, It is a lamentable fact that one can scarcely take up a newspaper without the pain of meeting with an accident that has arisen from a stage coach.

(May 25, 1822)

# CHAPTER TWO

# The Cotton Lords' Bible

*

Lancashire in the 1830s and 1840s was often a battleground for 'the two nations,' – the rich and the poor – whose struggles suggested to Disraeli the sub-title for *Sybil*, published in 1845. The *Guardian*, denounced as 'the cotton lords' Bible' by Richard Oastler, deserved its nickname both for its views and its standing. This chapter reflects life in Lancashire as Taylor, Garnett, and Harland saw it in those years. It was a one-sided view, but public-spirited.

Taylor continued to write the leading articles which fixed the paper's line on the Ten Hours' Bill, the Corn Laws, and the Chartists. His elder son, Russell Scott Taylor, was only 18 when his father died in 1844. For the next four years he and Garnett worked closely together. The paper took a new and, as it proved, a lasting interest in environmental problems. Young Taylor died in 1848.

## Masters and Men

### THE ASHTON TURNOUT

#### January 8, 1831

A most daring and extraordinary outrage was committed on Tuesday last, by a body of turn-outs[1] from Ashton and the neighbourhood, at the factory of Messrs. John and William Sidebottom and Co., of Millbrook, in Longdendale. On the forenoon of that day, a meeting of spinners was held at a public-house at Ashton-Underlyne, and, after it broke up, the persons composing it, with others, to the number altogether of five or six hundred left the town in small parties, and assembled on the top of the hill near Hollinworth, and then suddenly poured down upon the factory at Millbrook, the hands of which had turned out along with those employed at the other mills in the neighbourhood; but a portion of them had resumed their employment, and were at work when the turn-outs reached the spot. The overlooker of the mill, finding it surrounded by a large crowd, went to ask them

1. Strikers

what they wanted, and was informed that they had come to turn out the spinners who were at work; and they should certainly do so. The manager offered to send the hands away; but the turn-outs refused to allow this. They then forced their way in great numbers into the mill, and dragged the spinners whom they found at work into the road. They there *turned all their coats inside out, tied them together with cords*, inscribed the obnoxious price '3s. 9d'[1] on their backs with chalk, and then drove them along the turnpike road to Tintwisle, and over Tintwisle's bridge to Waterside, another factory belonging to the same firm, in which, also, a portion of the spinners had resumed their employment.

Fortunately, however, before the arrival of the turn-outs intelligence had been received of what had occurred at Mill Brook, and the hands had all been sent away, and no one remained about the premises except Mr. James Sidebottom, one of the partners, who demanded to know what they wanted. They told him they were to come to turn out his spinners; and, on being told that none were at work, they insisted on examining the mill, into which they forced their way, and searched it from the ground floor to the roof, upon which some of them mounted, for the purpose of ascertaining whether any of the spinners had concealed themselves in the gutters. Finding no one, they left the place, first informing Mr. Sidebottom that they would compel him to pay the price demanded. They also informed him, that if any of the spinners resumed their employment at any lower rate, they (the turn-outs) would come again, kill them, and destroy the machinery.

They then went off, still driving their captives before them; down the Derbyshire side of the river, to Woolley Bridge, which they crossed, and proceeded along the turnpike road through Mottram, and to the bottom of the hill near Stalybridge, where they halted, loosed their prisoners, after having driven them five or six miles, – and dismissed them, – but first informing them, that if they were found working again until they had obtained their price their lives would be forfeited. The turn-outs then dispersed, and returned home in small parties, as they had originally gone out. Notwithstanding the vicinity of Stalybridge to the place where the outrage was committed, not one of the offenders was known either to Mr. Sidebottom or to any of his workpeople.

We come now to what appears to us the most extraordinary affair, if the circumstances have been correctly narrated. It is stated to us, that when the turn-outs made their appearance at Mill Brook, they were joined by a person mounted upon a chestnut horse, who appeared to direct their movements, and who accompanied them as far

1. The price of piece work fixed by the makers.

as Tintwisle. He then turned back towards Mottram, and appears to have waited somewhere in the neighbourhood, for some time afterwards he rejoined them going up the hill to Mottram, and accompanied them to the place where they dismissed their prisoners. It has been stated to us that he there made a speech to them before they dispersed, but we do not know on what authority the statement rests; and we are really inclined to think that the whole story must have been founded on the accidental presence of some person mounted on horseback at (one) or two points during the progress of the rioters. However, whether that part of the statement may be well or ill founded, it is clear that the outrage was one of the most audacious that has ever been committed in this neighbourhood; and if it does not meet with the most signal punishment, there must be very great remissness on the part of the magistrates of the neighbourhood.

## CHILD SABOTEURS

### September 28, 1836

> Richard Oastler (1789–1861), 'the factory king,' was one of the group of Tory Radicals who strenuously opposed the mill-owners of the North. He led the agitation for the Ten Hours Bill. In 1836 there were many complaints that the existing law limiting the hours of employment of children was not being enforced. The *Guardian* was as opposed to evasion as Oastler was, but totally disapproved of his methods. It said so. Oastler replied in this letter.

*To the Editor of the 'Manchester Guardian'*
Sir,
    We are now no longer contending about the obtaining of a law. The Factories Regulation Act,[1] whether it be good or bad, is now the law of the land. It is indeed their [the mill-owners'] own law, it was opposed by all the friends of the ten hours bill; it was brought into the house of commons by the great whig leader, Lord Althorp, and it was supported by Mr. Poulett Thomson, and the bit of a parliament of mill owners, who assembled in Palace Yard. They, 'the mill owners' can therefore have no excuse whatever, in attempting to break the Factories Regulation Act. Now the fact is, that the mill owners are resolved to break that law, and I am resolved that it shall be enforced.

1. 1833. It limited the employment of children under 13 to nine hours a day, and provided for inspection. Poulett Thomson was M.P. for Manchester.

– The government are united with me: the magistrates, with the exception of those at Halifax, are assisting the mill owners, (they, themselves, being, in very many instances, mill owners, or the relatives of mill owners.) The question then now is, whether shall the law and the government, and myself be overcome by the mill owners and the magistrates, or shall the latter yield to the former. At present it is only necessary, that I should remark on part of the report, on which you have animadverted, and which you have marked in italics. That there may be no mistake, I copy the words. 'I will teach every factory child in the kingdom how to use a knitting needle among the machinery – I'm taking lessons now, to learn little children how to do more harm than good' [in the mills]. I have no doubt I used these words. I know that I intended to do so. Whether or no, I now adopt them: and am prepared to maintain, that, when the whole argument is fairly stated, I am justified by the soundest principles of justice and reason in this line of proceeding. You observe, on these words of mine 'a man who can use language like this – who can talk of teaching children to destroy the property of their employers – is either a madman or a most hardened and desperate villain.' 'It is high time – either that his friends should put him under some restraint, or that the law should interpose to check the career of wickedness, which he seems disposed to run.' Now, sir, this is plain speaking: I admire it, I hate your 'half and half,' your 'milk sop' politicians who use expressions, which may be turned to a thousand different meanings. I did use those words, and I will if circumstances require it, that is if the magistrates and the mill owners are more powerful than the law, and the government and myself, I will act upon them.

Depend upon it, sir, if there will be no law against the factory masters, there can be no law against the factory 'king.' – I was speaking, sir, at Blackburn of the time having arrived of which Mr. William Rathbone Greg[1] prophecies (see 40th page of his excellent work), the time when the system of social union would be undermined, when the silken bonds of amity, which unite all men to their kind, would be burst asunder, that is, to use my own words, in explaining Mr. Greg's, when the factory masters shall have succeeded, by the aid of the new reform magistracy, in defying the law and the government – then, of course, the army must be dismantled – the public ledger must be closed – nay the king himself must come down from his throne – for sure am I, he will never be content to reign over a smuggling and murderous banditti, who defy the laws. Now sir, let us suppose a case: – There is a law against assassination: some of the masters talk of assassinating

1. W. R. Greg (1809–1881) mill-owner and essayist – see pp. 93 and 107.

me. Suppose one of them were just now to enter my office and attempt to push his knife in my breast, should I be a 'madman' or a 'most hardened and desperate villain' if I attempted to break his blade and thereby destroy his property? Or, supposing that the law against assassination were as openly and as frequently broken as the factory law is, and that the victims were little girls and boys, and that the magistrates, being themselves either assassins or the friends of assassins, were to refuse to enforce the law – should I be a 'madman' or a 'most hardened and desperate villain,' if I instructed the little girls and boys how to break the assassins' blades and thus to destroy the property of the assassins? I really fancy they would be justified, in reason and law, if they were to destroy these assassins.

The cases are precisely similar: the machinery is the knife and those who are resolved to break the law, must not expect the law to defend their machinery any more than the assassin's knife. Depend upon it sir, the mill owners, who defy the law, are the real 'madmen,' the magistrates, who refuse to punish them, are 'the most hardened and desperate villains.' It is indeed 'madness' for men whose property is in machinery, to defy the law. – It is indeed 'villainous' for the men who are sworn to execute the laws, to wink at the transgressions of the rich.

If the magistrates and the mill owners defeat the law, the government and myself, why then, the old system of government is ended, and I will lay the foundations of a new one, by teaching the factory child the use of her grandmother's knitting needles. – Now, sir, I believe I am as much the friend of the mill owners as you are. I have plainly stated my position: I can maintain it in spite of their wealth and power. I have courage to go through with it, but as their friend I would advise them to yield. I would indeed. I remain, sir, respectfully your obedient servant,

RICHARD OASTLER.

*Fixby Hall, near Huddersfield. September 26, 1836*

### MR. OASTLER AND HIS SPEECH AT BLACKBURN[1]

We have given in another column a very extraordinary letter from *Mr. Oastler*, in which it will be seen that gentleman deliberately justifies the act of instructing children to destroy the property of their employers. We think no rational man who reads that letter can have any doubt as to the state of *Mr. Oastler*'s mind, or as to the propriety of his being placed under some restraint, to prevent him from involving himself

1. From a leader probably by John Edward Taylor.

and others in the commission of acts as little reconcileable with
morality and natural justice as they are with the law of the land; and
which, if detected, would inevitably be punished with the utmost
severity. The hypothetical case put by *Mr. Oastler* has all the ingenuity
which a diseased mind frequently displays in treating on the subject of
its hallucinations. *Mr. Oastler* maintains that he has as much right to
destroy the machinery of a mill-owner who breaks the law, as he would
have to destroy the weapon with which a man threatened his life; but,
in the estimation of a sane man, the cases will not appear to have the
slightest analogy to each other. In destroying the knife of an assassin, a
man acts strictly in self-defence; but what plea of self-defence can *Mr.
Oastler* set up when he destroys the property of a manufacturer? None
whatever. It is not necessary for his protection, nor for the protection
of the children because the latter can protect themselves, by staying
away from the factories where the law is broken. Society would very
soon be in a lamentable state if any man had the right to take into his
own hands the punishment of offences, or what he may choose to consider offences against the law. We believe *Mr. Oastler* has broken the law
by publicly recommending and inciting others to commit a wicked and
unlawful action; and, according to his rule of morality, the mill-
owners would be justified in committing violence upon him, in order
to prevent him from following up that incitement. We dare say *Mr.
Oastler* would be cool enough in his judgment to perceive the inconvenience and injustice of the rule if it were made to apply to himself; and the pity is, that he has not equal quickness of perception in the
case of others.

# The Chartists and the Anti-Corn Law League

The North of England provided the main support for the Chartists and the Anti-Corn Law League. The People's Charter had six points, all but one of which (annual general elections) is now law. At the time all seemed revolutionary, and the physical force wing of the Chartists proposed to use revolutionary means. From 1836 to 1848 the Chartists were the main working-class political movement.

The Anti-Corn Law League, Manchester born, was formed by merchants and manufacturers to fight the taxes on food, and in favour of Free Trade. It also had much working-class support.

The *Guardian* was frightened by the Chartists. It supported the League, but distrusted the tendency of its inner ring to treat Free Trade as a religion and themselves as its infallible priests. Its own attitude was put in a leader on January 23, 1839: 'A protection which applies to one class of persons, and not to another, cannot be very equitable; it is a mode of benefiting one class at the expense of another, landowners and farmers (at the expense of) manufacturers, especially cotton manufacturers.'

## BLOODY WHIGGERY

### Saturday, March 2, 1839

A meeting was held in the new Corn Exchange, Hanging Ditch, on Thursday evening last, in order to receive the report of the [Anti-Corn Law] delegates on their return from London. The doors of the room were besieged from an early hour; and when thrown open at half past six o'clock, the room rapidly filled, many of those present – perhaps from one-third to one-half being obviously chartists and tory-radicals.[1]

The report having been read by Mr. George Wilson,[2] the chairman said he had great pleasure in introducing to the meeting Dr. Johns.

Here Edward Nightingale, being recognised in the room, was loudly cheered by a number of the chartists, who forthwith began to create a disturbance by shouting, groaning, hissing, and cries of 'universal suffrage,' 'Stephens[3] for ever;' and 'three groans for the whigs.' The uproar continued to increase, and at length Edward Curran, a hand-loom weaver, who as one of the representatives of the trade was upon the platform, rose to address the meeting. He was received with

1. Followers of Oastler.
2. The 'boss' of the Anti-Corn Law League (1808–1870).
3. Rev. J. R. Stephens, Chartist (1805–1879).

mingled cheers and groans; on which he said, if working men would not hear a working man, one identified with them in sympathy and interest, his opinion was, that they would not hear common sense. The worthy chairman had told them that evening, that the house of commons would not listen to the prayers of the people. This was quite sufficient to satisfy them, that something must be done to put an end to that system of electing members of parliament. – (Cheers.) He remembered that nearly twenty years ago, when the brave men of Manchester and surrounding towns met upon St. Peter's Field[1] to ask for the repeal of those infamous corn laws; but while they were met there that day, innocent as lambs, but determined as men, and legally proceeding with their business, what was the result? They were cut down by an armed band of ruffians. Had the policy of our rulers that day taken a different course, we should not have had to meet this evening for the repeal of those infamous corn laws. But they persisted in violence and intimidation ('You're a hired whig'), and they had destroyed the nation as nearly as possible; and now it came to be the business of the people again to demand the repeal of those laws. He had heard a voice call him a hired whig; but he would tell that man that he (Curran) stood here an honest advocate for radical reform; he had been persecuted for his adherence to that cause, and he would say to the man that dared to insult him with such a lie, that the truth was not in him.

Richard Moore, an old hand-loom weaver, and another representative from that body, rose, and attempted in vain to be heard, though he said he had been a radical reformer for 45 years. (Groans and hisses.)

At this moment Mr. Nightingale made his way close to the reporters' table, in front of the platform, where he attempted to address the meeting; but, Mr. Prentice,[2] who was on the platform, said, that as Nightingale had prevented others from speaking, he should not be allowed to be heard. – Great uproar ensued, every one vociferating; both Moore and Nightingale attempting to make themselves heard, in a Babel-like confusion of voices, and cries of 'sit down,' 'pull him down,' 'hear him,' and sundry denunciations of 'bloody whiggery.' Nightingale, who looked very fierce and furious, shouted, 'I insist upon my right.'

At length the Chairman beckoned to Nightingale, who mounted the table of the platform, amidst the cheers of his party. The confusion still continued unabated; and, for some time, both Moore and Night-

1. Peterloo, 1819
2. Archibald Prentice (1792–1857) once Taylor's close friend but now his enemy. He ran the radical *Manchester Times* in opposition to the Whig *Manchester Guardian*.

ingale were standing on the table, one on each side of the chairman, and neither of them able to make himself heard.

At length Moore left the table to the sole possession of Mr. Nightingale, who said, 'Gentlemen I am not surprised at the partial conduct of the chairman, when I look upon the men who surround him.' (Hisses, cheers, and groans.) It is a matter of perfect indifference to me whether the chairman will – (Cheers and hisses.) – The Chairman: Gentlemen, I have no objection to hear Mr. Nightingale, although he is not here regularly as a petitioner against the corn laws.

Mr. Nightingale said, he was so used to the bullying of the whigs, that it was a matter of perfect indifference to him whether he was to be heard at eight or nine o'clock; but heard he would be. Indeed, he knew not whether, from the usage he had had, that even common courtesy demanded from him that he should respect he who was seated in the chair. – (Hisses and cries of 'Shame.') The chairman had questioned the propriety of his (Nightingale's) addressing him; but with equal propriety he (Nightingale) might ask upon what authority the chairman occupied that chair. – ('Hear,' and laughter.) He (Nightingale) was present at the commencement of the proceedings, and he pledged his honour – (laughter) – to those who were not, that it was not put to a show of hands that Mr. Harbottle should occupy the chair. – Mr. Alderman Cobden:[1] Then I call for a show of hands for the chairman. – (Owing to our position, and the circumstances of a number of persons standing upon the seats in the middle of the room, it was impossible to ascertain with any positive certainty, the proportion of hands raised; but they appeared to be a majority.) – Great confusion ensued, in the midst of which Nightingale amused himself with all sorts of grimaces, bawling out, 'Mr. Alderman Cobden, O Lord!' putting the thumb of one hand to his nose, and describing a circle with the other in a way and with a signification peculiar to people of a certain class.

At length, partial silence having been obtained, he said that, in his progress up the room, the only individual that he observed, to know personally, was an honest Irish lad, a laborious lad; he thought they called him Pat Murphy. If he were in the room, he would have the goodness to say 'Ay.' ('Ay,' was called from at least a dozen different parts of the room.) He was not to be thwarted, and he begged to move that honest Pat Murphy take the chair. – (Cheers and hisses.) At length, a man, answering to the appellation of Pat Murphy, made his way to the reporters' table, and at Nightingale's invitation he mounted it. He

1. Richard Cobden (1804–1865), the main exponent with John Bright of the Manchester School.

was a broad-set Irishman, apparently a labourer or carter's assistant; he wore clothes which scarcely served to cover him, and a ragged apron of coarse wrappering, which, with a little blue cloth cap on his head, and a huge pair of clogs on his feet, completed his attire.

Nightingale again proposed that 'honest Pat Murphy should take the chair,' – (Cheers and hooting.) – Mr. Prentice then mounted the table, close to Nightingale, and the uproar was, if possible, greater than ever. Besides the three persons standing on the table, another Irishman with a black beard was holding an angry colloquy on the platform; and in various parts of the room, persons were shouting 'Order,' 'Chair,' 'Go on, Nightingale.' – Nightingale then proposed 'Three cheers for Stephens,' which were, of course, given by the chartists; 'Three groans for Archibald Prentice,' which were also given; 'Three cheers for the national convention'; and, 'Three cheers for Oastler.' To increase the disorder, another Irishman, evidently intoxicated, mounted the table, and proceeded to harangue the meeting upon '*aquil* laws and *aquil* rights; and let us pay our *parlimint*, and bring in *mimbers* of our own.'

One of his own friends, being somewhat ashamed of this exhibition, attempted, by shaking him, to induce him to quit the table; but the orator politely intimated to his friend, that if he persevered, he would put his clogs in his friend's *chops*. – (Loud cries of 'Down, down.') Several Irishmen, working men, near the reporters' table, were highly indignant at this proceeding, and at the readiness with which Murphy had placed himself on the table at the command of Nightingale; and accordingly, amidst the general confusion, a sort of running expostulatory address to Murphy was kept up by these men, which, under other circumstances, would have been highly diverting. Amongst these appeals we heard the following: – 'Och, Pat Murphy, I'm ashamed of you.' 'Pat, don't make a fool of yourself and your country.' 'Come down, for the sake of Ould Ireland.' 'Don't be bought and sold by a *jerry-lord* like Nightingale.'

As Mr. Harbottle still kept his position in the chair, an attempt was made, on some intimation from Nightingale, to hand a chair up to the table for Mr. Pat Murphy to occupy. The first chair, handed up, was seized by some of the parties on the platform, and borne off into the ante-room behind, two of the shade glasses of the gas chandelier being broken by the chair in its passage over the heads of the persons on the platform. A second chair was handed up, and was also intercepted; so that it appeared doubtful whether Mr. Pat Murphy would not have to stand during the remainder of the proceedings. At length Nightingale got another, which he brandished over his head, menacing some persons near him, as if he would *brain* them. Several of the chartists had before this attempted to climb upon the platform at different points but had been repulsed; and all these appearances of personal collision began to arouse the pugnacity of numbers present, till at length a rush was made towards the platform, to which the reporters' table in front afforded an easy stepping-stone; and the reporters, after vainly endeavouring to keep their seats, finding themselves overborne from behind, made their way over their table, and the chairman's table, and across the platform to the ante-room behind.

For the last half-hour, the weight and pressure of a great number of men, standing on the benches, broke several of them down; and we observed that some individuals had armed themselves with the fragments; others seized the now vacated chairs of the reporters, and a general *mêlée* seemed to be at hand. The members of the Anti-corn-law Association, however, seeing that it was useless any longer to attempt to resist the violence, or to oppose the clamour of the chartists, retired from the platform to the ante-room, and thence through an entry to the street. The platform was speedily taken possession of by the chartists, who scaled the sides, and surrounded several of the gentlemen who remained.

Amongst others, Mr. Prentice was in this situation. – We believe that Nightingale, having been struck by some one, chose to accuse Mr. Prentice; and immediately about a dozen individuals raised their hands to attack him. One of them struck him a blow with the fist, on his right cheek just below the eye, which Mr. Prentice returned with interest; others struck at him; his hat was knocked off; and, finding he stood no chance against numbers, he retreated into the ante-room, without any personal injury beyond what we have stated. – Mr. Howie, his brother-in-law, seeing him attacked, came to his assistance, just as one fellow was wielding a chair, and fortunately prevented the descent of this awkward weapon upon the head of Mr. Prentice. Mr. Howie received one or two blows upon the face; and he then made his way into the ante-room, but succeeded in recovering Mr. Prentice's hat.

At length the parties convening the meeting left the room in possession of the chartists; Mr. Pat Murphy was installed in the chair, and Mr. Nightingale, the *Rev.* Mr. Jackson (who is said to be a methodist minister), and others, addressed the meeting. An amendment on the vote of thanks to the anti-corn-law delegates was moved, and of course, passed unanimously, to 'the national convention'; – 'the base, bloody, and brutal whigs' were most liberally abused in the choicest Billingsgate; and at length the chartists, after sundry cheers for their demagogues, and groans for those who do not please them, separated about half-past nine o'clock.

## ANTI-CORN LAW DINERS

In 1840 there was a week of political meetings in Manchester organised by the Anti-Corn Law League. A banquet was attended by 28 M.P.'s, including Daniel O'Connell who was met at the station by 'an immense crowd.' There were delegations from Aberdeen, Birmingham, Carlisle, Dunfermline, Edinburgh, Glasgow, Leeds, Liverpool, London, Nottingham, Paisley, Sheffield, Stranraer, Stirling, and Wolverhampton. A wooden pavilion was built for the occasion.

### Wednesday, January 15, 1840

The pavilion, we believe, is by far the largest building ever constructed for such a purpose in this (or perhaps we might say in any) part of the kingdom, and some idea of its extent may be formed from the fact that it is much larger than Exeter Hall.[1]

#### THE BILL OF FARE

In addition to their other numerous and multifarious engagements, the committee for this great dinner, consisting of only six gentlemen,[2] undertook the Herculean labour of providing the supplies requisite for the thousands of guests to be assembled on this interesting occasion. And this task, to them doubtless a strange and novel one, they performed with great judgment and discretion. Instead of the usual mode of contracting with some hotel-keeper to furnish the dinner at so much per head, the whole of the provisions were purchased by members of the committee themselves, and the requisite cookery was conducted under the management of able superintendents, in the kitchen and cellars of the building recently occupied as Bywater's Hotel. Orders were despatched to several eminent purveyors in Cumberland, for a supply of hams and tongues; other agricultural districts were laid under contribution for turkeys and geese; an experienced baker was employed to supply the dinner buns and bread; one of the committee proceeded to Liverpool, and purchased a number of hogsheads, barrels and boxes of fruit, either from the ship or the wholesale dealers; and to Mr. Wm. Ibbotson, of the Globe Works, Sheffield, was entrusted the order for the thousands of knives and forks required for

1. London's largest hall.    2. One of whom was Richard Cobden.

the occasion. Of the solid viands for dinner, such as beef and mutton, hams and tongues, turkeys and capons, veal and mince pies, bread, &c. not less than ten thousand lbs. weight, or in round numbers four tons and a half, were provided! This is wholly exclusive of the dessert, in which the fruit, biscuits, 'crackers,' &c. are estimated by chests, barrels, and boxes. The dinner service and other articles of earthen-ware number ten thousand pieces; the wine-glasses, bottles, decanters, and other articles of glass, about ten thousand more; the knives and forks about sixteen thousand pieces.

## VIANDS FOR DINNER

The dinner was by no means a sumptuous one, which, indeed, would have been unsuited to the magnitude of the festival, and the main object of the vast assemblage held within the walls of the pavilion. It had rather the character of one of the banquets of the olden times, where the chief food of the guests was the 'flesh of heaven,' the 'great beef of Old England.' As it would have been a physical impossibility to have placed such a dinner hot on the table, – the distance of the remote parts of the pavilion from the kitchen being great enough to cool a red-hot poker in traversing the intervening space, – the whole was in the shape of a cold collation, of the most solid and substantial character. The staple dishes were rounds, ribs, and sirloins of beef, and legs of mutton.

## THE WINES,

as we have stated, were supplied by Messrs. John Herford and Brother; and were, altogether, of qualities and price to do them great credit. The cost was port and sherry, at 5s. per bottle; hock 6s.; champagne and claret, each 8s.; and red hermitage 9s. The port was a fine old wine, of the vintage of 1830, which had been between nine and ten years in the wood. The sherry was also a fine old wine, of a very superior character to that usually supplied to public dinners, the hock was a fine, superior wine; the champagne (notwithstanding its price of 8s. instead of the ordinary one at 10s. 6d. per bottle) was, we believe, of the very finest growths of the most favoured vineyards in France; and the claret and red hermitage were of equally high character. Indeed the whole of the wines were such as are usually reserved for the select guests of a private dinner party, and such as, we can say, were rarely if ever equalled in any public dinner in this town or neighbourhood. The following were the quantities consumed,

|                | Bottles |        |
|----------------|---------|--------|
| Port           | about   | 1000   |
| Sherry         | do.     | 1300   |
| Hock           | do.     | 60     |
| Champagne      | do.     | 90     |
| Claret         | do.     | 24     |
| Red Hermitage  | do.     | 3      |
| Total number of bottles drunk, | do. | 2477 |

We should not here omit to state, that Mr. S. H. Slack, surgeon, apothecary, and soda water-manufacturer, Downing-street, Ardwick, sent (gratuitously) a large supply of very delicious distilled water.


## BRONTERRE O'BRIEN AND THE GUARDIAN

In 1840 James Bronterre O'Brien (1805–1864), a leader of the physical force Chartists, a graduate of Trinity College, Dublin, and a radical journalist, was tried at Liverpool Assizes and sentenced to 18 months' imprisonment. A *Guardian* reporter gave evidence:

### Wednesday, April 8, 1840

Mr. Thomas Thornhill Clarkson[1]: I am a reporter for the *Manchester Guardian*. I attended a meeting at Batty's Circus from seeing a placard. I got there about eight o'clock. The place was quite full. I took notes, but not full notes. This is an examined copy of my original short-hand notes, which I also produce. The next speaker (Clarkson said) was Bronterre O'Brien. He rejoiced that his hearers were up to the work, and proceeded to say that he would prove that the government deserved the epithet of robbers which he called them. He also alluded to the corn laws, which gave such undue prices to the corn lords. The system was nothing but wholesale damnable robbery. The speaker alluded to a leg of mutton; the argument being that the aristocracy got the meat, and the people the bone. He next adverted to the ejectment of 'honourable robbers' from the house of parliament, but whether by the door or by the window, he would not say. Let them be strictly legal till the time came. Let them be prepared for the crisis. They must protect themselves from robbing, and assassination by justifiable vengeance. Were they prepared? – (Cries of the meeting, 'We are.')

1. (b. 1817), a lawyer's clerk before he became a reporter on the *Halifax Express* in 1835.

They would trust their cause to the God of justice, and the God of battles.

Re-examined. – On the 16th July I was at another meeting at Batty's Circus. I saw Mr. O'Brien there. The place was full. I believe a John Campbell was in the chair. Mr. O'Brien first addressed the meeting. He considered the time for lecturing and discussion was passed. The petition had been sent to the parliament by the convention, but it had been rejected. If the people were as much up to the mark as he was, they would not again petition a house so corrupt. He proposed that they should take universal suffrage, and elect their own representatives. He knew of a plan, but it was a secret, by which they would accomplish this, and beat both the whigs and tories. The argument of the speaker was, that this would supersede the present legislature. If he were elected one of them, he would be ready with a little bill, which when passed into a law, would put a good coat on the back, and a good hat on the head of the working man. He should propose that the uncultivated lands in our colonies might be freely cultivated without payment.

He then went on to propose a national holiday[1] and cessation of labour, until the government had yielded to their wishes. It would be said, how would the people live without work? but how did their enemies live who worked not at all? There were various ways. They might beg, borrow, or steal. He would not advise them to steal or to beg. To beg would be of no use, because they would get nothing, unless they did as the beggar in Gil Blas did, who, when soliciting alms, had his hat in one hand, and the finger of his other on the lock of a loaded blunderbuss. They might, however, borrow. They should wipe off the 28 millions paid annually for interest on the national debt. He also pointed out other resources. The landlords and aristocracy had robbed the people of two millions of money, which they would have enjoyed if they had had the formation of their own situation.

Cross-examined by Mr. Wortley (for another defendant): – The report I have read did not appear in the *Manchester Guardian*. A short account only was inserted. I took the reports partly for my improvement in my short-hand, and partly because it was a rule with us to take full notes, whether they were afterwards written fully out or not. In some measure, it is the practice for reporters to make out their reports with a shade of the politics professed by the paper for which they report. We give what parts we think best suited to our readers. I gave such a report.

I never was friendly to socialism; quite the reverse. (A small pamphlet

1. This was the Chartist term for a general strike.

was here put into the witness's hand.) I know that book. It was written by me when I was nineteen years old. I repudiate the sentiments it contains, and was persuaded to them by others. It does not contain social principles. I once entertained an opinion that marriage should not be a religious, but a civil ceremony. At a great meeting at Manchester on the corn laws, Mr. O'Connell called the landowners 'robbers.' Mr. Cobden has also spoken strongly, in such language as that stated.

Cross-examined by Mr. B. O'Brien. – If a reporter practices for twenty years, he may still be improved. I deny distinctly that Mr. Protheroe, of Halifax, complained to me of my reporting. I reported a speech of a gentleman, in which I made a mistake of a word in place of 'Knickerbocker.' Mr. Harland is the senior reporter of the *Guardian*. Both of us are employed at large meetings; but the meetings in question were not thought of sufficient importance. I have said that I dissent from socialism. I consider socialists infidels, and I am the reverse. It is very likely that you are very unpopular with the parties called whigs. In reporting such meetings, I inserted those passages only which I thought the most interesting. I never stated to a reporter, that it was our practice to alter reports so as to suit our readers.

Your arguments on property were, that no man had a right to the soil unless to cultivate its fruits, but that, if it were improved in value, the value of such improvement belonged to the people. You also said that the spontaneous fruits belonged to the people, and that all raised beyond it belonged to the cultivator. You said no one had any right to take any land without giving the full market price, or something like it. You divided the land into three classes of value: – first, the general value; secondly, the additional value given by improvements; and, thirdly, the contingent and improvable value. You may have said, that what God created belonged to all men alike; but that what human skill created was the subject of private property. You admitted that compensation would be just in all cases, except such as grants to the Duke of Wellington.[1]

Here witness was required to read a passage from his report, in which the defendant said that he had found the people of Leigh were arming themselves, but that you did not advise the people to do any thing against the law. Some one alluded to Lord John Russell's letters to lord-lieutenants and magistrates, stating that the people should unite as volunteers, for the protection of life and property, and that he would supply them with arms at the public expense. You might have

1. Earlier in his evidence Clarkson had quoted O'Brien as saying that Wellington got his 'for cutting people's throats – making people die before their time.'

said this. (Mr. O'Brien here recited a long portion of his speech, referring to political events in ancient Rome and Sparta.) The witness did not remember. I cannot swear that you said they could have no chance of success unless they rigidly adhered to the law and the constitution.

At Halifax I was a reporter, and assisted in the shop. I was not a penny-a-liner, I had a regular salary. I don't remember seeing in the *Guardian* an article in which Mr. O'Connor and you were called 'two prowling Irishmen.'

> Three months later there was an unpleasant sequel to Clarkson's evidence:

## ASSAULT ON A REPORTER
### Saturday, July 11, 1840

On Tuesday evening last, a discussion on the corn-laws, between Mr. D. Ross, an occasional lecturer on that subject, and a person named Leach, a member of the Universal Suffrage Association, took place at Carpenter's Hall. Charges of 1d., 2d. and 3d. were made for admission to different parts of the room, which was nearly filled.

There was nothing in the discussion itself to require notice; but, at the conclusion of it, a most violent and disgraceful attack was made by a large party of chartists, upon Mr. Clarkson, a reporter from this office, on account of the evidence given by him on the trials of some of the chartist leaders, at the last Liverpool assizes. Mr. Clarkson was not only struck and kicked repeatedly in the room, but an attempt was made by a gang of ruffians to throw him over the bannisters of the stairs, in which case he would most probably have lost his life; but the attempt was defeated by the strenuous and praiseworthy exertions of Mr. Abel Heywood[1], the chairman of the meeting; Mr. Grant, a reporter from the *Advertiser* office, and one or two other individuals, most of whom suffered severely from blows and kicks; and Mr. Heywood narrowly escaped being himself thrown over the bannisters, in his efforts to protect Mr. Clarkson. At length they made their way, with great exertion, to the bottom of the stairs, and got out of the building, when there were some indications of a renewal of the attack; but, several other persons having come to Mr. Clarkson's assistance, the intention was frustrated.

1. Radical Manchester bookseller and newsagent, imprisoned for selling unstamped newspapers, treasurer of National Charter Association 1840-42.

# Crime and Punishment

## PUNISHMENT OF DEATH
### Saturday, July 18, 1840

If we know ourselves in the least, we believe we may assert that we are quite free from any thing of a sanguinary disposition, and should be as little disposed as most persons to prosecute to the last extremity crimes committed against ourselves. But we must say, that we gravely fear the effect of that wholesale abandonment which Mr. Kelly proposes to make in regard to capital punishment. He tacitly admits, that the public is not prepared to see the abolition of the punishment of death in cases of murder, by removing that crime from the operation of his bill. But it seems to us that he loses sight too much of the intention of acts; and we, ourselves, are wholly unable to perceive why an unequivocal attempt to commit murder should be punished the more lightly because it is unsuccessful. Nor, we confess, are we prepared to acquiesce in the propriety of the withdrawal from females of that protection which is involved in the subjection of the crime of rape, under certain circumstances, to a capital penalty. It is admitted that there are cases of rape of the most atrocious and aggravated kind; but in many more instances, it is said, the offences are not such as may be suitably subjected to capital punishment. The natural inference from this state of things would seem to be, that it is proper to leave the power of capital punishment in existence for extreme cases, but to mitigate the sentence where such a lenient course seemed justifiable.

It is true that objections are made, and made not without some reason, to the investing of judges with a discretion as to the punishment that shall be awarded to crime. But on the other hand, some of our recent legislation shows how preposterous it is, and how little conducive to justice, to fix absolutely the sentence for an offence, without any regard to the circumstances under which it may have been committed. We frequently see judges compelled by law to condemn a man to transportation for life for crimes that would be amply punished by a twelve month's imprisonment.

But if the investing judges with a discretion as to punishments be deemed seriously objectionable, why not give a discretion to juries? Why not let crime of the particular kinds under question be divided into two or three classes, and leave it to juries to decide to which of these classes any particular case belongs; the judge apportioning the penalty according as the crime was found to belong to the highest or lowest class in point of enormity? So long as a jury is considered competent to pronounce absolutely upon the question of guilty or not guilty, there can surely be no well-founded objection to permitting them also to assign the degree of guilt.

## THE PRISON CHAPLAIN'S REPORT[1]

### Wednesday, April 12, 1843

In consequence of the unusual influx of prisoners, occasioned by the late unfortunate riots in the manufacturing districts, I have been obliged to read prayers twice every morning in the chapel; I would again urge upon the magistrates the desirability of enlarging the building, in order that the whole of the prisoners might attend divine worship twice every Sunday, instead of devoting one half of that sacred day, as I am inclined to believe that so many do, to employments in every respect most reprehensible. With respect to the conduct of the prisoners in the chapel, I may certainly once more speak in terms of the highest praise.

It is melancholy to reflect on the alarming increase in the number of delinquents throughout the country, and their apparent indifference to the system of good discipline, as exhibited by their repeated returns to prison. I confess that it does appear to me, that much improvement might be adopted with regard to the punishment of young offenders, and that it is well worthy of consideration whether it would not be better, in many instances, to *flog them soundly and discharge them at once, or to give them a few days' solitary confinement, than, as at present, to keep them for months in one another's infectious society,* by night as well as by day, and giving them as much food as the strongest adult in the building.

There is one suggestion that I must be allowed to make to the magistrates which I am sure they will feel of much importance. It is this: that there are no cells at present in the building, adapted for persons sentenced to solitary confinement. It is the custom now, to place such prisoners in cells on the ground floor, from the windows of which they can freely converse with the prisoners in the adjoining yards, still untried, and consequently never absent. It is self-evident that every object of such a sentence is, by this means, thoroughly defeated. The darkened cells, appropriated to offenders against the rules of the gaol, commonly known by the name of 'Pompey,' have, I grieve to say, been frequently occupied; very often, too, by female

1. Kirkdale House of Correction.

prisoners, many of whom have been most unruly. Having been well drained, they can now be occupied during the night without danger to the health. The gaol has been remarkably healthy during the whole year, and only eight deaths have occurred during that period.

RICHARD APPLETON

## Clean Air: Fresh Air

In 1844 the *Guardian* ran a campaign for open spaces in the town. A series of leading articles were written by Edward Watkin (1819–1901), later the last of the great railway magnates. This campaign arose naturally from the work of the national inquiry into health in large towns. This report included a remarkably thorough investigation into part of Manchester by a surgeon, Mr. P. H. Holland. The first of these extracts is from a leader by Watkins; the second from one which the *Guardian* got Holland himself to write.

### THE NEED FOR OPEN SPACES

Saturday, July 20, 1844

Scantily as the large towns of this country are supplied with places for public recreation, Manchester stands forth in the unenviable notoriety of being almost the only town of importance in the kingdom *entirely* destitute of parks, promenades, or grounds of any kind, for the free use of its population. London has its magnificent parks, Derby its arboretum, the munificent gift of the late Mr. Strutt, Liverpool its parade, Glasgow its Green, stretching for nearly a mile along the banks of its river; yet our own Manchester, needing such public places more than any town in the world, offers its toiling inhabitants nothing better than the dirt and dust of streets and highways. This apparent absence of regard for any thing but mere work, strikes every observer from a distance with the greatest force. The stranger sees, and wonders at, our almost living machinery, and admires the perseverance and devotion of our people. Imagine his surprise when he hears, that this people, the makers and workers of this machinery, the rearers up of an industry which has astonished the world, leave themselves and their children, from year to year, without a yard of ground upon which they can be merry and happy in common! We remember the following passage in a letter from Thomas Carlyle, published last year in the *Guardian*: –

'I have regretted much, in looking at your great Manchester, and its thousand-fold industries and conquests, that I could not find, in some quarter of it, a hundred acres of green ground with trees on it, for the summer holidays and evenings of your all-conquering, industrious men; and for winter season and bad weather, quite another sort of social meeting place than the gin shops offered! May all this, and much else, be amended.'
And disgraced we shall be if it be not amended!

## THE NEED FOR FRESH AIR
### Wednesday, July 31, 1844

The existence of large towns seems to be an essential condition of the present state of English civilisation. Every year sees a larger and larger proportion of our countrymen become, whether for good or for evil, inhabitants of towns; and there seems every probability that this increase of the civic, and comparative decrease of the rural population, will continue. Fully allowing that some great and evident advantages accompany this change, it would be absurd to close our eyes to the fact that the evils also are enormous. Among the most serious of these is the high rate of mortality in all our large towns.

If this be an unavoidable evil, we must submit to it with gallant resignation, however dreadful; but if, on the contrary, it really be, as the commissioners represent it, in a great measure, if not entirely removable, the wickedness of allowing it to continue is equalled only by its immeasurable folly.

If the rate of mortality in the following towns of Lancashire, namely, – Ashton, Bolton, Bury, Liverpool, Manchester, Oldham, Preston, Rochdale, Salford, and Wigan, could be reduced to that of healthy localities, there would be a saving of between ten and eleven thousand lives a year, out of the thirty-two thousand who now annually perish It is believed that improved salubrity to this amount is really attainable, and that, too, by means easily within our reach.

What is the reason that three out of every hundred of the inhabitants of Manchester, for instance, perish every year, while, in healthy country districts, two only die out of the same number in the same period? Our fellow-townsmen are not worse fed, worse clothed, or worse lodged, than the generality of their countrymen, nor are their occupations more unhealthy; and yet three die where only two would in healthier districts! It is well worth our while seriously to inquire the reason, and earnestly to seek the remedy.

The great difference between a country and a town life, as regards health, are that in the latter we breathe a less pure air, and enjoy fewer opportunities of healthful out-door exercise. The purity of the air that we breathe is quite as important to our well-being as the wholesomeness of our food; indeed it is doubtful if it is not more so. All decomposing animal and vegetable matter gives out emanations which are absolutely poisonous, when concentrated; and always injurious, unless existing in exceeding small quantity. We can easily perceive how it happens that one set of streets, which are narrow, built up at their ends, undrained, unpaved, and filthy, may have a rate of mortality twice as high as other streets, open, airy, clean, and dry, though they are in the very same neighbourhood, and are inhabited by the very same classes of people, with similar employments, and rates of wages. The one set of people are living in the midst of foul air and filth – for dirty streets imply dirty houses, dirty clothes, and dirty personal habits; the other are breathing an air comparatively pure, for clean streets facilitate, though they may not cause, the contrary conditions. We need not then be surprised at the different results as to the health of their respective inhabitants.

A large extension of drainage is indispensable. Not only must every street be sewered, but every house must have its drain, and be provided with a plentiful supply of water, to render domestic cleanliness as easy as it is essential to healthful existence.

Besides these measures, which every one will allow to be required, a complete reform of faulty construction of dwellings, especially those for the poor, must be undertaken. An efficient control must be exercised over the builders of dwellings for the poor, to prevent any being erected in which healthful habitation is impossible. Provision for sufficient ventilation must be secured, and protection from cold and damp. If it be argued that this is a question between landlord and tenant, with which the public authorities have no right to interfere, we answer, that not only have they a right, but it is clearly their duty, to prevent the use of an insalubrious house, as clearly as it is to prevent the sale of insalubrious meat. The destructive influence of a bad dwelling-place is as powerful as that of bad food.

# 'Bitter' Observance of the Sabbath[1]

## Wednesday, June 5, 1839

On Monday evening last, a meeting was held of the (so-called) 'Manchester Lord's Day Society,' in the Corn Exchange, to which admittance was had by tickets only, to the following effect: – 'The person presenting this ticket pledges himself not to address or in any manner disturb the meeting.' The room was tolerably well filled; four-fifths of those present being ladies.

After speaking of the institution of a day of rest, as existing in Paradise, though the very toil of man was then but repose – 'the dressing the luxuriant branches of the vine, and training the lovely efflorescence of the flowers' – the Chairman[2] asked how much more *a fortiori*, was a sabbath necessary for fallen man? If lovely in Paradise, it was lovelier in the wilderness into which we were fallen; and if good for man while yet in a state of purity, how much more good for him, now that he was sunk in depravity, and immersed in woe. If rich men and bad men and unwise legislators should take from us the Sabbath, they would break down the barriers that protected the poor man; and hard as was his present toil, he would not then have one-seventh of his time left for himself; his weary bones and aching head and tired arms could not then rest even one day in seven. – After talking of his own delight at seeing the artisan in his 'decent black coat or blue coat with its gilt buttons, kept up against the Sabbath,' going to church, he said if we had not one given and determined day, rescued and redeemed for us by God himself, one would worship God on a Friday, another on Saturday, another on Monday and so on. The very end and intention of the society for promoting the better observance of the Lord's day was to try to rectify and resist the manifold abuses encroaching on that day, and to defend the poor man from the tyranny of the rich man that would make him work on the Sabbath day. (Mr. Stowell was loudly applauded by a number of working men at the bottom of the room.) It was to prevent the poor man from being robbed of that seventh of his time, which, as no man gave him, none had any right to take from him. He advised workmen, young men, clerks, &c. steadily to refuse to work for their masters on the Sabbath.

He did not see why the honest huckster's shop should be shut from Saturday evening to Monday morning, and that he was to be taken

---

1. An original *Guardian* heading with 'bitter' in italic.
2. Rev. Hugh Stowell (1799–1865), Vicar of Christ Church, Salford; noted Evangelical writer and preacher.

advantage of by his dishonest neighbour, who opened his door half-way on the Sabbath; or why the vendors of evil should have the whole Sabbath to themselves – why the public-house, beer-shop, and dram-shop, should be open on the day of rest. If a man were compelled, from necessity, to travel on the Sabbath, he would let him go to rest in an inn; but he would shut the beer-shops and gin-shops from Saturday night to Monday morning; they should not open one inch of their windows or doors. – (Cheers.)

There was now scarcely a large public-house in Manchester which had not got – what did they think? – an organ! To worship the devil with *God's own instrument*! Did he speak severely, or say more than the truth guaranteed and warranted? That organ was got, in order to lead into those houses the unwary young Sunday scholar, the member of the church or the chapel choir, under the fond and flattering pretext, – for it might perhaps afford an opportunity to the ill-informed conscience, or to the conscience willing to be stupefied, that the heart might follow its own lusts, – drawing them in under the pretence that they are going to keep the Sabbath holy by worshipping God there. He then told of a gentleman going into one of these 'synagogues of Satan,' and anything more shocking he had never witnessed. In one corner of the room, a number of persons perfectly drunk, some on the floor; in another, others, drinking and singing profane songs; while around the organ were a number of young people, some of them with babbling tongues singing solemn words. Did it hallow that dark scene that there the name of God was taken in vain under pretence of worshipping him? Now he thought this Sabbath Society, and he was quite willing to do his part in it, ought to ask our magistrates to order these organs to be discontinued; or, if they could not do that, to say to the landlords, 'If you have sacred music in your houses on Sundays, we will not renew your licenses when the license day comes round.' – (Cheers.) The people of Manchester had another noble opportunity of stepping forward; the directors of the Manchester and Leeds Railway were to take in to consideration whether that railway should be kept open on the Sabbath. He could not wish a prouder distinction to Manchester than that she should set the noble example to the nation of closing her railways on the Sabbath-day. Then every town would follow in her wake, and every railway would be closed. Keeping a railway open on the Sabbath-day was a most wantonly gratuitous and ungrateful desecration of the Sabbath.

He rejoiced to think that her Majesty's ministers did not now hold their cabinet councils on Sunday as once they did; he wished the time were come when Hyde Park should be deserted during the Sabbath, and that the Queen went nowhere on the Lord's Day, but to the worship of God, or to walk in her garden. (We are here obliged to stop, having already given ample specimens of the chairman's introductory speech.)

The Rev. Mr. Allen, from Bury, did not like a political priest in any sense of the term; he never had, and never should interfere in politics. But let him tell gentlemen of England, that the question at the next general election would not be corn laws or anti-corn laws; but the great question to candidates would be, 'How are your views upon the education question, and upon the Sabbath question?' Yes, the rallying cry of Great Britain should be, not 'Corn-laws,' nor 'Anti-corn-laws,' but 'Protestanism – No Popery, – Christianity!' – (Question, question.)

Popery belonged to this question. A very talented and very wicked countryman of his had said, that one fact was worth a whole bushel of arguments. The fact would be quite sufficient to prove that popery was not Christianity. – (Hisses.) Popery imagined that as she changed the Sabbath, so she had authority to abrogate it; but we would tell her, that what popery never established, popery should not ever destroy. Popery on the one hand, and infidelity on the other, had common ground of argument, against vital and practical religion. – Popery was a kind of theoretical religion; she was no practical religion at all. – ('Question, question.') (Here the Chairman interposed, intimating to Mr. Allen that he was a little deviating from the purpose and object of the meeting.)

## Arts

### 'FIDELIO'

#### Wednesday, January 30, 1839

The first performance of this splendid opera (though in its English dress) in the provinces, is in itself a sort of era in the annals of our musical history. It would be a theme, in no way flattering to our character as a music-loving people, to speak of the causes why this fine work of genius, unsurpassed probably by any other opera save the *Don Giovanni* of Mozart, has hitherto been to us of the north a sealed volume of the richest melody and harmony. At least a more pleasing task will be, briefly to notice some of the peculiarities of the mastermind whose production has afforded us so much pleasure.

*Fidelio* was first made known in this country, by the excellent

German company in London during the seasons of 1832 and 1833, – when Mademoiselle Schroeder Devroient's performance of *Leonora* showed an English audience what a depth of pathos and intensity of thrilling interest, Beethoven had woven around a simple tale of woman's tender but heroic fidelity. Subsequently the opera was brought out at Drury Lane, in an English dress.

We must now notice the performance of this opera at our theatre last week, – which we might at once characterise as full of beauties and defects; of beauties so far as the composer, and the efforts of Mr. and Mrs. Wood,[1] and we may add Mr. G. Horncastle, were concerned; of defects, so far as to the other principal vocal performers and the choruses. The orchestra contributed its share to both; excellent and correct in most of its music, but feeble from want of the numerical force requisite to bring out the massy grandeur of the author's conceptions. We question whether this opera was ever before left to the orchestral care of some 16 or 17 performers only; certainly it suffered much in effect, especially in the choruses, from this circumstance, though the able and judicious leading of Mr. Aldridge, and the generally good following of his corps, left little to be wished for, but additional strength. The opening duet 'How uninterrupted' was an utter failure; Mr. Barker is a feeble, inefficient tenor, and Mrs. P. Crowe's tones were to us any thing but pleasing; occasionally she was much out of tune.

But for the splendid scena, 'Oh monster,' was reserved her [Mrs. Wood's] full power to astonish, to thrill, and to delight her auditory. We have heard few things more full of the real power of music, linked with the drama, to awaken emotions, deep, varied, and rapid in their alternations. The mingled expression of fear, indignation, and love, driven almost to despair, – which are given in the fine, deep sustained notes which few we think of her auditors could have expected to hear, or remained unmoved on hearing, from Mrs. Wood, – gradually melts down into a strain of great sweetness, in which she apostrophises Hope, – beginning with the words 'Sweet hope I have no friend but thee.'

The closing piece of the second act 'Audacious dotard!' was given with spirit and effect. Indeed, the choruses were, on the whole, as well sung as could be expected, from the very short time allowed the vocalists for study and rehearsals. But still we cannot say that these choruses were of that high character which a Manchester audience is prepared

1. Mary Ann Paton (1802–1864), the best known English soprano of her time, had married Lord William Pitt Lennox, a journalist and author, in 1824, but divorced him in 1831 and married Joseph Wood the same year.

to expect, and which Manchester choral singers are qualified to maintain; and we confess we should have hailed with pleasure the strengthening of the operatic corps, on this occasion, with a number of members from the choral society.

We cannot omit giving another proof of the extent and power of Mrs. Wood's roles. The English words we do not recollect; but in the German score it occurs in the words 'Trost verderben dir!' After holding on E (dotted minim), she passes to G alt, and thence to B flat, in alt, also a dotted minim, which she sustained with a distinctness and fulness of tone rarely equalled. This note falls on the second syllable of *Verderben*, and the two succeeding notes are C sharp and D, the last a semibreve. The whole passage requires great physical power, and the triumphant way in which the vocalist's energy carried her through this succession of vocal efforts cannot soon be forgotten by the musical auditor. We are tempted to think, that Beethoven (possibly from his own privation, without being sensible of the immense exertion and consequent exhaustion, to the singer, of this piece) has laid a cruelly heavy load on the already heavily-taxed vocalist, in the immediately following duet 'No greater bliss,' (in the original '*O namen namenlose Freude!*'). Nevertheless, it was sweetly sung, though very differently from what it could have been, had the composer thrown some other piece between. We must not omit to mention the true nature and forcible effect of the hysteric laugh in which Leonora's over-wrought excitement finds relief, after she has driven the murderer off, and saved the life of her husband. Its effect was electrical; and many ladies were in tears.

We have thus noticed this opera, not so much from any wish to censure, where there was so much to admire, but because we think it impossible that *Fidelio* should not be represented here again and again; and we would have so noble a work treated with full justice, and allowed every legitimate means of making its way to the favour of the public. That this might be done without any large outlay would be easy to demonstrate, the principal *desiderata* being a few additional instruments in the orchestra, half a dozen extra singers for each part in the choruses, and a good powerful bass singer in the part of Rocco. All but the last are within the immediate reach of the management; and we trust that, having done so much and so well, the spirited manager will do a little more, to make *Fidelio* acceptable to the many lovers of music here, who are familiar with it in the language and music of Beethoven.

## SHAKESPEARE IN 1843

There were very frequent performances of Shakespeare at this
time at the Theatre Royal, Manchester. The violence of the
critical comments is the counterpart of the 'robust' political
controversy of the day.

### Saturday, August 5, 1843

#### ROMEO AND JULIET

Mr. Anderson,[1] though perhaps the best Romeo on the stage, does not
give us the same degree of pleasure here that we have derived from the
performance of his Huon, and other characters. The impetuosity
which carries this actor away, and which is admirably suited to the
portraiture of a man with lofty aspirations and of high soul writhing
in the bondage of the serf, or suffering from what he deems the cruel
pride of his lady-love, is in Romeo out of place. Thus it is not to be
wondered at that throughout Mr. Anderson was too loud; even his
soliloquies, in the orchard of his foe's house, were as strepitous as if
challenging the household to oppose him, and, while he overhears
Juliet's apostrophe of love to himself, his 'asides' are delivered in a
tone so loud, that it requires a great effort of imagination in the auditor
to suppose the lady does not hear them. We dwell the more on this
vicious practice in a talented actor, because not only is he the possessor
of a fine strong voice, which reaches over a large area without any
need of shouting, but also because other performers, taking the pitch
from him shouted and screamed in turn. Thus Juliet fell into the error
of answering her nurse (who calls to her from within the house) in a
whisper, while she replies to her lover in a voice so loud that it must
have been heard by the nurse, on all the principles of acoustics. These
things destroy the illusion which it should be the business of the actors
carefully to maintain – certainly not rudely to destroy.

Mrs. Bland's Juliet is not to us a pleasing performance; in the picture
she conjures up of the horrors she may encounter in the charnel house,
she quite out heroded Herod. The careful perusal of Mrs. Jameson's
*Female Characters of Shakespeare* would be of great service to Mrs.
Bland in arriving at the true idiosyncrasy of those beautiful creations of
the poet.

The afterpiece was also Shakespeare's – *The Taming of the Shrew*,
in which Mr. G. Vandenhoff enacted Petruchio, not so much to our

1. James Robertson Anderson (1811–1895), manager at Drury Lane 1849–1851.

taste as Mercutio, but still very ably. He seemed to fail most in representing that quality of firmness, which convinces the observer that to resist is a fruitless task. He was sufficiently boisterous, plied his whip abundantly, and showed his physical superiority over Catherine with great vigour: but he lacked the nice discrimination of that intellectual and moral supremacy which is the real victor of the shrew. Still we repeat, the performance was an able one, and free from any stiffness or want of vivacity. The acting of Mrs. Bland as Catherine was a too sweet sourness: she had rather the pettishness of a spoiled child, than the wilful reckless rebellion of a shrewish tempered woman.

## Wednesday, October 18, 1843

### A ROUGH TEMPEST

In our judgment, the *Tempest* is a play rather for the closet than for the stage. The fatal objection to the *Tempest*, as an acting drama, is, that it is not a play of the passions, but purely one of sentiment and poetic fancy; it contains nothing to call forth the deepest emotions of the heart; it can only please at best; – it can never awaken deep horror or intense sympathy, or open the sluices of joy or sorrow in the human heart. It is in fact, as put on the stage, a pageant dignified by the richest and most imaginative poetry. These circumstances will, to some extent, account for what we must call the general disappointment expressed at the performance of the play on Saturday evening.

But there were other circumstances contributing to this, which, however unpleasant, our duty to the public requires us to notice. We were glad to see the cordial greeting with which the audience recognised a favourite of last season in the garb of *Prospero*; but we must add, that the applause of his performance of that character was subsequently but partial; and, with every disposition to make allowances, we must say that Mr. Butler made a very large demand on the patience and forbearance of his audience. It has rarely been our fortune to hear Shakespeare so mangled by any actor as on this occasion.

One of the best sustained characters in the piece was the *Caliban* of Mr. Bass; it was the best monster we have ever seen. Mr. Davidge's *Stephano* was another able performance; he never forgot his mock gravity or intemperance, and his by-play was exceedingly good. We cannot say much for Mr. C. F. Marshall's *Trinculo*, and we must caution this actor against his coarse tricks, which savour more of a sawdust arena than of the boards of a theatre-royal. Any actor of taste and judgment would feel that, when the dramatist has a passage that may be offensive to a modern audience, the best treatment of it is to utter it quietly and as common-place; instead of which, Mr. Marshall labours to make the most of it, and seems to dwell on it with pleasure, as giving him an opportunity of currying favour with the gallery. This must be amended, and we shall not be disposed to spare any repetitions of this practice. His smelling of 'the monster' was a piece of the coarsest and most revolting acting ever endured by a respectable audience.

## POOR MARY BARTON

Wednesday, February 28, 1849
*From a Correspondent*[1]

If the work had met with the fate of nineteen out of twenty of the novels published now-a-days, I might have been well content to let it sink into oblivion, with its false statements unchallenged, and its doubtful logic unquestioned; but, possessing an internal force and vitality far above mediocrity, it has reached that height of a novel writer's ambition, a third edition, thus showing that it is being well read, and, consequently, that its errors have become dangerous. The authoress of this truthful tale of Manchester life acknowledges that the interests of both masters and men are really the same; and if her intention were to get both parties to act together for their mutual benefit, it would have been well to have considered whether her book would have that tendency or not. As a whole the tale is beautifully written; the characters introduced are graphically delineated; the events are so interestingly interwoven, and the groundwork is so artistically constructed, that whoever reads the two first chapters is sure to read the whole story, and will then be sorry that he can know nothing more about Jem Wilson and his wife Mary; or of Margaret, the once blind girl, and her grandfather, Job Leigh. The only fault of the book is that the authoress has sinned gravely against truth, in matters of fact either above her comprehension, or beyond her sphere of knowledge.

A meeting is called at which about 20 masters meet a deputation of weavers, which body being at the point of starvation, are desirous of arranging matters. Mark well the feelings, conduct, and words of the masters, according to our authoress. 'Some were for a slight concession, just a sugar-plum to sweeten the naughty child' – 'no one

---

1. *Mary Barton* had been first published in 1848. The author, Mrs. Gaskell, was married to a minister at Cross St. Unitarian chapel, Manchester which John Edward Taylor attended. The writer of the article is unknown. It may be W. R. Greg, a mill-owner, who in the 1850s was a regular contributor.

thought of treating the workmen as brethren and friends' – 'I, for one,' says one, 'won't yield one farthing to the cruel brutes; they're more like wild beasts than human beings.'

If such be their character and condition, heavy indeed are the responsibilities of the mill-owners, and great the neglect on their part of their Christian duties. But I deny that such is the case; and in this I am supported by the testimony of many intelligent visitors to the manufacturing districts, whose evidence goes far to show that in physical and intellectual condition, the manufacturing population is superior to that of the agricultural districts.

But to return to the story. At the meeting, a shilling a week more was offered (by the way, power-loom weavers were never paid by the week, but by the piece), which the men refused, and the meeting broke up. Before, however, the deputation left the room, Harry Carson found time to draw a caricature of the five miserable workmen who composed it, which he handed round to the other mill-owners who chuckled over it, and were highly amused. [One of the men got hold of it and] It was exhibited at a meeting soon afterwards, and caused such exasperation among the workmen, that they resolved to murder young Carson, and he was murdered. Every feeling of grief and tenderness in the heart of old Carson was totally absorbed by the thirst for revenge, to be gratified by the immediate punishment of Jem Wilson, the supposed murderer, whom he wished to see executed before his son was consigned to his grave, and followed up this atrocious project with a vindictiveness not to be exceeded by an Indian savage.

Can the authoress believe this to convey a truthful impression of Manchester life? It is a libel on the workmen of Manchester; they never committed a murder under any such circumstances. It is a libel on the masters, merchants, and gentlemen of this city, who have never been exceeded by those of any other part of the kingdom in acts of benevolence and charity, both public and private.

In a truthful 'tale of Manchester, or factory life,' it appears very strange that no notice whatever is taken of what has been done by the masters for improving the condition of the workmen: – for instance, of the day and Sunday schools attached to many mills, and where this is not the case, of the inducements held out for their becoming subscribers to extensive libraries founded expressly for their benefit, or to mechanics' institutions, the management of which are left entirely in their own hands. Nothing is said of the parks which have been purchased, and laid out exclusively for their recreation and enjoyment where thousands of happy and intelligent faces may be seen on Saturday afternoons and on holidays, delighting themselves in innocent games or athletic exercises, nor (when the mills are stopped for the want of a market) of the many instances in which the masters advance their workpeople a weekly sum for their subsistence, frequently given gratuitously. Not one word of all these is there in this 'true tale of Manchester life.'

## Death of Dr. Dalton[1]

### Wednesday, July 31, 1844

Our venerable and venerated townsman – one of the greatest philosophers of his age, and the father of the present race of chemical investigators and discoverers – is no more. Science has lost one of its most devoted sons; England one of its greatest *savants*, and humanity one of its brightest living examples of the wisdom of the philosopher, united to the purity and simplicity of the child; for truly he was 'wise as the serpent, harmless as the dove.' His long and useful life closed unexpectedly, but apparently without suffering, on Saturday morning last.

On visiting the chamber of death several hours afterwards, we were struck with the serene and placid expression of the countenance of the venerable man, which had the appearance of the healthy repose of a brief half hour, rather than the deep and lasting slumber of the grave. His fine massive head, venerable with the silvery hairs of age, and with the still more characteristic expression of a benevolent spirit, with which, even in death his brow was radiant, was a solemn but a gladdening picture. The aspect and features were those of the aged Christian philosopher, who, 'having finished his work' and closed his long and valuable labours, had laid down to rest, calm in the tranquil faith which ever distinguished him, and without one struggle of departing mortality, or one fear of the darkening gloom of 'the valley of the shadow of death,' clouding those features, which still seemed to beam with the light of wisdom, benevolence, and Christian philanthropy.

There follows a 3,000 word obituary.

He took and recorded three observations daily during a period of more than half a century, viz. at eight o'clock a.m., at one, and at nine o'clock p.m. The doctor's bedroom fronts Faulkner-street; and several

---

1. John Dalton (1766–1844), chemist. John Edward Taylor had been taught mathematics by him. The article is by John Harland.

of his instruments are in this room. In a recess, near a window, stands
a desk, on which lay the book in which the observations were regularly
recorded; and on an inner wall of the recess hangs his barometer,
which we are told was made by himself many years ago. It has a somewhat rude and antiquated look, and though doubtless a very accurate
instrument, few of those who judge by external appearances, would be
at all desirous to suspend it in sight, in their houses. Its graduation, too,
is not easily decyphered by a stranger, and besides the original scale,
there is a paper one pasted upon the frame by the side of the tube. On
another inner wall hangs a thermometer for registering the temperature indoors; and nearly every observation respecting the barometer
will apply with equal force to this instrument which was also made by
himself. Formerly he had a second and smaller thermometer, attached
to the brickwork outside a window, of the same room, but as this was
liable to some external influence from the wall, and as it was moreover
not very easily read, Mr. L. Buchan contrived a little apparatus, by
which the thermometer is kept isolated an inch or two from the
window, its tube fronting a pane, so that it may easily be read without
opening the window, by holding a candle close to the glass inside.
With these and other equally simple and apparently rude, but really
exact apparatus, Dalton made those observations, upward of *two
hundred thousand* in numbers, and extending over *half a century*, which
he recently presented to the Manchester Literary and Philosophical
Society. His mode of recording these was as follows: and we cannot
offer a more interesting exemplification of it, than in the three last
lines that were traced by that pen, which could scarcely be held in
the tremulous fingers, now cold and rigid in the grasp of death. The
book was of plain and even coarse paper, ruled in ten columns, as
shown below, and the observations of which we give a copy, were the
three recorded for, and on, Friday last: –

| Day of Month | Hour | Therm. In | Therm. Out | Barom. | Wind | Strength | Rain | Evap. | Remarks |
|---|---|---|---|---|---|---|---|---|---|
| (July) | | | | | | | | | |
| 26 | 8 | 65 | 75 | 30·03 | S.W. | 1 | | | |
| — | 13 | 63 | 73 | 30·10 | Sy | 1 | | | |
| — | 21 | 60 | 71 | 30·18 | S.W. | 1 | little | rain | |

In the column for the hour, the figures '13' and '21' imply one o'clock and nine o'clock, such being the 13th and 21st hours of the day, counting from midnight to midnight.

## The Grand National[1]

### Saturday, March 7, 1840

This event came off on Thursday last; the weather throughout the week had been clear, dry, and frosty. All anticipations were extremely favourable to the chase, though great anxiety was manifested lest it should freeze so intensely as to render the ground too flinty for the horses to run. Many prognosticated that such would be the case, but they proved false prophets. Though the morning of Thursday was keen, with a biting easterly wind, the frost was not so severe as to destroy the elasticity of the turf, and the ground was in the very finest order.

The course marked out by the flags was practically the same as last year. The horses, at starting, had a high bank to get over. Their first leap was over the brook where Conrad last year fell with Captain Beecher. The aspect of this leap had not at all improved in the meantime. A strong rail had been erected on the side from which the leap is taken, and the brook is somewhat more of a 'yawner,' from the circumstance of the banks on the opposite side having given way. The second brook, a very formidable-looking leap, has been narrowed, but as the leap was into a field of wheat, and as the artificial bank is new, the ground was particularly loose and dangerous. Beyond this some of the leaps have been rendered more teasing, as it was believed that the course was too easy after the second leap from the brook had been surmounted. This was merely a ditch with a rail on the opposite side. It is not of any great extent, but of particularly awkward appearance. The leaps from the field to the road near the canal bridge, and from the road to the race course, are both formidable, consisting of a stiff newly-cut hawthorn hedge, so strong that if not cleared both horse and rider would have to bite the dust. At each of these points crowds of people were stationed, the first and second brooks, and the canal bridge overlooking the double leap just described, being the favourite spots. A considerable crowd had also assembled at the starting place.

The betting, immediately before the race, was as follows: –

1. This was the second time the race, then called the Liverpool Steeplechase, had been run.

| | | |
|---|---|---|
| 3 to 1 against | The Nun |
| 4 to 1 ,, | Lottery |
| 6 to 1 ,, | Seventy-four |
| 8 to 1 ,, | Arthur |
| 16 to 1 ,, | Jerry |
| 100 to 3 ,, | Cruikshank |
| 100 to 4 ,, | Valentine |

The horses were started in a cluster, and scrambled over the bank in such a heap that it was difficult to say who was first in the field. The marquis, however, took the lead on The Sea, followed, or rather accompanied by Lottery, Seventy-four, and Valentine, all struggling to be first at the brook. There was some heavy ground, but light fencing to get over before the troublesome leap came into sight. The gallop up to it was over a considerable extent of heavy ploughed field. The first who came up to it, we believe, was Won on Columbine, who took it bravely. M'Donnough on Arthur, Mason on Lottery, Oliver on Seventy-four, the Marquis of Waterford on his horse The Sea, and Power on Valentine, followed almost together. Then came in quick succession Spolance, Jerry, Hasty, Augean, Weathercock, and Cruikshank. Weathercock took his leap well, flying clear over all; but he had scarcely advanced five yards from the brook when he fell heavily, throwing his rider, Barker, out of the saddle. Cruikshank, who was close behind, tripped over him, and rolled on the top of Barker. Both horses were, however, immediately on their legs, and Gray quickly mounted and continued the chase; but poor Barker lay insensible on the turf, and the general impression was that he had been killed on the spot. Mr. Whitty, who was on the spot, caused him to be lifted up and conveyed to a house in the vicinity, where he was attended by Dr. Collins, who happened fortunately to be present. It turned out that Barker had been only stunned, and that, though much shaken, he had not suffered any very material injury.

Meanwhile, the other horsemen pursued their way towards the second brook or artificial ditch. The first horsemen got over cleverly in nearly the same order as at the first brook. Hasty was pushed courageously at the fence, and he cleared all well; but when he got to the other side, he was unable to maintain his footing and he tumbled headlong over throwing his rider on the yielding soil. All the rest got well over. The next leap, a ditch and rail, was cleared gallantly by the whole field, and nothing of consequence remained between the horsemen and the race-course but the two road fences at the bridge, which were got over in good style. There was now a long gallop across the race course in the direction of the grand stand. Valentine, in the course of this run, acquired the lead, and came first to the stone wall, – a jump that was expected to try the mettle of the horses severely. Valentine went over pretty clear; but it was evidently as much as he could compass. Lottery and The Nun came next, and both went down, Mason and Powell being tossed sprawling on the turf. Neither was seriously hurt. A gap had now been effected in the wall, and the Marquis of Waterford jumped at the breach, and went clear away. Arthur and Jerry followed the example, and went close upon the heels of Valentine and The Sea. Seventy-four emulated the example of his old competitors, The Nun and Lottery, and came to the ground, placing Oliver on the list of invalids. The others got through tolerably well; but it was evident that some of them could not last through the race, though the efforts of those who had preceded them had left them little to do, so far as the wall was concerned, parts of it having been almost entirely swept away.

Only five horses managed to get round again to the first brook. Those were Valentine, Jerry, Arthur, Cruikshank and The Sea. The three first were nearly together; Cruikshank was a considerable distance behind, and Gray's face was bleeding profusely from the consequence of his fall. The Marquis was still farther behind, but apparently quite cool and taking it easy. All went over this difficult leap beautifully. M'Donnough, on Arthur, arrived first at the second brook. He bounded over it; but his horse immediately tripped, and tumbled almost heels over head. Jerry and Valentine cleared the ditch, and went away at a good pace towards the goal. M'Donnough remounted in a moment, galloped after them, and was in time to come in second. Jerry cleared the remaining leaps beautifully; and as he entered the course, it became evident that Brotherton must win the race. He kept the lead up to the winning post, and as we have stated above, Arthur, notwithstanding the check which he had received, came in second, Valentine being third.

# CHAPTER THREE

# The Second City of the Empire

*

Manchester men, and not least *Guardian* writers, relished the phrase 'second city of the empire.' It expressed their pride in achievement, their own and their country's. The achievements were not only material. This chapter illustrates some of the aspects of this proud position, and what the paper thought about them – and about less pleasant things as well – the Crimean War and the Indian Mutiny, for instance, and education's failure to keep up with the times.

For the *Guardian* the period divides at the end of 1860 when Garnett and Harland retired. Edward Taylor (1830–1905), the founder's second son, was active throughout both periods. He became sole proprietor in 1854, and was at least nominally editor throughout the sixties, though the greater part of his time was spent on the newspaper industry as a whole – founding the Press Association, for instance. H. M. Acton (1828–1907) joined the paper as a leader writer in 1848, and became the principal one in 1855. Both Garnett's and Acton's sympathies were Palmerstonian – and this was the age of Palmerston.

## The Duke and the Undertaker

### Saturday, November 20, 1852

We have no fear of seeming to speak irreverently, or of causing a jar to the tender feelings with which the whole nation still turns towards the bier of its greatest servant, when we say that it is a relief to be able to record that the Duke of Wellington's funeral is past. We confess that we have not succeeded in discovering, from the tone of public comment or conversation, that anything has been gained to the solemnity or impressiveness of the occasion, by prolonging 'the first dark day of nothingness' to nearly three months, and suffering genuine emotions of sorrow for the dead to be gradually displaced by sympathy with the anxieties of the undertaker. A longer delay than perfect taste would have desired was doubtless unavoidable. Yet, while there was a suspicion abroad that an attempt might be made to interpose the national grief between the deficiencies of statesmen and the censure of the representatives of the people, the warmest admirer of Wellington was the first to grudge every hour by which his last honours were delayed.

It would be vain for any of the present generation to hope again to see a spectacle of kindred and equal greatness; because the opportunities of accomplishing such a career as Wellington's can only occur rarely in the history of the world. Grand sights we may have, of even greater sumptuosity and brilliance – more yards of customary black, – more nodding plumes, – a longer array of marshalled warriors, – and a louder roar of earthly thunder; but the spirit which even the most sensual and ignorant man in that vast conclave could perceive moving over the heads of the funeral procession, will not be among us again until a fresh convulsion of the universe – may it be long distant! – calls to England for a mind of equal capacity, and receives an answer to the call.

In two successive years the inhabitants of the English metropolis have had the fortune to witness two of the grandest spectacles, as well as most impressive historical events, in recent history. There is much of apparent variance, but something also of real similarity, in the ideas evoked respectively by the opening of the Great Exhibition, and the burial of the great military chief. In the first instance, we flattered ourselves that we were performing the baptism of Peace; in the second, we may seem to have buried War, in the person of the last and most illustrious personage of a military age. Yet, it is not wholly so. We fear that we could not do the interests of peace a severer injury than by causing it to be believed that we had interred our martial strength and ardour in the grave of our greatest captain.

# The Crimean War

There had been no major war since Waterloo when Lord Raglan had been 27. Now he was 66 and commander-in-chief in the Crimea. When he died in 1855 the *Guardian*'s London correspondent wrote, 'very little confidence has been, of late, felt in his military genius and strategic ability.' To John Bright (1811–1889) the war was 'a reversion to barbarism.' The paper took a different view:

## THE TEACHING OF HISTORY

### Wednesday, December 19, 1855

With much that he (Mr. Bright) said it would be superfluous to affirm that we entirely agree. That education is a good thing and drinking a bad thing – that books are better than beer, and knowledge than delirium tremens, – with these and similar avowals we are, of course, at one. But all these truisms – valuable indeed and capable of advantageous reiteration though they be – were only a prelude to the real gist of the matter of Mr. Bright's speech. They were what the heavy dough pudding of a schoolboy's dinner are to the tender mutton and the fruit tarts – a sort of pilot engine, to smooth the way for the coming train of remarks. These last, of course – Mr. Bright's rhetorical cakes and ale – were directed in favour of peace, and against all war in general and the present one in particular.

'Read, study, buy books – ponder on them,' says Mr. Bright, 'and you will find that every war is a costly and criminal thing, entailing expense and damage on distant generations.' We say, 'Buy books, read them, study history; make yourselves acquainted with the rise and fall of nations; and thus enable yourselves to judge of the interests of your own country.' But no further do we go with Mr. Bright. Our corollary is not his. From the same data we arrive at a conclusion entirely different. Yes; we too say to the people buy books and read them. Buy books of history and study them. Study the masters who have enriched the mother-tongue of England with the splendid records of the old world's decline and the new world's youth. Study the translations of those older masters, whose truthfulness, comprehensive sagacity, and enlightened patriotism shine through the vault of ages and the dim atmosphere of a score of modern dialects. Then when you have read these golden works, 'golden and worthy of eternal life,' go to your own chambers, ponder over the deeds of the brave and the sayings of the wise, and ask yourselves this question: 'Has there ever lived on earth a people, from the Almighty's favoured race to the lively people of ancient Greece, or the impulsive stock of mediæval Italy, who were great in the arts of peace or strong in the possession of civil liberty, and not equally great in the contests of war, and hardened by its trials?' Why do we still read with undying interest the annals of that small Athenian state, whose whole free population never equalled that of the least of our metropolitan boroughs? Is it for the graceful verse of its tragedians, the rollicking wit of its comedians, or the glowing eloquence of its orators? Not a bit of it. All these treasures of literature are precious to us, because they are the legacy and the inheritance of a freedom gained at fearful odds from mighty hosts. It is because each choric song and each tragic lay breathes of the spirit which drew the sword at Marathon, and baffled the invader at Salamis. Each page of history tells us that it is only so long as a people retain the power of self-defence and the spirit of military resolution, that they can do these things for which the world will rank them among peaceful benefactors; and that, when that spirit and that power are gone, the gift of beneficent and humanising influence has departed also.

As yet the nationality of England is intact. Her national spirit is not dead. The traditions of the past are not lying rusty in the lumber-rooms of men's memories. The greatness of the empire is not become a thing indifferent and of small concern to the mechanic or the peasant. And if they will only so far obey Mr. Bright's directions as to study the comprehensive history of the past; if they will but read and examine these things, we are not afraid even of Mr. Bright's perverse eloquence deadening in them the genial emotions of English pride, and stifling the expression of English patriotism.

## SOLDIERS' LETTERS

For its war news and reports the *Guardian* had to rely on extracts from the London papers, but it kept its eyes open for soldiers' letters home and made good use of them.

Saturday, February 3, 1855

*From a Private*:                                    Scutari Hospital, Turkey,
                                                     28th December, 1854
My dear mother, – It is with the feeling of the sincerest gratitude to an almighty and merciful God, that I am so long spared to write you these few lines. When we got to Balaclava, all of us were eager to land,

we had six miles to march, we had not got many yards before we had to pick our way through the mud. Our guide said to us, 'Never mind the mud, you will have plenty of that by and bye,' and we very soon found it out, for we were up to the knees in sludge and mud, there were three or four poor fellows actually had their shoes and stockings torn from their feet, and were compelled to go barefooted. Some of us not being able to keep up with the remainder, stayed behind; some lay down in the mud exhausted, and it was pouring with rain. Twenty-one of us got lost, and we determined to go no further, we pulled our blankets off, and lay down in the open air for the night. We had not lain long before we were drenched to the skin. Just when one of our small party awoke, there was a French officer passing on horseback; he spoke English, and said he would take us to the 77th's camp; we went with him, and glad enough we were to get into a tent. You may judge my feeling when, in the morning, instead of vineyards and all kinds of fruit being there, it was nothing but complete desert, covered with tents. We had to go about three miles to get a bit of wood to boil our breakfast, and we had to burn the coffee and then pound it on a cannon ball. We had to go a great way for water, such water that you would not look at, so thick with mud. We were turned out the other night about one o'clock; the Russian had advanced into our batteries, but in less than half an hour we were all at it, cannon balls, shells, grape, and canister flying in all directions. It was the first engagement ever I was in; I shall never forget it; but we very soon drove them back. We are now within 200 yards of the walls of Sebastopol, in our advanced works, but no more about that until my next.

The next day I was taken ill with cholera, I was carried into the hospital tent, I got better of that, and then came pains in my feet and swelling, and pains in my chest. I was blistered and sent down to Scutari, about $1\frac{1}{2}$ mile across the water from Constantinople in Turkey; it is a splendid place. I get plenty to eat and drink; I get $1\frac{1}{2}$ lb of bread per day, two pints of tea, one pint of port wine, one pint of arrowroot, one pint of porter, and one fowl or one pound of mutton chop, which I please; but I generally choose the fowl, so you see I live like a king. I am not able to walk, but I have a pair of crutches, I am very weak and in great pain at nights. I like those kind-hearted ladies that are come out here from England, they wait on us just like mothers, and make us lemonade, and anything we can fancy. I often offer up a prayer for you in the middle of the night when pain breaks my slumbers, and wish you were here along with these old widows (?)[1] Dear mother, you must excuse my bad writing, as I write whilst lying on a bed of sickness

1. The question mark is in the original *Guardian* copy.

which is very uncomfortable. I shall not go up to the Crimea before next April, if I am ever able to go up again. We have not received a halfpenny in pay since we came out, so that it is impossible for me to pay the postage, which is only 3d. I am very sorry but I cannot help it, we have no money for anything. I hope you will write to me as soon as ever you receive this, as it will be such a comfort for me to hear from you; send any old newspapers you can get. The troops are dying by scores in a day up at the Crimea, but they will not let you know, the men and horses are just like skeletons. There is a ship in the harbour all in one complete mass of fire, loaded with wine and spirits for the hospital here, – all lost. We had a very rough voyage down the Black Sea. Paper is 2d. per sheet here; I had this by me, or I do not know what I should have done. Good-bye, and God bless you, is the constant prayer of your affectionate son

JOSEPH STRETTON.

*From a Sergeant*:

Headquarters, before Sebastopol,
December 19, 1854

Dear mother and sister,

Many thanks for the stamps, paper, and pens that arrived so timely. My pens and paper were quite done. I can provide paper, but the pens I am so proud of; for English pens cannot be provided. I have been promoted sergeant since the 1st November, over the heads of about twelve lance-sergeants; all quite down in the mouth because they were not promoted. Don't you think it looks well to see your two brothers, one a colour and the other a platoon sergeant. The medal and three clasps that we have to get for the three general engagements will shine on our scarlet coats when we come to see you next year. You must not imagine, my dear mother, that we are starving, or at all in want of provisions. Since I came to the country the wet weather makes it disagreeable to cook our victuals, and fills the trenches with water, where we have sometimes to hide from the Russian cannon. But there is no one fit for the army but a soldier; and it is an old saying, that a soldier should live three days on the smell of an oily rag. Arthur joins in kind love to you; and I am, dear mother, your affectionate son, and your loving brother, Eliza. Direct for Sergeant Robert Stuart, 1st Battalion Royal Regiment, headquarters before Sebastopol, Crimea.

*From an Officer*:

On board Transport – , at anchor in the Bosphorus,

January 17, 1855

My dear——,

I am certain you will be glad to get a few lines from me, so I sit down and tell you all the news. I am now on board ship, in charge of sick soldiers and the attendants. Poor fellows! they are very ill, and we lose many. I read the service over two and three a day; it is, indeed, a very unpleasant duty. I fear that the hard winter out here will ruin our army; and the work is very hard on the men. Often we are only off duty for nine hours at a time. As for myself, I thank God that I have kept up; but my health is not good – I cannot stand the cold and wet. For five days, I had not a dry stitch on me, and I slept in wet blankets. We never take our boots or trousers off, except to get a wash; and that is very seldom, for the water is a long way off. My plan has been to walk to the spring, and strip and wash there; but it is too cold for that, now the snow is on the ground. I really hope Lord Raglan will do something soon, or he will have but a small army left; it is now greatly reduced by sickness. Our companies at first went into the trenches 90 strong, and now we cannot find more than from 25 to 30 men per company; all are sick, and unfit for duty. We are also often obliged to go and fetch our own rations, a matter of 16 miles; and then these poor fellows are for duty or perhaps they had only just come off duty. Now, I should like to know what men can stand such hard work, in such weather – so wet that no fire can be lighted, so they can get nothing warm? The coffee is given to us in a raw state; we have to roast it and grind it ourselves, which we do with a round shot. The pork, if left in water for a few hours, is not so bad; and the biscuit is nearly always very good; the salt beef is not so good. We should get fresh meat once a week, but we have only had it twice since we came to the Crimea; and, I am sorry to say, half rations of provisions and rum is not uncommon with us. Lord Raglan I have not yet seen, but the French general, Canrobert, often rides through our camps; sometimes twice a week. I think if his lordship would show himself to the men now and then it would cheer them up.

Ah, my dear——, I had often heard about the misery of war, &c. but I never thought it was half so terrible. In England the people little know what we go through; the sights you see are fit to break the hardest heart. Only fancy, a few months ago, the Crimea was a lovely spot covered with fine trees and noble mansions. Now all is levelled to the ground, and the roots we are now getting up for firewood. The other day, when we were attacked in the trenches, one of our gallant

fellows bolted home and got into his blankets. Luckily the sergeant of
the tent was in, and he said, 'Where have you come from?' 'Why,' says
he, 'them Russians made such a noise they frightened me; so I came
home.' He was, of course, confined, tried, and flogged. Well, at the
parade, I just cast my eye around me, and I could see poor fellows on
stretchers going to their long homes, others being assisted to the
hospital tent, men dragging dead horses away, and a man being
whipped, all this at one view. Oh, I sincerely pray God that the war
will soon come to an end.

Yours affectionately, ―― ――

## The Indian Mutiny

When Lord Canning became Governor-General of India in
1855, the *Guardian*'s 'private correspondent' in London wrote:
'He will become, personally, one of the most popular and conciliatory governor generals and these personal qualifications are
not unimportant when the modern theory imposes on the
governor general the duty of gaining the confidence of the
natives of India by cultivating a friendly, social intercourse with
the educated class of Hindoos.' Two years later came the Indian
Mutiny. 'Those disasters and troubles,' a *Guardian* leader remarked, 'are not wholly devoid of a character of a reasonable
retribution' since they were caused in part by the fact that 'the
English officer, from being the friend, the comrade, and the
adviser of his native followers, has become, in too many instances, haughty, insolent, and vain, looking at his military profession only as a stepping stone to dignified civilian employment, and the speedy acquisition of wealth.'     August 1, 1857.

## 'THE SPLENDID PRIZES OF AN INDIAN CAREER'

*Monday, December 10, 1855*
*From a Private Correspondent*[1]

London, Saturday
Very few persons in London, and scarcely one of your readers perhaps, have ever paid a visit to the East India Company's military
seminary, at Addiscombe. Twice a year the chairman and directors
issue their invitations to a few of their private friends, to distinguished

1. The writer is most likely to have been W. R. Greg.

Indian officers who may happen to be in this country, and to the ministerial functionaries charged with Indian affairs, requesting their presence at the half-yearly examination of the gentlemen cadets. Yesterday I had the honour to be included among the invitations.

What Addiscombe is for the Indian army, the college of Haileybury (in Hertfordshire) has been for the civil service, viz. the nursery from which the East India Company draws its supplies of young men who administer law and justice among millions of Hindoos. But, while Addiscombe escaped intact from the reforming provisions of the recent East India Act, the fiat went out against Haileybury, which, in a year or two, when present nominations have expired, will be shut up. The government bill, as originally brought in, contained a clause throwing open all the nominations to the Indian army, as well as to the civil service, to public competition. But it was represented to the ministry that, if the nominations to Addiscombe were thrown open, young Hindoos or Mahometans might be sent over to compete for them, and having once gained commissions in the Indian army, might rise to high rank and commands therein. It seemed to be assumed that English rule is not so popular in India, that a Hindoo Napoleon can be safely trusted with the command of any large force of Sepoys. The government, giving way to these hints, made no alterations in the existing regulations of Addiscombe. The chairman and directors of the East India Company still, therefore, possess the right of nominating gentlemen cadets to Addiscombe; and a most valuable piece of patronage it is, since, if a lad is able to pass the necessary examinations, the splendid prizes of an Indian career are open to him, and he enters at once upon pay and allowances sufficient to support him in comfort and respectability.

It is impossible to put a money value upon a presentation to Addiscombe or Haileybury; but, in by gone days, when society was more corrupt than we believe it to be now, very considerable sums used to be given for nominations to the two colleges; and directors have been arraigned in our courts of justice for trafficking in these appointments. The gentlemen cadets are not educated at the sole expense of the company, since it is estimated that every cadet costs his friends £200 a year while in the college. At Haileybury, the term fees and personal expenses exceed this sum. But the East India Company pay their officers, both civil and military, so liberally; and talent and integrity in India, may in the long run look so confidently for a satisfactory reward, that every engine of influence has been brought to bear upon the directors to obtain presentations. Influential holders of East India stock knew so well how to make a bargain with a candidate for the honour of a vacant seat in the direction, that when he found himself successful, he usually discovered that his patronage was pledged for many years to come; and that great London bankers and retired Scotch East Indians had first to be served before he had any patronage to bestow upon his own sons, nephews, and dependents.

Let the reader now imagine himself in the large schoolroom of the college. A hundred and fifty English lads, glowing with health and exercise, and wearing the handsome uniform of a gentlemen cadet, – dark blue, with red cuffs and collars, and decorated with gold lace, – are seated upon forms placed longitudinally along an oblong room with an open space in the centre. At a table at one end, are seated the chairman, deputy-chairman, and directors of the East India Company, who are invested, in the imagination of these lads, with majesty indescribable; for are they not the dispensers of collectorships[1] and commands, and has not each director more solid good things in his gift than many a petty potentate in a German principality? Upon the right of the chairman sit the professors, an awful band of grey-headed men whose nod is fate. A little nearer to the boys is the public examiner, always an officer high in the Queen's army, who in all the glory of full regimentals, with his medals and decorations, is the living impersonation of the glories of a successful military career.

When all are seated and silence is called, the public examiner calls the name of some cadet in his last term, and tells him to demonstrate some mathematical problem of demoniacal abstruseness and difficulty. The cadet leaves his seat, and goes to the end of the room, opposite to the chairman, where several large black boards are reared upon stands. Here, provided with a piece of chalk, he commences under the eyes of all beholders to arrange his squares and cubes, his forces and equivalents. When Mr. Brown is under weigh, Mr. Jones is called upon to expound some theorem of even greater perplexity; and he is followed by Mr. Robinson, until every black board is in process of being covered with white hieroglyphics, at which Œdipus would have stood aghast, seeing that mechanical philosophy was not much cultivated in that day, in its relation to the laws of projectiles. As soon as Mr. Brown is ready he takes a wand, and demonstrates his problem, the public examiner being careful to see that every link in the chain of reasoning is complete. Mr. Brown is rewarded by a 'very well'; and his schoolfellows look at each other, and think him safe for the Engineers. Mr. Jones is more nervous – has to be told to 'speak a little louder,' if he pleases – omits some of the intermediate steps of the demonstration, and is dismissed with 'that will do, sir.' Mr. Jones is known to be a

1. 'Collector of Taxes' – a grade in the Indian Civil Service.

good mathematician; but the lads suspect he will find himself among the artillery, and that Madras or Bombay may be his lot, instead of the golden presidency of Calcutta.

## THE INDIAN MERITOCRACY

Open competitive examinations for the Indian Civil Service had been introduced just before the Mutiny, fifteen years before they were applied to the Home Civil Service. According to the *Guardian* of March 21, 1862, the successful candidates included

| | |
|---|---|
| Sons of | |
| Church of England clergymen | 21 out of 38 |
| Gentlemen | 8 out of 15 |
| Physicians | 4 out of 6 |
| Mechanics | 3 out of 7 |

| | | |
|---|---|---|
| Surgeons | 2 | |
| Missionaries | 2 | |
| Cheesefactors | 1 | number entered not stated |
| Confectioners | 1 | |
| Wrights | 1 | |

## A SURGEON AT CAWNPORE

*To the Editor of the 'Manchester Guardian'*

Monday, February 8, 1858

Sir, – I herewith forward you extracts of a letter from my brother,[1] who is an assistant surgeon in the Company's service, and now doing duty at Cawnpore. I wish you to make what use you think proper of this news from the hospital at Cawnpore; and am, Sir, your obedient servant, Henry Planck, 10 Lever St., Manchester, Feb 6.

Cawnpore, Dec. 14, 1857

During the six days we were in the intrenchments, I had tremendous work. All the wounded in the two previous battles outside were brought in. The first day I amputated eight limbs, dressed more than eighty wounds, and so on every day, eating biscuit and beef and drinking tea, or water, when the opportunity offered. Three round shot passed through my hospital roof, bringing down plenty of tiles

1. Charles Planck

and dirt, but injuring no one. The bullocks and camels suffered most, several being killed. Plenty of bullets pattered against the walls, but they were too high for mischief, because the earthworks protected the lower part. The hospital has again been removed to what was formerly the dragoon barracks, nearer the intrenchments than the place I told you of last. We have now 800 sick and wounded, with one surgeon (Dr. Dioper) and eight assistant surgeons. The work I have done lately no one would credit: during the time we were in the fort, six days were but as one of incessant toil. The hard work had one beneficial effect upon me, that I felt almost indifferent to the proceedings of the enemy, though, towards the end, I was almost done up. Jaller's (his Indian servant man) expression was, 'Sir, the works has dried you up. If mem sahib (the mistress) could see you now, she would indeed cry.' However, thank God, I am all right again. All my clothes were spoiled with blood. I went about in my shirt sleeves and bareheaded; my hair was matted with blood; my hands and arms covered with blood; blood spited from arteries into my mouth and eyes; indeed I was covered with blood. How many bullets I extracted – how many wounds I probed, and stanched and dressed – how many operations I performed or assisted at – I cannot say; but, certainly, I saw more surgery than most surgeons witness in a life time; and I trust I am proportionally improved by my experience. I cannot spare one thought to the future as regards my own prospects. It has pleased God to separate me from those who are near and dear to me; but of one thing I am sure – I am only doing my duty; here in my place amongst those who fight, and bleed, and die; they are noble fellows, and whilst I have strength I will work for them with my whole might. Ay, these country-men of ours are indeed noble, noble fellows. Trust me in this, I have cause to know the truth of what I say; for I am with them in their pain, and misery, and death, and I am always impressed with their noble courage and patient endurance.

At present my horizon is not bright; the dangers encompass us on every side; the enemy are all around, intent on killing, and death walks hourly by my side, so I must be prepared lest my time should come; and should it please God so to cause it, my greatest comfort in that sad hour will be that you and my precious children are safe in happy old England, and my brave little son must be taught that his father's last wish was that he devote his whole life to love and protect his mother.

## ATROCITY-MONGERING

What actually happened in India during the Mutiny was bad enough; what was reported to have happened was infinitely worse.

Saturday, February 6, 1858

Treacherous and cruel as have certainly been the enemies who have started up from the ranks of our dependents, the error of imputing to them an excess of infamy from which they shall hereafter be proved to have been substantially free, must be held to reflect discredit on our national fairness as much as it has disturbed our policy and needlessly lacerated our feelings. Much of the reproach for this strange mistake, should it really have been committed, may be thought to rest upon the public press in this country and India, but only because they are the channels through which impressions of passing affairs are communicated to the world at large. Belief in horrible stories of torture, mutilation, and dishonour worse than death, inflicted on our countrymen and countrywomen in India, has been universal. Every organ of opinion has echoed it. In as well as out of Parliament, it has been professed as an article of unfaltering faith. If anywhere there has been a man who has doubted that the general course of the mutiny has been stained by crimes perpetrated with the object of inflicting on the English race not only loss of dominion but ineffable shame and humiliation, we do not know where the head of the sceptic has been concealed. The sources from which the common conclusion of the public has been derived are too well known to require to be indicated. Countless letters from the scene of disaster and suffering, confirmed, as it seemed, over and over again, by the testimony of witnesses of the visible consequences of Indian savagery, both in Calcutta and England, have strengthened the painful impression day by day.

Cause for misgiving was furnished some months ago by the authoritative denial given by the *Lahore Chronicle* to the story that Miss Jennings – whose name is associated in this country with exposure to indescribable insult – and Miss Clifford were outraged previous to their murder at Delhi. But these isolated instances of disputed statement were little heeded in the prevalence of the general impression. The leadership of the change of opinion which has visibly set in, is due to a correspondent of the *Times*, apparently filling a judicial position in India, and writing with an unquestionable sense of the gravity of his theme. He declares his total dissent from the belief that the incensed Indian soldiery, besides murdering their English victims of all ages and sexes, inflicted upon them torture and disgrace. 'Having visited almost every place from which such stories could have come,' he says, 'I have not learnt one instance in which anyone has survived to tell of injuries suffered. I believe there is not one mutilated, tortured, or, so far as I can gather, dishonoured person now alive.' 'I will say positively,' he adds, 'of my own knowledge, that nine tenths of the stories told are not to be heard at all on the spots to which they have reference; it is only as we get farther and farther off that they grow and acquire force and circumstantiality.' Specific instances of the disappearance of revolting narratives, as they were traced to their ostensible origin, are adduced in example.

The effect produced was apparent a day or two afterwards, in a statement published by the desire of the General Committee of the Mutiny Relief Fund. The members of this body wished it to be known that they had ascertained that no cases of mutilation by the Indian mutineers had come down the Ganges in any of the vessels of the Inland Steam Navigation Company at Calcutta, nor had any come to England in any ship belonging to the Peninsular and Oriental Steam Company. This declaration may well have affected those who read it with astonishment only less than their thankfulness; for, surely, we have had detailed accounts of the arrival of persons barbarously mutilated, not only at Calcutta, but at Southampton. Where is the workshop of horrible fiction by whose ingenious manufactures we have been so monstrously deluded?

# Machines and Men

The Great Exhibition of 1852 set a fashion. In 1855 it was the turn of Paris. This involved a State visit by the Queen and the Prince Consort to Napoleon III. The first of these three extracts is by the *Guardian*'s first regular foreign correspondent, the mysterious 'M.X.', whose identity is hidden even in the ledgers by initials. It sets the ceremonial scene, and adds a pertinent social comment. The second deals with that aspect of the exhibition which really caught the imagination of the age. For this the *Guardian* had sent over Grenville Withers. The third extract describes the launch of *Leviathan*, an occasion which might be compared with our Concorde's first flight. It was held to justify the unusual expense of a really long telegram. The last extract is from an early travel article.

## LIBERTY AND EQUALITY

Monday, August 27, 1855
*From our own Correspondent*

Paris, August 24

I confess to being still under the impression of last night's fête, than which anything more splendid can never be offered to mortal vision. One is almost unable to pick out any one distinct object. No, I am wrong there; there is (or rather was) one which, were I to live a hundred years, I should never forget. I mean the staircase, built up in the Cour de Louis XIV. That is, without exception, the most beautiful thing, in the way of decoration, that I think the human imagination can conceive. How to describe it I really know not. Fancy a double staircase, somewhat after the fashion of the famous one at Chambord, winding upwards from a gigantic vestibule, or covered court, and leading at once into the throne-room. In the centre is a group representing France and England united, and below this group a fountain, or rather *bassin*, of clear water, wreathed round with flowers, and whose waves are fed from the urns of two reclining statues, representing one the Seine, the other the Marne. I cannot paint to you the charming effect of these two water-nymphs, in the midst of the broad-leaved water plants, the lilies, flags, and rushes that seemed with their very aspect to cool the air. But above everything lovely was the chandelier that lighted the staircase. I could have imagined nothing so exquisite, and I confess to being haunted by this beautiful invention. This is the staircase which I told you would be used only by the Queen and the two courts, and then destroyed. With the exception of such decorative inventions as the one I have just spoken of, all these kind of fêtes are the same; fine rooms, stirring music, flashing lights, glittering jewels, pleasant refreshments – these constitute everywhere the materials for such pageants; and, after all, when you have seen some dozen of them, you have seen all.

There is, however, something which may perchance not get in the London papers, and which I cannot help thinking very interesting for the readers of so-serious a journal as the *Guardian*. You may think I have latterly often referred to the *Siècle*, the paper you hear least of in England; but I do so for what seems to me a very good reason. The *Siècle*, which, whatever people may say of it who perhaps never read a column in it in their lives, is an essentially moderate journal, and it is now, in France, the only popular paper. The *Siècle* is the paper of the shopkeeper and the ouvrier – the paper without which no man of the lower orders ends his day. It has 45,000 subscribers, and may fairly boast that there is not a hamlet in France where it is not read. It is now the only journal which the lower orders trust; they believe in it entirely; and I must say it does but very little in any way to mislead them. I, therefore, hold that the words of such a paper are entitled to attention: 'England, who to-day visits us in the persons of the Queen and Prince Albert, is possessed of all her liberty. Nay, more than merely possessing, she has no fear of it; and every day causes its benefits to be more widely spread – one proof of this is sufficient: the satisfaction expressed by ministers, in the speech from the throne, at having abolished the stamp duty upon newspapers, and thus enabled instruction to penetrate everywhere more largely into the popular masses.[1] But if England, in coming to visit France, can in no way salute a sister in freedom, we, at the same time, do possess certain things which, by a strange contradiction, are wanting in the English. We are a nation of democracy and equality. With us the soldier becomes a general – the peasant, proprietor – the clerk, minister. If to our equality we could add liberty, with all the vast developments it enjoys in England, we should be very near to the realisation of the principles of our immortal revolution of '89. – On the other hand, England could only gain in imitating our principles of equality.'

M.X.

---

1. It had made it possible, and indeed necessary, for the *Guardian* to become a daily.

## ENGINEERS – THE STRONG MEN OF THE AGE
### Tuesday, August 28, 1855

Figure to yourself a gallery upwards of 4,000 feet long, in one straight line, covered by a semi-cylinder of glass, and decorated through its entire length with many-coloured star-spangled flags, union-jacks, and tricolours. Such is the 'Annexe.' Every nook of the immense place is filled with objects and materials indispensable to arts and manufactures; not a corner is there to spare for the display of articles of mere luxury. It is a temple dedicated to industry, and filled with the *chefs d'œuvre* of labour and genius. Every machine for locomotion, from a railway engine to a wheel-barrow – every utensil, from a vacuum sugar refiner to frying pan – every tool, from a Whitworth's duplex lathe to a black-smith's asp – is there, the best of its kind in existence. Such a sight was never seen before. The magical effects of the Crystal Palace have not been attempted. The senses are not bewildered by an undefined, almost painful astonishment; there is absolutely nothing to dazzle or amaze – all is positive. You are here shown the means, in every known combination, by which materially 'we live, and move, and have our being,' the sources of a people's wealth and an empire's strength. You witness the whole results of what has been discovered in science and art from the first man, Adam, until now. You get the actual measure of the human mind, the data for observation of its future growth, and, by the aid of a lively imagination, the formulae for calculating the time when there will be no more to discover nor invent, and the great designs of creation will be known and accomplished.

Before taking special notice of the engines and machines in the 'Annexe,' let us say a word or two of the engineers and machinists; the really strong men of the age; the improvers and inventors of those metallic wonders which, without possessing the faculties of sight and touch, do the work of hands and eyes with unerring precision, and neither get drunk nor turn out. Those worthies – not the machines, but the machine inventors – of whom the world has such cause to be proud, are now in congregation at the universal exhibition in anxious competition for the meed of distinction to be awarded by the judges of constructive excellence, whose verdicts, as is well known, are not always according to the evidence. It may be told beforehand, without pretension to the gift of prophecy, that, unless the miracle of the loaves and fishes be repeated on the exhibition medals, there will be much heart-burning, gnashing of teeth, and abundant explosions, not loud but deep, of the vulgar tongue.

The jury have a difficult task to learn for themselves, and a still more delicate one to teach the exhibitors. They are honest men and sincere; but human judgment is frail; and no man living is quite impartial in his awards to the merits of others. They are charged with an unenviable duty, and feel they must [do] the impossibility of satisfying themselves or doing full justice to fair claims. There is learning enough amongst them; but the real merits of an invention, and the machine that best realises the inventor's meaning, are not to be determined by algebraic signs. These are not ill-natured remarks, quite the reverse. The intention is to show the folly of giving rewards to engine and machine makers. With the highest respect for the jurors, let it be asked if, amongst the whole brigade, there are a dozen who can distinguish a Whitworth's duplicate lathe from a grinder's polishing wheel? Are there three amongst them really capable of pointing out, or truly appreciating, the very remarkable perfection of Mason's slubbing and roving frames. To see the jurors 'dressed in a little brief authority,' as I see them every day, scrap-book and pencil in hand, wandering in search of something, peeping at machines and jotting down notes, looking all the while as knowing and as pompous as a stoker's pupil; to see this, I say, is an incident for a six months' laugh. It is subject of common remark that, excepting one or two practical men, the rest are as much puzzled to understand the complex combinations of mechanical transmission before their eyes as our plain, simple, honest George III was to divine how the apples got into the dumpling. Under such circumstances, no inventor, or machinist, need be surprised at being passed over by an 'honourable mention,' or forgotten altogether. He must expect to see the gold and silver distinctions carried off, for the most part, by that curse to mechanical genius, brain stealers – men who grow rich and insolent by piracy, and never praise or encourage an improvement they cannot or dare not steal.

But whilst whipping partial wrong, let us console ourselves with the certainty of general good. The universal exhibition at Paris is a great, a glorious reality; it will, because it must, be followed by mighty results; the advancement of industrial art, the increase of social happiness, and a more logical appreciation of public freedom.

GRENVILLE WITHERS

## THE LEVIATHAN AFLOAT AT LAST

Brunel, the great railway engineer, was also a steamship man. His wooden paddle-wheeler, the *Great Western*, in 1838 crossed the Atlantic in 15 days. In 1845 his iron, single screw *Great Britain* knocked half a day off this record. In 1858 he built the *Leviathan* (renamed the *Great Eastern*) which was far larger than any ship of the time and comparable in size with the Atlantic liners of fifty years later. She had both paddle wheels and a single screw. On her maiden voyage an explosion killed five men; Brunel died a few days later. The *Great Eastern* was used mainly as a cable-laying ship.

Monday, February 1, 1858
*From our own Correspondent*

(By British and Irish Magnetic Telegraph)

London, Sunday Evening
The metropolis below bridge has forgotten, to-day, its usual strictness of Sunday observance, in its anxiety to see the monster ship take the water. The high wind of yesterday prevented Mr. Brunel from taking advantage of the spring tide. Captain Harrison, as the sun went down, wished for wind and rain enough to knock his hat in, and a storm of the desired pitilessness broke upon the metropolis in the night, and cleared the atmosphere, exactly as the captain had foreseen. The wind fell, and a day of April warmth and brilliancy succeeded, to welcome the Leviathan into her native element. The river was covered with innumerable two-oared boats, which were laden to the water's edge with reckless sightseers. Five tug steamers were at hand to tow the big ship from her cradle and were sailing round her as circumstances rendered necessary. The Greenwich and Woolwich boats reaped a rich harvest; for, as the news spread, every boat up and down was densely crowded, and every available point on both sides of the river, from which people on shore could see anything of the launch, was occupied. Flags waved from the taverns and ships, and the cheerful sounds of church bells, and the occasional cheers of the crowd, would have led a stranger to suppose that some day of great festal rejoicing had arrived.

About noon the men in the yard began to work the rams, and at half-past one o'clock the Leviathan had been propelled along the rails no less than 60 inches. During all this time the engine continued to discharge water on board, a little before two the monster craft began to show unmistakable symptom of liveliness at the stern. As her buoyancy became more marked the steamers in mid-stream pulled her broadside on towards the river. As she slowly sailed away from her shore cradle, the workmen in the yard set up a hearty cheer, which was responded to by those on board. Two steam tugs were then stationed at her bow, and took up the pulling, and the last chain cable that held her to the shore was let go with a noise that reverberated through the iron mass like thunder. An extraordinary spectacle was now afforded by the stern cradle, upon which half the ship's huge weight has so long rested. These massive baulks of timber were only kept together by the superincumbent mass, and when the Leviathan floated away from her cradle the huge timber darted up about 20 feet above the surface of the water, in a perpendicular direction, falling about in alarming proximity to some of the pleasure boats; the cockneys in which might be pardoned if for a moment, they regarded them as sharks, or other monsters of the deep, springing out of the water at them.

The scene on board the Leviathan was exciting, and to strangers somewhat bewildering. Captain Harrison, who has been playing an amphibious part hitherto, as soon as the ship became lively in the water, took his speaking trumpet and became thoroughly at home and in his element. Now he was at the bows telegraphing to the steam tugs or making the workmen haul in the cables with a will; anon he was amidships, calling for axes or sledge hammers, and directing men to cut ropes with their knives, or do anything else that a critical emergency invited. Mr. Brunel, who had now changed places with Captain Harrison, was also very busy on deck, giving orders to the shore people, and catching hold of a speaking trumpet – performances which he varied by occasionally tumbling over ropes, and having narrow escapes of precipitating himself into the ship's hold or over the sides. The Marquis of Stafford, Mr. Henry Bentinck, M.P. with other noble lords and gentlemen, were on deck, in everybody's way of course, but delighted to be on board during the launch. Mr. Howlett, the eminent photographer of Bond-street, who has taken a variety of exquisite photographs of the Leviathan in all stages of her progress, and who has photographed the engineer, the shipbuilders, the directors, the visitors, Mr. Trotman, the celebrated inventor of anchors, the press, and everybody and everything connected with the ship, was on deck with his camera, giving the last finishing scene of the work, and taking Mr. Hope, the chairman of the company, in with a view of the deck.

The steamers and boats which covered the river, the marines who thronged together to see the launch from the Deptford dockyard wharves, the crowds everywhere observable in the streets and on the jetties, the music of the bells, and the beautiful sunshine, the trampling of workmen fore and aft, the roaring noise of steam from the tugs, and the hoarse cries exchanged between the Leviathan and her little satellites, made up the assemblage of sights and sounds which, considering that the day was Sunday, a man would scarcely wish to see and hear more than once in his lifetime; but which the necessity being conceded he would be sorry to have missed.

Slowly the gallant ship moved away down the river from the Ship Yard, which has so long been impatient of her presence, and which was piled with timbers, the *débris* of the launch. 'I wish,' exclaimed Captain Harrison, as she made way, 'I had her rudder up, that I might move her as I like. I am afraid of the paddle wheels coming in contact with the barges.' In two minutes, the fear was shown to be well grounded. Two barges at the bows on the river side had been employed as a purchase to hold the chain cables. The paddle wheel on the river side drifted against the first of these barges, and all attempts to extricate the wheel or remove the barge were useless. In vain the steam tugs pulled the ship ahead; in vain a tug attempted to drag the barges away. The moment was critical, for three o'clock had arrived, the tide was on the turn, and in a few minutes the monster ship might be drifting helplessly into the river broadside on, and swamping every craft between Millwall and London Bridge. Sledge-hammers were sent for; the sturdiest artisans hammered away at the iron paddle wheels of the Leviathan without making the smallest impression. Again the tug shifted her position. The barges were immovable. 'Axes,' cried Captain Harrison; they were brought, and one of the barges was soon scuttled; another judicious tug from the little steamer and the paddle wheel cleared the remaining barge. A mighty shout from the boats and shore welcomed the victory, and again shout after shout rent the air as the mighty Leviathan, now fairly afloat, and clear of all obstacles, was towed to her moorings in the middle of the river. The Leviathan was launched at last, and the news, quickly circulating throughout the metropolis, has diffused as much joy as that of some great victory. The view of the monster ship in the water confirms the anticipations of those who declared that her bulk would never be properly realised until she was afloat among other craft, – the beauty of her lines, the sharpness of her bows, the amazing length of hull, which strikes the eye as it runs along it with a new sensation, the magnitude and solidity of her stern, will render her an object of admiration to the nautical man, and of ceaseless wonder to the public.

## THE MID-VICTORIAN TOURIST

By 1850 railways and steamships had enabled people to get about quickly and come back on time. Middle-class people were going farther afield for their holidays, and newspapers catered for and helped to create the habit. Harland, for instance, wrote travel series on the English Lakes and Paris as well as Ireland, where he 'did' Killarney in 1852.

### Saturday, August 7, 1852

From Cork to Bandon, the tourist usually travels by rail, 19 miles; the line was opened on 6th December last. I was sorry to find along the country manifest symptoms of the potato disease, and I saw some exceedingly bad cases. Still, however, the mischief is neither so slight on the one hand, nor so severe on the other, as you find asserted in different localities. The solution of the discrepancy is this: – The early potatoes, in the vicinity of large towns, are so much in advance of the disease, that though it affects the haulms, which die down and exhibit every symptom of the rot, it does not reach the tuber before that is ready for gathering. Hence in the neighbourhood of Bandon they tell you that the potatoes are not so bad as they look. But in the rural districts between Cork and Bandon, where the soil is luxuriant, and the farming very superior, the late potatoes, which are the kinds more generally planted for the great supply of the country, are suffering very much from the disease.

Bandon is a small, neat and comparatively prosperous town, and parliamentary borough, for which Viscount Bernard, son and heir of the Earl of Bandon, has just been re-elected. The parliamentary influence which returns his son is not his, but that of the Earl of Shannon, the purchaser of the property of that nobleman, recently in the market. Here the shoal of tourists seemed to have exceeded the means to float them onwards to the Killarney lakes; and nearly an hour was lost in packing them inside and outside (everyone of course preferring the outside) of coaches and outside cars at the railway terminus. At length, by dint of shouting and swearing and doing and undoing, waiting for a drag-chain gone to the smithy for repairs, and (just at starting) breaking a splinter-bar, which gave an opportunity for procuring from a neighbouring inn a bottle of Bass, almost a necessity under a sun whose fervour excited unpleasant apprehension of a coup de soleil to those who sat impatiently on coach tops and outside cars, waiting for a start, – we got off. We had a long and weary drive to

Bantry, through undulating and but half cultivated country; making a long stop at Dunmanway. Here a small grocery store found a market amongst thirsty tourists for sour porter and for 'potheen,' which native manufacture he vended at a penny a glass, as much as would be charged 8d. or 1s. in England.

A good, large inn is at length reached, the new inn at Glengariff, which has only been erected a few months. At Glengariff is a poor, half-witted young man, who gets a few pence by reciting a list of what he calls 'the fish in the say.' His catalogue is rather curious, and, omitting numerous repetitions, runs somewhat as follows: –

'Then there's the hakes, and the haddocks, and the glishogues, and the rogahauns, and the cangers [conger eels], and the lings, and the throuts [trout], and the sawmons [salmon], and the brames [bream], and the mackarels, and the phytings [whiting], and the flat-fish, and the skadhawns [anglicé, herrings], and the pilchards, and the shprats, and the maywanns [a sort of rock weed], and the trepauns [another seaweed], and the barnicles, and the oyshters, and the mushills [mussels], and the peritinkles, and the sayweed [seaweed], and the liak [a sort of moss], and the crabs, and the lobshters, and the monseens, and the cravaunes, and the talabars, and the dolomans [I could get no translation of these names], and the turbots, – and that's all.'

Above the old inn, in its grounds, is a steep woody eminence, half grove, half orchard, from which a splendid view is had of the whole extent of the bay, as it lies stretching its lake-like, placid surface to the sea, where its entrance is some 12 to 14 miles wide. I saw it before sunset, and again under the radiance of the almost full moon, and I know not under which light it is most beautiful.

### Wednesday, September 1, 1852

And now adieu to Killarney. We secured outsides on one of the coaches for Mallow; for the flood of the tourists over-flowed two coaches, even to filling an outside car in addition. The road gradually became less interesting, as we put more distance between us and the scenes of beauty we had left behind, till at length we rolled along between bogs and peat mosses, barren moors and stone hedges, with here and there a mud cabin; the only accompaniment of our ride, one which never grew scarce, being the tribes of beggars, that on the noise of wheels, came rushing down hills and over bogs to the road, running alongside the coach, barefoot, for miles, the young ones screeching for a 'a harp-penny,' the elders in whining tones imploring 'the price of a loaf,' for 'the lone widdy,' or 'the mother of six children and nivver a bite to give them'; and so on. Many of these beggars are clever artists and actors in their own way, both in their piteous appeals, their witty replies, and their admirable 'make-up' of rags.

## Arts

## ART TREASURES FROM AGNEW AND DEBRETT

The Art Treasures Exhibition in Manchester in 1857 was unique. The Queen, the Dukes of Bedford, Buccleuch, Hamilton, Manchester, Marlborough, Newcastle, Northumberland, Portland, Richmond and Wellington lent exhibits as did four Marquises, twenty Earls, and twenty-two Barons. Manchester merchants were great collectors, especially of the English school. The exhibition was opened by the Prince Consort. More than 1,250,000 people visited it.

### Tuesday, May 5, 1857

'What in the world do you want with art in Manchester? Why can't you stick to your cotton spinning?' So a noble is said to have inquired when applied to for a contribution from his gallery to the Exhibition which will be opened to-day. Many both in and out of our town will be inclined to ask the same question, though few are likely to word it so bluntly.

Manchester is the centre of a district more populous than any other in the Queen's dominions. The wealth of this population is proportionate to its density, and its laboriousness is at once the source and the measure of its wealth. There was a time when labour alone sufficed for the serious hours of Manchester masters and Manchester men. What leisure they had was given to animal enjoyments; to abundant feasts, copious potations, rough pleasures, and brutal sports. Thus, even in those days, the life of this population showed that man will not brook continuous, unrelieved labour. But such employment of leisure was more degrading than the most grinding toil. The time for such misuse of the hours of rest is gone by. From the highest to the lowest of us this fact is apparent. The spirit is daily usurping upon the flesh; culture spreads among all classes. Travelling is every day easier; books grow daily cheaper and more accessible; we have yearly more and more public parks, athenaeums, and reading-rooms, popular lectures, and schools of design. Our children are better taught; our adults seek higher amusements; our Agnews and Grundys are among the most enterprising of art-traders; our manufacturers are the best patrons of living artists.

Looking, therefore, to the fine arts as unconnected altogether with manufacturing design, we need be at no loss for reasons why Manchester should trouble herself about pictures and statues. The craving for the beautiful has grown up even in this great workshop. Were there no more than this, then – we repeat it – Manchester has good reason to gather together her exhibition of art treasures. But the fine arts have their application, also, to design. It is not easy to overestimate their importance, in this respect, to a district which contributes so largely to the textile productions of the world.

### GAINSBOROUGH[1]

#### Wednesday, May 6, 1857

Here we may note the full spring of portraiture in the hands of Reynolds and Gainsborough. Here we may measure them one against the other, in some of their choicest examples. Reynolds was so ignorant of chemistry, and so careless of consequences, in his eager search after the means of immediate effect, that he never scrupled to blend colours mutually destructive, or to mix unequally drying mediums and varnishes. To this we have to attribute the ruin of many of his finest works and the serious damage of almost every portrait that ever came out of his studio. But comparing the two masters as they hang on these walls, we are not sure that the two portraits by Gainsborough, which adorn the east end of the gallery, are not superior – the one in painting, the other in all the requisites of a female portrait – to anything we have here from the hand of Reynolds.

Everyone knows the story of the 'Blue Boy.' Sir Joshua had maintained that the predominance of blue in a picture is incompatible with a good effect of colour. There was no love lost between the painters. Gainsborough never forgave Sir Joshua for describing him as 'the first landscape painter of the day.' He painted this picture, perhaps, as much to show his claims to be considered the first portrait painter of his time, as to disprove Sir Joshua's theory about the predominance of blue. At all events, the picture goes almost as far in proof of the one fact as of the other. The boy painted was a Master Buttall, of whom we know nothing; but Gainsborough has given us a face of rare shrewdness and humour atop of the blue jacket and continuations, and has so set his solid, life-like, easy figure in a landscape grandly suggestive in its masses of lurid sky and its sweep of broken ground and woodland, that the whole work rises into the ideal of portraiture. It is a story; it is a poem; you may look at it till you build a future for the boy – and you

1. This and the following extracts are by Tom Taylor.

find yourself speculating as to his character and belongings. Look closely at the picture and there is infinite freedom and facility, but no carelessness in the sweeping brush-work of the dress, in the strong yet delicately-managed shadows of the face, in the stately swell of the landscape, and the lighting up of the stormy sky. Go to a distance, and the power still makes itself felt. From half way up the gallery the Blue Boy still stands out like a solid piece of healthy flesh and blood. It does not need distance to be enjoyed, and yet enjoyment is enhanced by distance. And if the 'Blue Boy' be the very incarnation of youthful manhood, when was ever the daintiest and most delicate class of womanhood more sweetly put into form than in that lovely girl, – we beg her pardon, she is Mrs. Graham, – that lovely young woman by his side.

TURNER

## Wednesday, May 13, 1857

Turner, happily for all lovers of nature and art, is here represented by no fewer than 19 pictures (in oils) – to say nothing of the magnificent series of his drawings in the Water-colour Gallery.

The 'Barnes Terrace' was exhibited in 1827 [as] 'Mortlake Terrace, seat of William Moffat, Esq.; Summer Evening.' The day that closed as this picture represents, should have been a happy one. The broad light of the evening sun still lies upon the river, and casts the lengthening shadows of the lines over the golden sward, where a garden chair and a portfolio speak of the artist who has just left the spot, and the gilded barges and glancing wherries tell of holiday-makers upon the river, and the dog has awakened from his doze in the sun to leap upon the parapet, and bark at the passing boats. This dog is one of the often-quoted examples of Turner's reckless readiness of resource and carelessness as to means of effect. There was no dog in this picture originally. Turner thought, or somebody suggested to him, that a dark object on the parapet would throw back the distance, and enhance the aerial effect of the whole picture. So Turner cut out this dog in black paper and stuck him on the wall, and satisfied with the effect, either forgot how it was produced, or did not think it worth while to replace his paper dog with a painted one; and there the paper dog remains to this day.

Another work here catalogued under the name 'Pas de Calais' – but which we presume to be the picture exhibited in 1827, by the title ' "Now for the painter;" – Passengers going on board,' – is by very much the most powerful example of Turner's sea painting here exhibited; and, indeed, one of the very finest of seas we have ever seen from his hand. It shows what an immense advance he had by this time made upon the work of those days when Van der Velde furnished his ideal of marine painting. Here is liquidity and lustre as well as true drawing of waves. His seas reflect as well as rock the craft that roll and pitch upon them as naturally as ever. We may see, too, how much larger and grander his seas have grown – how much more awful in its expression of power is even this quiet and harmless channel sea, than the storm-lashed ocean which is grinding the Minotaur to splinters.

## CONSTABLE

### Thursday, May 14, 1857

Constable's heart was in East Bergholt all his life; and a circle of a few hundred yards around Flatford, near his native village, comprised the scenes from which his best pictures were painted – the lock, of which two pictures may be seen in our Exhibition, and the landscape called 'The White Horse', among the number. Of the scenery round about this centre Constable was an intense and genuine lover. All his pictures here exhibited illustrate this intense sympathy with the nature in the midst of which his eye was educated and his mind was formed. Of all aspects of nature he most felt the beauty of clouded skies and sudden gleams. It is such 'greatcoat' weather, as Fuseli christened it, in all his pictures here. In all of them we stand, as the painter loved to stand, by the margin of the brimming river, with its luxuriant growth of burdock, and plantain, and sedges, its fringe of sallows, and its eyots with their thick growth of aged willows. We seem as we look, to see the pulses of the stream as, stirred with languid strokes of the oar, it waves all its lazy lilies, or to hear the cheerful dash of the skull race, or to mark the rise and fall of the water in the lock, among the glistening piles and slimy sluices, and weed-grown fissures of the dank brickwork. And always the low cloud, grey with its weight of rain, or leaden with its brooding freight of thunder, hangs over our heads, and all the light comes in fleeting bursts, or falls in pencils from a shrouded sun. Always the same earth – the same sky – the same spire – the same mill – the same meadows – the same river. Constable was a true snail. He carried his home upon his back.

The 'Salisbury Cathedral' was another of Constable's favourite pictures. It is contributed by our townsman, Mr. Samuel Ashton. He may congratulate himself on the possession of a genuine, plashy, willowy, weedy, rain-clouded Constable, with more than is agreeable to us of his peculiar blackness and dirtiness of colour.

## THE PRE-RAPHAELITES
### Monday, May 18, 1857

Criticism, artistic or unartistic, may deal with these men and their works as scornfully and spitefully as it will. It is, nevertheless, a fact beyond dispute, that besides drawing into their ranks the most distinguished of the rising painters, this school has decided the tendency of all the art of the day, – by which we mean, the painting of all men not too settled in practice to acquire any new habit, men alike past learning or unlearning.

Mr. Hunt appears here as the real corypheus of the school. His 'Claudio and Isabella,' from Shakespeare's *Measure for Measure* – to speak our own mind of it – is far and away the most impressive work.

Mr. Hunt's scene from *The Two Gentlemen of Verona*, though a far more marvellous work in colour, and a much more difficult achievement in all technical respects than the 'Claudio and Isabella,' contains no such perfect example of expression as that face of Isabella's. But most touching and most lovely is the Julia, who leans against the tree, unwilling witness of the degradation of the man she loves. Most persons, when they first come upon this picture, with eyes accustomed to the conventional scale of colour all about them, will be inclined to protest against it as garish and overpowering. Let them wait awhile, and then contemplate the picture from some little distance. They will find, in a very short time, that the eye will recognise a brightness not beyond that properly belonging to such materials and objects as the painter has represented. When these are seen under full southern sunlight, even the light reflected from the crimson velvet mantle of Julia upon her chin and cap are perfectly to be accounted for under the circumstances. The drawing of the background is as admirable, in the way of landscape, as is that of the figures, in respect of action and expression.

### LANDSEER
#### Thursday, May 21, 1857

We may trace Landseer here from his earlier and more careful stage of practice up to his perfection of free and masterly power. It is only in the course of nature that we should be able to follow him some steps in his decline from culmination, for Sir Edwin is not a young man, and can never again be what he was. Among those earlier works is 'The Shepherd's Grave' that pathetic tribute to the fidelity of the dog. How delicate and careful is his painting of this picture: Here is no dash, no bravura, no parade of breadth or mastery, but honest close rendering of every object and effect. And the sentiment is worthy of the work-manship; like it, true to nature, delicate, and unobtrusive. So Landseer worked as a young man. And now let us pass to the work of his per-fected power. As examples of this, we will select for force his 'Alpine Mastiffs rescuing a Traveller from an Avalanche.' Here the dog is all alive with a feeling which, while not untrue to canine nature, yet belongs to that part of the dog which is most akin to man. With what passionate energy these noble brutes are scratching away the snow from the half unburied body – what solicitude there is in the expression of the one which is licking the frozen face – and how the other's deep-mouthed bay seems to be pealed out like a bell, calling for succour in that howling wilderness! For strength of hand and mastery over animal anatomy and colour, this picture stands far and away at the head of all else of Landseer's here exhibited, and the whole work is one by virtue of which Landseer may safely rest his claim to a place by the side of the greatest animal painters the world has yet seen – Rubens and Snyders; and even above them, in that he has ennobled the brute in his painting of it, while they seem rather to have lowered their humanity in order to [give] more perfect apprehension and representation of the brute.

## THE BIRTH OF THE HALLÉ

Charles Hallé, a Rhinelander, settled in Paris in 1836 where he became a friend of Chopin and Berlioz. He moved to Manchester in 1848. He quickly found an enthusiastic supporter in Charles Sever (Sigma), the *Guardian*'s music and dramatic critic. Sever (1807–1888), a Yorkshireman, had served an apprenticeship to a letterpress printer, worked as a reporter and sub-editor on the radical *Manchester and Salford Advertiser*, and set up as a general printer in 1836.

### Wednesday, August 29, 1849

#### CHARLES HALLÉ AT THIRTY

Monday Evening, the 27th of August, 1849
DRESS CONCERT
    The Gemini (for happily we have had to speak of Hallé and Ernst[1] so frequently in conjunction of late, that the name of the one now-a-

1. Heinrich Wilhelm Ernst (1814–1865), violinist and composer, born at Brno, disciple of Paganini. He lived in Paris 1832–1838, and settled in London 1855.

days suggests that of the other) enriched the scheme enormously with
their inimitable performances. Nothing can be more distinct than the
physique and temperament of the two. Hallé is all quietness and tranquillity – unsophisticated in person and movement – and nothing to
indicate the poet-musician till you see him seated at the instrument,
– listen to the divine strains of Beethoven, delivered with an expressiveness that ravishes the fancy as if some new faculty for enjoyment
had been imparted, – and mark the slight inflection of his head (the
face all radiant with intelligence and feeling) at some exquisite turn
of the melody, or some phrase of more than common beauty is delivered. Ernst is the embodiment of all that is sombre and intense. The
olive complexion, the dark moustache, and eyes which seem to emit
fire as he draws forth some of the impassioned tones from his almost
sentient instrument, present a whole which might realise one of
Salvator Rosa's gloomiest conceptions – he seems like a stern recluse
suddenly drawn from his solitude, to be again in the world but not of
it. And yet their playing seems to be directed by one intelligence and
one genius, so perfectly does it blend and harmonise in finish and
sentiment. Their first duet was one of the subjects from *Semiramide*,
and was principally for violin. It was full of brilliancy both in composition and execution. Ernst's tone was purity itself, but was bright
rather than full. The sonata of Beethoven (in G) was fraught with
alternate fire and tenderness, and was played with a sympathetic expression and identity which were wondrous as well as delightful. The
respective solos of the two accomplished artists were deserving of
equal praise. We need not say that all they did was enthusiastically
applauded.                                                          Σ

Saturday, November 27, 1852

THE CHAMBER CONCERTS

The opening of another season of these charming classical chamber
concerts – (the alliteration is forced upon us) – is quite a musical era
and festival in Manchester. And large and brilliant was the assemblage
on Thursday evening, that graced the first public appearance this
season of Charles Hallé, the gifted, amiable, and accomplished musician,
– one of the greatest classical pianists of our day. As our Manchester
readers are aware, a scheme was recently announced for establishing
these subscription concerts on a permanent basis, like those of Ella in
the metropolis, the subscribers being strictly limited to 350; as this
description of music cannot be heard to advantage in a very large room.
So general was the desire to become subscribers that last week the

entire list was filled up, and from 40 to 50 applications were received which could not at present be entertained; the names being registered for admission hereafter, as vacancies may arise. The season is to include eight concerts from November to March, single season tickets £2 2s. and family tickets (admitting four) £7 7s. each.

Another new feature was as acceptable to many of the audience, as it cannot fail to be interesting and indeed instructive to all. We mean the descriptive and illustrated programme, so far as relates to the concerted pieces – descriptive in letterpress of each movement, and its peculiar character and beauties; illustrated by a few bars of typeprinted music, so as to indicate the opening passage, the subject or motivo, of each movement. In such an assembly as the subscribers to these concerts, there can scarcely be an individual present who cannot read this musical notation sufficiently to comprehend the character of the movement which it so neatly and compendiously indicates; while, even to the well-read and accomplished musician, whether professional or amateur, these indexes to what is coming are most agreeable 'notes' of preparation, either recalling at once to remembrance a whole piece, or (if new) furnishing him with a key to its interpretation, of which he cannot fail to feel the advantage. To all, the description and notes together furnish full and agreeable information, which enables an auditory to meander through music's mazes more pleasantly with the artists, than could possibly be the case where (as heretofore) all the information given is the time of each movement in a few Italian words.

Nothing was lacking which the highest resources of practical art could give, – either in the quality of the instruments, or the style of performance, – to present it [the Kreutzer Sonata] in full and perfect proportions to the delighted audience. Some of the effects produced on the piano were as wonderful, as the means by which they were realised seemed easy and effortless to the gifted performer. Nothing could be finer than the rich, full, singing of Molique's[1] violin, and the finished skill of his double stopping. The applause at the close of the piece and of the first part of the concert, was most enthusiastic.

Herr Molique selected, for his solo performance a composition of Sebastian Bach's, termed a 'Bourrée and Double,' – the former being a French term for a lively dance in common time, beginning with an odd crotchet. With this light and merry theme, Bach, in his own peculiar way, interweaves deep harmonies, fraught with legitimate difficulties enough to call for the skill of a master in grappling with and

1. W. B. Molique (1802–1869), German violinist and composer, had settled in London in 1849.

overcoming them. To say that Molique did this triumphantly is a simple acknowledgment of an obvious truth. The piece was quite a musical curiosity; but, amidst all its intricacies, never violating those canons to which Bach religiously adhered. Lastly, we had a deliciously wild and plaintive nocturne, followed by a brilliant polonaise, both compositions of Chopin,[1] – a living master, whose genius expends itself in these graceful little productions. These were played as only Hallé can play them; and they closed a most excellent concert about half-past ten o'clock.

## Monday, February 1, 1858

### THE SYMPHONY CONCERT

The institution of these concerts[2] is quite an event in the musical history of Manchester. The experiment is a bold one, but we are not without hopes that it will meet with such an amount of public support as will fully remunerate the undertakers of it (for these things, it is almost needless to say, cannot be done without large pecuniary means), and show that the musical taste of Manchester is sufficiently advanced to welcome the introduction of the higher compositions of musical art. No provincial town except Manchester, we venture to think, is in a position to make such an experiment; partly from the fact that no other town has so large a body of resident instrumental musicians but more, perhaps, from the fact that no other town possesses a resident musician of Mr. Hallé's calibre. Thoroughly acquainted with the powers and resources of an orchestra, and with all the great instrumental works written for it, unrivalled as a pianist, and with manners and bearing that attract and inspire confidence and esteem from the members of any orchestra submitted to his control, as was shown by the handsome acknowledgment made to him by the Art Treasures band, he has every qualification that could be wished for in carrying out the undertaking in which he is now engaged.

We have on a previous occasion, when speaking of the present band, stated it to be identical with the Art Treasures band in point of numbers. It is, however, much superior. That band numbered 50 performers only; the present one numbers 60, the increase being in the most important element, namely, the strings. For the information of our musical readers, we give them the constitution of Mr. Hallé's band; those versed in such matters will see how admirably it is adapted for

1. Nocturne in F minor (Op. 55) and Grand Polonaise in A flat (Op. 53).
2. A series of Saturday subscription concerts. The programme on this evening included Beethoven's First Symphony, the 'Ballet des Sylphes' from Berlioz's 'Faust' ('encored unanimously') and three of Mendelssohn's 'Songs without Words' with Hallé as the soloist.

orchestral effects: – The strings are 36, viz. 20 violins, 10 first, headed by Mr. Seymour; and 10 seconds, headed by Mr. Buck; six tenors[1] headed by Mons. Baetens; five violoncellos, headed by M. Vieuxtemps; and five double basses, headed by Mr. Waud. The 24 remaining instruments are two flutes, two oboes, two clarinets, two bassoons, four horns, two cornets, two trumpets, three trombones, ophicleide, kettle drums, bass drum and cymbals, harp, and piano forte.

The effect of this band, as heard in the Free Trade Hall on Saturday evening, is very beautiful. In a room with so much resonating surface, it might have been feared that such a powerful mass of wind instruments would be felt to be too prominent; but it was not so, for both the wind and stringed instruments are in excellent hands, the former having the power of playing with the utmost delicacy, and the latter with plenty of sonorous force, so that on no occasion, even when the full force of the wind instruments was employed, did the strings ever lose their supremacy, and this is a great matter. Anyone who heard Mons. Jullien's band on Wednesday evening (and this is a comparison almost forced upon us), and Mr. Hallé's on Saturday evening, will understand the matter better than from any words we can use.

## THEATRE: A SEASON OF FAREWELLS

Charles Sever was as reluctant to say farewell to old favourites in the theatre as he was keen to welcome new talent in the concert hall.

### Saturday, September 29, 1849

#### MACREADY

The retirement of Mr. Macready[2] from the stage is one of the most untoward events which could befall it. He has stood alone in the attempt to elevate and sustain it. Scene painting, costume, and stage mechanism were carried to perfection; the tainted atmosphere of the green room and the saloon was purified, and he made manifest, for the first time, in the modern history of the stage, that the most delightful representations of art, – the most picturesque and classic exhibitions on the stage were

1. Violas.
2. W. C. Macready (1793–1873). Earlier in 1849 the rivalry between Macready and the American actor, Edwin Forrest, who were both playing Macbeth at the same time in New York, had led to riots in which seventeen people were killed. Macready's last appearance was as Macbeth at Drury Lane in 1851.

quite consistent with – received an added charm from – the strictest maintenance of the social proprieties.

## Wednesday, October 3, 1849

*Othello* was performed on Monday evening, Mr. Macready taking the part of Iago. We have seen all the Iagos from Mr. Charles Young downwards, and we consider Mr. Macready's to be the most perfect of them all. We mark in his performance the subtle, treacherous villain, even while talking with Othello, though the manner is sufficiently plausible to impose upon the latter; while in his soliloquies he shows himself the malignant, revengeful being, with an occasional outburst of hatred, which is perfectly startling. The common error is to make Iago a barefaced villain, to be imposed upon by whom is to betray a more than average credulity and weakness; while a dash of humour is given to his character which takes away from its odiousness. Mr. Young's conception, on the contrary, was the really 'honest Iago,' to the audience as well as to Othello and it was only in the soliloquies and in some occasional byplays, that we detected his real character. Mr. Macready, on the contrary, makes that most difficult distinction – the letting the audience see the villain at the same moment that he plausibly imposes upon Othello. Treachery is developed to the audience in every tone and attitude, while to Othello all may *reasonably* appear honest. The concentrated malice with which Iago tortures Othello is perfectly fiendish; while the passionless tone in which he expresses his concern – 'My lord, I see you are moved,' is enough to freeze the blood. Mr. Graham's Othello was respectable: we cannot award it specific praise. His style is turgid. Miss Kemble wants warmth and passion for Desdemona; but it was eminently a lady-like perform-ance, offending the taste in nothing, pleasing it in many things.

Σ

## Wednesday, October 10, 1849

### MRS. GLOVER

On Monday, another actor, also inimitable in her way, commenced a farewell engagement, – we mean dear old Mrs. Glover.[1] This lady is associated with the palmiest days of English comedy – with what is now called the old school of English acting, in which the nicer touches of art were aimed at and relished by audiences, rather than the rude and crude conceptions and the broad effects which seem to be the

1. Mrs. Julia Glover (1779–1850). She had played Mrs. Oakley for the first time in 1802. She also took the parts of Mrs. Candour and Mrs. Malaprop during this Manchester engagement.

'be all and the end all' of comedians now-a-days. In those days some of the most delightful actors on the stage would not refuse the sub-ordinate parts, which they portrayed with a degree of elaborate finish not less than that of the leading cast, thus producing a completeness worthy of the French comic stage. Of this genuine school Mrs. Glover is the last member; – one *disciple* remains, Mrs. Charles Kean, who though happily much too young to have 'flourished' in the Augustan period of the comic drama, has inherited the conceptive power and acquired the highly-finished manner of that bygone school.

Mrs. Glover's name will ever be associated with some of the leading parts of English comedy, in which Mrs. Candour and Mrs. Malaprop will ever stand most prominent; and we have heard of her even play-ing Hamlet with a truthfulness and grace which left little to be desired. We do not think her selection of Mrs. Oakley, in *The Jealous Wife*, a happy one for an opening appearance. Of course it was exquisite as a piece of art, but the dear old lady cannot look the self-willed, over-indulged wife of – say forty or less.                                        Σ

## A FREE LIBRARY

In 1850 the Public Libraries Act had authorised a halfpenny rate for public libraries subject to a poll of local ratepayers. The result of the Manchester poll was overwhelmingly in favour. It was at this time that the *Guardian* started the regular reviewing of books.

### Saturday, August 14, 1852

On Friday next the burgesses of Manchester will have to answer by their votes, ay or no, to the question, 'Will you have, on the sole con-dition of a small yearly expenditure for its maintenance, one of the most magnificent gifts, one of the most admirable institutions, ever offered to the acceptance of a great community?' Let us suppose, for a moment, that some benevolent millionaire were to say to the people of Manchester, 'I will give you a spacious and handsome building, fitted up specially for the purpose of public libraries and reading rooms; and in that building two libraries including together 21,000 volumes, in every department of literature and science, carefully selected with especial view to the requirements of Manchester. This building and these books have cost me upwards of £12,000. They are yours and your children's to all generations for ever. All I ask is, that you shall guar-antee that this valuable property shall not be useless; that you will set aside a small sum yearly to maintain the library. Not to buy books, for that is forbidden; but to maintain a librarian and necessary servants;

to secure the cleaning, lighting, and watching of the building, and its repairs when needed.' Well, this offer is made to Manchester; with this difference, that instead of being that of some benevolent but perhaps crotchetty individual, who might err in his views of the requirements of Manchester, it is made by a large number of our fellow-townsmen, cognizant of the circumstances and needs of the community in which they dwell, and therefore less likely to be in error as to the utility and value of such an institution as a library free and open to all. It is said by some carping and captious individual, that a few wealthy individuals have given considerable sums; but that the library will be a failure; that the working men, for whose benefit it is mainly desired, do not care for it, and will not resort to it! Let us take the quaker's test, 'Friend, how much dost thou feel for it?' The working men of Manchester cannot feel in £5 notes, as more than 400 of their wealthy neighbours have done; but they have felt for this institution, in pence and in shillings, to an aggregate amount of more than £800. Upwards of *twenty thousand* working men in Manchester have given of their hard earnings towards the establishment of this Free Library, – to which we are modestly asked to believe they will not resort; and did the vote of Friday next rest with this class alone, it would be given in favour of the library by an overwhelming majority.

The only objection we have heard which is likely to weigh with any class of burgesses, – and we hope to a very small extent with any, – is the old bugbear of 'another rate.' Let us take it at the very worst; let us suppose there is a halfpenny rate every year, – a most preposterous and unlikely supposition. On an assessment of £10 the burgess would, in that extreme case, have to contribute *fivepence* yearly to the library, – the price of one copy of a Manchester newspaper. On an assessment of £15, he would have to find *sevenpence half-penny* every twelve months; and on a £20 assessment only *tenpence* a year! Why if it were only to secure reading for himself, – a common, calculating, selfishness ought to be satisfied with access to a library of 21,000 volumes, at a cost of less than a penny a month.

Any one who reads at all knows that books (especially on the terms to be offered in the Free Library) are the cheapest luxury, the most rational enjoyment, within the reach of all classes, that in this nineteenth century can be presented to mankind. Who does not feel and know, that reading is a perennial pleasure, enjoyable alike in winter and summer, not dependent on weather or seasons; available whether travelling or at home; on steamer or in railway train, almost as completely as by the family hearth. Of all material things, books come nearest in universality, variety, and perennial verdure and freshness, to the immaterial thought which man carries everywhere with him and invokes at pleasure. A good library has been called a winter park; it is rather a garden of delight, where perpetual summer reigns.

## Bigotry in the Streets and on the Bench

### ANTI-CATHOLIC RIOT IN STOCKPORT

#### Saturday, July 3, 1852

We regret to have to record one of those disgraceful riots which exist only where the lower class Irish dwell in considerable numbers – arising out of the perpetual feuds between the Irish catholics and the lower class of English factory hands.

For some time past, there has been in Stockport a bad feeling between the two classes indicated, partly on trade quarrels, partly on national grounds, but chiefly the result of religious differences between ignorant Irish catholics on the one hand, and as ignorant English protestants on the other. Collisions have frequently occurred, which have come before the magistrates – charges and counter-charges have been made – the English have been attacked by the Irish; the Irish have been assailed by the English; and it has been obvious for some time past that there only needed the spark to fire the train and explode these inflammable materials in some extensive and bloody fray. That occasion has arisen under the following circumstances: – Sunday last was the anniversary of the usual procession of all the Roman catholic scholars connected with the three chapels in Stockport. The recent royal proclamation against Roman catholic processions was much discussed.

When it became known that the procession would not be prevented, party feelings amongst the lower classes ran high, the catholics boasting they would not be stopped, and the protestants declaring that their processions ought to be put down. The procession, however, did take place on Sunday afternoon, and, on the whole, passed off quietly. The procession was headed by the priests, next followed a number of Irish labourers, walking six a-breast; then came the numerous boys and girls in the Sunday and day schools. There were no banners in the procession; the priests did not wear canonical vestments, but appeared in ordinary attire; even the girls' handkerchiefs or veils, which they usually wore on these occasions, were laid aside; and they only wore white frocks, and little crosses suspended round the neck by ribbons. The only badges or symbols that might be supposed to contravene the proclamation, were a ball and cross, and a gilt dove. As we have said, the procession passed along its course, from first to last, without the slightest disturbance, beyond occasional groans and hisses from zealous protestants, and they finally dispersed without any breach of the peace of which we have heard.

> But on Tuesday one of the Roman Catholic priests warned Mr. Sadler, the chief constable, that he feared angry Irish Catholics would assemble that evening in considerable numbers.

The police force of the borough is obviously too small for such a population, consisting only of Mr. Sadler himself and ten constables, with two or three assistants, or at most half a dozen, for duty on Saturday nights and Sundays, the seasons when there is most disorder and brawling in Stockport.

Very suddenly considerable numbers of English and Irish had simultaneously made their appearance in Hillgate, and had commenced fighting with sticks and other weapons. Which party commenced this fray Mr. Sadler was unable, either then or subsequently, to ascertain.

> The police were attacked; the military sent for.

Meanwhile the form of declaration, the reading of which is usually called 'reading the riot act,' was copied out in readiness (printed copies of this ought always to be in readiness in populous towns). A considerable number of men and youths, who were known to have taken part in some of these riotous proceedings, were conveyed to the Court House. Many of these were severely wounded, and from four o'clock in the morning till noon, four medical men were more or less engaged in dressing their wounds and hurts.

Thus far we have given a semi-official account of the riotous proceedings of the night. But as the police force was generally too late to come up with the rioters, while their reckless acts of destruction were being committed, we have endeavoured to obtain from other sources, how the proceedings arose.

After the police had dispersed the mob in the Hillgate, the Irish, in a tolerably compact body, retreated towards Rock Row. At the corner stands the residence of Mr. Alderman Graham, surgeon, who, we believe, has in some way incurred the hatred of the Roman catholics. They assailed this house with volleys of stones and brickbats, smashed most of the lower windows, and the servant man received a severe wound in the forehead from a stone. In this attack, the next house, belonging to Mr. White's factory, also suffered considerable injury in the lower windows. The mob, which at this period appeared to consist mainly of young men and lads, then turned their attack upon the Sunday school connected with St. Peter's Church, and they had broken some of the windows in the building, when they were overtaken by the English who attacked and drove them up Rock Row, and who then seem to have proceeded in retaliation to Edgeley, gutted the Roman catholic chapel and priest's house there, and thence to St. Michael's catholic chapel in the Park, which they also sacked. Fights between small bodies of both factions continued for some hours afterwards. In these fights, one life has been taken, and it is not improbable that other very severe injuries may terminate fatally. About ten o'clock, some men brought to the Court House an athletic young Irishman, named Michael Moran, about 23 years of age, who was knocked down by the mob, and was subsequently struck on the head with a thick stick, while, in a helpless condition, he was being led between two men, in search of surgical aid. It was found that he had received a severe fracture of the skull and other injuries, and as he was evidently dying, he was removed from the prisoners and placed in a room below the Court House, where he expired about a quarter before two o'clock on Wednesday morning.

Another case is of a very distressing nature. At an early part of the evening a man named James Ogden, an operative block printer, was charged by Mr. Sadler to assist the constables in preserving the peace. He found a number of Irish and others fighting in a low cellar. Finding himself in danger, he attempted to escape, and laying hold of the door for that purpose, some one behind struck at his hand with a sickle or reaping hook, and completely severed from his right hand the whole of the forefinger. The poor man went direct to the Stockport Infirmary where his hand was dressed, and he then returned to the cellar, which he found deserted, and, looking about, he picked up his finger, where it had fallen behind the door. He was in great distress, as he told us it was the very finger he most needed in his trade, and he was afraid he could work no more. To add to his sufferings, he is a married man, with a family of six children, and his wife will shortly again be confined; and so much was he afraid of the effect upon her, that at first he dared not acquaint her with what had befallen him. We trust this case will have the benevolent consideration of all the well-disposed.

The scene which presented itself on Wednesday morning in the large room of the Court House, used for the daily purposes of a police court, cannot easily be described. Within a rail separating the lower end of the court, from that where justice is administered, were penned together some sixty or seventy youths and men, nearly all Irish, and most of whom had bandages and plasters on their heads, faces, hands, arms and legs. One with a fractured shoulder blade was yelling in pain under the manipulation of the surgeon, and another young man lying on the floor was also shrieking under the pain caused by handling a dislocated ankle. Others were moaning and bleeding, and the whole formed a scene not unlike that of a military hospital after a battle.

We have purposely left for separate description the three chief outrages on property, viz. the cottage dwellings in Rock Row and Carr Green; the Roman catholic chapel and adjoining priest's house, Edgeley; and St. Michael's catholic chapel, Park-street.

The scene in Carr Green, Rock Row, and the neighbourhood, almost defies description. The first house is occupied by a man named Shaughnessy, who, with his wife and family, were in the house when the windows were smashed by volleys of stones; subsequently the door was broken in, and every article of furniture was taken into the road and demolished. In the next house Michael Moran was taking shelter on a bed in an upper room, when the mob rushed in and smashed the furniture, &c. The interior of the house is a perfect wreck, and not a sign remains that there was ever any furniture in it. The adjoining house, occupied by William Riley, was entered through the lower window, the frame of which was entirely smashed; the door resisted all the attempts to break it open; but it is almost covered with deep indentations, caused by a hammer-head, or some other iron instrument. Timothy Finnigan, who lived in the next house, was at work in the country on Tuesday; but his young wife, who is in an advanced state of pregnancy, was in bed upstairs. In addition to the furniture, two trunks, filled with clothes, are said to have been taken out of this house and destroyed. Michael Tully, a widower, with two sons and two daughters, were in an adjoining house with some of their neighbours. After the windows and doors had been smashed, Tully was seized and dragged into the street; he escaped severe injury, as did also his children, but his furniture, including a good clock, was utterly destroyed.

It might be about a quarter before nine o'clock when the crowd came up [to Edgeley Roman Catholic chapel], chiefly boys and young men, armed with pick-axes, hatchets, hammers, crowbars, &c. and they began by throwing stones at the two parlour windows of the priest's house. Almost immediately afterwards they threw stones at the chapel windows next Chapel-street, and having broken most of the front windows of both the chapel and the house with hatchets, pick-axes, and sledge hammers, they then forced in the front door of the chapel and rushed in. When the attack on the priest's house became fierce, the Rev. R. Frith, and four young men who were with him, entered the chapel from the vestries, and concealed themselves in the bell-turret, the door of which was locked after them by one of the attendants. Here they remained for some time, while the wrecking of both the house and chapel was proceeding; till at a later time, when attempts were made to set both the house and chapel on fire, and then the priest and his friends succeeded in getting upon the chapel roof, traversing it on the side next the house, descending upon the house roof, and through a window into the house; and then through the yard and over a wall into the next garden.

On effecting their entrance, they (the rioters) rushed up to the altar rails, which are of iron, broke them with axes and sledge hammers; made their way up to the altar and tabernacle, and rapidly destroyed these; females, it is said, being as eager and active in the work of destruction as males. The rioters proved themselves zealous iconoclasts, for they destroyed every cross and crucifix, picture, image, statue, candlestick, etc. with which the chapel was adorned. One large body of the rioters, armed as already described, and some having butchers' cleavers, the others the legs and backs of chairs which had been broken up in the priest's house, proceeded to smash up the benches or seats on the floor of the chapel, which work of demolition was carried on till not a lineal foot of seating remained. Another party was doing a similar work in the gallery, all the seats of which, on the side next the school, were similarly destroyed. In the centre of the large gallery stood a large organ. The instrument was speedily demolished; all the side and back windows of the chapel were broken, and in many places even the frames were destroyed. The chapel was lighted by bronze gas pendants from the gallery. Only one of these remains; the rest have been torn down or unscrewed, and the burners and portions of piping carried away.

We never saw the interior of any building exhibiting such utter demolition and destruction as do the chapel and the adjoining house at Edgeley.

## COMMENT

In strict and rigid truth, the riot appears to have been the direct offspring of Lord DERBY's proclamation against Roman catholic processions and costumes. As soon as this paltry electioneering device was before the public, it was turned by the anti-catholic agitators of Stockport against the Sunday School procession known to have been fixed for last Sunday, and which, it was therefore contended, should not take place. Under these circumstances, we cannot think the catholics blameless in persisting in their procession, – harmless and inoffensive as they desired it to be.

We have spoken as we think, of the apparent occasion of this disturbance. But, whatever rashness or imprudence may be laid to the charge of the unfortunate sufferers, the irretrievable disgrace of the affair belongs to the bullies and ruffians who abuse the name of Protestants. The appearance of the whole town at this hour testifies on which side the guilt has lain. The loss of life and property is almost wholly on the side of the catholics, while of violence on their part, scarcely a trace is visible. The sacrilegious ransacking of churches, the fiendish destruction of houses and furniture, and the most cruel and cowardly murder, are memorials of protestant zeal and enlightenment alone. The affair was more like a *battue* than a fight. Judge from the names of the prisoners[1] in the hands of the police, and the first inference would be that the object of the mob's fury must have been something particularly hateful to Celtic catholics; but ask what of this description has been destroyed, and your attention is directed to a few squares of glass! The bloodshed, the violence, and the rapine are protestant handiwork, not in self-defence, but in brutal and licentious phrenzy. Had not the tory government, by a popularity-hunting attack upon Roman catholic ceremonials, and had not its admirers and imitators in the country, by a series of provocations addressed to the same quarter, wilfully cast about to stimulate the sectarian passions of the electors, for their own selfish purposes, we should have been free from the shame and danger.

## A HUMANIST DEFENDED

### Wednesday, December 8, 1852

We wish permission to refer as briefly as possible to an exhibition of judicial misconduct which has unaccountably escaped comment from the London press to whom it properly belongs, but ought not to pass entirely unnoticed. An insolvent tailor, having applied to the court over which Mr. Phillips presides, to be discharged on bail till his hearing, Mr. George Jacob Holyoake, well known as the editor of the *Reasoner* and the author of various speculative writings, presented himself as one of the proposed sureties.

Mr. Commissioner Phillips: Pray what do you call yourself?

Holyoake: A 'secularist.'

Do you (demanded the learned commissioner) believe in a God?

1. Most of the 113 arrested were Irish.

Holyoake: I am not prepared to say.

'Mr. Commissioner Phillips indignantly declared that he would not hear him. "Not prepared to say," remarked the learned commissioner, "whether you believe in a God. You put yourself forward in a court of justice, and bring scandal upon it by saying that you are not prepared to say whether you believe in the Deity! Go and attend to your 'secular' business".'

So the scene terminated. The unfortunate sceptic was ejected out of a court of justice like a thing too foul for human contact; and the insolvent, in default of bail, went back to prison.

Mr. Holyoake's religious peculiarities have as good a right to be treated with respect as those of a Quaker, a Jew, a Hindoo, or any other witness who may come before a court of law. We need hardly say that we differ from him on almost every point respecting which his opinions are publicly known; we consider his condition and his career as unenviable and distressing. But he has this claim on respect, that he has suffered deeply for his convictions,[1] which is more than we are aware that Mr. Commissioner Phillips has done, and more than we think he is likely to do.

## Education

### THE THUNDERCLAP FROM THE NORTH

In 1852 a Select Committee report had shown that a smaller proportion of Manchester children were then in school than in 1834. The *Guardian* promised that, in spite of 'arithmetical calculations of repulsive aspect,' readers 'would not be long in losing all consciousness of distasteful labour in an overwhelming sense of the importance of the discussion.' But in 1864 things were even worse. Edward Brotherton (1814–1866) made a thorough investigation. He described what he found in the *Guardian*. H. A. Bruce (1815–1895), the minister responsible for education, described the result as 'the thunderclap from the North.'

Tuesday, January 5, 1864

#### THE NEED FOR EDUCATION

I have lately been exploring the less public districts of Manchester, with a view to understanding thoroughly whether any progress in

1. G. J. Holyoake (1817–1906) was the last person imprisoned in England (in 1841) for atheism.

social economics or education is being made. The result is that I have been shocked and alarmed to find vast masses of people rotting and festering in ignorance and corruption. I do not exaggerate. No words of mine are strong enough to convey any idea of the truth; and the most fearful sign is that the evil is rapidly increasing. We look at the census returns, find every ten years a large increase of population, and look upon it as an index to the prosperity of the district. Now I believe that, at present, nearly the whole addition which is being made to the population is of this ignorant, half-starved class, who are constantly spreading into districts that formerly contained only the moderately well-to-do classes. These latter are now extending only outside the limits of Manchester.

It seems to be overlooked entirely that in a manufacturing and commercial city like Manchester there is very little chance of success for any man who has not the germs of education, so as to be able to read and think for himself. In rural districts it is of comparatively little importance. A man can do, and generally obtain, labourer's work. But here there are continual changes of manufacture, changes of fashion, and every change throws out of employment many who had learnt to do some specialty work. If the worker has never had his intellect awakened, he cannot take the same wide and intelligent view of his position; he cannot obtain the needful information as to what he ought to do; his range of possibility is bounded by what he sees with his eyes; he has no mental range at all. The probability is that he just sinks into one of the dens of misery, and he and his family slowly die there – die by inches.

But this is one of those things that is not seen by the intelligent classes, because they do not know Manchester. Nowhere – even in London – is the separation of classes so complete as in the great commercial towns of England, and it is one of the most fatal and ominous conditions of the situation. It is one of the changes which have insensibly crept upon us, as the result of railways and the manufacturing system of modern times.

I speak far within compass when I say that in Manchester and Salford there are more than 50,000 children who ought to be at school and are not. These must almost of necessity, grow up idle, reckless, and many of them criminal.

Most people in Manchester believe that progress is making, and that this vast mass of ignorance is being reduced. I confess I had a vague idea of this kind myself, until I began to investigate. My conclusion now is, that this ignorant population is growing at the rate of more than 2,000 per annum. There are a few more being taught each year, but the increase of education is so much behind the increase of population, as to leave this result: ignorance, vice, and misery are constantly growing.

At present the matter stands as follows: –

1. Of the civilised world, England is the only important country that has no thorough system of education for the bulk of the people.

2. Vice and crime are making rapid strides, side by side with rapidly increasing wealth.

3. We know, perfectly well the remedy for this state of things. In the words of the Royal Commissioners appointed in 1858, 'the moral and religious influence of the public schools is greater than even their intellectual influence. A set of good schools civilises a whole neighbourhood.'

4. Criminals and paupers are educated and cared for, in body and mind. The children of the honest poor, who can barely subsist, are left unprovided for.

Saturday, January 9, 1864

THE MOST FAVOURED DISTRICT

I will speak first of the district of Deansgate, not only because it is central and densely peopled, but because it possesses school advantages beyond all other districts of Manchester. There are two schools in this district – one in Peter-street and the other in Lower Mosley-street – which not only stand very high in public opinion, but gain the highest praise from the Government Inspector. The district contains, also, the only free school which Manchester possesses, four Church of England schools, and one Catholic school. In short, I can conceive that a stranger coming to Manchester, who should be conducted from one to another of these schoolrooms, and see the rooms only, so large and so near each other, might imagine that there was certainly no want of education in this district. I have visited all these schools, and have obtained from them the following particulars.

In the two first-named, the Peter-street New Jerusalem School and the Lower Mosley-street Unitarian School, there are of boys, girls, and infants, 1,300 scholars. But their high and long-established reputation draws these scholars not only from every part of Manchester and Salford, but from Eccles, Irlam, Chorlton-cum-Hardy, Newton Heath, Holt-town, Stretford, Cheetham. Altogether the two schools can scarcely count 400 as belonging to the district.

Altogether there are 1,980 of the children of all ages residing in this district in attendance at the day schools in the district.

According to the census of 1861, the population of this Deansgate district is 29,029. Taking the average proportion, according to the census, of those under 15 years of age, there must be more than 9,700 children in the district under 15. But leave out those under 2½ as too young, and those above 12½ as able to work, and there remain 6,471 who ought to be at school. I do not by any means endorse the notion that after 12½ there should be no more schooling. But make every allowance to those who do think so, and they have 6,471 to provide for, either in infants' schools or boys' and girls' schools. Now, there may possibly be one or two private schools or dame schools in the district that I have not heard of though I do not think there can be. But allow for these 200 scholars, and allow that there may possibly be a few who reside in this district, yet go to schools in other districts, and say 200 for them, we then account for, – 1,980 going to school in the district, 200 for supposed private schools omitted, 200 for supposed scholars going out of the district. We have thus 2,380 going to school out of 6,471; leaving uneducated 4,091; and this in a district where schools are best and most numerous, and where also exists the only Manchester Free School. Why do I say these things? I am not asking for bread for these poor. No, but I ask for that which would make them independent of your help. They perish and will continue to perish in spite of all you can do for them in the way of relief funds or poor-laws, if you will not give them power to use those faculties which, in Manchester, are indispensable to life.

The other day I visited, in company with a friend, a cellar in the Deansgate district. It was dusk, and when our eyes grew accustomed to the dimness inside, we could not but wonder how the inmates lived in it. It was very small and the whole middle of the room was filled with lumber consisting of broken and old furniture. The husband had been a carpet weaver, but could get no work. He could not read, and neither he nor his wife dared to go out of Manchester to any other town where carpet weaving might be found. They had always lived here, and knew no other place. To them removal was an idea more weighty than emigration would have been to an intelligent man. His present occupation is that of a porter, chiefly for one of the auctioneers who sells broken-down furniture in Campfield. This man sometimes gives him credit for a few articles which he manages, in a rude way, to patch for sale. But he dare not take credit for more than £3 worth of goods, which nearly fill his cellar. He is strictly honest, and afraid to owe money, lest he should not be able to pay it. In this miserable, wet cellar, crammed with lumber, live the man and his wife, and two children, with another shortly expected. He earns sometimes 4s., sometimes 6s. or 7s. per week. Now to anyone who will talk with this man or his wife, it is evident that there is the basis of thoroughly honest, good character. But the man's ignorance causes all his views of life to be absurdly cramped. If it were not so mournful, it would be ridiculous to hear his account of his views and position. He feels cowed, and afraid to lose his hold of the miserably small foundation he has in the world, lest he should be altogether swallowed up and lost. He has become so convinced of his own helplessness that he has lost all faith. It was touching to hear his wife tell of his going every day to the man who occasionally employs him who reads for him the advertisements of other sales where he goes to look for portering.

I have thus, following Sterne's example, taken 'a single captive' of ignorance, and shown him in his dungeon. But he is one of many thousands.

### Tuesday, January 12, 1864

#### THE NEED FOR FREE SCHOOLS

The same difficulty exists everywhere. The people cannot pay. And almost everywhere a certain proportion of the scholars are paid for, or partly paid for, or taken at less than the ordinary rate. The principle is admitted, practically, that many must be educated free, or that education must almost come to a stand. Sooner or later this work of education will have to be done. The longer it is delayed the more costly it will be; the longer it is delayed the heavier our burdens in the meantime. Does any reasonable man think that if a general plan of education had been adopted ten or twelve years ago, the cotton famine would have been felt so severely as it has been? I for one do not. A good education for the masses would have wrought like magic in their general elevation.

But your readers know these things well. Will none of the many wealthy and benevolent men of Manchester resolve to take this matter to heart? If a system of schools can but be once thoroughly established, there can be no doubt they will soon be so rooted in the people's hearts that they must be kept up. There would be no greater difficulty in supporting them by a public rate than there is now in the case of the Free Library or the people's parks.

There are good schools to be had in all parts of Manchester; and in the neighbourhoods where they are most needed they are to be had at low rents. No new buildings would be needed. Many fine and lofty rooms, now used only as Sunday or Ragged Schools, are unoccupied during weekdays. Surely there is common ground on this matter with men who have one standard of virtue, one language and literature, one science, one political and social interest, one country, and one city as the centre of their interests and affections. Surely those who have one hope of immortality, one bible, and who own one Christ as Master and Lord, need not differ as to who should save the drowning while the drowning perish.

But if there cannot be union, there can surely be separate efforts. At present there is utter stagnation and forgetfulness, because almost all who can do anything have left the doomed city.

Saturday, January 16, 1864

THE EDUCATION OF GIRLS

There is not, I believe, in Manchester or Salford a single free school for girls of the working classes. There are girls whose education is assisted, their parents paying a part of the expense; and I doubt not there are a few, in different schools, who are paid for entirely by benevolent individuals. But these are so few as to be practically out of the calculation, when we consider the many thousands who are not receiving any education.

In a poor family with three or four children, when the income will not admit of the schooling of all, of course the boys get the preference. It is a general feeling that as the boy has to go out and wrestle for his life with the world, education is far more necessary for him than for his sister, to whom it is looked upon rather as an accomplishment, desirable, but not indispensable. The same feeling is manifest in the founders and supporters of schools, to some extent. If a school is to be commenced, the boys are first thought of, and the girls' claims are looked upon as less urgent.

Whatever justice there may be in this instinctive feeling, it is evident that, in a town like Manchester, the neglected education of girls is fraught with the most disastrous consequences. Great numbers of the present mothers of families have, almost from childhood, been compelled to earn their own livelihood in mills, workshops, and warehouses. They have consequently never had any of the household training which is so necessary to a mother of a family. Very often, when one of this class marries, she cannot read, or can read only so imperfectly that the effort is painful to her, and gives her no intelligible ideas. She cannot sew, she cannot wash, she cannot cook. When she first attempts to clean up her little house, her cleaning is what an old-fashioned Lancashire housewife would call 'cat-licking.' She is improvident, for the simple reason that she has never learnt what calculation and forethought are. Those who condemn her for improvidence ought to reflect that providence is the result of the culture of a number of faculties trained to a distinct use. One might as justly blame her for not being able to play the piano.

She marries as other people would take a day's holiday. Her wedding is a pleasant little incident in her life, and the next day she goes to her work as usual. Until children begin to come she and her husband are well off, and, according to their notions, happy, perhaps. Both are earning money, and they live extravagantly, without thinking of the future, often getting 'relishes,' cooked meat from the cook-shop, beer, or spirits, and spending all as it comes. But with the children, their troubles begin. The wife's income becomes irregular, or ceases; there is additional expense, there is sickness, poverty, misery, discontent, and often quarrelling. The husband comes tired to his cheerless, dirty, unfurnished home, in a dingy street or court. Both he and his wife feel there is something wrong, but neither of them know what. They have an instinct which tells them this is not a reasonable and proper state of things. One blames the other, and then the husband seeks refuge in a beerhouse.

The children grow up inured to rages and neglect. As soon as they can be made to earn something they are sent out – the girls, probably, to follow the mother's footsteps, – only each generation sinks into a lower degree of wretchedness and vice. Among their companions in the mill and in the streets and courts where they live there is profligacy in its most hideous forms. The girls constantly hear miscreant words – forged by fiends, and hot with the fire of the nether pit. They learn to utter language revolting to any sensitive ear. The young women whose lot appears to them the most enviable are the Magdalens who live all round them, whose names they know, and whose talk they often overhear. They see that these have no work to do, are well fed, have as much gin or rum as they care for, and seem to be the most notable and influential women in the neighbourhood. From a sort of admiration for these women, akin to that of a boy for a highwayman, the girls begin unconsciously to mimic their shameless showy dress and swaggering gait. If you meet three or four such girls, of fourteen or fifteen years of age, walking together in the evening, each one outbraves the other in some loud and coarse remark, the one who most outrages modesty being rewarded by the applauding laugh of the others; and, in innumerable instances, virtue is lost before it is known what virtue is.

## Tuesday, January 19, 1864

### THE QUESTION OF COMPULSION

I will say a word about compulsory education, in favour of which the feeling is clearly growing. To me the matter presents itself thus: – We have two classes of parents to consider: – 1, those who would educate their children, and cannot; and 2, those who could and will not. Let us not confound the two.

Now, it seems to me that the first thing to be done is to provide education for all those who cannot do it for themselves.

As soon as this needy class is provided for, we shall be in a doubly advantageous position for taking the next step. In the first place, we shall have cleared the ground and shall find out the residuum who are able but not willing to pay. I think we shall then find this remainder exceedingly small, because the fact that all the children of the lowest working classes are receiving education will stimulate those who can pay, and they will, for very shame, and from the compulsion of public opinion, be generally obliged to educate their children.

But at this time, another very powerful remedy can very properly be applied, which I believe will be sufficient, without any legal compulsory power, to set the whole matter right. If, when the poor are provided with means of education, the employers of labour will resolve not to employ any child who has not been educated, all parents will at once bestir themselves, under the pressure of a compulsion that no one can lift a word against, which will search, with Argus eyes, in every house. If it be thought needful, a public officer might be appointed to examine children and give certificates to those who are fitted to go to work. And if the parents once knew that without this certificate there were a hundred chances to one against the obtaining of employment, the whole matter would be settled.

## Tuesday, January 26, 1864

### THE GUARDIAN SUMS UP

Repeatedly the Committee of Council have laid down the principle, that the aid of the State is only intended for those classes which can pay but a portion of the cost of educating their children in the bare rudiments of knowledge. The instruction to be given was to be purely elementary, and the assisted schools were not to compete with others not receiving State aid, and designed for pupils of a somewhat higher station. But it has been found almost impossible to maintain the desired distinction. The education given in the assisted schools has been so good that they have been largely used by persons whom it is certain the State never intended to help in the instruction of their children, and which ought, perhaps, to be above seeking such help at their neighbour's expense.[1]

Now, it may be feared by some persons that a corresponding difficulty would follow the establishment of free schools. Regulations could hardly be devised which would succeed in preventing the descent into the new schools of a portion of the pupils whose payments are now supplemented by the Privy Council grants. The assisted schools may perchance suffer to some extent, and it is perhaps well that this result should be kept in view. But similar consequences follow every effort designed to benefit the poor, and ought never to be allowed to interfere with the carrying out of a work of such importance as the education of the most ignorant of our population. It is true, too, that free schools, to be efficient, can be little less costly than those which are already established; and the serious question then arises, how are they to be supported. In a wealthy community like this, animated too by an unusual share of public spirit, we do not despair of seeing an extended system of free and unsectarian schools instituted, and supported by subscribed funds. But such could not be the case through the country at large, and there, at least, for the effectual and enduring support of free schools, we must ultimately look for taxation, national or local. For this, no doubt, the country at large is not prepared, but it is to that achievement that the friends of popular education should always direct their efforts, and we are not sure that in districts like our own the day when it shall be feasible need be considered far distant.

## THE SCHOOL OF EXPERIENCE

### Friday, May 28, 1858

The love of horse racing is naturally one of the most powerful feelings in an Englishman's heart, not only is this feeling quite excusable, but it is one of which no man need be ashamed. A very significant anecdote from the report of the Rev. W. Brookfield, inspector of schools in some of the southern counties, affords a proof of the correctness of our views. Mr. Brookfield requested one of the most intelligent boys to write down a description of a racehorse. The boy wrote as follows: – 'The racehorse is a noble animal used very cruel by gentlemen. Races are very bad places. None but wicked people know anything about

1. The growth in the number of pupils in grant-aided schools had been partly at the expense of private dames' schools.

races. The last Derby was won by Mr. I'Anson's Blink Bonny, a beautiful filly by Melbourne, rising four. The odds were twenty to one against her; thirty started and she won by a neck.' We venture to assert that nine boys out of ten would have written something very similar in substance. There would have been the same platitudes and vague assertion in regard to races in the abstract; the same completeness of information, and vigour and animation of style, in all that related to any particular race.

## SO MUCH FOR THE PUBLIC SCHOOLS
### Tuesday, November 8, 1864

We are decidedly of opinion that a well-educated mechanic could, by giving two or three hours each evening to the instruction of his boys, enable them to pass these Oxford and Cambridge local examinations with credit at the usual age.[1]

1. November 8, 1864 – from an article on the Public Schools Commission – one of a series of 'Social Papers' by Antony Pentland.

# CHAPTER FOUR

# The Astonishing Contents of a Gladstone Bag

*

This chapter starts with Mr. Gladstone's first government and ends on the eve of his last, the twenty-four years from 1868 to 1892. In *Guardian* history it covers the first period of C. P. Scott's editorship. The earliest article included was written just twelve months before he joined the staff; the latest four years before he went into Parliament. For the first half of this period H. M. Acton was still the principal leader-writer, while from 1873 to 1875 Richard Whiteing brought a new touch to the paper's descriptive writing. In the second half, W. T. Arnold became second-in-command and senior leader-writer.

## The Condition of England Question

### IN THE SLUMS

Wednesday, February 16, 1870

#### ANGEL MEADOW

'The slums' may be described as that border land which interposes between our homes and our avocations. Pushed from the centre of our city by commerce, expelled from the circumference by civilisation, 'the slums' form an intermediary zone severing the two; not in a continuous circle, it is true, else they would be seen, and being seen, would attract attention, and then perhaps be inquired into. Stray voyagers would now and then penetrate it; strange revelations would from time to time be made, and our duty as explorers and chroniclers would have been performed by others. Public opinion would be brought to bear upon it, and private interest would have to fall before it. Private interest! Yes, private interest; 'the slums' are strictly preserved for private interest. Avarice is head keeper there. He fences them off from the highways and broad streets, by warehouses and ginshops, shutting out public view, and fresh air. These are both too valuable to be given freely, and neither is deemed good for those whose dwellings are in 'the slums.' Breaking through this cordon, strange sights, strange sounds, and strange smells assail one, and the traveller requires to be armed with the triple combination of patience, strong resolution, and a cold in the head.

Scarlet fever blossoms in perennial bloom, and delicate and insinuating typhoids spread with marvellous rapidity and diversity. Under the warm moist shades of this Upas tree which we nurture so carefully, Death's fletchers are busy winging his arrows – arrows to be shot as from a bow drawn at a venture, and who can tell which joint of whose armour they will enter at? On many a granite and marble tomb, which sets forth by its cost the wealth, and by its inscription the virtues, of a lost one, might be inscribed with perhaps greater truth, 'He died of "the slums".'

Very few of our readers probably ever entered a 'common lodging-house.' Still a common lodging-house plays a very important function in the life of thousands in Manchester. It is the home of many an industrious artizan, as well as the lair of the thief and the den of the prostitute; and the law of natural selection seems to develop itself even amongst common lodging-houses. Indeed they resolve themselves into particular lodging-houses, each quarter having its own class of lodgers; and though we have found here and there the rare exception of a well ordered and carefully tended house, the enormous preponderance of the evil is most remarkable. We see how hard it is for the poor to be either decent or moral; and there seems to be a cruel irony in the preamble of that act which declares that 'it would tend greatly to the comfort and welfare of many of Her Majesty's poorer subjects if provision were made for the well-ordering of common lodging-houses.'

Here is an average specimen of one of the better sort in Charter-street. We enter out of a bright frosty air direct into the common room, – a room which looks as if it had once been a shop. It is dark and cold outside – inside it is ruddy with a glowing fire, and reeking with the damp of drying clothes and perspiring humanity. Eighteen adults and several babies of both sexes are here, seated on backless benches in a room about 14 ft. square. In one corner are the itinerant tinman and his wife, busy soldering up the pastry cutters which, by their leaf-like forms, suggest that the days of pork pies are at hand. It is about eleven o'clock at night, and little Maggie, their seven years old daughter, who ought to have been in bed long ago, is busy watching, and fetching the soldering irons. There, half asleep, propped up by the wall, sits a woman knitting cheap mats for ornaments; and in front of the fire is a vagrant blind singer, who says he gets his living in the streets by 'singing a few patriotic songs in the ould Irish style.' One woman is brewing tea in a basin, and stirring it with a knife to give it a flavour. As for the rest, they are 'cadgers' of all sorts and conditions, dozing in front of what they are pleased to call by the singularly inapt epithet of a 'rousing' fire. Listless, moody, almost sullen, they certainly do not talk, and scarcely seem to think, and their chief object appears to be to postpone as long as possible the terrible ordeal of going to bed. Nor do we wonder at this when we have seen what bed is like. Passing through what once was the 'shop parlour,' where there is a bed to be occupied presently by the 'deputy' and her husband, we ascend to the bedrooms. Of these there are four and in these four there are ten beds, each bed to hold two persons. As to the beds themselves they present every possible variety of archaeological interest, the old four-poster being decidedly the favourite, for, with the top removed, the posts are very available as a hanging wardrobe, on which such garments as are either too good or too bad to serve as additional covering are arranged for the night. The attic ceiling is black with damp and mould, and the wet drops through on to one of the beds. There is neither gas nor fire here, and the cold damp chill which strikes us as we enter, explains the desire evinced by the occupants to take as much heat up to bed with them as possible. What the effect of this change must be is told by the racking cough of some of the huddled-up inmates who have already retired.

So much for the physical effect of the bedrooms. As for the moral effect what can be expected where the beds are placed as close to each other as they well can be? There is no screen, no curtain, no provision for the common necessities of life – not even any appliances for washing; and 'they washes when they wants to in a bowl on one of the forms in the kitchen,' is the information we obtain in answer to what is evidently deemed an impertinent question. This house seems to be a favourite, for the 'deputy' says she is 'mostly allus full,' and only had 'a half bed empty' last night, 'and reckons to make her five shillings every night.' The standard price in Charter-street seems to be threepence per night per person, and 'they mostly sort themselves' for sleeping partners, anyone who comes in late taking the first vacant place.

## Wednesday, February 23, 1870

### THE GERMAN COLONY

From Charter-street we pass to Angel-street. Here too the property is in the most neglected state. We will take two adjoining houses, both of which are registered, as fair illustrations. In both of these the wet streams through their roofs, and in one we could actually see through a large hole into the open air. A broken spout conveys the water from the one side of the roof to the other, and by its overflow drenches the house from attic to kitchen. During a recent heavy storm the tenant was up till three o'clock in the morning ladling up the water as it came in. In the back yard the only access to the privy is by crawling over the ashpit, and when there there is neither door nor seat. About four feet from the kitchen window is a slaughter-house – registered, too, we presume by the local authority – and the maddened and infuriated animals have to be driven into this narrow back yard before they can be slain. No repairs have been done for a long time, and the only notice taken of the complaints made has been to raise the rent. A year or two ago the weekly rent was 6s. 6d.; it was then raised to 7s. 3d.; it is now 7s. 6d. This rent is not called for, but has to be taken every Saturday morning to the landlord, who, we were informed, but we hope erroneously, is a member of the Town Council.

In Crown Lane is a block of four houses forming the lodging-houses of the wandering Germans, and very much more cleanly they are kept than are the common lodging-houses of the wandering English. The walls are gay with coloured prints which have come from 'Fatherland'; the benches and tables, instead of being black with dirt, are white with scrubbing, and, so far as the internal economy of the houses is concerned, there are many more appliances for comfort and decency than we have seen elsewhere. But here, too, the roof and walls are in much disrepair. There is no window nor ventilator in the stair-case, and the smell ascends from the kitchen into all the upper rooms. As German cooking is somewhat pungent, and as German smoking is pretty constant, a good deal of smell does go up there. These four houses have but one privy amongst them, and through each of their yards flows an open gutter, carrying through each the 'swill' and refuse of the other. They have no water laid on, and it has all to be fetched from a tap in the street. When we think that at least fifty people occupy these houses, we wonder how it is they are so clean, and leave them with a very high opinion of their keepers.

Style-street and Back Mount-street run parallel to each other, but Back Mount-street is on a much higher level than Style-street, consequently the houses are built over one another. Opening out of Style-street, on the left hand coming townwards, between the houses, are here and there narrow entries. There is only one outlet to these, and in the half-dark places thus formed are four privies in such a condition that it is almost impossible to enter them. The floor is a flood of urine and a mass of ordure. The ashpit is overflowing with decaying vegetable refuse, and rendered more than usually disgusting by receiving the filth from Back Mount-street as well. What ventilation there is here is into the street, and immediately under the windows of inhabited dwellings. In order to exhaust at once the horrors of this place, we will go to Back Mount-street and look at the second storey of these latrines. Here, to enter them, we descend into a cellar passage, and find a low range of privies with not a door nor a seat amongst them; often, too, without the stone support on which the seat rested, and to add to all these horrors comes up the reeking stench from those below. Our courage requires the aid of brandy, and our nostrils that of strong tobacco; yet this is all the 'accommodation' afforded for 11 houses, in which dwell well-nigh 200 people. Very bitter and very deep is the outcry of the poor who are compelled to live here – live here, too, from year end to year end – at this enforced indecency; and, indeed, we learned to consider those as the most decent people who openly used the public street.

We have not done with this fever pit yet. Over it people live! Yes, there are houses over this, and the stench from this reeking mass of festering filth is the air they breathe, in which they sleep by night, and which poisons the little food they get by day. We go into a house in Mount-street. On the ground floor, over the entrance to these latrines is a small room, occupied by a man, his wife, and their child. It is bedroom, kitchen, parlour, and all; and the wife and child must spend almost all their time in this atmosphere – an atmosphere, 'which is enough to knock you down of a morning,' as a visitor there says, and which even now, when the fire is burning and the door open, is much too strong for even our hardened lungs and nostrils. Up stairs more people live, and up stairs more stench goes, and fever follows it.

## Thursday, March 3, 1870

### DEATH IN THE STEWS

Women standing about in the doorway, or coming in with some drunken man whom the ginshops of Deansgate have half maddened, betoken the nature of the place and its traffic. Crouching round a fire are six or seven women, silent; there is no sound heard but sobbing, and the sibilance of long-drawn sighs. The change from the noise and riot elsewhere, to this oppressive quiet, makes us enter on tip-toe, and ask with bated breath the cause. It soon reveals itself. On the knees of the centre figure of this strange group lies a little month-old baby, dying, – the last of twins. It is miserably thin, and the yellow skin shows the articulation of its frame in plainest and most repulsive manner.

The eyelids are drawn close down, and a long bony arm weakly and painfully raises itself, the scraggy hand, unfolding itself convulsively, points upwards, and then, as a faint sigh escapes from the little one, falls slowly down, and rests apparently for ever. A cry of sorrow breaks forth from the mother; tears glisten in the fire light, and plough literal, not metaphorical, furrows down the painted cheeks of the sorrowing harlots. We could not sorrow; to us it seemed a matter of rejoicing that the poor child's miserable parenthesis of life should be so short, and that the cradle and the grave should be so close together. The mother said she had been turned out of one lodging the night before, for fear the baby should die in the house and 'interfere with business.' A drunken soldier, with his uniform buttoned all awry, leant frowning against a screen, and a gaily coloured portrait of Pius the Ninth smiled from its frame on the wall on this sad scene in the drama of life and death. But no, not death unfortunately. The child lives, or did a few days ago; its little spark rekindled, and yet flickers doubtfully. Turned out from here because the child didn't die, the wretched mother sought refuge in that last and most vile of all places – an ex-public-house, now trading on vice under the sanction of the police, protected by the common lodging-houses acts.

### Thursday, March 10, 1870

#### THE SINGING PUBS

How prolific of vice the Deansgate quarter is, a few facts and figures will painfully demonstrate. There are 151 common lodging-houses, giving a total of 519 rooms, and making up 1,612 beds, affording accommodation for 3,224 persons. There are also 46 houses registered as houses of ill fame, and 73 as the known resort of thieves.

In one house, devoted to sporting notabilities, we saw no fewer than six card sharpers, all of whom had been many times in prison, and who were evidently engaged in the concoction of some new trick by which the unwary might be plundered more easily. It was a picture worthy of Teniers. The cards thrown aside, excepting a few held in the hands of the demonstrator; the closely gathered heads, of villainous expression and many shades of dirt, lit up by the light of the fire and one guttering candle; the strong contrast of light and shade, and the low villainy of the scene, were quite worthy of the Dutch master; and we found ourselves involuntarily criticising it as a work of art, till a strong oath, prefacing an inquiry as to who was wanted, woke us up to the reality of our position, so relieving their minds by informing them that it was none of them this time, we wandered away.

But the most startling feature of Deansgate is the enormous number of its ginshops, its public-houses, and its singing saloons.

Here is a place opening out of the main thoroughfare. Outside and on the ground floor, it is a ginshop; inside and upstairs it is a singing saloon. It is a long, low range of rooms thrown into one another, tiers of benches run longitudinally down the room, with very narrow tables in front of them, then more benches until the room is full. At the time of our visit it was crowded with men and women – not respectable artizans taking their wives for a little outing, but young men scarcely of age, chiefly apprentices to trades, by the look of their hands, with here and there a young man from a warehouse, who, with a short stick, short jacket, and short hat, looks quite as great a snob as he thinks himself a gentleman. The women were of Deansgate. There is a sodden, suffocating air of would-be gaiety in the whole thing, which is most intensely depressing; and not even the sporting coquetry of the well-developed damsels who occupied the centre seats, after the manner of their kind in the 'market row' of a more fashionable assembly, could relieve its tedium. Song followed song in wearisome monotony.

A youth of perhaps eighteen, the son of the proprietor, presided, and announced in regular succession that 'he had no doubt our friend Mr. Langley, or Mr. Kilvert,' as the case might be, 'would faver the cu'pney with an inkhore song.' As the work of the evening seemed to rest upon these two vocalists, they invariably did, but as for the audience, they took it placidly and bore it without a murmur. Never a muscle did they move, and it was only when some particularly rampant chorus could be evoked, that anything like a sense of animation exhibited itself. As for wit or humour, it was not to be found. There was scarcely an idea exhibited during our long stay, and we were very hot and very weary when we came away.

Not far away, in one of the streets leading from Deansgate, is another singing saloon, a saloon boasting a drop scene and proscenium. A grey, dirty, blind old man is strumming away with mechanical regularity at a cracked piano, and a tolerable voice is singing, with considerable taste, an air from *Don Giovanni*. Who the singer is no one knows – not even the proprietors.

His hair was very short, and he had evidently been making a longer sojourn in a larger establishment. His vocal efforts were not much applauded. They ranged much too high for his audience, and he was succeeded by a faded vulgar female, with not very much limp muslin in her dress, who brought down the house with innuendoes broadly put. By entering into a sort of omnibus box on the side of the stage – a box which served as a green-room also – the aspirant to fame amongst his fellows could enjoy the distinguished privilege of treating the prima donna to 'three pen'orth o' gin 'ot,' and other similar luxuries. It was curious to see how proud the young fools were of this distinction; the entrée to the green-room at the opera never sent the hearts of young swells bounding with more glee, than the entrance into this mystic recess did the young silly ones here. As for the singing usually given at these places, it was so admirably criticised by a slightly-inebriated habitué of this place, that we cannot refrain from quoting him: – 'Anything,' says he, 'is good enough for a drunken man, but this is a'most too bad for that.'

## Thursday, March 17, 1870

### THE ITALIAN ORGAN-GRINDERS

Running parallel with Market-street is Cannon-street. It is quite a relief to turn into a quiet house at the corner. It is a common lodging-house of an uncommon character, being one of those occupied by the Italian organ-grinders who raise our ire and our children's glee so frequently. The front room is occupied by the instruments of torture. Here are the villainous 'kists o' whistles' that have driven us to the verge of madness, and a longing desire to rush in and take our revenge is strong upon us, but it is restrained by a laudable effort, and we enter the back room instead. The *padrone* is in Italy, but his deputy steps forward to do the honours of the establishment. There are some eighteen or twenty people seated in the kitchen – bearded men and black-eyed women – the men mostly eating, the women knitting or sewing. There is plenty of merriment and laughter going, and the contrast between the stolid sullen silence of a common lodging-house occupied by eighteen tramps, and this, is startlingly great. Nor does the contrast terminate here; upstairs it is even greater. The beds are scrupulously clean and are provided with clean washing curtains, so as to screen each bed; and *mirabile dictu* there are appliances for washing! We never found such things in the common lodging-houses devoted to the vagrant English. The rooms for married couples are divided off by partitions affording every privacy; the decency, order, and cleanliness manifest themselves everywhere. One particular feature struck us much. On a shelf round each room was ranged an enormous number of piccolo pianos we used to see carried by our enemies some time ago. We inquire the cause of such number being here, and the answer startles us. 'Ah, signor, since they have shut up so many public-houses they are of no use. They are not loud enough for the streets – in fact, they could scarcely annoy anyone – so no money would be forthcoming to induce them to move on, and they find their limbo in the sleeping-rooms here.' Our guide did not know what he should do with them; perhaps when the *padrone* came back they might go into the country for the summer, but he regretted much the closing of the smaller public-houses. 'If they would close the singing saloons, signor, there would be some sense in it'; so diversely do we look upon things in this life! Descending into the kitchen again, and inquiring after the present conditions of Lucca, Genoa, Pisa, or wherever else our friends may come from, we leave with a pleasant 'a rivederci, signor,' uttered by a score of lips, pleased very much with all we have seen here.

These Italian lodging houses form a strong contrast with the cheaper English ones, and yet they are even cheaper. You may lodge for eighteenpence a week here.

---

We regret to announce that, owing to the illness of our contributor, – an illness directly traceable to his explorations of the 'slums' already described, – the regular weekly publication of this series of articles may have to be suspended for a week. We anticipate, however, being able to resume them on the 31st inst.

---

The investigator's illness proved more serious than expected, and the series was not resumed until April, 1871. By that time C. P. Scott had joined the paper. It is not perhaps surprising that in the summer he gave up a week of his holiday to canvassing for sub-scriptions to a housing association – 'of all useful enterprises it seems to me to be the one in which one may hope to do the largest amount of good, both physical and moral, with the smallest risk of incidental harm.' (Hammond, *C. P. Scott*, p. 37.)

## A WALK WITH A SCHOOL BOARD OFFICER

The 1870 Education Act established directly elected School
Boards with powers to make attendance compulsory in their
area and to pay the fees, if necessary, of those who could not
afford them (4d a week in Manchester). The writer is unidentified,
but is likely to have been Richard Whiteing.

Wednesday, September 17, 1873

'I'm glad we've got that boy at last,' says the officer, looking at one of
the names on his list. 'The father had to go to prison for him for seven
days, and I believe it was pretty nearly as much the lad's fault as anybody's.' The hopeful child had an almost invincible repugnance to the
pursuit of knowledge, and for a long time cherished in his mind a
rich preserve of the weeds of ignorance. The officer (sometimes in a
quite unofficial way) had taken all sorts of trouble with him, and once
seemed to have him well in hand. But it was only for a moment; the
next the bird had flown – not from the school alone, but as it seemed
from the neighbourhood, until he was found in company with others
of the feathered tribe in a pigeon fancier's loft pretty far from his own
home. What the birds said to him is not known; but it is conjectured
that they set him an example of docility under instruction which was
not without its effect. At all events, here he was, in school, his demeanour marked by all the meekness of the doves whose associate he
had lately been.

Some of the excuses for non-attendance are plausible enough; but
are they true? There is an alleged case of quinsy a few streets off. The
house lies in our way, and there will be no harm in making an inquiry
after the patient. Signs are not wanting on the road that the officer has
come to be popularly recognised as one of the district authorities. A
stout matron makes for him from her doorway. 'Here, I say, are you
the School Board? because I think it's a great shame you don't look
after Mrs. ——'s children as well as mine.' If we care to dive beneath
the surface of things for motives, we may find that the ladies have
simply fallen out, and that of two confederates formerly leagued against
the Board one has now turned informer on the other, in the good old-
fashioned way.

A weird figure of a child crosses our path – a small head and feet in
proportion peeping out from either end of a huge shawl – presumably
'mother's' – which seems to serve as cape and bodice and skirt and
petticoat all combined to be in another sense than motley the only

wear. This infant is not unknown to the Board. There is, indeed, a mutual recognition, and as soon as it has passed, the shawl – it is absurd to speak of the insignificant mite of a child inside it – is seen flying like 'the sail before the wind' which it so much resembles. 'I shall have you yet,' says the officer gloomily, and he keeps the even tenour of his way. The boy with the quinsy is at home, and in compliance with a friendly rather than an official request, puts the quinsy in evidence with a completeness that leaves nothing to be desired, save his speedy recovery.

These matters settled, there are defaulters to be warned. 'If I've told you once, Mrs. ——, I've told you twenty times,' says the officer, talking through a cottage doorway, 'that you'd get into trouble about that boy. And now you see your husband's summoned, and worst must happen if he don't attend.' 'What am I to do,' says the woman querulously – 'up from my confinement only a fortnight, and no one to run errands.' – 'I can't tell you, but you'll have to send that boy to school.' – 'He can't go; his boots are bad, and he has sore feet.' ('How can he run errands then?' – Visitor, *aside*.) 'You don't send either of them,' pursues the officer, 'if the girl doesn't make up three days and a half the rest of this week, you'll have a summons for her too.' 'The lies I've had from that woman,' he mutters as we walk away. 'If it isn't one excuse it's another; but in one thing she's always the same; she won't let the boy go to school. He hasn't attended for a month in all since Christmas last. They've been fined for him already, and I know they'll have to be fined again.'

He was talking a moment ago. He is now in nimble chase of the little animated bundle of shawl that we met a while ago. The shawl had turned out of a side street, and, seeing the officer, had once more fled before his face with all the speed its strangely muffled limbs could command. It is soon run down. It proves to be a truant, sent to school by its parents, and doing its persistent little best to get them fined. The shawl being now fairly cornered grows wet with tears, and from within it come promises of amendment in a broken voice. 'Don't let me ever catch you running away again when I call you,' says the officer. 'Never,' sobs the shawl, and, as soon as he has turned his back, it scampers round the corner rather faster than before.

Some women have watched the little comedy, but they don't interfere. 'It's only the School Board.' Everybody seems to know him. And he certainly knows everybody. In all this vast district there is not one child failing to attend school that is not familiar to him by sight and by name. At a rough estimate there should be about 5,000 names on the books, and of these all but about 50 are now duly entered. On a given day last November there were 4,177 children so set down; on the same day of the month this September there are 4,830, so the attendance has been increased by over 650 in two months short of the full year. How many of our grand conquerors might envy this one the solidity of his triumph.

'It's of no use to have anything to do with school board work unless you have a love for it.' He repeats that again and again. Finding out educational deficiencies is with him something more than a duty; it is a hobby. Years ago before the Board employed him, and before it existed to employ anybody, he visited some thousands of poor families to find out how many of them could read and write, and mainly for the love of the thing. The result, finally embodied in a report, showed that of the fathers of the rising generation but 25 per cent, and of the mothers but 34, could read or write, and that about 50 per cent of their children, aged from 14 to 20, were in absolute ignorance. The French have never invented so droll, yet at the same time so respectable, an example of the English passion for work.

## ETON BOYS

### Tuesday, July 15, 1873

The Eton and Harrow match has this year proved, no doubt, a highly profitable affair for the proprietors of Lord's Cricket Ground; but there the profit ends. It is difficult to say which is most painful – the fulsome slang in which the *Daily Telegraph* gloats through three columns over the incidents of the great 'event,' or the disgraceful fight of excited schoolboys with which the match concluded. It is bad enough that the University crews should every year be crowned by the sporting papers and the sporting public with the doubtful honours formerly reserved for racehorses and prize-fighters. They are old enough to take no great harm from such unenviable notoriety, and most of them heartily dislike it. But it is a different thing when mere lads are seized upon for the same kind of treatment, when their names are bandied about with all the vulgar familiarity due to important sporting characters, and their points and performances minutely criticised by gushing special reporters and masters of turf slang. What kind of ambitions are likely to be bred among schoolboys who find all London eager to see them play a cricket match, 10,000 people wild with excitement at the game, the London newspapers in fits of sympathetic emotion, and a successful champion on the winning side treated to an ovation simply frantic in its enthusiasm? The first result was, as we have seen, that the partisans on either side so far forgot the restraint of gentlemanly feeling, not to say of common decency, as to belabour each other, and the police and the bystanders into the bargain, with fists and sticks. The second result, if the authorities of Eton and Harrow have the courage to perform what they must know perfectly well to be their duty, is that the school match will not again be played in London.

### Wednesday, July 30, 1884

Mr. Warre has been elected to the Head Mastership of Eton. The new Head Master has been assistant master at the school for over twenty years; he is probably the best rowing coach in England. He has done more to mould the Eton of to-day than any living man, partly owing to his native force of character, partly owing to his boundless popularity among the boys. The question, therefore, of the goodness or badness of his appointment depends on the further question whether Eton is a good school or the contrary. If it is really true that the moral tone of the school is bad, that idle and luxurious habits are fostered instead of being sternly repressed, as they were at other English schools by an Arnold or a Bradley, that the boys are contemptuous of discipline, and have developed to a high degree that youthful insolence for which it is hard to find an exact equivalent outside the Greek language – then the appointment is probably not a good one.

## JOSEPH ARCH AND THE FARM WORKERS

### Friday, January 16, 1874
*From our Special Correspondent*[1]

Sheffield, Thursday

A man was smoking a pipe outside the Temperance Hall to-day during the dinner hour. He had the strong frame of one who had done much work, and his face showed that he might still do at least as much more – a sturdy labouring man of middle age, one would have said at a first glance, with nothing very remarkable about him in any way. It was Joseph Arch, who spoke at this Congress last night, and was speaking again to-day.[2] Joseph did not go into the public-house to smoke his pipe, because he is a total abstainer. He is however no bigot in these matters, and though he would cheerfully consent to enter a gin palace

1. The Congress was reported by John Turner. This sketch may be his or Richard Whiteing's.
2. Joseph Arch (1826–1919), Liberal M.P. for N.W. Norfolk 1885–1886 and 1892–1902. The village inn at Barford in Warwickshire is now called the 'Joseph Arch.'

to further the business he has in hand, nothing would induce him to break his temperance pledge. It has been said that there is nothing remarkable in the face, but the moment one *knows* this is Joseph Arch one begins to look for the signs of power, and finds them in the large mouth with its thinnish lips capable of closing very tightly on a resolution taken. There is something of the same meaning in the rather cold blue eye, or the novelists who lay down the laws for us in these matters are all at fault. For the rest, the best thing that can be said about the face is that it is essentially English, in not promising finer achievements than brain and hands are likely to perform. It has had to be examined somewhat curiously, not to say impertinently, to show any expression at all, and at first view it is simply a good, plain, serviceable collection of features, such as belongs to so many men in this island who have the knack of doing the most astonishing things.

Some of the delegates here have an odd but impressive habit of calling out, not their names, but the number of men they represent, when they rise to speak – as thus, '90,000,' which means that so many busy fellows who are now hammering or stitching away in this or that great town have sent me with this message to you. Were Arch to adopt that practice he might announce himself as '100,000,' for that number of agricultural labourers look up to him as their hero and their chief. Yet about a couple of years ago and not a hundred of these were organised for obedience to his or any other man's summons. At that time he was a field worker himself, living in the neighbourhood of Leamington. He was something more than an agricultural labourer and something less. He did all kinds of odd things. In his boyhood he had followed his master to the hunt with the led horse; as he grew older he picked up some knowledge of carpentering, and when there was nothing else to be done he could take a hand at most kinds of field work. He was in short a general handyman, and was reputed to be pretty thorough-going in whatever he undertook.

Besides all this he had gained some local fame in another kind of labour – the preaching of the Gospel. As a Methodist he had been rather unpopular with the parsons long before he had the good fortune to give special offence to the squire. At one time he had found it very hard to get work in his own neighbourhood, and he had been obliged to travel from place to place not so much in search of work alone as in search of work and independence together. Hence, in great part, his general aptness; hence, too, another acquisition of infinitely greater value – the fortitude to endure petty persecution. This, he maintains, is a virtue only to be had through practice, and one likely to be found in its greatest perfection in modern days in the 'Methody' man. The Methody man has in many cases to pay for his popularity among the poor by becoming an object of contempt and aversion to the classes above them. The parsons do not like him, and the squire, as in duty bound in things spiritual, takes their word for it that he is a person who ought not to be liked. The Methody gets used to this state of things; hence a good three fourths of the emissaries now working under Arch are of that persuasion, and, like him, have done their little bit of wayside preaching in the teeth of all sorts of odium and of hindrance from the keepers of the agricultural conscience. One of his agents, trying to speak at Leighton Buzzard on fair-day, had a narrow escape of his life, and had to be marched back to the railway station by an escort of policemen to save him from the wrath of the farmers – who had dined – and the rowdies supposed to be in their pay.

It was on a day in 1872 that Arch was destined to become famous. He was staying in his cottage for two reasons; for one it was a wet day, for another his soldier son was home on furlough, and the father wanted to spend some time with his lad. On that day the farm labourers, acting under some mysterious influence, which Arch declares is the secret of Divine Providence, and not his, made up their minds to combine for the bettering of their condition. He had said nothing to them, and as far as he knew, they were wholly uninfluenced from without. It was a case of spontaneous combustion, and the fire broke out in three places at about the same time. The labourers were dumb, and they wanted a spokesman. They remembered the 'Methody,' and they came to his cottage just as he was finishing a box to hold the 'traps' of his son. He was asked to speak. At first he declined, but after a while they seized him good humouredly by the collar and dragged him out into the open, and there and then he had to begin his first social, political, economical oration as best he could. The thoughts were in him, and under this pressure of circumstances they came out. From that moment to this, heart, hand, and head have been given to the work.

COMMENT

Thursday, January 1, 1874

The impression which Mr. Arch's speech produces as a whole is one of thoroughly honest conviction on his part. Even when he said hard things he usually said them in a homely way which was indeed extremely telling oratorically, but at the same time smacked of a certain good nature very wholesome in controversies involving class interests, into which it is fatally easy to infuse a leaven of bitterness. What, for instance, as a retort against the plea often set up against raising wages, that if wages are increased the increase is likely to be misspent, could be better than this: – 'Would any landlord like to hear of his tenants saying, We owe you so much, but we will pay you 40 per cent less, because you are a horse racer and a gambler, and on such and such a horse race you lost £40,000, and we do not like you to spend your money like that. Would those gentlemen like to be treated like that?' This is a sort of argument which will appeal to both sides.

Now, a man who can talk like this, who can express in a vigorous, homely way the wants and the wishes of a great class whose language hitherto has with us, been somewhat inarticulate, and in other countries has become articulate chiefly in the burning of ricks and the shooting of landlords, certainly deserves to be heard with respect.

## THE 'NEW UNIONISM'

The Dockers' Strike in London and a gas workers' strike in Manchester, both in 1889, were part of the movement to organise the low-paid unskilled workmen. In Manchester, the Dean, John Oakley (1834–1890), a Christian socialist, wrote two letters when the strike failed which the *Guardian* gave on the main news page. They were based on interviews which he and the Rev. H. T. Smart (Methodist) and the Rev. Bernard J. Snell (Congregationalist) had with the men.

### Monday, December 16, 1889

#### THE STRICKEN STRIKERS

*To the Editor of the 'Manchester Guardian'*

Sir, – There seems to be room for a brief summary of the whole story of the gas stokers' strike, told by the men. This I got from them yesterday evening, with the benefit and assistance, as friendly questioners, of the Rev. Messrs. Smart and Snell. Most of the following sentences were written or dictated by the men who met us.

I. Some Manchester gas stokers, having read in the summer that a union had been formed in London, came to the conclusion that they ought to form branches in their own district. They consulted the General Secretary in London, Mr. Thorne,[1] with the result that on August 23, 1889, the first branch was formed. So eager were the men to join, that the officers had difficulty in supplying cards and books of

---

1. Will Thorne (1857–1946), founder of the National Union of General and Municipal Workers.

rules. Over 5,000 men were enrolled in the Manchester district in the first three months.

II. After the men had got rule-books and had time to read them (note the ingenuous chronology) they found that the object was to establish a system of an eight hours' working day in all gasworks. This raised discussion here, as such an alteration in working would make a reduction in wages in many cases. But it was agreed that 'the rules should be adhered to,' the reduction of wage being accepted for the sake of reduction of time and the probable employment of other men. This great gain was achieved in comparative peace, but not without the men being told by one of the managers that if they did get the eight hours they would not have it long; and further, that 'before the Gas Committee would be bested with us' (beaten by us) 'they would commence with the watchmen at the gates and discharge every man.' In fact, he said the Gas Committee would spend £50,000 or £100,000 before they would be beaten. This view and language explains all the subsequent suspicion on the men's part.

However, the terms were granted, and all seemed well until the first pay-day.

A period of confused negotiations led to a strike or lock-out (it was threatened as one and developed into the other), mainly over the question of non-unionism.

### Tuesday, December 17, 1889

1. There is no room for doubt that the whole treatment of the men by the two Gas Committees was throughout what the French call '*de haut en bas*' – the attitude of stooping from a great height. I avoid the common adjectives which imply contempt or scorn, for of any conscious air of these there is no trace. Nobody meant to be unfair or unkind, I am willing to believe. But there it is, in every line and phrase of the communications, that the men had no right to do what they were doing – viz., to dictate to their employers, – and that before all things it was necessary in the public interest to convince them of this. For one, I traverse this position absolutely. We ought all to welcome the growing independence and power of the workman – his ability to make by means of combination his own terms and conditions with employers, on an equal footing. It affords the only hope of those fundamental social reforms affecting the lives, health, wages, moral welfare, mental progress, and recreations of the poor – in which hitherto our Parlia-

ments, Governments, corporations, companies, and committees have been either sterile or ineffective.

2. The second fact that stands out is the fear, and the grounds for it, on the part of the men that they had to face settled hostility on the part of the subordinate rulers of the gasworks. In the interest of all of us, this spirit should be firmly stamped out. Nothing is so certain to lead to the renewal of strife. Obviously true tales reached me which it would do no good to put in print. But I desire to note the confirmation of them by Sir J. J. Harwood in the act of denying that any hostility existed. So far from this, he said, we have been used to engage our new hands at the office in the Town Hall *lest any prejudice* on the part of the overseers or foremen *should lead them to reject union men*! If the Corporation knew it to be necessary thus to provide against it, who will wonder that the men feared it?

3. This leads to the difficult question of the relations between union and non-union men. In the interest of employers as well of employed, it is probably to be desired that the habit of combination amongst the workers should become universal. And many of the former hold this strongly. But my present point is rather to help candid people to realise what is meant by compelling them to work side by side. To begin with, the unionists *cannot* imagine a favourable reason for refusing to join them. They know their own intentions and the good results for all of their action. And they find the minority who are led to hold out in no way backward to accept the benefits procured by the courage and self-sacrifice of the unionist majority, who have, of course, only succeeded by *being* a majority. And they accordingly regard these men as aiming at their own interest and trying to 'stand in' with the employers and their foremen.

4. One passes naturally to observe how this and all the other incidents of the local controversy illustrate the need for self-protection on the part of the men, and bring out the true purpose of a trade union. Its objects are mainly two – to provide pacific means for the settlement of labour questions, and to enable the men not only to protect themselves but to help one another.

Strikes are utterly foreign to the spirit of a trade union. Strikes are the mere ultimate appeal to force which is the final resource of all of us in the presence of the footpad or the burglar. Every true trade unionist *hates* them. His union exists to facilitate mutual knowledge and communication and to provide modes of arbitration and conciliation between those whose interests tend to clash. There would have been no strike here if both sides had been willing and accustomed to meet and negotiate upon equal terms. The habit on the men's part of considering one another was touchingly illustrated. When some of us, before the mediation, tried to arrive at an irreducible *minimum* of their demands, we were met by this plea, amongst others: 'But we can't ask for our own reinstatement, upon any conditions, without also asking for the reinstatement of those who have "gone out" simply in order to support us.' And this real 'altruism' has cost them dear. Some of us think that several other kinds of association – political, municipal, and ecclesiastical – may have something to learn from the disparaged and despised trade unions.

5. I cannot refrain from speaking with the most deep and sincere respect of the simplicity and inexperience and readiness to confide even in their avowed enemies displayed by the men. I have tried to deal in no hard words. And if I speak of 'taking advantage,' it is because I can literally find no others to describe the policy of the Gas Committees of the two boroughs when it became clear to them that they were dealing with an infant, unorganised, and impecunious union, led by ignorant and simple men. And I would not use them now if I could not honestly add that I know they do not describe the conscious aim of any individuals – certainly of none known to me. But I am sure they do describe the unconscious bias and the consequent line of conduct of a group of public officials who had come to believe it to be a public duty to defeat the gas stokers; and to do so, almost *per fas aut nefas* – by silence, or suppression, or delay, or official and impersonal proclamation; or by the threats or cajolery of underlings. My point is that the men met all this with the courage of clear consciences, and the openness and frankness of gentlemen. No doubt they showed cards which they might have more prudently concealed. But if the masters have got the tricks, the men perhaps have won by honours.

*Deanery, December 16*                                     Yours etc.,

J. OAKLEY

# The Condition of Ireland Question

The *Guardian*'s lasting concern for Ireland came about ten years after its commitment to radical social reform in England. It arose in the same way – from careful study of the conditions in which people lived. This led it after six years to a belief in Home Rule.


## WHEN THE CROP FAILS

The winter of 1879–1880 was one of great distress in Ireland through the failure of the potato crop. The *Guardian* sent out W. T. Arnold, a newcomer to the staff, to inquire:

Monday, February 16, 1880

Clifden, Sunday

Brown bog and purple moor hold more than their fair share in Connemara. This state of things may be partly due to the imperfect means of communication, a subject to which I shall return presently, but there is no doubt that the line of country from Galway to Clifden would present a far better appearance than it does if the landlords were resident and energetic as improvers, instead of being, in the main, mere rent-receivers and absentees.

The first ten miles of my drive from Galway through the rain were enlivened by the endless stream of red petticoats pouring into the town for the weekly market. The women were of all ages – some young and shapely, with here and there a really beautiful face; others old and withered, but all clothed in the picturesque Connemara dress, the flowing folds of thick white stuff wound round the body and covering the head, and the petticoats of all shades of red, from vermilion to claret. The shades of red were sometimes superb, and it was a perfect feast to the eye to have all this bright colour to contrast with the universal greyness and mistiness of the rest of one's surroundings. The great majority were quite guiltless of shoes and stockings; but some more careful or better off than the rest were carrying a good pair of boots and woollen stockings in hand, as well as their loads of butter on their backs, intending to put them on before entering the town. It looked rather melancholy to see all these women trudging into town their eight or ten miles along the highway in the rain; but I trust they sold their eggs and butter well, and came back home with lighter loads and heavier purses. Oughterard is a decent little town on Lough Corrib, much frequented by anglers in the summer, and was a fortnight or three weeks ago the scene of very severe distress. Since then a good deal of relief has come, and for the moment the people are better off. But there is the usual lack of seed potatoes, and no employment to be had. In a poor country like Connemara, where there are no substantial farmers worth mentioning, there is nothing to look to for the support of the people except the employment that is to be had in England. Great numbers of people go every year from this district to work in the dockyards on the Clyde, and one of the causes which have combined with other more obvious evils to depress the condition of the people is the slackness of the ship-building trade for the last few years.

Eighteen miles further along the road in the neighbourhood of the Recess Hotel I found a certain amount of much-needed employment being given by the public-spirited landlord of the Recess Hotel, Mr. Macredy. He has 100 men at work making a road and an enormous boon the employment certainly is. From here to Clifden, however, nothing is being done, and the result is an amount of distress which makes itself very visible in the town.

The whole of this coast is very badly off. Their potatoes have failed, their oats have failed, even the fish have failed. As to the fisheries it is the usual story of the fish remaining outside in the deeper water, and the fishermen not having the necessary boats or gear to enable them to face the open sea. The low price of cattle has further aggravated the distress and though there is an upward movement in certain kinds of stock, at present it would be unwise to draw too sanguine deductions from it. Well bred yearlings are readily sold this year, as any year, by jobbers, who buy them up throughout the country for stall feeding; but the ordinary small cattle of the country, which are what alone the poor farmers possess, command as yet no sale at all. The people all along the coast and in the many islands off it must be helped to live for the next few months, for, as far as those best acquainted with their circumstances can judge, there is little prospect of their being able to support themselves. The islands are in some cases particularly badly off. There is much distress in Inishturk and Terburt for instance, and the same applies to the larger Boffin Island off Cleggan Point. I had hoped to pay a visit to Boffin Island and see the state of the people for myself, but it is a nine mile row from the mainland, and the wind getting up I took warning by the experience of an unfortunate commercial traveller who went to the island last year intending to stay a night and was weather-bound for a week, during which he subsisted on potatoes and buttermilk – the Irish commercial's ordinary diet being as far as I can judge of a decidedly liberal character, and consisting mainly of chops and whisky – and finally came out a thinner and wiser man. But I learnt enough of the condition of the people to be properly thankful for the expedition of the *Goshawk* which has set off with 50 tons of meal on board to visit the islands off the coasts of Galway and Mayo. Most of these islands are far too thickly populated, and there can be little doubt that if facilities for emigration were offered they would be largely accepted, but in a month or two the fisheries by which the islands mainly live will be in full swing again, and their urgent distress may fairly be hoped to be of a temporary character.

There is a lawless spirit still visible in Clifden and the surrounding district. The people are very excitable and fond of a row, and the police have been strengthened into quite a formidable body. A large farmer in the neighbourhood of Letterfrack, who was suspected of having paid his rent without the reduction demanded by the rest of the tenants, had a hundred of his sheep drowned one night a few weeks ago. Some other tenants of a small Clifden landlord had not only carefully abstained from paying any rent but had decamped from their houses altogether, first easing their minds by totally demolishing the roofs and windows appertaining thereto. The poor landlord told me of this with a very rueful countenance, and as he was by no means severe on his tenants, it was rather a hard case it must be allowed. One of my drivers, a rakish-looking old man, who really was like the Hibernian in a play, told me half a dozen such stories with intense gusto, breaking forth after his narration of each exploit into a long senile chuckle, which was a source of great enjoyment to himself and great amusement to me. However, on the whole, things are beginning to quiet down. Where a fair reduction has been given the rents have been paid. An agitator would say that this is because the spirit of the people has been crushed out of them by their tyrants. My own impression is that the people are rather to be compared to schoolboys who have tried hands successfully at a barring-out, but having won pretty much what they wanted or expected to get, if not all they asked, do not care to push their resistance any further.

It is not 'rack-renting,' to use a spouter's phrase, that is bringing the people down – though I fully hold that, unless there is a great improvement in the seasons, rents must be generally reduced below the level fixed at a time of high prices – but the general lack of employment. A proposal is on foot, and has been on foot for the last half dozen years, which would give employment to thousands. I refer to the Galway and Clifden railway. The line would not be difficult to make, and would be probably remunerative. If the country is ever to be developed at all, it can only be developed by a railway. Merely for governmental purposes it is very necessary that the communication between Galway and Clifden should be improved. In the late disturbances the amount of inconvenience and delay which had to be endured before the police at Clifden and the neighbourhood could be reinforced was almost incredible. But the line would be an immense benefit in more ordinary and more important respects. At present Clifden is supplied with all heavy articles by ship from Galway, and when the weather is bad no ship of moderate size can venture to face Slyne Head. The consequence is that there are times when there is hardly anything to be bought in the place. As for any trade in the Connemara marbles or such weighty goods it is out of the question. Now that the kelp trade seems to have gone away from the coast, I am afraid never to return, it is necessary, if we are not to have a partial famine in Connemara every dozen years, either to emigrate the people to a large extent or to give them a chance of a market for anything they have to sell. At present it is not an uncommon thing to buy a splendid turbot in Clifden for a half-a-crown that at a Dublin fishmonger's would fetch a sovereign. So much for considerations of permanent utility. The urgent reason, however, for such a work is that it would give the people employment for the next six months, and if they do not get any such employment I for one am at a loss to understand how they are to live.

## THE YEAR OF DECISION

In 1886 Gladstone introduced a Home Rule bill for Ireland, split his party, and lost a general election. Most of the great regional newspapers had been Liberal; many now went Unionist. The *Guardian* took Gladstone's line. Behind its decision lay the careful study of Irish conditions which Arnold had begun in 1880, and which was continued in such inquiries as that which Spenser Wilkinson (1853–1937) now undertook. He had joined the paper in 1882. The leader writing on Ireland remained in Arnold's hands.

Tuesday, February 16, 1886

Ballaghadereen, County Mayo

A miserable footpath left the road at right angles. 'Shall we go along the *boreen*?' said Father Dennis, the parish priest, whose car had brought us; and along the *boreen*, or sidepath, we picked our way to the first of a

group of cottages which here studded the hillside. The tenant, a
healthy, clear-eyed man of six and thirty, stood in front of the door and
welcomed my friends. At once he began, unasked, to tell them the
story of his rent. The tenants on the estate to which he belonged had,
it appears, agreed to act together in refusing payment unless a reduction
of half a year's rent were agreed to. The agent offered a reduction of
15 per cent, which they refused, and he began to 'process' them. At
once the combination broke down. Our sturdy tenant appeared
ashamed of himself. He evidently felt that he had done a mean thing;
as he said, 'I've paid the rint, sorr, £5 – £4-10s. for the year's rint and
10s. for costs.' He explained that the holding was of 14 acres, of which
he had half and his brother half, the total rent being £9. The borders
of the plot were pointed out, and a more miserable piece of land eyes
never saw. It had been an unclaimed mass of bog and rock; years of
labour had given it the appearance of fields, and portions of it had
borne potatoes and possibly oats. But a strong imagination would be
needed to see value in it.

> Wilkinson went on to describe the cottages and the poverty he
> found there.

But to return to the hillside and the moors; it is there that the words
'holding,' 'rent,' and 'eviction' can be interpreted, for these words in
Ireland cover realities unknown in England, and the ordinary English
interpretation of them would give rise to a notion of Irish life that
would be no better than a caricature. A mile from where the dying
man lay was a widow's cottage. She, too, had paid her rent. I was shown
over the holding. I spent half an hour in noting the crops that had been
grown, their values, the value of the seeds – all the data, in fact, out of
which the value of the land might be inferred. They seemed to confirm
the evidence of my eyes, that the land had no value whatever. I wanted
to know how the rent had been paid. The widow has six sons – two
are in England; four were at home and talked to me. The youngest, a
fine strong boy of twenty, stays at home and works on the holding.
The other three were a large part of last year in Cheshire, working as
farm labourers. Their wages averaged 12s. to 13s. a week each, and out
of this during the year 1885 they sent home between them £12. That is
the whole history of the rents of these holdings. They are not paid out
of the land, for the simple reason that that is impossible. The plots I
have described are cultivated at a loss. After returning from our drive
we dined with our friend the priest, and met at his table three other
priests, a well-to-do farmer, and a gentleman holding an official
position here. All of them knew well the holdings I had visited, so I

produced my figures for discussion and elucidation; the conclusion, from which there was no dissent, was that no business man would undertake to cultivate these bogs even if they were given to him.

'Why, then,' I asked, 'do these poor people stay there?' This seemed to all my Irish friends a ridiculous question, as the answer to them was obvious. The people have nowhere else to go. If they leave their homes they must starve. To emigrate they cannot afford, and they are attached with a passionate attachment to their homes. Even from America and Australia their children send money to keep them in 'the old home.' On these holdings, miserable as they are, the tenants' improvements have conferred such value as they possess. The houses I saw had been built by their inmates. The tenants have drained what is drained, cleared what is cleared, tilled what is tilled of the land. The very road was made by the tenants when the great famine obliged the Government to find employment for a starving people. The landlord lives in England, and I cannot find that he has ever seen his Mayo property.

Saturday, May 15, 1886

COMMENT: LOOKING AHEAD

Ulster Protestants cannot destroy geography; they cannot dissolve the thousand ties that bind them to the Irish homeland. Represented in an Irish Parliament, they could effectually protect Irish Protestantism; if they hold aloof from such a Parliament, they will repent it. They will have refused to throw in their lot with their fellow-countrymen, and their fellow-countrymen will have a right to regard them as aliens. There will inevitably be a constant invasion of the special rights and privileges of Ulster, which Ulster can only resist by appealing for the help of England. If England listens to the plea, good-bye to the hope of friendly and peaceable relations between the two countries.

# THE PLAN OF CAMPAIGN

The special articles which the *Guardian* commissioned in 1889 were much more political in tone than the 1880 and 1886 series. The name of the writer is unknown.

## THE CLANRICARDE ESTATE

### Wednesday, September 4, 1889
*From our Special Correspondent*

Portumna, Galway

The late Marquis of Clanricarde was one of the noblest of this great race. A man of commanding presence, a favourite in society, and a statesman of high rank, yet found time to live for part of the year at Portumna Castle, where he kept up a continual round of gaieties. The country folk were as merry as they could be while he was at the Castle and always regretted his departure. There were quarrels no doubt between him and his tenantry, but even now you may see his portrait hung up in the houses of those who most abhor his son. And now the last of the line reigns. When the present Marquis of Clanricarde[1] dies the family of the Burkes will be extinct in the male line. It seems strange that with such ancestry Lord Clanricarde should be what he is. He hates his people sullenly and intensely. His delight is to wring money out of them, and when he cannot do that, to injure them and cause them sorrow. Except when his father was buried, he has never been near the estate. He would only accompany his mother's remains as far as Holyhead. So careless is he about the traditions of his family that to this day the late Marquis and Marchioness lie in neglected graves without the smallest memorial stones to show where they rest. He has never spent a five-pound note on the estate, which till lately was bringing him in £22,000 a year. Of all Irish landlords he is in the worst odour. Even Dublin Castle looks coldly on him; even Mr. Balfour[2] has not dared to hold him up as an example of maligned virtue.

As soon as I arrived in Portumna I was placed under the strict supervision of a detective sergeant and another constable. These were stationed opposite my hotel from the time of my arrival till my departure. It is rather a novel sensation for an English citizen, not con-

1. Second Marquis and 15th Earl of Clanricarde (1832–1916), Liberal M.P. for Galway 1867–71, succeeded father 1874; estates compulsorily transferred to Congested Districts Board 1915.

2. A. J. Balfour as Chief Secretary for Ireland 1887–91 undertook 'resolute government.' Prime Minister 1902–05.

scious of having committed any offence against the law, to be watched as if he were a notorious burglar or pick-pocket. But in a little time I rather enjoyed this police *espionage*. It gave one the feeling of being in Russia, without the trouble and expense of travelling thither. Another curious sight was Lord Clanricarde's bailiff walking up the street with a Winchester rifle in his hand, and two constables by his side with loaded rifles. My first business was to call on Father Pelly, the parish priest of Portumna. He proved to be an exceptionally good witness. He is the son of a land agent, and by education, connections, and personal interest belongs to the landlord party. Moreover, he is only a mild Home Ruler, and neither belongs to the National League nor approves of the Plan of Campaign. Therefore whatever he has to say on behalf of the Portumna tenantry may be received with ready credence. Now nobody could speak more strongly than he did. 'If,' he said, with humorous exaggeration, 'Mr. Balfour could have seen what I have seen during the last five years by this time he would have become an Invincible.' He told me that he regarded the situation with the utmost dismay. There is now no chance of the dispute being settled as between the landlord and the tenants. It will have to be settled compulsorily from without.

Meanwhile the exasperation of the people is rising to a dangerous point. They are getting out of hand, and the secret societies, which are the curse of Ireland, are gaining strength every day. Only lately Father Pelly had to dissolve the Gaelic Athletic Club of the parish because he found that it was being used for secret society purposes. It must be remembered that the people, who have suffered so cruelly and so undeservedly, have no outlet for their passions. If they could cheer and groan at public meetings and hear the cruelty of their landlord denounced, while they themselves were exhorted to patience and lawful behaviour, that would be a safety valve of enormous utility. As it is, the older men can only scowl and mutter curses, and the younger men are being continually tempted to plot revenge. Till lately Portumna, though not far from Loughrea of evil fame, was the most law-abiding parish in Galway. But some serious symptoms have recently made their appearance.

In the morning I drove out with Father Pelly to the scene of the late attack on Mr. Tener, Lord Clanricarde's agent. A large field of wheat here borders the road. It is about a hundred and fifty yards long from the road to the next fence, and there is not a tree or a bush of any kind of cover in it. Mr. Tener, armed with a Winchester rifle, drove past this field in broad daylight, and he was followed by a car holding three policemen. Of these the sergeant had a Winchester rifle, and the other men ordinary police carbines. As the cars approached two bands of men rose out of the corn, one of which attacked Mr. Tener and the other the police car. I stood exactly where each band had stood and examined the line of fire. A worse place than that chosen to attack Mr. Tener could not have been selected by any assailants anxious to succeed. The road is much lower than the field, and when I caused the driver of my car to pass along it I found that I could only see his broad shoulders. In fact, nearly all the shots intended for Mr. Tener struck the bank, and were either buried there or were taken by the ricochet over his head. Moreover, after the first volley, he was protected by a thick bush, and next by a much higher bank. He was actually hit by one or two small shots, but he was not hurt. It is reported that he wears chain mail, and at any rate no shot penetrated, and the next step of his horse took him out of danger. The police fared worse. The mare that drew their car was brought down by several shots in her neck, and when she attempted to rise she was shot again in the same place. This would seem to show that the men in the field did not desire to kill the policemen. When the mare fell the driver and the policeman on his side were thrown violently out of the car and both stunned for the moment. The sergeant and the remaining policeman were unhurt, and as soon as they could collect their scattered senses they rushed to the roadside, and the sergeant with his Winchester rifle and the constable with his carbine fired fourteen rounds at the retreating men in the field. These were stooping under the corn as they ran and the two policemen could therefore only fire at the moving grain. It is believed that their fire was ineffectual, and that the men got safe away to Lough Derg, where they took boat and so escaped.

The attack was curiously insensate, if the object of the men was to kill Mr. Tener, for only a single snap-shot could be obtained at a very small portion of his person. Therefore many people think that this was a bogus outrage got up by emergency men. I am convinced that it was not so. The fearful risk which the assailants ran, the fact that Mr. Tener was actually struck, the great danger that one of the shots aimed at the mare might kill a policeman – all these things show that the outrage was a genuine one. I believe that it was perpetrated by young men belonging to one of the secret societies, who were quite prepared to lose their own lives if anything went wrong. In short, it is a sad proof that in this unhappy part of Ireland the people can no longer keep their rage within lawful bounds.

Subsequently I visited the farmhouse from which Thomas Minogue was lately evicted. No more mournful sight could be seen in Ireland. Minogue was obviously a man who took great pride in his farm. The outbuildings were large and substantially built. In front of the house was a pretty little flower garden, with neat box edgings and little gravel walks. But the house itself was pulled to the ground, and thatch and walls were tumbled together in hopeless ruin. It seems that after Minogue had been evicted and his furniture tumbled into the road his wife and daughter crept back into an outer room to sleep. At three in the morning Mr. Tener, with an armed force of emergency men, came to the house and turned the unhappy women out – dazed and bewildered. Then the band applied levers and crowbars to the corners of the house, and in a very short time brought the whole building to the ground. There was not the slightest reason for this barbarous act. As Father Pelly said, it was 'nothing but an incitement to outrage.' Every Galway man who now passes by that house hisses a curse through his teeth.

## Foreign Affairs

### AFTER THE COMMUNE

#### TRANQUILLITY

C. B. Marriott had been inside Paris throughout the siege and reported the street fighting as the government troops slowly made their way in. His last message after a week of street fighting laconically reported 'All men and women taken with arms in their hands are immediately shot. Such is the order and it is rigorously executed.' He had not been unsympathetic to the Commune. In an earlier message he had written, 'It is extraordinary how popular all Englishmen have been with the Communists. In all my connection and transactions with them I have never been treated with anything but the greatest courtesy.' When all was over a *Guardian* leader regarded the present with disgust and the future with dismay:

### Thursday, June 1, 1871

'Tranquillity' has been restored, and Paris begins once more to assume its 'usual aspect.' The shops are being opened, coffee and absinthe are sipped as of old upon the Boulevards, and but for the smoke from the ruins of nearly a quarter of the city and the reek from a few thousands of yet unburied corpses, it would be almost possible to forget the horrors of the past week. The insurrection has been remorselessly trampled out. Its fires have been quenched in blood. The exasperation of the Versailles troops was extreme, and no attempt appears to have been made either by the Government or the officers to restrain their excesses. We are distinctly told that no quarter was given to man, woman or child found with arms in their hands, and the wounded were butchered as they lay. The very fact of being wounded served as a sufficient condemnation. When the actual fighting was over, a systematic search was started for those who were in hiding. Three shambles were appointed, and a system of wholesale and summary execution was commenced almost unparalleled for its reckless barbarity. A veritable reign of terror commenced. No man was safe from malicious denunciation or groundless suspicion. It is difficult to say whether the wholesale butcheries or the individual barbarities of which we hear are more horrible. Many of the incidents recorded by eye-witnesses are so utterly atrocious that they appear almost incredible.

Meanwhile M. Thiers[1] has spoken, not of moderation, but only of 'expiation,' and has applauded the worst excesses of this outbreak of military brutality as merely forming part of a 'glorious campaign.' The position of M. Thiers is no doubt difficult. He probably feels that his hold of power is daily becoming more precarious, and dares not oppose the revengeful appetites either of the army or of the Assembly. But it is likely that his reign, do what he will, will be brief, and it would have been well for him had it not been sullied by crimes which he will be held to have sanctioned because he did nothing to prevent them.

For the moment the triumph of the Assembly – that is to say of the peasants and the soldiery, guided by the priests – appears complete. The Red power has received a mortal blow at its very heart and centre. The Republic is felt on all hands to be on the point of giving way to some form of personal government. The often renewed struggle between the towns and the country has been decided once more in favour of the country. Yet, for all this, nothing has been really settled. France remains as she was before – two nations. One of these has for the time been weakened, but it will atone for diminished numbers by added hate. Its turn of success must one day come, and then it is terrible to think of the appeal that will be made to recent precedents. This party includes the miserable and the lawless in all the great towns of France. It includes also much of the boldest intellect and the most ardent popular sympathy in the country. At any time it may find leaders as capable as they are fanatical. Was it wise to drive such a party to desperation?

1. L. A. Thiers (1797–1877), leader of Liberal opposition to Napoleon III; first President of Third Republic 1871–73; defeated by Right wing and retired 1873.

### THE PILGRIMS AND THE REDS

The Catholic reaction against the anti-religious excesses of the Commune expressed itself symbolically in the building of the church of Sacré Coeur on Montmartre. The devotion to the Sacred Heart sprang from visions seen by a nun in Paray-le-Monial in 1685. The English contingent of an international pilgrimage to Paray was accompanied by the *Guardian*'s Paris correspondent – probably Arthur Ory who had been its war correspondent with the French army of the Loire. The *Times* was also represented – 'I was near forgetting to mention that after we had prayed for the conversion of sinners, the Canon proposed that we should say a few decades for a very hardened sinner who was in the same train with us, one that ought to be a Catholic, he said. This son of perdition was no other than the *Times* special.'

Thursday, September 4, 1873
*From our own Correspondent*

Paris, Tuesday 10 p.m.

I have just arrived with the main body of the pilgrims from Dieppe. There are at least 600 of us in all, so that I may be excused for forgetting or omitting many English noble and eminent Catholic names.

The whole town had come down either to welcome or examine them. A hand was laid on my shoulder, and on turning round I recognised an old acquaintance whom I first met on one of the battle-fields of the Loire, and a year later fighting in the streets of Paris against the Communards. He was promoted to a lieutenancy on the field of Coulmiers, and is now a captain. 'Have your countrymen no pilgrimages at home?' he asked. 'Yes,' said I; 'but there are international pilgrimages as well.' 'That's just it,' he interrupted; 'international is the word, and those people would do much better to remain in England, for,' he continued solemnly, 'will you have my opinion?' I said I desired nothing more earnestly. 'Well, the majority of those so-called pilgrims are rank Communards, and nothing else. But let them beware,' he went on. 'I have combated them once. If I have to do so again, God help them, that's all.' As he was getting excited I wished him good-bye till the *revanche*, and went to see the misunderstood pilgrims land. The first pilgrims I spoke to after the steamer was cleared were some honest Preston folk, who were horrorstruck on hearing my friend the officer's opinion of them, and inquired anxiously whether that was an opinion generally received in France. I was, of course, happy to assure them that it was not. I learned from them that they had had neither bite nor sup since 5.30 this morning, and it was then nearly four in the afternoon. On this hint I spoke, and we adjourned to the railway refreshment-room, where I had their corporal wants attended to.

## Saturday, September 6, 1873

Paray-le-Monial, Thursday

The special train which brought the English pilgrims here left yesterday morning about 7.30, and did not get to Paray till 10 p.m. The journey, instead of lasting twelve hours, which is quite sufficient, lasted fifteen. I attribute the delay chiefly to the ill-will and anti-pilgrim sentiments of the men employed on the line. They are most hostile to the movement which is to regenerate France, and the principal business of the special police commissary attached to the line running from Mâcon to Moulins is to keep the railway employés within the bounds of decency and common good behaviour towards the pilgrims to Paray. This holy shrine lies in the very centre of a Radical district of the reddest dye. Within a few miles we have the Creuzot Coal, Iron, and Engineering Works, employing 15,000 hands. Nearer still we have the mines and foundries at which other tens of thousands are employed. All these workmen are Radicals in politics and Socialists in religion, for Socialism is with them a dogma. Not very far away is St. Etienne, which has the speciality of murdering its prefects. At Mothard, a village about ten miles off, the Radical Mayor has just been committed for trial for swindling his *administrés*. He got the schoolmaster's salary raised, but on condition that the master should pay him 50 per cent on the increase.

On reaching Paray I saw one of the prettiest sights it has ever been my lot to behold. It was night already, but there was a splendid moon, and the sky was overcast with clouds just thick enough to moderate the moon's light without obscuring it, and to form the richest and most variegated halos one can imagine. There was not a breath of air stirring, and this allowed the lampions lit round the base of the church spire to burn steadily, and with a mild light. At a distance, when the moon disappeared for a few minutes, the black mass of the church could not be discerned, and then the lights formed a large halo such as we see over the heads of saints, apparently floating in the air. The little town itself was all ablaze with candles stuck with great prodigality on the window sills in the open air, but the most effective display of all was the hundreds of lights flitting round the station and glimmering through the trees.

At 10.30, immediately the bell pealed forth, the banners and lights got into motion again *en route* for the station, and once more we sang 'Sauvez Rome et la France. au nom du sacré coeur.' Besides the Bishop of Beverley, there was also waiting on the platform, with his mitre on, the Bishop of Oran, in Algeria. A ringing British cheer, three times repeated, such as the echoes of the night never heard before, and which did my heart good to hear, ushered the train into the little station. The English pilgrims now unfurled their banners, and that of 'the Catholic Association of Sheffield' took the lead at the head of the procession.

Physically the British pilgrims are a credit to Old England; that's a fact. In spite of their weary, tiresome ride they were, both men and women, as fresh as daisies. They walked, head erect, with an elastic step, and must have appeared a race of giants to the comparatively diminutive French pilgrims. Such chests, such shoulders, such beards (on the men), had they been a picked thousand chosen purposely for the occasion they could not have more astonished the French. Nearly all the pilgrims bought tapers, which they lighted and carried in their hands. Picture to yourself Chat Moss in the olden time, with thousands of will-o'-the-wisp's flitting about the morass, and you will be able to realise to some extent the fairy-like aspect of the scene as the procession wound slowly up the streets of Paray at midnight on its way to the church. In the dark corners of a bridge a deputation of the International had ensconced themselves. As soon as the gendarmes who had escorted the procession were out of hearing, these fellows sent up a shout of 'Vive les membres de la Commune.' The Frenchmen, who were evidently prepared for a manifestation, at once replied with a thundering 'Vive l'Angleterre Catholique.' 'A bas les Pèlerins' was the retort of the Communists. 'Vive les Pèlerins Anglais,' uttered with stentorian vigour, silenced them and the manifestations came to an end, probably without a single Englishman being aware that he had just assisted at what the French papers call 'des troubles.' We reached the church at last, but not till our countrymen had added one more proof to the French belief that we are not a musical nation. While some of us were singing the litany of the Blessed Virgin, others were chanting the Magnificat, and further on it was the English Hymn of the Sacred Heart. The effect of the whole was unsatisfactory.

# THE TURKS AND THE YUGOSLAVS

## AMONG THE REFUGEES

Wednesday, August 1, 1877
*From our Ragusa Correspondent*[1]

Spalato, Dalmatia: July 9

The prospect that opened before me on surmounting the last rocky summit that concealed the glen of Kamen (so this spot is called) could hardly be surpassed in picturesque and romantic beauty. Imagine, after spending hour after hour in toiling over the monotonous steeps of a wilderness of white disintegrated rock that seemed to redouble the pitiless glare of the sun above, coming upon a fresh green oasis, a beautiful gorge overgrown with fine beech trees, from amidst whose verdure, and partly clothed by it, started up endless peaks and towers and pinnacles of what from a remote point of vision might have been mistaken for the ruins of some quaint Düreresque stronghold of the Middle Ages, but which was, indeed, nothing but a rock citadel of Nature.

In the shade of the trees in the green glen below, the refugees had put together the wretched little wood shanties that served them for shelter against the elements; and here in miserable groups, as we approached each homestead, the various households clustered around us to receive our alms. English help has been reaching them now for some weeks, but their sufferings have been frightful. Here and there beneath the trees, with no doctors to attend them, with no bed to lie on but the kindly bosom of mother earth, lay victims of hunger, typhus, and small-pox, from which latter disease there had been one death that day.

About eight days before, the Turks had first appeared in the district. This region, according to information of my own received before any of the outrages took place, had been evacuated, weeks before, by the troops of Colonel Despotović, and the refugees were unanimous in stating that there was no insurgent in the neighbourhood when the Turks came.

But the fact that the villagers were rayahs – that they had once held allegiance to the insurgent commanders – was quite sufficient to provoke the Turkish hordes who appeared among them only ten days ago to a savage revenge. Cottages were burnt, the usual outrages took

1. A. J. (later Sir Arthur) Evans; Ragusa is now called Dubrovnik; Spalato, Split.

place, cattle were driven off, and after murdering five individuals, including a village elder, the Turks collected twenty-six villagers, 'house-fathers' and others, threw them into irons, and drove them off like a herd of cattle in the direction of Travnik. Nothing has since been heard of them.

This driving off of captives is perhaps the most terrible feature in the present Reign of Terror in Bosnia. Rarely indeed do men so driven off return to their homes. Many sink under the fatigues of the march alone, and the cruelties perpetrated on them by their armed captors surpass belief. Those who arrive at their destination are thrown into Turkish prisons, and are there subjected to the visits of Mahometan fanatics, who mutilate them with their sword-knives. Many are starved to death, and others are assassinated outright.

Glutted for the moment with vengeance and plunder, the Turkish troops left this district for a while; but two days before my visit to Kamen they had returned, and a ferocious act of savagery which they perpetrated on their arrival at the village of Stekerovatz had driven Christian inhabitants who still remained in the district to seek refuge by flight.

The Turks on their arrival in the village collected thirteen of the villagers – peasants perfectly unarmed, who had never joined in the insurrection – and, falling on them then and there (driving them off to a more lingering fate was, it seems, this time too much trouble), shot some and butchered the rest with their 'hand-jars.'

About this atrocious massacre there is no room for doubt. I have the details from a variety of witnesses – from men who escaped from the scene of the outrages, and from two witnesses who after the departure of the Turks buried some of the mutilated remains.

The Turks, after plundering the village, carried off the heads of the victims with their loot in the direction of Glamoš.

I cannot close this ghastly chronicle without the mention of two relics of the normal state of things in Bosnia in the period immediately preceding the present uprising. One of them is an implement, the other a victim of the feudal tyranny of the Mahometan Begs.

I have lately held in my hand an instrument, the use of which might well excite the curiosity of a spectator. It is like a heavy hammer, but the pointed extremity is shaped like a beak or claw of iron. With one end you might fell an ox; with the other you might dig three inches into the trunk of an oak tree. This mysterious and deadly weapon is called a 'nadjak'; and its use is only too well known to the Bosnian rayah. The 'nadjak' is the inseparable companion of the worst of the Bosnian Begs when he goes amongst his Christian serfs, and woe to the man who on such occasions shall fail to satisfy his worst behests. With a blow from this terrible instrument he can brain his victim or tear his flesh; he can murder outright, or maim for life, or simply inflict severe bodily pain. I am happy to be able to record that this 'nadjak' is at present only used by the worst of the Mahometan landlords. Used, however, it still is. That under notice was taken by the insurgents from the country-house of a neighbouring Beg – if I mistake not, a member of the Kulenović family. The iron of its material is most artistically inlaid with silver; among the ruling caste in Bosnia refined taste can co-exist with refined cruelty.

The other relic that I spoke of is a living monument of the ferocious tyranny which provoked the present outbreak. A short time since I saw among the Bosnian refugees at Ploča, in Croatia, an aged cripple, and heard the story of his wrongs. A few years ago there was no more hale old man near Stari Maidan than Lazar Czernimarković. He was then the house-father of a family community which, owing to its superior industry, was better off than the other rayah households of the neighbourhood. But the mere fact that he was comparatively well-to-do marked him out for the special extortion of his Mahometan landlord, who, suspecting that his serf might have some hidden hoard, made an exorbitant demand for a hundred ducats. The poor man was at his wits' end; he brought out all the little savings of his lifetime, which did not, I believe, amount to a fifth of the sum demanded. But the Beg would not be satisfied. As old Lazar persisted in his assertion that he had nothing more, the Beg had recourse to the bastinado. The aged house-father received a hundred strokes, but this did not add to his ability to pay. He was beaten more horribly than before, and left almost inanimate. He was then buried up to his neck in dung and left three days, the Beg giving orders to his apparitors to strangle the wretched man if at the end of that period he should be found alive and still refused to pay. Meanwhile the friends and relatives of the victim collected among them a sum sufficient to buy off the Beg. Lazar Czernimarković was dug out, and lives still, a wreck of his former self. Even when I saw him he could scarcely hobble with a staff, and his toe-less stumps bore witness to the pitiless rigour of his torturers.

## NEWS OF VICTORY

### Friday, November 2, 1877

It was half-past two when the glad tidings reached the small palace at Cettinje. Heralds were sent to tell the citizens that the Princess had something important to communicate to them. In five minutes the whole place was astir, and the people thronging before the palace gate.

The Princess now stepped forth on to the balcony and informed the crowd, amidst a breathless silence, that Nikšić was taken. She had intended to read her husband's poetic telegram [a quatrain],[1] but was cut short by a tremendous 'Živio!' (Evviva!) and a simultaneous volley from the guns and pistols of her loyal subjects, and retired kissing her hand.

The scene that followed almost baffles description. The people surged along the street, firing, shouting, singing, leaping with joy. It is an enthusiasm, an ecstasy, unintelligible, impossible in a civilised country – hardly to be expressed in civilised terms. Yes, these are children! – children in their primitive simplicity, in the whole poetry of their being; children in their speech, their politics; their warfare; and this is the wild, self-abandoned delight of children.

Ancient veterans, grim, rugged mountain giants, fall about each other's necks and kiss each other for very joy. The wounded themselves are helped forth from the hospitals, and hobble along on crutches to take part in the rejoicings; men, in the ambulances, dying of their wounds, lit up, I was told, when they heard these tidings, and seemed to gain a new respite of life. Crowds are continually bursting into national songs, and hymns, broken at intervals with a wild 'Živio! Živio!' and ringing hurrahs which Czernogortzi, as well as Englishmen, know how to utter. The big ancient bells of the monastery, and the watch-tower on the rocks above, peal forth. The bronze cannon – a gift from the sister Principality – is dragged out, and salvoes of artillery tell every upland village that Nikšić has fallen; the thunder-tones of triumph boom on from peak to peak; they are redoubled in a thousand detonations across the rock-wilderness of Chevo; they rumble with cavern-tones through the vine-clad dells of Cermnitzka and Reika; they are caught far away in fainter echoes by the pine woods of the Morača – dying and re-awaking, till with a last victorious effort they burst the bounds of the Black Mountain, and roll on to the lake of Skutari, the lowlands of Albania, the bazaars of Turkish Podgoritza.

The Metropolitan of Montenegro, most unsacerdotal of prelates – have I not seen him any summer evening, undeterred by his long robes, 'putting the stone' with athletic members of his flock? have not

---

1. A quatrain which Evans put into English thus:
   'Mine is the standard that floats to-day above Onogoski's castle;
   Plamenatz, leader in war, quaffs the red wine cup below;
   Shrieking like mountain eagles, the standard bearers around him
   Gather; but Nikšićs mourns, captive to-day of my arms.'

tuns of ale been flowing at his expense for the last half-hour? is it not written in his face? and shall I hesitate about the epithet? – the *jolly* Metropolitan of Montenegro proceeds to form a ring on the green-sward outside the village capital, and there – between the knoll that marks the ruins of a church destroyed centuries ago by the Turks, and the Elm of Judgment, where of old the Vladikas sat and judged the people – the warriors dance in pairs a strange barbaric war-dance.

In the evening the dance is renewed before the palace. Little Cettinje illuminates itself, and the palace walls and entrance are brilliant with long rows of stearine candles. It is here, before the palace gate, that the people form a large circle, the front rank of the spectators holding lighted tapers to illumine the arena. On the palace steps sits the Princess amidst her ladies, and little Danilo, the 'Hope of Montenegro,' stands in the gateway, almost among the other bystanders.

Two old senators, whose dancing days were over, one would have thought, a generation since, step forth into the ring, and open the ball amidst a storm of cheers. Younger warriors take up the dance – the 'dance!' but how describe it? Of this I am sure, that a traveller might cross Central Africa without meeting anything more wild, more genuinely primitive.

The warriors dance in pairs, but several pairs at a time. In turns they are warriors, wild beasts, clowns, jack-o'-lanterns, morris dancers, teetotums, madmen! They dance to one another and with one another, now on one leg, then on the other. They bounce into the air, they stamp on the ground, they pirouette, they snatch lighted tapers from the bystanders and whirl them hither and thither in the air, like so many Will-o'-the-Wisps. In a Berserker fury they draw from their sashes their silver-mounted pistols, and take flying shots at the stars; their motions slacken; they follow each other; they are on the war-path now – they step stealthily as a panther before it springs – they have leaped! but are they bears or wild cats? They are hugging one another now; they are kissing one another with effusion. Other pairs of warriors enter the arena, and this bout is concluded.

At every turn in the dance they give vent to strange guttural cries; they yelp like dogs, or utter the short shrieks of a bird of prey. Was there a time – one is tempted to ask – when the dancers consciously impersonated the birds and beasts whose cries they imitated? Did they, too, once, as the American Indians do still, disguise themselves in the skins of wolves and bears, or the plumes of a mountain eagle?

Perhaps, after all, that was originally a hunting dance, and has been transferred later on to the god of war. Perhaps – but the most fascinating of interludes cuts short our speculations! One at a time, in light white Montenegrin dress step forth from the palace gate a bevy of fair damsels. These are the relations of the Prince himself come to honour the people's representatives by dancing with them. The scene is of Homeric times, and these are the pure, true forms of antiquity. 'Hero' their dance is called, and it might have been a *choros* of some Hellenic festival divine.

## 'BRUTAL AND DOMINEERING BOERS . . . LIVING IN SLUTTISH PLENTY'

### Monday, September 23, 1876

There would appear to be little doubt that the native war in which the Boers of the Transvaal Republic have involved themselves is one altogether beyond their power to cope with. The vast extent of their territory would render a single defeat in a remote district in itself of little consequence; but they have shown such cowardice and incompetence that the numerous warlike tribes who dwell among and about them may be encouraged to a general rising, under which the scanty and half-civilised white community would not improbably succumb. It is hardly necessary to observe that we should not intervene in the matter for the sake of the Boers themselves. These men represent a portion of the Dutch inhabitants of the eastern district of the Cape Colony, who about the year 1835, having some legitimate grounds for dissatisfaction with the British Administration, but in the main impelled by disgust at the abolition of slavery, swarmed northwards and eastwards in order to enjoy a savage independence. The Transvaal district which is now in question has never been under our sovereignty. Over this territory, larger than Great Britain and Ireland, are spread a native population computed at a quarter of a million and about forty thousand Dutch. These Boers lead a lazy pastoral existence, living in sluttish plenty among their flocks and herds. They appear to have very little tincture of civilisation left, are stolidly unenterprising, and occupy a magnificent country without attempting to develope in any way its resources. Towards the natives they have been brutal and domineering, dispossessing them of their lands and reducing many of them to slavery. The war from which they are now suffering is entirely of their own provoking, and we cannot affect to pity them for the chastisement which they have most richly inherited.

Unfortunately, however, diamond fields extend into the Transvaal and have attracted a large number of British immigrants. These, however, are close to our own frontier, and could be protected without much difficulty. But there is also a British population far away to the north in the gold district round about Leydenburg, close to which the war is going on, and to their fate we cannot remain altogether indifferent. Moreover, if the tribes were to continue their victories so as altogether to drive the Boers back, there would be great danger of violations of our frontier, and in any case a long-continued struggle would have a disturbing effect on the whole native population, who are already a source of great anxiety and possible danger. It would seem, therefore, to be the wisest policy at once to endeavour to secure the pacification of the Transvaal district. But unless the Boers are thoroughly frightened and cowed, it may be taken for granted, that they will endeavour to drive as hard a bargain as possible, and they may probably propose confederation on equal terms. It appears to us that such an offer would be altogether unacceptable. We should take great risks and responsibilities without any corresponding power or advantages. We should of course nominally have the direction of the native policy all along the frontier. But the Boers require keeping in order with a strong hand; and if they were allowed any great degree of local independence nothing would prevent them from displaying the same spirit and the same conduct that have involved them in their present troubles. In fact having the assurance of protection from a strong Power, they would probably become more turbulent and aggressive than ever.

If we are to annex the Transvaal, it should be on terms of absolute submission of the inhabitants to the British sovereignty. A wild region with a scattered and lawless population of diggers, squatters, and savages is by no means ripe for the more liberal representative institutions which may come with more stable and organised conditions of society. The great addition to our native subjects would be a source of much anxiety. But the greatest element of doubt which the question presents is the indeterminate nature of the work that we should be undertaking. We have not, in fact, to consider merely the limits which may at present mark the furthest advance northwards of white occupation. The Orange and the Vaal provide at present a well-defined and safe frontier line. If we cross them we are taking the first step towards the annexation of all South Africa, as far as soil and climate will permit white colonisation to extend. It may be that we have no choice in the matter. If the northern country is anything like so rich in mineral and agricultural wealth, as it is said to be, nothing will prevent swarms of restless pioneers pushing forward to it. It is better that this process should take place under imperial restraint and protection than that gangs of white adventurers should herald the progress of civilisation by acts of rapine and outrage of which we should ultimately have to incur the responsibility and bear the consequences.

> The Transvaal was in fact annexed in April, 1877; regained its independence 1880.

## Arts

## WALTER PATER AND THE RENAISSANCE

> Book reviews were still anonymous. The principal literary reviewer throughout this period was George Saintsbury (1845–1933).

## Wednesday, April 16, 1873

It is not often that we have to welcome a book like this, which brings its readers into fresh and intimate relations with remote phases of life and art, informing these with the vivid glow of a new personality, and alluring the melody and clearness of such a style as has not been written before. From the fertile soil of life and passion the genius of the poet, the creative artist, rears blossoms at will. But the time comes when these flowers fade, as the melody of poetry is marred in the changes of the years and of men's speech. That is the moment for such criticism as Mr. Pater's, and as Mr. Arnold's. They perform, by some 'alchemy of art,' such a change as Paracelsus thought was possible to revive the ghost of a faded flower, raising from the dust the perfect image in its ancient hues and fragrance. And this is done by an indefinable skill, which is something more than the cunningest analysis and the most accurate notation; a skill scarcely ever possessed except by a genius, which can employ also, and naturally prefers to employ, the higher, but hardly less rare, faculty of original creation. The exercise of this magic brings the charm of the unseen picture, of the song never listened to, before the reader as surely and strangely as the magic of Wordsworth or Keats brings him into the presence of unfamiliar scenes and tones of cloud and sea.

It is hard to analyse the results of analysis, and to criticise criticism. But if it is necessary to look for the secret of Mr. Pater's success, it might be stated as lying in a peculiar exquisiteness, distinction, refinement, occupying itself with artistic subjects somewhat remote in character. By this we do not mean that he seeks for interest in *bizarre* and out of the way places, values a soul merely because it is strange, a period merely because it is little known. Mr. Pater's themes are connected by the fact that they form links in the great movement of the Renaissance, 'the desire for a more liberal and comely way of conceiving life.' And from this movement he does not choose the obscurer names, nor admire the works of art that were done in a corner. Michelangelo, Leonardo, Joachim Du Bellay are central figures, names known of all men. The impression of remoteness, novelty, refinement comes from the way in which the lives and works of these artists are studied; the subtlety which tracks the most hidden and most powerful of their impulses; the wonderful clearness with which the result of this exploration is expressed; the mastery of character which makes the study of Sandro Botticelli as valuable as Mr. Browning's 'Fra Lippo Lippi.' With all this, there is a command of such a style as has not before been written, a wonderful style that sometimes threatens to overstep the limits of prose, delicate, dainty, impassioned, yet certain and chastened.

Throughout Mr. Pater is true to the philosophy of his own conclusion that 'a taste for metaphysics may be one of those things which we must renounce if we mean to mould our lives to artistic perfection.' Other things than a taste for metaphysics, it appears, must be given up in this quest. For after a brief and passionate description, on the Heraclitean text, 'all things change, and nothing abides,' of the vanity of life, Mr. Pater announces that 'our one chance is in expanding our interval, in getting as many pulsations as possible into the given time.' All passions and enthusiasms give this quickened sense of life, but art the most; for art professes to 'give nothing but the highest quality to your moments as they pass, and simply for those moments' use.'

Perhaps it ought to be counted as a merit in Mr. Pater's book that it invites to such reflections and to such questioning of life. In this way it acquires the moral interest which is all it might seem to lack to set it on a footing with Mr. Arnold's *Essays in Criticism*, as one of the two most stimulating and delightful books of criticism which this generation has produced. It is a work that no one can afford to overlook, and that no one with any care for art can read without a certain *nostalgie*, an affection which will draw him to it again and again.

## HENRY IRVING AS CHARLES I

Theatre notices also were unsigned throughout this period. A. W. Ward (1837–1924), later editor of the *Cambridge Modern History* and the *Cambridge History of English Literature*, had come to Manchester in 1866. Scott soon recruited him as a dramatic critic, a position which he shared in the 1870s with A. G. Symonds.

### Friday, July 25, 1873

Henry Irving,[1] if he may not to be said to have had his early training among us, was an actor of recognised intelligence in Manchester before his general reputation had been achieved, and his friends here have never failed to follow with interest the steps by which he has risen to eminence in his profession. Mr. Wills's play, with some faults, among which a too prevailing sombreness of tone and an almost total absence of construction are conspicuous, has many excellences. It contains several striking situations; the characters, however wide of accordance with historical truth, are consistent in themselves; and the versification has a natural declamatory flow which serves well the purpose of the rhetorical passages of the dialogue.

It would be a great omission not to mention here another recommendation which the play is supposed to possess. We are at a point of time, it seems, at which the people appear to be recovering their respect for ancient national institutions, and the revived feeling of loyalty which finds suitable expression in *Charles the First* is characteristic of a day of wholesome 'constitutional reaction.'

We refer to the real or supposed excellence of the polemical element in the play chiefly in order to say that we think it may very advantageously be dispensed with in writing for the stage. The invitation to applaud implies in simple justice permission to condemn; and there are fully as many fine phrases to be used in defence of liberty as in defence of divine right. If Cavaliers and Roundheads are to be pitted against each other, it will only be a question of strength of lungs or impudence which party is to prevail, and a larger section of the public, more worthy perhaps of consideration than either, may be in danger not only of being offended, but – what may even be worse – of being bored. Moreover, if the theatre is to be made the means of seriously teaching the people how to estimate the events and characters of a past day, it

---

1. Sir Henry Irving (1838–1905) had been a member of Charles Calvert's company at the Theatre Royal, Manchester from 1860–1865. He was the first actor to be knighted, in 1895. The play was by W. G. Wills (1828–1891), a portrait painter as well as a dramatist.

must be required studiously to conform its lessons to established facts; and that is not only a test to which we do not think historical plays ought to be rigidly subjected, but one which we are pretty sure Mr. Wills's play will not bear.

Dignified and impressive throughout, he (Mr. Irving) rises on the call of certain occasions to a height of power which will surprise even those who have seen him in the intensely melodramatic part of the murderer in the *Polish Jew*. The ease and grace of his playing with the children in the first act makes us the more regret the absence of comedy in the later scenes. His indignant denunciation of the Commons' envoy in the second act – the best, we think, of the four – was tempestuous in its vehemence without a trace of rant. To say that Mr. Irving has become, or is on the road toward becoming, faultless would be to overlook a monotonous chant into which he is the habit of falling, especially in the more subdued passages of his part. He has some obvious mannerisms which will be in danger of being confirmed by indulgence; but no one was ever less 'stagey.' His look, intonation, and gesture are his own, and they are strikingly true to nature. He possesses above all that *intensity* which is perhaps the one heaven-descended gift which actors who attempt to depict the play of the higher emotions should desire.

## MAMMON AND MUSIC

'Manchester – a thing of the past, a political Carthage, given over to Mammon and music.' George Dawson, M.P. for Birmingham, reported in the *Guardian*, February 2, 1874.

Charles Hallé was knighted in 1888. He remained conductor of the orchestra which bears his name until 1895. His death that year, a few months after that of George Freemantle, the *Guardian*'s music critic since 1867, ended an era. The first of the next two extracts may well be by Freemantle; the second is certainly his.

### THE FIRST BAYREUTH FESTIVAL

Monday, August 14, 1876
*From a Correspondent*

Bayreuth, August 9

Portraits of the composer and the singers who are to take part in the approaching festival adorn every shop. From each window frame his characteristic features stare one in the face. The cigar shops are selling but one form of pipe, meerschaum carved with the heroic features of

Bayreuth's present idol; wines, cigars, hats, collars, cravats, etc. are all of the Wagner brand; and from the windows float snatches of Nibelungen music.

Wagner has laboured for very nearly thirty years upon the work he is now producing, slowly approaching his ideal; much of the music was composed more than a quarter of a century ago. For the Bayreuth festival is the legitimate outgrowth of two desires on the part of its originator: viz. to found a distinctively national type of opera (*i.e.* dramatic music) and then to produce this opera free from the trammels which have been created and fostered during a century and a half by the nonsensical *libretti* and the 'machine music' that marks much of the work of the Italian and French schools. The German musician, as Wagner says, looking down from his own field – that of instrumental and choral (*i.e.* symphonic) music – saw no finished and imposing form in the operatic *genre*, for which Gluck, Mozart, Beethoven and Weber had only introduced partial reform such as cropped character-istically out of their nature and gave most satisfaction to their indi-vidual poetic sensibilities. Whilst the oratorio and symphony presented him a nobly finished form, the opera only offered a disconnected mass of undeveloped, illogical, and inartistically arbitrary rules, encumbered by conventionalities quite incomprehensible and most inimical to freedom of development. Further, Wagner had been deeply impressed with the fact that an ideal perfection of the opera such as so many men of genius had dreamed of could in the first instance only be attained by means of a total revolution in the character of the poet's participa-tion in the work. Building on these ideas, he has produced his musical dramas, which bid fair to fulfil the first of his desires and certainly have accomplished the second.

A pleasant stroll brought me to the 'terraced' front of the great theatre building; a rambling, no-style building, resembling rather two buildings, large and small, joined together, stood before me, and a single glance sufficed to show that all fancy form had fled in the face of stage demands. Entering one of the ample portals, we find ourselves in an exceedingly plain auditorium. The cane-seated chairs, large and comfortable, rise in 30 rows one above the other as in an ancient amphitheatre, and are 1,350 in number. The rear wall – that opposite the stage – is semicircular in form, and at each side is a granite stair-way leading to the sole gallery the house contains, a gallery given up to those entitled to free seats, wives of artists, singers, &c. Below this gallery are the royal boxes, three in number, destined to serve the Emperor William, the Emperor and Empress of Brazil, King Louis of Bavaria, and a host of lesser royalties. These boxes are the only places in the house that exhibit any luxuriance in fitting. The stranger will have noticed the apparent absence of an orchestra, and here we find the practical execution of another of Wagner's favourite ideas. For the orchestra is sunk from the sight of the audience, but its director is in plain sight of the singers, and faces the men under his *baton.* The shape of the orchestra – which is almost a hall in itself, for it seats 130 performers – is best compared to the sole of a high-heeled lady's shoe minus the heel, the toe part of the shape being well under the front of the stage. The musicians sit in ranks, and the sound is thrown first against the sounding board, which divides the audience from the orchestra, thence to the back of the stage, whence it travels to the audience.

Herr Brandt, the master machinist, from the Royal Theatre at Darmstadt, offered politely to explain the mysteries [of the stage]. The roof above my head was composed apparently of a mazy myriad of ropes, sticks, pulleys, and canvases, and I could see the sides of some snow-clad hill in what seemed sad juxtaposition with the glowing interiors of princely palaces. In fact, above me were the pieces and sections of many a wonderland Herr Brandt will produce in the coming festival. There is a height of 108 ft. from the stage to the flies, and the sides are occupied by five machine galleries, the first being forty-five feet from the boards. The bowels of the stage have a depth of forty feet, a descent to which discovered a most distressing labyrinth of ropes and traps and awkward elbowed joists that resembled a section of some universal motor. There were, in addition, two immense long wooden drums for working the machinery by means of steam, a steam pump, and other requisites for the production of vapour, which in some portions of the *Nibelungen* drama covers the scene from sight, so that while the fleecy clouds are radiant with reflected coloured lights the transformation necessary to the story will take place. The nymphs who swim from rock to rock in the Rhine do so with the most perfect of motions, and apparently without support from above or below. In fact, the Lehman sisters and Fraulein Lammert, who personate the Rhine daughters, refused at first to submit themselves to the clasp of the dreadful skeletons; but Wagner was imperative, and now they are said to like the motion. Their movements are guided by an accomplished musician in time to the music's rhythm. The dwarf Prince Alberich, who clambers from ledge to ledge, moves with positively frightful rapidity on a base of machinery, in and out, here and there, like a flash, in pursuit of the evading Rhine daughters.

The first grand dress rehearsal took place on Sunday night. Joining the band of profound-looking music lovers, I groped my way to my seat in the gallery. The anxieties of a nervous spectacled gentleman, who was afraid that sufficient support had not been placed beneath the gallery, were hushed at the appearance of Herr Wagner. A curt bow, a few immaterial words in a low monotone, hardly audible from where I sat, a pause, then a rap, and the wonderful waves of undulating music which introduce the prologue to the trilogy *Das Rheingold* came floating up from the mysterious depths beneath the stage. The sinking of the orchestra gave a mellowness and unison to the music, without in the least diminishing the volume or dulling the tone. It seemed to flow and follow, growing fuller and grander, like the current of some mighty stream, until the curtain parted and the realistic effect of the scenery was added to the impressive power of music, and one really thought he saw the lonely depth of the Rhine, each crested wave lit with a golden light. Of course there were the inevitable hitches and pauses consequent on any rehearsal, yet they were few and far between, and everything went most smoothly.

Wagner, as stage director, sat normally in a chair at the side of the stage. He was dressed in light clothes, and wore his velvet cap. Suddenly he would shuffle across the stage with his hands beneath his coat tails, gesticulate violently to put more force into the orchestra, or rush up to a singer in the midst of his or her part and say, in a light sharp voice, 'No, no, no; not so; sing it so'; and, suiting the action to the direction, would sing the part as it should be, or throw the necessary dramatic fire into the acting. All his directions were given with the aim of producing the greatest naturalness and through this, the most perfect power. The delighted audience sat in silence, and as they streamed out of the theatre onto the terrace and into the beer-room in their festal dress, the only word heard was 'Herrlich' (glorious).

## BERLIOZ'S FAUST

### Friday, January 13, 1882

Now that *Faust* has been heard three or four times its merits are more obvious than when it was first given. One can hardly say that the execution is better than it was, for, in truth, Mr. Hallé had so carefully rehearsed it that full justice was given to the music when he introduced it to his audience. But we are certainly better able to survey the work as a whole as we gradually become familiar with it. The plan is laid out to no recognised system. The composer has presented us with his own idea of the *Faust* legend. Berlioz's musical forms are his own also. We do not either enjoy or comprehend at first much that we hear. It is only as the work becomes gradually known that we discover symmetry as well as design in what originally seemed both fantastic and formless. But we must grasp the whole compass of his various scenes. They do not admit of subdivision, and he has so keen a sense of what is dramatic that it is impossible to separate any portion from the whole without injury to the general effect. The 'Ballet des Sylphes' has an infinitely greater interest when heard as part of that mystic and unholy scene of enchantment of which it is a portion, than when given as a member in a miscellaneous programme; and even the soul-stirring 'Rakoczy' March – almost dragged into *Faust* as it is – has a wonderful *éclat* there which proves how true the instincts of the composer were.

The sudden transitions are amongst the chief elements of success. The 'Easter Hymn' would probably not impress us as it does but for the contrast which it receives, first in its opposition to the Mephistophelean idea, and later, from the roystering revelry in the Leipsic beer-cellar. When this has passed away, a scene of pastoral life enables us to enjoy perhaps the most thoroughly musician-like portion of the whole. Faust's dream is a creation of exquisite loveliness, sufficient to justify the claims of its composer to rank amongst the great composers. The 'King of Thule' ballad has a setting of the tenderest beauty, wonderfully set off by the wailing reiteration of the theme by the solo viola, as later in the work, Margaret's other song gains half its effect from a similar *obligato* accompaniment by – we think – the Cor Anglais. Of the picturesque use of the orchestra generally we need scarcely speak. Whatever Berlioz may not have been, he has always been recognised as a master here. Even his contemporaries who denied him much else, admitted so much. Instances of original treatment are everywhere to be found. The discord which announces the presence of Mephistopheles comes on us with almost the force and suddenness of a pistol shot. The uncomfortable sensations suggested so vividly by the detached violin phrases in the 'Flea' song we have before alluded to; while the curious cross *tempi* in the fiend serenade and elsewhere are used with a boldness which almost produces a new musical sensation.

Perhaps the love scene in the third part is the least successful effort in this remarkable work. We feel here the need of scene and action. With Faust and Margaret before us in flesh and blood we cannot help comparing the poverty of effect with that superb scene where Gounod has told the tale of the maiden's fall. And yet, while we still adhere to our preference to the version of *Faust* which the latter composer has given us, it is only just to add that we are now able to discover also how much he owed to the earlier setting of Berlioz. Every now and then we discover something which without being quite like anything in Gounod, is suggestive of movements of his which, hitherto, have been thought to be not only original but unique. The 'Chorus of the Soldiers' in Berlioz's *Faust* is a striking instance of this. It is not the air certainly which we can accuse Gounod of having appropriated in his own chorus, but we cannot doubt that the rhythm and general swing, if we may so express it, are derived from Berlioz.

Our readers have opportunities of forming opinions such as have never before, or elsewhere, been afforded. The fame of Berlioz is in the hands of the present generation. The revival now going on presents his claims to consideration with a completeness which admits of no possible extenuation. Whether it will pass away leaving little trace behind or establish the fame of Berlioz beyond doubt or cavil remains to be seen. Possibly another generation may elapse, and another revival give our children sensations still new as now.

## Court and Personal

### FIFTY YEARS A QUEEN

#### Friday, July 1, 1887

G. W. E. Russell, a radical who knew everybody, an Anglo-Catholic, a bachelor, a member of an old Whig family, a devoted Gladstonian, and a man of great friendliness, began his long connection with the *Guardian* with this article.

##### THE QUEEN'S GARDEN PARTY

A falling glass, a leaden sky, a breathless atmosphere – all threatened rain. 'This is the break up of the fine weather,' cried the croakers. 'Nothing but the Queen's presence can stave off the rain,' said the more hopeful; and the hopeful people were right. The invitations to the Royal Garden Party summoned their recipients 'from five to seven,' but long before the appointed hour all the avenues to Buckingham Palace were besieged by strings of carriages. Not only the great entrance facing the Mall and the privileged side-door opposite Buckingham Palace Hotel were opened, but the private entrances in Grosvenor Place threw back their accustomed doors. Not for full fifteen years had the Palace Garden witnessed such a function, and six thousand invitations – so rumour had it – were issued. Few Londoners even, and certainly no stranger from the provinces, have any notion of the extent of the handsomely wooded park or pleasure-ground which modestly styling itself a garden, covers a square enclosed by St. James's Park, Constitution Hill, Grosvenor Place, and Buckingham Palace Road. It is only just over the tops of the towering belt of trees that one can discern the topmost windows of Belgravian houses bounding the distant view. In the forefront stands the stately though rather ponderous façade of the Palace, a classical design in white stone which London smoke has long since subdued to its own tint. The wide lawn is encircled with thick plantations, where Lord Beaconsfield's peacocks, transported from Hughenden, dispute the territorial ascendancy of the Queen's pheasants. A large piece of water bears an abundance of light craft manned by the Royal watermen in their picturesque uniforms of scarlet. One long marquee contains every variety of light refreshment; a smaller one facing it on the other side of the lawn, and banked up with the choicest flowers is destined to house the Queen and her family and guests. The Beefeaters, with their quaint doublets and ruffs, keep guard on the Terrace. The band of the Royal Marines discourses delicious music, and a vast and variegated crowd is dispersed over the lawn. As an effect of colour, it is unfortunate that the men's black coats and hats are not relieved by any vivacity in the ladies' costumes. White is almost universally worn by the younger ladies and black or purple or deep green by their elders. A lady who has ventured into pink or yellow or crimson, or even displays a red parasol, is a public benefactor to the aesthetic sense.

The sombre effect of these costumes is deepened by the darkening sky. The air is deathly still and there are ominous rumours of an impending storm. Suddenly there is a rift in the clouds. The sun bursts out; a light breeze moves the Royal Standard, which, floating from the Palace roof, announces that the Queen has arrived. There is a sensation, a flutter, a sigh of relief. The Royal charm has triumphed over the barometer. It is Queen's Weather again, and the Queen comes with it. There is a flash of scarlet in the distance as the Royal carriages drive into the garden. Sir Spencer Ponsonby-Fane, secretary to the Lord Chamberlain's Office and virtual dictator of all courtly revels, hurries up to Lord Salisbury[1], who, badly dressed and looking jaded, is surveying the animated scene through his characteristic eyeglass. He is summoned to greet his Sovereign; and now *God Save the Queen* bares all heads. A long lane is formed across the lawn. The Lord Steward and Lord Chamberlain, with their subordinate officials, walking backwards, prepare the way. Bareheaded we all are as the Prince conducts his mother. Dressed in slight mourning, supporting herself with her folded

1. The Prime Minister.

parasol, and wearing a happy smile, the Queen advances with that inimitable mixture of grace and dignity – that swimming, sweeping gait, which reminds one of some old-world figure-dance, and which compensates for the want of height and the departed elasticity of youth. Deep are the obeisances on either hand. The magnificent Countess of Lonsdale seems to sink into the earth and to reappear. Indian Princes, one blaze of scarlet and gold embroidery and diamonds, make their beautiful salaams. Right and left the Queen bows, pausing every few minutes to make more deliberate acknowledgments, and shaking hands with old friends whom she recognises in the crowd. And so she gradually makes her way to her tent, and behind her files the long row of her children and grandchildren and princely visitors, all decorated with the new Jubilee medal and brightly but not sumptuously apparelled.

The dusky Queen of the Sandwich Islands walks with a singular freedom and dignity, and makes up by benignity of bearing for conversational deficiency – her only English being contained in the brief sentence, learned by rote. 'How do you do? Pray sit down.' All eyes are fixed on the Crown Princess of Germany, looking very young, and plainly dressed in black and white, as she holds an animated conversation with the Papal Envoy. The Envoy, a slight man of middle age, has the typical countenance of the Italian priest – subtle, intelligent, refined, and inscrutable. His curious costume – a cassock and a tall hat – attracts amused regards, but it is no joking matter, depend on it, which is the subject of conversation between him and the sagacious and politic daughter-in-law of the great Protestant Emperor. The same subject probably engages them which has been present to the minds of all who noted the Envoy's reception at Marlborough House and his invitation to dine and sleep at Windsor – the renewal of diplomatic relations between England and the Holy See, with a special reference to troubles in Ireland.

Meanwhile the victorious sun streams down upon what Lord Beaconsfield called 'a brisk and modish scene.' Everyone who is known in politics, in the Church, in the services, in art, in literature, in mere society, is here. The grouping is interesting and picturesque. Mr. Chamberlain displays a white orchid. Lord Hartington strolls by with an umbrella. Conversation is rapid and exhilarating. Hunger and thirst, in delicately modified forms, assert their claims. Some people seek coolness on the water, and some rest on the too few garden seats. Rapidly the gay minutes pass and suddenly, almost before we are aware, we see the Royal procession reforming; again the Queen goes smiling and bowing and scattering her gracious greetings. *God save the*

*Queen* announces her departure. The Royal Standard disappears, the vast gathering breaks up, and at 8 p.m., though darkness is falling on Belgravia, the streets have scarcely ceased to echo the hoarse shouts of linkmen or the thundering chariot-wheels of belated guests departing from the Jubilee Garden Party.

## DOING THE LAMBETH WALK

### Friday, October 17, 1890

#### THE NEW BISHOP OF ROCHESTER[1]

The Dean of Windsor is an amiable pietist with a great knack of standing well with people in high places, and a considerable love of negotiating, arranging and wire-pulling. The Queen's fondness for Archbishop Tait secured the Deanery of Windsor for his son-in-law, and there this very fortunate young man's promotion might very properly have ended. The spiritual charge of South London requires quite other gifts and experiences than his, and, I may add, quite another theology. Mr. Davidson is a Broad Churchman inclining to Low, and this is a type of teaching more congenial to princes and dignitaries than to the toiling masses of Southwark and Bermondsey. This is pre-eminently an appointment which Mr. Gladstone would not have made, but Lord Salisbury has not the moral fibre which is requisite for withstanding the royal volition.

## MR. GLADSTONE'S GOLDEN WEDDING

### Thursday, July 25, 1889

We all know what we owe to Mr. Gladstone, or some of us at least know, but perhaps no one but Mr. Gladstone himself knows what we owe to his wife. We shall best express our sense of what we owe to the lady who completes her fiftieth year of married life to-day by declining to regard her as apart from her husband, and rather uniting them in our thought as they have been united in purpose, in labour, and in sympathy.

And what a fifty years it has been! In the marriage register Mr. Gladstone is described as member of Parliament for Newark, where he

---

1. Randall Davidson (1848–1930), Archbishop of Canterbury 1903–1928. In 1890 the present diocese of Southwark was included in Rochester. This London Letter paragraph is almost certainly by G. W. E. Russell.

had sat for half-a-dozen years as the friend of Sir Robert Peel and the nominee of the Duke of Newcastle. Already he had held office as an Under-Secretary of State, and men pointed to him as destined to do great things and as the rising hope of the Tory party. One half of that forecast has been fulfilled in ample measure, but the other has been strangely falsified. Nothing is more wonderful, where there is so much that is wonderful in this long career, than the unceasing growth and expansion of Mr. Gladstone's mind. It is this which marks him out from other statesmen who have been content to grow old. Lord Palmerston lived to a greater age than Mr. Gladstone has yet attained and held power to the last, but long before then he had reached the limits of his political tether, and the world waited to move on till he should have passed away. But to Mr. Gladstone it would seem to have been given to carry forward to the limits of his age the privilege of youth – its elasticity, its hopefulness, its readiness to embark on new and great undertakings. It is a heroic prerogative, but it carries with it its allotted penalty. To spirits so touched time brings no release, and where others would discover the occasion for retirement they find only the opportunity for action. Had Mr. Gladstone retired from political life even ten years ago he would already have accomplished more things and greater than any other statesman of the century. To have borne a great part in the battle of Free Trade, to have reformed the tariff, to have compelled the enfranchisement of the householders in the boroughs and to have carried their enfranchisement in the counties, to have given protection to the voter by ballot, to have laid broad and deep the foundations of a system of national education, and to have dealt in no half-hearted spirit with the great and thorny questions of the Irish Church and Irish land, this surely would have been praise enough and labour enough for any single man. Yet to all this Mr. Gladstone has added the greatest by far of the tasks of his life – the reconstruction of the political relations of Ireland to the remainder of the United Kingdom. The undertaking is vast, it is urgent, and it is critical. Of all living men, by experience and authority he is best able to carry it to a happy and a fruitful issue. Amid the good wishes and congratulations which will pour in upon him to-day there will be mingled the prayer, deep and earnest, that his long life may yet be prolonged and his strength sustained for the accomplishment of a great and patriotic purpose.

It has been usual amongst Mr. Gladstone's opponents and detractors, amongst those who hate and those who fear him – we fear a numerous and highly placed company – to denounce him as the great innovator, the breaker of images, the destroyer of institutions and of interests.

As often happens with great men who embody and give effect to the movement of their time, he has been made responsible for a good deal more than by right belongs to him. It has been Mr. Gladstone's lot to become the author of many great reforms, but the bent of his mind has remained to the last conservative. It has been his part not so much to mould as to give effect to the advance of opinion, and he will always rank as a Parliamentarian acting upon the political forces which he found in play, rather than as one who sought to infuse into the nation the spirit and the purpose which make up the forces on which politicians act. It is this which has made him powerful. It is this also which has made him feared. He has embodied the movement of a time, embodied as no other could, and enforced it with extraordinary power. To the unthinking he has seemed to originate what he adopted, and because a movement became powerful in his hands he was thought to have invented it. His latest great act of policy is no exception to this rule. Mr. Gladstone did not invent the Irish movement; he found it. He has watched it and coped with it for fifty years. Neither did he create the conditions which now have for the first time rendered its fundamental solution possible. They have come in the fulness of time, and he has merely recognised through and through the significance of facts which others saw but whose lesson they have yet to learn.

> Three years later Gladstone formed his fourth and last government, resigning in 1893 after the defeat of his second Home Rule bill.

## Oh! Mr. Scott

### Saturday, June 29, 1878

Bicyclists, it is to be hoped, will not fall into the mistake of supposing that the highways are laid down for their especial benefit. The lordly air with which they expect foot passengers to get out of their way indicates a sense of indefensible superiority which it may be desirable in some way to weaken. It is intolerable that men, women, and children should be constantly exposed to the risk of being run over by reckless young fellows.

# CHAPTER FIVE

# Land of Hope and Glory—
# A Dissenting Judgment

\*

In 1895, six months after Lord Salisbury became Prime Minister and Joseph Chamberlain Colonial Secretary, the Jameson Raid failed to overthrow the Transvaal Republic. The Diamond Jubilee in 1897 brought imperialist sentiment to a climax which lasted throughout the South African War (1899–1902). The Russo-Japanese War brought an opposite mood in Europe.

Throughout these ten years C. P. Scott was M.P. for Leigh and frequently absent from Manchester. The principal leader-writers were C. E. Montague (1867–1928), who had been appointed in 1890, L. T. Hobhouse (1864–1929), who was in Manchester from 1897 to 1902, and, on military subjects, Herbert Sidebotham (1872–1940), who joined the paper in 1895. Scott and his paper were throughout on the small Radical, anti-imperialist wing of the Liberal Party.

## The Meaning of Empire Day: South Africa 1899-1902

### THE PERSONALITY OF PRESIDENT KRUGER

Tuesday, October 3, 1899
*From Our Special Correspondent*[1]

Pretoria

It is utterly impossible for a casual visitor to get beneath the outer husk of this grim old man, with the massive, furrowed face, who sits upon his stoop, puffing a huge meerschaum pipe and growling out disconnected sentences between the spits. You ask yourself as you sit waiting for his Dutch to be put into English (Kruger speaks no English), what manner of a man is this? A pious patriot, soldier, farmer, driven by sheer circumstances into high politics and adapting some natural bucolic cunning to the purposes of diplomacy in the defence

1. J. A. Hobson. Paul Kruger (1825–1904) had taken part in Great Trek (1836); President of the Transvaal since 1883: spent the war in Europe trying to secure support.

of his country, or a scheming old hypocrite, who has richly feathered his nest by every art of political corruption, and who employs every trick of evasion and falsehood in defence of his monopoly of the public power and purse, using for these purposes the single genuine passion of his life – hatred of the English? Even those who have associated intimately with the old man for many years differ widely in their estimate of his nature and his political power; indeed, this inscrutability is itself a strong factor in the situation. There are even those who, upholding Kruger's personal and political honesty, yet think he may be prepared to wreck his country by war in order to maintain the supremacy which might fall from his hands under reform. A brief personal impression of such a man is not worth much; even corrected and filled out by the freely expressed opinion of many of his friends and enemies, it only warrants some general conjecture. To strangers Kruger is not often communicative; the State Secretary, Mr. Reitz, who took me to him, told me he had a few days before introduced a well-known member of the British Parliament, but could extract nothing but an occasional grunt and a 'Yes' or 'No' from the old man, who had buried himself behind a cloud of tobacco smoke. Sometimes, however, he dilates and opens out in free narrative. Olive Schreiner tells me of a talk she had with him a short time ago, in which he warmed up with a long, animated, and wonderfully picturesque account of the hunting and fighting of his adventurous youth. Even now his reserve of physical force is immense; by his sheer power of voice and presence he cows the Opposition in the Raad; in ordinary talk he exercises little self-restraint; if any point of controversy rises, he will bring his big fist down upon the table with alarming force.

I was somewhat fortunate in my reception. When the old man was told who I was, he himself expressed the desire to make a statement to the English people upon the matter of the broken promises imputed to him.

The allusion is to the promises of 'equal treatment' which he is said to have made in the negotiations previous to the Convention of 1881. He passionately insisted that he had given equal treatment so far as all civic rights were concerned, and that as regards the rights of burgher-ship he had all along sought to practise the same policy, but the foreigners who came in refused to accept the duties of burghership while seeking to gain its privileges. He cited to me several instances where instead of helping the burghers to defend the country, settlers had preferred to register themselves as British subjects or to make an appeal to the power of Great Britain so as to escape the commando. 'I have,' he said, 'always striven to bring these people into the full rights of citizenship by inviting them to help our citizens to bear the burdens, but they always refused; they wanted the rights without the duties.' Historically there is some substance in this defence. But the real interest lies in the light it throws upon Kruger's conception of politics; fighting has played so essential a part in the making of the nation that it seems to him that such personal service is the only basis of burgher rights. Animated by such feelings one can understand how he regards the agitation of the speculators and the counter-jumpers of the Rand, who look on the burghership not as linking them with the destinies of a country for which they are prepared at twelve hours' notice to mount their horse and fight to death, but rather as a means of helping them to develop the industrial resources of the country and make a pile. I do not say this view is correct, but it is inevitably the view which such a man as Kruger must take.

Such a view expresses the whole dramatic antithesis of the situation; the old seventeenth-century countryman, with his crude, belated politics and his stern Old Testament direction is brought all of a sudden face to face with a culminating type of modern capitalist civilisation in the luxurious, speculative, cosmopolitan life of Johannesburg. If to a Londoner this golden city fairly staggers the imagination with its dizzy artificialism and the rapid transformation of its life, how must it appear to Kruger and his following of inexperienced Boers? Is it any wonder that they think these brilliant, tricky strangers intend to take from them the control of their country, and that they view an extended franchise as a political and moral cataclysm? 'Yes,' it may be said; 'but this assumes Paul Kruger to be the honest, simple-minded peasant which he is not.' It is idle to shirk the accusations brought against the President; they are not merely the vague whispers of agitators on the Rand. Many Transvaalers not hostile to the general policy of Kruger are evidently staggered and perplexed by certain aspects of that policy and certain incidents in his career. Enemies boldly cast in his teeth personal corruption, insisting that he has taken large sums of money, that he has allowed some members of his family and a little clique of personal friends to enrich themselves by abuse of official power and by lobbying. Upon this matter I have probed many well-informed persons, and can get no sure conclusion. One thing is certain, that Kruger has not what we should call a 'nice sense of honour' in these matters.

The only quite specific charge, however, that has been made against Kruger is in the dynamite affair, when even in the Raad it was plainly insinuated that certain shares entered in a fictitious name were really owned by the President, who had received them as a consideration for giving favourable terms to the concessionaire.

A study of the entire history of the dynamite concession indisput-ably supports a *prima facie* suspicion. On the other hand, high officers of State – as the State Attorney, whose honour no one impeaches – and who alone have direct access to the documentary evidence, assure me that there is absolutely no foundation for this charge. It must be allowed that the allegation of corruption against the President is based on purely hypothetical evidence, and those who are aware of the reckless way in which imputations of fraud are supported here will be slow to endorse this charge.

Other accusations of 'feathering his nest' are lavishly made. In large measure these accusations appear to be based on the admitted fact that Kruger has grown rich during these later years, and enemies trace these riches to a foul source. Yet it is certain that a perfectly clean explanation of Kruger's wealth exists in the land operations by which, in common with many leading citizens, he has made money. For instance, not long ago he sold his Geduld estate for £120,000, which was at once disposed of to a company for half a million, and is at the present time worth between two and three millions. A shrewd business man owning land in mining districts has these chances. Joubert, Vice President, against whose honour no whisper has ever been heard, is considerably richer than the President, and has made his money by similar dealings. Kruger's lax notions about 'presents' and a disposition to screen certain friends who have indisputably yielded to corruption, coupled with a good deal of nepotism, have not un-naturally brought grave suspicions upon his personal honour. But under cross-examination these charges are found to rest upon mere conjecture. The strongly religious character of Kruger spells hypocrisy to those unaccustomed to analysis of character.

That religiosity is consistent with certain curious ethical per-versities is a commonplace of which perhaps Kruger and the Boers furnish instructive illustrations. But the deep, passionate genuineness of his belief in the Bible and an inner light derived from its study can only be questioned by inveterate 'malignants.' Kruger is a fanatic, a narrow-minded bigot, if you will, but no hypocrite. His strong con-fidence in his monopoly of spiritual truth is illustrated by a charac-teristic story which I have not seen in print. Some little time ago he was induced to go to Johannesburg to open a Jewish synagogue, and an immense reception was prepared for him. On entering and taking his place he removed his hat and paid no heed whatever to the sugges-tion of his secretary, who explained the Jewish custom of covering the head. Rising to speak, he ejaculated a few brief sentences, in which he said that it was a pleasure to him to declare the synagogue open, but he would be still more pleased if his audience would give up the Jewish faith and accept Christianity, adding that he was preparing a little treatise which he hoped would have the desired effect of converting them to the truth in Jesus Christ.

In politics, as in religion, Paul Kruger is governed by a few simple, deeply rooted notions. The notion that he is a far-sighted, foxy politician seeking his own ends seems to me quite unwarranted, and arises from the situations, which often force him to give reasons and arguments for actions which are really based upon sentiment, intuitive caution, or set prejudices. Kruger is really fighting for the independence of his country, as he conceives it; warding off the danger of an over-whelming rush of alien influences. When called upon suddenly for a set defence of his position he has no ready dialectic, but often blurts out reasons which are not the real actuating forces. His evasions and dilatory bargaining are not really a conscious statecraft so much as a rude instinctive fence which is successful against a sophist like Mr. Chamberlain, because the latter, by a characteristic fallacy, supposes his antagonist to be the same manner of a man as himself. At the same time able men who know him tell me Kruger is a powerful thinker, who drives right down to the bed-rock of an issue, has a keen nose for fallacy in argument, and is even willing to admit an error when it is clearly pointed out to him. There is, however, one weakness in his position which deserves notice. He reads nothing except the Bible, neither books nor newspapers, though extracts from the latter are read to him. The result is that he depends upon the friends around him for all his knowledge of the larger world; even in regard [to] the most material facts which reach his mind there is thus a constant danger of unfair selection and misrepresentation. Kruger is not the self-sufficing man he is sometimes painted. Dominated by certain passions and experience, he is never shaken by threats or by violence, but he is very amenable to the influence of friends. This, too, is a characteristic of his race which English Jingoes ignore. The concessions which seem to them to have been wrested by fear of war have really been made under the urgent pressure of friendly representations. Of Kruger's actual power it is hard to judge. The Boer is a free-spoken man, and there are signs that he is not prepared to give absolute confidence even to the President. But there is no strong man in or out of the Raad who can really stand up against the President or can rally a powerful party against him in a national emergency like the present. Boers do not like the notion of dictatorship, and are strenuous in their insistence on extreme forms of democracy. But my conviction is that Kruger is virtually endowed with a dictatorship. To this extent the Transvaal may be regarded as a one-man State, but one explanatory fact must be borne in mind – namely that Kruger's power is not created by his sole will and authority, but it is the self-conscious recognition by the people that he is the true repository of the Boer spirit and traditions, and that he will fight with all his mind and all his might for the independence of his country.

## SPION KOP: AN ACRE OF MASSACRE

Tuesday, February 27, 1900

J. B. Atkins describes an unsuccessful attempt to relieve Ladysmith:

Spearman's Farm Camp, January 30
If you looked up from the Tugela to the hills where Sir Charles Warren fought, you would say that they rose in a continuous slope to the top. But South African hills are like the sea; at a distance they seem smooth, but look close into them and you will find unexpected valleys and crests. Nothing on the face of South African nature is what it seems. You see the British trenches up there seeming to lie immediately under the Boer trenches, but if you go up you will find that they are on different hills and a deep valley lies between them. You see troops march out on to a sheer plain, and when they have disappeared suddenly on their march you learn for the first time that the plain is no plain, but is full of dips and rises, dongas and unremarked kopjes. From the river it seemed for almost a week that Warren's troops were within charging distance of the crest of all those hills; really they remained from the crest the distance that separates a victory from a retirement.

Spion Kop, properly used, was the key of the position, and the key that would open the door of Ladysmith. Patrols had reported that there were only a few Boers on it. Soon after dusk on Tuesday a party set out to make a night attack on the hill. It was a hand-and-knee march up the southern face – a climb over smooth rock and grass. It was necessarily slow; it is to the great credit of the party that it was steady. The force was three-quarters of the way up before it was discovered. Then a Boer sentry challenged it for the password. 'Waterloo!' said an officer. The sentry turned to flee, but fell bayoneted where he turned. 'Fire and charge,' came the order. The Fusiliers went forward at the deliberate conventional trot; Thorneycroft's, with the untrained, admirable enthusiasm of volunteers, rushed forward in a frenzy. Only a picket

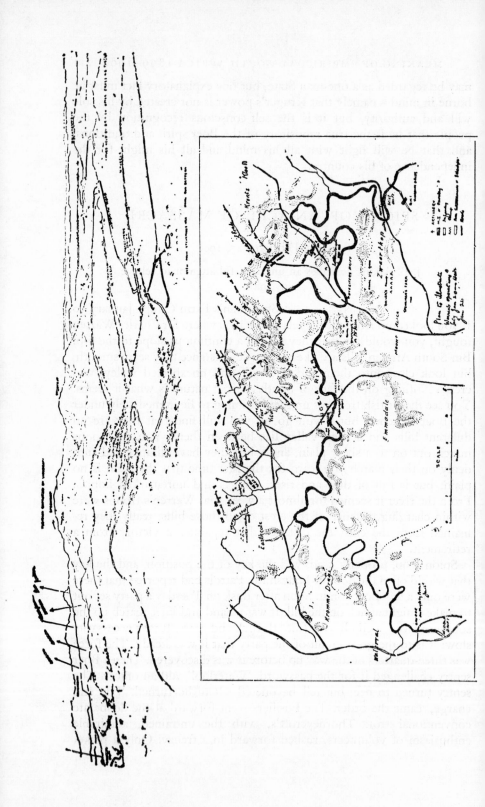

was behind the sentry and it vanished. But the crest was not reached till dawn. When dawn came the party found that it was in the clouds. It could see nothing but the plateau – 400 yards across – on which it stood. Trenches were made, but it was difficult to determine the right place for them. The Boers were invisible; our own troops below were invisible; for three hours the party lived on a fog-bound island in the air. At last the mist lifted.

The curtain rose upon the performance of a tragedy. The Boers – need I say, upon another ridge of Spion Kop? – began to fire heavily, and our men seemed to have no sufficient protection in the trenches. The space was small; they were crowded together. I will describe the scene as I saw it from below. I shall always have it in my memory – that acre of massacre, that complete shambles, at the top of a rich green gully, with cool granite walls (a way fit to lead to heaven), which reached up the western flank of the mountain. To me it seemed that our men were all in a small, square patch; there were brown men, and browner trenches, the whole like an over-ripe barley field. As I looked soon after the mist had risen (it was nine o'clock, I think) I saw three shells hit a certain trench within a minute; each struck it full in the face, and the brown dust rose and drifted away with the white smoke. The trench was toothed against the sky like a saw – made, I supposed, of sharp rocks built into a rampart. Another shell struck it, and then – heavens! – the trench rose up and moved forward. The trench was men; the teeth against the sky were men. They ran forward bending their bodies into a curve, as men do when they run under a heavy fire; they looked like a cornfield with a heavy wind sweeping over it from behind. On the left front of the trenches they dropped into some grey rocks where they could fire. Spout after spout of dust bounced up from the brown patch. So it would go on for perhaps half an hour, when the whole patch itself bristled up from flatness; another lot of men was making for the rocks ahead. They flickered up, floated rapidly and silently across the sky, and flickered down into the rocks, without the appearance of a substantial beginning or end to the movement. The sight was as elusive as a shadow-show.

The Boers had three guns playing like hoses on our men. It was a triangular fire. Our men on Spion Kop had no guns. When on earth would the artillery come? Guns were the only thing that could make the hill either tenable or useful. When on earth would they come? No sign of them yet; not even a sign of a mountain battery; and we who watched wriggled in our anxiety. The question was whether enough men could live through the shelling till the guns came. Men must have felt that they had lived a long life under that fire by the end of the day, and still the guns had not come. From Three Tree Hill the gunners shelled the usual places, as well as the northern ranges of Spion Kop where the Boer riflemen were supposed to be. Where the Boer guns were we did not know. If only they had offered a fine mark, like our own guns, we should have smashed them in five minutes. The British gunner is proud of the perfect alignment and the regular intervals which his battery has observed under the heaviest fire; the Boer gunner would be sorry to observe any line or any interval. He will not have a gun in the open; he is not proud, but he is safe. You might say that in this war the object of the Boer gunners is to kill an enemy who cannot see them; that of the heroic British gunners is to be killed by an enemy whom they cannot see. The European notion of field guns is that they should be light enough to be moved about rapidly in battle and not hamper the speed of an army on the march. Now, does it not appear that the Boers will change all that for us? They have dragged heavy long-range guns about with them and put them on the top of steep hills, and we, of all people, know that they have not hampered the speed of their army. Some dunderhead, perhaps, proposed that such guns should be taken by the army into the field – some fellow who had never read a civilised book on gunnery. But how many fools in history have led the world? Let us make ourselves wise men by adding another to the list.

Reinforcements were ordered to Spion Kop. They were needed. The men on Spion Kop were crying out for them. I could see men running to and fro on the top, ever hunted to a fresh shelter. Some Boer riflemen crept forward, and for a few minutes fifty Boers and British heaved and swayed hand to hand. They drew apart. The shelling did not cease. The hollow rapping of the Maxim-Nordenfelts was a horrid sound; the little shells from them flapped and clacked along the ground in a long straight line like a string of geese. But the reinforcements were coming; already a thin line corkscrewed up the southern slope of Spion Kop. Their bayonets reflected the sun. Mules were in the column with ammunition, screwing themselves upwards, as lithe as monkeys. The Dorsets, Bethune's, the Middlesex, the Imperial Light Infantry – volunteers destined to receive a scalding baptism – were on the climb. From left to right of the field, too, from west to east, infantry moved. Hildyard's Brigade and the Somersets emerged from behind Three Tree Hill in open order, and moved towards the Boer line on the north and towards the west flank of Spion Kop. The Boers sniped into them. A man was down – a shot rabbit in the grass with his legs moving. The infantry went a little way further east and north, halted and watched Spion Kop for the rest of the day. General Woodgate had been hit over the left eye about ten o'clock in the morning; the command came by a natural devolution to Col. Thorneycroft. And this big, powerful man, certainly the best mark on the hill, moved about fearlessly all day and was untouched. The reinforcements poured up the steep path which bent over suddenly on to the plateau at the top. It was ten steps from shelter to death. The Scottish Fusiliers came over the east side of the hill from Potgieter's. The men were packed on to the narrow table under the sky; some were heard to say that they would willingly go forward or go back, but they could not stay where they were. But no order was given to go forward. If there were few orders, it was because the officers had dwindled away. In the Lancashire Fusiliers only three officers were unwounded; in Thorneycroft's eleven were hit out of 18. Of Thorneycroft's men only about 60 came down unwounded out of 100. Late in the afternoon the 3rd battalion of the King's Royal Rifles advanced up the eastern slope of Spion Kop from Potgieter's and seized two precipitous humps. The left half battalion took the left hump; the right half the right hump. Never was anything more regular, and seldom more arduous. One hundred men were lost in the brief advance. I did not see it, and I am told I missed the most splendid thing that day. English people are fond of praising, with a paradoxical generosity, the deeds of Irish and Scottish regiments. Here is a case for praise, without affectation, of an English regiment.

Night fell, and still no guns. The shell fire continued and the sniping. The Boers still had the range. At eight o'clock Colonel Thorneycroft decided to retire. We were to give up the key to the position and the key to Ladysmith – and no one will ever be able to find anything but praise for what Colonel Thorneycroft did that day. He had been sitting on a target for thirteen hours, and now he was going. It was necessary. Some men had fought there for twenty-one hours without water. In England you have not the physical proof of what that means. The Mountain Battery was already up; two naval 12-pounders were half way up. But Thorneycroft was going; it was necessary. When dawn came the officer in command of the naval guns on Mount Alice looked through the long telescope. He looked long before he answered someone who asked how our men were on Spion Kop. 'They are all Boers or Red Cross men there,' he said. That was the first we who had slept at Potgieter's knew of the retirement; it was the first the Headquarters Staff knew of it. In a few hours Warren's force was coming back across the Tugela. 'The way round' had failed. No; let me say one of the ways round has failed; another must be found.

J.B.A.

## THE RELIEF OF MAFEKING

### Monday, June 18, 1900

Filson Young (1876–1938), whose brother was the *Guardian*'s commercial editor, set out from Vryburg on May 10 with the relieving column. On the way a runner reached them from Mafeking, asking their strength. Having no code, they improvised one – 'Our numbers are the Naval and Military multiplied by ten (94, Piccadilly = 940); our guns the number of sons in the Ward family (6); our supplies the O.C., 9th Lancers (Col. Small-Little).' It was not a great force, and it ran into trouble as the convoy straggled.

### THE FIGHTING NEAR THE MARITSANI
#### *From our Special Correspondent*

Monday, May 14

It was then 4.45, and a bewildering moment for the Brigadier, who had a great bulky convoy to protect and had it at the moment in a defenceless position. I think I would not take any reward to bear the responsibility of acting at such a moment. The shots were sounding quicker, but one could see nothing except the surrounding trees. Colonel Mahon looked coolly round. 'We must try with the guns,' he said, and ordered another squadron out on the right. The convoy was moving on now on as broad a front as the shrubs and trees would permit of; it raised a cloud of dust, which the level rays of the sun lit like a rainbow, and the bullets began to come in a hail. Well, that is rather exaggerated – not a hail. But on a summer day after oppressive heat and dark clouds the big rain-drops begin to splash on the ground; and this fire, which many old stagers who have been through several fights describe as the hottest they have known, was something like that. There was no cover; everyone was under fire; so there was nothing to do but to dismount and lead one's horse along beside the convoy. Every now and then among the clear high 'phit' of the Mauser bullet would come the hideous twisting whistle of the Martini – really a horrible sound. There was something like a panic amongst the native drivers; they walked along bent almost double, taking what shelter they could; one I saw crawling along on his belly, and the sight made me laugh, although I had at heart too much sympathy with him to be really amused. The mules and horses, alarmed by these strange whistlings in the air, began to neigh and scream, and they added to the general tumult. One gave up wondering whether or no one would be hit, but merely wondered if it would be a graze or a 'plug.' There were the usual number of miraculous escapes; the driver of the waggon beside which I was walking tumbled off his seat like a sack, stone dead; a mule in the waggon behind me leapt and kicked, and sank on the ground; my horse jumped as a Martini bullet smote the sand at his heel; yet I think there was never a bullet nearer me than a dozen feet. Major Baden-Powell, who is accompanying the expedition for his brother's relief, had his watch, worn in the left breast-pocket, smashed to atoms, but his skin was not even scratched. They were ten very long, and, to put it frankly, very hateful minutes that passed until M Battery opened with a roar. It was a welcome sound, and still more welcome the 'pom-pom-pom-*pom*,' like the bark of a good dog, that sounded immediately afterwards. And it was like oil on water, or water on fire. Immediately the enemy's fire slackened; in two minutes it had almost ceased; in five it had stopped entirely, and one began to get one's breath. There were men lying all round and about the wood, and the small ambulance staff had more work than they could do; my cart made three trips, carrying wounded men from the column to the dressing station. Only ten minutes of fighting, and twenty-six casualties; five killed, twenty wounded, one missing. But when one had been through those ten minutes, it was not the men lying stark and still in the grass beside the ambulance that made one astonished; it was the sight of people walking about and talking that made one wonder whether or no one had been dreaming.

## Mafeking, Friday, May 18

### MAFEKING AT LAST

They were twenty-four very exciting hours. Many miles were travelled, a great enterprise was brought to a successful issue, a tough battle was fought, men received wounds and died, Mafeking was relieved – enough incident and adventure to fill months of ordinary life. The bare events I may describe, but the emotional history of those twenty-four hours will probably never be written, simply because there is no one here able to set it forth. But read the narrative, put yourself in the place of those to whom it was not a story but a piece of life, and then perhaps you will realise something of what it meant to them.

The country consisted of a succession of ridges lying at right angles to our line of march, and as each one rose before us the staff galloped forward to the summit, only to see another lying beyond. But at last, while some of us were buying eggs at a Kaffir kraal, a more adventurous person climbed upon a rubbish heap and shouted 'There's Mafeking.' There was a rush for the coign of vantage, and a great levelling of glasses. There it lay, sure enough, the little town that we had come so far to see – a tiny cluster of white near the eastward horizon, glistening amid the yellowish-brown of the flats. We looked at it for a few moments in silence, and then Colonel Mahon said, 'Well let's be getting on'; and no one said anything more about Mafeking, but everyone thought a great deal.

There was one more brisk engagement to be fought.

The commando that had been holding on for days on our right had effected a junction with a force sent out from Mafeking to oppose us, and had just arrived in position near Israel's Farm when we came up against them. From the large outline of their attack there must have been at least two thousand of them, and from the cleverness with which they were disposed we at first estimated them at twice that number. We held them on our right while we sent a strong force working round on our left, which ultimately got out far enough to turn their right. Of course we were too few to do more than dislodge them; surrounding was out of the question; so when we had fairly turned them we 'let go' on the right and they fled in that direction. The house at Israel's Farm they held until the very end, shelling our rear-guard briskly. The engagement lasted close on five hours, during which our casualties amounted to less than forty. It seems strange that there are five hours of fighting to be accounted for. Five hours! Was it for so long that one listened to the voices of guns and rifles?

The fight was over, but as the convoy began to work its way cautiously through the bush in the dusk we began to talk about it, and to fit it together from the pieces of our individual experience. What had they been trying to do? The Boers had once more given us a lesson in tactics, and we had given them one in dealing with a nasty situation. They had bluffed us by extending their attack round a large perimeter, leading us to suppose their strength to be far greater than it really was, and but for the really excellent fighting on our side might have held us where we were until the want of supplies forced us to retire or surrender. As we had so few casualties, it is probable that they had not many; but it is possible to have very warm fighting with few casualties. Our cover was excellent; so was theirs; and Colonel Peakman, who with the rearguard bore the heaviest burden of the fight, lost hardly a man, although he lost heavily in horses. Everyone is agreed that the honours of the day fall chiefly to this gallant business man, who in his spare time has made himself so good a soldier.

Major Karri-Davies had ridden on into Mafeking, and, with the luck which rewards daring people, had found the road clear and sent back a messenger with that information to Colonel Mahon. I think people were never so willingly awakened from sleep; not even the wounded grumbled, who had also to be roused from their beds on the grass and repacked into the stuffy ambulance. At about 12.30 we were ready to start, but during the first mile there were long halts and delays while the guides argued and boggled about the roads. At last the strain became too great, and Major Gifford, Captain Smith, and I resolved to ride on and trust to finding the right road. We knew the direction by the stars, and started across the veldt a little south of east. It was bitterly cold, and we were all both sleepy and hungry, but there was an excitement in the air that kept us easily going. After about half an hour we heard voices ahead, and descried the shapes of horses and men. Our hearts sank for a moment, only to rise again when we recognised Colonel Peakman, who, having been in command of the rearguard on the previous day up till nine o'clock at night, was now taking his turn at advance guard at one o'clock the next morning. As a Kimberley man, it had long been his ambition to lead the relieving force into Mafeking, and I think no one grudged him the honour. Amongst all, indeed, there was a certain amount of competition, and the four correspondents who survived to the end of the expedition became strangely silent about their intentions for the evening. I pinned my faith to Peakman, as I knew he was as anxious as anyone to be in first. For an hour we jogged on at a fast walk, until we had clearly 'run the distance,' as they say at sea. Still no sign of the trenches or forts which should mark the outward boundary of the defended area. We pulled up, and the guide was questioned. 'Two miles more,' he said. We rode on for another quarter of an hour, but still found nothing before us but the rolling veldt; not a light, not a sound except the beating of the horses' feet. Again we halted, and this time Colonel Peakman himself questioned the guide, and the man had to admit that he had mistaken his way, and that we were on the lower road, longer by a good three miles than that originally intended. We had no connecting files with the main column, and, as it had a guide of its own, it was certain that it would take the shorter road, and probably be in before its own advance guard.

So we went on again, this time at a trot; the excitement seemed to extend to the horses, so that even they could not be restrained. In ten minutes we saw men sitting by the roadside, and found a hundred very weary Fusiliers, who had been sent to Israel's Farm at the end of the fight and told to go on afterwards. 'Had anyone passed along the road before us?' 'No'; and with a gasp of relief we hurried on. In a few moments the group in advance pulled up, shouting, "Ware barbed wire!' We all stopped, and there were frantic calls for wire-cutters. With four reports like the snapping of big fiddle-strings the last barrier before Mafeking was removed, and we passed on again, this time at a hand canter. In a few minutes we heard the sound of a galloping horse on the road, and a mounted man challenged us. 'Halt! Who goes there?' 'Friend.' 'Who are you?' (The excitement was too high for the preservation of the proper formula.) 'Colonel Peakman, in command of the advance guard of the relief column.' 'By Jove, ain't I glad to see you, sir!' It was an officer sent out by Colonel Baden-Powell to meet us and bring us in. We left the squadron, and the five of us went on, this time at a gallop, over trenches, past breastworks and redoubts and little forts, until we pulled up at the door of the headquarters mess. Ah, the narrative is helpless here. No art could describe the hand-shaking and the welcome and the smiles on the faces of these tired-looking men; how they looked with rapt faces at us common-place people from the outer world as though we were angels, how we all tried to speak at once, and only succeeded in gazing at each other. One man tried to speak; then he swore; then he buried his face in his arms and sobbed. We all gulped at nothing, until someone brought in cocoa and we gulped that instead; and then the Colonel came in, and one could only gaze at him, and search in vain on his jolly face for the traces of seven months' anxiety and strain.

After an hour we went out and found the column safely encamped just outside the town. Everyone was dog-tired, and although it was half-past five in the morning and the moon was sinking, we lay down and were immediately asleep – in Mafeking.

F.Y.

## JOURNEY IN CAPTIVITY

### Thursday, September 26, 1901

#### THE DIARY OF A BOER FAMILY

(The following extracts from a diary, of the authenticity of which we have obtained sufficient assurance, illustrate in detail one aspect of the process of 'clearing' tracts of the country occupied by the enemy.)

Amsterdam, New Scotland, Thursday, February 14, 1901. This morning about eight o'clock the cavalry of the enemy entered the town by the Glen Aggie road. They soon spread all over the town, the infantry following. In a short time every garden and tree was stripped of everything; not even a green peach remained. All the live stock was taken; the cattle and horses were collected by natives and driven off, while the poultry, pigs, &c. the soldiers made off with. We locked up all the doors and remained in the house looking on. At about 11 a.m. two intelligence officers came to search the house; they took away a revolver and cartridges we had. About 3 p.m. General Campbell arrived with his staff; he was very abrupt and the reverse of pleasant in his bearing. He said they, the English, had come to give us food and protection. Mother replied that we were quite satisfied with the food and protection our own people afforded us. Then he said we were to be ready to leave the following day at 10 a.m., and after a deal of talk and argument he left, highly offended.

Friday [Feb. 15]. Worse than ever. Another column has come through Sweede Poort. At about 11 a.m. the Provost Marshal, Capt. Daniels with four others, entered the house and began searching the place again. Mother was absent when they came. It would be impossible to describe how they rummaged and pulled everything about; the mattresses and pillows were felt, doubled up and patted; every box, great or small, was thoroughly overhauled and searched to the very bottom; the fireplaces, book-shelf, kitchen, pantry, loft, every nook and corner was ransacked, and they took what they wanted – soap, candles, mealies &c even to white sewing cotton. When mother came in, Capt. Daniels turned to her and said, 'Those devils of Boers have been sniping at us again, and your two sons among them, I suppose. If I catch them, they will hang.'

Sunday [Feb. 17]. At dawn Capt. Ballantyne came and said that a waggon would arrive in a few minutes and we would be allowed a quarter of an hour to load, and only to take the most necessary things, as fifteen were to go on one waggon, and once in the English camps we would be supplied with everything that we required – food, medical comforts &c. So we were one of three families in the waggon. The Mullers, from Middleburg district, living in Mrs. Davel's barn, sixteen in all, including an old woman over eighty years of age and a baby not three months old, were put on to a trolley with a half tent fixed at the back. There was not even room for them all to sit. We – that is, all the people – were taken across the spruit to the English camp. The waggons were drawn up in rows and each one thoroughly searched by a party of men, everything taken off and each box and bag carefully looked through. Not a thing, however small, escaped inspection; even housewives' needlecases were opened and looked through. What the men considered you did not need was taken. Feather beds, clothing, mattresses, chairs, chests &c, odds and ends of all kinds were piled in heaps and burnt. Foodstuffs – flour, sugar, tea &c – were also taken.

In the afternoon we trekked about twelve miles. There were over 400 waggons. We would trek a few yards, when there would be a block so that most of the time was spent in waiting for the way to clear. It rained all day, and, almost without exception, every waggon leaked. Many people had not a dry thread in their waggons by the evening. No halt was made; no food partaken of since 6 a.m. At 9 p.m. we outspanned at the top of a bult in a hard rain, no food to eat, and not even a drink of water to be had. It was pitiful to hear the children crying all night in the wet waggons for water and food and not to be able to get a thing for them. The oxen were just tied to the yoke in the mud – no grazing.

At dawn the next day the oxen were inspanned as they stood from the yoke, we trekked past Volve Koppies and outspanned about 9 a.m. Here we found out that we had to furnish the driver and the leader of our waggon with food from what had been left us. We received no rations at all, no food of any kind, no wood or water. The driver had to walk fully a mile to fetch water, and we had some planks that we made fire with. It rained all day. This evening Lt. Pratt came and told mother he had had instructions to remove our waggon from the others, and that a guard was to be placed over us to prevent our speaking to other people. So we were drawn away from our trek, and four armed soldiers were put by the waggon.

Tuesday, 19th. We reached Piet Retief to-day. The English have a large troop of cattle and horses, which are driven into every mealie field or cultivated ground as we pass – generally Kaffir lands – and in a few minutes everything is destroyed. Also the cattle, goats &c. are taken, as they might furnish food for the Boers. At Volve Koppies we saw a Kaffir hut on fire and the troopers warming their hands at the blaze. This evening we received a leg of mutton, the first food of any kind supplied to us since leaving on Sunday morning. We are, of course, on one side with our guard. Our guards have pitched their tent beside the waggon; there is always one on guard at night. During the day, while we trek, one is by the waggon, and at the outspan all four.

Sunday [Feb. 24]. We are on a very dirty spot. Heaps of sheep, the only food we get, are killed every day by the people and the Kaffirs, and the skins and insides are left all over the place, just where the sheep are killed. The stench is almost unbearable. We have been here several days, and are in a ring of English camps. No convenience of any kind is put up for the women or children, and it is impossible to go out in the daytime without being seen.

Sunday [March 3]. We trekked as far as the Red Paths, where we slept. The Red Paths is one of the worst bits of road on one of the worst roads in the Transvaal. Monday – We went up the Red Paths to-day. The waggons only had bedding and clothes on, and it took three spans to take our waggon up; the trek-tow broke four times; the mud is dreadful; it is all the oxen can do to drag themselves along. Tuesday – Annie very sick. Must be the food, as we have only meat, and mealies when we can pick them; no bread, not even meal for porridge, and not able to get anything for love or money. Our guard was removed to-day. They were always willing to help in any way, and we had nothing at all to complain of from the men; they were good to us.

Wednesday [March 6]. Annie very ill all day. A driving misty rain. We are about twenty miles from Utrecht, unable to obtain anything in the shape of food, not even meat, as the sheep have been left behind. We have three spans of oxen on, and one ox fell down from exhaustion, and was beaten and dragged out of the road in a dying condition. Oxen with lung sickness are made to pull until they fall down in the yoke to die.

Monday [March 11]. Left Newcastle yesterday afternoon; arrived here (Volksrust) 9.30 in the rain. The station a sea of mud and slush. No provision of any kind made for the women and children, over 300. We bought what we require at the refreshment room, but many had no money. The rooms formerly used by the Z.A.R. (South African Republic) as Customs offices were thrown open and the women and children herded in until there was scarce standing place. Those left out, ourselves among them, were loaded on to two trolleys and taken to what was formerly the Volksrust Hotel, where 14 of us spent the night in a small single bedroom. It contained nothing but a table. One of our party brought two rugs with her, which we spread on the floor and sat down until morning.

Sunday [March 17]. A week of rain and misery. We are still at the Volksrust Hotel – eleven of us in a small verandah room; barely room to sleep; we eat and live outside. The camp is quite close to us in the town among the houses. Many of the tents are standing in mud pools; the only concern of the laager commandant seems to be that the tents should be put up neatly in rows – where does not matter; two bell tents between three families. Mother would not take those shown to her, one single, one lined, standing in mud pools; the rain had washed right through, in one side, out the other. She told Supt. Nixon they were not fit even for a dog, and declined to move into them.

Friday [April 19]. At half-past eight last night, just as mother was going to bed, message that Major Watt, Assistant District Commissioner, wanted to see her at once. Mother replied, 'Impossible; she would come in the morning.' The man said he did not dare to take such a message, so eventually mother, Annie and Polly Coltzer went with the policeman, who took them to Major Watt's house, where they were shown into his bedroom. Major Watt was in a dreadful rage. 'You are Mrs. Cameron?' 'Yes.' 'You are a most dangerous woman, you have been speaking against the British Government. You are an Englishwoman.' 'All my sympathies are with the Boers.' 'Policeman, make a note of that. All the concessions we intended making you will be withdrawn. You will not be allowed to receive any parcels.' Some days later the two families in the room with us – Mrs. Strauss and Mrs. Coltzer – were removed to the new camp beyond the railway station, outside of the town.

Thursday [April 25]. Late this afternoon we received the following: – I beg to inform you that you are to proceed to Maritzburg to-morrow, 26th inst. by the 11 p.m. train. A waggon shall convey your luggage to the station.' We did not leave until the following Sunday evening as no waggon was sent until then. We arrived here on the 29th April, and are at present still here. Green Point, Pietermaritzburg, Natal. B. R. Cameron, Prisoner of War, May 31, 1901.

## WHAT MISS HOBHOUSE SAW

### Wednesday, June 19, 1901

In December, 1900 Emily Hobhouse, the sister of L. T. Hobhouse, went out to South Africa to visit the concentration camps. Lord Milner, High Commissioner for South Africa, allowed Miss Hobhouse to go only as far as Bloemfonteyn. Her report, in the form of a diary because of the constantly changing conditions, covered the period from January 22 to April 22. The following is a typical extract from the *Guardian's* four and a half column summary.

January 31: Some people in town still assert that the camp is a haven of bliss. Well, there are eyes and no eyes. I was at the camp to-day, and just in one little corner this is the sort of thing I found. A girl of 21 lay dying on a stretcher – the father, a big, gentle Boer, kneeling beside her; while, next tent, his wife was watching a child of six, also dying, and one of about five drooping. Already this couple had lost three children in the hospital, and so would not let these go, though I begged hard to take them out of the hot tent. 'We must watch these ourselves,' he said. I sent – to fetch brandy, and got some down the girl's throat, but for the most part you must stand and look on, helpless to do anything because there is nothing to do anything with. Then a man came up and said, 'Sister, come and see my child, sick for three months.' It was a dear little chap of four, and nothing left of him but his great brown eyes and white teeth from which the lips were drawn back, too thin to close. His body was emaciated. The little fellow had craved for fresh milk, but of course there had been none until these last two days, and now the fifty cows only give four buckets. I can't describe what it is to see these children lying about in a state of collapse. It's just exactly like faded flowers thrown away. And one has to stand and look on at such misery and be able to do almost nothing.

> Miss Hobhouse returned to South Africa without permission, was not allowed to land, and deported under military guard.

## 'EVERY STEP IN THE PROCESS COULD BE ACCURATELY FORETOLD'

> Most of the *Guardian*'s political leader-writing on South Africa was by Hobhouse or Montague. This one on the concentration camps reads to me like Hobhouse; the following one, on Rhodes, like Montague.

### THE MORTALITY IN CONCENTRATION CAMPS

#### Friday, September 27, 1901

Two thousand three hundred and forty-five persons – men, women, and children – died during August in what the Government, with grim humour, calls the 'Camps of Refuge' in South Africa. One thousand eight hundred and seventy-eight of them were white, and of these more than fifteen hundred were children. The remainder, 467, were natives, whose promised career of happiness under British care has thus sadly been cut short. They are ugly figures. It would be pleasant to forget them, and it would be as well to do so if the fate of thousands more did not hang upon the British Government and the British public. Since, however, our Government is responsible for the camps and the concentration policy of which they are a part, it is a painful necessity to dwell upon these figures and see what they mean. This is the third complete monthly return that has been issued. The return for June showed a death-rate of 109 per thousand per annum. This was rightly regarded as terrible, and supporters of the concentration system were at pains to explain it away as due to temporary causes. There was an epidemic of measles, it was said, and we were assured that the July figures would show a reduction. The July figures were published in due course, and showed a rate of 183 per thousand. On these figures Field Marshal Sir Neville Chamberlain[1] wrote to us as follows: – 'These figures, reduced to a few simple words, imply that about ten women and children have died in the concentration camps in July as compared to one who would have died in London. Who is guilty for the excess of the nine?' Measles, and pneumonia supervening, were put down officially as the causes. Now come the August returns, and we find that the rate has risen to no less than 213, a rate equal to or greater than that of the worst week of the plague at Bombay. Altogether 4,067 white men, women, and children have died in these camps in the last three months. If this rate is maintained over 16,000 will die in the year.

People have not hesitated to heap insult upon injury by accusing the Boer mothers of neglect and incompetence. It is a cruel accusation, and no less cruel than absurd. The death rate varies according to the good or bad management of the camps. We are told with unblushing effrontery that the women and children have all and more than all their usual comforts in these camps – that is, we suppose, that the children of well-to-do farmers are accustomed to lie on mattresses, or without them, under canvas, on the ground, often in mud and sometimes in water. If these unfortunate people have their usual comforts why are they dying? It is useless to deceive ourselves. The cause of the mortality is manifest.

It is not merely that the food is often bad, the overcrowding worse, the fuel scanty, the protection from the weather insufficient. We might multiply detailed illustrations of these defects from Miss Hobhouse's account and from other sources. But let us take the official excuse – an epidemic of measles. How does this affect our responsibility? There is an epidemic raging of which children are dying by dozens, say, in a Transvaal camp. A General sallies forth and 'sweeps' so many square miles of country. The women are turned out of their houses. They are given a few minutes to collect what they can. The rest of their goods may or may not be burnt there and then. They, with their children and scanty belongings, are huddled on to trucks with a crowd of other 'refugees' and, after one or two more days of exposure, arrive at the pestilence-stricken camp. Here the new-coming children, already

1. Sir Neville Chamberlain (1820–1902); commissioned in East India Company's army, 1837; defended Delhi during Indian Mutiny. He was not related to Joseph Chamberlain.

weakened by exposure, quickly take the measles from the sick. With bad food and insufficient protection from the weather, pneumonia supervenes and they die in turn. Every step of the process could be accurately foretold. The concentration policy may or may not have contributed to the success of our arms, but let us at least be candid and recognise what it has meant and still means in human suffering. Bishops may approve of it, but soldiers like Sir Neville Chamberlain have told us that there is nothing approaching it in the annals of British arms.

## THE DEATH OF CECIL RHODES

### Thursday, March 27, 1902

Mr. Rhodes, who died yesterday near Capetown, had that in him which makes men do either good or evil on a great scale. He could frame very strong wishes and fairly long plans, and would work hard and cunningly to bring them about. He understood weak men and the special qualities of their weakness – how some are best driven with a bit and others drawn with a ring in the nose, or a carrot, or by perseverance in patting them. And he knew not merely individuals but crowds and the special accessibility of crowds to certain forms of collective emotion. He saw that in modern politics intrigue, if it is to succeed, must be democratised and whole populaces excited or frightened or misled; hence the careful concocting and timing of the 'women and children' appeal to English sentiment for the furtherance of the Jameson Raid and the subsequent purchase of the control of the greater part of the British South African press when the agitation for a more official war against the Transvaal succeeded the former conspiracy. Of course all this knowledge and this power are neither good nor bad, morally, in themselves. They are like a ladder, that may be used to save a child from a burning house or to commit a burglary. Mr. Rhodes's extraordinary power of getting things done in the political world he lived in cannot in itself be counted to him either for righteousness or unrighteousness. It was an attribute neither moral nor immoral, but non-moral, like being six feet tall. He must be judged not by his knowledge and command of those means, but by the quality of the ends for which he used them. What were those ends, then?

We cannot find the truth in the assumption sometimes made that Mr. Rhodes was simply a very rich man with a strong desire to grow richer, or even that he was merely a very strong man with a great relish for the use of his strength. He had, as it seems to us, a real though a shallow patriotism. He seems to have wished with great vehemence that his country might gain what he thought to be best for her. It was his idea of what was best for her that was at fault. It was, to all appearance, a greatness purely physical. That she should own more and more square miles of land, that her flag should be, as he called it, 'the greatest commercial asset in the world,' that she should hold in the hollow of her hand the lives of more and more men of other races – this we fully believe that Mr. Rhodes fervently and constantly desired for England. It was an ideal purely dynamic, a wish not so much that England should succeed in achieving this or that great and worthy thing in the world as that she should be able to do anything she liked. In individuals this longing to have the command of wealth and influence simply as forms of force, and not as means to any predetermined end beyond them, is common enough; but it is seldom entertained so unreservedly and uninquiringly on behalf of a man's country as it seems to have been entertained by Mr. Rhodes. Had the adequacy of the conception of patriotic duty and aspiration been questioned in Mr. Rhodes's presence he would probably have stared and wondered what the questioner was at. Any kind of political idealism would probably have seemed to him fantastic or mawkish; territory was solid; gold and diamond mines were realities; a map of South Africa wholly red was something that you could see; this was the 'robust' reasoning fashionable in his day and his career has been the most striking example of its application.

For a great number of his countrymen this embodiment of a purely materialist patriotism had a remarkable fascination. From a shallow study of the outlines of the theory of evolution a surprisingly large number of people had recently derived the notion that to get the better of everybody one can, nationally if not individually, is a piece of laudable conformity to natural tendencies which make for the perfection of the world. The idea is as remote from science as from morals, but its vogue in our period of half-educated transition from general popular ignorance to – let us hope – general intelligence has been tremendous; and Mr. Rhodes was hailed with delight as a statesman openly and bluntly unconcerned with the ideals held up to the nation by such different thinkers as Burke, Pitt, and Gladstone. Here at last was a man 'with no nonsense about him.' With a touch of positive enthusiasm the most robust of these moderns dwelt on the business-like cynicism with which Mr. Rhodes had told the falsehoods needed for the Jameson conspiracy and how he had tried to bribe one, if not two, political parties in the House of Commons. If the nations of the earth were to be as 'dragons of the prime, That tore each other in their slime,' here indeed was a dragon efficient in tooth and claw. Mr. Rhodes before he died had outlived the warmest of the admiration that he thus won. For one thing, his exclusive preoccupation with purely material considerations had led him terribly wrong, and, through him and his press, had led this country terribly wrong too, as to the cost and length of the war. On the eve of his success in bringing about its outbreak Mr. Rhodes used to predict confidently that the Boer resistance to conquest would break down at the first blow. He was probably absolutely incapable of comprehending the idea of a whole population, men, women, and children, determined to fight to the death against overwhelming odds rather than surrender their country's liberty, a thing not material. This indisposition to allow anything for the effect on others of ideals not entertained by himself was always apt to futilise his calculations, and the spectacle of anarchy, ruin, and hatred that filled South Africa at the time of his death offers a tragic warning to the practitioners of narrowly materialistic statecraft. With a real inclination to serve his country and with powers that would have enabled him to serve her effectually, the judgment of history will, we fear, be that he did more than any Englishman of his time to lower the reputation and to impair the strength and compromise the future of the Empire.

## Russia in 1905

### BLOODY SUNDAY IN ST. PETERSBURG

Friday, January 27, 1905
*From our Special Correspondent*[1]

St. Petersburg, Friday
In a low hall on the out-skirts of the city stood a dense crowd of working men who impatiently awaited the coming of the priest. The majority of the faces were open and sincere and the expression of some was almost childlike. Father Gapon appeared in a cassock, with flushed face, and eyes sparkling with unnatural excitement. He waved his hand to the crowd, and there was silence. 'I greet you,' he cried. 'We greet you,' responded the crowd. 'I wish you success in your battle for your rights.' Then the priest began speaking in a quick, nervous manner, about the behaviour of the Putiloff directors. In short, simple sentences he told the men they were being exploited and downtrodden, that the factory inspectors were in the pockets of the capitalists, and

1. H. W. Williams

the men must struggle for their rights. All his sentences were punctu-
ated by shouts of approval from the crowd, which frequently repeated, parrot-like, the speaker's phrases. He declaimed against the
Government officials, saying that these were withholding from the
people their freedom. 'Freedom' shouted the crowd with tremendous
enthusiasm. 'If,' he continued, always in the same hurried, but impressive way, 'if the Tsar does not satisfy our demands there will be no
Tsar,' 'No Tsar,' cried the crowd. Then, summoning the men to the
grand demonstration on Sunday, Father Gapon read the petition which
was to be presented to the Tsar on that day – a strange mixture of the
well-known Liberal demands with others of the most naive and impracticable character. Father Gapon made a superficial attempt to
explain some of the more unusual phrases but it was evident the crowd
did not understand the significance of the petition, and the enthusiasm
with which they responded was almost painful; they seemed like men
under a hypnotic spell. The concluding sentence of the petition declared that the sufferings of the petitioners were so great that the only
possible issues were freedom or death. After reading this sentence
Father Gapon raised his hand and bade the men swear to appear armed
at the place of meeting on Sunday. 'We swear!' cried the men with
raised right hands. 'If they touch us, if they hurt one of us,' said the
priest, 'we shall fight to the death.' 'We'll die!' shouted the crowd joyfully, 'we'll die!' And the speaker after saying a few parting words
left the stage, followed by shouts of 'Thanks, father.' It was a strangely
exciting meeting, yet there was something terrible in the thought that
this crowd of ignorant, unintelligent men were ready to fling themselves
upon almost certain death at the bidding of this priest, who talked so
lightly about wringing concessions from the Tsar.

In conversation, Father Gapon said he was sure the men would be
able to make their way to the Palace Square, and that the police dared
not prevent them. He himself had written that day to the Minister of
the Interior pledging his own life and the lives of his supporters that
the person of the Tsar would not be touched. His own immunity from
arrest he explained as the result of the fear of the police, and it is true
that the workmen on strike have enormous power in their hands at
present. When asked what the crowd would do if the Tsar did not
appear, Father Gapon declared they would wait till he came. 'Tsarskoe
Selo is not far away,' he said, and 'the telegraph is still working.' 'And if
still he does not come?' 'Then we'll see,' said Father Gapon. What
chiefly struck one in Father Gapon's conversation was the careless way
in which he spoke of the possibility of his own death or the butchery
of his followers, and the lack of a sense of the grave responsibility he

was taking upon himself. His immediate followers seem to be devoted to him. He travels about with an escort of twenty workmen armed with revolvers, and moves through the throng like a chief.

The hypothesis that Father Gapon is an *agent provocateur* seems incredible, though his career is by no means free from suspicion in this regard. One prefers to think that ambition has carried him beyond the limits of the activity marked out for him in society's statutes as sanctioned by M. Plehve, and that his unexpected success has led him to take advantage of a moment of popular excitement to make himself the leader of a labour movement on a sensational scale.[1]

Saturday, January 28, 1905

St. Petersburg, Sunday Night

The morning was very fine; the sun shone from a sky of pale blue in which there were faint traces of cloud. There was a bracing frost, and a light breeze blew from the north-west. One woke in the expectation of great events, but up till after ten the Nevsky was quieter than on an ordinary Sunday morning. When I went out about half-past eleven with Dr. Dillon, the correspondent of the *Daily Telegraph*, the scene had already changed, and scores of people, chiefly working men in black overcoats and black lambskin caps, were streaming northwards in the direction of the Neva. This was astonishing. We knew that troops were posted on the outskirts of the city, and wondered why the men had been allowed to pass. It almost seemed as though the Government were going to allow the demonstration to take its course, perhaps for some ulterior end of its own. But as we passed on further we saw bands of Cossacks riding by, big ruffianly looking fellows, in caps with red bands and beaver overcoats. They sat their horses splendidly, and smiled as though delighting in the prospect of a day's sport. We soon heard the news that there had been firing at the Navisky Zastav, one of the entrances to the city from the Schlusselburg industrial region. Some workmen had been killed, and the others, it was said, had run away. So far things were fairly clear. It was shown that the authorities intended to keep the working men away from the Winter Palace. The probable behaviour of the workmen was still a riddle.

Dillon and Williams hired a sleigh and drove round the city.

1. In April, 1906, John Dover Wilson gave an exclusive report in the *Guardian* of Gapon's secret execution by his comrades who had discovered he was a police spy. Plehve, the Minister of the Interior, had been assassinated in the summer of 1904.

Down the Kromberg Prospect, we suddenly came face to face with a black mass of people who were marching slowly along towards the garden. We turned off into a side street and watched them go by. The workers were marching to the Tsar to demand their rights, a grand and moving spectacle. Most of the men were in black overcoats and caps, their hands deep in their pockets. They walked along with a shambling gait, and smiled awkwardly at the bystanders, as though their sudden and unaccustomed conspicuousness made them shy. They marched in three sections; several students were in the front ranks, and there were ladies among them. Some angrily called upon the bystanders to come and join their ranks. And so they moved slowly on. We drove quickly around a back way, and came out again to the right of where the Cossacks were drawn up. We suddenly met a band of Cossacks on foot, running and laughing at the prospect of the excitement. A bugle call rang out. We turned swiftly back and followed the fleeing crowd. By this time the workers' procession had entered the garden and was within about two hundred yards of the Cossacks. Suddenly there was a rattle of rifles – one volley, followed by a second and a third and a fourth; an interval of silence, and then we heard shouts and cries. We learned afterwards that several were killed and wounded.

We approached the Winter Palace from the east, and found the neighbouring streets dense with crowds. Cossacks rode about, and lines of Cossacks and gendarmes kept back the people from the Palace Square, which lay white and clear, a few soldiers who were posted in the centre playing at fisticuffs to warm themselves. The great red front of the Palace showed no sign of life, and the balcony on which so many thousands had expected the Tsar would appear to grant his people the gift of freedom was empty; the Tsar seemed very far away. A dense crowd was coming from the Alexander Garden, on the west side of the square, and trying to force their way through the line of mounted police. These urged them back, and, as the crowd continued to press on, finally charged them, driving them along the footpath of the Nevsky and beating them with their fists. The temper of the crowd looked ugly, and it seemed as though the worst might happen.

In the big reading-room of the Public Library the *intelligentsia* (educated literary classes) had improvised a meeting to discuss what was to be done. Someone began reading the workmen's petition, but was interrupted by the arrival of a man who stated that three volleys had been fired upon the crowd in the Alexander Garden, and that many had been killed. 'A fight is going on in the streets,' he cried, 'and it will be an everlasting disgrace to the St. Petersburg *intelligentsia* if it does not go out and join its lot with the workers.' And the assembly rose as one man and hurried down to share the workers' fate. They were pale, but they had no fear; lawyers, authors, professors, students, women, old men and young went out to die with the people. But when we came out into the Nevsky again we found the crowd in great excitement, and had not gone very far before we were driven back by a squadron of Cossacks, who were forcing the whole mass up the street. No one could go anywhere near the scene of slaughter. As we drove we were overtaken by a sleigh followed by working men running along bareheaded and who cried out bitterly against the Government. In one of the sleighs was a wounded student and in another a fearful and sickening sight, the dead body of a student with a bullet hole in the left side of his head; his brains had been blown out. A comrade sat supporting him, and workmen joined in the terrible procession, crying and crossing themselves as they ran.

'Caps off,' they shouted angrily to all whom they passed, and all bared their heads in reverence before this great sacrifice to the cause of the people.

All doubt was over now. The Tsar had given his answer in blood. and the people who had been so peaceful and confident all the week, now suddenly broke out into a passion. All the afternoon the riots went on on the Nevsky. The cavalry charged the crowds again and again, and finally soldiers were drawn up in squares at intervals along the streets. The workmen broke open shops and began to attack the isvostchiks. When we came out again in the evening it was a strange, wild scene. People were running at full speed along the Nevsky, one could not tell why or whither. Of looting just then we could see no sign.

During the evening I saw some of the working men. They were fine, simple fellows. One, who was unhurt, said, 'We came to him to ask him to give us things and this is the way he answers us. Now we shall see.' Another who lay so badly wounded in the leg and thigh that there seemed little chance of his recovery smiled bravely and refused to accept money from some compassionate Russians who tried to press it upon him. He even wanted to pay for a postcard that had been given him. He spoke with great enthusiasm of Gapon. 'Plucky fellow! There are not many priests like him,' he said. Of Gapon it was difficult to learn anything. Some declared he had been killed; others said he had been wounded in the morning at the Navrisky Zastav. In the evening we heard he was safe. On a quiet street I saw three soldiers, half drunk, reeling along embracing a workman who seemed to be their friend. 'We are going to the death,' the workman said, 'aren't you ashamed to shoot your own brothers?' 'We don't want to attack a brother,' said one of the soldiers; 'but what can we do? There's the oath.' This is a new thing for the Russian people. It was only students who were shot before. Now it is their own brothers, and they are full of grief and bitter indignation. The great opportunity came to the Tsar of receiving the unbounded loyalty of his people, and with colossal folly he rejected it. And of those who were supposed to advise him one cannot write fittingly now. We are simply watching from hour to hour the issues of this tremendous wrong.

## A VISIT TO COUNT TOLSTOY

Thursday, February 9, 1905
*From our Special Correspondent*[1]

Saturday

I reached Yasnaya Polyana on Thursday morning. A snowstorm had blown over, and the sun shone from a wind-swept sky on the rising ground upon which stands the plantation enclosing the well-known homestead. Yasnaya Polyana seems a very haven of peace. And about Tolstoy's own personality the atmosphere of peace seemed to be resting continually. He was very calm, with the calmness of one whose time of struggle is past, and though he talked freely about current events and was kind and courteous after the gracious manner of Russian noblemen of the old school, one knew that his real life was hidden in some remote world of quiet contemplation.

Tolstoy walks with a brisk step, but stoops slightly. He has not abandoned his habits of vigorous exercise, spending nearly every afternoon in riding or walking and in spare moments indoors plays battledore and shuttlecock with his daughter or amuses himself with cup and ball. He is in excellent health, though a doctor living in the house assured me he was very liable to catch cold. He is as firmly convinced as ever of the value of a vegetarian diet.

It was with the Constitutional movement that our conversation naturally began. Tolstoy's opinion of it was very summary. 'It is dangerous,' he declared, 'and useless because it diverts men's activities from the true path. A Constitution cannot improve matters; it cannot bring freedom. Governments are maintained by violence and the threat of violence, and violence is opposed to freedom. A man is only free when no one can force him to do that which he believes to be wrong, and the right course of action for every man is to abstain from

1. H. W. Williams. Tolstoy was 77 at the time of this interview.

all participation in the acts of the Government, to refuse to serve in the army, to refuse to accept a position under the Government, but every day and always to do good. The agitation for a Constitution can only lead to false results.'

He was greatly interested in hearing of the recent events in St. Petersburg, and was particularly anxious to learn more about Father Gapon. He deplored the massacre and was horrified to hear the details, but declared it was only what might be expected of the Government, which must maintain itself by violence.

'Do you think, then,' I said, 'that it is the agitation amongst the workmen that is responsible for this result?'

'No, no,' he exclaimed. 'I could not go so far as to say that. I only say that the whole movement for a Constitution is a movement in the wrong direction. The people does not want a Constitution. But those who are agitating for it do not know the people. With all their professions of care for the people, they have no real care for it, they simply despise it. The people wants one thing – that is, land. Have you read Henry George's works?'[1]

He would not admit that the particular form of government prevailing in a country made any essential difference in the lives of its citizens.

'Don't you think,' I asked, 'that it is better to live, say, under the English system than under the Russian? Look at the passport system here, for instance; the censorship, and the banishment of political offenders.'

'It is not a whit better in England,' he stoutly declared. 'Wherever there is violence people are deprived of their freedom. Why, my friend Tchertkoff, who lives outside the town of Christchurch, is compelled to pay a tax for the maintenance of a band which plays inside the town, and which he himself would much rather never hear at all. And as for banishment, that affects a man very slightly. I have been awaiting banishment for the last twenty years, and if it came I should not be disturbed. Banishment cannot prevent one from living the true life. And freedom of the press? Does the people need the freedom of the press? These gentlemen may have freedom of the press, if they will, to air their own views, but that is a small matter.'

It should be added that Tolstoy himself suffers keenly from the effects of the censorship. Even such a distinguished writer as he is not spared the indignity of having many passages blacked out in the books and papers that are sent him from abroad. And the existence of the

1. Henry George, advocate of a single tax on land, author of 'Progress and Poverty' (1879).

censorship prevents him from receiving copies of many works of his own that are published in England or Germany.

He spoke of strikes, and said the most effective would be a strike of those who provided the nation with bread. I mentioned a report I had heard in Moscow, to the effect that all the physicians in rural districts intended striking.

'All the better,' said Tolstoy, with a smile.

'But then,' I said, 'all the peasants will be without medical help.'

'So much the better,' he declared; 'forty or fifty years ago, when I was young, there were no doctors among the peasants, and the peasants got on very well without them. No, sickness is not an evil; death is not an evil. The one evil is that men do wrong.'

In the evening, after dinner, we forsook the thorny ground of politics, and Tolstoy began speaking of questions that affect him more nearly. Speaking of the choice of a profession, he said that a man's mode of life is the resultant of the action of two opposing forces – his own effort to reach the ideal, and the inertia of his past. 'There is a terrible saying of Kant's,' he said, 'a saying that for a long time I did not dare to accept, but which I now see to be true, to the effect that a man who does good merely from habit is not a good man. But it is a fact. When we have reached one stage of goodness we dare not rest there, but must strive to reach a higher. You reminded me,' he added, turning to the family physician, who sat close by, 'of a saying of Sutaieff's. It was not Sutaieff but another peasant who, when it was pointed out to him that divorce was un-Christian, said that to continue living with his wife must be, after all, the work pleasing to God, because it was so hard.'

'I am an old man now,' he said again, 'and must soon die, and for me it is more important to think of the eternal life than the forms of the world. And, moreover, as other men do not know how soon they will die, it seems to me important that they too should concern themselves with the life eternal. When I am asked about the future life, where I shall be after death, I can only refer again to my dear old Kant, who pointed out that the conceptions of space and time are merely formative principles of the human intellect. The question "where" involves a consideration of space, "shall I be" one of time. And in the eternal life there is neither space nor time. We are each one of us a part of the universal life that is above space and time.'

Tolstoy has a poor opinion of Russian literature, and, in fact, of most other literatures of the present day. 'Formerly,' he says, 'art was like chamber-music, and appealed to the few; now it appeals to the taste of the great commercial and industrial classes. It will never come to its own until it appeals to the people as a whole.' He drew illustrations of his thesis from contemporary English literature. 'Look at Rider Haggard,' he said; 'he writes the most extraordinary fables'; and he proceeded with great gusto to relate to an artist who was of the company the contents of *She*. His estimate of Miss Corelli and Mr. Hall Caine, particularly of the latter, was extremely unfavourable. For Dickens he has an unbounded admiration; and has lately re-read with delight his *Child's History of England*. Ibsen is not to his taste, and he strongly criticised *When We Dead Awake*, which had recently been given in a Moscow theatre.

Anatole France's *Crainquebille*, too, seems to have evoked his special admiration. He expressed his wonder at the perfection to which the technique of novel-writing had been brought. 'Why, the Russian ladies,' he said, 'nowadays write excellently – far better than Turgenieff or any of us; only, they have nothing to say.'

Our conversation was frequently interrupted; part of it was held over lunch, part in the study, part, again, at dinner and over the evening glass of tea. He spoke simply and kindly, without the least pretence at dogmatism, and was always ready to listen to an opinion opposed to his own. And one never lost the impression of his inward calm, as of a man who had faced the deepest problems and had found in their solution peace.

I left him at midnight, and next morning was back in Moscow, hearing of agitation in the Nobles' Assembly, the radical resolutions of a meeting of lawyers, and excited discussions as to the probability of a conflict between the terror from above and the terror from beneath. Involuntarily I thought of Tolstoy's words – 'The Constitutional movement is a noisy movement, and this is not in its favour. God's work is wrought in stillness. To Elijah the prophet God spoke not in the earthquake, not in the wind, but in the still small voice.'

And yet it is in the stormy life of the cities that the battle of Russian freedom is now being fought out, and not, though one would like to believe it were, in the happy, peaceful haven of Yasnaya Polyana.

# A Parody of Education

In 1898 C. E. Ratcliffe made a survey of school conditions in Middlesex, Buckinghamshire, Kent, Lincoln, and Cornwall. At the end C. P. Scott in a leader (January 2, 1899) wrote: 'It is a remarkable story; no impartial person having the good of his country at heart can have arisen from its perusal without a sense of indignation and of shame. It is a scandal and a folly by the side of which all other abuses and failures in our administration sink into insignificance.' The articles were reprinted as a pamphlet and circulated to many knowledgeable people whose comments formed the basis of a further series of articles. The National Union of Teachers sent the paper an official letter of thanks.

## Saturday, November 26, 1898

Lincolnshire is Nonconformist to the backbone; yet two schools in three can be claimed by the Church of England.

Without disrespect be it said, the clergyman is in a great proportion of cases the despot of the village. He may be a benevolent one or the reverse. Unless I have been unfortunate in my selection of villages, he is benevolent only so long as he gets his own way in everything. It does not pay anyone to cross him. The parish is 'his,' the church is 'his,' and, above all, it is 'his' school. He appoints the managers of the school, who may always be trusted to do as he wishes. Relatives, curates, church-wardens, and tenants are those whom he most favours when making a selection. They don't 'manage' at all; they just do as he tells them. This results in the teacher being completely 'under the parson's thumb.' I shall deal with this matter by and by. But see how it affects the religious question. The teacher is the only man as a rule, who knows the facts and who would have any chance of victory in a conflict with the clergyman. If he says anything or does anything contrary to his master's wish the invariable result is notice to quit. Hence we see in Lincolnshire villages where 80 per cent of the children are of Dissenting parentage that all are compelled to learn the following: – Apostles' Creed, Lord's Prayer, the Ten Commandments, the Baptismal Covenant, the Desire, order of morning and evening prayer, to find the places in the Book of Common Prayer, and have to attend church during Holy Week and on saints' days. The only protest that is ever made is against the weekday church.

The first school I visited was an excellent one in every way. It was just outside a well-known small Lincolnshire town. It calls itself 'higher grade.' That means you pay a fee to attend; it means that the school is 'select,' and it means little else. Four miles further on we come to the kind of school which is typical. The head master was busy with his books, while the little ones were being 'taught' by a girl of fifteen. Of these thirty-four children some were in Standard VI[1] and others did not know their alphabet. In the same and only room, being 'taught' by an illiterate girl of fifteen, were girls and boys of thirteen and little mites of three. There were eighteen children absent, most of whom were working in the fields. For the maintenance of this school of fifty-two children the total income for a year is £70 16s. This is spent in the following way: – Salaries, £59 3s. 7d.; drill master, £1 8s. 3d.; books and stationery, £5; fuel, light and cleaning, £1 2s. 9½d.; repairs to building, £6 17s. 9d.; other items, £3 3s. 7½d. For the fifty-two children the whole income of the school amounts to £1 10s. per child. It costs more per head to work a small school efficiently than a large one. The London Board school child is none too lavishly treated, but it costs the Board £3 12s. 3d. per child to keep the school going. What, then, can be the character of the work being done in this school? More money would provide at least one other room, in which the lower half of the school could be taught. It would also give them a separate teacher. It would give the head teacher a 'living wage.' A man who passed high in the 'Queen's Scholarship' examination, who graduated high in one of the best training colleges, and who has had twenty years' experience in teaching children, should be receiving more than £59 3s. 7d. per annum: £59 3s. 7d. would not be an extravagant pension for a superannuated police constable. Can it be regarded as adequate pay for a 'leader of the democracy'? More money would alter all this. The man is not alone in his poverty; 19,969 fully certificated teachers are in receipt of less than £75 for a year's hard toil. More money would abolish the broken chair with a cracked basin on it which does duty for a lavatory. But the master had little hope of any more money. No one in the village visited the school or took the slightest interest in it. There were three chapels, and the people were mostly Nonconformists. But there were no withdrawals from the religious teaching. Catechism was taught. The children, however, learnt little of it. They only attended about seven times out of ten. Whenever work was to be had – leading horses, planting or 'lifting' potatoes, or in the harvest field – the parents sent their children to work, and defied the law. The teacher thought that if the parents knew they could withdraw their children from the religious lesson they

1. Normally the top of an Elementary School – promotion depended on attainments.

might, but he was not sure that they cared sufficiently about the matter to take that step.

The next school is owned by a private gentleman, and is let to a school board. There are eighty children on the roll, who break the law every time they absent themselves. For the previous year the average attendance was fifty-three. For the previous week it was only forty-eight. It will not improve until there is no work to be got in the fields. That is to say, that half of this school of eighty children are being illegally employed without let or hindrance. The room in which the children are taught was a failure as a house, so it was made into a school. People would not support it as a British school,[1] so it ceased to exist under that name. Revived as a Board school, it exists, but it certainly does not thrive. The by-laws have not been revised since 1870. The children have neither water to drink nor a lavatory in which to wash their ofttimes dirty hands. The principal 'manager' has been educated only sufficiently to sign his name. For assistance the master has his wife and a monitress. His wife, under cover of Article 68, deludes the inquirer with the idea that her services are of value. She is needed at home with a family of small children. Cooking and other household duties demand her attention, but they do not get it. The home is sacrificed for the school, and when she breaks down, or leaves, or dies the master will have to leave also. For this 'white slavery' they are remunerated with £100 per annum. The school rate is three-pence in the pound, and the five illiterate men constituting the Board, of whom only one can read and write, will not allow it to be any more, come what will.

When I asked these teachers what they would do if the income of the school was augmented, they echoed the general wish of the country teachers – (1) Above all, the master would take his wife out of school – 'It is killing her,' he said; (2) build a new school – and he was right there too; (3) buy furniture worthy of the name; (4) ask for a 'living wage.' In the next village to this there was a Board school for girls and a Church school for boys. The Board that controls this school also controls two others in neighbouring villages. This is strangely unlike our English way of managing village Board schools. There is generally one Board for one school. Some Lincolnshire genius discovered, however, that there would be a saving of rates if one Board managed the three schools, and that settled the matter. To keep down the rate is the be-all and end-all of the rustic school board member. This Board happens to consist mainly of Wesleyans. A Frenchman would stand as

1. 'British Schools' were set up by a Nonconformist society; 'National Schools' by the Church of England.

much chance of appointment to one of their schools as a man who was not a Wesleyan and a local preacher. What is taught matters nothing; how it is taught matters less. What the inspectors say is disregarded. This Board will neither raise the rate of a penny to employ teachers in place of makeshifts, nor will it perform the elementary duty of seeing that children attend the schools it has erected. Take specific cases in the schools under review. When the inspector called there were present in one school fifty out of ninety-six children. His report is – 'It is impossible for the school to be worked efficiently under such conditions.' What does the Board care for that? Nothing further happens. One boy attended 63 times out of 338 possible, another 64, another 54, and so on. A girl who ought to be at school now is at work in service in this very village. She was absent from school 207 times in 1892, 207 times in 1893, 261 times in 1894, 279 times in 1895, and has only attended seventeen times since that time. Taken before the magistrates, the summons was dismissed, and she is still in service. In Switzerland the family would have to leave the village. Out of the number of children reported in one week as illegally at work eight are employed by members of the School Board – weeding, hay-making; or fetching beer for the men. The official who is responsible to the Board for the attendance of this locality must cover twenty-six miles merely to walk across his district once and home again. His remuneration is £2 per annum. This is paid him *to do nothing*. A more zealous officer would soon be removed.

Is the 'National' school here any better? It is worse, as only boys attend, and they have not the excuse for irregularity in the home calls which, not without reason, are often made upon girls. Sixty-five attendances out of a possible 401, or two out of a possible 108, are sufficiently suggestive. I do not know that they lose so very much, after all. One of the teachers in this school, under the notorious Article 68[1] was a girl who was an extremely handy, clever *servant girl*. What do the sapient managers conclude? Reasoning *a fortiori*, I suppose, they say, 'Bright, clever servant – make a good teacher.' They confess now that they made a mistake. Fifteen years ago the head-master of this school, a teacher who has since proved his ability, a teacher who provided the managers with a certificated assistant mistress in the person of his wife, a teacher who brought the school up to a pitch it had never before reached and which it has never reached since, was forced to resign because he contradicted the vicar on a point of

---

1. Under which 'Additional Women Teachers' could be employed. It used to be said that an Additional Woman Teacher was 'a woman of 18 years who had been successfully vaccinated.'

fact. The next man drank himself to death, and his wife is now in a lunatic asylum. Two miles away the wife of another master, wearied out with six children and housework and Article 68 work, simply died. Some of us were not sorry to hear it. No finer testimonial to the rural teacher can be found than that he retains his sanity and is not – as a rule – more than a moderate drinker. If he is a wise man he will sign the 'pledge' when he takes a country school.

I have not mentioned the early age at which children leave school for some time. Let it not be forgotten that this is a permanent factor in the problem. The children who attend school so irregularly, the children who are at work when they ought to be at school, who when at school are taught by unqualified teachers, leave school altogether at any age from ten to thirteen. Out of every hundred children attending English day schools sixty-five leave before they are eleven years of age, never to return. If anyone should be disposed to think that the facts about the school attendance in Lincolnshire are so bad that I must have selected an extreme case, let him remember that Lancashire is lower in the scale than the worst division of Lincolnshire. The district I have been writing about stands seventeenth on a list of fifty counties, while rich Lancashire, urban Lancashire, is forty-eighth.

## Ireland's Poorest Parish

Wednesday, June 14, 1905

BETWEEN THE BAYS OF CARRAROE

*by J. M. Synge*

*Illustrations by Jack B. Yeats*[1]

In rural Ireland very few parishes only are increasing in population, and those that are doing so are usually in the districts of the greatest poverty. One of the most curious instances of this tendency is to be found in the parish of Carraroe, which is said to be, on the whole, the poorest parish in the country, although many worse cases of individual destitution can be found elsewhere. The most characteristic part of this district lies on a long promontory between Cashla Bay and Greatman's Bay. On both coast-lines one sees a good many small quays, with, perhaps, two hookers moored to them, and on the roads one passes an occasional flat space covered with small green fields of oats – with

1. One of a series of articles on the West of Ireland written by J. M. Synge (1871–1909) and illustrated by J. B. Yeats (1871–1957).

whole families on their knees weeding among them – or patches of potatoes, but for the rest one sees little but an endless series of low stony hills with veins of grass. Here and there, however, one comes in sight of a fresh-water lake, with an island or two, covered with seagulls, and many cottages round the shore, some of them standing almost on the brink of the water, others a little higher up, fitted in among the rocks, and one or two standing out on the top of a ridge against the blue of the sky or of the Twelve Bens of Connaught.

At the edge of one of these lakes, near a school of lace or knitting – one of those that have been established by the Congested Districts Board – we met a man driving a mare and foal that had scrambled out of their enclosure although the mare had her two off-legs chained together. As soon as he had got them back into one of the fields and built up the wall with loose stones he came over to a stone beside us and began to talk about horses and the dying out of the ponies of Connemara. 'You will hardly get any real Connemara ponies now at all,' he said, 'and the kind of horses they send down to us to improve the breed are no use, for the horses we breed from them will not thrive or get their health on the little patches where we have to put them. This last while most of the people in this parish are giving up horses altogether. Those that have them sell their foals when they are about six months old for four pounds, or five may-be; but the better part of the people are working with an ass only, that can carry a few things on a straddle over her back.'

'If you've no horses,' I said, 'how do you get to Galway if you want to go to a fair or to market?'

'We go by the sea,' he said, 'in one of the hookers you've likely seen at the little quays while walking down by the road. You can sail to Galway if the wind is fair in four hours or less, may-be; and the people here are all used to the sea, for no one can live in this place but by cutting turf in the mountains and sailing out to sell it in Clare or Aran, for you see yourselves there's no good in the land, that has little in it but bare rocks and stones. Two years ago there came a wet summer, and the people were worse off then than they are now, may-be, with their bad potatoes and all; for they couldn't cut or dry a load of turf to sell across the bay, and there was many a woman hadn't a dry sod itself to put under her pot, and she shivering with cold and hunger.'

A little later, when we had talked of one or two other things, I asked him if many of the people who were living round in the scattered cottages we could see were often in real want of food. 'There are a few, may-be, have enough all times,' he said, 'but the most are in want one time or another, when the potatoes are bad or few, and their whole store is eaten; and there are some who are near starving all times, like a widow woman beyond who has seven children with hardly a shirt on their skins, and they with nothing to eat but the milk from one cow, and a handful of meal they will get from one neighbour or another.'

'You're getting an old man,' I said, 'and do you remember if the place was as bad as it is now when you were a young man growing up?'

'It wasn't as bad, or a half as bad,' he said, 'for there were fewer people in it and more land to each, and the land itself was better at that time, for now it is drying up or something, and not giving its fruits and increase as it did.'

I asked him if they used bought manures. 'We get a hundred-weight for eight shillings now and again, but I think there's little good in it, for it's only a poor kind they send out to the like of us. Then there was another thing they had in the old times,' he continued, 'and that was the making of poteen (illicit whisky), for it was a great trade at the time, and you'd see the police down on their knees blowing the fire with their own breath to make a drink for themselves, and then going off with the butt of an old barrel, and that was one seizure, and an old bag with a handful of malt, and that was another seizure, and would satisfy the law; but now they must have the worm and the still and a prisoner, and there is little of it made in the country. At that time a man would get ten shillings for a gallon, and it was a good trade for poor people.'

JACK B YEATS

As we were talking a woman passed driving two young pigs, and we began to speak of them.

'We buy the young pigs and rear them up,' he said, 'but this year they are scarce and dear. And indeed what good are they in bad years, for how can we go feeding a pig when we haven't enough, may-be, for ourselves? In good years when you have potatoes and plenty you can rear up two or three pigs and make a good bit on them, but other times, may-be, a poor man will give a pound for a young pig that won't thrive after, and then his pound will be gone, and he'll have no money for his rent.'

The old man was cheerful and seemingly fairly well-to-do, but in the end he seemed to be getting dejected as he spoke of one difficulty after another, so I asked him, to change the subject, if there was much dancing in the country. 'No,' he said, 'this while back you'll never see a piper coming this way at all, though in the old times it's many a piper would be moving around through those houses for a whole quarter together, playing his pipes and drinking poteen and the people dancing round him; but now there is no dancing or singing in this place at all, and most of the young people is growing up and going to America.'

I pointed to the lace school near us, and asked how the girls got on with the lace, and if they earned much money. 'I've heard tell,' he said, 'that in the four schools round about this place there is near six hundred pounds paid out in wages every year, and that is a good sum, but there isn't a young girl going to them that isn't saving up, and saving up till she'll have enough gathered to take her to America, and then away she will go, and why wouldn't she?'

Often the worst moments in the lives of these people are caused by the still frequent outbreaks of typhus fever, and before we parted I asked him if there was much fever in the particular district where we were.

'Just here,' he said, 'there isn't much of it at all, but there are places round about where you'll sometimes hear of a score and more stretched out waiting for their death; but I suppose it is the will of God. Then there is a sickness they call consumption that some will die of, but I suppose there is no place where people aren't getting their death one way or other, and the most in this place are enjoying good health, glory be to God! for it is a healthy place and there is a clean air blowing.'

Then, with a few of the usual blessings, he got up and left us, and we walked on through more of similar or still poorer country. It is remarkable that from Spiddal onward – that is, in the whole of the most poverty-stricken district of Ireland – no one begs, even in a roundabout way. It is the fashion with many of the officials who are connected with relief works and such things to compare the people of this district rather unfavourably with the people of the poor districts of Donegal, but in this respect at least Donegal is not the more admirable.

# General Booth's Victory March

Friday, August 11, 1905
*From our Special Correspondent*

In 1905 General Booth (1829–1912), founder of the Salvation Army, undertook a long tour throughout England in a white motor-car. The *Guardian* followed his journey for most of its way. The following extracts by E. W. Record are typical:

Rotherham, Thursday

Claycross is a place where the Salvation Army is very active and where, amongst a turbulent class, it has accomplished much good work. General Booth showed that he knew something about the district when he began to speak in his brusque, straight-from-the-shoulder fashion to the men. 'God bless you all,' he said; 'You are a beautiful looking lot,' and when there was a ripple of laughter he checked it sternly with, 'I mean you men. I want to talk to you more especially. Mind you make good husbands. Some of you, don't you, nurse your wife before the wedding and thrash her afterwards? Love your wife, each one of you, and never thrash her. Nurse her as much as you used to do when you were swearing all those sweet things in her ear.' They were very earnest words, spoken with an obvious purpose, and women's voices softly said, 'Thank you, General; God bless you.' The Claycross meeting was short, but it was the most impressive that the General has addressed to-day, and the pale upturned workers' faces upon which they looked from the platform were full of pathos, and to them the well-known looks of what they call soul-hunger. General Booth's visit to Belper had for him a personal interest, because it was his first visit to his father's birthplace. He stopped his car at the work-house as he entered the town in order that he might address what he called some cheer-up words to the inmates. They waited for him at the gates, the women in red bodices and white caps and the men in corduroys, and waved their feeble hands to him in greeting. His message to them was not to bemoan their present state but to count on the employments and enjoyments of the world to come, and when he had offered them this comfort he offered a prayer that they might exchange their condition of hardship and poverty for the joys that are the hope of believers.

Everywhere along the route General Booth is feted with splendid enthusiasm. The women to-day have pelted him with flowers and rice, and the children have assembled in groups to wave flags and shout the

'*Yours for God and Humanity, William Booth*' – *a drawing
by Francis Dodd published on August 21, 1912.*

General's motto, 'Glory for me.' At one town General Booth was
greatly touched by the speeding word of a superintendent of police.
'Good-bye, sir,' the policeman said, 'would to God there were more like
you.'

Saturday, August 12, 1905

Brighouse, Friday Night
In his speeches to-day at Barnsley and at Wakefield General Booth
has talked very interestingly about his colonisation schemes. He tells
us that he is going to devote all the leisure of his declining years to the
work of pushing these forward and of seeking a solution of the prob-

lem of the unemployed. 'It is not right,' he says, 'to leave people to starve to death in a land of plenty, and the poor people ought to be furnished with the means by which they can get their daily bread. All that is wanted is a scientific, systematic transfer of the distressed people to those distant lands which are hungering for workers.' General Booth is rather severe on the childish impracticability of the emigration systems of the past – systems which have dumped the emigrant without resources on a piece of barren land, with the result that in a few years he has given up in despair and gone to swell slumdom and the prisons or returned home broken-hearted.

'My idea of the way to treat the emigrant,' General Booth says, 'is this. Build him a cottage, prepare his garden, put him up a hovel for his cow and a sty for his pig: put a cow in the hovel and a pig in the sty, and if he does not understand the ways of the country show him how to carry on, find him employment or furnish him with a certain amount of money until he gets his feet and can obtain a livelihood by his own exertions. If you do that you will make a small farmer of him, and he will succeed. You can do all this and still keep the man under the Union Jack.'

Of course the General recognises that much money is wanted to carry through a scheme of colonisation on this system, but he has been a financial optimist for sixty years and is not worrying about the ways and means. The chief thing, he says buoyantly, is that the land is available, and he talks of the thousands of acres across the Atlantic and in Australia waiting for workers. A Frenchman wrote to him the other day: – 'I have 70,000 acres in the United States. If you will work it you shall have half the profits. What I want is men and women to go and live on it.' General Booth thinks that the State must take up colonisation, and he is looking to the demonstrations of the unemployed as levers to speed the realisation of his expectations. 'Men and women will not starve in silence. They will make their claims known; and, if I am not mistaken, we shall hear their claims more emphatically in the coming winter than we did in the last.'

General Booth's audience appeared to be deeply interested on this colonisation topic, and he himself seems to be treating it more and more thoughtfully in each succeeding speech.

This evening we have witnessed two magnificent demonstrations in compliment to the aged Salvation Army leader. We left Wakefield at six o'clock, hymned on our journey with 'God be with you till we meet again,' and our route lay through Dewsbury to Brighouse. The General's hands never ceased to wave their acknowledgments to greetings from the roadsides. When the crowds thickened, the tall green-coated veteran sprang to his feet, doffed the big motor-cap from his snowy head, and stood with waving, outstretched arms, smiling his delight.

When we descended the hill into Dewsbury we came upon thoroughfares choked with people, and the Square before the Town Hall was packed with thousands. On a high tier of steps the scarlet-robed Mayor and a company of violet-robed councillors awaited the General, and when he arrived he climbed up amongst them and added his picturesque figure and picturesque coat to a grouping of civic colour which was finely lit up by the setting sun. The Mayor's welcome was delightfully unconventional and full of Yorkshire heartiness. 'We are right glad to see you, General. You're a big man and you've a big work, and we hope you'll live another twenty-five years to carry it on. But you know, General, you can't go on for ever, and we are hoping that you will find the right man to succeed you when the time comes for you to take your rest.' We left the crowded streets of Dewsbury echoing with cheers, and a quarter of an hour later were in the more crowded streets of Brighouse.

The Mayor met us at the borough boundary, bringing with him his mace-bearer, a number of councillors and aldermen in robes and a company of mounted police officers. General Booth transferred himself to the Mayor's carriage, and made his entry into the town standing upright and bareheaded as usual, and waving to the right and to the left. Again the spectacle was full of picturesque colour, for the low, slanting sun caught the silver mace and the silver hair and beard, and beside the tall figure in Lincoln green sat the Mayor, glowing with scarlet and gold.

Brighouse gave General Booth the finest reception he has had since he left Dover. The whole population was in the streets, and the cheering was continuous. They welcomed their visitor not only because of his position, but because long years ago, before the Salvation Army was thought of, the Rev. William Booth, as he was then styled, was stationed here. Mindful of this, the Mayor and the citizens took the General to-night to a little clearing in the houses where he could see the chapel of which he once had charge and the little house in which his early married life was spent, and there they gave him a beautifully designed address of welcome and congratulation, and listened, as their reward, to the General's reminiscences of Brighouse forty odd years ago.

# Sport

## THE SEASON OF THE MAY-FLY

Monday, July 3, 1905
*By the Hon. R. C. Drummond*

It is only on certain favoured rivers of the South country that the beautiful May-flies hatch out in any considerable numbers. Regarding the sport obtained with the artificial imitation opinions differ. Purists of the dry fly – or some of them – are averse from using it on the ground that little skill is needed to make good baskets with the artificial May-fly. But by the majority the brief period during which these insects are on the water is eagerly anticipated as providing the most enjoyable outing of the year. And truly when all things are favourable the sport has much of fascination. Trees and bushes have assumed their fresh verdure of early summer. The world of the riverside teems with life. Where in the sunlight the burnished river flows past the meadows, the swallows flit forth and back in pursuit of their insect prey. Among the trees the song birds answer one another, and now and then the surface of the smooth current is dimpled by the circles born of a rising trout. Arriving from the towns amid these scenes, it is no wonder that the angler should retain pleasant memories of the 'Festival of the May-fly.'

Mindful of enjoyable feasts in the past, one would think that the trout would greedily seize upon the delicate May-flies immediately they made their appearance. But this is not the case. At first they allow the insects to float past them unheeded. As the rise grows stronger and the flies come by in greater numbers the trout overcome their strange timidity and set steadily to work to enjoy the plenteous banquet. This is the opportunity of the fisherman. But he must not suppose that in their eagerness for the feast the trout altogether lay aside the wariness that so often has saved them from disaster. Let the cast be bungled but a little, the invitation awkwardly presented, and the great trout that erstwhile was sucking in the dainty morsels minute by minute will be seen no more. He has detected the fraud – in fishing parlance has been 'put down,' – and some time will elapse before he will think it safe to recommence feeding. Favoured by an upstream breeze the veriest tyro may contrive to kill fish with an artificial May-fly, but it is another matter when the wind is in the wrong 'airt.' The size and bulky outspread wings of the imitation render the task of presenting it accurately by no means easy of accomplishment, and the difficulty is vastly increased when the fisherman has to contend with an adverse wind.

This year the May-fly season was disappointing, rain and cold winds rendering the rise fitful and uncertain. Nevertheless many good trout were landed, including one of $3\frac{1}{2}$ lb. on the Test, and a beauty of $4\frac{3}{4}$ lb. taken in a Hertfordshire stream.

## HARDLY CRICKET

### Monday, October 29, 1900

#### THE FOOTBALL FIELD

In the match at Bury M'Latchie, one of the Sunderland forwards, was ordered off the field for misbehaviour. Later some unnecessary vigour was noticeable in the Sunderland play, and the referee found it necessary to tell the players collectively that he would have no more of it. The incident is not creditable to the Sunderland team, and it is well that Mr. Kingscott took a strong course in dealing with it. The discipline of football must be most carefully preserved, or the game is bound to suffer. A referee, as it is, has an office which is often a troublesome one. He is not infallible as a referee, of course, but the traditions of sport give him a right to claim respect from the player, and he is vested with powers to enforce his authority. Firm action in matters such as that at Bury always has a salutary effect, and the more isolated these examples are the more impressive do they become. All football authorities are in agreement that the future of the game depends in a very large measure on the preservation of discipline. The recent severe punishment meted out to a Northern Union[1] player is a case in point, and its effect is bound to be far-reaching. In that case the offence was a more serious one than that of the Sunderland player – it was for deliberate roughness in play. We want no return to the days when football was correctly spoken of as a sort of 'friendly fight' – a form of recreation in which 'when the exercise becomes exceeding violent the players kick each others' shins without the least ceremony.'

Apart from the disagreeable incident the match at Bury was one which gave a large amount of pleasure to a moderately large crowd. It was played to a draw without a score, and in the first half, at any rate, there were some capital passages of football.

1. Now known as Rugby League.

# Arts

## EARLY DAYS AT THE ABBEY

Monday, January 2, 1905
*From our Special Correspondent*[1]

With these young, unselfish Irish artists it is only the play that counts. With an art of gesture admirably disciplined and a strange delicacy of enunciation they perform the best drama of our time in the method of a lovely ritual.

In moments of deep emotion the best among the company express not only the human accident but its idea. When Miss Maire Nic Shiubhlaigh as Cathleen-ni-Houlihan (the personification of Ireland in Mr. Yeats's play of that name), or as Nora Burke, the herd's wife (in Mr. Synge's *Shadow of the Glen*), was before us on the stage our thoughts ran upon greater matters than a distressful country and a stunted life. Any clever actress with either of those parts could have been moving, or passionate, or appealing, but very few could have moved us, as her acting moved us, to such poignant memories and tragic pity for the lonely. As Cathleen-ni-Houlihan she was the grey and ancient Eire, 'keening, keening' for 'the friends that are gone' in the old battles and the old gallant risings. Her speaking of certain lines and her mournful crooning of a ballad (itself a pitiful thing and one of the most touching of modern poems) was of an infinite sadness, as though the words were as flowers laid upon the graves of patriots. I have seen no acting more delicate nor heard more touching speech, save in this lady's performance of the lonely glenswoman. Her Nora Burke is perhaps the finer performance of the two. It is a part less fraught with meaning, but the character is subtle, difficult to play justly, easy to play wrongly, easy to misunderstand. Mr. Synge's play is a little tragi-comedy, full of bitter truth and always nearer tears than laughter. Perhaps the greater number of those that read the play or see it played will regard it as a comedy. It is far from being that, though parts of it are excellently comic. It is 'the bitter old and wrinkled truth,' expressing the tragedy of an emotional nature. Nora Burke, the wife of an old coarse man, passes her days in a lonely cottage, in a lonely glen, among the hill-mists and the sheep. It is her tragedy that the only other man she sees is something of a sheep and a good deal of a craven. Mr. Synge has expressed her

---

1. John Masefield who recalled his time on the paper (1903–1905) as 'a most romantic delight.'

character with much discrimination. She wins our sympathy, for she is lonely and beautiful and full of the vague sorrow that is in all deep simple natures for 'all things uncomely and broken, all things bowed down and old.' Played as Miss Maire Nic Shiubhlaigh plays her, the lonely woman in the glen, left desolate by her lover and driven into the rain by her husband, becomes one of the high women of tragedy, a calamitous and wretched figure, dignified in sorrow, like a queen born.

Mr. Yeats's play *On Baile's Strand* was played on both the nights I was there, and its final scene stays in the memory as one of the most moving passages I have seen performed. Though the pitiful horror of the end, where the Fool (Mr. W. G. Fay), with his whining cunning, is showing the hero, Cuchullain (Mr. F. J. Fay),[1] that he has killed his son, must remain in the mind like an effect of nightmare, I shall not forget the musical and ringing declamation, beautiful like a stricken bell, with which Mr. F. J. Fay made magical his part.

I came away from their opening performance glad that a company of such talent should have met with such encouragement and with a patron so generous as Miss Horniman.[2] Their art is unlike any to be seen in England. It is never common, it is never derivative. One thinks of it as a thing of beauty, as a part of life, as the only modern dramatic art springing from the life of a people.

1. F. J. Fay and his brother W. G. Fay with Yeats and Lady Gregory were among the founders of the Abbey Theatre. F. J. Fay's son, Gerard Fay (1913–1968) was the last 'London Editor' of the *Guardian*.

2. Miss A. E. F. Horniman (1860–1937) subsidised the Abbey Theatre and helped with its productions until she quarrelled with Yeats. In 1907 she moved to Manchester and made it a major theatrical centre with her foundation of the Gaiety Theatre there.

# EDWARD ELGAR AND HANS RICHTER

Sir Charles Hallé's place was not easy to fill, but in the end the most distinguished conductor of his day came to Manchester. Hans Richter (1843–1916) appeared as a guest conductor in Manchester in 1897 and finally settled in the city in 1900. Elgar (1857–1934) was giving English music an altogether higher reputation abroad than it had enjoyed for centuries, and Richter proved himself a sympathetic and persevering interpreter of the composer's work in England.

The *Guardian* had had to find a new musical critic. Arthur Johnstone (1861–1904) had been teaching at Edinburgh Academy when he was appointed in 1896. He was both a Richter and an Elgar enthusiast. He was also an adventurous man. In 1897 he went out with J. B. Atkins to cover the Greco-Turkish war for the *Guardian*.

## WHY RICHTER CHOSE MANCHESTER

### Thursday, October 18, 1900

It is an admitted fact that the occasion on which Dr. Richter rehearsed Beethoven's C minor Symphony for the first time with a London orchestra, in the year 1877, marks a new era of orchestral playing in this country. His manner of dealing with the symphony caused extreme astonishment, and even some ridicule, at first. The London players had never encountered before a conductor who knew the score by heart down to the minutest detail, frequently singing passages to show how they should be rendered. But though the performers laughed at first, they discovered ere long that the young German's conception was a revelation of such beauty and grandeur in the work as they had never before suspected, and at the present day there is not a self-respecting conductor in the world who has not been influenced by it. Thus began that 'troubling of the waters' – previously rather stagnant in the musical life of this country – which led to the wonderful modern development of public interest in great orchestral music. Whatever we may think of Wagner's own music, it is absolutely certain that the Wagnerian school rediscovered the Beethoven symphony for us, just as, at a later date, they rediscovered the Mozart musical drama – for it is glaringly obvious that those wonderful Mozart performances at Munich in which for the first time justice has been done to Mozart's dramatic works are a simple outcome of the Bayreuth idea. The original group of executive musicians, whose genius of interpretation formed the necessary complement of Wagner's creative genius, consisted of three men – Liszt, Bulow, Richter. There is no need to discuss which of them was the greatest, for of the three Dr. Richter alone survives. At the present day there are a good many able conductors in Europe and America; but every man of them learned his business from that school which Dr. Richter alone personally represents, and it is amusing to find fanciful writers pushing the claim to be considered 'best living conductor' of this or that individual whose real relation to Dr. Richter is best defined by the German proverb *Wie die Alten sungen so piepsen noch die Jungen.*[1]

The question why Dr. Richter should have left Vienna and settled in Manchester – a question which is doubtless exercising a good many minds – can only be partially answered. Personal matters that are not suitable for public discussion had much to do with his decision. One very important point that influenced him can, however, be mentioned. In his own words, he was 'opernmüde' – tired of conducting opera – and he felt that so long as he remained in the Austrian capital he would never be rid of the opera. That he should be 'opernmüde' is not hard to understand. No conductor ever before brought such conscientiously minute study to the work of interpreting a score, and the strain upon the conductor's attention is more severe and prolonged in an operatic performance than in any kind of concert. His work at the Imperial Opera was also beset with personal worries which Dr. Richter had long regarded with growing distaste. The same motive – dislike of operatic conducting – probably had much to do with his preference of Manchester among the many places from which he received brilliant offers when it became known that he meditated leaving Vienna. In St. Petersburg, in Buda-Pesth, in New York, or in Boston he would have doubtless been required to conduct opera, while here there is no opera for him to conduct. Thus it seems that, by one of 'life's little ironies,' the one great and grievous defect in our musical organisation has actually helped to bring us a gigantic piece of luck.

We do not, however, mean to suggest that the want of an opera in Manchester was Dr. Richter's only reason for coming here. That would not only be unflattering but quite untrue. He fully appreciates the work done by Sir Charles Hallé in educating public taste. He finds the Manchester audience appreciative and enthusiastic, and holds that such a body of men as the Hallé Committee is better to work with than some agent who necessarily regards music from a purely business point of view.

1. As the old birds sang, the young ones chirp.

## THE DREAM OF GERONTIUS

Arthur Johnstone's notice of the first performance (under Richter at Birmingham in 1900) brought out the quality of Elgar's work which the imperfection of the performance hid from most of the audience. 'I am more than usually troubled,' he ended his notice, 'by the sense of utter inadequacy in these notes, and can only hope that I may have some opportunity of doing better justice to a deeply impressive work.' He had. He was present at the first adequate performance – that at Düsseldorf in 1902. At the previous Lower Rhine festival he had been the only English journalist. This time there were several London critics.

### Thursday, May 22, 1902

Düsseldorf, Tuesday

Rightly or wrongly, Germany and the Continent of Europe in general did not feel that serious English music was a thing to be taken seriously, and to that fact the writer (of the programme notes) refers with ingenious delicacy, going on to say that about the turn of the century a change began to be noticeable. Everyone concerned with musical affairs knows how that change was brought about, though not everyone on our side of the Channel cares to admit what he knows. It is in the main to Edward Elgar – a man who has done his best work living quietly in the Malvern Hills, without official position of any kind, remote from commercial distraction and the strife of commercialism – that the change is due. It is not accidental that on the present occasion the names of Handel, Mendelssohn, Schumann are absent while Bach is very abundantly represented, Beethoven's name figures in connection with the most modern in feeling of all his works (the C minor Symphony) and Liszt's with his revolutionary *Faust* Symphony. Nor is it accidental that the preference is given to Strauss among German and Elgar among English composers. For those are the men who really carry the torch, and the Germans are not to be deceived in such matters.

But 'Gerontius' still had to wait for a satisfactory English performance. At last Richter gave it at the Hallé:

### Friday, March 13, 1903

Originality is disadvantageous to a composer at first in two ways. The more obvious is that listeners find the music speaking to them in an unknown or partially unknown tongue, and are displeased; and the less obvious that players and singers cannot, as a rule, do justice to an unfamiliar style. When it is a case of winning recognition for something new and original a thoroughly adequate rendering is half the battle. Such a rendering carries with it a sense of enjoyment and satisfaction in the performers, and there is always a chance that this may to some extent communicate itself to the public; whereas in the other case the embarrassment of the performers will certainly communicate itself, and the audience attribute everything unsatisfactory to the unknown or insufficently guaranteed composer. In Elgar's 'Gerontius' the originality is strong and unmistakable, and the performers find their technical skill severely taxed. But fortunately the composer has a clear head; he knows the technique of each instrument and he never miscalculates. Performers therefore find that their task, though often difficult, is always possible and, further, that the result is always satisfactory. For Elgar has an ear; he is a man of tone, and does not care for music that looks well on paper but sounds muddy. These points made it possible to hope that the Manchester performance of his great oratorio would be a striking success and perhaps even throw new light on the merits of the composition, and it can scarcely be questioned that the experience of yesterday evening fulfilled these hopes.

## 'LAND OF HOPE AND GLORY'

### Friday, October 3, 1902

To the Coronation Ode I listened with great curiosity, remembering the ordinary fate that overtakes patriotic composers and wondering what Edward Elgar would make of the subject. I find he has let himself be inspired by the nymph of the same spring whence flowed those two delightful Tommy Atkins marches known as 'Pomp and Circumstance.' It is popular music of a kind that has not been made for a long time in this country – scarcely at all since Dibdin's time. At least one may say that of the best parts, such as the bass solo and chorus 'Britain, ask of thyself,' and the contralto solo and chorus 'Land of Hope and glory.' The former is ringing martial music, the latter a sort of Church parade song having the breath of a national hymn. It is the melody which occurs as second principal theme of the longer 'Pomp and Circumstance' march, which I beg to suggest is as broad as 'God Save the King,' 'Rule Britannia', and 'See the Conquering Hero,' and is perhaps the broadest open-air tune composed since Beethoven's 'Freude schöner Götterfunken.' Moreover, it is distinctively British – at once beefy and breezy. It is astonishing to hear people finding fault with Elgar for using this tune in two different compositions. I find it most natural in a composer, to whom music is a language in which, desiring to say exactly the same thing again, one has no choice but to say it in the same notes. Besides, such tunes are composed less frequently than once in fifty years. How then can one blame Elgar for not composing two in six months? The chorus enjoyed themselves over it, and so did the audience. As to the sentimental parts of the Ode, frankly I find them uninspired.

## BELLOC ON THE SHORT STORY[1]

### Wednesday, June 14, 1905

The short story is a very modern thing. What brought it into being has not been discovered, though the subject has been discussed at great length. It may or may not last. Another confused, eager, and creative time, the Renaissance, produced the essay and the essay (though perhaps it is dying to-day) has had a good three hundred years' run for its money. Perhaps, in spite of prophecies, the short story will survive. Anyhow it is here now, and probably the best writer of it in English (at this moment) is Mr. Masefield. The examples which this one presents are familiar to readers of the *Manchester Guardian*, the greater part of them having first been printed in these columns; but I will venture to quote a little that I may prove this judgment not to be extravagant. It is in the very essence of a good short story that its metaphors should be clean and sharp, doing a lot of work in a very little space. Now read this from 'The Devil and the Old Man': –

It was still dead calm – water all oily blue – with shark's fins astern cutting up black and pointed like the fingers on them things called sundials.

There is an error in realism, for no old sailorman would ever have thought of such a comparison – it is the metaphor of a highly educated and observant man; but errors in realism are, if anything, an advantage. As a metaphor it is quite of the best, and no one who has seen a sundial, or the triangular dorsal fin of a shark cutting above a calm sea will ever forget it. Again, of a strong man struggling with several adversaries (in 'A Monthly Allowance'): –

Sometimes he was like a sail being furled, or a rope being tautened, or a cart being driven to market.

All these three are very good, especially the first.

There is another element in Mr. Masefield's manner of writing which is admirably suited to the short story – the very short – story.

1. A review by Hilaire Belloc (1870–1953) of John Masefield's *A Mainsail Haul* – 'back-pagers' from the *Guardian*.

It is the trick of saying a thing once and no more. In most literary work such terseness is an affectation. In much - in lyrics, for instance – it is a vice. But in the short story it is a necessity, and one which a very great many writers forget.

But there is something else. The short story demands poignancy, and there is a great temptation to take short cuts to poignancy – to bring in violent emotions which, precisely because they are violent, are not 'matter of art.' When men are jaded in their emotions they demand things monstrous to arouse them. Perhaps this demand has created the modern supply of the monstrous in letters, but also largely the facility which is thus afforded to the writer of producing an effect. I repeat, it is not 'matter of art.' Violent dread, violent cruelty, violent lust – all these things are outside the drama within which humanity is permitted to draw. There is no power of development about them; no recurrent fruitfulness, which in letters as in agriculture, follows upon wisdom and restraint. If I may draw a metaphor from my little farm, they 'pull the land.' They lead to nothing. You soon reach the end of them, and beyond there is a blank. But you never reach an end of true tragedy, of sublime awe, of pain that is sacrificial and majestic; such 'matter of art' is capable of an indefinite extension. There is an endless competition in it between the great masters of the pen.

Mr. Masefield is not blameless in this regard. He has done nothing so paltry as Kipling's worst in the same field; there are no tortures, and you never smell the coward. But there is an occasional hint of bullying as a subject to arouse the reader, of ecstasies of terror. It is a pity, for in such a rhythm as 'The Port of Many Ships' one sees that it is not native to Mr. Masefield but only to the time he lives in; one sees that he could without anguish have omitted such sentences as 'a mass of bloody bodies lay horrible on each side of the hatch' or 'there was a foul smell of blood.' I wish he had been the first to do so. He is strong enough to start a new fashion.

H. BELLOC

## MASEFIELD GOES DOWN TO THE SEA AGAIN

Monday, October 23, 1905
*From Our Special Correspondent*

Portsmouth, Friday

I am in Portsmouth in the Blue Posts Tavern, listening to an old sailor who is telling of the spring tide floods. A spring tide, it seems, sometimes floods the Blue Posts, so that the customers have to wade to their tankards, a circumstance which must give a zest to the morning draught. It is hard to be reminded of reality in this haunt of romance. One wishes that the old man would be quiet. The Blue Posts can have changed very little since the midshipmen came here for their 'tea and toastesses.' If the old man would smoke quietly one could think of them as they were a hundred years back, when they filled these old rooms and paid their bills with the fore-topsail.

I have been to the Sally-Port and to the Point, for these were the two places I had most longed to see. I tried hard to picture them as they were when the cutters of the king's ships rocked there in the clear green water 'in eighteen hundred and war time.' The quiet places must then have been rowdy enough. One of Rowlandson's prints has immortalised the 'dear old blackguardly Point,' and one can recognise the place to-day from the drawing, though the ships in the water beyond are no longer wooden. Poll and Bet have vanished. The little gravel beach is no longer thronged with boats. There is no more jesting and ribaldry between the women of the town and the boats' crews, nor do the man-of-war boats come thrusting past the wherries of the watermen, shoving them aside with boat-hooks amid a general cursing. The little quaint, oddly built houses at the Point are now peopled with discreet householders. The old lieutenants in their white lapels and white silk stockings and athwartships hats would miss the ancient profanities. The midshipmen in their little blue coats with the white patches on the collars would perhaps find it difficult to get tea and toast in their old haunt.

From the Point I took a wherry and sailed out to the Victory. She was painted black and white, like 'a Lord Nelson's chequerplayer,' though her upper topsides were no longer dark blue and she lacked the lines of blue and scarlet which once decorated her. But for this and for the facts that she stood very high out of the water and had a harbour rig she was much the same as she was a hundred years ago when Nelson ate his last dinner aboard her. I thought of how she must have looked a hundred years ago, and longed that the cluttered decks, with their cabins and obstructions and general odds and ends, could be made clear for a moment, so that I might see her as she was. It would have been 'light airs and baffling winds,' I thought, that day a hundred years back, and the great wooden hull would have been rolling and the great sails slatting and jangling and the cannon creaking and the china cups of the messes skidding over to leeward. The hammocks would have been lying in the nettings, neatly stowed ready for the night, when many poor fellows would take their last sleep in them. The guns would have been secured to the ship's sides, and the busy hundreds of

*A drawing of H.M.S. Victory by F. E. Emanuel which
illustrated Masefield's article.*

the crew would have been walking and stamping on the planks. Some
would have been asleep between the guns, and some would have been
playing chequers or yarning in the deep voices of sailors about battles
and home and the chances of the service. As I came aboard some seamen were standing at the gangway, and I thought of the countless men
the old ship had known – men gathered, God knows how by the press
or the quota bounty, and scattered, God knows where, in battle and
chance medley and by 'the act of God.' Then there would have been
'the warrants,' with pigtails a yard long and scarlet ribbons sewn on
to the seams of their clothes. There would have been all manner of
officers and strange guests and visitors. The ship must have played a
part in the lives of thousands. I wondered what was the happiest
memory she had ever left in the mind of men or women who had

known her. I wondered what master shipwright had designed her, and whether he had followed her career after she had left his hands.

When I had gone about the decks and seen the guns and the cockpit and the cable tiers I got aboard my wherry again and sailed away up the harbour with a fair wind.

Saturday

In the bright morning I walked down to the Point and set sail into the harbour. The Victory was flying her famous signal, and there were laurel-wreaths at her yardarms and mastheads. She was surrounded by shore-boats, and there was an admiral aboard her. I could see the bayonets of the guard glittering above her nettings. A hundred years before she had been clothed to her trucks with canvas. Her ports had been opened and her guns run out, and she was running slowly down, a leaning and lifting thing of beauty, with the allied fleets ahead of her. We slipped past her at speed, and caught a glimpse of a scarlet tunic through one of the bow ports. She alone of the ships in harbour was gay with flags.

We sailed past many ships of war, grey and great, on our way to the Hazard. Their men looked down at us as they paused at their polishing of brass. The familiar pipes sounded over us. Boats came and went from the holystoned teak gangways. A little past Prinny's Hard we came to an old coal hulk, a decayed ship of the line, which had been supplanted by the new erection and now awaited the breakers. After so many visions of efficiency all the way up the harbour, it came as a shock to see the old ship, once so stately, now so lonely and ruinous. Her sides were broken about and her ports gone, and they had nailed canvas on parts of her where her poor seams gaped most. She had once been a splendid vessel, with a glorious carved stern and colours at her peak. Now she was all falling apart, a thing infinitely melancholy. I cannot view an old ship without sentiment, and the old man who was with me was quite overcome. We agreed that on such a day the ship-keeper should have strained a point and hoisted a flag aboard her and fired a salute from any firearm he possessed.

Portsmouth itself is not taking the centenary very deeply to heart. Some shops have the tricolour and the white ensign in their windows, but the event of the day is undoubtedly the Welsh football match. Once or twice during the afternoon I have seen a small boy pause outside the George Hotel to read the inscription on the wall. The inscription tells us that within the George Lord Nelson passed his last hours in England. I confess I had not expected more of Portsmouth. The town is peopled by those who express their patriotism in their lives. They show their patriotism and their sense of Nelson's victory, not by hanging out a banner and singing in the roads, but by going down to the sea in ships (which are sometimes submarines) and manning the vicious little guns which are to be seen along the walls. To-night, as a work of supererogation, they are going to illuminate the Victory so that she will appear upon the night in fiery outline. I have been to the Point and to the Hard to see her thus, but as yet she lies darkly, save for her riding lights and the gleam from her after-cabin windows. A hundred years ago to-night she was rolling like a hulk upon the sea with her spars crippled and her sails torn to rags, and her great Admiral dead in his cot. At this time a hundred years ago they were busy knotting and splicing, and the men who had fought the guns all day were weeping for their dead leader. One can picture the confusion of the moment. So many men were killed or wounded that each division of the crew must have needed reorganisation. And there was all the work to be done, and few effective hands to do it, and the ruling brain stilled like a quenched fire.

But I must be leaving Portsmouth, with her sailors and ships and her street posts made of sea-cannon. She is an unchanging town, full of character and charm and jolly people. They have started electric cars, but there is even now a merchant service brig in her little dock. They cannot change such a town, for the nature of her inhabitants cannot change. But I must be leaving Portsmouth. In the grey, silent streets upon which I gaze move certain figures, vague figures in clothes of an unreal blue. They are phantoms of her ancient sailors, ghosts of a press-gang, each beautiful with a special pigtail. If I do not get away at once, goodness knows – .

J. Masefield

Tailpiece: Whatever will they think of next?

Friday, March 20, 1903

# CHAPTER SIX

# Unfinished Agenda
## 1906—1914

\*

The country gave the Liberals an overwhelming majority in 1906 and, with their allies, a sufficient one in the two 1910 elections. They had a programme of sweeping social and political reform. Much was accomplished. The foundations of what was to become the Welfare State were laid in Old Age Pensions, health and unemployment insurance. But things moved more slowly than made sense. The great constitutional struggle over the powers of the House of Lords monopolised the middle years. This chapter starts with the Lords defying the Commons. It goes on to show that, far from being the golden age of wistful hind-blindness, the pre-war years were full of violence and threats of violence – industrial, feminist, Orange. On the eve of the 1914 war it even seemed that the government of the day could not rely on the army to obey orders.

In *Guardian* history the period was marked by the return of C. P. Scott, now a widower, to the full-time, active editing of the paper of which he had now become the proprietor. He had retired from Parliament but, through his friendship with the leading radical ministers, he and his paper occupied a position of greater political influence than ever before. Montague's reputation was at its height both as a leader-writer and as a dramatic critic in a city where Miss Horniman's Gaiety Theatre gave a critic everything he could possibly want to write about.

## The Commons and the Lords

Wednesday, December 1, 1909
*From our Special Correspondent*[1]

Westminster, Tuesday Night
It was the sixth and last day of the Lords' debate on the Budget. This was the day of action and decision, and after to-day nothing in British politics will ever be quite the same. All the doubts and hesitations and

1. Harold Spender

rumours of the last weekend had now been dispelled. It was clear that the 'backwoodsmen' had come back from their woods and the wild peers from their fastnesses. They meant killing. There they were in their long, unmistakable, ruddy-faced rows – not unpleasant men, but profoundly undistinguished, tremendously ordinary, just the victims of passion and prejudice that most average men are.

The murmur of talk died down, and the Clerk of Parliament, rising, called out, 'The Lord Archibishop of York.'[1] Then, from the corner seat where he had been sitting beside the Archbishop of Canterbury, there advanced the wise, grave, youthful-looking man who fills so mighty a place in the national Church. The Archbishop of York has been sitting all through the debates at the further corner of the House, and one has had time to observe his face. It is a serene and unruffled countenance, and there lurk in the eyes and mouth great reserves of strength and resolution. He faced the House of Lords very quietly and nobly this afternoon, prefacing his speech with a slight and graceful apology for his youth. Then without more ado he told the House why he had felt compelled to alter his first intention of taking no part in the debate.

'Since the debate began,' he said, quite simply, 'I realised that I could not conscientiously refuse to give my vote, and that if I were to give it I was compelled to give it against the amendment.' Then, with convincing simplicity, he went on, 'No man could have approached this matter with a more open mind, and it is only the course of the debate which has convinced me.' Gloomy silence seemed to penetrate the Tory ranks. They had had many blows but this looked as if it was going to be the worst – the blow from this calm young Daniel come to judgment, so fearless and so wise. The House of Lords as a rule does not very much love the bishops, but this was not an episcopal style at all. Archbishop Lang did not raise his eyes or wash his hands. He faced them quite simply, and spoke to them like a man and a brother peer.

'There have been many arguments to prove that this is a bad Budget, but not enough to convince me that it is right for us to throw it out. For this is an unprecedented course. Never before have you refused a Finance Bill. Never have we refused supplies to the King's government.' Worse and worse – the gloom deepened. Dr. Lang stepped with measured and impressive march into a long and convincing statement of the reasons why they should not reject the Budget. He brushed aside almost contemptuously the argument that they were not rejecting it, and only referring it to the people. Actions must be judged not by

1. Cosmo Gordon Lang (1864–1945), archbishop of York 1909–1928, Canterbury 1928–1942; this was his maiden speech.

what is intended but by what is done. 'To refuse supplies for the year is to reject the Budget.'

I need not follow Dr. Lang through the course of his weighty argument. There was only one point at which he raised a Tory cheer. That was when, with some gravity, he turned for a moment from rebuking the Tories to rebuking Mr. Lloyd-George. But, he argued, the House of Lords had nothing to do with Mr. Lloyd-George's speeches. They could only deal with what was in the bill. So even on that the Tories did not get very much help.

The Archbishop passed to a suggestive passage on Socialism, which, curiously enough, has received more sympathetic treatment from the Bishops than from any other part of the House. He consoled the Lords by telling them that the British workmen were not logical, and therefore not likely ever to become Marxian Socialists. Then came an even more suggestive touch. 'The logic of one generation is not the logic of another,' but the worst attitude towards Socialism was to fight it with harsh weapons. 'It is in an atmosphere of hopelessness that Socialism has its best chance.' 'It is to the moral rather than the political feelings of workmen that Socialism makes its appeal.' 'The truest system is not to alienate and embitter it by mere undiscriminating talk' – a very wise and humane rebuke to the foolish language of Lord Rosebery.

Dr. Lang ended and stepped back to his corner seat. That grave restrained figure in the long flowing robes gave place to a very different man. Lord Curzon advanced to the table from his seat next to Lord Lansdowne – a well-groomed, straight-backed figure of an Englishman, alertness and self-confidence in every line of his face and figure. He made a brief apology for his health, received with sympathetic murmurs. But there was no sign of weakness in what followed. On the contrary, never has Lord Curzon been more himself – more ready, more self-assured, more self-confident, more self-complacent. You felt that he was conscious of a great occasion and a great opportunity, and it is pleasant to see a speaker so frankly enjoy himself. But as compared with the Archbishop's speech here was tinsel unto gold, water unto wine. Beneath that flamboyant manner and that histrionic utterance there seemed no sense of the gravity of the occasion, no glimpse of the solemnity of the issue. And accompanying every phrase was that manner – or should I say mannerism? – which has driven so many respectable Anglo-Indians into violent Radical courses. How shall I describe that manner? The imperial glance round his audience, the stately prance backwards and forwards from the bench to the table, the stately shrug and lifting of the hands – but why need I describe it? For perhaps the most remarkable passage in the speech was that in which Lord Curzon exhorted his fellow-peers to stump the country in their own canoe, and offered himself, 'so far as my health will permit,' to lead the van. So the country will soon see this inspiring exhibition for itself.

For the rest, the speech was the most daring expression of reaction that the House of Lords has yet heard in these debates. Lord Curzon asserted without any shadow of hesitation the Lords' right to control finance, and put forward without flinching the amazing theory that they were taking their revenge for Mr. Gladstone's success in preventing them from keeping on the paper duties in 1860. 'There is still in this House,' he said, 'a peer who heard the famous Lord Lyndhurst defend the House of Lords in 1860. That peer is my father. He and his son will go readily into the lobby to support Lord Lyndhurst's views to-night.' A very pretty personal touch, but think of its political meaning! It is almost as if we were exhorted to go back on the Reform Bill! And this will be applauded by at least half of a press which owes its very existence to Mr. Gladstone's victory!

But that was the size of the claim throughout. It was to be an aristocratic counter-revolution, a return for all the shames of three centuries. 'I will endeavour,' Lord Curzon began, striking one hand on the other three times, and raising his voice to its highest pitch, 'to place before you reasons why we ask you in perfect confidence and perfect integrity to support this motion.' And then the argument developed, taking as it moved onwards every variety of protean shape – now as an appeal to the people ('It is in the interest of the social welfare of the nation that we ask you to vote') – then as the cry of an angry landlord ('This intolerable inquisition!') – and finally as a protest of the House of Lords itself – ('We are asked to vote like a number of puppets, just to nod our heads!') – but always as the same, the claim to control the people from the House of Lords.

The only note that was not sheer reaction came at the end, and it was a very significant note. Perhaps the strangest conclusion ever given to a speech was that in which Lord Curzon, after placing the claims of the House of Lords at their very highest, admitted that it needed reform. 'I think it is quite likely that we are at the beginning of a long and arduous struggle – perhaps two elections – and that the component parts of the Constitution will emerge in an altered form. Some of us will welcome the proposal that we should have a reformed House of Lords, and I hope it may be reserved to my party to carry such a reform – a real Second Chamber and not a mere phantom, ridiculous because of its paralysis – independent and fearless and strong.' And then Lord Curzon, suddenly stopping, stepped back and sat down.

The House then relapsed into a period of quiescence covering the dinner hour, and did not wake up till the return at nine o'clock. Then the Chamber rapidly filled until there was scarcely sitting room left for a new-comer.

The scene at this moment was memorable. The whole floor of the House was packed with black-coated peers – a mass of dark-coated figures, except for a splash of white here and there (the white shirts of the diners) and that little waterfall of black and white in the far corner where the bishops sit. The impression of crowd is increased by the group of peers on the woolsack in the centre of the House. But the great mass of figures is in front of the throne. On those steps there is standing room only. In the very centre of this great group stands Mr. John Burns, his iron-grey face just below the Royal arms. The steps up to the throne make a natural amphitheatre. All round this chamber, on the narrow little railed balcony which stands out against the fretted panel-work, sit the peeresses. It is a sign of the stress this evening that scarcely any of those ladies are in evening dress, and their dark cloaks give a sombre touch to the scene.

It was at a quarter past ten that Lord Crewe rose – smooth and serene, the politest man that ever led 'a predatory party.' Lord Crewe is not a great speaker. He lacks fire and fluency. His gestures are poor – he cannot separate the hands, and he bows too often. And yet somehow he gets on easily with the Lords, and they listen to the Liberal gospel from his lips more readily than from others.

But at last, at eleven o'clock – for it was the eleventh hour and the House was thirsting for a division – Lord Crewe came to the real push of pike.

'In tearing up the ancient charters and removing the old landmarks you are all making a tragic blunder. I know you are not afraid, but you are just the least bit afraid of being afraid.' Then followed a touch of autobiography – a description of his own experience for fifteen years as an Opposition peer. 'During that period I cannot remember ever having been of the smallest use to this House, ever affecting a single vote or carrying a single amendment.' That was intolerable enough, but things were getting worse.

What was the result? Why, that after to-night these two Houses, which had jogged on together in a sort of way, would no longer be on speaking terms. What was the result? From that time forward 'we must set ourselves to obtain guarantees, not merely the old guarantees, but if necessary guarded and fenced by statute, which will prevent the indiscriminate destruction of our legislation, of which your work to-night is the climax and the crown.' With that threat Lord Crewe sat down.

Then the Lord Chancellor rose from the Woolsack and put the question, reciting Lord Lansdowne's amendment very slowly and carefully.[1] 'Those who are on behalf of the amendment will cry "Content" and the contrary "Not Content".' 'The Contents have it,' cried Lord Loreburn. 'The Not-Contents have it,' sputtered the Liberal peers. 'Clear the bar!' cried the Lord Chancellor, and then the deluge began. It came from the Tory benches – a steady torrent of ruddy-faced unknowns voting down the people's rights. A crowd of members of the Commons watched from the galleries, and from the steps of the throne Mr. Burns and Mr. Winston Churchill looked on. The deluge went on – five minutes, ten, fifteen. Then the little knot of Liberal peers rose together as if for company, and walked down the House to the right of the throne and disappeared. The stream of Tories ceased, and the House was left empty, its scarlet benches glaring up at the electric lights.

There was a minute of emptiness, and then the door to the left of the throne opened and the Tory peers began to come back. They returned silently, the two tellers counting them with the white wands. The Duke of Northumberland came in with his hands in his pockets, Lord Halsbury jaunty and light-hearted for all his years. The returning stream flowed on – five minutes, ten, fifteen. One looked for some familiar faces in that crowd – the Duke of Norfolk, Lord Burnham, the Duke of Devonshire – here a duke, there a duke, scattered amid a flood of noble barons. Now they seemed more cheerful. It all seemed so easy once you tried it – just a little walk through a lobby and then an end!

The Lord Chancellor sat chatting to a peer, seemingly quite nonchalant. Then suddenly there was a stir, and through the crowd round the Woolsack the tellers come pushing and hand him a piece of paper. The Lord Chancellor takes it, puts on his glasses, reads – 'The Notcontents 75, the Contents 350 – so the Contents have it.'

> The following day Mr. Asquith announced that the King had agreed to dissolve Parliament. The government won the general election with a reduced majority and eventually, after a further crisis and another election, carried the Parliament Act of 1911 which curbed the power of the Lords.

---

1. 'This House is not justified in giving its consent to this bill until it has been submitted to the judgment of the country.' The Lord Chancellor was Lord Loreburn, the close political friend of C. P. Scott.

# Towards A Welfare State

## THE FIRST OLD-AGE PENSIONERS[1]

Wednesday, November 11, 1908

An application for a pension begins at the Post-office. Here forms of claim may be obtained, and if you cannot write very well or are not a good hand at understanding print the postmaster will help. The questions to be answered are fairly simple. They include name, position, place and date of birth, income, and particulars of residence outside the kingdom, if any. The form also states some of the grounds on which a person is disqualified for the receipt of a pension, among which are: the receipt of parish relief at any time since January 1, 1908, habitual laziness or improvidence, imprisonment without the option of a fine during the past ten years, the existence of an order of disqualification issued by a court. The applicant, of course, must have reached the age of seventy, or reach it before the New Year. Each form bears an official postage stamp, and is addressed to the Inland Revenue Office, so that all that remains to be done when the form is filled in is to post it. The Inland Revenue and the Poor Law officials (in case of relief having been received) first take steps to verify the answers given by the applicants as to age, &c.

In cases where no birth certificate or other certain evidence is forthcoming this is often not an easy matter, and now and again it is only by the exercise of a good deal of ingenuity that anything like proof of the applicant's bona-fides can be obtained. For example, one of the applications received in Manchester came from a Jewish resident in Cheetham, who claimed to be 70 years of age and a naturalised Englishman. But no naturalisation papers could be found. The applicant was asked if he had ever exercised the franchise, and he said he remembered voting for John Harwood in 1865. This, of course, was before the Ballot Act came into force. The papers for that year were turned up, and there it was found that the applicant had the right to vote.

After verification, in so far as that is possible, the applications are submitted to the Old-age Pensions Committee. This is split up into 15 sub-committees. At present three of these committees are sitting every day at the Town Hall, considering cases and interviewing personally applicants about whose claims there may be any doubtful

1. By Basil (later Sir Basil) Clarke

points. Only yesterday afternoon one of the committees had before them a Darby and Joan, very tidy-looking in their black clothes and respectable, who must both have been getting on for eighty. It took them several minutes, each helping the other, to get up the Town Hall steps. It seems that they had lived out of the country for some years – in America – and absence from the country is in some cases ground enough to disqualify an applicant. It is fairly safe to assume that the authorities administer the law in as broadly liberal a spirit as they can under the Act, but there is no doubt that a number of deserving old people have forfeited their claim, unknowingly perhaps, through only slight failure to comply with the conditions. Thus the 'no Poor Law relief since January 1, 1908' clause has been the means of stopping a number of grants, for it has been a hard year, and there have been a number of quite new-comers on the Poor Law lists. The residence rule, too, sometimes works hardly, but absence from the country is not inevitably fatal.

## THE DOCTORS AND THEIR COUNTRYMEN

The next major step, the National Insurance Act, met with bitter opposition. Mistresses – the word had a wider range of meaning then than now – said that they would never lick stamps for their servants' cards. Doctors threatened a boycott. Two leading articles, both probably by Montague, were firm in their opposition to the wreckers, but conceded that some of the difficulties might perhaps have been avoided.

### Monday, July 15, 1912

The passing of this Act has been one of the wonders of modern politics. Mr. Lloyd George's handling of reform, like Romeo's wooing, often seems too sudden and tempestuous; it lacks deliberation; he carries by storm at great cost positions to which a more cautious but less brilliant generalship would be content to lay siege by sapping and mining. But if there have been drawbacks, the compensations have been great beyond comparison. No one else and no other methods could have accomplished so much in so short a time.

### Monday, July 22, 1912

Service under the [National Insurance] Act is national service as much as service in the navy or army and so deadly is the chief enemy in the field that a general refusal by doctors to take part in the new campaign against it might even be compared with a general refusal of

Englishmen to volunteer – at anything less than a certain rate of pay – against an invader already landed in Kent.

We do not say that these facts make it the duty of doctors not to stand up for such pay as they think to be fair. Indeed, we think there is some clear gain in any controversy that helps to dissipate the common and mawkish gush about the doctor as the angel in the house, &c., and puts him on a more sane and honourable footing in people's minds as a man who works to live, like others, and, like others, ought not to be sweated. At the same time there is no getting over the distinction in most of our minds between ordinary employments and the great directly national services among which the nation has now invited medicine to enrol itself. There is no question but that the Act, when in full work, will do good in many ways; for one thing, it will tend to bring cases into the doctors' hands at an earlier stage; it will, as every sensitive doctor would prefer, make it more profitable to him that the public health should be good than that it should be bad; it will release doctors in the poorest districts from much of the hateful functions of adjusting fees, of collecting accounts, of practising complaisances and concessions which honesty longs to withhold. Private practice in a poor quarter, though there be no club work in it, is not now a career satisfying to a man with high professional and personal ideals. The Insurance Act, when well in force, must help to cleanse it of many features painful to self-respecting men; it will become a career in which first-rate men may feel that they need abate nothing of the candour and dignity of men of science and trusted public officers.

That this good may come it is, we fully believe, needed that all the doctors working the Act should be fairly paid, and we think the pay at present offered is not high enough. It is not so high as the corresponding pay in Germany, where professional incomes generally are lower than here. We would gladly have seen the income tax charged with the sum required to render the pay liberal, and should support any other reasonable means taken to do so. But such support is not facilitated by the inclination of the doctors' combination to talk in ultimatums and ultimatums only. As far as we gather, the chief reason offered for the ultimatum policy on Saturday was that the combination was remarkably strong and could enforce it. The doctors have the most drastic and advanced trade union in the country, the one whose 'peaceful picketing' is the most effectual, the one with the least mercy for 'blacklegs,' the one most ruthlessly prepared to brush aside considerations of general public interest, and even to arrest a national campaign against consumption, in order to advance the financial interests of its members. The question now as it seems to us, is whether the pay offered under the Act is to be raised by the nation freely or under compulsion. The doctors began with a good deal of public sympathy on their side. There is some of it still left. But the ultimatum recommended on Saturday was an ultimatum to the public, and the strike it foreshadows would be a strike against the public; and ultimatums and strikes do not exactly conciliate sympathy in those against whom they are aimed. It is conceivable that the doctors' union might defeat the nation, and force it to yield the whole of the doctors' uncompromising demand. A trade union of which you may say that it holds life and death in its hands is a formidable opponent, even for England. But such triumphs are not things that the victor can rest on.

> Six months later the first benefits began to be paid. 'This morning,' the *Guardian* began its story on January 13, 1913, 'at the stroke of midnight, the sickness and maternity benefits became operative; on Wednesday the first medical benefits will be claimable; and on January 24, the first unemployment benefits will be paid.'

## CASTE AND EDUCATION

### Monday, March 20, 1911

A London secondary school has decided that it can no longer put up with the 'Board school' scholarship boy, and has renounced a considerable annual grant from the London County Council paid for the education of these boys. The school is the University College School at Hampstead, and apparently it has taken action at the behest of the parents of the paying boys themselves. We are afraid that there is only one explanation possible. There is a fear, no doubt, among the parents that the 'Board school boys' may communicate to the other boys some taint of faulty pronunciation or inelegant manners. It is a pity. If these parents valued the right things instead of the wrong things they would be only too glad of a stiffening of scholarship boys – that is, picked boys of special ability from the popular elementary schools. They would see in it a guarantee that their boys would have the stimulus of a keen intellectual rivalry and a high standard of earnestness and accomplishment. One would not like to see our chief Manchester secondary school[1] deprived of the scholarship boys from the elementary schools. The superficial elegancies and refinements of life are only too easily learned by boys in and out of school. In the serious things, they should learn from the beginning that the realm of intellect and endeavour is a

1. Manchester Grammar School

democracy. The republic of letters, in the widest sense, should be a conception familiar to them as soon as they are introduced to the world of letters. In the United States a piece of news like this would arouse vehement public indignation, and any of the parents and authorities responsible who had any part in public life would be made to pay the penalty. The son of the President is expected to sit down on the same public school bench as the son of the bootblack. It would probably be the better for us if there were the same democratic jealousy here. For with the attempt to keep particular secondary schools a preserve of a particular class will always go the attempt to keep the higher walks of life in the professions and the public services a preserve for the same class. Apart from this material danger, the caste system in education is a bad ideal. It would be far better if the Spartan ideal of poverty were imposed on all the youth of the nation until their education was finished.

Saturday, March 25, 1911

*To the Editor of the 'Manchester Guardian'*

Sir, – From the tone of your article on the above subject, I gather that it is with regret that you have noted the exclusion of Board School Boys from the University College at Hampstead – this is on purely democratic lines, and I presume, with no regard to the feelings of the paying boys in question.

I wonder whether you have ever considered the matter from the side of a gentleman who is thereby forced to come into daily contact with the innate vulgarity of the lower orders.

I think you will agree with me that the refinement in sons of gentlemen is distinctly a national asset and as such is surely worth cultivating. Is it not more probable that the sons of gentlemen will be levelled down rather than the sons of Pork Butchers levelled up by continual daily contact. The lessons of the gutter are more easily learnt than the traditions of caste.

The fact that by keeping particular secondary and Public Schools a reserve for a particular class keeps the higher walks of life in the professions and public services a preserve for the same class, is surely a great argument in its favour. The lower classes never were a Governing class and why should the master sit side by side with the servant. The British Empire has been built up under the class system and so surely as this is done away with, so surely will the decline of our great Empire commence.

I am aware of course that we live in a democratic age, but in this and other things (for instance, one has only to look at the present position in Parliament to see the result of extensive pandering to the lower orders), we are surely going too far in bowing so low to the God of Democracy. – Yours faithfully.

*Kensington, London, March* 20                                   Public School Boy

(This letter is, we gather, written seriously – though it would be charitable to suppose that it was not – by one who has himself had a public school education. Most people will be inclined to think that if his state of mind were to be taken as exemplifying the results of the system, nobody need regret not having passed through it. – Ed. 'Guard.')

Wednesday, March 29, 1911

*To the Editor of the 'Manchester Guardian'*

Sir, – The value of the testimony of personal experience is not enhanced by anonymity. If, however, I were to sign my name, it would involve me in vain discussion and difficulties which would only detract from the real good I can do in my ordinary work, and it might do harm to the school which, as it were, I govern in trust.

The real difficulty is not the social or the pecuniary inferiority of the elementary boy, but his enormous moral inferiority. Most of the other boys that come to us have a very definite idea that certain actions and thoughts are 'caddish' or 'bad form' or 'blackguardly.' The knowledge of such terms and the recognition that among wrong actions there are some to be very specially avoided, and the dread of the loss of caste and self-respect that will follow upon them, help a master immensely. Their reasoning may be defective, but it is an incalculable advantage to feel that, if once you can convince a small boy that a certain action is a 'blackguard' thing to do, that only a 'hopeless cad' would think a certain thing, more than half your battle is over.

Now I have been dealing with a certain proportion of elementary boys for some years, and I have failed to find any parallel idea or word that I can appeal to. I have to begin *de novo*. Your readers may hold up their hands in righteous indignation, but the sad truth is there for me and others that I know of my profession. The virtues of the elementary boy are industry and obedience, which are, in our opinion, secondary virtues for a boy. For cribbing, meanness, cowardice, cruelty he has just as much feeling of abhorrence as for unpunctuality – perhaps rather less.

We have now had some years' experience of the working of the 'free place' system, and can see something of the results. My own experience is as follows. We have no County Council scholars, but in order to earn the grant of the Board of Education we admit every year from the local elementary schools 25 per cent of the number of boys who have joined the school during the past year.

My first complaint is that the proportion is too large, and that there is no real demand for so many 'free places.' On one occasion there were fewer candidates than there were 'free places' offered.

Now our experience of the 'free placers' after their entrance into the school is that some 20 per cent or 25 per cent rise to very good positions in the school, take a full and creditable share in the out of school activities of the school, and are, in a word, such boys as I should choose for prefects if they should stay long enough in the school. I should say, however, that this *élite* of the 'free placers' almost always are sons of parents who for social and pecuniary reasons ought never to have applied for free places. Fifty per cent of the 'free placers' reach a fairly creditable position in the school as far as work is concerned, but gain little or no benefit from what is perhaps the most important feature of secondary education – *i.e.*, the formation of character through various activities out of school. They only join in such games as are compulsory, and return home as soon as they can.

Lastly, about a quarter of the 'free placers' are quite undeserving of their position, either intellectually or morally. We do very little good to them, and they do decided harm to us. Their position in the school is below the average, and, although with difficulty one can keep them outwardly in the path of honesty, one can never trust them.

Yours &c.,
Head Master

## Strikes and Disturbances

### TROUBLE AT TONYPANDY

Wednesday, November 9, 1910
*From our Special Correspondent*[1]

Tonypandy, Tuesday
The centre stretch of the Rhondda Valley, where it lies deep between mountain slopes all autumn brown and ashen grey, was in wild turmoil late last night and early this morning. Strikers and policemen were in furious conflict, stones were thrown in showers, truncheons were drawn and vigorously used, colliery property was smashed, and

1. J. V. Radcliffe

more than a hundred strikers and six or seven policemen were injured, some of them badly. What set the bad spirit abroad cannot be known. It seemed to fall with the gathering darkness. High above the Llwynypia pit is a frowning head of rock, which the clouds wrapped round last night in sullen gloom, and if they had distilled riot and fury down its threatening front the effect in the valley could scarcely have been more sombre and wild. The first mutterings of trouble were heard about nine o'clock. Four thousand men marched to the pit and halted at its gate. This was a repetition so far of the morning and midday marches, but the temper of the men underwent a sudden change. Some youths showed the first symptoms of what was stirring. They made a rush towards the gates, where the police kept guard. It was not a formidable movement, and the police withstood the shock without a tremor, but the repulse set more evil designs on foot. A sober-minded collier very bravely ventured to set himself against the current of feeling. Climbing a bank, he began a speech of counsel to his fellowworkmen to act humanely and justly. The counsel was too quiet for distempered minds, and if it had any effect at all it was only to divert attention from the colliery gates and their police guard to the long line of palisading that shuts off the pit yard from the road.

One common motive actuated the thousands of men massed together. It was to get to the electric power-house, to drive out the men in charge and stop the machinery. The power-house since Sunday has been manned by under-managers and other officials of the Glamorgan Colliery Company, with Mr. Llewellyn, the general manager, at their head. The regular enginemen and stokers have been frightened away. The power station is the citadel of the situation so far as the Glamorgan Company is concerned. It supplies the power for pumping and ventilating five pits. The pits, at any rate, will be in danger of flooding, the ventilation has already ceased, and as a consequence the fate of hundreds of horses is only a matter of hours. To stop every bit of work at the collieries, to stop the pumping as well as the ventilating, was what one man called the trump card that the strikers were now to play. They rushed at the palisading to tear it down. They dare not push it before them lest they should fall with it on the railway below. It had to come down on the road. Thick stumps were snapped and props and stays torn up by the pulling of thousands of hands, and the men began to swarm into the pit yard. The brightly lighted power-station was in front of them, and to hinder their advance only the railway, a line of trucks, and a score or two of policemen advancing in scouting order. Not one of the strikers got behind the line of trucks. Big, active men more than their match physically drove them violently back, and they did not try that way any more. Worse things were in store. Stone-throwing began. The road that skirts the colliery is cut low down on the hillside. Another road descends the hill to join it fast by the colliery, and for a hundred and fifty yards it overlooks the colliery entrance. A band of strikers had taken up places here as well as on the slope between the two highways. Stones were plentiful, and big and small, just as they came to hand, they were hurled at the policemen at the gates.

The policemen were unfortunately conspicuous. The light from the power station, without which the men there could not work, shone on the silver facings of their helmets and made them an easy mark. Man after man was hit, and when the line was weakened and another attempt was made to carry the pit by storm the policemen gave way, and the strikers were already within the gates when reinforcements came from another part of the yard. These men had their truncheons drawn, and laying freely about them they drove the crowd beyond the gates and some distance along the lower road. The men on the higher road were at the moment beyond reach, but when the stone-throwing commenced Captain Lionel Lindsay, Chief Constable of the county, called his men together and led them in a charge up the hill. The attacking force consisted of 118 men, every one of them 6 ft. tall or thereabouts. With their truncheons in their hands they advanced with long swinging strides. The colliers did not wait. They preferred throwing stones from a distance to a personal encounter, in which, indeed, they would have been completely overmatched. They scuttled off as fast as their legs would carry them, but not fast enough for all to escape the horrid thud of truncheons on their heads and shoulders. It was a wild, headlong flight for safety, only limited by the necessity for the policemen to remain in touch with their base. Even after this there was no quietness. The strikers re-formed once and again, and other though minor charges were made. The night passed into morning, and still the road was in turmoil. About four o'clock there was a second but this time half-hearted attempt to storm the power-house. It was easily defeated.

Daylight revealed in a striking manner the part of the conflict that darkness had hidden. Most fearful-looking of the wreckage was the litter of stones, half-bricks, and bits of rock that lay all about the colliery gate. It was appalling to think of enduring that merciless, invisible hail. In less profusion, the missiles lay a considerable distance along the road, and a walk up to the hill showed where the supply had come from and the commanding position the throwers held. The best-placed would be thirty or forty feet above the heads of the police and scarcely more than a street's width from them. Standing in a body, as they were obliged to do, and picked out by the colliery lights, the police were completely exposed, a mark for any coward who chose to aim from a distance.

The power-house itself, though it stands well back from the road, had not escaped scot-free. A number of its windows were perforated by stones, but no one inside was hurt. Those of its garrison who were struck were hit while passing to and from the boilers. Twenty men who are really prisoners in this building are waging a hard, unresting struggle against a flood of water in the mine. Amateurs at stoking as they are, they find it almost beyond their power to keep a sufficient head of steam to run the pumping machinery. None of them has slept since Sunday night, and weariness compels them to lie down sometimes on the hard concrete floor, but the rest is brief. They are doing all that men can do to save the pits, and are just keeping the water down. If it overflows the dam it will invade the steam coal pit, and incalculable damage may be done and some three hundred horses drowned. As it is three fates threaten the horses – by starvation, asphyxiation, or drowning – and one can scarcely tell which is coming fastest.

I was permitted this morning to enter the power-house. I found its occupants as eager to gain news from outside as I was to know what had happened within. We therefore exchanged information. Their great physical needs, I ascertained, were first sleep and second cigarettes. The strain of the past thirty hours' vigil and the constant exertion were marked in weary lines on their faces. Some of them were on duty and alert, and the remainder were getting some relief in the easiest attitudes they could assume on the floor. There was not a chair or a form in the place.

There was hope for a time during the afternoon that troops would not be necessary to enforce order in the Valley. The morning had passed quietly, and the afternoon was occupied chiefly, so far as the strikers were concerned, with a mass meeting at which ten thousand were present, and a huge parade round the district. The long delay in the arrival of troops known to have started for the coalfield caused wonder and surprise, and the explanation came later in the afternoon. The strike leaders received a telegram from Mr. Winston Churchill inviting them to meet him in London to-morrow. The Home Secretary's telegram added (according to a statement made by the strike leaders) that he was reluctant to have troops quartered in the Valley, and that if quietness were maintained the troops on the way would not be sent to their destination. It was extremely unfortunate that this telegram had not arrived in time to be read at the mass meeting. The strike leaders met immediately afterwards to consider what reply they should send, and decided to accept Mr. Churchill's offer and to advise the men to keep the peace.

There were, however, no effective means of promulgating their decision, and to-night Tonypandy has been the scene for hours of a terrible uproar. Rioting broke out again as soon as twilight fell. It began down at the Llwynypia (Glamorgan Colliery) pit. The police in strong force were again on duty at the gates and in the yard concentrating their force so as to defend the power-house. A great crowd drew up in the road. All at once stones began to hurtle through the air. Another attack was made on the palisading, and the wreckage of last night was piled up in the road to prevent the mounted police from charging. The fusilade on the police was unendurable. The Chief Constable took advantage of a temporary cessation of the onslaught to make a last appeal for order. The reply was another volley of stones.

The Chief Constable himself was hit and knocked to the ground. There was a menacing rush to the gates, and the police replied by drawing their staves and charging. They drove the men before them until they had cleared a good space, and just the same as last night it was necessary to clear the higher road with truncheons. This space the police resolved to defend. Their line was weakened by being extended, but they were in a less vulnerable position. On each side of them was a desperate crowd, but for a time they won a breathing space. The tale of the injured has yet to be told, however. Nobody knows how many are injured, but news comes from the pit that nine constables are lying there in a serious condition. The riot is spreading throughout the town, and it is unsafe to venture into the street. A fellow-journalist has just come in bleeding from a wound in the head, inflicted by a stone. He was a stranger, and that alone seems to account for the attack. A reckless crowd is marching through the streets. There seem to be no police about. The rioters swarm down the main street.

A number of men started a short time ago on a mission of wanton destruction bringing half bricks with them. They hurled them right and left into the shop windows. I followed safely in their tracks and saw the damage they had done. Some shops have not a particle of glass left in their fronts, and it is impossible to say how many windows are smashed. There has also been unrestricted looting. In the central square of the town a dozen shops have had their fronts completely broken out, and the goods that filled the windows three hours ago are now lying in the street. Companies of strikers have climbed to the upper floors and are rifling the stores, throwing them out of the windows to the people below, who are bearing them away in armfuls.

The square is littered with clothing, millinery, groceries, confectionery, and chemists' wares. It is an amazing sight and quite undescribable.

The scene in the centre of the town is one of utter confusion. People stand about in small groups, either silent or discussing under their breath the events of the past few hours. The looting of shops is still going on. I have just seen a man standing behind the broken glass of a clothier's window emptying a broken bale of goods. He called out, 'Who wants a waistcoat?' and handed one to the man who first spoke; then a pair of trousers, then a coat; in this way the goods were distributed until the bale was empty. To assist the distribution the gas in the shop window had been lighted. Everything was done openly. There are no police about. Carpenters are already at work boarding up the broken windows.

### Thursday, November 10, 1910

Tonypandy, Wednesday

The town was awake all night. Excitement and fear kept many out of bed, and only the dawn scattered the prevailing alarm. All night long men were boarding up the shattered shop fronts and carts were going round for the sweepings of plate glass that littered the main street for three quarters of a mile. Now and again there was the heavy tramp of large bodies of police going or returning from the Glamorgan pit at Llwynypia, but nothing occurred to remove or increase the anxious suspense. To-day is also full of fear. The few shops that escaped damage yesterday are being barricaded to-day, and the night is awaited with dread. Soldiers have arrived. A squadron of the 18th Hussars reached Pontypridd early this morning, and after a rest a troop came here by road, a distance of seven miles, while the other troop went to Aberdare. Their places at Pontypridd were taken by another squadron brought from Cardiff, where they had been overnight. The troop here rode through the town about one o'clock to their quarters at the New Colliery offices. The Metropolitan Mounted Constabulary have also arrived. Superficially there is nothing but curiosity in the minds of the slow-moving crowds that are in the streets, but the same could have been said yesterday, and those who know the temper of the Rhondda miners predict more trouble. Let us hope the prophets of evil are wrong.

Ten o'Clock

Tonypandy to-night and Tonypandy last night are not like the same town. Even within the past two hours there has been a great change.

There is not even a crowd about except in the square, where the number of people is perhaps large enough to be called a crowd. At first the disappearance of the strikers caused misgiving. It seemed as if they had acted on a common understanding, and the fear was that they might be congregating elsewhere. A good effect was produced by a proclamation in the square inviting all well-disposed persons to avoid associating themselves with riotous assemblies. I have walked to Llwynypia and as far as the grounds of Mr. Llewellyn's house. There are only curious sightseers about. The colliery is brightly lighted, and the loud hum of the machinery in the power-house shows that it is running at full speed. The police, chilled by the cold night air, are stamping up and down to keep themselves warm. Mr. Llewellyn's house looks as secure as Buckingham Palace. No doubt there are many police guarding it, but they are all hidden by the darkness, and it has not been thought necessary to secure the gates.

## A STRIKE THE 'GUARDIAN' SAVED

Nineteen-thirteen was another bad year for labour troubles, but there was one strike which the country was spared thanks to an interview given to a *Guardian* reporter. The Midland Railway dismissed a goods train guard because he had refused oral orders to take out a train which was over-loaded according to the written regulations (the 'Appendix' of the following extract). The unions – the National Union of Railwaymen was in process of being formed out of four existing unions – took up the case strongly. The Company was adamant. A national strike seemed inevitable. Then Walter Meakin saw Guard Richardson and got his account of what happened when he was seen by the directors. The chairman of the company offered to reinstate the guard if he would repeat to the directors what he had said to the *Manchester Guardian*. The dispute was settled more or less in the way indicated in Meakin's second message.

Tuesday, March 4, 1913
*From our Special Correspondent*

Normanton, Monday
I had a conversation with Guard Richardson to-night at his home in Normanton about the Midland Company's version of the events which have led up to the present railway crisis.

'Did you know,' I asked Richardson, 'that an order was given by the

General Superintendent to the control officers in November that the loading on this section between Chesterfield and Sheffield was to be varied?'

'I did not know it,' he replied, 'and no such instruction was issued to the men.'

'Do you remember when the last issue of the Appendix was?'

'Yes; it was in June last year, and a supplement was issued in January this year. This supplement does not contain a word about the loading regulation on the Chesterfield to Sheffield section having been altered, and I called attention to this when I was before the directors. I asked why the printed regulation had been kept in operation if it was not intended to be worked to. The statement that I said I should have refused to obey the verbal orders of the General Manager is not quite accurate, when put in that way. I was naturally rather out of my element, being alone before six of the directors, and I do not remember the actual words I used. But what I had in mind and tried to express was that I should not obey such an order unless specifically freed from any responsibility. I do not think it was quite fair that I had to meet the directors alone. I asked permission to be accompanied by a fellow-worker, so that there could be a witness as to what transpired, but this was refused, and I am in the position of having to put my own word against that of the official statement. It is true that I said I had acted on principle, and I still hold that as no printed notice had been given to us that the regulation was altered, and as there was no reference made to it in the supplement – which we take to record all alterations of the Appendix regulations – I was bound to carry out this particular regulation, in view of the gradients over which I had to travel.'

Putting the merits or demerits of his case aside, Richardson impresses one favourably as a man. He is as far removed as can be imagined from the aggressively defiant type of worker who is sometimes a thorn in the flesh of railway officials, and his reputation as a workman in the Normanton district is indicated by the ease with which he obtained temporary employment at a colliery on the outskirts of the town within a day or two of being dismissed by the Midland Company. Speaking of his railway record he said, 'I have never had a black mark, nor have I been suspended during the whole of my twenty years' service, and the only time I have had to go to Derby to answer a complaint was four years ago, about a very trivial matter.'

Thursday, March 6, 1913
*From our Special Correspondent*

Normanton, Wednesday Night

I have seen Guard Richardson again at Normanton to-night, but I gathered from him that he had been advised by the union leaders to make no further statements at present. He was obviously worried and feeling the nervous strain of the last two or three days. He does not withdraw in any way from the statements he made to me on Monday, and I am to say that he shares with virtually all the other trainmen employed by the Midland Company the conviction that the condition laid down by the Executives of the unions to-day respecting written orders to vary rules and regulations is essential for the protection of the men. A settlement on these lines would entirely remove the uncertainty which at present fills the minds of the men. I spoke to several engine drivers and guards who were leaving their work at Derby before the decision of the unions was known, and they unanimously fixed upon this point of responsibility as the all-important thing to be settled. 'We must know where we stand,' said one of the drivers. 'What we do understand now is that if anything went wrong owing to a regulation being broken it would be the trainmen who would be blamed. If we were all told from headquarters that the foreman or control officer who gave us the instruction to work against the Appendix would be responsible it would make all the difference.' The others said that this statement entirely expressed their own feeling on the matter.

In Normanton I met a group of goods guards, and when I told them of the union terms they agreed that a settlement on these lines would meet the difficulty so far as they and the majority of their colleagues were concerned. 'I don't want to be a boss,' said one of them. 'I am always willing to obey reasonable orders, and if we had a written order when an Appendix regulation had to be altered we should know exactly where we stood and feel secure that we were not to be held responsible for the alteration.' 'It will be a jolly good thing if it can be settled like this,' said another. 'We don't want to strike, but there seemed to be nothing else for it until the Company's offer came this morning. We who know Richardson well can easily understand that he would not be able to say just what he wanted when he was before the general manager or the directors. He is not a man who is used to talking, and it isn't an easy thing for one of us workmen to face the directors. When he was talking quietly to the newspaper men he would be much better able to make himself understood.'

# Women's World

## VOTES FOR WOMEN

The demonstration described in the following extracts was organised by Mrs. Pankhurst's militant suffragettes. The Women's Social and Political Union protested against the proposed Manhood Suffrage Bill as 'a grave and unpardonable insult to women,' and 'firmly refuses to allow the political enfranchisement of women to depend on a mere amendment' to the Bill (which Mr. Lloyd George proposed to move). During the evening 223 arrests were made, including three men. The first story is by Francis Perrot, the second by G. H. Mair.

### Wednesday, November 22, 1911

#### A MILITANT TRICYCLIST

There was a policeman outside Caxton Hall last night who told us that a year ago he was at Tonypandy. 'A year ago to the day,' he said, 'and a bright, cold night like this, but there was blood flowing then. This job'll be child's play to it.' Saying which he gently shepherded away a quiet little group of women who had come out of the hall and were trying to get into Victoria-street by a forbidden path. That was the beginning of it. All who set out from the hall reached the danger zone without much difficulty. They walked arm-in-arm and close together for companionship. The crowd was only small round the hall, and it was far from excited. There was a little cheering and some jeers, but the people were for the most part simply curious, as they would be at any street happening.

It was getting on for eight o'clock when the women began to penetrate into Parliament Square. The policemen had been ready for them for well over an hour. As usual all the approaches to the House were guarded and double guarded by thick hedges of men. The roadway by St. Margaret's had not only a treble line but some mounted men also who took the first brunt of the attack. By Old Palace Yard there was another embattled line, and all the minor approaches had their defences. It was not surprising therefore that with one exception none of the women ever got near the doors of the House. The exception was a woman who calmly rode through the lines on a tricycle. When she got to the members' entrance there was a puzzled police debate as to what should be done with her, and a sergeant finally decided that she would be safest where she was. And there she stayed – alone in a great empty expanse.

But before this the women had begun the attack at the St. Margaret's approach. One or two women hung desperately to the bridles of the horses, but were easily shaken off. These were the first arrests. Anything like a concerted attack was out of the question. The women had to squirm their way through the crowd to the police by great efforts, and they were arrested for the most part singly. The onlookers formed a sort of buffer between the women suffragists and the police ranks. You saw the woman come silently up to the line and push feebly against it, and in another moment she would be seized by a policeman by each arm and marched away. These arrests were repeated with melancholy monotony. I myself saw at least a score of them made at this point and at the entrance to Old Palace Yard.

In no case was there anything which could reasonably be called violence or ill-usage on the part of the police. They seemed indeed to use the greatest forbearance. In at least one case it was not until a policeman had been struck in the face by a woman that she was taken away. Sometimes they struggled in the officers' hands, but usually, in police court language, they went quietly. Everyone looking on noted the unnatural calmness of the women as they pushed themselves with dull persistence against the broad chests of the policemen. 'Hysterical' was the common description, but there was none of the wildness of hysteria in it. Some smiled foolishly and seemed oblivious of what they were doing. All this time other suffragists were coming up in taxis, but they were always promptly hauled out.

I caught a strange glimpse of these doings from a balcony over Westminster Bridge Road. Behind the police stretched the dim and desolate roadway round the House. By the pompous line of yellow lights on the parapet there was not a soul, but on the other side of the barrier was this restless, nearly silent mob, with very few women in it, so it seemed, and quickly getting less.

As time went on the novelty wore off. The street population tired of these performances. Soon after nine a fresh police regiment with mounted men came up and began the work of clearing the crowd away, driving it up Whitehall, and the drift began to set homewards. The M.P.'s, having seen all there was to see, went back to hear what Mr. Lloyd George had to say for the servant insurance. The raid was even more of a failure than earlier raids as far as getting to the House was concerned.

The part of the evening's proceedings which did succeed as militancy counts success was the window-smashing.

## THE REASON WHY

It was not later than a quarter-past-six when I saw a double line of policemen drawn up in front of Westminster Abbey; by the Caxton Hall groups of them were standing in the roadway; behind, near St. James's Park station on the Underground, police were forming up. There were squads of policemen in Downing-street, in Whitehall, and Victoria-street. As events proved later there must have been thousands in reserve. One saw with some surprise respectable looking men in bowler hats holding up the traffic and then one realised the presence of the plain clothes man. Then every man in a bowler hat seemed to take on an air of authority, and one saw, or fancied one saw, plain clothes men everywhere. Most of the police that I saw were strangers, and one or two who were put to the test proved themselves unable to give the simplest directions to buildings in the neighbourhood.

It was about a quarter to eight when the first deputation left the Caxton Hall. Twenty yards from it – in front of the gates of the St. Ermin's Hotel – a line of police drawn across the roadway held it up and the process of dispersal began. The leaders were allowed to go forward, their followers broken up into small parties and impeded till the little band who passed must have been far on their way down Victoria-street. Then they were let forward, too, but in twos or threes. There was never a march in a body during the whole evening.

In Victoria-street in their wake expectancy reigned, men and women – the crowd seemed mostly composed of couples, and everywhere I saw it was absolutely orderly – hung about the roadway waiting for more to come. Far ahead under a luminous yellow haze thronged the crowd. There was no noise to break the monotony of the traffic's roar. Cabs and 'buses passing continuously assured us that whatever else was happening the road was open. Only the soundless flashes that shuddered and winked in the sky – not the signal lights of the police, as I heard someone say, but, more romantically, the flashlights of the press photographers – hinted at events. Then we came on the first arrests. A tinkle of glass – the panes in the door of Victoria-street Post-office – and then, walking very quickly, four policemen, each with a woman by his side, hurrying off to the police station in Cannon Row. A trotting crowd of loiterers, and then more policemen and women, then the rush of a photographer, a flash, a report, a puff of white smoke, and we had the nearest thing to action we saw the whole evening. In all I saw about twenty women taken to Cannon Row by Victoria-street. There was no sign of disorder either in the arrests or in the making of them, and as an inspector passed in animated conversation with a white-haired old lady, whom he had apparently just taken, the crowd raised a sympathetic cheer.

Opposite St. Margaret's the crowd grew denser, swaying backwards and forwards, and rolled up the pavement and against the railings as the bays of the mounted police edged and shouldered them down the roadway. 'Buses passed perilously, top-heavy with craning passengers on tiptoe on the roof, taxi-cabs bulging with sightseers, lines of capes and helmets pressed up and down the street. A little knot of women, there could not have been more than five, passed on into the densest part of the crowd. They came back singly, policemen by their side.

Then a girl quite close by me began to speak to the crowd on the pavement. She spoke very softly, but very bravely and clearly: 'I suppose you know why we are doing this, you men. All the laws in the past have been men's laws, and we women, though we've been citizens as far as taxpaying went, haven't been allowed to vote how we want to be taxed.' And then she went on to talk about all the women's suffrage bills that had got their second readings and how they had all been dropped and how now they wanted to put a measure of manhood suffrage before the Conciliation Bill.' It was all just the simplest statement of the deputation's case, and we must all have heard it many times, but everybody listened and nobody jeered, and at the end a little old woman who had worked quite evidently for her living spoke kindly to the speaker. There was nobody but was orderly, nobody but seemed to sympathise with the strength of purpose that can make such things be. I think the London crowd is beginning to do what crowds so rarely do. It is beginning to understand and respect an idea.

The disorder, if it could be called disorder which was so silent and orderly, was at its height before nine. By ten it had almost ceased. During all the time I was in the Square and its neighbourhood I saw nothing whatever in the way of violence. The police were uniformly good-humoured, though they plainly did not like the job. Arrests were wisely made quickly, and, as wisely, not resisted. And though there was much to regret in the stupidity which broke windows indiscriminately as far east as Bouverie-street and sunk a cause in exasperation and hysteria, there is at least nothing graver for London to charge itself with. For that one may feel genuinely grateful.

G.H.M.

COMMENT

C. P. Scott was a life-long advocate of votes for women, but a determined opponent of the militants' way of attempting to get them. He called the leader he wrote that night 'Some Suffragists and the Government.'

The enthusiastic but unreasoning section of suffragists who follow the lead of the Women's Social and Political Union yesterday made their protest in riot and window-breaking against what they denounce as the insult of a proposal to enfranchise about seven million of their sex. Unhappily the organisation of the Women's Social and Political Union is an extraordinarily narrow one. It is completely dominated by at the outside four persons; it is as complete an autocracy as the Salvation Army itself, which in many respects – in its emotionalism, its unconventionality, and the secrecy of its inner councils – it closely resembles. To these characteristics it no doubt owes much of its success. Discipline, continuity, swiftness must in any militant organisation carry with them conspicuous advantages. But in a political society they have their corresponding defects. Too much depends on the judgment and temper of a very few persons, and these almost necessarily move in a too narrow circle of admirers and devotees, and the sense of reality is lost.

# THE DERBY AND THE SUFFRAGETTE

## Thursday, June 5, 1913

'They had just got round the Corner, and all had passed but the King's horse, when a woman squeezed through the railings and ran out into the course. She made straight for Anmer, and made a sort of leap for the reins. I think she got hold of them, but it was impossible to say. Anyway the horse knocked her over, and then they all came down in a bunch. They were all rolling together on the ground. The jockey fell with the horse, and struck the ground with one foot in the stirrup, but he rolled free. Those fellows know how to tumble. The horse fell on the woman and kicked out furiously, and it was sickening to see his hoofs strike her repeatedly. It all happened in a flash. Before we had time to realise it was over. The horse struggled to its feet – I don't think it was hurt – but the jockey and the woman lay on the ground.

The ambulance men came running up, put them on stretchers, and carried them away. Most of the other jockeys saw nothing of it. They were far ahead. It was a terrible thing.'

This was an account given to me (writes a representative of the *Manchester Guardian*) by a man who was standing behind the rails quite near to the place where the woman rushed out. It conflicts in some detail with descriptions given by other people in the tightly-packed crowd at the Corner. Another version has it that the woman did not come from behind the rails, but had managed to stay outside when the mounted policemen cleared the course, and had concealed herself by crouching down, and that she ran towards the horse bending low without trying to seize the reins.

All the accounts agree that she was struck with terrible force by the galloping horse, and that she rolled several yards before the horse lost its footing and fell upon her. The jockey, said one man, 'flew from the horse's back like a stone from a sling,' and it was doubtless only owing to his jockey's skill in knowing just how to fall that he was not far more seriously injured.

Anmer was the last of the string, and the last but one was Mr. Bronson's Agadir, ridden by Earl. The woman just missed Agadir, and Earl was the only jockey who got a glimpse of what happened. The race had been over for some moments before the news reached the stands and the King learnt what had befallen his jockey. He was standing in the Jockey Club at the time, and soon afterwards he looked on with great concern at the spectacle of the jockey, bleeding and with closed eyes, carried past on a stretcher towards the hospital. The King then went to tell the Queen what had happened. The doctor afterwards reported to the King that Jones had had a wonderful escape. One of his arms was injured and he was bruised all over, and one of his ribs was broken.

The woman was far more seriously hurt, and the first report that spread about the course was that she was killed. She turned out to be one of the best known of the militant suffragists, Miss Emily Wilding Davison.[1] It is said that underneath her jacket was found a suffragette flag tied round her body. A house surgeon at the Epsom Cottage Hospital a couple of hours after the accident reported that she was suffering from severe concussion of the brain. 'She has lain unconscious since the time of her admission,' he said, 'and it is impossible to say for a few hours whether her life will be saved.'

1. A member of the militant wing of the Suffragettes since 1906; in prison seven times 1909–1912, term usually curtailed by hunger strike; frequent contributor to *Guardian* correspondence columns. She died of her injuries.

The first clue to her identity was the finding of a paper in her possession bearing the words 'W.S.P.U. Helpers.'

The people who were near enough to see what happened could not believe at first that the woman ran out deliberately. They thought she must have had the idea that all the horses had gone by, and had rushed on the course, as everyone does, as soon as the racers have passed. The only alternative to this theory in the mind of the crowd was that it was the deed of a mad person or a suicide, for it was about as dangerous a thing to do as it would be to throw oneself in the track of an express train.

## THE PIT-BROW GIRLS[1]

### Friday, August 4, 1911

'Well, I don't know!' I can almost hear the well-known phrase, expressive alike of surprise, consternation, and indignation, going up from a hundred homes well known to me as it becomes realised that the younger daughters now at school are to be debarred from 'working on the screens,' and that the occupation of their elder sisters, their cousins and aunts, and even their mothers is to be officially scheduled as degrading and improper. The proposal is a perfect example of the type of legislation which is prompted by the most admirable intentions and marred only by an ignorance more or less complete of the conditions with which it proposes to deal. I can remember a vague unpleasant feeling that there was a race of abject and distorted men, half savages, who necessarily worked under horrible conditions underground in order to provide coal for the consumption of society.

Of course there are brutal and debased colliers as there are brutal and debased doctors, or stockbrokers, or artists or cab-drivers. But what comes as a surprise, almost as a disillusionment, to the newcomer, is not only the comfortable, well-furnished houses and the high standard of comfort among the majority of colliers, but their almost painful respectability. It certainly came as a surprise to me to find the young married collier taking his full share of the burden of the babies, donning a frock-coat and a top-hat on Sundays, expert at bowls and billiards, keen and well versed in politics, and as a rule either strictly orthodox in religion or a militant agnostic. What I have said is a fair description of the majority of colliers I have known in Nottingham-

1. Prohibition of this employment had been suggested in 1886; investigated and rejected by the *Guardian* in five articles between April 24 and May 13 of that year. The illustration on p. 295 appeared on May 10, 1886.

shire and Lancashire, and the majority of the women working on the pit-brow are the daughters of such men.

Now what is the pit-brow lass really like? In Lancashire, at all events, you may always tell her, if you meet her coming away from work, by the scarlet band of flannel across her forehead, which gives her a strangely foreign aspect. The bandage is worn to protect her hair from the coal dust while she is at work, and as she swings along homeward in her clogs you see but a triangle of it under the shawl which invariably covers her head and shoulders. It is a curiously becoming head-dress, and one would not willingly miss from our monotonous streets the sight of these light-hearted home-coming girls. For their superior health and vigour is no fairy tale. How could it be other than it is? They work almost in the open air though sheltered from rain. Their work is arduous enough, but it is not high-pressure work, and does not involve the kind of strain, either muscular or nervous, that is particularly injurious to the physique of women. The coal as it leaves the screens passes slowly before them on an endless band, and as it travels along they remove the 'dirt,' and deftly handling large lumps and smaller ones send the mineral duly clarified to its proper destination. Compare this with the strain on the 'four-loom weaver' or the card-room girl, ever on the alert to keep time with machinery that almost every year speeds up, and working in the artificial atmosphere of the factory, an atmosphere necessarily humid and at a temperature often approaching 90 degrees, and inhaling the cotton 'fly,' that is certainly as dangerous as coal dust. I have not the figures before me as I write, but a good index of the comparative healthiness of different occupations is the incidence of phthisis among those engaged in them, and judged by this standard there is no doubt as to the advantages in health enjoyed by the pit-brow girl over her sister in the mill, and this conclusion would be more than confirmed were figures available as to the prevalence of anaemia and allied conditions.

In fact, on the ground of health there can be no conceivable reason for the proposed with-drawal of women from this particular class of work. The further suggestion has been made that this employment is undesirable on moral grounds, and again those who know the colliery districts are left wondering why.

FRED E. WYNNE

## 'THE MOST DESPISED FORM OF EMPLOYMENT'

Wednesday, May 28, 1913
*From a Correspondent*

The inquiry[1] into the conditions of domestic service has been conducted by means of two series of questions circulated respectively
among mistresses and maids. The servants were addressed by a set of
twenty-four questions, of which two of the most striking were – (1)
'Would you advise any young friend to go into service? If not, why
not?' and (2) 'What do you think could be done to make domestic
service a more desirable occupation?' and the answers so far received,
especially in reply to these cited questions, provide an unequivocal
condemnation of our whole system of household organisation. The
enquiries were sent forth broadcast throughout the United Kingdom,
and have reached every grade of domestic service, from the 'between-

1. Conducted by the Women's Industrial Council. The *Guardian* gave some advance
results in two articles.

maid' earning £12 a year to the butler who has visited fourteen countries, and who, according to his wife, a cook-housekeeper, 'is an
honoured correspondent of many of the intellectual giants of the
world.' From these varying social levels the answer returned is clear,
decisive, and, for the most part, reasoned; the profession is felt to be
undesirable, if not repulsive, under its present conditions.

A cook of 24 years who has been ten years at work laments: 'When
you are in domestic service you are not treated as human beings, and
you are never able to go anywhere for a pleasure-trip the same as your
girl friends, but have to stay in and work while your mistress takes her
pleasure.' And then, with unexpected organising instinct, she adds
that Sunday work might be better arranged, 'for if they (i.e., the family)
had cold supper we could have everything ready, and we could take it
in turns and one come in early one Sunday and the other the next to
clear and wash up, and then we should have Sunday a little different to
a weekday.'

A children's nurse, aged 32, replies to the question 'How long
holidays have you in the year?' 'One day in two years,' and sets down
as her 'free time' in the day 'an hour if the baby is asleep, not unless.'
A lady's maid who has been 15 years in household service, prompted
thereto by 'a great desire to travel in foreign countries,' remarks: 'For
many nights in succession I do not go to bed till the early hours of the
morning, but the day's work is expected just the same, and you are not
expected to be tired.' And in answer to the question 'How much free
time have you each day in the house?' she states laconically, 'None.' A
maid in a country vicarage has no time to herself on Sunday, but is
constrained to attend church three times in the day, which necessitates
changing her dress eight times. She notes that she 'cannot get out at all,
not allowed even in an adjoining garden from the house,' yet she would
advise any young friend to go into service when she 'can get a little
more liberty.'

Modern 'unrest' in the household can no longer be explained as an
unreasonable revolt proceeding from elementary school education
with a top dressing of Women's Suffrage Movement since a high degree
of thoughtfulness characterises these replies, while in some cases a
remarkable impartiality in judgment and a sense of fair play are displayed. There is, moreover, frequent allusion to the 'better living' in
domestic service and occasional recognition of the advantages of an
employment which fits a woman for married life, 'what lies before the
majority of us,' as a young cook sagely remarks. Still, the unanimous
opinion is that present restrictions render domestic service 'the most
despised form of employment.' 'We are treated much as though we

were in prison'; 'we are kept in the house from week's end to week's end'; 'servants have it continually impressed upon them that they are inferior, and eventually do come inferior to what they were'; 'a girl in service is ignored by people in her own social scale,' 'the servant girl has less chance of marriage than any other' – such is the monotonous dirge that resounds through these papers.

A somewhat unexpected fact that comes to light is the resentment against the modern Sunday with its influx into the household of week-end visitors, varied entertainments, and resultant extra work for the servants, and the desire for 'a quiet old-fashioned Sunday where there is not so much company going on' seems pretty general. Indeed, there appears to be a stirring of sentiment in several directions with regard to Sabbath observances. 'A girl should be allowed to follow her own religion,' remarks a kitchen-maid of 20 years, and a housemaid, aged 21, says, 'We should not be asked if we have been to church.' Another young maid comments plaintively, 'We should not be made to go to church in bonnets,' and an upper housemaid of demurer years thinks that a servant ought not to be 'compelled to wear black to go to church.'

A more serious indictment against the employers is voiced in the oft-repeated assertion that mistresses lack in consideration for and courtesy to their maids, complaints which culminate in such observations as – (1) A parlourmaid, who remarks, 'I think in our days dogs are treated far better than human beings, as we are not allowed to use the bath, but in my last situation four dogs were bathed weekly and my share of the bath was to keep it clean after them,' and (2) a cook, who states, 'My sister and I were in separate situations in the Midlands. Though we knew no one else, yet we were not allowed to have each other in the kitchen.'

# Orange and Green

## ASQUITH IN DUBLIN

### Saturday, July 20, 1912

Backed by the Parliament Act the government set out to secure
Home Rule for Ireland. The prime minister, Asquith, received a
hero's welcome in Dublin – the first visit ever paid by a prime
minister. Haslam Mills carefully captured the occasional intimate
moments – the talk to a few representative Liberals, for instance,
in the Chief Secretary's drawing room in a voice so quiet 'that
the angry fuss of a bee imprisoned in the window pane behind
Mr. Asquith's back was quite a loud accompaniment.' But
mainly he was concerned with two great demonstrations – an
open-air meeting when the Nationalist leader, John Redmond,
'with the lightest motion of his hands kept the cheering within
such bounds as to punctuate and not obliterate the Prime
Minister's speech'; and a full dress affair on Friday in the Theatre
Royal, which suffragettes had tried to burn during the performance the night before.

Dublin, Friday night

Mr. Asquith was almost swept off his feet when he rose to speak from
the rostrum in the Theatre Royal. In a considerable experience of
public meetings I have seen nothing to equal and few things to compare
with it – nothing so terrific as the crouch and then the sudden leap of
the gigantic and impassioned living thing which this audience was; the
rising of this plain of men, the tempest of the waving hats, the gleam
of the jewelled women in the circles and the boxes on their feet with
the rest; the passion, the hunger of the throng. It seemed that the
audience would never be satisfied. Again and again it broke out. A
statistician next to me said that for seven minutes the demonstration
went on, rising to a higher and higher rate of passion and resolve. And
then suddenly it ceased, and Mr. Asquith launched himself upon a still
surface of unbroken silence and attention. Nothing has been more
striking in these memorable two days than the instinct of the Irish race
for public meeting, their gift for listening, their self-suppression, their
tact. A city which can amid so many difficulties carry off two great
meetings like that of last night and to-night is fit to be the seat of
government; it can govern itself.

The meeting in the Theatre Royal to-night was a concentration within four walls of the passionate spirit which overran the streets last night. But it was more than that. It was the Irish people in epitome and ordered representation of the civic and social life of Ireland. Behind Mr. Asquith and Mr. Redmond on the stage were ranged file after file the members of the county councils – those living arguments for Home Rule whom Lord Salisbury had the ill-luck or the ill-management to call into being. Among them were the lord mayors and mayors of every city and town in Ireland, except two. The chairmen of Irish county councils on the stage were 28 out of a possible 33. On the pit floor of the theatre was a compressed assemblage of the average man, but the theatre as a whole was representative of every class of Irish social life. Great numbers of men were in evening dress; and in the boxes and in the circle it looked like an opera night. A battery of opera glasses was turned on Mr. Asquith's ruddy face and silvered hair when his speech was on its way, but all classes joined in the overpowering demonstration. The passion with which the great audience was possessed was no respecter of persons.

Mr. Asquith might have had an easy night feeding the roaring fire, but he chose instead to damp it down with matter which will not immediately burn – with a review of the past relations of the two countries, with an expository account of the bill.

At the end, however, there was another great demonstration. For his peroration Mr. Asquith improvised on a passage of Burke. 'No reluctant tie can be a strong one.' The purpose in hand was to substitute for the reluctant tie one that should be voluntary and affectionate, light as air and yet stronger than links of iron.

### MILITANTS AT WORK

But even in Dublin Mr. Asquith, an opponent of women's suffrage, was not free from demonstrations. A party of English militant Suffragettes had followed him over.

Dublin, Friday

The suffragette outrages on the occasion of Mr. Asquith's arrival in Dublin last night had a sequel this afternoon at the Dublin Police Court. Gladys Evans and Mary Leigh, 33, addresses refused; Lizzie Baker, 66, Chatham-street, Stockport; and Mabel Capper, 23, of 21, Oxford-street, Manchester, were charged with having unlawfully conspired to commit grievous bodily harm and malicious damage and to cause an explosion at the Theatre Royal of a nature likely to endanger life and cause serious injury to property. The charge further alleged that Mary Leigh last evening threw a hatchet at a carriage in which was Mr. John Redmond, who was thereby cut and wounded. The court was crowded, and the speech of the prosecuting council was punctured with applause.

Sergeant Cooper, of the 2nd Connaught Rangers, said that as he was leaving the Theatre Royal with his wife he saw a fire in front of the cinematograph box. There was petrol on the carpet, and a woman was striking matches and throwing them down. The witness with a comrade's assistance put out the flames, and an explosion then occurred, causing a report and a cloud of smoke like those of a field artillery gun. A woman opened the door of the cinematograph box and threw matches into the interior. The witness closed with her, and in the struggle they fell downstairs together. The woman said, 'That is only just the start of it; there will be more explosions in the second house.' Afterwards a canister which smelt of gunpowder was found near the scene of the explosion.

John O'Brien, chief marshal in the procession on Thursday night, said he was walking beside the first carriage in which was Mr. Asquith, Mrs. Asquith, Mr. John Redmond, and the Lord Mayor. As the carriage passed along O'Connell-street the prisoner Mary Leigh came towards the carriage and 'fired' something, but he could not say what. She clung to the carriage, and when the witness tried to remove her she hit him on the face for all she was worth. – (Laughter.) The witness took her away from the carriage after a struggle during which she tore both epaulettes from his coat. – (Renewed laughter.) The witness then handed her over to two men. The thing she threw struck Mr. Redmond on the ear. The witness afterwards found it was a hatchet which the prisoner threw at the carriage.

Detective Forrest said that he took possession of Mrs. Baker's bag, in which he found a pair of rubber gloves and an envelope containing gunpowder. There was also a letter in the bag. In Miss Capper's suitcase he found a blue bag which contained a book called *Flames*. – (Laughter.)

Miss Capper said she only bought the book on coming across. It had no bearing on the case. – (Laughter.)

Counsel: Another of the books found was *The Devil's Disciple*. – (Renewed laughter.)

[The militants were sentenced to five years' imprisonment for arson. Scott in a leader on August 8 wondered] whether a truer diagnosis would not rank these women rather as morally insane than as criminals. They have been fooled and misled by the muddy incoherence preached day by day and week by week as a kind of political inspiration by persons of some education and no sense who pose as leaders of the cause which they degrade and futilise.

## KING CARSON

### Thursday, September 26, 1912

But there was, of course, as always, another Ireland. In the autumn H. W. Nevinson (1856–1941) covered the campaign which led up to the signing of the Ulster Covenant under Sir Edward Carson.

Portadown, Wednesday evening
Never had General, or rather King, Carson such a day as this. Here is a largish town of 12,000 population in county Armagh, about 25 miles south of Belfast, on the river Bann, flowing from the Mourne Mountains into Lough Neagh. Like most Ulster towns, it lives on linen and its developments, but it is more strongly Protestant than most. Roman Catholics claim one-quarter of the whole population but probably the proportion is rather less. As the train with Edward Carson's party approached just before noon the usual detonators on the rail fired a battleship salute. The saloon carriage was shunted round to a special platform on which half a company of the 'riflemen of the Portadown Unionist battalion' was drawn up in two ranks. They wore khaki hats trimmed with yellow leather, and carried brown haversacks of military pattern. They were all armed with dummy rifles with solid wooden barrels and real triggers, but with no breech. All, however, had rifle slings, which is a distinct advance upon the Lisburn infantry, who had dummy arms but no slings. When the saloon carriage came to a stand a bugle sounded the general salute, and the order to present arms was given. At the same time a standard was lowered in salute, as is only usual before royalty, and the National Anthem was played. When the Anthem was over the command to order arms was given, the flag was raised, and the troops stood to attention while two addresses were read. Standing on the step of the carriage Sir Edward Carson graciously acknowledged his reception and addressed encouraging words to his faithful army of the clubs and lodges on whom, he said, the real work of the battle would fall, but he was sure that they would make any sacrifice for him in the hour of danger. He then inspected the half-company, who again came to the present. King Edward then emerged from the station to a carriage and

pair, the coachman of which held his hat in his hand as for royalty. In front and behind the carriage mounted troops formed an escort, carrying bamboo lances hung with Union Jacks. They were under the command of Captain Holt Waring, who, I am told, holds a commission in the Yeomanry known as North of Ireland Horse. As he was receiving the King of Ulster, of course, no one could object to his presence.

So the carriage bearing King Carson, Mr. F. E. Smith, Lord Londonderry, and another advanced into the town and made a complete circuit of its main streets, passing under a triumphal arch displaying the symbolic shut gate and cannon, with the eternal dates of 1688–1690. This parade occupied about an hour, after which the royal party withdrew to the Imperial Hotel for lunch. At two, however, His Majesty took up his position at a saluting base close beside a statue of old Colonel Saunderson[1] at the top of the main street. He witnessed a march past of the Unionist clubs and Orange lodges, many of which had been brought into town by eight special trains. As each detachment passed the commands 'Eyes right,' 'Eyes front' were given, and the colours were dipped as to the King, most of the men also raising their hats, and King Carson standing bareheaded in the carriage and acknowledging the salute, with Mr. F. E. Smith standing at his side. Perhaps the troops from Edenderry, the lower part of Portadown across the river, carried off the prize for military grandeur, for their contingent had two field guns made of painted wood and mounted on large open wheels with them, the gunners dragging them with ropes. Behind followed a mock ambulance van with a white hood marked by the red cross and six nurses in army nursing uniform. This had also a full piper band in a sham military uniform with the Gordon Highlanders' tartan, scarlet jackets, and feather bonnets, enough to sicken any Highlander in the army with shame. During the march past Carson's Cavalry kept the route, being drawn up in line opposite his carriage, and when all the troops had passed they again formed an escort before and after the royal carriages on the road up to the place of meeting. In a long experience I have never seen so shameless a travesty of royalty or of national grandeur, but neither of the King's counsellors in the carriage appeared to perceive either the absurdity or insolence of the proceedings.

The procession arrived on the agricultural show ground half a mile south of the town at three, and was again received by a salute of

1. Edward James Saunderson, Whig M.P., opposed every Irish reform bill from the Disestablishment of the Irish Church onwards. F. E. Smith, later Lord Birkenhead, prosecuted Casement 1916, supported Irish Treaty 1921. Sixth Marquis of Londonderry, Viceroy of Ireland 1886–9.

mounted troops. A platform was erected in front of the stand, and two sentries with dummy rifles were set to guard it, walking up and down beside the press table with sloped arms. The crowd covered about a third of the open ground, the Union Jack being unfurled in the centre opposite the platform. Sir John Lonsdale, M.P., took the chair and announced the customary hymn. He said 'We will lay down our lives rather than our birthright. We are on the brink of a darker tragedy than ever before if the bill is carried.'

Sir Edward Carson then addressed the meeting. 'Are you prepared to give me a mandate and follow me to the end?' – (Great cheers.) 'Next Saturday you will bind yourselves to me, and come what may you will never desert the flag. Let the flag fly in every loyal house in Ireland, England, and Scotland next Saturday.' Sir Edward Carson was then presented with a blackthorn stick from North Armagh, and he promised that if he had to use it, he would use it to the best of his ability.

Mr. F. E. Smith was the last speaker on the programme. He referred to next Monday's Liverpool meeting, where they would find the same inflexible resolve; to whatever steps they might be driven they would be supported by English sympathisers. In vain the Nationalists would appeal to the British army which they had so often reviled. He predicted that the Government had not the nerve to give the order to the British army to coerce Ulster. If they gave such an order the populace would lynch them on their lamposts.

The meeting soon afterwards ended. King Carson and Mr. Smith resumed their places in the Royal *cortège*, the sham lancers trotting before and behind, and the general mass of troops following, with bands, the cannon, the ambulance, nurses, and stalwart infantry bearing dummy rifles, all in due order.

# THE CURRAGH MUTINY

By the spring of 1914 the Home Rule bill was about to become law; Ulster was preparing its shadow government to take over power. It was clear that the army might have to be used. Troops were to be sent from the Curragh, the Irish Aldershot, to guard military stores in Ulster. At this point Brigadier-General Gough and the majority of officers of the Cavalry Brigade made it clear that they would rather be dismissed than obey. The *Guardian* in a leader, probably by C. E. Montague, called their behaviour 'contingent mutiny.'

Tuesday, March 24, 1914

### CONTINGENT MUTINY

The contingent mutiny of the cavalry officers in Ireland has raised political questions that make even Home Rule seem small by comparison. These officers asserted the right to lay down for themselves the conditions under which they would continue to serve the King. Has that right been recognised or has it not? That is the question to which the answer was anxiously awaited all yesterday. If the answer had been a plain 'No,' plain men, irrespectively of what their views on the merits of Home Rule might be, would all have had this cause for thankfulness, that the supremacy of law had been vindicated and that the Government, not the army – or a small section of fashionable men who happened to be connected with it, – were our rulers. If the answer had been a plain 'Yes,' then these same men – and that without any reference to the particular views that they might happen to hold on Ireland – would have had cause to fear the worst. They would have known that when any future crisis came no Government could feel sure that the weapon with which it is accustomed in the last resort to enforce respect for the law of the land would not break in its hands. The officer has no rights in these matters that the private soldier has not. If the officer may resign when he is threatened with work which he or his friends do not like, so may the private soldier. The civil Government would have ceased to exist except in so far as the army approved what it is doing, and the real sovereignty of the country would have been transferred from the people to a military caste. Had Mr. Asquith's answer been an emphatic 'No,' he would have been enthusiastically supported by every Liberal in the country and by every Conservative who still believes in the old ideals of his party. He has, in fact, said neither 'Yes' nor 'No,' but his answer is much nearer 'Yes' than 'No.' We say it with the deepest regret and some shame, but the facts must be faced.

The duty of the Government was as plain as that of the officers. When they threatened to resign (that is, to desert or to absent themselves without leave) they should have been dealt with exactly as private soldiers would have been dealt with under the same conditions. They should have been tried by court-martial, and punished as the rules of discipline dictate. They have not been so treated, first, because they were rich men; secondly, because they had the prejudices of their class. Not only, then, is there one law for the rich man in the army and another for the poor, but there is one standard of a Tory officer's loyalty to his oath and another for a private with Labour sympathies. For a Liberal Government to acquiesce in that interpretation of military duty is not only to deal a serious blow at the army but to be false to the whole conception of democratic progress. What worse risks were there that compelled the Government to take a risk like this? We cannot imagine.

Wednesday, March 25, 1914

THE KING NAMED IN PARLIAMENT

John Ward, trade unionist, ex-private soldier and radical M.P., raised the same issue in the Commons. James Drysdale described the duel between him and Leo Amery.

*From our Parliamentary Correspondent*

Westminster, Tuesday Night

'Is it proposed,' demanded Mr. John Ward, 'that Brigadier-General Gough should form a Government?' With the suddenness of an explosion the question was followed by a reverberating roar of applause which echoed backwards and forwards for some time between the Ministerialist and the Nationalist benches.

Afterwards, on the Army Estimates, Mr. John Ward obtained a ruling from the Speaker, that it would be possible to discuss (in Mr. Ward's uncompromising phrase) 'the recent mutiny among officers at the Curragh.'

To Mr. Amery's[1] perplexity his paeans in praise of the political action of the officers had been listened to in obvious discomfort by his

1. L. C. M. S. Amery (1873–1955), Conservative cabinet minister, 1922–1929 and 1940–1945.

friends – several of them officers themselves – while, on the other hand, many of what he doubtless conceived to be its most telling points had evoked rounds of ironical Liberal applause. At last came Mr. John Ward's turn – the turn of the ex-private soldier, the spokesman of Labour, the veritable voice (for as such it sounded at the moment in all ears) of an awakened scandalised democracy. Scarcely less remarkable than the speech itself was its reception by the different parties. Not for the first time in this controversy, the Opposition sat strangely mute, except when irresistibly moved to raise some anguished yet feeble protest against the almost intolerable severity of the onslaught. Even so, the cheering was almost continuous, for in sentence after sentence the orator – possibly amazed at the electrical effect of his own rugged and purely natural eloquence – stirred the benches behind him to a tumult of excitement and delight.

As the storm rose and fell Mr. Bonar Law[1], who had visited his place for a moment, hastily withdrew again, as if to escape its retributive vehemence, while almost simultaneously Mr. Asquith, together with troops of other members, came hurrying in as if in search of an explanation of the unwonted and far-resounding clamour. What they heard, to begin with, was a startling recital by Mr. Ward of the cordial welcome that had been extended by a Syndicalist newspaper to the Unionist party for their aid in 'destroying the military fetish and breaking up the British army.' 'What right have you,' cried the accuser, concluding his reading and addressing himself directly to the Opposition, 'to spread sedition any more than these men?'

Mr. Amery protested that the officers had acted in obedience to their consciences. 'Is it only the officers who have consciences?' indignantly demanded the ex-soldier, proceeding to instance the case of the Dublin Fusiliers, who, despite the notorious dislike entertained by many of their rank and file to the Boer War, never dreamed of shrinking from their duty on the battlefields of South Africa. 'But they were soldiers,' was his scornful comment; 'they were not officers.' What, after all, he added, was the question now before the country? 'It is simply this – whether the people are to make the laws absolutely without interference either from King or Army.'[2] In this sentence came the climax alike of the speech and of the passionate enthusiasm with which it had been followed from the opening sentence to the last.

1. Leader of Conservative party, 1911, Prime Minister, 1922–23.
2. Col. Seely, the War Minister, had been called away from a cabinet meeting to an audience with the King. On his return he added on his own responsibility a sentence to the document which had been under discussion to say that the government had no intention of using its right to employ troops to preserve order as a means 'to crush political opposition to the policy or principles of the Home Rule Bill'. He was forced to resign.

## Wednesday, March 25, 1914

### THE ARMY AND THE COUNTRY

The *Guardian* was as delighted with John Ward's speech as it was horrified by the army officers and their supporters. This leader too is probably by Montague.

Among civilians this challenge from the Tory cavalrymen has produced an instant blaze of indignation. It is reflected in the extraordinary animation and enthusiasm with which the House of Commons listened last night to the spirited and thoroughly reasoned speech of the Labour member Mr. Ward. Of course the challenge is the one theme of talk in every barrack-room too, and a whole army of men drawn from the class to which strikers and the unemployed belong are everywhere discussing the suggestion of General Gough and of Mr. Law that it will be their 'duty' to throw in their lot with rebels or rioters of their own class when called upon to control them. Our more 'exclusive' cavalry regiments, with their inflated social pretensions, their anti-popular tone, their obtrusive expensiveness, and, relatively to these things, their professional inefficiency, have long been one of the settled objects of contumacious wit in all our colonies. It is something of a standing joke against us that, with serious work for an army to do, we maintain such institutions at all. But a veritable peal of derision would go up from the whole Empire if we went further now and set up these spoilt children – these almost obsolete spoilt children – as political dictators over us. In a phrase that sticks in one's mind an Australian visiting England during the last general election said that the colonies would think the mother country 'ripe for any degradation' if she submitted to the domination then sought by the House of Lords. What would the colonies think of us if, after we had curbed the Lords, we allowed a committee of lancers and dragoons to put bits in our own mouths and to say which of our laws shall be enforced and which shall be left for anyone to break who will, with the passive complicity of our army? The thought is unendurable. No Englishman with any warmth in his blood will be able to take a lively interest in any other question until this question of civic self-respect and national safety is settled beyond all revival.

# Ind. Imp.

## IN THE RED SEA

### Wednesday, January 8, 1913

'But why do you do it?' said the Frenchman. From the saloon above came a sound of singing, and I recognised a well-known hymn. The sun was blazing on a foam-flecked sea; a range of islands lifted red rocks into the glare; the wind blew fresh. And, from above,

> *Nothing in my hand I bring,*
> *Simply to Thy cross I cling.*

Male voices were singing; voices whose owners, beyond a doubt, had no idea of clinging to anything. Female voices, too, of clingers, perhaps, but hardly to a cross. 'Why do you do it?' I began to explain. 'For the same reason that we play deck-quoits and shuffle-board; for the same reason that we dress for dinner. It's the system.' 'The system?' 'Yes. What I call Anglicanism. It's a form of idealism. It consists in doing the proper thing.' 'But why should the proper thing be done?' 'That question ought not to be asked. Anglicanism is an idealistic creed. It is anti-utilitarian and anti-rational. It does not ask questions; it has faith. The proper thing is the proper thing, and because it is the proper thing it is done.' 'At least,' he said, 'you do not pretend that this is religion.' 'No. It has nothing to do with religion. But neither is it, as you too simply suppose, hypocrisy. Hypocrisy implies that you know what religion is, and counterfeit it. But these people do not know, and they are not counterfeiting. When they go to church they are not thinking of religion. They are thinking of the social system. The officers and civilians singing up there first learnt to sing in the village church. They walked to the church from the great house; the great house stood in the park; the park was enclosed by the estate; and the estate was surrounded by other estates. The service in the village church stood for all that. And the service in the saloon stands for it still. At bottom, what that hymn means is not that these men are Christians, but that they are carrying England to India, to Burma, to China.' 'It is a funny thing,' the Frenchman mused, 'to carry to 300 million Hindus and Mahometans, and 400 million Confucians, Buddhists, and devil-worshippers. What do they do with it when they get there?' 'They plant it down in little oases all over the country, and live in it. It is the shell that protects them in those oceans of impropriety.

And from that shell they govern the world.' 'But how can they govern what they can't even see?' 'They govern all the better. If once they could see, they would be lost. Doubt would enter in. And it is the virtue of the Englishman that he never doubts. That is what the system does for him.'

At this moment Coryat's voice was borne down the breeze, and it appeared as he approached that he was discoursing to the captain on the merits of Dostoievsky's novels. Coryat is no respecter of persons; he imposes his own conversation, and the captain, though obviously puzzled, was polite, for no one can resist Coryat. 'Russians may be like that,' the captain was remarking as he passed, 'but Englishmen aren't.' 'No,' said Coryat, 'but don't you wish they were?' 'I do not,' said the captain with conviction. I looked at the Frenchman. 'There,' I said, 'behold the system.' 'But your friend?' 'Ah, but he, like myself, is a pariah. Have you not observed? They are quite polite. They have even a kind of respect – like our public schools boys have – for anyone who is queer, if only he is queer enough. But we don't belong, and they know it. We are outside the system. At bottom we are dangerous, like foreigners. And they don't quite approve of our being let loose in India.' 'Besides, you talk to the Indians.' 'Yes, we talk to the Indians.' 'And that is contrary to the system?' 'Yes, on board the boat; it's all very well while you're still in England.' 'A strange system – to perpetuate between rulers and ruled an impassable gulf!' 'Yes.' But, as Mr. Podsnap remarked, "so it is".'

We had penetrated to the bows of the ship and hung looking over. Suddenly, just under the surf there was an emerald gleam; another; then a leap and a dive; another – a pair of porpoises were playing round the bows with the ease, the spontaneity, the beauty of perfect and happy life. As we watched them the same mood grew in us till it forced expression. And 'Oh,' I said, 'the ship's a prison!' 'No,' said the Frenchman, 'it's the system.'

DON[1]

## ULSTER IN INDIA

### Friday, January 17, 1913

'Are you a Home Ruler?' 'Yes. Are you?' Instantly a torrent of protest. He was a Mahometan, eminent in law and politics; clever, fluent, forensic, with a passion for hearing himself talk, and addressing one

---

1. Goldworthy Lowes Dickinson. 'Coryat' of this sketch is a character, 'a poet,' in Lowes Dickinson's *A Modern Symposium*, so is the Audubon of the second sketch – 'a man of business.'

always as if one were a public meeting. He approached his face close to mine, gradually bucking me into the wall. And I realised the full meaning of Carlyle's dictum 'to be a passive bucket to be pumped into can be agreeable to no human being.'

It was not, naturally, the Irish question for its own sake that interested him. But he took it as a type of the Indian question. Here too, he maintained, there is an Ulster – the Mahometan community. Here, too, there are Nationalists, the Hindus. Here, too, a 'loyal' minority, protected by a beneficent and impartial Imperial Government. Here, too, a majority of 'rebels' bent on throwing off that Government in order that they may oppress the minority. Here, too, an ideal of independence hypocritically masked under the phrase 'self-government' (Swaraj). 'It is a law of political science that where there are two minorities they should stand together against the majority. The Hindus want to get rid of you, as they want to get rid of us. And for that reason alone, if there were not a thousand others' – there were, he hinted, but, rhetorically, he 'passed them over in silence' – 'for that reason alone I am loyal to the British raj.' It had never occurred to me to doubt it. But I questioned, when I got a moment's breathing space, whether really the Hindu community deliberately nourished this dark conspiracy. He had no doubt, so far as the leaders were concerned, and he mistrusted the 'moderates' more than the extremists, because they were cleverer. He 'multiplied examples' – it was his phrase. The movement for primary education, for example. It had nothing to do with education. It was a plot to teach the masses Hindi, in order that they might be swept into the anti-British, anti-Mahometan current. As to minor matters, no Hindu had ever voted for a Mahometan, no Hindu barrister ever sent a client to a Mahometan colleague. Whereas in all these matters, one was led to infer, Mahometans were conciliation and tolerance itself. I knew that the speaker himself had secured the election of Mahometans to all the seats in the Council. But I refrained from referring to the matter. Then there was caste. A Hindu will not eat with a Mahometan, and this was taken as a personal insult. I suggested that the English were equally boycotted; but that we regarded the boycott as a religious obligation, not as a social stigma. But, like the Irish Ulsterman, he was not there to listen to argument. He rolled on like a river. None of us could escape. He detected the first signs of straying, and bucked us back to the flock. 'Mr. Audubon, this is important.' Coryat, at last, grew restive, and remarked rather tartly that no doubt there was friction between the two communities, but that the worst way to deal with it was by recrimination. He agreed; with tears in his eyes he agreed. There was nothing he had not done, no advance he had not made to endeavour to bridge the gulf. All in vain! Never were such obstinate fellows as these Hindus. And he proceeded once more to 'multiply examples.' As we said 'Good-bye' in the small hours of the morning he pressed into our hands copies of his speeches and addresses. And we left him perorating on the steps of the hotel.

A healthy mistrust of generalisation prevents me from saying that this is *the* Mahometan point of view. Indeed, I have reason to know that it is not. But it is a Mahometan point of view in one province. And it was endorsed more soberly by less rhetorical members of the community. To a philosophic observer two reflexions suggest themselves. One, that representative government can only work when there is real give and take between the contending parties. The other, that to many men, and many nations, religion means nothing more than antagonism to some other religion. Witness Ulster in Ireland, and witness, equally, Ulster in India.

DON

## CIVIS BRITANNICUS SUM

### Tuesday, February 18, 1913

'Allow me to introduce you to a deportee.' I was talking, before dinner, to a group of young Indians, all Oxford and Cambridge graduates, when this little bomb was exploded. It was a very little one, though clearly it gave satisfaction to the audience; and the occasion of it did not look as if an Imperial Government need have been afraid of him. It may, or may not, have been wise to deport him; I do not pretend to pronounce. But neither ought anyone to pronounce – even the Secretary of State himself – until he has estimated the strength and tenacity of the resentment every deportation leaves behind it in the Indian community. The laughter which greeted this incident was not pleasant for an Englishman to hear. It was not the first time I had heard it; and it will not be the last.

At dinner the conversation flowed freely on art, literature, philosophy, religion. All these men were saturated with English culture. 'They say we hate England and the English,' one of them said. 'It is not true. We love England; we owe to her all we are; but England is not the English Government.' 'No,' said another, 'neither are the English at home the English in India.' And as he spoke, my mind went back to my yesterday's evening among Anglo-Indians – to the talk of polo, racing, and golf, and to the welcome euthanasia of bridge in which these banalities were too tardily extinguished. 'Neither were the English at home the English in India.' I hoped they were not, all of them. But I kept discreet silence.

'To talk to an Englishman from England,' one of them pursued, 'is like breathing fresh air to us. We are in prison. We cannot act our ideas, Government forbids that; we cannot even talk them, except to ourselves. We are cut off from both communities.'

'But do you not associate with the English in India?'

Again that bitter laugh, and then a torrent of anecdotes. This one, of New College, Oxford, had been ordered out of a railway carriage by a subaltern. That one, of Trinity, Cambridge, had been addressed as a 'damned baboo.' Another had been asked what the devil he meant by appearing in English clothes. Another, paying a visit of courtesy, had been summarily shown the door.

I suggested that such episodes were rare. But they would not admit it, nor does it really matter. For one is enough to poison the minds of thousands. I took refuge in England, confident that there at least an Indian gentleman would be treated with courtesy. 'In the universities for example?' Alas! It was the same story. 'Damned nigger' was the undergraduate phrase that had stuck most obstinately in their minds. 'Had they not made friends with English students?' No, they had been left to themselves, happy only if they were not molested. It used to be different, they had heard; but things had changed for the worse. I could not deny it. For even at Oxford and Cambridge the New Imperialism is undermining the Empire.

I fell back upon India itself; I talked of the *pax britannica*; of the efficiency of the Government; of its public works; of its justice; of the growing material prosperity of the country. They would have none of it. When I said 'irrigation,' they replied 'malaria.' When I mentioned railways, they countered with the export of wheat; when I praised the trade returns, they pointed to the dying crafts. I pleaded British justice; they answered, Midnapur and Lajput Rai[1]. There was nothing good the Government has done for which they would give credit. There was nothing evil for which they are responsible themselves for which they did not blame Government.

'Unreasonable.' 'Impracticable.' 'No sense of fact.' Oh, yes, all that! But why? Because they are members of a conquered race, smarting under the sense of it. That first; but that cannot be altered; history is responsible. What can, and must be altered, if the British force in India is to be anything but a soldier smoking on a powder-barrel, is the

---

1. Lajput Rai, an extremist lawyer, from Lahore, was deported in 1907 under a regulation of 1818.

attitude of the conquerors to the conquered. No one who has not been in India can realise the gulf that separates Anglo-Indian[1] from Indian society. The Englishman does not make himself formidable by his overbearing and exclusive ways; he makes himself only hateful and ridiculous. The majority of civilians in India, I believe, are aware of this, but the minority more than neutralise all their efforts. And as to the army! I myself have heard this simple solution propounded – 'to turn the Pathans loose on Bengal to play with the baboos with the bayonet.' Political reform is good and is being pursued on good lines, but it will be useless unless there is also a reform in manners. But a reform in manners means a change of heart.

DON

## The Negro Boxing Champion

Thursday, January 22, 1914

We do not say that the *Times* and others are not right in crying out against prize-fights and boxing shows in which Jack Johnson, the negro pugilist, takes part. But they have rather odd ways of putting it. It all reads as if there were something more which they do not quite like to say. What they most dread is that Johnson should be matched against an Englishman. In that case, as they feel, the Englishman might be beaten; indeed he almost certainly would; and they fear that this would make negroes uppish in British Africa. It has always been a sacred tradition among us that the negro, on the whole, is no good with his fists, and the tradition has the support of numberless cases in which British colonials have related in British bars and smoking-rooms that with one well-placed blow they sent some contumacious nigger spinning, and that the nigger then curled up at once and was permanently improved. This tradition the negro race has been pretty widely asked to imbibe, and it is feared that the good work thus done might be partly undone if it were known that the best negro boxer had beaten the best Englishman. The negro might then begin to extract from the *Times* and adapt to his own case the great anti-suffragist argument that the only proper basis of the right to a vote, and to political power generally, is personal physical strength. Bombardier Wells, the anti-suffragists argue, ought to have a vote, and Mrs. Humphry Ward ought not, because – to put it briefly – Bombardier Wells could knock out Mrs. Humphry Ward when it came to fisticuffs. It is feared that the

1. In 1913, Anglo-Indian did not mean a person of mixed descent, but an Englishman whose career lay in India.

Kaffir might adopt this philosophic doctrine and begin to argue that if
Jack Johnson or Sam Langford were to knock out Bombardier Wells
the negro's title to political power would similarly be established.

## Arts

## THE KNIGHT OF THE BURNING PESTLE[1]
### Saturday, December 26, 1908

Nearly all of *The Knight of the Burning Pestle* was still such good fun on
Thursday night that one felt it must have been wonderful fun in 1611.
Thursday's audience laughed most of the time; imagine how they
would have laughed if the play had made game not of the London
train-bands of 300 years ago, but of the Territorial Army. For *The
Knight of the Burning Pestle* was even more topical than our pantomimes;
it was more like a modern French *revue*, in which the topics of the day
are touched not only by the way, but are the very theme. It says much
for the humour of Beaumont and Fletcher – Beaumont chiefly, we
suppose, as he did the joking part of the syndicate – that all the bur-
lesque part, the parody of tall and steep romance, can still be made so
droll as Mr. Esmé Percy made it at the Gaiety. It is the last triumph of
genius spent on parody to go on living and amusing long after its
victim is dead and buried. You need not read *Amadis de Gaul* to enjoy
*Don Quixote*, nor *Pamela, or Virtue Rewarded* to enjoy *Joseph Andrews*
nor Heywood's *Four Prentices of London* to enjoy *The Knight of the
Burning Pestle*. In each case the parasite has outgrown the thing it grew
upon, until now the places are changed, and what was once the original
work tends to become in turn a parasitic survival, partly kept alive by
the vitality of a jest at its own expense and looked up now and then
by students curious about a great wit's butt.

    The first performance, too, brought out a new, compensatory
interest in the farce, to make up for the staling of some of its allusions.
When staged it is a most vivid 'document' in social and theatrical
history. From all the part about the spectators sitting on the stage,
from the semi-maternal relation of the city man's wife to the apprentice,
from the military passage, and from a score of the critical remarks by
the Citizen and his lady, any amount of authentic learning is to be im-
bibed in an agreeably uneducational-looking manner. One sees now
why historians with a tincture of the artist in them, like Macaulay, and

1. One of Miss Horniman's productions at the Gaiety Theatre, Manchester.

artists with a tincture of the historian, like Scott, went, above all, to old plays for local or temporary colour. On seeing *The Knight of the Burning Pestle* acted whole passages of Macaulay's famous description of seventeenth-century England, their atmosphere and colour, come to the mind, as a portrait does when you see the original, or as Scott's *Fortunes of Nigel* does when you first read Shadwell's *Squire of Alsatia* and come upon the pit from which Scott digged. Whatever the causes of their selection, the smaller touches of life and circumstance that you get in a play, quite by the way, when the dramatist's thoughts perhaps are on some larger matter, seem pre-eminently charged with their time's lifelike expression.

Mr. Hugh Freemantle has painted the pre-Fire London as it is usually painted for modern plays assigned to that period, prettily and quaintly, a little too prettily and quaintly perhaps, in a kind of May-day spirit, like an American's dream of Chester before landing; there is an air of *bijouterie*, a slightly over-cosy snugness and 'contraptiousness,' a slightly over-frisky play of fancy in the building, a vein of sentiment akin to that which equips the 'arty' villa of our time with so many sepulchral little ingle-nooks and bashes so many little window-holes in the wall, anywhere and anyhow, as if by artillery fire from a distance. But will no one give us on the stage a vision of the old London or Paris with its mire and harsh gloom, presented perhaps with an art less explicit and circumstantial and with more half-seen and half-suggested things to set imagination working?

Of the acting, Mrs. Theodore Wright's was best. Besides all her humour and spirit and clearness of characterisation (as the Citizen's wife) she seemed to hold the whole piece together and to create single-handed, against all difficulties, a vehement impression of the genuineness of her spectatorship and, through it, of the genuineness of the theatre within the theatre. It was a splendid illustration of the way in which the best acting not only makes a character live, but sheds reality over everything and everybody round it. Mr. Esmé Percy was the man for Ralph. He brought to it a chubby face, all curves, like an infant Bacchus, and the effectiveness of Ralph's thunderous rant issuing from the principal dimple of this pleasing countenance was a lesson in the value of contrast. It was as funny as the terrific baying that sometimes proceeds so unaccountably from the person of some little dachshund.

C.E.M.[1]

1. C. E. Montague

# THE WINTER'S TALE[1]

Monday, January 16, 1911

Mr. Flanagan has sometimes been accused of eking out Shakespere with irrelevant delights, and on Saturday evening he gave us a taste of his quality in procession and dance before we got to the real stuff of the play. But the strictly dramatic action of *A Winter's Tale* would hardly grip a popular audience, and still less, perhaps, a sophisticated one, so we must not blame Mr. Flanagan for making Shakspere go. This is his business, and he does it splendidly. Shakspere, no doubt, saw that he had some responsibility, too, for making things go, and to this we owe Autolycus. He is one of the glories of the play, but he has very little to do with it. Shakspere, we may surmise, did have his audience very much in mind, and Autolycus did not come on before he was wanted. The jolly lyrical impulse that he gives is invaluable, and Mr. Ryder Boys enjoyed himself so thoroughly in the part that he infected the audience. Mr. Flanagan could hardly have looked at the play if it had not been for Autolycus, and we may conceive Shakspere stretching a hand across the centuries to the enterprising manager. We are always conscious of this collaborator, and in one of the stage directions he must have seen the chance of a lifetime. We remember his herd of deer and perfect realism of stones in the running brooks in the Forest of Arden, but, the famous 'Exit, pursued by a bear' is a greater test of a manager's resources, and it can never have been more nobly met. It was a real bear – small, perhaps, but formidable – and it appeared to be making straight for Antigonus. After that we could forgive a *première danseuse* in a pastoral.

Everything went finely on Saturday, and the machinery was in wonderfully good order for a first night, but the acting was not very good. It would be a pleasure to praise a Leontes who worked so hard as Mr. Percy Rhodes, and we may in part blame Shakspere if he did not give us much pleasure. Leontes falls short of the tragic quality, and it must be less difficult to act tragedy than to make something approximately human of such a blusterer. Mr. Rhodes does violence to his speeches, and we could forgive him if he did some kind of violence to his or Shakspere's conception of the character. Perhaps, however, the performance all round suffers from the natural desire to make the most of things. There were times when we felt that unstressed words were best and that the actors would do well to discard gestures that may have carried some meaning once but have lost it. The performance of

1. Richard Flanagan's production at the Queen's Theatre, Manchester.

Shakspere is very much traditional, and perhaps there is, too, something of tradition in our reception of *A Winter's Tale*. It was with some
sense of personal failure and insufficiency that one made so little of it
on Saturday, while others, it seems, could fall naturally into the attitude
of reverence or enthusiasm. Mr. Flanagan's scenery and dresses and
properties were all very fine and grand on the scale that we have come
to expect from him, and everyone seemed to be delighted with the
production.

The trouble is that the poetry hardly came home to us, and the rest is
paraphernalia.

                                                                 A.N.M.[1]

Nevertheless the production ran till after Easter at the Queen's
Theatre, Manchester.


# GILBERT MURRAY ON MONTAGUE[2]

## Thursday, February 9, 1911

Mr. Montague never lets the wish to be amusing predominate over the
wish to make a true judgment, neither does he mind showing quite
frankly that in the main dramatic movements of the day he is firmly on
the side of the angels. Not that his tastes are narrow. In the chapter on
good acting he gives Mr. Robey of the music halls a high place between
Coquelin and Janet Achurch. But in the general distribution of the
book you find that the few plays which really matter – Ibsen's, Shaw's,
Synge's, Masefield's, and the like – bulk large, and those which do not
matter scarcely appear.

Mr. Montague has judged fearlessly and sincerely, and has earned, if
any of us have, the chance of feeling some time or other before we are
dead that at some real turning point in the history of the English
theatre we were on the side that was right then and that afterwards
won.

If we are to search for points on which to criticise or supplement Mr.
Montague, we might argue that perhaps he is a little carried off his
balance by the Irish drama; that, with all its sincerity and eloquence, it
remains an instrument of very restricted range, not capable of dealing
with large regions of life, and even that, like all brilliant and vital
movements, it must now look carefully lest it fall into mannerism and

---

1  A. N. Monkhouse
2.  A review of *Dramatic Values*, a collection of Montague's theatre notices. Murray
was professor of Greek at Oxford, translator of *Euripides*.

affectation. In another place we might suggest that Ibsen the permanent artist suffered from Ibsen the pioneer. He invented so much that he never had time or peace of mind to make his work smooth. Every living playwright has to learn from him, but his own plays strike one as out of date or at least old-fashioned.

The last essay, on 'The Wholesome Play,' gave me such intense enjoyment that I hardly dare to add a word to what it says. Its analysis of the wholesome play as the play which flatters the egoistic dreams of man in his lazy and well-fed hours completely convinces me. But I have a kind of sympathy – a remote intellectual sympathy, like that of a naturalist with snakes – for our natural enemy the Philistine who craves for 'wholesome plays.' For one thing, as Mr. Montague sees, we ask too much of him. We artists put the whole of our working day into our craft, and want it to be a great thing and sincere, and such as to fill our souls. But he, poor man, comes to it, as he explains, when he has finished his work and only wants play. If he had nothing else to do he would not mind working hard at Meredith or Ibsen, as we have done, but how should we like, after working at literature till four o'clock, to be set adding accounts – even the funniest or most illuminating accounts – in the evening? No, the question where an artist can safely or reasonably look for a proper audience is a question too painful for these columns. And, again, when the Philistine calls our problem plays 'unwholesome' I am naturally annoyed, yet I always remember a stout, straight-backed man at a performance of the Stage Society's who waved his hand towards the audience, intelligent and Bohemian-looking as usual, and said: 'I don't mind reconsidering my moral code, but I'm blowed if I will take my new one from these people.' From his tone I think he did us a wrong, but still – . However, I do not suppose Mr. Montague would repudiate these mild pleas in mitigation of sentence. In any case, at a time when Shaw and Galsworthy are silent and Masefield has retired into the fortress of the Stage Society and Granville Barker is driven from the theatre to the music hall and William Archer writes chiefly about Spain and reformed spelling, and there seems hardly a bright spot on the horizon, this book shines like a good deed in a naughty world.

GILBERT MURRAY

# THE GUILT OF MR. CHESTERTON
## Wednesday, August 9, 1911

'The criminal is the creative artist; the detective only the critic,' mourns Valentin, chief of the Paris police, on the ninth page of this blood-red fairy-book. There's a nasty implication in the thought perhaps – yet it isn't mere professional resentment that makes one sternly retort that *The Innocence of Father Brown* fairly proves the guilt of Mr. Chesterton. He has been accused of many crimes by our literary Valentins – of undue flippancy, of undue earnestness, of a proneness to platitude, of a weakness for paradox; but perhaps the true charge against him, underlying all these, is that he is too big for his books. That, on the face of it, might not seem much more culpable than palming off sovereigns for shillings – and, indeed, there are extenuating circumstances. For the first four or five of these dozen 'detective' tales are really simply golumptious; *The Blue Cross, The Secret Garden, The Queer Feet, The Flying Stars* – their names alone are enough to set the blood simmering as it used to do on Boxing-nights, when the pantomimes were pantomimes still; – and the tales themselves beat their titles as easily as the harlequinade did the simpering ballets. The centre of each is some madcap, incredible crime, worked out with a lunatic exactness and intricacy, and then hidden cunningly away in the midst of conspicuously meek and mild accessories – among sweetshops in Camden Town, placid villas in Putney, policemen and postmen and matter-of-fact porters. This done – solution safe, and relying on his own ready wit to bring the wildest irrelevance to heel – 'G. K. C.' fairly lets himself go. Round we are rattled, pelted with puns and wild poetry, at the heels of little moon-faced Father Brown, till at length in some blind alley, with reason on the verge of revolt, the baffling eye of the problem blandly opens and executes a solemn wink. And the effect of fantasy is famously heightened, just as it is in a harlequinade, by the vivid realism of the figures and scenes. Mr. Chesterton has the poet's gift for seeing the most commonplace things – moons or men's faces, hills, street lamps and houses – with a startling freshness and suddenness, as though they had been but that instant made; and since epithet and object leap into his mind together – since he has, undeniably, the power of seizing the one golden word and planking it down with a rollicking bang – the old familiar places past which the rout pours shed their old shabbiness wondrously, shine out with the sudden significance of places washed by a dawn.

It is when he (the reader) is half-way through the book that he becomes aware of a sudden change – a change so sinister that he may very well wonder whether the madness has not mounted to his head. He gets the dark indescribable sensation of being in the presence of something actually evil. All the violence and vividness become horribly akin to the insane lucidity of nightmare. Yet, queerly, as he perceives on reflection, this change coincides with another which seems a pure triumph of virtue. Flambeau, the great criminal, the author of the fantastic crimes he has been tracking hitherto, suddenly repents; and Father Brown is at liberty to roam more largely about the world, holding Flambeau by the hand, a brand snatched from the burning, like a little dumpty Dante tripping beside a big blond Virgil. But instead of the light from this Flambeau falling on sins of an ever-increasing freshness and fantasy – outrages so utterly outrageous that we laugh at them as at the red-hot pokers and battered policemen of pantomime, – we pass into places where things unspeakable prowl and spawn as though we were indeed winding down the circles of some hell.

It is a violence that seems somehow daemonic. It is a vividness like the unclean clarity that comes with drugs. It is like moving in a world of gargoyles, among the devils on Notre Dame. It is the evil of ugliness, of deformity – and the deformity is fundamentally due to the disparity between energy and outlet. It is this inadequacy that drives the perspectives mad and fills the trees with a frightening energy, – hints at solemn significance where there is none and darkens impossible crimes, till they swell into symbols of Sin. 'Pooh!' cries Mr. Chesterton cheerily. 'You are too easily terrified nowadays. The men who carved gargoyles did it out of jollity, sitting in the sun and drinking ale like brothers.' Maybe; but at least they did it to lighten an ancient faith, not to give weight to a joke. Perhaps it isn't such an innocent thing to give away sovereigns for shillings. There is such a thing as degrading the currency. Something might surely be said about images and superscriptions.

And, instead? Well, we suppose it is true that we can never hope to see Mr. Chesterton clinging to the face of some cathedral cheerily chiselling away; and the vision of him booted and spurred, leading his men at the charge is doubtless also doomed to remain just a figure in a dream. And to speak of poetic dramas is also perhaps too optimistic; Mr. Trench leaving the Haymarket and all. But there is one fine form of art – a little ailing just now, it is true, but immensely capable of revitalisation – which would give him just the scope he requires. It calls for pageantry, poetry, and puns with an equal distinctness; it could both tower up into great symbols and sprawl into boisterous

jokes; it ought to be as merry as a Christmas party; and it is a true
child of the grim old moralities. Exactly! Come down, O Chesterton,
from yonder madcap height, and write us – the perfect pantomime.

DIXON SCOTT[1]

## THE LANSDOWNE REMBRANDT
### Friday, March 3, 1911

A wealthy American offers the enormous price of £100,000 for a
famous Rembrandt landscape;[2] and the owner, Lord Lansdowne, a
prominent statesman, the political spokesman of a majority of the
peerage, and one of the greatest figures in the nobility, offers it to the
nation for the same figure, with the generous promise that he himself
will contribute £5,000 to the purchase fund. That is to say, Lord
Lansdowne, instead of accepting £100,000 from America, will give his
picture to the nation for £95,000. How long this munificent and
patriotic offer remains open we do not know, for the casual and meagre
announcement by the Director of the National Gallery to the *Times*
gives no particulars, but already the National Art Collections Fund
Committee is considering a public appeal for funds.

We are to have a repetition, it seems, of the strange episodes which
accompanied the proceedings of the Duke of Norfolk and Messts.
Colnaghi over the Holbein portrait. In that affair a dealer was concerned as well as a duke, and Messrs. Colnaghi were actually the
vendors. But in the present case a marquis in high position, one of the
leaders of half the nation, is acting alone. About the comic process of
Lord Lansdowne's 'subscribing' part of the purchase money which
will go to himself there is nothing to be said, except that it would have
been better frankly to have offered the picture to the nation at the
lower price and left the question of subscription alone. But what are
we to think of the kind of public spirit which coolly prepares to send
abroad what, though it is in private hands, is one of the nation's
treasures, and makes no better acknowledgement of the virtual
trusteeship which belongs to every possessor of an art treasure than a
limited option and a 5 per cent discount? As the *Telegraph* well and
wittily remarks, *noblesse oblige* must henceforward be written *noblesse
n'oblige plus*. And what kind of hope can we have now that the public
spirit and pride which have restrained many poorer and not less
honourable owners from parting with their treasures will survive
when such an example is shown? An old master to an American

1. Pseudonym of Walter Scott.          2. 'The Mill'

millionaire is a passport of social eminence, and as such acquires a
huge and unreal value dictated by scarcity and by no relation to artistic
merit. To Lord Lansdowne it ought to be a treasure held in trust for his
country and with its special dowry of pleasure and pride to himself.
But our great nobles are teaching us that this is an old-fashioned view.
We are now expected to buy the art treasures that we thought belonged to us because their owners were our countrymen in the open
market with a 5 per cent preference. *Noblesse n'oblige plus.*


## Manchester and Thirlmere

Tuesday, January 31, 1911

*To the Editor of the 'Manchester Guardian'*

Sir, [The Lord Mayor of Manchester] is reported as saying, 'Ruskin
in the past had talked about the spoiling of scenery; but if Ruskin could
come to life again he would admit that the City Council had actually
improved the scenery instead of damaging it.' It is pleasing to note
that Ruskin, if he could have accepted the Lord Mayor's invitation,
would have taken the City Council's view of the situation. It is well,
perhaps, that Ruskin cannot accept it. If he could return to meet the
Corporation, I should much like to be present at the interview. I do
not know what my dear old friend and master would say. But I can
imagine that he would at once ask what mandate Manchester obtained,
when it got its Water Bill, to set about the improvement of Lake
District scenery. He might ask very pertinently if heavy stone copings
and iron railings and dressed gate-posts of red Arran stone and the
tops of stone walls, disfigured by cement, and blue Welsh slates imported into a countryside within hail of the Borrowdale slate quarries,
and suburban laurel shrubberies trimmed and cut round the approaches
to their water well-tower had done anything to improve the natural
scenery of the vale. He might further inquire in what way the destruction of the wild beauty of Shoulthwaite Moss, got rid of in the process
of tidying up, had added to the scenic charm. I am sure he would have
congratulated the Lord Mayor on the result of his three weekends in
Thirlmere last summer and be glad to know that he was thereby
enabled to assure his audience that he was delighted with the scenery.

But Ruskin, as I knew him, dealt not only with generalities but
would descend to particulars. He would ask the Lord Mayor what the
inhabitants of the Lake District used to think about the beauty of
Launchy Ghyll and whether, having visited Launchy Ghyll last sum-

mer, the Lord Mayor had visited it since the destruction of the oak wood on its banks. Perhaps he would refer to the pictures of that destruction which appear in the *Manchester Guardian* of to-day. He might then perhaps have gone on to ask if the Lord Mayor seriously contended that any one of the oak trees under Fisher Crag overhung the Lake, or were in any real way a menace to the purity of their famous water supply, whether, as a matter of fact, there was not a whole strip of fell-side meadow land intervening between the wood and the Lake. He would inquire next what was meant by his assertion that 'they had to cut down trees that were of no use to them,' and if he really believed that it was any answer to those who objected to the wholesale destruction of the most beautiful thing they had on their property, not for gain and against the wishes of a minority of the Waterworks Committee, to say that for every oak that had been cut down they had planted magnanimously somewhere else upon the estate ten larch or spruce seedlings. For, after all, that is the only answer that has been given as palliation for the cruel outrage upon the fairest bit of Lakeside scenery in the custody of Manchester.

I think Ruskin would have gone further. He would have said: 'If you think that by treating your Manchester Corporation property at Thirlmere or as much of it as is not available pasture simply as a nursery of serviceable timber for the wood merchants and, if regardless of scenic effect, you have determined to afforest your land throughout with spruce and larch, at least you should have remembered that there are tens of thousands who prefer the bare shoulder and the unrobed splendour of Helvellyn and the lower slopes of Armboth Fell unhidden and undisfigured by monotonous belts of conifers.' He might have added, 'Do you really believe that you have added to the beauty of the scene by so cutting down your woodland as to expose to view the new quarry that you have just opened by the side of the road near Launchy Ghyll? You say that you are cutting down all trees that are of no use to you, but you are subject to the Sawfly pest and you need all the birds you can get to fight your battle with it. If this oak grove did nothing else for you, it tended to foster bird life.'

And he would, I believe, have emphatically have added that the use of these venerable oaks was not only for bird life, but for the rejoicing of the eyes of passers-by and the strengthening and refreshing of the souls of weary men. 'Your own expert,' he might finally have replied, 'reported that his instructions were to improve the old woods and plantations.' 'Do you seriously contend then,' Ruskin would say, 'that it is any improvement to old plantations to clean up the trees from ground to head and leave them under bare poles, and was it contemplated that the only improvement of the old oak wood that appeared possible to the Manchester authority should take the form of improving it from off the face of the earth?' Yours, &c.

*January* 30                                                    H. D. RAWNSLEY

# Election Talk 1910[1]

## Monday, November 21, 1910

It tickled Shakspere once to work out the contrast between the usual talk of men ripe for victory and the usual talk of men ripe for defeat – between the firmness, restraint, and directness of the chief speakers in the English camp on the eve of Agincourt, and the fantastic vaunts, insolences, and scurrilities in the camp of the French. It is a misfortune for Shakspere, as he had this interest, to have died before he could have read the *Observers* and *Daily Telegraphs* of our day. Read Mr. Garvin. It seems to be all about 'charlatan partisanship,' 'hypocrisy in hysterics standing on its head,' 'hacks,' 'gangs,' 'baggage-smashers,' 'Buffalo bagmen,' 'dollar domination' (he means no offence to the Lords), and 'humbugs in convulsions;' at every few sentences somebody 'wipes his feet upon the Government of grovel' or the country 'is going to spew out of its mouth' somebody with whom the polite writer very slightly disagrees. 'I will trot a mile to-morrow,' says Shakespere's French prince before Agincourt,' and my way shall be paved with English faces.'

---

1. From one of Montague's almost daily General Election leaders. J. L. Garvin was editor of the *Observer*.

# CHAPTER SEVEN

# A Liberal at War

*

The chapter begins with the outbreak of war and ends, not with a peace treaty, but an armistice. It starts with Lloyd George, C. P. Scott's closest political associate, as Asquith's most powerful cabinet minister; it ends with him as prime minister and the nation's hero. Meanwhile the foundations of a Jewish National Home in Palestine had been laid, two revolutions in Russia had shaken the world, and the end of the real United Kingdom was assured by the obtuseness with which, for example, leaders of the Easter Rising were nursed back to life in order to be executed, as the *Guardian* put it, 'in a tribute to that sense of symmetry which stands in place of justice.' At home conscription brought the problem of conscientous objectors and, contrary to normal English experience, our practice proved less humane than our theory. Labour unrest of a new kind was apparent before the end of the war. On all these matters there was a characteristic *Guardian* view which is reflected in the following extracts.

In *Guardian* internal history the most marked feature was the absence of C. E. Montague who boyishly dyed his hair and enlisted. In 1916 Scott reached the age of 70 in the middle of the busiest period of his editorship. Military commentaries kept Sidebotham fully occupied until he went to the *Times* in the last months of the war. L. T. Hobhouse wrote many leaders, but Scott himself was his own principal leader writer.

# Prospect of War

## DEATH OF A SOCIALIST

### Saturday, August 1, 1914

#### M. Jaurès,[1] the French Socialist leader, has been assassinated in Paris

*From our Correspondent*[2]

Paris, Friday Night

Grave as is the international situation even the probable imminence of war has been overshadowed for the moment in Paris by the appalling crime this evening of which I was an eye-witness. It is impossible to one who knew M. Jaurès, whom one could not help loving, to write about it calmly with the grief fresh upon one. I was dining with a member of my family and a friend at the Café du Croissant, the well-known resort of journalists in the Rue Montmartre close to many newspaper offices including that of the *Humanité*. M. Jaurès was also dining there with some Socialist deputies and members of the staff of the *Humanité*. He came in later than we did. I spoke to him just as he entered and had a short conversation with him about the prospects of war and peace. Like everyone else, he feared that war was probable, but he still had some faith that Sir Edward Grey might succeed in inducing Germany to be conciliatory. If some sort of conference could be arranged, he thought, peace might even yet be secured; and if the French Government would bring pressure to bear on Russia and the German Government on Austria an arrangement might be possible. He added, however, that he feared the French Government might not do that. What a crime war will be and what a monstrous folly. The last words that he said to me was an inquiry about M. Anatole France, who, he said, must be deeply distressed by the situation.

At about half-past nine, when we were just finishing dinner, two pistol shots suddenly resounded in the restaurant. At first we did not understand what had happened, and for a moment thought that there was shooting in the street outside. Then we saw that M. Jaurès had fallen sideways on the bench on which he was sitting, and the screams of the women who were present told us of the murder. It should be explained that M. Jaurès and his friends were sitting on a bench with

1. Jean Jaurès (1859–1914), leader of French Socialist party and editor of *Humanité*.
2. Robert Dell.

their backs to the open window of the restaurant, and the shots were fired from the street through the window. M. Jaurès was shot in the head, and the murderer must have held the pistol close to his victim. A surgeon was hastily summoned, but he could do nothing, and M. Jaurès died quietly without regaining consciousness a few minutes after the crime. Meanwhile the murderer had been seized and handed over to the police, who had to protect him from the crowd which had quickly collected in the street. At that hour in the evening the Rue Montmartre is filled with newsvendors waiting for the late editions of the evening papers.

It is said that the murderer is a member of the Royalist society Action Française, but I have not yet been able to discover whether this report is true or not. A more cold-blooded and cowardly murder was never committed. The scene in and about the restaurant was heartrending; both men and women were in tears and their grief was terrible to see. It is as yet too early to say what the effect of the murder will be, but it may be considerable. M. Jaurès has died a victim to the cause of peace and humanity.

In any case the French Chauvinists and reactionaries cannot escape a large share of the responsibility for this murder. For years their organs in the press have been denouncing M. Jaurès as a traitor sold to Germany, and the language used by the *Action Française* has been almost a direct incitement to his assassination. Even such comparatively moderate Chauvinist papers as the *Temps* have bandied the charge of treason recklessly. I have known M. Jaurès well, and a more simple-hearted man I never met in my life. He was absolutely free from personal vanity and personal ambition, and gave up the whole of his life to the cause of Socialism and peace. His death is a terrible loss to the Socialist party in France which cannot replace him without the very greatest difficulty.

It is the intention of the Government to issue a proclamation to the people of Paris expressing the national mourning at the death of M. Jaurès and calling upon the people of Paris to remain calm.

A register has been opened at the offices of the *Humanité* in order that the people may express their sympathy. Hundreds of people are outside the office waiting to come in.

# THE LAST DAY OF PEACE

Tuesday, August 4, 1914
*From Our Parliamentary Correspondent*[1]

Westminster, Monday Night
Rather less than two hours sufficed to-day for the essential passages of
the strangest, the most moving, and in every sense of the word the
most fateful sitting of Parliament within living memory. In some of its
accessories the scene was almost theatrical. Although there have been
half-a-dozen occasions this session when the House has been more
crowded, it had been thought necessary to revive a precedent not
previously invoked since the Home Rule Bill of 1893, and to cover the
centre of the floor with double rows of chairs. Moreover, the peers
had been admitted to their gallery before prayers, a privilege which
spared them the indignity of a rush-and-tumble invasion in common
with the general public.

Sir Edward Grey rose to take the nation into the confidence of the
Cabinet. Every word of his skilfully phrased and profoundly moving
argument had been committed to manuscript, the pages of which now
lay open before its author on the box at the corner of the table. As
could be perceived from the placidity with which they endured the
suspense of a narrative that kept less privileged hearers in an agony of
alternating encouragement and despair, the Opposition leaders were
already aware of what was coming. Consequently they took no part in
the rival demonstrations – neither in the faint applause of the Minis-
terialists as some fitful gleam of hope seemed to brighten the horizon
nor in the fierce outbursts of acclamation with which the Unionists
hailed every additional portent of the gathering storm. Ministers sat
through it all in the tense attitude of men oppressed by a sense of heavy
and solemn responsibility.

For a long time the Foreign Minister kept his hearers in a state of
almost torturing uncertainty. On the surface the earlier part of his
statement seemed to be a justification for neutrality, or relative in-
action. It was made clear that until Sunday we had given no promise of
more than diplomatic support. Not only so, but we were not parties
to the Franco-Russian Alliance and did not even know the terms of it.
Even so, our longstanding friendship with France – 'And with Germany,' interjected a Liberal member – had led to arrangements which,
in Sir Edward's opinion, involved us in certain responsibilities.

1. James Drysdale

Of these the heaviest turned out to be the undefended condition of the northern and western coasts of France due to the withdrawal of the French fleet to the Mediterranean. Here a hypothetical case was presented – the possible event of an attack on these coasts by the German fleet and of ourselves looking on as dispassionate spectators. With greater energy than he had hitherto shown, Sir Edward, raising his voice and speaking with unusual emphasis, declared that in such an event we could not possibly stand aside. 'Hurrah for France!' shouted Mr. William Redmond[1], while, swayed by the same impulse, Mr. Arthur Lynch half rose to his feet and waved his handkerchief.

Strange to say, those ebullitions of feeling were succeeded by an obvious sense of disappointment on the Opposition benches as the Minister went on to explain that help was only to be forthcoming in the event of hostile operations by the German fleet against France in the Channel or in the North Sea. Soon, however, the war feeling was revived. Faint Liberal and Labour cheers welcomed the disclosure of Germany's undertaking in return for a pledge of British neutrality not to attack the northern coasts of France. 'I only heard that offer just before I came into the house,' Sir Edward observed, 'but it is far too narrow an engagement' – words promptly cheered to the echo by the Opposition. In any case, there was the more serious question of the invasion of Belgian territory, culminating this very afternoon in an impassioned appeal by the King of the Belgians to the British Government for yet further diplomatic intervention.

From this point on Sir Edward Grey's tone became more and more determined, almost, as the Opposition seemed to assume, more and more warlike. To the integrity and independence of Belgium the highest and most vital importance was attached. If that went, we were solemnly warned, the independence of Holland would follow, and then what of the fate of British interests?

Mr. Redmond, who spoke amid frequent outbursts of Unionist cheering, testified to the accuracy of an observation by Sir Edward Grey as to the state of feeling in Ireland – that it was 'the one bright spot in the whole of this terrible situation.' So true was this tribute that, according to the Nationalist leader, the Government might withdraw all their troops from Ireland to-morrow and Catholics and Protestants would be found united in the common defence of their country against foreign attack.

If a section of the Opposition could have had their way no further

---

1. (1861–1917) younger brother of John Redmond, the Irish Nationalist leader; killed in Flanders on active Service. Lynch (1861–1934), Nationalist M.P., had fought for the Boers in 1900 and been Paris correspondent of the *Daily Mail*.

speeches would have been heard. Some impatience was shown when
Mr. Ramsay MacDonald, in his firm yet temperate manner, was giving
voice to the determination of the Labour Party to have no part in a
policy of war, and a little later other critics of the Ministerial position
were threatened for a moment or two with closure by clamour.
Happily this tendency to intolerance soon wore off, and for the rest of
the night the House listened in sombre stillness to speech after speech
from the Liberal benches, all, with scarcely an exception, severely
critical of the Foreign Minister's arguments and actions.

## War Observed

## BY H. W. NEVINSON ON GALLIPOLI

In 1915 Nevinson accompanied the expedition to the Dardan-
elles, was wounded, but returned to Suvla before the evacuation.
Throughout the war the work of many leading war correspondents appeared in the paper but, except in this instance, the
*Guardian* was sharing the cost of other papers' men. Here it took
the lead.

### Friday, April 14, 1916

#### THE WITHDRAWAL

December 21, 1915[1]

The stores began to go first, slowly. Various ruses and accidents served
to deceive the enemy, who even thought that the increased number of
ships off the bay signified a strongly renewed attack about Christmas.
To maintain this apprehension, parties of our men were taken off at
night and returned by day, like a stage army. On the final day, an ironic
order commanded that the immemorial custom of our men showing
themselves on the skyline should be carefully maintained, and we all
did our best to serve our country by walking everywhere round Suvla
in the enemy's sight. Orders were further received that mule-carts
were to be driven slowly up and down. The mules were singular fine
animals; happily all were saved at Suvla, and nearly all at Anzac.
Native Indians managed them as though mules were well-trained dogs,
and served with great patience and fortitude, even under the severe
trial of tempest and frost.

After the strain of carefully organised preparations, the excitement

1. Held up by the censor for four months.

of the final hours was extreme, but no signs of anxiety were shown. Would the sea remain calm? Would the moon remain veiled in a thin cloud? Would the brigades keep time and place? Our own guns continued firing duly till the moment for withdrawal came. Our rifles kept up an intermittent fire, and sometimes came sudden outbursts from the Turks. An aeroplane whirred overhead, but was invisible. We could not be sure it was our own until we saw a green star blaze for a few seconds just below Saturn. On the earth a few fires still blazed where camps or dug-outs were once inhabited, but gradually they went out. Only far off the hospital tents along the curving shore showed lights, and there were only two of these. The sea glimmered white through a moonlit haze, and over its surface thin black lines kept moving. Could an enemy see, or could he possibly miss the significance of those thin black lines?

Mules neighed, chains rattled, steamers hooted low, and sailor men shouted into megaphones language strong enough to carry a hundred miles. Still the enemy showed no sign of life or hearing, though he lay almost visible in the moonlight across the familiar scene of bay and plain and hills to which British soldiers have given such unaccustomed names. So the critical hours went by slowly, and yet giving so little time for all to be done. At last the final bands of silent defenders began to come in from the nearest lines. Sappers began to come in, cutting all telephone wires and signals on their way. Some sappers came after arranging slow fuses to kindle our few abandoned stores of biscuits, bully beef, and bacon left in the bends of the shore. Silently the staffs began to go. The officers of the beach party, who had accomplished such excellent and sleepless work, collected. With a smile they heard the distant blast of Turks still labouring at the trenches – a peculiar instance of labour lost. Just before three a pinnace took me off to one of the battleships. At half-past three the last-ditchers put off. From our familiar northern point of Suvla Bay itself, I am told, the General commanding the Ninth Army Corps was himself the last to leave, motioning his chief of staff to go first. So the Suvla expedition came to an end after more than five months of existence. I do not discuss policy, but the leaving of the existence well became it.

At six on Monday a bugle rallied the battleship crew to quarters for action. The darkness was illuminated by great fires of our stores and rubbish. In the morning at seven the Turks were evidently puzzled, but not realising the truth, they poured shells into the fire, with purpose obscure. Meantime our picket boats had searched the shore, but found no stragglers, not even an army doctor, left behind. At nine she (the battleship) turned and left the scene, passing westward to an island harbour over the tranquil sunlit sea, and I think we are unlikely to land at Suvla again.

One could mention names if names were allowed, but the whole army and navy engaged in the operation must share the honour. Besides, one must include the fortune which attends adventure. As it was, the movement was hurried forward by one day. It ended at nine yesterday morning. At nine to-day a south-west wind is raging, the sea roars upon our coast, and rain falls in a deluge. What if the decision had been delayed those few hours?

## BY HERBERT SIDEBOTHAM FROM CROSS ST.

### Tuesday, July 18, 1916

#### SOME NOTES ON THE OFFENSIVE
#### *By a Student of War*[1]

Sir Douglas Haig, in his despatch of yesterday, announces the surrender of the remnants of the garrison of Ovillers. What its original size was is not stated, but the number of prisoners is two officers and 124 Guardsmen. Even if we suppose that the original was twenty times that number, it means that some 2,000 to 3,000 men have delayed many times their numbers for a fortnight. General Haig compliments the garrison of Ovillers on its bravery, and no doubt the compliment was deserved. But what their prolonged resistance really means is that we have not yet found an answer to the machine-gun. The attack was equally brave, but it has been held up all this time, and its losses have been equally great if not greater than those of the defence. Is not the true moral that for special work like this of capturing a ruined village held by a handful of desperate men with machine-guns we need some special equipment? To expose human flesh and blood to the malignity of machine-guns is not scientific war but the untutored valour of the savage. What we seem to need for operations of this nature is some kind of armour which would enable the attack to get to close quarters with the defence without suffering such heavy losses. The defence is in effect wearing armour – the armour of a wall of bullets from their machine-guns besides the wall of masonry. The attack should have armour too, and as in these close operations the support of heavy artillery is out of the question the real parallel is not with anything known in field operations but with street fighting. In Dublin

1. Herbert Sidebotham. This comment on the battle of the Somme antedates the first use of tanks in warfare by two months, and of helicopters by a generation.

street fighting one of the most successful devices was mounting a Scotch boiler filled with men with a machine-gun on a motor. With this protection they were able to go down the narrowest streets and gain access to the tenements which the rebels were defending.[1] This Scotch boiler was in effect an example of collective armour, like the testudo which the Roman soldiers used in their assaults or the still more primitive Trojan horse. The Russians are said to have used enormous steel shields in some of their attacks in this war. The popular mind always conceives success or failure in war in terms of individual valour or moral qualities. The scientific spirit holds that there is very little difference between the moral qualities of civilised nations, and thinks of victory or defeat in terms of equipment or of tactics. The whole history of infantry tactics is capable of being written in these terms. By equipping our army with steel helmets we have given away the principle of light equipment. If you have steel helmets there is no reason why you should not have breast-plates and greaves, and certainly no reason why the attack should not use shields – whether mounted on wheels or carried by the individual soldier is a question for detailed experiment. The future war will almost certainly see two types of infantry – the heavy armed hoplite with shield and body armour, who will be used in storming, and the light infantry for rapid manœuvre in the open. We could imagine quite a small army of this kind with heavy armed infantry and a light infantry, mounted on aeroplanes for preference, beating ten or a dozen times its number of conventionally armed soldiers. We are too ready to call on valour to make good the faults of equipment, too ready to call on moral qualities to redress the stupidity of our conservatism; and it is arguable that the very worst enemies of advancement and progress in the art of war are those whose minds and souls do not revolt against the enormous casualties of modern war, but apologise for crass conservatism by endowing it with moral virtues.

1. See page 342-3

## IN SOLDIERS' TALES

The *Guardian* 'back page' gave young men in the Forces a chance
to keep their hand in and transmute their experience into words.
The first 'back-pager' is by a reporter from another paper who in
later years, now himself a *Guardian* man, recalled with gratitude
and delight the letter he, an unknown private, had received from
C. P. Scott. The second is by a *Guardian* sub-editor who had been
killed in action before his story appeared.

### MÈRE LAGNIER

#### Friday, December 15, 1916

She was portly and vigorous, like most of the women of her race. A
shade over fifty, there was none of the marks of age upon her, and her
day-long activities in the little café where foregathered the English
soldiers from their reserve billets confirmed the impression of essential
youth.

But in her eyes dwelt the look which belongs to all the women of the
invaded provinces – the women, proud and staunch as their menfolk,
who have seen civilisation ebb away from their farms and their artisan
dwellings and yet have remained. It is the expression of a soul that has
known war, that has lived in the very throes of it, and tasted all its
horrors only a little less fully than the soldier himself. A look of pene-
trating sadness, it may never be effaced from the present generation of
Frenchwomen in Flanders, in Artois, in Champagne.

The 4.7 battery by the slag-heap would open, and the explosion of
the charge would rattle the shattered windows of the untenanted
dwellings.

'It is the English who bombard, then, to-day? Is it not so?' Mère
Lagnier would inquire, without raising her eyes from the eggs splutter-
ing in their pool of melted butter on the stove. 'What is it that you say?
Coffee and some butter and some bread? Toute suite, mon enfant.'

The German guns would be teased into reply. One – two – three
shells would plough the ground around the wrecked colliery shaft, and
the repercussion would vibrate through the abandoned village. The
search for the battery would continue. Suppose the search should extend
to the village itself. It wasn't improbable. It had happened before, and
with what consequences Mère Lagnier knew full well. But her native
tranquillity had never deserted her in presence of these dread un-
certainties. And so now. If it came, it came. Meanwhile, Mère Lagnier,

her strong, competent arms bared to the elbow, goes about wiping the oilcloth table-tops against the coming of her English soldier clients – mes enfants.

One enters. There is a coffee to be served and a tale to be told. It is told in English, but it is an old tale and easy of comprehension. A shell has fallen by the coal sidings, and two gunners of the Royal Garrison Artillery have gone to their last bivouac. Mère Lagnier pauses from her duties as the narration proceeds and, resuming her ministrations at the eternal stove, murmurs 'Les pauvres garçons.' And then, as in an anger of recollection, 'Les sales Boches!'

'Yet another coffee, my friend? But yes, at once.'

That is all. These incidents have lost their power to shock. They awaken in that motherly heart but a dull pain, unexpressed, perhaps inexpressible.

And how well we remember her on that September morning – the morning of the great battle. Mes enfants had gone up a few days before for the attack, and strange, fresh units were moving up in their place. The artillery, furious for days, had swollen to a terrific diapason during the night. The flash of the guns and the flare of the starlights all seemed intended to reveal in its utter abjectness the derelict village of P———. That tragic jumble of half-wrecked miners' dwellings, caught in the vivid glare, epitomised every brutality of war. Of its once thriving, happy population there remained but Mère Lagnier and the caretaker of the colliery, his wife and three children.

Like the sudden passing of an October gale the roar of the guns ceased. It is the moment of the attack. And it rains. Old now in the ways of war, Mère Lagnier takes her steaming cafetière into the rain and slush. She knows that soon some of mes enfants must come down that way, and their least need will be a hot drink. That dramatic interlude of the guns was eloquent of what was happening away up there. There is not long to wait. Down they come – a trickle of maimed and bandaged men soon swelling to a considerable stream. Mère Lagnier waits for them in the shadow of the torn houses that once rang with the glad laughter of children and knew the deep, strong voices of men. Mes enfants, their tartans and tunics bloodied and muddied, smile in their pain at this veritable mother as they receive from her the cup of a nation's gratitude.

'Tout va bien, là-bas, mes amis?'

'Yes, mother, we've got 'em running this time. They're parteeing, toute suite. We've taken trois lines of tranchees, and they still allee. Yes. Oui, blessé in the arm, but pas beaucoup.'

'Ah, c'est bien. Au revoir et bon voyage, mon brave.'

Twelve months have passed, and I am back in P——. It is even more tragically desolate. Decay has set in about the mine shafts. The derailed waggons have taken on a deeper rust, their sides are more than ever pierced by shell splinters. Newer shell-holes tell of a bombardment. Many dwellings that a year ago were near enough whole to serve as billets have foundered in dust and debris. The Estaminet du Progrès is a sign and a serrated façade only. And the dwelling of Mère Lagnier? I am not astonished. One becomes incapable of astonishment. It is little more than a rubble heap, and among the litter of wallpaper and broken furniture is the twisted stove at which we warmed our hands on winter nights.

A cross and tinsel wreath in the civil cemetery of N——, back in the ways of peace, mark the resting-place of Argentine Lagnier, 'tuée par un obus.' Brave, constant, amiable Mère Lagnier! Your memory flowers in the heart of many a British soldier with whom you shared the perils of war in the tragic strip that separates that nightmare land which is the front from the security of the world at peace. Not least of the glories of France are her Mère Lagniers. And we – soldiers of a foreign land – salute them.

H. BOARDMAN

Thursday, May 24, 1917

#### THE ROADMAKERS

It was an infantry working party driving a road across what had once been a battlefield. The French had fought there, but now the English had taken over the line and were opening up a half-destroyed road.

A soldier, working in front, leaned on his pick and called across to his mate.

'Say, Tom, give us an 'and with this 'old 'Un, and shift 'im off the road.'

'What 'ole 'Un?'

'This 'ere. See 'is boots a stickin' out of the ground.'

'Oh, shove some stones on 'im.'

'Dunno, 'e might 'ave bin a decent cove for all you know. Don't be so 'Unnish. 'E seems to 'ave put up a decent scrap, anyway.'

''Ow can yer tell that, Mr. Knowing?'

'Well, look at the 'ole 'e's in. Them there Mauser cartridges – dozens 'o 'em 'e must 'ave fired – lying about. There's 'is steel 'elmet, too, with an 'ole in the front – bullet at close range looks like. An' there's 'is baynit broken. An' look at them Frenchies' graves just 'ere. Reckon 'e strafed some of 'em before they did 'im in. 'E must 'ave been left behind when they retired like. Not much bloomin' "Kamerad" about 'im, I reckon.'

'Oh, 'orl right. Gimme a spade. We'll shove 'im in by these Frenchies. P'raps 'is pals 'll do the like to us some day, I *don't* think.'

They worked for a while and placed the remains under the shadow of the nearest wooden cross. Then said the first man, 'Wot do these 'ere 'Uns 'ave on their graves – wording like?'

"Ere's one. "An Allemand," it says.'

'That's French, I believe.'

'You'd best put, '"Ere lies an 'Un. Rest in peace." Then you'll know what yer talkin' about. 'Ere's an inky pencil.'

So there is a wooden cross in France which bears the name of a French soldier on one side and the rough English tribute to a brave foe on the other.

H. FEATHERSTONE[1]

## BY CROZIER OUT OF BARBUSSE

From 1914 to 1918 the *Guardian* published a fortnightly History of the War to which Sidebotham and Crozier were the principal contributors. Crozier's share alone was as long as this Omnibus. He was not only a perceptive commentator on operations, but one who could enter sensitively into 'War As It Is,' the title the paper gave to his review of *Le Feu* by Henri Barbusse.

### Monday, September 3, 1917

This book won the prize of the Académie Goncourt in 1916. It has had a great success in France, and has been translated and published in Germany. M. Barbusse had fought at the front for over twelve months, and had broken down in health. His story appeared first as a serial, sharply cut by the censorship; then as a book, with no or few deletions. It is said that the author was astonished at this immunity, and no one who knows for what purpose the censorship exists will read the book without sharing his astonishment. Perhaps it was only an oversight, for censors not only nod but sleep; or perhaps it was because the

---

1. Pseudonym of Lt. H. F. Clark, who had been killed in action on May 3, 1917. 'He had,' so the writer of his obituary said, 'an exact and wide knowledge of the craft of the countryside. Fishing, shooting, hunting, and the habits and haunts of the creatures of the river were as familiar to him as ships and the sea to a sailor, and he could write and talk about them with an ease and fulness of knowledge and a kind of unsentimental joyousness that no one who was privileged to know him can ever forget.' (*Guardian*, May 10, 1917.)

censor did not really read the book, thinking that books are less dangerous material than newspapers; or perhaps it was that he read it and for the time was not a censor but a man.

The book is an unrelenting portrait of the ugliness of war. This little, humble squad of men, companionable and patient – one had almost said homely, but that here the epithet would be derisive, – whose number diminishes steadily by dreadful deaths, live an existence of squalor and misery which is almost unrelieved. To M. Barbusse the life of the trenches is one of gloom and mud and filth and stench, of infinite fatigue, infinite waiting for the horrors that lie around and for the moment of action that brings intoxication for the moment, to be succeeded again by the familiar round of wretchedness.

M. Barbusse writes with a fierce sincerity. He says the things that in our polite world of spectators are suspected but not said. His picture is of another existence than that drawn for us by the eloquent war correspondents, who cannot describe the soldier's life because they have not lived it, and would not be allowed to describe it if they had, and than that of the camera, whose neat, bright pictures, with their pretty bursting shells and rising smoke and falling buildings, lie the more easily because they bear the imprint of reality. M. Barbusse would say that these things tell nothing of what the war does with the bodies and minds of men, the material with which it is waged. His world is that of which we only hear in the whispers that from time to time ruffle the smooth agreement by which the 'horrors of war' are taken for granted but, as the saying is, mercifully concealed. M. Barbusse has no mercy, and he does not conceal them; he recreates with a pitiless imagination every phase of the interminable torment that, to his mind, makes up war.

(His) men, arguing among the desolation and the dead, think that if after the war, when they had escaped from suffering, they could only remember with unblunted edge what war had meant to them they might make an end of it. Which is perhaps why M. Barbusse wrote the book.

It is a poignant and arresting work, with its tale of simple-minded men bound to an endless chain of suffering. Some parts are pitiful in the extreme. Some are horrible and gruesome to the last degree. Some march as in a nightmare. There is a picture of a 'Poste de Secours,' deep underground, a cavern peopled by strange spectral figures, of mingled dead and dying, wounded and raving mad, all indistinctly seen through a gloom which is only broken by the eruption of an iron hail of German shells. M. Barbusse would accept this suggestion of a nightmare, for he himself makes it more than once. When, in the great attack, he and his comrades have at last passed through the German

*Hill 304 at Verdun by Jacques Souriau, an officer in the 5th Regiment of Artillery. Reproduced in the* Guardian *on May 8, 1917.*

barrage, then 'we recognise each other, confusedly, in haste, as if in a nightmare we had met again one day face to face at the bottom of the shores of death.' Others, too, who have written of their emotions in a great attack have had this feeling that they were moving in a ghostly world of dreams.

It is an impression, of course: one aspect of the truth, not the whole of it. M. Barbusse knows that he has not said the whole when he has unveiled the misery of the face of war. He works this out in the words of his own characters. 'War must be killed,' says one – 'war itself.' A second objects that all that matters is to win the war, but the others will not have it – the end matters too, the result of it all; and there is one who says of his children: 'I'm going to die, so I know what I'm saying, and I say to myself "They will have peace at last" '; and another, 'Perhaps I shan't die but I shall suffer. Well, I say "So much the worse"; aye, and I say "All the better" too, and I'll know how to suffer again if I know that I am suffering for something.' Dimly these men apprehend that they are passing through the fire for something bigger than a military victory, but it is the very dreadfulness of their sufferings that drives them to look beyond the crushing of the enemy to a war that is waged against the things and the men who make war, in whatever country they are to be found. So 'it would be a crime to display the noble side of war even if there were any,' says one of the soldiers, speaking for M. Barbusse himself. Such relief as M. Barbusse gives is to be found in the sympathetic handling of his characters, the very human victims of the fire.

It will be said by some that books like M. Barbusse's should not be written, that the nature of war, the mangling of body and soul in the extreme of agony, is too much for the human mind to contemplate. But that would be to say that the human mind must not realise what it has itself created – an impossible position. War may be necessary and may imply no guilt to some of those who wage it, but those who refuse to recognise its true character must share the blame for its continuance in the world. Behold it for what it is, says M. Barbusse, and it is less as a master of the art of polished writing than as one charged with a mission that he hammers out his message, stroke on stroke.

A perfect translation is not to be expected; one would not envy a Frenchman the task of rendering the racy idiom of men from half a dozen English counties, not to mention that M. Barbusse's vocabulary is not an easy one to handle. We admire Mr. Wray's zeal to stick to his author, but we cannot commend the result. 'The scene is picked out in sketchy incipience' is not a reasonable translation for the sharp, concise 'Le décor s'ébauche et pointe.' And what shall we say of 'The great event of these foreign teeth's establishment' for the simple 'L'événement de ses dents étrangères,' which turned an old Poilu into an 'élegant'? Mr. Wray's translation is rather like a Tank. Too often the translator dulls the fine edge of M. Barbusse's blade. But its power remains: so much we must admit in fairness to Mr. Wray. Only, to translate M. Barbusse really well it would be necessary to be stirred by his passion and to taste with him the salt of human tears.

W.P.C.[1]

# Ireland in 1916

## DUBLIN AT EASTER

George Leach got into Dublin on Wednesday in Easter Week, when the Rising was two days old. How he did it was told in *Guardian*, pp. 389-390. This extract picks up his story on Friday.

Tuesday, May 2, 1916

Dublin, Sunday

In the evening we learnt the significance of an increasing fire on the west side of Sackville St.[2] The Post Office was on fire. It had been shelled and was now ablaze. Its garrison were helpless, but would they

1. W. P. Crozier
2. Now O'Connell St., Leach's headquarters were in the Gresham Hotel in this street.

surrender or would they try to escape, running the gauntlet of the almost encompassing troops armed with machine-guns and rifles? I have learnt something of the spirit of the garrison from two or three different sources. On Monday night, I am told by a priest who was admitted to the building, it contained 500 or 600 men and a score or so of young women, who proposed to cook and nurse. The priest heard the confessions of many of the men, and they told him they were going to die for Ireland. He counselled the young women to leave, but they replied that they would stay and die with the men – a spirit too good for so bad a cause.

When the end came and the fire drove the garrison out they sought to escape by rushing in a body from the rear of the building. The street at the back bends a little, and beyond the bend was a machine-gun which, as soon as the rout began, discharged its volleys into the flying rebels, whose idea was to break into the nearest houses and make a way through. My informant believes that about 150 men were in the stampede, and that many of them achieved their purpose. A few wounded and helpless men were being carried.

It was to be expected that the fall of the Post Office would have an immediate effect on the course of the battle in our district. In this we were not disappointed, for Saturday morning opened much more quietly than the preceding days had done. Hour after hour went by, and the local lull continued, and in a mysterious way, at a quarter to four, the word came from nowhere and spread everywhere that the rebels had surrendered and that there was to be peace in the city.

The effect of the rumour was wonderful. Empty streets became full. Women and girls made their way boldly to the bakeries to satisfy households on the verge of starvation, and a glance at the military picket at the end of Sackville St. seemed to corroborate the rumour, because the soldiers were walking about carelessly, and a platoon was assembled in the very centre of the roadway. It was another good sign that the fire brigade came round to attack the fires, which up to now had gone on unchecked, and the next vehicle to arrive – curiously and beautifully out of place it seemed – was the van of the Little Sisters of the Poor, driven by an aged and feeble old man. Milk carts came through with a cheerful rattle, and all hearts hereabouts were uplifted with hope.

Then there came a reaction of misgiving caused by the presence of two men who have frequented the locality all the time and have been the disseminators of many fantastic stories. They said it was not peace but a truce to allow of people getting bread. It was a plausible story, because the provisioning of the city had become a crucial question.

There was no food in the houses. In my hotel we had had a small allowance of porridge and a half slice of bread for breakfast, and a rasher of bacon and two potatoes for a mid-day dinner. For tea the previous day there had been a handful of biscuits. It must have been much worse than that in many a private house.

Therefore these men – who had been pointed out to me before as ardent Sinn Feiners – might have been right. Only they weren't, although I did not positively know that till Sunday [*when he saw a copy of Commandant Pearce's surrender order*].

But although 'Commandant General P. H. Pearce, commander-in-chief of the army of the Republic' had surrendered, the rebellion was not quite at an end. Cannon were firing during the night, and there was some amount of sniping even in our quieter neighbourhood.

I have traversed part of the line of battle and have had revealed to me the tremendous task before the troops in face of a desperate resistance. It will be in the knowledge of all who have visited Dublin that the homes of even the poorest in the central area of the city are in lofty three and four storey houses. Garrison these houses with armed Sinn Feiners, and the roads become deep trenches loopholed with windows from which to attack a cramped and exposed foe. It was into wall-bounded gullies of that kind that the soldiers had to advance, taking the individual houses by storm. The precise methods of the advance varied according to the locality, but they were all according to a general scheme, and it will be sufficient to give one example.

Parnell Street at its western end joins Capel Street at a right angle. The Sinn Feiners seized the houses in Capel Street commanding Parnell Street, as well as the houses at the corners, and put men in a number of other houses on both sides of Parnell Street all the way to Sackville Street, and further on still up to Summerhill, where there was a slight barricade. The side streets also had their snipers, so that the attacking party was involved in a fortified labyrinth against which it was not possible, on account of the non-combatant and friendly citizens, to employ artillery. But it was imperative that the road should be cleared. In the early attacks the soldiers suffered dreadfully. They were without cover and subject to a cross-fire which was unbearable. I was told by an officer who took part in the assault that one battalion had very heavy casualties in an hour at the entrance to Parnell Street, and from the look of the place it was clear that if it was to be taken by open assault the cost must be tremendous.

Happily someone hit on the device of an armoured motor-car – not the scientifically contrived weapon that does service in France, but a rough-and-ready improvisation. First he got a heavy motor lorry with solid tyres. Then he put a steel boiler upon the lorry and riveted it securely. The driver and the engine he protected with rectangular plates of steel. It was an innovation in war machines as sensational in its effect upon the battle as the invention of the ironclad Monitor was in the American Civil War.

The boiler was loopholed for rifle and machine-gun fire and became a mobile fort. Being impervious to the enemy's bullets, it could go with impunity into the hottest rifle fire, and it was taken into Parnell Street and stationed in turn opposite each house that had to be captured. Its machine-gun opened on the windows, and under this covering fire a party of infantry dashed up, smashed the door, and disposed of the defenders. The manœuvre was repeated many times, and house after house was captured. Steel fort was pitted against brick, and the victory was with the better armed of the two.

The side streets were another problem. Progress would have been too slow if they had had to be cleared one by one, and the forces employed must needs have been much larger. So a barricade was thrown across every opening, and the main route was held secure. This method of attack, as it progressed, had the good effect of isolating the enemy snipers and confining them to limited areas. By and by the Sinn Fein strongholds were unable to communicate with one another, and each was left to make an independent fight.

It is not explained how the rebels were able to accumulate such large stores of ammunition for the different kinds of weapons they were using. They added to their stock of arms by raiding police barracks, commandeering arms, and gave receipts such as: 'Sixty rifles taken by the Irish Republican Army. ——, captain.' Or, 'Received 50 bayonets, commandeered by the Irish Republic. Will be paid for.' And again a captain's signature.

The insurgents also had three machine-guns which have a rather interesting history. They were purchased from Germany some time ago – were imported in coffins, and, to delude the police, mock funerals were held in different parts of the country. From then to the outbreak of this revolt those guns were never seen or heard of. They were, I believe, a good match for the machine-guns on the military side.

The rebels also had dynamite, which was taken on Sunday by a contingent of the Citizen Army from a quarry and stored in Liberty Hall.[1] The police were aware of the theft, which was, as it now seems, the first overt act of the rebellion.

1. The rebel forces were drawn from the Sinn Fein 'Irish Volunteers' and from the 'Citizen Army,' founded by James Larkin during the Transport Workers' Strike. Liberty Hall was his old trade union headquarters.

As on Sunday the rising was virtually at an end, the way seemed to be open to England. It had been a fairly simple thing to enter Dublin on the Wednesday, but it was plainly going to be far from simple to get out.

## SHALL ROGER CASEMENT HANG?

### Friday, June 30, 1916

#### SENTENCED TO DEATH

On the eve of the Easter Rising, Casement (1864–1916), knighted for his exposure of atrocities in the Congo and in Peru, landed in Ireland from a German submarine, but was arrested.

London, Thursday

At half-past four this afternoon the Lord Chief Justice sentenced Sir Roger Casement to be hanged.

After listening for a very long time to the prisoner's gentle, wistful voice, reading his amazing apologia, one's attention had wandered for a moment. A little usher in black, like a verger at a funeral service, broke the feverish silence of the court, croaking out 'Oyez, oyez.' Looking up, at this signal, one saw with a shock of terror that the three judges had thrown over their wigs black squares of cloth, and, as small things are often noted in a terrible moment, it was seen that Mr. Justice Avory's 'cap' dangled grotesquely awry over his prim face.

For four days we had been staring at those three scarlet figures until they had become familiar and even intimate presences. Now in an instant they were changed into something remote and forbidding. Sunlight fell from the lantern windows on the three silent judges and searched the ashen face of Lord Reading, which seemed all at once to have grown old.

Another long pause, and the strong nasal voice of the Lord Chief Justice was heard reading from a paper the half-dozen emotionless sentences in which he sent Sir Roger Casement to death. 'To be taken hence to a lawful prison and thence to the place of execution and there to be hanged by the neck till you be dead.'

Sir Roger Casement heard these words, and smiled wanly, looking down, one thought, as if to reassure his friends who were near the dock. Then, erect and quite self-possessed, he turned and disappeared behind the green curtain. He had kept his dignity, his almost incredible detachment, to the last. It was all over.

The jury had been out so long that there were murmurs of a disagreement. They came back just under the hour, and, after the prosaic interlude of answering to their names according to form, returned him guilty. Then the 'Master' of the court, from his place under the presiding judge, asked the prisoner in a matter-of-fact tone what he had to say why he should not die according to the law. Sir Roger Casement was standing at the dock rails with his arms spread along them, looking through the scene before him with that strange, thoughtful gaze in his smouldering eyes.

Yes, he had much to say. Stretching out his hand, he took from the warder behind him, a manuscript, and, leaning well over the dock, began to read it with the air of a rather diffident speaker at a public meeting. So fast did he read, and in so low a voice, that the jurymen, anxiously straining to hear, must have lost a good deal of it.

The historic statement, and the one that followed it, were addressed, as he explained, not to the Court at all, but to the audience of Ireland and America. It was a beautifully phrased essay, full of wit and sarcasm, the work of a rich and cultivated mind that dwells among ideals and great emotions. It was neither defence nor defiance, but an elaborate political manifesto in which personality – the personality of a man condemned to be hanged – was secondary to an abstract passion of principle. Sir Roger Casement sought to escape from his judges, and took his stand on a simple refusal of the right of the 'foreign' jurisdiction of England to try him. Like all Irish patriots brought under English law, he repudiated the claim of an English tribunal to test his loyalty at all. 'I made no appeal to Englishmen,' he said, 'I asked Irishmen to fight for their rights.' He put himself forward as the victim of what he called 'a judicial assassination,' and taunted the Crown with being afraid to bring him before an Irish jury.

A warder brought him a glass of water, and thus refreshed he went on more vigorously with the interminable reading, all eyes watching with fascination his lean, brown hands as they flicked over the pages of his manuscript. He turned the last page, and people began to stir, thinking it was the end, but the prisoner said with a smile, 'I haven't done yet,' and taking a second and more recent essay from the warder he began again.

The second essay was a closely reasoned vindication of his work in arming the Irishmen in Germany to fight, as the defence maintains, 'for Ireland only.' Most notable was the bitter passage on the Ulster faction and its leaders. Looking towards the Attorney General, he said; 'Their treason' – the treason of the Ulster leaders – 'lay on the way to the Woolsack; mine lay on the way I knew it must lead – to the dock. I am proud to stand in the traitor's dock in the place of my honourable accusers.'

Sir Frederick Smith, who sat with his little wig tipped over on his forehead, did not raise his eyes from his brief. With a final extempore appeal to the jurymen to put themselves in his place as a foreigner tried before an alien tribunal Sir Roger Casement ceased.

> There followed a large number of letters to the editor, most of which vainly urged a reprieve. The following extracts are typical. The 'unconvicted and indeed unprosecuted traitors' of Bernard Shaw's letter include, of course, Carson and F. E. Smith (Lord Birkenhead) who, as attorney general, had prosecuted Casement. Nevinson's letter refers to the officially inspired 'leaks' of homosexual passages from Casement's diary.

## Saturday, July 22, 1916

I presume I may count on a general agreement that Casement's treatment should not be exceptional. This is important, because it happens that his case is not an isolated one just now. There are several traitors in the public eye at present. At the head of them stands Christian De Wet.[1] If De Wet is spared and Casement hanged, the unavoidable conclusion will be that Casement will be hanged, not because he is a traitor, but because he is an Irishman. We have also a group of un-convicted, and indeed unprosecuted traitors, whose action helped very powerfully to convince Germany that she might attack France without incurring our active hostility. As all these gentlemen belong to the same political party, their impunity, if Casement be executed, will lead to the still closer conclusion that his real offence is not merely that of being an Irishman but of being a nationalist Irishman. I see no way of getting round this. If it was proper to reprieve De Wet, whose case was a very flagrant one, Casement cannot be executed except on the assumption that Casement is a more hateful person than De Wet; and there is no other apparent ground for this discrimination than the fact that Casement is an Irishman and De Wet a Boer.

The reasonable conclusion is that Casement should be treated as a prisoner of war. I believe this is the view that will be taken in the neutral countries, whose good opinion is much more important to us than the satisfaction of our resentment. In Ireland he will be regarded as a national hero if he is executed, and quite possibly as a spy if he is not. – Yours, &c.,

G. BERNARD SHAW

1. (1854–1922), the most successful Boer general in the South African War; led un-successful rebellion, 1914; convicted of high treason, but soon released.

## Tuesday, July 25, 1916

One word more. It is common knowledge that insinuations against Casement's private character have been passing from mouth to mouth. These insinuations have no bearing on the charge of which he is convicted, nor have they been established or mentioned in court. They are said to be founded on documents discovered by the police among Casement's property. How the alleged contents of these documents came to be whispered abroad I cannot say. In certain Continental countries one could imagine the police, or even the Government, spreading such rumours with the object of poisoning the public mind against a man whom they wished to destroy. I am told that this was a common device also of the Inquisition in old days. But in the case of an English Government and English legal or police authorities such conduct is, of course, unthinkable. I can find no explanation. I can only say that anyone who may have attempted by such means to blacken the character and prejudice our feelings towards a man who stands in acute danger of a degrading and hideous death is, in my opinion, guilty of a far meaner and more loathsome crime than the worst which could possibly be unearthed in the career of the criminal himself. – Yours &c.,

HENRY W. NEVINSON

## Thursday, July 27, 1916

### A QUESTION OF POLICY[1]

Almost every State, certainly every free State, that has ever dealt out severity to rebels has wished afterwards that it had been less severe. Every nation when criticising other nations condemns their severity in political matters and applauds their rare leniency. All the world can see the wisdom of General Botha's reprieve of De Wet. Mrs. J. R. Green, in a letter to us this morning, points out that every belligerent nation accepts the rebellious from the recalcitrant subject nationalities of their enemies. We may be quite sure of the way in which our friends in France will regard this question. We may be quite sure of the hopes and fears of our friends in the United States. We may equally be sure that our enemies the world over will rejoice if Casement is executed. To the Germans Casement living is worth nothing. He is just a broken tool. But Casement dead is to them worth, at a low valuation, an army corps.

1. From a leader probably by L. T. Hobhouse.

## Conscience in War-Time

### PETER GREEN AND BERTRAND RUSSELL'S
### BURGLAR

Thursday, March 15, 1917

For 44 years Canon Peter Green (1871–1961) was, as 'Artifex,' a
regular *Guardian* columnist. He was perhaps the best-loved
parish priest who ever declined a bishopric – Lincoln, after the
death of Bishop Hicks, his predecessor in his parish and as a
*Guardian* columnist. Green was also the best-known Anglican
writer of his generation on ethics. The war gave a personal point
to many of his articles. One such was prompted by an anonymous
letter, anonymous only because 'if anyone gets to know where
(the writer) is, he will be in gaol very soon.'

I cannot do as he asks and either blame the conscientious objector or
declare him to be in the right. I wish indeed that life was such a simple
thing that one could say of every action either that it was absolutely
right, a 100 per cent of pure rightness, or absolutely wrong, a 100 per
cent of pure wickedness. But that is not so in this world. I should
suppose that everyone would admit that in most actions there is a spice
of what is good mixed with the wrong or of wrong mixed with the
right. It is very seldom that of two alternatives one is altogether right
and the other altogether wrong. Even the most convinced conscientious objector would probably admit that, while nothing could possibly make him take an active part in war, there were elements in his
position which he regretted. I know that many hundreds of young men
who are to-day fighting for their country detest war, and would have
found it hard to respond to their country's call if Germany, in her mad
folly, had not first violated and then tortured Belgium. What I mean is
that of two men who hate war and believe it to be morally wrong one
attaches so much value to those deep moral considerations which led
England to enter the war that he thinks the way of war the lesser of
two evils. The other feels so strongly the evil of war that rather than
fight he accepts many other things from which his conscience would
otherwise revolt. I may not agree with the decision at which a man
arrives. But if he is following the dictates of his conscience, above all
if he is so following them at great cost to himself, why should I blame
him?

If I were a layman, and of military age, I should fight. I could not accept all my life the advantages of citizenship and in the moment of crisis say, of war alone, out of all the evils with which our civilisation is inextricably bound up, 'With this I will have nothing to do.' I think that to be a real conscientious objector a man must be, consciously or unconsciously, an extreme individualist with little sense of the solidarity of mankind and of our membership one with another. I could not, as a member of the community, say 'I will not fight, but I will let others fight for me. I will not fight, but I will accept protection from the police and from penal laws, and pay taxes which support not only the gaol but the scaffold.' I know war is an evil. But I cannot regard it as the only, perhaps not as the chief, evil of our modern civilisation. I cannot say 'I will accept all the benefits of citizenship and acquiesce in all the evils of civilisation, but with war alone I will have nothing to do.' I do not wish to condemn the man who takes that attitude, nor to doubt his sincerity. But it is not my own attitude.

Monday, March 19, 1917

*To the Editor of the 'Manchester Guardian'*

Sir, – There are no doubt many kinds of reasons which lead men to become conscientious objectors, but I am convinced that the chief reason, and the most valid, is precisely that sense of 'the solidarity of mankind' of 'our membership one with another,' which 'Artifex' denies to us. It seems to me that when he wrote 'mankind' he was thinking only of the Allies. But the Germans, too, are included among 'mankind.' The conscientious objector does not believe that violence can cure violence, or that militarism can exorcise the spirit of militarism. He persists in feeling 'solidarity' with those who are called 'enemies,' and he believes that if this feeling were more widespread among us it would do more than armies and navies can ever do to prevent the growth of aggressive Imperialism, not only among ourselves, but also among potential enemies.

'Artifex' repeats the argument that the conscientious objector accepts the protection of those who are willing to fight and that he will accept protection from the police and from penal laws, and pay taxes which support 'not only the gaol but the scaffold.' But the conscientious objector only 'accepts' that 'protection' because there is no way of avoiding it. He has not asked for it and does not believe it necessary. For my part, nothing would induce me to prosecute a thief, and if there are any burglars among your readers they are welcome to take note of this announcement; but I shall be very much surprised if I lose as much through them as I have lost through the operation of the law. And is it not rather ironic to speak of the protection of the law to men whom it has deprived of the means of livelihood and shut up in prison for the duration of the war, with only occasional brief intervals for fresh courts-martial? Is there really such a vast gulf between Wormwood Scrubs and Ruhleben?

Yours, &c.,

*57, Gordon Square, London, W.C.*                    BERTRAND RUSSELL

Thursday, March 22, 1917

[Artifex replied:]

Several letters make the point, which Mr. Bertrand Russell makes, that I am wrong in calling C.O.'s extreme individualists, since most of them are moved rather by a sense of the unity of all men. It is an honour to cross swords with Mr. Russell, and I have a special interest in doing so since our paths have not met since our names stood next to one another in a certain final class list at Cambridge.[1] But he cannot be ignorant of the way in which opposite opinions often produce identical results, and of the way in which any doctrine pushed to extremes tends to fall over into the opposite. We have an example of that in the familiar connection between the views of the Socialist, who sees in the State the source of all power and authority, and those of the Anarchist, who refuses to recognise any authority in the State at all. Indeed Mr. Russell, while claiming for the C.O. a deep sense of the solidarity of mankind, himself declares that he would never prosecute a thief, a position which seems to be that of the philosophic Anarchist.

Mr. Russell and many other correspondents complain of my saying that the C.O. accepts the advantages of the State, which include protection by the army and navy. What else can we do? they ask. Quite so! What else can they do? Which emphasises my point that it is not in a man's power to divest himself of responsibility for the acts of the nation into which he is born and in and by which he lives.

Several people cannot understand why I can neither blame the C.O. nor declare him to be right. This is because the writer and others do not distinguish between the different meanings of the word right when we say a man is right. It may mean 'free from moral blame,' and any man is that who is acting according to his conscience. Or it may mean 'acting in accord with an objective standard of right, which should be recognised as right by all who judged correctly.' If everyone who is sincere is judged to be right in the latter sense, then two men who hold opposite opinions may both be right. And in that case there can be no objective right at all, and morals are a department of the natural history of taste. But I hold that there is an objective standard of right,

1. Moral Sciences Tripos Part II 1894 in the First Class.

and that it is the object of the science of ethics to determine what it is. In the meanwhile to praise the C.O. and declare him 'right' merely in the sense of 'sincere' would seem to me an impertinence. I should not suppose that any sane man doubted their sincerity.

# G.B.S. ON PERPETUAL HARD LABOUR

## Tuesday, June 12, 1917

The *Guardian* had opposed the introduction of conscription on strictly practical grounds, but accepted it as morally legitimate – especially since it was accompanied by guarantees for genuine conscientious objectors. Experience soon showed, however, that these guarantees were not working.

*To the Editor of the 'Manchester Guardian'*

Sir, – The announcement that a sentence of two years' hard labour has been passed upon Mr. Clifford Allen[1] raises the question whether the press and public, in accepting the news without protest or comment, are acting advisedly, or only in that ignorance of public routine of which we have had so many staggering examples during the war.

In point of severity imprisonment with hard labour is the most severe form of incarceration practised in England. A sentence of two years is regarded as reaching the limit of endurance; only when the offence is of such a nature as to provoke the court to do its worst is it resorted to. When terms of imprisonment exceeding two years are called for the prisoner is sent to penal servitude. The difference is that a prisoner at the end of two years' hard labour is in a state of exhaustion which could not be prolonged without endangering his life, whereas penal servitude has to be so ordered that men can endure ten or even twenty years of it without physical collapse.

It must therefore be clearly understood that a prisoner can be killed by sentencing him to hard labour for a continuing offence and renewing his sentences as they expire. Thus Mr. Clifford Allen, having already served a severe term of hard labour, on the expiration of which he is immediately sentenced to two years' further hard labour, and will presumably be sentenced to two more if he survives it, and so on for the rest of his life, is virtually under sentence of death by exhaustion, starvation, and close confinement.

Is it the intention of the Government, the military authorities, and

1. Clifford Allen (1889–1939), later Lord Allen of Hurtwood; general manager, *Daily Citizen* 1911–1915; director, *Daily Herald* 1923–1930.

the nation? If so, there is nothing more to be said. It may be so, for it is a matter of daily experience that many people who are taking advantage of their age and sex to do not less public work than Mr. Clifford Allen and Mr. Stephen Hobhouse[1] did long before the war put any pressure on them, but no public work at all, think that such a death is too good for a conscientious objector, and do not hesitate to say as much. But are these vicarious zealots in the majority? May not the absence of protest be merely the ignorance of the respectable man who knows nothing of prisons and criminal law and has no idea that Mr. Allen is being treated with a new and quite abnormal frightfulness?

One other point. Why are the scruples and personal rights of the objectors treated with pedantic respect when they operate to the disadvantage of the objector, and overridden by force when they have the contrary effect? Mr. Stephen Hobhouse is sharing Mr. Clifford Allen's fate because he refuses to submit to medical examination. Why was he not examined by force? Objectors refusing to put on uniform have been forcibly clad. Women refusing their dinners have been forcibly fed. Your columns have just reported the case of an invalid recruit who was stripped naked for an hour and a half and forcibly prevented from sitting near the fire. He is now dead. Yet when Mr. Hobhouse objects, his wishes and his person are regarded as sacred, and the authorities, deploring his obstinacy, consign him to hard labour for life.

Anyhow, here are two gentlemen in a fair way to be killed because the public has no knowledge and the authorities no sense. If we wish to kill them, cannot we shoot them out of hand and have done with it, Dublin fashion?

Yours, &c.,

G. BERNARD SHAW

## THE CASE AGAINST PERSECUTION[2]

### Thursday, July 19, 1917

MR. BRIGHTMORE's plea of conscience having been rejected, he passed eight months in prison. After that he appeared to have been returned to the army, where on maintaining his refusal to serve he was sentenced to 28 days' confinement, and was placed in a narrow pit ten feet deep, the bottom of it full of water. The prisoner had to stand upon two

1. Stephen Hobhouse (1881–1961), nephew of the *Guardian*'s L. T. Hobhouse; engaged on war relief work in the Balkans 1912–1913; chairman, Quaker committee for helping enemy aliens and prisoners 1914–1916; co-author with Fenner Brockway of *English Prisons To-day*.

2. A leader by L. T. Hobhouse.

strips of wood all day just above the water-line. 'There is no room to walk about, and sitting is impossible. The sun beats down, and through the long day there are only the walls of clay to look at.' Here he stood for eleven days and nights. This is not punishment, but torture. In the opinion of the War Office it is even worse. It is an 'irregularity.' For the facts are admitted. MR. MACPHERSON yesterday 'regretted to state that the allegations were substantially correct.' It is fair to the War Office authorities to say that as soon as they heard of the case[1] they despatched a staff officer to Cleethorpes camp to make investigation, and as a result 'the irregularities ceased.' This is good so far, but unfortunately we now know that an allegation of gross cruelty is not to be set aside as incredible merely because it is an allegation of gross cruelty. What we deemed incredible we must no longer deem incredible. We must keep an open mind and insist on the examination of accounts of this kind, and we must also insist on clear prohibition and, where wrong has been done, on sharp punishment.

There are many views of the conscientious objector and the treatment proper for him. Some say 'Shoot him out of hand' to prove that we are free Britons and not even as these Prussians. Others say he is a saint and a martyr to the cause of liberty, not caring to ask themselves by what methods in the history of the world liberty has in fact been won and maintained. Between these there are many intermediate views, but none that we know of such as would justify torture or the gross degrading bullying that approaches physical torture, and to the mind is perhaps worse than physical torture. Shooting is at least decent. Repeated ducking in the foulness of a horsepond till a man's will is broken is another matter. How is it that these things occur? They are bad for the army, they lower the moral of the nation and impair its whole-hearted confidence in its leaders. Our national endurance is being subjected to a severe test in these months. Its strength depends on the virtual unanimity of the nation in the belief that our cause is that of justice, of freedom, and of a humane civilisation. Of one thing the Government may be sure. If there is anywhere the beginning of a doubt which might undermine that faith of which we have spoken as the basis of all our endurance, that doubt is being nourished by nothing so much as the treatment of the conscientious objectors, and would be removed by nothing so readily as the complete and final stoppage of the persecution.

1. The *Guardian* had published a letter from Mr. Brightmore on June 30.

# The Home Front

## WHY NOT TO BE A FARMER'S BOY

Wednesday, March 27, 1915

### A CRISIS IN AGRARIAN HISTORY
*By J. L. Hammond*
(Joint author of the *Village Labourer*)

Mr. Asquith's speech in the House of Commons resigning to the discretion of the local authorities the Government's responsibility for the administration of the education laws may come to mark as definite and unhappy a crisis in the history of the agricultural labourer as that fatal day, a hundred and twenty years ago, when the nation slipped, almost as casually, into the slough of the Speenhamland system.[1]

Our great war to-day has reproduced one of the effects of our great war a century ago. It has raised prices; in the South of England to the extent at least of 3s. or 4s. in the pound. But it has also taken off a number of agricultural labourers who are now serving their country in the Flanders mud. In 1795 there was one question before the governing world: how were the labourers to live? To-day there are two: How are the labourers to live, and how are the farms to be worked? The two questions are bound up together and the answer that is given to them will have consequences no less grave than the answer our fathers gave in their generation.

Two years ago it was the contention of the principal members of the present Government that the position of the agricultural labourer, his low wages, his want of freedom, his inability to secure decent terms for his labour, the bondage of his home and life, were a public scandal, and a scandal that the Government was resolved to bring to an end at all costs as quickly as possible. No small part of this description was accepted by political opponents, and Mr. Leslie Scott and a group of his fellow-Unionists introduced a bill to set up wages boards. The need for reform is undisputed. And it is these employers who have now asked the Government to allow them to take the children from the schools, because they cannot find men to work their farms. The natural answer surely is that they must first of all remove the conditions that make their employment unattractive. What wages do you give your labourers? Do you allow them a Saturday half-holiday? On what terms do they occupy their cottages? Have you let them know

1. The subsidising of wages out of poor rates.

that you have no objection to their joining or starting a union? These are a few of the questions that must first be asked and answered. Until they are asked and answered satisfactorily any proposal to release children from school for the service of these employers is a proposal for a subsidy from the nation, and a subsidy of a very terrible kind, in aid of sweating, and sweating by a set of employers who are making an uncommonly good profit.

Unhappily, if Mr. Asquith's speech represents the last word of the Government, this is precisely what the Government are doing. Miss Susan Lawrence, writing in the *Labour Woman*, reports that the Education Acts are now in abeyance in no less than twenty counties. Now what shadow of a guarantee has the nation that all other resources have been exhausted and that the farmers in these counties will not take advantage of the system to oppress their labourers still further? We know from the history of Lancashire what happened in the early days of children's employment in the cotton industry. What is there to prevent a Wiltshire farmer from saying to his labourer, 'No, I won't give you another 2s. a week but I will take your boy into my employment, and, what is more, if you don't bring him there will be no work for you either and you will have to leave my cottage'? To introduce this system of child labour into an employment conducted on the lines on which agriculture is conducted in England is to invite a terrible aggravation of all the evils on which leading members of the Government used to speak with such indignant eloquence. And when is it going to end?

Let proper wages be guaranteed to men and women, and make the labourers' unions a recognised and essential part of the machinery of organisation and labour-recruiting.[1] If it is still found necessary to employ children, arrangements must be made to secure that these children are themselves compensated for what they lose in education. To leave this revolution to take its course without check or control is to commit treason against society, which has not made its education laws for fun; against the agricultural labourer, who is to find his bondage made still tighter; and against these children, for we should prevent them from entering on any other employment than agriculture, and we should at the same time be helping to make agriculture more than ever an employment from which every enterprising and high-spirited boy would wish to escape.

---

1. In 1917 an Agricultural Wages Board was set up. It was abolished in 1920, but restored by the Labour Government of 1924.

## THE UNREST AMONG THE ENGINEERS

'The strike on the Clyde last year was the first sign of a general discontent, which seems to have increased. In the earlier part of this year there were strikes at Liverpool, on the Tyne, and at Barrow. A month ago strikes occurred simultaneously in London, Manchester, Sheffield, Leicester, and Coventry. Obviously a state of affairs which produces these strikes in an industry essential to the prosecution of the war is very serious whatever the causes may be.' Thus J. V. Radcliffe, who had himself covered several of the strikes, began a series of articles in which he thoroughly investigated the nature of the men's grievances. Walter Runciman who had recently been President of the Board of Trade thought well enough of Radcliffe's work to write to Scott, 'Have just finished a second reading of the *Guardian* special articles about the industrial troubles, and I presume to send you a strong word of commendation for publishing the articles at all and for selecting as your investigator a man who has powers of observation which put him well below as well as over the surface.' The last of the five articles appeared on

### Wednesday, June 27, 1917

SHOP STEWARDS AND THE FUTURE
*From our Special Correspondent*

North, south, east, and west I find that men are physically weary, nervously exhausted, and spiritually depressed. In addition, although the number of active pacifists is negligible, there is everywhere a great longing for the end of the war and the return to peaceful ways and avocations.

The hours worked for nearly three years have been long. They are still long. Seven shifts a week continue to be the rule in some places. I heard of one large works in Scotland where men are working 90 hours a week. A working week of from 70 to 80 hours is common. The arrangement to pay men mealtimes in order to keep the machinery running incessantly involves the taking of food as quickly as possible, and there is not even a dinner-hour relaxation of mind and body. The continuous strain has produced a more or less chronic state of 'nerves' – all the irritable effects of neurasthenia. What I have described as spiritual depression may be in part a reaction from the physical condition. It is also a consequence of the falling away of the ideals that swayed men's minds when the war began, and the obsession with the daily horrors of the conflict and the harassing troubles of the work-shop and the home. The desire for peace is very real, but it is a desire with little hope, because there is no sign that the German people – German labour – is changing its attitude towards its Government and the war. There is no evidence of pacifist movements among the workers.

It is apparent that some of the causes of unrest are not industrial, and a change of industrial conditions cannot therefore wholly remove them. Certain aspects of the industrial questions of the hour are political, and perhaps the most difficult necessity is to promote con-fidence in the Government. The decision to abolish leaving certificates and to require arbitration awards to be made within a fortnight[1] will ease two of the most glaring causes of irritation, and if the Govern-ment will go further and restore 'freedom of action' to the trade unions they will probably get rid of many legitimate workshop grievances that ought not to exist at all, and would not exist if, in the last resort, the sufferers were at liberty to resist them. It is desirable that the leaders of the trade unions should at the same time be in closer touch with the members than the requirements of the Government have lately permitted them to be. Another strong reason for discontent would be removed if there were an effective control of food supplies and prices. Still another would go if the Government would reconcile their assertion of the need for dilution with the simultaneous demand for skilled men for general military service.

This attempt to gauge the extent and the depth of the unrest in the engineering works would be incomplete if it did not at least indicate that a change is coming over the mind of the workers and that new aspirations are shaping themselves. Labour questions have not stood where they were since August, 1914. Neither has labour thought remained where it was. Labour politics are going to be much more advanced. There is at the moment no new labour policy, but the old programme will not hold the new thought. The same is true of labour's industrial policy. I could not fail to be impressed by the assumption everywhere – it was equally marked in the steady-going trade unionism of Birmingham and in the constitutional Socialism of Glasgow, and it was taken for granted in Manchester and Sheffield and on the Tyne – that after the war the worker must have a real share in the control of workshop conditions. This is a fixed and positive idea. There is in most localities an equally confident belief in the continuance of the shop

1. In effect, men had been bound to one employer by the need to obtain a 'leaving certificate,' while employers had been free to sack men. Arbitration had been substituted for the right to strike, but delays had been long and numerous.

stewards system for the representation of the unions in the workshops. This is a different thing from the shop stewards' 'movement' as it has developed during the war, and the difference ought to be maintained. It will be necessary for the trade unions to capture the shop stewards' organisation or it will capture them. All the more reason therefore why the trade union executives should get back to the leadership of the workmen.

The shop stewards' system has already been recognised at Coventry on lines that subject the stewards to the discipline of their unions but make a considerable departure from precedent. At Coventry each shop is entitled to elect its own steward, but the election must be ratified by the district committee of the man's union. In a large works the shop stewards will belong to several different unions, and in the committee of shop stewards, which is almost certain to be established, there will be a local court for the discussion of works grievances that will tend to rival in authority the district committees of the several unions acting independently.

It has been the aim of these articles to be practical and definite. One thing about which it is impossible to be definite is the influence that will spread in this country from the Russian revolution. Something will most surely come of it, and in an uncertain way one gets to feel that the forces which made for revolution in Russia are stirring here too, but vaguely. However that may be, the plans that are made to allay the unrest in the skilled engineering trades must take account not alone of the particular grievances alleged, but also of the altered state of mind and the new thought among the workers.

## A CRYING SCANDAL AT BARROW

Wednesday, August 29, 1917
*From our Special Correspondent*[1]

Barrow-in-Furness, Tuesday
The Industrial Commission, over which Judge Parry presided, reported that the housing problem at Barrow-in-Furness had become 'a crying scandal'. The denunciation is strong, but it comes short of what the conditions call for. The overcrowding is worse even than those who gave evidence before the Commission thought it to be, and far worse than anybody elsewhere can believe possible. The wonder is that the town has escaped serious epidemics.

1. J. V. Radcliffe

It is impossible to give an exaggerated idea of the overcrowding. In a great many cases whole families live and sleep in one room. People inhabit cellars and back kitchens, and a few have caravans. Any family that has arrived in Barrow during the last eighteen months is lucky if it has the use of two rooms. Births and deaths occur in the common room that is crowded night and day. I was assured by a woman investigator that she knew of a number of cases in which immediately after the birth of a child the other children had had to share the mother's bed. It is a more common thing for the landlady to insist that an expectant mother shall leave the house till after the baby is born, and as Barrow does not possess a maternity hospital this means that mothers have to choose whether they will go into the workhouse or to friends at a distance. I heard of a case in which the only place for a coffin was on the table and the family gathered round the dead body to eat their meals.

Neither decency nor cleanliness is possible. The houses are of two general types, one being a four and the other a six-roomed house. There may be a tiny back kitchen as well, but there are no bathrooms. The rooms are small, and, after being in them, one is more astonished than before that families find their cramped quarters tolerable even for a week.

A father and mother and four children (one over 16 years of age) sleep in the same bedroom. They live in a damp and dimly lighted cellar in the daytime. For this accommodation (unfurnished) they pay 7s a week. The mother told me they had lived in this fashion for three years. A second room in the same house is let for 6s. unfurnished. In another house thirteen persons, old and young, occupy two small bedrooms. There are houses in which each of the four rooms is tenanted by a separate family. Eight families live in a house of a larger type in Duke Street. It is not uncommon to find 16 and 17 persons living in four rooms. A man gave me the following details of the place in which he lives. A woman and six children sleep in a back room; another woman and four children in the middle room; a lodger has a third room; a woman and three children have the parlour; the old landlady sleeps on the sofa in the kitchen and he and his family have the remaining room. There is a six-roomed house (two living rooms, two bedrooms, two attics) that has 19 occupants, including a family of nine, six of whom are over 16 years of age. This family has two rooms. A man, his wife, and three children live in the kitchen in a two-roomed house in Ship Street, and five persons occupy the other room, which can only be reached through the kitchen.

In Latona Street six men lodgers sleep in a room which three beds fill so completely that there is nowhere to put their personal belongings except beneath the beds. The window is directly over one of the beds, and in wet and windy weather it cannot be opened. A man and his wife and four children are in an adjoining room. One of the occupants of a two-roomed house told me that he and his wife and two children and his brother-in-law and his wife sleep in one room, which they divide with a screen. The tenant and his wife and two lodgers sleep in the kitchen. A woman complained to me that she and her up-grown son are obliged to sleep in the same room. For decency's sake many families have divided, the father taking the boys to one house while the mother and the girls remain together. I could multiply cases not less shocking but these are surely sufficient.

Famine prices are being charged for apartments and lodgings. Two unfurnished rooms may be sublet for more than the rent of the house. The worries of housekeeping have become so great that landladies are declining to board their lodgers, and after charging 5s. per head for the share in the use of a bed are leaving them to feed themselves as best they can. The Increase of Rent and Mortgage Interest Act forbids the raising of rents, as it also forbids the ejectment of tenants except when the owner himself wishes to take possession. In Barrow the sale of houses is going on rather rapidly on unusual terms. The purchaser pays a deposit of as little as £10 or £20 to the seller, and the balance of the price (invariably high) is converted into a mortgage repayable by weekly instalments of an amount considerably in excess of the former rent. Whether this is merely a way of evading an Act of Parliament may not be certain, but there is no doubt of the evil results when the new purchaser takes possession of a room or two and farms out the rest of the accommodation at an unholy profit. Here is an instance which I had from the man concerned. He rented a house at 9s. 6d. a week. It was bought over his head, and the purchaser went to live there and let apartments. She charged my informant 6s. 6d. a week for the use of one unfurnished room. There are now twenty persons living in the house.

At last the Ministry of Munitions admits that something must be done, and it is going to build 250 houses, which will be handed over to the Town Council at a valuation five years hence. But 250 houses will not do. I asked the Medical Officer of Health, who is greatly concerned at the dangerous overcrowding, how many new houses the town needs, and he answered 1,500 for the permanent population and another 1,500 if the war population is to be properly housed. The Ministry of Munitions must be stirred up to do more and do it quickly. It will be too late when an epidemic comes.

## Russia in 1917

When the Tsar abdicated on March 16 the *Guardian* was represented in Russia by Philips Price who was at the Grand Duke Nicholas's headquarters in the Caucasus. 'I want to tell you,' the Grand Duke said, 'that what happened in Russia in the last twenty-four hours is final and cannot be reversed. I would regard anyone who tries to do so as an enemy of our Fatherland.' (*Guardian*, March 20, 1917.) Scott sent out David Soskice from England to Petrograd – he had been the Petersburg correspondent of the *Tribune* in 1905. When he and Philips Price met, they agreed to split the work, Soskice taking the capital, Price the provinces. This lasted from June to September, when Soskice became Kerensky's secretary and Price was again on his own.

## THE KRONSTADT COMMUNE

### Tuesday, July 17, 1917

Petrograd, June

Lately Petrograd began to get alarmed about the state of affairs in Kronstadt. Rumours circulated that this important island fortress guarding the sea approaches to the capital was in the hands of the most dangerous type of Anarchists, who had destroyed the fortifications, were selling secrets to Germany, and were preparing to spread terror and destruction all over Russia. Knowing that there are people in Petrograd who spread rumours for sinister purposes, I decided to go down to Kronstadt and investigate for myself.

After an hour and a half's ride from the mouth of the Neva across the blue waters of the Gulf the steamer pulled up alongside the quay of a long, flat island. I got out and walked along the little streets of an old town. Life was going on just as usual, and I saw no outward signs of disorder. In a large house in one of the main streets I found the headquarters of the Kronstadt Council of Workers' and Soldiers' Delegates, which controls the fortress.

With some little misgiving I passed by the sentries and asked to see the president of the Council. I was taken into a room, where I saw a young student with a red badge on his coat looking through some papers. This was the president of the Council, elected by the revolutionary soldiers and sailors and workers of Kronstadt. His hair was long, and his face bore that expression of mingled sympathy and mystery, which is so often seen in the Russian student.

'Well,' he said, 'they seem to be very frightened of us in Petrograd, but we are doing nothing more than putting our house in order after the chaos and terror of the Tsar's regime.'

I asked him if the Council recognised the Provisional Government of Russia, and he replied: 'Of course we do, if the rest of Russia does, but that does not prevent us from having our own opinions as to what the Government ought to be. We would like to see the whole of the government in the hands of the All-Russia Council of Workers' and Soldiers' Delegates.'

I was taken to see the prisons where the agents of the Tsar's tyranny were sitting. In the first prison I found about 100 gendarmes and secret police agents. The quarters were very bad, and many of the cells had no windows at all. Great hulking men with coarse animal features were lounging about dark and narrow corridors. Some of them still had on the uniform of their former profession. 'I am afraid you must be very uncomfortable here,' I said to one of them. 'Ugh!' he grunted, 'if only they would let us go to the front and fight or work and do something.'

In the next prison I found a number of admirals, generals, and naval and military officers of all ranks. They told me stories of how they had been arrested as soon as the news of the events in Petrograd had become known to the revolutionaries in Kronstadt. They all complained that they had been kept for three months without any trial or examination of their cases. But the young sailor who accompanied me chimed in: 'I sat in this very prison not for three months but for three years for having been found with a Socialist pamphlet in my possession. All that time I never had a trial of any kind whatever.' I pointed out to the sailor that the prison accommodation was unfit for a human being. He answered, 'Well, I sat here all that time because of these gentlemen, and I think that if they had known they were going to sit here they would have made better prisons!' This attitude of the revolutionary Kronstadt sailors, if not justifiable, is explicable. These officers are now being tried by a commission sent from Petrograd.

Revolutionary ideas have always been strong in the Russian navy, and the great naval fortress in the Baltic has been the centre of the force which the Tsar's Government created to crush them out. Almost every sailor in Kronstadt has at one time or another been in these Government prisons and been lashed with the knout. Several of them that I met that afternoon told me how they had been sent to Siberia for life and had escaped from there in order to come back to Kronstadt, in spite of the terrors of the place, and carry on revolutionary propaganda there. They were always treated like dogs. They were not allowed to walk in the boulevards or go into any public places of amusement, and for the smallest offence they were beaten. On the first day of the revolution they went to the Admiral's House, dragged him out, shot him, and tried to burn the body. It was a law of blood and iron that ruled in Kronstadt, and I fear during the first days of the revolution the sailors gave back what had been given to them.

That evening I was taken to the house of Admiral Veren, who had been murdered as I describe. I found the Anarchists in possession. In the sumptuous halls where once councils of war were held by medalled officers I now saw unkempt, long-haired revolutionary students and sailors. I was introduced to their leader, a veteran fighter, who had taken a prominent part in the mutiny of the Potemkin on the Black Sea in 1906. I expected to find the most desperate characters among this lot, but I confess that they turned out very harmless. Their revolutionary ideas did not go beyond the speedy application of Marxism and the class war, while the Anarchists I found to be peaceful Tolstoyans who would refuse to shed blood on principle. As it was already late they invited me to supper and to sleep the night.

Next day I was taken to visit the battleships and training ships in the harbour. I first went to the Naval Staff. The commander of the fleet I found was now a young lieutenant. He received me very cordially, called me 'Comrade,' and took me to his cabin to lunch, which consisted of the same food as that eaten by the sailors. He wore no epaulettes on his uniform, he was not saluted by the sailors, and when they spoke to him they called him 'Comrade.' All the officers of the fleet in Kronstadt are now elected by the crews of the ships on which they serve, and the Council of Sailors' Delegates elects the officer commanding the fleet. My first question was how did this new principle of electing officers affect the work and efficiency of the fleet. The Chief of Staff, although himself an old sailor, and not accustomed to this new way of doing things, said that on the whole he thought it worked well. At first there was some difficulty. The sailors elected officers just because they liked them and not because they knew their job. But after a while, he added, the men got to know who were efficient as well as those who were nice to their men.

On the following day I was taken to see some of the factories where war material is made and ships repaired. I found all the men working busily, and the rumours of disorganisation prevalent in Petrograd quite unfounded. All the private works and shops are put under the control of the Council, and the profits divided with the workers. Most of the private owners, however, left after the revolution, so that now the works are run by the committees of the men. An eight-hour day is compulsory throughout the island, with three hours' overtime for special and urgent work. Trade unions are being formed among the different grades of artisans. I came across a meeting being held by the Union of Strikers in the ship-repairing yards. The men were discussing a plan of mutual insurance against unemployment and sickness.

M. PHILIPS PRICE

# HOW THE BOLSHEVIKS TOOK THE WINTER PALACE

## Thursday, December 27, 1917

(The following article by Dr. David Soskice gives the first connected account, and the first account by an eye-witness, of the last days of the Kerensky Ministry, and of the scenes in the Winter Palace, where Ministers were besieged and captured by the Bolsheviks.)

When I left the Palace on November 6 I was under the impression that the new Bolshevik rising had completely miscarried. But the next morning the situation changed almost miraculously. It appeared that all the reports which the generals had given to Kerensky were misleading. Hardly a single unit in the Petrograd garrison executed the orders given them on Kerensky's instructions. The troops guarding the arsenal joined hands with the Bolsheviks, who got possession of all the artillery and ammunition and enormous stocks of rifles. Every regiment or company of soldiers in the city had passed a resolution supporting the Bolsheviks, who accused Kerensky's Government of wishing 'to surrender Petrograd to the Germans so as to enable them to exterminate the revolutionary garrison.' The Bolsheviks spread the rumour that the Government was preparing to move to Moscow. Although a very small minority in each regiment took part in these meetings the effect was to paralyse the Government, because the vast majority of soldiers remained passive. They said they would not interfere in the struggle for fear that 'brotherly blood' might be shed. In this way the telegraph and telephone passed into the hands of the Bolsheviks almost without fighting during the night of November 6, and there were no armed forces upon which the Government could rely for its defence. Personally I am under the strong impression that there was a strong element of disloyalty among the military command in Petrograd.

When I arrived at the Palace on the morning of November 7 I found that its food supplies had been stopped, so that the guards had left, being unable to get food. Kerensky had set out on a dangerous mission to bring loyal troops from outside the city. The new commandants began to organise the defence of the Palace, and for that purpose I, too, went to that wing of the Palace in which the offices of the Palace administration were situated to obtain a plan of the immense building in order to place guards at all possible entrances. But to my great amazement I found the vast offices absolutely deserted by the administration, and the doorkeeper informed me that none of the officials had even put in an appearance that day.

Some of the old servants of the Palace, who had formerly served the Tsar and were well acquainted with the vast building, volunteered to serve as guides.

'You will find no traitors among us,' they said to me, and they proved loyal to the end.

Fresh units of cadets were called into the Palace. Food was ordered by telephone, but on the way to the Palace it was commandeered by the Bolsheviks.

I was sitting in my study. The next room to mine was that of Konovaloff.[1] The Ministers gathered from time to time in his room or mine, and through the window watched the crowds on the bridges. The situation grew more and more critical. Five thousand sailors arrived from Kronstadt, and the cruiser Aurora entered the Neva and lay with guns directed upon the Winter Palace. The Fortress of SS. Peter and Paul was now in the hands of the Bolsheviks, and its guns were also turned upon the Palace. The Government offices on the other side of the square were gradually surrendering to the Bolsheviks, whose troops were little by little surrounding the Palace itself. The palace guards had erected a huge barricade along the principal gates and façades leading to the square from accumulated reserves of timber, and the two opposing forces were awaiting the final onslaught.

Within the Palace the Ministers were almost all by now assembled. All our telephone lines were already disconnected except one, through which we occasionally received some disturbing tidings. It began to grow dark. During the day I had several times been obliged to warn the members of the Government from crowding to the windows, as by so doing they were likely to attract unwelcome shots. And now we

1. The senior minister in the absence of Kerensky.

carefully drew the curtains to hide the few electric lights we were obliged to make use of.

At seven o'clock the Cabinet held its last meeting, which was of a memorable character. It was held in the famous Malachite Hall, where the sittings were usually held. This meeting was held in darkness except for the rays which shone through the open door from a lighted vestibule which had no windows. The Minister of Labour, a Socialist, raised the question whether some of them should not leave the Palace to mix with the populace and try to influence them. Some other Socialists supported him. But after a close debate it was decided that the Ministry should stand and fall together. The welcome news that some food had been scraped together was brought, and at about eight o'clock the Ministers went upstairs to Kerensky's apartments to partake of a scanty meal. By arrangement I was to leave the Palace at eight o'clock. When that time came all the ordinary exits were either besieged or barricaded. My faithful attendant, who was well acquainted with every corner of the Palace, managed to get me through into the central courtyard, which was filled with loyalist guards, and thence I was conducted to the huge iron gate, strongly guarded by loyal sentinels. In front of the gate was a high wooden barricade. A stout female nurse was just being hoisted over this barricade to proceed to her duties in the military hospital situated in one part of the Palace.

I stood for a moment gazing into the darkness. A hand touched me, and somebody said: 'Don't stand here. You may be hit by a bullet.' I thanked the sentinel and went along by the barricade in the direction of Millionnaya Street, the only passage still kept by the loyalists. They were barring the street, but they allowed me to pass through. When I had proceeded a short distance I heard the order given behind me 'Take aim!' I heard the click of the rifles, and two big soldiers who were proceeding some steps in front of me gathered up the skirts of their coats and took to their heels. I looked back and saw the line of loyalist soldiers aiming straight before them in my direction. I realised that the two soldiers in flight were Bolsheviks. Luckily for me they had disappeared in the darkness, and the soldiers did not shoot. I went on, and when I reached the next corner I found it guarded by the Bolshevik Red Guard. These were ordinary young workmen, wearing belts and rifles slung across their shoulders. They did not stop me, and I went on in the direction of the Hôtel d'Europe, where I was staying. Everywhere at the street corners were stationed Bolshevik soldiers or sailors or detachments of the Red Guard. I reached the hotel unmolested.

Later in the evening, when I was ready to return, I learned that the

General Staff had already surrendered to the sailors before I left the Palace, and that the Palace itself had been completely surrounded, so that it was impossible for me to enter it. I learned that a friend of mine who had gone with Mme. Kerensky in a cab to the Palace had been arrested, with her, by the Bolsheviks and taken to the Smolny Institute. During the night the booming of guns began. I knew they were the guns of the Aurora bombarding the Palace. An ultimatum was sent to the Ministers to surrender. They refused. Bolsheviks began to penetrate into the Palace through some unknown entrance, and from the upper floor, where the apartments of Kerensky and of Babushka (Mme. Breshkovsky, the grandmother of the Russian Revolution) were situated, they began to throw hand grenades into the hall below. These Bolsheviks were arrested by the loyalists. The Aurora discharged a number of shots at the Palace. A violent fusillade of machine-guns and light artillery was also directed against it. A battle ensued, during which there were some hundred casualties on either side. Gradually the Bolsheviks forced an entry and invaded the Palace. On their way they pillaged every room they entered. The Ministers retired from one room to another, until at last they were arrested and conveyed to the fortress.

The Palace was pillaged and devastated from top to bottom by the Bolshevik armed mob, as though by a horde of barbarians. All the State papers were destroyed. Priceless pictures were ripped from their frames by bayonets. Several hundred carefully packed boxes of rare plate and china, which Kerensky had exerted himself to preserve, were broken open and the contents smashed or carried off. The library of Alexander III, the doors of which we had locked and sealed, and which we never entered, was forced open and ransacked, books and manuscripts burnt and destroyed. My study, formerly the Tsaritsa's salon, like all other rooms, was thrown into chaos. The colossal crystal lustre, with its artfully concealed music, was smashed to atoms. Desks, pictures, ornaments – everything was destroyed. I will refrain from describing the hideous scenes which took place in the wine-cellars, and the fate to which some of the captured women soldiers were submitted.

## AT THE SMOLNY INSTITUTE

Saturday, October 21, 1967

While Soskice was in the Winter Palace Philips Price had been
with the Bolsheviks in the Smolny Institute. Unfortunately his
message was one of many that miscarried. Fifty years later, however, the *Guardian* gave what was substantially the missing 'story'
in an extract from Price's autobiography, *My Three Revolutions*.

The Second Soviet Congress was starting at the Smolny Institute at
eight o'clock. I managed to squeeze in and I heard that the Congress
consisted of delegates from all over Russia elected by the local Soviets.
It was a very different gathering to the Petrograd Soviet. The latter
delegates were hardened proletarians and very class-conscious. The
delegates to this Congress were country people, peasants and small
town workers who were not indoctrinated and were mainly concerned about ending the war and getting the landlords' land.

Many of them had been at the First Soviet Congress in June and had
supported the Mensheviks and Socialist-revolutionaries. Now these
same delegates had come to the conclusion that the Bolsheviks were the
only people who would get them what they wanted. This Congress
clearly marked the revolt of the workers and peasants in the poor lands
and forests of North Russia with the passive consent of the more
prosperous peasants of the south who, though not starving, were land-
hungry, as I had seen in the Volga provinces.

The chairman of the Congress was Dan, the Menshevik leader, still
in office as elected in the First Congress in the summer. Actually conditions were rather chaotic because the Socialist-revolutionary delegates in the Congress were now split into a Left and Right wing, the
Left being ready to cooperate with the Bolsheviks. It was soon clear
how the land lay because the first thing the Congress did was to elect the
Bolshevik leader, Sverdloff, as chairman in place of Dan.

The next thing I remember was that a member of the Right wing of
the Socialist Revolutionary Party now rose to a point of order. 'We are
living in strange times,' he began. 'Three of our party comrades,
members of the Government, are at this moment besieged in the
Winter Palace, where they are being bombarded by a gunboat, manned
by the supporters of the majority of this Congress. We demand their
immediate release,' he roared, thumping his fist upon the table, while
derisive shouts arose from the body of the hall.

When he had finished, up rose Trotsky. 'That sort of speech comes badly from a member of the Socialist-Revolutionary Party,' he began, 'for that party has shared joint responsibility for a Government which has, during the last four months, kept under arrest a number of our party comrades and has put to watch over the rest of us the members of the old Tsarist secret police.' General sensation and tumult throughout the hall followed, while the Menshevik and Socialist-revolutionary delegates of the Right left the Congress in a body, accompanied by groans and hisses. When they had gone, it was possible to see by the empty places that they represented about 20 per cent of the whole Congress. Such had been the revolution of opinion during the year.

Now I saw on the platform the short, bald-headed little man that I had seen six months before leading the small Bolshevik group at the First Soviet Congress. It was Lenin without his moustache, which he had shaved off in order to change his appearance during his period of forced concealment. I thought his voice was weak, apparently with excitement, and he spoke with slight indecision. It seemed as if he felt that the issue was still doubtful and that it was difficult to put forward a programme here and now.

A Council of People's Commissars was set up, he said, and the list would be submitted to the Congress. The Council would propose to the Congress three resolutions upon the basis of which three decrees would be issued. The first was that steps should be taken to conclude an immediate armistice on the front as a preliminary to peace negotiations. The second decree would secure for the Land Committees of the peasant communes the right of temporary possession of the landlords' estates pending detailed legislation. The third decree would give the factory workers power of control over all operations of employers and managers. 'We appeal to our comrades in England, France and Germany to follow our example and make peace with their fellow workers over the heads of their capitalist governments,' concluded Lenin. 'We believe that the nation which gave Karl Marx to the world will not be deaf to our appeal. We believe that our words will be heard by the descendants of the Paris Communards and that the British people will not forget their inheritance from the Chartists.' When he had finished, I heard a delegate sitting near me say the word 'slaby' (weak).

By this speech, however, Lenin struck me as being a man who, in spite of the revolutionary jargon that he used, was aware of the obstacles facing him and his party. There was no doubt that Lenin was the driving force behind the Bolshevik Party and so of this second Russian Revolution. He was the brains and the planner, but not the orator or the rabble-rouser. That function fell to Trotsky.

Trotsky was always the man who could say the right thing at the right moment. I could see that there was beginning now that fruitful partnership between him and Lenin that did so much to carry the Revolution through the critical periods that were coming. What would have happened if they had not been there, particularly Lenin, is one of the riddles of history. Probably there would have been the same result in the end, but only after long periods of chaos and distress. There was to be plenty of that anyway, but without Lenin there would have been much more of it.

The Congress dragged on into the night. The only practical thing done that I remember was the passing of a motion expressing confidence in the Government of the Soviets and the establishment of socialism in Russia. Hope was expressed that the workers in the countries of Western Europe would follow Russia's example. In those days it was part of the Bolshevik theory that revolution must break out in the rest of the world to save the Russian Revolution. I remember talking to a delegate who asked me what would happen in England when the news from Russia was known. When I told him that I did not think it would have any effect on the internal affairs of the country, his face fell and he said, 'Then Russia is lost.'

Soon after this, news arrived that the Winter Palace had been taken and the Ministers of Kerensky arrested. This, of course, aroused fresh enthusiasm among the delegates, everyone standing up and cheering. No more business was done and sometime after midnight I left the Smolny and went out to see what I could before trying to catch an hour or two's sleep in my flat. All around the Smolny were gathered groups of soldiers round log fires. They were the guard, but so far had nothing to do. Picturesque confusion reigned everywhere. I went towards the Neva, already beginning to freeze in the shallows along the wharfs. A raw November fog was blowing up from the Gulf of Finland. Opposite the Yassily Ostroff lay the cruiser Aurora with guns trained on the Winter Palace. I crossed the Neva bridge and approached the Petropavlovsk Fortress. The Red Flag was flying from the tower of this 'bastille' of Tsarism.

At the Winter Palace I found everything was quite quiet. It was occupied by sentries from the garrison of the city who had gone over to the Bolsheviks. From conversations I had with the soldiers who, though not expansive, were nevertheless ready to say something, it appeared that they were not all class-conscious proletarians. If things had gone the other way, there is no doubt their loyalty to the Bolsheviks would have wavered. But there was a strengthening of Red Guards from the factories among them who were dedicated revolutionaries. According to all the information that I could get, there had been no fighting in and around the Winter Palace and there were certainly no signs of any. Once the Palace was surrounded, it appeared that the Ministers of Kerensky had surrendered to avoid bloodshed.

It was clear that power in Petrograd was actually in the hands of the military revolutionary committee. I remember walking about the streets of the capital and feeling an atmosphere of unreality everywhere. The middle-class press was being sold in the streets as if nothing had happened. Its tone, however, was subdued. The Cadet 'Retch' appeared too staggered by the shock to be able to do more than moan about the fate of Russia.

Soon I, too, was beginning to feel that the whole thing might be a mad adventure. How could committees of workmen and soldiers, even if they had the passive consent of war-weary and land-hungry peasants, succeed against the whole of the technical apparatus of the still-functioning bureaucracy and the agents of the Western Powers?

On the following day, however, there was a different feeling in the air. It seemed as if there was, for the first time for many months, a political force in the country that knew what it wanted. This view was clearly reflected in the common talk in the streets. Mingling with the crowds, I heard comments from different types of people, shopkeepers, students and members of the professional classes. I heard no word of criticism about the violent methods which the Bolsheviks had used in coming to power. The questions which really interested these people were whether the new Government would be able to bring food to the towns and make an end to the war. The Tsar's Government could not do it nor could Kerensky's. Perhaps these people may.

Towards evening I went to the Smolny. The Second All-Russia Soviet Congress was just ending. Upstairs in the office of the Soviet official paper, 'Izvestia,' I found the Bolsheviks already in possession. The editor, Stockloff, was engaged in earnest conversation with someone. Axelrode was trying to put some order into a pile of papers. Somebody else was fiddling with a bradawl at the lock of a drawer from which the keys had evidently been removed by the Mensheviks when they had left. Along one side of the room I saw Lenin walking up and down sunk in deep thought. I looked at this scene at the centre of the new authority and again began to wonder, could it last? Was this really the intellectual nucleus of a new ruling power in the world, or was it only a passing incident?

# Zion: a Dream Comes True

## THE NINTH OF AB

### Wednesday, March 7, 1917

To me it was merely an early day in August. Up there in the dusty camp, miles away from Salonika, how should it be anything else? In that completed ceremonial of modern war that evolved hourly among the hills what was there to remind me of the immemorial and pathetic ceremonial of the Ninth of Ab? Day after day the limbers came down empty from deeper Macedonia, and creaked back loaded to those remote trenches which the vans could not reach. And always at evening, when the shadows of a wind came with the other shadows and the wind shepherded the sheep-bells into a fold of music, you could see the rustics in their dingy fustanellas leading home their ponies and hear them singing their uncanny songs.

What was there in these things to remind me of Jerusalem fallen? But I had spent the whole of this day in the town of Salonika, and nothing had brought the imminence of the anniversary into my mind. Perhaps I was not looking for omens. If I was conscious of anything, it was a determination to get into my blood some abiding memory of the strange old town which after a few days I should see no more. I had passed under the hoary gate built by that other Constantine[1] and had spent the day in the more spacious east side of the town. When night fell and the searchlights began to be busy I returned centrewards along the quay. The fishing-boats were rocking against the breakwater and the half-naked fishermen were arranging their nets as pillows. But Floca's, the Hotel Continental, the Hotel d'Angleterre were ablaze. The officers of five armies sat together talking a wonderful joint language. The tassels of fez caps drooped amorously a few inches from smart little French toques that drew back archly. Fat proprietors loomed benignantly among the liqueur bottles, their eyes full of a golden glow like Grand Marnier and their souls as sea-green incorruptible as Crème de Menthe. I loitered here a little while, and then went on along Venizelos Street into the 'Ignatian Way.' The drinking slums of the west side were awakening into life. Outside the doors of the cabarets in 'Piccadilly Circus' were gathered ragged crowds, whose eyes glistened as they looked in on the red-clothed women

1. i.e. Constantine the Great, Roman Emperor 306–337. In March, 1917, Constantine I was King of the Hellenes. He abdicated in favour of his son, Alexander, later in the year.

singing and dancing on the platforms. (And the names of these places – Heliconian, Parnassian, Olympian!) I went on through the welter of the Monastir Road. Under the glare of the naphtha lamps gleamed heaps of melons, beside which the sellers counted their coppers into a fold of their sashes. Little boys fluttered lottery-tickets on a long pole. In every cabaret the shabby-booted little infantrymen of Constantine were showing their teeth over the greasy packs of cards which are with them night and day. Here and there an Albanian shepherd who had come down from the hills lay drunk under a table, with his dog mounted guard beside. From every corner came the thump of bronchial pianos and the gasp of consumptive violins, and, drowning it all, the insistent song of the women.

This was the region, then, into which I went deeper and deeper, for only thus, I understood, could any vision I should retain of the town be at all complete. The process of walking from street to street became almost mechanical. I lost sense of direction and identity and became an automaton, registering correctly but unconsciously the sights and sounds. I realised now I was in the ancient cities which the Lord destroyed utterly by fire, but which, phoenix-like, have always risen from the ashes of their destruction. The half-drunken soldiers who staggered and bawled past me were too frequent to distract me from my mood. So I went on until at the bottom of a dark and evil street I saw a light burning which was somehow different from the other lights I had seen, and I heard a sound, a wailing sing-song, which struck a new note in the extraordinary symphony of that evening. When I came to the end of the street I found that the light came from a miserable lamp which hung from a nail driven into the wall of a crumbling and wretched house. Round it in a dimly-seen semicircle was a group of thirty or forty people, sitting close to the ground on pillows and low stools. Underneath the lamp sat an old man with a parchment scroll between his hands, from which he was reading in a dolorous and uniform chant. Now and again he broke down for a moment or two and the wailing of the people round him became less and less restrained. The huddled shapelessness of the old man seemed to tell of some incomparable despair. He looked like a woman fondling and crooning over her dead child.

Whilst I stood there in the darkness a conviction grew upon me. Somewhere and sometime I had heard that chant – not once, but often. I looked more carefully into the faces of the group. There were girls, dark, with long lashes and patient faces. One I remember particularly, her pallid face standing abruptly out of the blackness, like a figure of Caravaggio. Her hair foamed round her forehead in black waves.

There were little boys, very indifferent to the solemnity of the time. One ran a pin into another and took to weeping to hide his guilt. There were old women seamed like the moon, too old to weep almost, and they were wearing the caps peculiar to the older Jewesses of Salonika, from which hang the cushioned pads of green silk, fringed at the end with a pattern of pearls. But I no longer needed this outward sign of their race. The chant had linked up many memories, with the sorrow I had heard reiterated every year, perhaps never to be assuaged. It brought back to me a little synagogue over a river in a certain sombre and indifferent town, and the unextinguished sorrow and the inextinguishable hope of the exiles who had drifted there. For it was the Ninth of Ab, the day on which over the far countries of the earth the Jews were bewailing the loss of the Temple – prosperous Jews in Fifth Avenue, desolate Jews behind the German lines in Poland with all their household goods bundled into a bed-sheet, Jews awaiting the order to charge in Flanders.

Now and again a group of soldiers lurched by; but the sorrow which brooded here, like a bird whose wings can be heard flapping over the empty nest, stilled them, and they stole away quietly. The little boys had begun to notice me. 'British Johnny, British Johnny!' they whispered to each other excitedly. I still waited in the shadow, and the old man went on with his reading. Then the murmur went round 'Israelite Johnny, Israelite Johnny!' The girls looked out of the corners of their eyes. The old women put their heads together and nodded and whispered. The old man looked up a moment, but his eyes were dim with tears, and he looked beyond me into the night. Then a youth rose from his stool, and with the courtly Spanish grace of four hundred years ago came to me and led me into the circle of the lamplight. So I sat among the others, and together we remembered Zion.

L. GOLDING

## PALESTINE AND THE JEWS[1]

### Wednesday, November 7, 1917

We speak of Palestine as a country, but it is not a country; it is at present little more than a small district of the vast Ottoman tyranny. But it will be a country; it will be the country of the Jews. That is the meaning of the letter which we publish to-day written by Mr. Balfour to Lord Rothschild for communication to the Zionist Federation. It is at once the fulfilment of an aspiration, the signpost of a destiny. Never

1. A leader by C. P. Scott.

since the days of the Dispersion has the extraordinary people scattered over the earth in every country of modern European and of the old Arabic civilisation surrendered the hope of an ultimate return to the historic seat of its national existence. This has formed part of its ideal life, and is the ever-recurring note of its religious ritual. And if, like other aspirations and religious ideals which time has perhaps worn thin and history has debarred from the vitalising contact of reality, it has grown to be something of a convention, something which you may pray for and dream about but not a thing which belongs to the efforts and energies of this everyday world, that is only what was to be expected, and in no degree detracts from the critical importance of its entry to that world and the translation of its religious faith into the beginnings at least of achievement. For that is what the formal and considered declaration of policy by the British Government means. For fifty years the Jews have been slowly and painfully returning to their ancestral home, and even under the Ottoman yoke and amid the disorder of that effete and crumbling dominion they have succeeded in establishing the beginnings of a real civilisation. Scattered and few, they have still brought with them schools and industry and scientific knowledge, and here and there have in truth made the waste places blossom as the rose. But for all this there was no security, and the progress, supported as it was financially by only a small section of the Jewish people and by a few generous and wealthy persons, was necessarily as slow as it was precarious. The example of Armenia and the wiping out of a population fifty-fold that of the Jewish colonies in Palestine was a terrible warning of what might at any time be in store for these. The Great War has brought a turning-point. The return of the Turk in victorious power would spell ruin; the rescue of this and the neighbouring lands from Turkish mis-rule was the first condition of security and hope. The British victories in Palestine and in the more distant eastern bounds of the ancient Arab Empire are the presage of the downfall of Turkish power; the declaration of policy by the British Government to-day is the security for a new, perhaps a very wonderful, future for Zionism and for the Jewish race.

Not that it is to be supposed that progress in such a movement can be other than slow. Nor does the British Government take any responsibility for it beyond the endeavour to render it possible. The Government have indeed laid down a policy of great and far-reaching importance, but it is one which can bear its full fruit only by the united efforts of Jews all over the world. What it means is that, assuming our military successes to be continued and the whole of Palestine to be brought securely under our control, then on the conclusion of peace our deliberate policy will be to encourage in every way in our power Jewish immigration, to give full security, and no doubt a large measure of local autonomy, to the Jewish immigrants, with a view to the ultimate establishment of a Jewish State. Nothing is said, for nothing can at present be said, as to the precise form of control during the period of transition, which may be a long one. Palestine has a special importance for Great Britain because, in the hands of a hostile Power, it can be made, as our experience in this war has shown, a secure base from which a land attack on Egypt can be organised. Our interest and practically our sole particular interest, in Palestine is that this danger should be effectually guarded against, and that no Power should be seated in Palestine which is or under any circumstances is likely to be hostile to this country. That condition would be fulfilled by a protectorate exercised by this country alone or in conjunction with, say, the United States, or by the United States alone, or by an international body designating us as its mandatory on conditions to be mutually agreed. Such may be the ultimate development of our policy, but in any case the fundamental principle now laid down will condition it. We recognise, and we shall continue to recognise, the Holy Land as the 'national home of the Jewish people.'

Other conditions are involved, and are stated or implied in the present declaration. The existing Arab population of Palestine is small and at a low stage of civilisation. It contains within itself none of the elements of progress, but it has its rights, and these must be carefully respected. This is clearly laid down in the letter, which declares that 'nothing shall be done which may prejudice the civil and religious rights of existing communities in Palestine.' There is, again, the question of the custody of the Holy Places, in which Russia and France are alike warmly interested. This is not expressly referred to, but will undoubtedly have to be carefully considered, and, with goodwill, should present no great difficulties. The final words of the letter may not, at the first glance, be perfectly intelligible. Not only are the rights of existing communities in Palestine to be protected but it is also declared that 'the political status enjoyed by Jews in any other countries' are in no way to be prejudiced. That may appear a rather far-fetched precaution against an imaginary danger, and so perhaps it is. But if anxiety is anywhere felt on this score, it is well that, so far as we are concerned, it should be allayed. And anxiety, though it may not be widespread, no doubt there is. But in any case what is this for the Jewish race compared to the hope and the promise of re-entry on their birthright? A small people they must be, for Palestine will hold but perhaps one-fourth of the scattered Jewish race; but they were a very small people when they gave two religions to the world, and, seated in their old land, they may yet become the vital link between East and West, between the old world and the new.

## Letters in War-Time

### ELIOT ON DOUGHTY[1]

Monday, July 24, 1916

This is an epic dealing with the creation of the world, the battle of Titans against gods, their defeat and their final subjugation in the service of man. One does not find fault with Mr. Doughty for writing an epic. No literary genre, once established, is ever outworn. But mythology is dangerous literary material. It should either be a mythology in which the author more or less believes or a mythology in which some people once believed. A mythology cannot be created for literary purposes out of whole cloth; it must be the work of a race. Mr. Doughty's mythology is neither Greek nor Hebraic nor Scandinavian; hence it lacks outline, it lacks tradition, and it lacks concreteness.

The theme suggests Milton and Keats. But Milton and Keats at their best communicate a feeling, the one of titanic revolt, the other of titanic silence and despondency. When they fail they suggest Mr. Doughty. Mr. Doughty's Titans have bulk without meaning. When Dante says 'Mi parve veder molte alte torre' an image arises; one feels the reality of immense bodies with something like human spirits in them. The Titans of this poem have violence, but no passions.

> Leaned to time-fretted cliffs
> Is entered weariness, in each marble corse.

In 'Hyperion' the weariness is made actual; here it is stated. One does not know quite why such creatures should be weary at all, unless from the boredom of their inactivity. One cannot understand them. Not being human, they have not even the reality of definite abstractions. Bios and Kratos in 'Prometheus Bound' succeed because they are boldly and intentionally abstract, and as such produce their effect by contrast with a passionate suffering human being. Æschylus was a master of effects of abstract and concrete; he never fell into the error of the vague.

1. A review by T. S. Eliot (1888–1965) of *The Titans*, one of two known reviews by Eliot in the *Guardian*.

As for Mr. Doughty's style, one is puzzled; one wonders whether he was himself quite sure what he wanted to do. He aims at the ruggedness of the Saxon tongue. If he were thoroughly and consistently Anglo-Saxon he might arrive at giving a total impression; even employing, as he does, many words of which one does not know the meaning. But there are heavy Latinisms too. One turns from the harsh

> *From the mount's knees, up to his frozen*
> *breast*:
> *Eotons and rime-giants strive mainly and sweat*

to

> *the adamantine Elements*
> *Couched indivisible particles . . .*
> *Shall his* mathesis, *through unerring thought,*
> *Discern . . .*

with a touch of Browning at the end.

One can enjoy a style of excess – Sir Thomas Browne, or Lyly, or Mr. Wyndham Lewis, or Browning – if it is excess in a peculiar and exclusive direction. Mr. Doughty's style is not archaic; it is not the style of any time or the style of any intelligible pose; it is eccentric, but not personal. Thus it recalls several writers without being imitative of them. It recalls especially Blake; not the Blake of extraordinary creations of phrase springing at a leap from the unconscious, but the Blake of such verse as 'America.'

T.S.E.

## LAWRENCE AS POET[1]

### Friday, September 1, 1916

Mr. Lawrence's poetic garden is none of those discreetly ordered, old-world pleasaunces whence English lovers of the old style gathered posies of verse for their mistresses. It is a luxuriant wilderness of sumptuous and fiery blooms, rich in the beauty that 'the sense aches at,' but often running to seed and sometimes touched with poison. As his title imports, he is a lover in many fashions – for child and sister, and the old mother, for the boys he teaches, and for mistresses wooed in many diverse tones of mingled soul and sense. The influence of Whitman is obvious, not only in the audacities – disguised, however,

1. A review by C. H. Herford (1853–1931), Professor of English at Manchester, of D. H. Lawrence's *Amores*.

in phrases more curiously recondite than his, – but in the wayward yet captivating rhythms. Without precisely abolishing the traditional metres – they sound fitfully through the verse like a tune through jangled bells, now taken up and eloquently carried on, now capriciously broken and tossed aside, – he seems, like Whitman, deliberately to have attempted to make his rhythmical vesture follow and vary with the moods of his sinuous thought. Thus in 'Week-night Service' he makes the night and the moon and the 'wise old trees' listen in ironical amusement or derision to the clangour of the peal:

> *The Patient Night*
> *Sits indifferent, hugged in her rags;*
> *She neither knows nor cares*
> *Why the old church sobs and brags;*
> *The light distresses her eyes, and tears*
> *Her old blue cloak, as she crouches and covers her face,*
> *Smiling perhaps, if we knew it, at the bells' loud*
>     *clattering disgrace*

In a graver mood he indulges 'dreams old and nascent' – now the dreams of the master over his boys as they bend over their books in the hot afternoon:

> *Oh my boys . . .*
> *In you is trembling and fusing*
> *The creation of a new patterned dream, dream*
>     *of a generation*
> *And I watch to see the creator, the power that*
>     *patterns the dream*
> *The old dreams are beautiful, beloved, soft*
>     *toned, and sure*
> *But the dream-stuff is molten and moving*
>     *mysteriously*
> *Alluring my eyes: for I, am I not also dream-*
>     *stuff,*
> *Am I not quickening, diffusing myself in the*
>     *pattern, shaping and shapen?*

In these passages the impression of eloquent prose-rhythm is hardly quite escaped. But in many pieces, like the powerful 'Scent of Irises' a music irregular but unmistakably of poetry is won with flawless felicity. In other pieces there are strangely mingled notes of a realism that would be grotesque in another context, but is caught up into the subduing atmosphere of pathos. So in the 'Ballad of Another Ophelia.'

The 'Mother' pieces are full of a tender exaltation. In the finest of them the son sees her dead form on the bier – his love, looking like a girl, but old, with hair of silver and uncanny cold:

> *Nay, but she sleeps like a bride, and dreams*
> *her dreams*
> *Of perfect things,*
> *She lies at last, the darling, in the shape of her*
> *dream*
> *And her dead mouth sings*
> *By its shape, like the thrushes on clear evenings.*

Mr. Lawrence's gift of poetry is beyond question; his discretion in the use of it not quite equally so.

C.H.H.


## EMINENT VICTORIANS[1]

### Tuesday, June 4, 1918

Present-day critics of the nineteenth century are numerous, and the younger ones mostly supercilious. Among them are a few apologists. Ordinarily they run the gamut of the moods, from contempt to indulgence, as in front of something absurd if not unamiable. Mr. Lytton Strachey is too intelligent for abuse, too independent for apology; and he makes no unfair or unhumorous exhibition of his abundant wit. Let Victorians come up for judgment, but in a just and magnanimous court, he seems to say; and his selected specimens, Manning, Florence Nightingale, Dr. Arnold, and General Gordon, he treats neither as waxwork models nor criminals nor fools. He only claims the right to place them so that they may not flinch from his very direct and searching gaze. No undertaker's biography for him. The result is an unusually interesting volume in a department of literature, which in England, has fallen to a grievously low level.

With one exception, his subjects are handled with a mild justice. He has a warm and humorous appreciation of the individuality, the originality of the English character, and surely his candour about some of the weaknesses so inextricably mixed up with Gordon's genius can offend none save the blindest worshippers. The marvellous and incalculable man, so impossibly heroic, so impossible, was never better portrayed. Also the studies of Florence Nightingale and Dr. Arnold could hardly be bettered. Mr. Strachey refuses to see the great per-

1. A review by Anne MacDonnell of Lytton Strachey's book.

sonality obscured by the 'lady with the lamp' legend. Acknowledging her gifts of pity and love, he persists in thrusting on our notice the fiery fighter, the woman of irresistible, relentless will who made all her helpers tools, minions – for the cause. And without forcing the point he lays his finger on the limitations which prevented Arnold from using his great success as a reformer of schools for the enfranchisement of English upper-class education, which he left still bogged in the mediaeval tradition.

Only in the study of Manning do we guess temper. The uneasy conscience of the man struggling with the worldliness of the ecclesiastic he shows, but never the worldliness conquered. And though he owns the marvellous attraction the old Cardinal had for the populace, does he gauge the full meaning of it? Perhaps the instincts of the labourers and the oppressed were quicker and truer.

A.M.

# Journey's End?

## GUILDHALL ON THE EVE

Monday, November 11, 1918

London, Sunday

During its long and remarkable history the London Guildhall has surely never been the scene of such a momentous gathering as that of last night.

As the guests assembled there was a tense feeling of expectation. The late editions of the evening papers had announced the abdication of the Kaiser and the Crown Prince, and the guests hardly believed it. 'Do you think it is true?' was the question that met one at every turn, and the gathering as a whole certainly did not trust the news absolutely until, at a late hour, the Prime Minister announced it as the climax of the events of the last fortnight. Then there was a storm of cheering such as has not been heard, at least in that hall, for many years.

But I am anticipating. The Prime Minister's speech always comes late at this banquet, and there was much to hear before we reached it. The note of victory was all over the gathering. When the toast of the King was honoured a most unusual thing happened. Usually the band plays the National Anthem, and that is all, but this time the guests insisted on singing it. Then we had a speech from Mr. Balfour, who, in proposing 'Our Allies,' travelled from Siberia to the United States, and rather wearied some of his audience. The French Ambassador, a picturesque yet dignified figure, the *doyen* of the Diplomatic Corps, replied in French. He never speaks English – in public. His theme was the perfect unity of military effort and political aim among the Allies. After this came the toast of the 'Imperial Forces,' proposed, according to custom, by one of the Sheriffs. There were three replies, and two of them were very long, the audience became visibly impatient at the prospect of having to wait so long for the Prime Minister.

It was ten minutes past ten before Mr. Lloyd George got his opportunity, and as the guests had assembled at six o'clock it was small wonder that they had been showing signs of restiveness. But they received the Prime Minister tumultuously. He knew what they were expecting. Nearly everybody had some idea that he might have in his pocket the reply of the Germans to the armistice terms.

He told them at once that he had no news of the sort, and then went into a comparison between the state of things a year ago, when Italy had just suffered a great defeat, and now. He reminded us of our own danger 'in the springtime,' a phrase he repeated over and over again, and then he sketched the position 'at the falling of the leaf.' Turkey, Bulgaria, and Austria had gone, while the great Empire that threatened civilisation was headless – thus leading up to his announcement of the abdication. 'Was there ever,' he asked, 'a more dramatic (here he paused) judgment?' and again the cheers were loud and long.

But unquestionably the part of the speech which was most to the liking of the audience was that in which he discussed what Germany would do with the terms of the armistice. 'She has her choice to-day – she will have none to-morrow' was a declaration which seemed to produce great delight, as did also the suggestion that the German people had been behind their rulers in their crimes against humanity and would have cheered them to-day if only they had won. He promised 'a stern reckoning' for the horrors. A glowing tribute to the fighting men – 'leaders and men' (though he never mentioned Sir Douglas Haig) – led up to a very moving passage about what we owe not merely to the men but to the mothers and wives and fathers who have grown grey in anxiety.

The speech was real Lloyd George all through – the touch of poetic fancy, the joy of scoring over critics, the moving references to family sufferings, and the appeal for national support. But it disappointed those who had gone to hear the note of final triumph. They heard the note of triumph, but not of final triumph.

## LONDON ON THE DAY[1]

### Tuesday, November 12, 1918

London, Monday Night

The maroons that had in the bad nights of the past beat like blows on the drum of Fate gave the news to London at eleven o'clock this morning, and sounded the overture of rejoicing.

This idea of using the maroons came right out of the humorous mind of London, and the once terrible sound was like a huge Cockney chuckle of delight. The guns boomed over the heavy grey sky, and everybody knew that the last guns had been fired on the home front.

Before the sound had died away innumerable people everywhere rushed into the streets, from house, factory, and workshop, and children helter-skelter from the schools crying 'The war is over!' In a few minutes all over London the little boys in red with the bugles, who used to send us to bed when the Gothas[2] had gone, were starting out blowing the cheery 'All clear' for the war. These chubby little angels of good-will were greeted everywhere with affectionate laughter as they blew away the four years' nightmare and all its horrors. The trains on all the lines carried on the note with a wheezy shriek of delight. The fat tugs on the river tried to play a tune on one note, and with all these noises mingled the first thin wail of cheers that in a very short time grew loud enough to drown the maroons.

Then the bells, that we have never dared to ring but once on any great day of war, burst into a confident ringing, Big Ben over all, letting themselves go, like all London below them. The bells acted like a beaten tin summoning a swarm of bees.

Looking from a Fleet Street window it was curious to see how instantaneously the swarm rushed out. The crowd gathered momentum in a most extraordinary way. In five minutes there was not an office window without a glaring new flag, till the street looked as if prepared for a mediaeval pageant. Hawkers appeared as from trap-doors with handfuls of hand-banners. The school children each had one in a twinkling, and went singing and dancing westward, leading a long procession from east to west that went on getting busier and more cheerful all day. Like magic the 'buses converted themselves into moving grandstands for the show. Within ten minutes I saw on the hood of a 'bus over the driver an officer, a private, a Wren, and a

1. By Francis Perrot     2. German bombers

W.A.A.C. dancing a peace dance. Nobody paid any fares – indeed very soon the conductresses gave up hope of collecting them.

Motor-cars came along, with people sticking to every inch of them like flies on treacle. Inside might be a small selection of the Allies, some dark Italian officer with cameo face, a blonde English staff officer, a land girl on the bonnet, all mixed up with accretions of Australians wearing Union Jacks instead of their slouch hats, a gorgeous Indian in a turban, and perhaps a bright blue Frenchman. A little later the munition workers joined the throng, doing the solemn East End dance down the Strand or clustered in the heavy army waggons. And all this motley mob went shouting, waving, in complete abandonment, down towards Whitehall, wounded soldiers with flags draped over their hospital blue stumping cheerily after.

The first instinct of the crowd took it to the seat of government and to Downing Street. They had not long to wait before Mr. Lloyd George appeared. He came out on the door-step of No. 10 almost before the maroons had finished, and stood there with uplifted head, smiling at the crowd. As soon as he could be heard he said: 'I am glad to tell you that the war will be over at eleven o'clock to-day.' He waved his hand and disappeared.

But the crowd wanted more of him. He was seen again at a first-floor window with Mr. Bonar Law and Mr. Winston Churchill – who had had an ovation all to himself as his car was pushed by the crowd down Whitehall. 'You are well entitled to rejoice.'

The housemaids of Downing Street waved their dusters and feather mops overhead. All the government clerks, men and women, lined the windows and balconies, and even ridged the roof of the Foreign Office, and they all followed Mr. Lloyd George's lead and rejoiced.

# CHAPTER EIGHT

# Disenchantment of
# A Liberal Newspaper

\*

This short period of Nemesis starts with the peace conference in Paris and ends with the resignation of Lloyd George, who was never again to hold power. Behind the unrest in Britain and the fighting in Ireland and in Europe there had been an idealism which gave way to frustration. By the end of 1922 something like normality was returning to the world and for the time being both fears and dreams were being put away.

Nineteen-nineteen saw the return of C. E. Montague to the staff, and the rapid emergence of E. T. Scott, C. P.'s son, as a principal leader-writer. J. L. Hammond gave more and more of his time to work for the *Guardian*, while a future editor, A. P. Wadsworth, made his reputation as a reporter. Another future editor, W. P. Crozier, consolidated his position as the indispensable lieutenant without whom the paper might, perhaps, on occasions have failed to come out. For the first time the *Guardian* had a regular body of full-time foreign correspondents, while 'the troubles' in Ireland gave reporters from Manchester work worthy of their skill and devotion. Nineteen-twenty-one was the *Guardian*'s centenary year for which C. P. Scott wrote his best remembered words – 'Comment is free, but facts are sacred. It is well to be frank; it is even better to be fair.'

## Britain at Peace

### MILITARY OCCUPATION OF GLASGOW

Monday, February 3, 1919
*From our Special Correspondent*[1]

Glasgow, Sunday Night
Glasgow found itself yesterday morning under military occupation. One's rest was disturbed in the small hours by the noisy tramp of feet and the hoarse yell of sergeants' orders. By morning some thou-

1. A. P. Wadsworth

sands of troops had been distributed all over the city. At the railway station approaches stood sentries in full field equipment, complete with tin hat and fixed bayonet. The Municipal Buildings might have been some French château before the days of long-range guns, expecting a revolutionary attack. Sentries stood at the gates. The interior quadrangle was filled with soldiers. Machine-guns, piles of rifles, and rolls of barbed wire lay about.

In other parts of the city things were the same. The post office, railway and river bridges, electricity stations, tramway depots, and gasworks were heavily guarded. One hears of carefully worked-out military plans which told how quickly troops could be rushed here or how long it would take to plant a machine-gun there, for troops had been steadily brought in through the early hours of the morning. They chiefly belonged to Highland regiments, but there were a few English battalions from regiments of the Durhams and the Surreys. They were, many of them, soldiers just returned from France who had been hurriedly drafted here from demobilisation camps.

To approach the City Chambers yesterday was as difficult as to approach G.H.Q. You had elaborately to explain your business, and then you passed through to an office. You found it occupied by soldiers, apparently busy on the clerical duties of a campaign. Piles of kit lay in the corridors, men were stretched out sleeping on the bare marble floors, stores and ammunition waggons rumbled in. Wireless apparatus was fixed to the central tower of the building.

Glasgow views these excited preparations with indifference and curiosity. To anyone who watched closely the disorder of Friday such lavish and pretentious display of force seemed altogether disproportionate and a trifle ludicrous. One doubts very seriously whether more than one or two hundred of the strikers in Friday's crowd took part in the assault, and they were easily dispersed by a comparatively small number of police.

The interference of the police was certainly within legal limits. They were within their rights in keeping the free passage of the tramcars, but it is quite probable that if a little more latitude had been allowed to such a great mass of people, violence might have been avoided. One cannot understand why the police could not keep the tramway route clear from the start instead of letting the crowd gather and completely block up the street before they forcibly opened up the traffic line. The subsequent rioting followed on this first exercise of force by the police.

Still the city authorities had evidently the highest official sanction for determined action, but it will be a great mistake if the impression goes forth that the Glasgow trouble was the beginning of an abortive

Bolshevik movement and the country has been spared unspeakable horrors by the intervention of the troops. It is true that Glasgow is the home of a few political extremists who have talked noisily of a class war on Russian lines. Some of these may have taken part in the strike, although one heard nothing of Bolshevism in their public speeches, and the most prominent of them, John McLean, never appeared in the strike at all.

The Clyde trouble, one is convinced, sprang from economic and industrial causes. The whole argument of the strike, and that which brought out more than 50,000 men, was the proposition that shorter hours will absorb the unemployed and demobilised workers. Where the movement has run up against established order has been in its assertion that official trade unionism works too slowly and needs supplementing by a newer form of industrial action and organisation, but unless the State is prepared to prescribe the forms which working-class association may take the agitation within trade union ranks is a domestic matter with which the Government can have no direct concern. That is why the arrest of the three leaders – Shinwell, Gallacher, and Kirkwood[1] – by no means ends the trouble. They are all of them more industrial than political agitators. The parade of military force may have unpleasant reactions. It may stop the more violent and intolerant manifestations of the strike – the intimidation of mass picketing, the threat to the municipal services, and the stupid street hooliganism of a few youths, – but it has not ended the strike. The employers clearly view the trouble as the work of a small faction who are being used 'by Continental Bolsheviks as a catspaw to discredit the sane element in trade unionism, create chaos in the industrial world, and upset the existing structure of society for ends which are not entirely unselfish.' The remedy proposed is for the union executives to deal with recalcitrant officials and members, and for the civic authorities to enforce order.

This statement of view has the merit of simplicity, but it is much too simple to explain the complex causes which have produced the ferment on the Clyde.

1. Gallacher, a Communist, Kirkwood and Shinwell all became M.P.s and Shinwell, Minister of Defence.

## PEACE CELEBRATIONS

A *Guardian* leader-writer, almost certainly Montague, expressed
the mood in which many soldiers came back from France in these
words – he was writing about the way in which they would react
to an anti-Bolshevik crusade in Russia – 'As a body they have
come or are coming home in such a state of scepticism about
official politicians as has probably never before possessed any
great mass of men in the world. From men so utterly sick of war
as to be impatient and derisive of any touch of rhetoric, even
innocent rhetoric, about it, such a proposal would meet with
angry or contemptuous repudiation.' (April 5, 1919.) He was
writing then about manual workers, but he was expressing his
own views in a later leader.

### Friday, June 27, 1919

There is a part of the population, shallow, luxurious and vulgar-
hearted, which seems to be trying as hard as it can to give to English
life that special quality often found in Empires that are over-blown
and ripe for degradation. It was seen in Paris in 1870 and in Berlin in
1914 – a kind of grandiose insolence of self-indulgence; the ancient
Greeks had a special word for it, and read it as a symptom of nearing
ruin. That part of our population no doubt would find a record glare
and blare of noise and illumination very much to its mind. So, perhaps,
would a few dealers in bunting, rockets, and refreshments. But scarcely
anyone else.

An extraordinarily large number of soldiers had the idea that they
might first learn that peace had come by hearing a joyful peal of bells
from the nearest unruined church tower in their rear. Many of them
did hear this, with an effect they are not likely to forget, within a few
seconds of the commencement of the Armistice.[1] Such men do not
want to hear any more guns or to see any more signal rockets. Still less
do they want any such 'portions and parcels of the dreadful past' as
formal musters and reviews. For them the general ringing of bells, one
of the most ancient, beautiful, and moving expressions of a common
joy, pretty well exhausts the possibilities of congenial demonstration
on this occasion. It costs almost nothing, and, as to results, you cannot
go one better than perfection.

Men and women are learning, each with his own measure of bitterness, the element of disillusion that there is in nearly all success. You

1. Montague had himself heard the bells at Mons on November 11, 1918.

fight the good fight, and, lo!, the prize itself has changed while you fought, and alloy has crept into the gold. You finish the long race, and only then you find that the 'you' who has won it is not the same 'you' who once had it to win. Everywhere, in all classes, you find a vague disappointment that the victorious England is not the England of August 4, 1914, simply with her desire attained; that Europe to-day is not the Europe of then, with the simple excision of Prussian militarism; and that in the peace now coming to birth there will not breathe simply the public passion which animated the free world less than five years ago. It may be that Prussianism, in its own fall, has infected its executioners; we cannot tell. Anyhow, something seems to be lost of the spirit which fired us then, and we cannot get it back any more than the parents can get back their sons. It is a delicate business to tell a nation so full of disquiet, so little at peace with itself, how to rejoice that it finds itself where it stands. There is a time to rejoice and a time to refrain from rejoicing, and also there is a time not to refrain wholly but to be sober and rather humble in one's joy.

## ECONOMIC CONSEQUENCES OF THE PEACE

*The Economic Consequences of the Peace* and Hitler's *Mein Kampf* were perhaps the two most influential new books in shaping the political outlook of the inter-war generation. J. L. Hammond, who had been the *Guardian*'s principal correspondent at the Peace Conference, reviewed Keynes's book in this leader page article. Keynes himself was a frequent contributor to the paper in 1921, and in 1922 he edited the important Reconstruction supplements for the *Manchester Guardian Commercial*.

Wednesday, December 24, 1919

Mr. J. M. Keynes was the most important of the advisers of the most important of the Governments represented in the great Conference of Paris. An economist of high repute, he was taken into the Treasury during the war, and the reputation to which he owed his selection for this special employment was so much enhanced that he was chosen to speak for that Department when the Allies met to arrange the terms of peace. He took the leading part in the long and difficult deliberations over reparation that occupied so much of the time of the Big Four, and he sat in Mr. Bonar Law's place at the Supreme Economic Council when the Chancellor could not attend. He resigned when the policy of the Council took a course that seemed to him fatal and irrevocable.

The publication of this book is, therefore, not merely an act of conspicuous courage and public spirit: it is an infinitely more important event than any speech that has been made on the peace by any of its authors. He tells us what he thinks; they tell us what they force themselves to think. As a piece of literature it is beyond praise; if many economists had his wit, his eloquence, his easy address in stating and analysing confused and intricate problems, their science would never have been called dismal. His portraits of the three chief figures[1] are masterpieces. But the book which would live by these qualities alone is yet more valuable, because it tells the world how the peace looks to the best minds that were engaged on its problems. Its appearance is a political event of great moment, for it gives to all the men and women who know that Europe has gone wrong at this crisis in her history clear and definite guidance on the measures that can and should be taken to retrieve those errors so far as it is still possible to retrieve them.

A story was going round Paris last spring of a famous dialogue between Lord Robert Cecil and one of the most intransigent of his French colleagues. 'You want to destroy Germany, and you want at the same time to enrich France,' said Lord Robert. 'Unfortunately, revenge and avarice are in this case incompatible.' A good part of Mr. Keynes's book is really the demonstration and illustration of this thesis. The peace ruins Germany, and at the same time it promises to the Entente Powers an indemnity which is not put into figures in the treaty, but which is meant to correspond in the public mind to the fantastic sums that were named on Coalition platforms a year ago. Now it is a simple thing to ruin Germany, but to ruin Germany or any other industrial State without ruining her neighbours is a less simple or straightforward matter; to ruin her and then to bleed her is the dream of a madman. The peace in its present form satisfies the desire for vengeance at the cost of the welfare of the world; it is not tenderness for Germany but care for mankind that makes every reasonable man condemn it when he realises its character.

Not, of course, that this is the only standard. Peace was promised on certain terms. Mr. Keynes's comparison of the terms on which the Armistice was arranged with the terms of the Treaty will not be read by any self-respecting Englishman without acute discomfort. Those of us who were following the proceedings from the outside regarded the moment when the President was brought to accept the charge for separation[2] allowances as falling within the reparation which the Armistice terms recognised as the most definite moment of capitulation.

1. Lloyd George, Wilson and Clemenceau.      2. i.e., marriage allowances to soldiers.

It is interesting to see that this is Mr. Keynes's view. His analysis of the casuistical processes by which the more subtle minds of his colleagues persuaded the President that his words meant less and less until they came to mean nothing at all makes one wish that we had similar intimate pictures of the play of character in other great debates in the history of the world. As a human drama it is an absorbing spectacle. But for us Englishmen, whose reputation for centuries will depend on these events, the history of these transactions is a painful exhibition of the easy transitions by which a nation that started with lofty scruples and high-minded ideals may be brought by its leaders into a fatal compromise of all its principles.

Why did the treaty go wrong? The leading cause is given in a passage towards the end of Mr. Keynes's book:

> It is an extraordinary fact that the fundamental economic problem of a Europe starving and disintegrating before their eyes was the one question on which it was impossible to arouse the interest of the Four. Reparation was their main excursion into the economic field, and they settled it as a problem of theology, of politics, of electoral chicane, from every point of view except that of the economic future of the States whose destiny they were handling.

This problem was pressed on the Four by their most competent advisers. If America can claim credit for Mr. Hoover, we may remember with some satisfaction in this dark hour when famine is no longer a shadow on the horizon, when whole peoples are dying because the great statesmen who met in the President's mansion had no time for such trifles, that Sir William Goode, Sir William Beveridge, and Mr. Keynes himself, to mention only some of the British Staff, were not less insistent on the urgency of this problem. French sentiment never forgave the President his reluctance to visit the devastated districts. That was one of his capital mistakes. But he and Mr. Lloyd George made a greater, for if they had seen with their own eyes the misery of the world of Central and Eastern Europe, with whose calamities they were toying, these advisers would not have been put on one side, nor would General Smuts and Lord Robert Cecil have pleaded in vain with the masters of the fate of Europe.

Why was the sum that Germany was to pay left indeterminate? The answer is no longer a secret. Week after week the Big Four wrangled over the share that France and England were to take. Mr. Lloyd George did not dare to tell the British electorate, who had been told that the whole cost of the war could be got out of Germany, that they had been deceived by their Government at the December election.

M. Clemenceau did not dare to mention a figure to his countrymen, because no figure that could be stated would come up to their expectations. It looked as if the treaty must wait indefinitely. Then a happy thought struck these statesmen. Let us name no figure at all, but let us draw up categories of obligation, make Germany accept them, and then go on year after year taking whatever we can get out of her. In other words, the fate of the peace was sealed when Mr. Lloyd George decided to make the indemnity the election cry, for he went to Paris the prisoner of the most reckless pledges ever given by a statesman. In December he could have saved Europe.

J.L.H.[1]

## THE MAN WHO WON THE WAR

### Thursday, November 11, 1920

A WARRIOR OF THE GREAT WAR KNOWN UNTO GOD

This was written on a wreath of laurel picked in the gardens of Ypres that was laid on the coffin in Westminster Abbey to-day. In the quiet, quiet spaces, in the exquisite ritual in between the flights of holy song, the prayers, the quiet speech by the graveside, one had time to let the mind busy itself with thoughts of what manner of man he was. Known to God, yes, and though his name will never be learned, known surely to us all by long intimacy in the years of war. Whatever is forgotten and unknown, the soldier as we knew him will never be, and this man stands for the type for ever. Such a man, one liked to think, as those honest-faced Guardsmen waiting there by the pillar to let the coffin down, an ordinary man, full of weakness, as we all are, but going through with the job as a plain matter of duty. The man who won the War.

They have given him for burial place the fittest that could be found. He lies apart from the great-named, the people of real or imagined importance in their day, right in the middle of the nave. The nave from ancient times was the people's part of a great church. This was a man of the people, and his stone will be trodden by everyone's feet. It is the true centre of the Abbey.

Sunlight came through the painted armour of a medieval warrior greeting a fellow-soldier with uplifted spear in a window over the grave. It made a bright patch on the yellowish columns and lit gro-

1. J. L. Hammond

tesquely the pompous effigies of eighteenth-century nobodies by the wall. A soft bell tolling in the misty height was the only sound for a long time.

A thousand bereaved women were sitting waiting, their mourning lightened by the flowers and wreaths on their knees. About a hundred V.C.s came in and formed an avenue from the choir gate – the Unknown's guard of honour. The heroes were ranged without distinction of rank. A naval commander, stiff with gold braid, would be next to an A.B., and among the soldiers you saw a famous officer like Freyberg[1] shoulder to shoulder with an ex-private in civilian clothes. It was a little democracy of valour. Fourteen wives and mothers who received the V.C. for their dead men folk had places of honour.

Looking up this avenue there was a vague glimpse of distant richness, of colour and golden lights about the high altar, and down the long church poured elegiac music from a soldiers' band – soft fluty music that wandered to and fro like the pulses of thought. Quietness was the note of all.

After a long time the choir, a procession of floating white and scarlet, moved up the nave into the choir, the Dean, solemn, and erect in his stiff mourning cope, walking last. They were singing the hymn:

> *O valiant hearts who to your glory came*
> *Through dust of conflict and through battle flame*

with that unearthly wistfulness of cathedral choristers. The sound diminished and became a faint bell-like resonance in the distance. Then from the remote altar came a murmur of words. The precentor was intoning the Lord's Prayer.

Silence. The bell tolled eleven, one heavy stroke after another, and at once all of us in the church became part of the multitude outside in the same mood. Out there in the street some loud word of command followed the last stroke. All sound ceased in a strange intensity of stillness. For two minutes it lasted, so that a creaking chair or a cough jarred intolerably. The cathedral seemed to breathe as in sleep.

The singers broke the silence at last, breathing out like a sigh the opening of the Contakion of the faithful departed:

'Give rest, O Christ, to Thy servants with Thy saints where sorrow and pain are no more, neither sighing, but life everlasting.

'Thou only art immortal, the Creator and Maker of man, and we are mortal, formed of the earth, and unto earth we shall return.'

Although the body had not yet come this seemed the most beautiful

---

1. Bernard Freyberg (1889–1963), New Zealand general and governor-general of New Zealand 1946–1952.

moment of the service, the purest in emotion, the most favourable to memory and aspiration.

The service was interrupted for a time while the clergy and the choir went to the north transept to usher the Warrior into his resting-place. As they went gusts of diminishing song floated back to us. The door opened, and there was a rush of sound from the outside, where the King was waiting. The guns were firing the Field-Marshal's salute for the unknown, like nineteen soft bangs on a big drum.

At the end of this we heard, still from the outside, a band rolling out the Chopin march, the weeping ghost of a tune. Drums rolled, trumpets shrilled.

The bells pealed louder; as the procession turned and advanced through the choir towards us the funeral march swelled potently. The choristers led the way, pacing very slowly behind the golden cross, singing with many pauses the 'I am the Resurrection and the Life.'

Down the lane of khaki and naval blue and hospital blue – what thoughts of War days that unfamiliar colour gave – the Guardsmen carried the coffin. On it lay the man's steel helmet and a laurel wreath. The soldiers set it down over the grave.

The King stood at the foot facing west. The Dean with the Archbishop, and the clergy clustered behind them, were at the head of the coffin, facing the mourner for a nation.

The customary ritual of burial took only a few more minutes: the Twenty-third Psalm, the recital of the chapter that tells of those who have come through 'the great tribulation,' and as we were singing 'Lead, kindly Light' the Guardsmen lowered the soldier into the grave – with the words 'The night is gone' he disappeared.

The Dean handed the King a silver shell in which was soil brought from France. The King cast it upon the coffin. Last of all, in the secular key of warning, Kipling's cry against 'the frantic boast, the foolish word' rang through the church.

From the east came a reiterated roll of drums, then the clear call of the reveille – a cheerful challenge carrying us on to the life that must be lived in action. The King's wreath lay at the head of the grave. It was over.

The King and his following went out at the west door, that yawned now to let the chilly mist of the London day and the noises of the street in upon that warm-coloured splendour, that calm of recollection. The Unknown Warrior lay there wrapped in his purple. There was a pause, and the cathedral bells alone rang silverly high in the air. Soon the throng of dignitaries, statesmen, soldiers, and sailors who had followed the King went by, casting each a look into the grave as they passed.

Then the congregation moved and became a crowd pressing with one impulse towards the coffin. The V.C.s broke the solemn ranks and became just comrades looking their last on a comrade. The bandsmen, carrying their instruments, came along sheepishly and gazed.

Then the women left their seats and began that long file past of the bereaved that was to last all through the day. West End and East End, all was one in this democracy of memory. The rich woman and the poor – for all the open grave meant exactly the same thing. A woman plucked a white chrysanthemum from a bunch she carried and threw it in the tomb. This example was quickly followed, and soon the purple carpet was thickly scattered with flowers white and red.

> The drums and the trumpets give you music,
> But my heart, O my Warrior, my Comrade,
> My heart gives you love.
>
> F.P.[1]

## SIR ERIC GEDDES AND HIS AXE

### Tuesday, February 21, 1922

Amid paeans of applause from the greater part of the press, Sir Eric Geddes, Lord Inchcape, and their colleagues have at length produced their much-advertised report. Instantaneous approval of 'the Report, the whole Report, and nothing but the Report' is preached as almost the first of patriotic duties. The judicious reader, who has passed the stage of swallowing documents whole because they appear in blue covers, will begin his examination of the Report by distinguishing critically between them [its different elements].

With the administrative proposals of the Report it is not necessary to deal at length. The invitation to local education authorities to reduce teachers' salaries is a much more serious matter.

The Report recommended a reduction and the placing of pensions on a contributory basis.

It must be remembered that the teaching profession has only just been rescued from a condition of things in which it was actually a 'decaying trade,' the annual entrants to the profession up to about two years ago being insufficient to replace the normal wastage. The

1. Francis Perrot

real salaries of teachers fell enormously during the war, when most other classes of workers received advances corresponding (of course very roughly and with many exceptions) to the rise in the cost of living. When, very tardily, the Burnham scales were fixed, it was understood that the teachers were to have the benefit up to 1925 of any subsequent fall in prices.

The teachers' organisations, however, will look after the question of salaries, and it may be doubted whether the Cabinet will risk a fall with them. The really tragic business is the menace to those who have no organisation and no votes, the children themselves. If the proposals are carried out as they stand, the result for millions of children will be a real catastrophe, which will leave its scar on our national life long after Geddes and Inchcape, and the critics of Geddes and Inchcape, are mercifully forgotten. The schools, which in the seventies were a kind of educational factory, were on the way to becoming places of natural and many-sided growth. All that movement, with its infinite possibilities for body and spirit, for the individual and society, is to stop.

> Geddes recommended the raising of the age of admission to six, the raising of class sizes from 32.4 per teacher to 50, and a big reduction in expenditure on special services such as medical provision.

Life in the twentieth century for the children of the poor is still a dangerous business: how dangerous the figures of child mortality and, still more, of child sickness, reveal. Now, up to six, in colliery village and factory town, in overcrowded tenement and foetid slum, they are to scramble along unaided. All the delicate skill which was gradually laying the foundations of a new way of life for young children is, so far as any but the rich are concerned, to be suddenly demobilised. All the recent improvements in the primary schools – nearly all in the direction of one form or another of 'auto-education,' of freedom, responsibility, initiative for the individual child – are to be swept away. The abolition of all free places above 25 per cent [in secondary schools] will ruin the pioneer work of Durham and Bradford and a score of other enlightened authorities. That, with higher fees and fewer schools [the Report recommended a 'substantial' raising of fees, and a reduction in the number of grant-aided schools], will go far to make secondary education what it was before 1902 – the privilege of the rich. Nor, once the programme is put into force, will matters stop there. Education is not a machine which can be taken to pieces and then re-assembled. It is a living organism. When it is starved it dies, and when it dies Sir Eric

Geddes himself could not recall it to life. The whole *moral* of public education will run down.

The Report confronts the nation with a moral issue of a very searching character, and more than is commonly realised depends upon the response to it. For consider the philosophy behind its proposals. It does not actually state, in so many words, that the children of the workers, like anthropoid apes, have fewer convolutions in their brains than the children of the rich. It does not state it because it assumes it. Its authors cry aloud that 'the condition of things when taxes and local rates were drawn on *only* to pay for the *elementary* education of the children of the working classes has been abandoned.' They lament, without adducing a shadow of evidence to prove their contention, that 'children whose mental capabilities do not justify higher education are receiving it' – though I do not observe that they propose to reserve endowed schools and universities for 'children whose mental calibre justifies it.' While most decent men have viewed with satisfaction the recent considerable development of secondary education, they deplore it as a public catastrophe, and are indignant that education, unlike the services supplied by Sir Eric Geddes and Lord Inchcape,[1] is sold 'below actual cost.' They think it preposterous that the reduction in the size of classes – how rarely, alas! carried out – should give common children the chance of individual attention. They propose to increase them, to raise fees, to convert what are now grant-aided secondary schools into private schools reserved for 'children whose parents can well afford to defray the whole expense themselves,' to abolish the system of state scholarships which has recently made it possible for a slightly increased – though still very small – number of working-class children to pass on to the universities. Their programme in short is 'back to 1870.' Their aim is to re-establish and perpetuate the organisation of education upon lines of class which has been the tragedy of the English educational system, as of English society, since its inception, and from which it was just beginning to escape.

Swift once suggested killing babies and tanning their skins, which, he shrewdly observed, would make excellent leather, and could be sold by business men at a profit. Is it much more humane to 'save' money by reducing height, weight, vitality, and mental development of children between 5 and 14?

R.H.T.[2]

1. Railways and shipping.    2. R. H. Tawney

# War in Ireland

The old Irish Nationalist Party was wiped out in the 1918 general election and replaced by Republican Sinn Feiners. On January 22, 1919 they met for the first time in Dublin as Dail Eireann. The same day two members of the Royal Irish Constabulary were assassinated in County Tipperary. 'The troubles' had begun.

## TERROR IN GALWAY

Friday, October 22, 1920
*From our Special Correspondent*[1]

Galway, Thursday
The Chief Secretary is good enough to suggest that English journalists who have written of the reprisals in Ireland draw their facts from the tainted source of the Irish Republican army or are persons of such 'anaemic and hysterical disposition' that they can see something to be condemned in the partial burning of half a dozen villages and a score of farmhouses. Sir Hamar Greenwood, to the discredit of his office and of the good name of the Government, knows less about the real state of Ireland than any English businessman who has travelled the country and met all sorts and conditions of its people. On the occasions when he comes to Ireland he remains in the seclusion of his Lodge or the Castle, perhaps paying an odd visit to Belfast. Of what happens in the South and West – in Cork, in Limerick, or in Galway – he knows nothing but what his police and military advisers tell him. He has instituted inquiries into some reprisals and he complains that the evidence is insufficient to convict anyone. Well it might be when the persons called on to report on the reprisals are policemen and soldiers themselves, whose natural concern is to screen or to explain away the excesses of their comrades. In the cases – and they are not few – where inoffensive civilians have been shot through some military or police stupidity there is a secret military inquiry at which, again, the evidence is wholly official.

One had thought that Sinn Fein's casuistry about police murders was bad enough, but the Chief Secretary outrivals it. There is no need to repeat the facts of the 'alleged reprisals' which one gathered on the spot while the ruins were still smoking and the people still too terrified

1. A. P. Wadsworth

to have had time to concoct any wicked libels on the police or soldiers. One can point to the murders and woundings of civilians that have taken place in the last week as evidence too plain to be tainted that the Chief Secretary is either suppressing or ignoring facts when he denies that his servants are pursuing a calculated policy of frightfulness. These are the acts not of men who have 'seen red' when a comrade has been murdered, but of his police and their auxiliaries as part of their police duties. The murders of the men in the reprisals are completely authenticated – Gibbons and Lawless at Balbriggan, Connolly, Sammon, and Linnane at Ennistymon and Lahinch, Quirke at Galway, three Sinn Fein leaders in Belfast, and a man and a boy at Bruree, Limerick. There have been numerous cases of people who have lost their lives owing to a policeman's or a soldier's rifle going off before they could reply to the challenge; a number of others where men were pulled out of their homes and shot. Three such were reported on Monday night alone – that of the brothers O'Dwyer at Ballydavid, Tipperary, and a man at Ballinagare, county Roscommon, while the same night a man was shot in the street in Drogheda by 'uniformed men.'

In none of these cases was there armed resistance, and only in the first group immediate provocation. But when one comes to acts which do not result in death, but only in wounds and loss of property, the indictment is longer. One need only take one county. Below are some examples taken down by myself[1] from the lips of the men attacked, who were cross-examined and cross-questioned, and corroborative evidence sought from others. No man who has had any experience in the sifting of evidence could doubt the general truth of their statements.

Michael Furey, Oranmore, County Galway, – At twelve o'clock last Thursday night I heard two shots fired outside the door and voices shouting 'Get up! Get up! Get a move on!' My father jumped up, but was not quick enough, because the door was smashed in before he reached it. They said to him, 'Who are you?' He replied, 'Roger Furey.' 'Is that right?' said one of the men, turning to another, who said, 'Yes.' They asked him to show them where his sons were sleeping, and told him to get back to bed. They came to where my brother Pat and I were in bed and said: 'We're told you're "Shinners." Get out!' We jumped up and I went to get my trousers, but they would not allow me to dress. We were both of us taken out, and beaten with revolver butts on the back of the head as we were going. Then we were told to go to the wall, getting another 'belt.' There we were asked if we had any prayers to say, and told, 'We give you three minutes to say your prayers.'

1. In Galway hospital.

We got on our knees, but they did not give my brother much chance to pray. They put questions to him, 'Were you responsible for the death of Constable Foley?' He said he was innocent of that. A revolver was put down his throat. They came to me and did the same thing. I was told to open my mouth and a revolver barrel was thrust into it. I was then hit on the lip with the revolver. 'I am going to do for you now,' one of the men said. He put out his hand and fired close to my left ear. The bullet grazed the ear, cutting it. We were ordered to get on our feet. A man said, 'Close them up together!' We jumped together and a man in front of us stepped aside, and I could see him raising the light about six yards away. He fired, and I received about 15 pellets in the left leg below the knee. They shouted to me to keep standing. Two more of the men came up and said, 'Captain, you have done enough to these two men; let them go to bed.' We were then told to get to bed, and as we were going into the house two revolver shots were fired at the door. 'Put out any lights or we will call again in an hour,' was shouted at us. I went to bed. Blood was running from my legs and face, and with the light of a shaded candle I tore a piece off the bed sheet and bandaged myself. An hour afterwards they came again and threw a bomb into the kitchen, shaking the whole house, knocking down dressers, milk pans, and crockery, making a good-sized hole in the cement floor and knocking plaster from the ceiling. There were from ten to fifteen men in the party. The man with the revolver wore a grey cap and a trench coat.

The next three cases were connected with the kidnapping of Patrick Joyce, a National School teacher, from Barna, near Galway, last Friday. One may say by way of preface that on Saturday R.I.C. auxiliaries went to Barna and put up notices that if Joyce were not returned by six o'clock they would blow up the village. Six men were held up and questioned and kicked and beaten, including Dominic Fagan, Vice-chairman of the Board of Guardians. The men in the County Hospital are: Thomas Carr, a simple kind of man who has never been known to belong to any political organisation, and William Connolly. Their story was:

Thomas Carr: I was met by police about three in the afternoon and told to put up my hands. My pocket was searched. They found rosary beads and a small knife. They took the knife. My mother came crying: 'Don't kill my son. Don't kill him because he is the only help I have. Give him a chance.' Four other men came up. They said: 'Shoot him! He's a Sinn Feiner.' I was hit on the jaw with a revolver. They asked me about Joyce, and I said I knew nothing about him and that I had no connection with him. A shot was fired over my head. I think they told me to clear off inside to my mother, who was crying. As I got to the door I was shot just above the knee by a revolver bullet.

William Connolly, of Moycullen, ten miles north of Galway: On Monday about one o'clock in the afternoon I was working with four other men on the peat in a bog off the road, when a lorry came up and men asked us if we knew anything of Joyce. I said I didn't know the man. 'Take off your waistcoat,' they said, for I had no coat on. Then they beat me with whips. As I was going away they fired, and I got pellets in the right leg and one in the face below the right eye. The other two men were also beaten. Some of the men in the lorry wore khaki, some had police caps, some trilby hats.

In these cases one had ocular evidence of the men's injuries – bloody faces and bruises where they had been wounded or struck – and the word of the doctors and nurses as to the genuineness of their shot wounds. One heard further details of the activities of the raiders who attacked them, but as the stories were not first-hand one does not give them. The most graphic narrative of all was given me by Lawrence Tallan, manager of the Moycullen Co-operative Society, and an educated man – the others were intelligent peasants – and a man who is not an active Sinn Feiner. He said:

On Monday afternoon, about twenty minutes past twelve, a lorry load of the 6th Dragoons and mixed police [i.e. police in ordinary uniform, police with black caps and khaki uniform, police in civilian clothes], with rifles slung across their shoulders and revolvers, halted at the cross roads. They surrounded our store, a large building 60 feet square, with a cordon of soldiers with fixed bayonets. A man walked in and, holding up a rifle, told all the men to come out and put up their hands. One employee upstairs was a little time in coming, and a shot was fired in the corridor to bring him down. The staff of four men and myself were ordered outside and searched and then put with our backs against the wall. A policeman asked me my name and position. He wore khaki with a black cap, and said: 'Understand, if Joyce is not returned before six o'clock to-night 100 Sinn Feiners will be shot and this village and this house will go up in flames with the rest of them.' They then turned to the first man of the row, Walter McDonagh, and asked him if he knew anything about Joyce, who was missing. He replied he did not, and was hit on the face with a butt of a revolver. 'On my honour,' he said, 'I know nothing of the man, I have heard of him, that is all.' 'Well we will make you know something,' was the reply. The questioner was a man carrying in one hand a revolver and in the other a whip and a leather thong. He wore khaki breeches, a blue guernsey and a round, soft, knitted blue cap. He spoke with a slightly

Cockney accent. 'I know nothing.' McDonagh repeated, 'Take off your trousers,' he was told. He was slow about it, and a man pulled them down for him. His waistcoat was torn off, and the man with the whip lashed him unmercifully, while two policemen stood with pointed rifles, one on each side.

Tim O'Connor was put through the same ordeal, asked the same question and thrashed in the same way with trousers down. I protested 'That man is absolutely innocent,' but they would not listen to me. A bayonet was shoved into my face and I was told to 'Shut up, you ——.' 'We want Joyce or blood!' one shouted. They then said to us 'Clear out immediately!'

As I was going away a policeman asked me my name. I said I was the manager. He said nothing but walked away, and just as I was crossing the road he turned like lightning and raised his rifle. I put up my hand. He fired and pellets struck me on the hand and on the neck and on the upper part of the arm, 32 altogether. I went inside the store where the girls were in a terrified state, kneeling on the floor praying. The police sat on a wall across the road. After a few minutes they laid their rifles on the wall and emptied their magazines into the building, there being several volleys of rifle bullets and some rounds of small shot, for I heard the pellets dropping round. Several bullets pierced the roof, which is of composition. There were about twenty soldiers in the party, but I did not see an officer, as I looked for one to appeal to.

McDonagh was in a bad state. He fainted and when he came to himself, tried to cycle home, but fell off the machine.


## THE DAY THEY BURNT THE CUSTOM HOUSE

Thursday, May 26, 1921
*From our Special Correspondent*[1]

Dublin, Wednesday
Sinn Fein to-day in broad daylight burned down the Custom House, ambushed several lorries of Crown forces, and held up the Central Fire Station. This *coup*, which must have been planned with much care, happened shortly after 1 p.m.

Before that hour a force of Sinn Feiners walked into the Custom House – a large, impressive building – ordered the staff out, and set fire to it. Under the arches which support the Great Northern Railway

1. D. F. Boyd

an ambushing party remained. Three lorries, unaware of the affair, passed and were engaged. Furious fights followed, both here and on the quays, where a tender full of Black-and-Tans had been passing.

A business man who was indoors at the moment says he heard three explosions and then a continual roar of small arms. He looked out and saw the police in the tender firing towards the Custom House and shouting madly. Another spectator, who was looking in the same direction but down Lower Abbey Street, saw the exchange of shots and saw one man, presumably trying to get out of harm's way, dash across the square in front of the Custom House. He was within a few feet of safety when he dropped on the pavement.

Meanwhile flames and great columns of smoke were bursting out of the Custom House windows. There were a few explosions and showers of cindered papers. The fight was still going on, and re-inforcements of military and police began to arrive, but the fire call was not answered.

At the precise moment when the incendiaries began their work six or seven men entered the Central Fire Station, which is only a few yards from the Central Police Barracks, and held up the staff.

Not long after another journalist and myself in search of news knocked at the door of the fire station, and after a moment's scrutiny were allowed in. Firemen in their scarlet shirts and blue caps were standing about. One of them was attending to the telephone in the usual way, and among them moved a number of inconspicuous civilians, one of whom was a boy of perhaps fifteen or sixteen. After a few minutes one of them asked our names and occupations and wrote them down, but it was not until I noticed that one of the men had a bomb in his hand that I guessed what had happened. The party had locked one man in a room but touched nobody else, and behaved with politeness.

It appeared likely then that the military or police would come to the station to inquire after the brigade and that there would be a fight, for the 'phone man could be heard answering constant calls and offering no explanation. A loud knocking sounded at the door. It was opened and a policeman, dishevelled and very shaken, came in and walked to the watch room. The boy produced a large six-chambered revolver, and told the officer to put his hands up. At first the order seemed to amuse him, but he complied when the situation was explained by another raider. It was then learned that he had come for the brigade, but had been forced by the intense fire to take cover on the ground for nearly 20 minutes. Meanwhile the men ordered the motor ambulance out, filed into it, telling us not to move for ten minutes, and so went.

They had scarcely left when a party of Auxiliary police in a car drove up and ordered the brigade out. It was just 1.45 when they got away, about three quarters of an hour after the firing of the Custom House. The latter was now well alight. Great crowds had gathered on the O'Connell bridge and down the quays and side streets to watch it. Every now and then they retreated in panic before the Auxiliaries, who constituted the cordon, and still at half-past two an occasional shot was fired, and there appeared to be no chance of saving the building, said to be worth a million pounds.

It is surmounted by a dome sheathed in copper, and on the top of this stands a huge statue of Hope in stone. At the time of writing flames ring the dome, which springs directly from the entrance hall. At five o'clock the dome was still standing, but the front of the building was apparently absolutely gutted. The inside must be in the same state from front to back.

The Custom House, besides fulfilling its normal functions, also housed the Crown administrative departments of local government, income tax, and old age pensions. It is, therefore, to a great extent the instrument of English government in Ireland, and shares such honours as there are with Dublin Castle.

### COMMENT

Since the burning of central Cork by the Black-and-Tans there has been no single act of arson so destructive as the systematic burning of the great Dublin Custom House by Sinn Feiners yesterday afternoon. The Custom House was the most striking building in Dublin and one of the finest, at any rate of its own ambitious kind, in the United Kingdom. If the procedure in force during the past year is followed, we now may expect some of Sir Hamar Greenwood's irregulars to go out, drunk or sober, in a lorry and burn some public building belonging to people who have no connection with the incendiaries at the Custom House, then the Sinn Fein criminals will probably rejoin in kind, and so the process will go on of razing to the ground at the same time the buildings of Ireland and the reputation of England. The prospect is not cheering.

No foreign nation is likely to go to war with us merely because our relations with Ireland have sunk into a shabby bandying of murder, arson, and robbery with a base and cruel Left wing of a misgoverned and rebellious nation. The harm that we suffer abroad through all this record of dead failure and shame is more insidious than that. It consists of gradual world-wide loss of caste in the eyes of civilised people;

a hastened decrease in the satisfaction with which many Australians, Canadians, and South Africans still acknowledge a close kinship and political connection with us; a progressive disablement of those well-disposed Americans who stand out against the sinister movement in American politics for running as a 'manifest destiny stunt' the idea of an ultimate war with England. We are all able to read now in book form, in English, not only the report of Lord Bryce's commission of inquiry into the German excesses in Belgium, but the German Government's official defence of those black acts. The defence cannot make them white, and yet it makes peculiarly mortifying reading for an English reader. The hands that sign it are German hands, but the voice is the voice of Sir Hamar Greenwood.[1]

Soon after, on July 11, a truce was signed and after difficult negotiations a peace treaty followed on December 6. It came up for ratification in Dail Eireann in January, 1922.

## PEACE – OR ANOTHER WAR?

Monday, January 9, 1922
*From our Special Correspondent*[2]

Dublin, Sunday
In this new drama of Ireland which is now being written the curtain has fallen on the last scene of the first act. It is only that. It is not the end of the play. All through it the action has lain between four chief actors. On either side has been a deeply pondering mind and a mind of ready speech and action – on this side Mr. Erskine Childers and Mr. De Valera, and on that Mr. Arthur Griffith and Mr. Michael Collins.[3]

In the last moments, as the curtain was going down and the throng of minor players were pressing noisily and excitedly off the stage, Mr. Childers was in eclipse; Mr. De Valera – after a brave fight to say what was on his mind – had broken down utterly half way through a sentence, and sat with his face buried in his arms; Mr. Griffith, a little flushed and with heightened colour, sat back in his seat, his thumbs thrust into the armholes of his waistcoat, his chest expanded belligerently. Mr. Collins the man of action, was standing erect, his broad, burly frame and massive dark head dominating the assembly. His good-humoured face was grave in this moment of triumph. He was calling

1. Chief Secretary for Ireland.     2. Howard Spring
3. Within the year three of these four men had been killed. Only De Valera survived the civil war that followed the treaty.

on the other side to join with him in forming a committee of public safety. There was no response.

Other players who will occupy the stage in the coming scenes began to emerge in that last moment, the black, baneful figure of Miss MacSwiney, speaking words of terrific eloquence, bitter words boding rebellion and hate. And the dry, acrid face of Mr. Charles Burgess, who has controlled the Sinn Fein army, floated up for a moment, thin-lipped and white.[1]

Mr. Charles Burgess, the War Minister, was to say the last word against the treaty and Mr. Griffith was then to say the last word of all. For those two speeches everybody was waiting. Mr. Burgess had been kept in the background all through the recent weary days. The Republican party looked to his speech with hope; the treaty party with apprehension.

Mr. Burgess, a stocky, clean-shaven little man, a defiant, dry-faced little man, began to speak in Gaelic. His voice was pitched on a high brassy note, and he split his sentences into little staccato bursts like the rattle of a machine-gun. When at last he broke into English he was soon launched on the full tide of a violent polemic directed against Mr. Michael Collins. There were cries of dissent and disgust. 'Order, order. Let him go on,' shouted a deputy, 'he's making a good speech for the treaty.'

I believe that was literally true. The slow moving of the fateful balance over to the side of the treaty I timed from the opening of that attack. The Irish people know Michael Collins's record, and many were uneasy at the slow-dropping acid of Mr. Burgess's words. He said he proposed to examine three matters – the real position Collins held in the army; what fights he had taken an active part in; did he ever fire a shot at an enemy of Ireland. Having suggested these last two questions Mr. Burgess made no further reference to them, and there was a general sense that was unfair.

He went on to speak of the legendary figure which the press, he said, had made of Mr. Collins. There were hisses and cries of 'Get on with the treaty,' but Mr. Burgess was blind to the wisdom of restraint. He went on like a upas tree in free perspiration. He accused Mr. Collins of trying to make himself a sort of romantic hero, which he certainly was not, and of telling fabulous stories of the price that was on his head.

I think little that the War Chief said after that mattered.

Mr. De Valera was solicitous for Mr. Griffith's comfort, and suggested that tea should be taken before the final speech of the debate was

1. Miss MacSwiney's brother was the Lord Mayor of Cork who died on hunger-strike. Burgess is now often known by the Gaelic form of his name, Cathal Brugha.

made. In the basement canteen of the University all those who were so soon to be in deadliest opposition on the matter of a nation's destiny chatted and laughed together.

Mr. Griffith was the embodiment of pugnacity as his small, tough figure stood facing towards the Opposition bench.

If my name is ever known in history, he declared, amid a storm of applause, I want it to be associated with the name of Michael Collins.

Thereafter, in a speech he has not equalled in the Dail, Mr. Griffith confined himself to examining the treaty. He displayed its solid advantages and the negation of statesmanship that was opposed to it, offering the Irish people no alternative. He spoke of the poverty of Ireland and her need of peace, and emphasised the claims of the living – claims as strong, he said, as those of the dead or the unborn.

When Mr. Griffith had finished, Mr. De Valera, ignoring the rule of debate which gave his opponent the last word, sprang to his feet like a lean prophet and made a passionate harangue, saying the Irish people would rise in judgment if the treaty were carried.

Then, in a tense silence, the roll was called, and in Gaelic each deputy answered yes or no. The Speaker, who does not vote, announced that there were –

|  |  |
|---|---|
| For the treaty | 64 |
| Against | 57 |

All order broke down. The hot room was filled with excited hubbub, till Mr. De Valera rose again to say significant words.

It will be my duty to resign my office (he said), but I don't know that I shall do it just now.

Then he declared that the Irish Republic established by the will of the people still existed. The mere approval of a certain resolution could not alter that.

Then Mr. Collins got up and made his appeal for a joint committee of public safety.

The President knows I have always tried to do my best for him (he said earnestly), and he has exactly the same position in my heart now that he always had.

The President did not answer and Miss MacSwiney undertook the task of dashing away the proffered hand. There was deadly hate in her face as she spoke of the betrayal of the Republic.

When her terrible eloquence was stilled Mr. Collins appealed again for an understanding. Then the President rose again for the last time and looked round the scene of his defeat. He was a worn, weary man, muffled in a thick brown overcoat with a heavy collar that fell down behind his head like a monk's cowl. He struggled with his emotion for a moment, and then managed to say brokenly:

My last word is this. We have had a glorious record, four years of magnificent discipline, with the world looking on, and now –

He stood palely for another moment, trying to urge his trembling lips to frame further words. Then, with a despairing gesture of the arms, he sank down utterly broken.

## BELFAST'S COMPETITION IN ARSON

Thursday, June 15, 1922
*From Our Special Correspondent*[1]

Belfast, Wednesday
The familiar clang of the fire engines accompanied city people to their offices this morning, but only the stranger's head turned round to watch the furious progress of the engines. A fire engine in a Belfast main road is as common a sight as a milk cart in a Manchester suburb. Its presence is accepted with a fatalistic complacency which is not a little bewildering in a Western business city.

There is no great outcry against the daily and nightly burnings, no overwhelming demand on the part of the whole community that the guilty parties should be caught and appropriately punished, and no general reprobation of the fact that the first conviction for the crime of arson has not yet been obtained. It is still more strange when one remembers that the haunts and the political associates of the petroleurs are matters of common knowledge. On the one hand there is the Sinn Fein 'soldier,' slipping about unadvertised with his petrol can or fire bomb; on the other hand there is the group of Orange corner boys concocting in its self-constituted Soviet the destruction of more Roman Catholic houses.

No doubt Belfast has citizens who could help the police in detecting Sinn Fein and Orange incendiaries, but they dare not. It is fatal to interfere in any way with the activities of a gunman or a fire-raiser, and a sound maxim for a citizen who would try to do his duty in all respects would be: 'Tell the police and say your prayers.'

1. Matthew Anderson

Recently a young woman was brave enough to give evidence against a bomb-thrower. She was murdered a few days ago on her own doorstep. That was her reward for performance of a public duty. Another instance. A woman and her husband were called from bed one night by someone on the street. They opened the door, and a man said to the wife, 'You have been carrying information to the mill.' 'Me,' she exclaimed. 'Never!' but she got no further. Two shots rang out, and she fell dead at her husband's feet.

This afternoon the press representatives were asked by a high military authority to suppress if possible the names of persons with whom they might have interviews, for those whose names appeared were at once marked down by the other side for attention. That is the atmosphere of terrorism in which people live and in which the police are expected to do their work. I am unable to send you photographs of the burnt-out Catholic houses, as the photographers whom I have approached prefer their personal safety to a little present profit. A prominent Unionist firm declined the commission on the grounds that the Orangemen in the district would certainly resent the exhibition of the ruined Catholic homes and that a man armed with a camera would be in danger of losing his life. You may have as many pictures of destroyed Unionist business premises as you please, but none of the Catholic dwelling-houses. The mob won't let you.

A police official admitted to me that the police were unable to prevent the intense campaign of incendiarism. 'You must,' he said, 'smooth down the old hates, create a better political atmosphere, and get back into people's minds a real desire for the rule of law and order before you can expect the police to function effectively. So long as you have one section of the public condoning these offences and another section afraid to assist in combating them you cannot expect peace in Belfast.'

It was in July or August of 1920, following on the expulsion of the Catholics from the dockyards, that the seed of to-day's incendiarism was sown. The mob took to burning business premises owned by Catholics and the houses occupied by them. Then it rested and there were intervals of peace between occasional fresh outbreaks.

This year there was a fresh scourging of the Catholics, and at the beginning of May an organised reply was made by the desperate minority, strengthened by men from the South who came with more than the idea of reprisals in their minds. Once more the burning of Catholic houses has been resumed, and where previously the burning was a rather one-sided affair it looks to-day like a competition between the two sections. From the business point of view the Unionists, who hold 90 per cent of the business houses in the city, are in the more vulnerable position – they can be attacked by the fire-raiser at so many points. In the nine days from May 20 to May 29, for instance, 77 business premises were set alight, and that takes no account of the numerous Catholic dwelling-houses which were burnt and wrecked.

The Northern Government took over a legacy of disorder, and that legacy has not dwindled in its hands. Before the new Government entered into office the mobs, thriving on their comparative immunity from the results of law-breaking, had been growing bigger and bolder and better organised. It is, of course, open to question whether the Northern Government has adopted the best method of restoring order, or even whether by its composition it is not handicapped in the difficult matter of dealing with partisans who have got out of control.

## Reds and Whites in Central Europe

For several years after 1918 Central Europe remained wildly un-settled, a land of famine and violent revolutions. J. G. Hamilton was first sent by the *Guardian* to Berlin and then given a roving commission in Central and Eastern Europe. Early in 1920 F. A. Voigt was posted to Berlin where he stayed until Hitler came into power.

## THE LAST INTERNATIONALE

Friday, October 31, 1919
*From our Special Correspondent recently in Budapest*[1]

A mixed crowd of women and children crowded the platform, and as they stood they sang. It was the first train to Budapest after Bela Kun's[2] fall, the first for quite a long period. The city itself was still some few miles away, for the station belonged to one of those outer industrial suburbs that are all factories and slums. Distant rifle shots and an occasional thud signalled the approach of the dreaded Rumanians from the parent city, of which they were by then in occupation. Under the flickering lamps one could see the strained expression on the faces of

1. J. G. Hamilton
2. Bela Kun (1885–1937), had led a Communist government which held power in Hungary for several months in the summer of 1919. It was overthrown with the aid of Rumanian troops.

these poor working folk as they anxiously stood there and waited. There was no talk. All were singing. They sang with intense earnestness, and the chant was repeated again and again. It was the 'Internationale.' The passengers, leaning out of the windows, listened quietly and unsympathetically. They were exclusively business men returning to Budapest in the hope – how illusory events have shown – of retrieving their lost fortunes.

Heard in England the 'Internationale' sounds strange and somewhat revolting with its banal melody and almost unintelligible sentiment. On the Continent of Europe in the year 1919 it catches the ear very differently. You recognise it as the 'Marseillaise' of a tremendous and dangerous revolutionary movement that, unlike that of over a century ago, seems to know no frontiers and to be unconscious of nationalism. It becomes unpleasantly familiar, and – I can speak for myself – always brings a certain sensation of fear. I had heard it in the streets of Paris on the First of May, when masses of workmen in the Place de la République had 'barked' it hoarsely and savagely into the faces of the Cuirassiers; in Berlin again and again, sometimes to the accompaniment of machine-gun fire; in Hamburg.

Here it had a pathetic note. It was, almost certainly, the last time that it was to be sung in this unhappy country; it was, as it were, Bolshevism's swan-song. Behind us we had left the White Terror raging in its full fury. White Guard officers had raided our train up the line for Red fugitives. At Raab the hue and cry was still on. In front of us lay the occupied city. A few hours later even this last pool of Bolshevism was to be scorched dry.

The incident, slight as it is, has this importance. It testifies to the sincerity and strength of the Bolshevik – or whatever other word one cares to use – faith among these working masses. During the next few weeks I had many opportunities of testing working-class feeling in Budapest. All the leaders were in prison or fugitives. Life was made hideous by the ceaseless and thorough search for arms and for suspects that went on day after day in the poor quarters of the town, by the tide of denunciation and espionage, and by the fierceness of the Terror. You would suddenly find whole blocks of the town shut off by a cordon of Rumanian troops. Within the cordon no one was allowed to go out of doors, while a house-to-house search went on. Well-dressed Hungarian civilians or officers often accompanied the Rumanian search parties with lists in their hands. Issuing from the cordon, one would see groups of men being marched off.

Yet throughout all this hard time the working class remained stalwart. They held aloof from the anti-Semitic fury. A Jew, of whatever class, was as safe in the working class quarters as he would be in London, though for a Jew to enter the aristocratic quarter in Buda, where the Allied Missions had their headquarters, and their soldiers, was to court death.

I will give a piquant instance of the state of working-class mentality – even after the overthrow. 'What do you think of Bolshevism?' I asked bluntly of a chief waiter, an efficient, deferential man who had served for years in one of the greatest London hotels. Most of the other guests, by the way, were English and American officers. 'No doubt it was bad, sir. But I am a working man, and things were much better then than now. Then I got as much to eat as other folks. Now I serve food to others that I cannot get myself.' He added that he had not tasted meat for weeks, and that his family was starving.

The mass psychology has undergone a vast transformation. Freedom is its dominating motive; freedom to live, which means shorter hours and more leisure, and freedom to live a full life, which means wages enough to permit enjoyment of leisure. It may be egoism, but it has its good side. The worker is hardly conscious of any change of mentality. He believes in his right to freedom and a full life just as innocently and unselfconsciously as he formerly accepted his relatively inferior human status. Nor can he understand any denial of this right. Proletarian governments may be crushed or fall by their own weight. But a mass psychology is not so easily dealt with. On the contrary it has to be taken into account if social stability is to be regained.

## TEN MONTHS LATER

When Hamilton returned to Budapest ten months later one Right-wing government had succeeded another, but the Terror continued. In March Admiral Horthy (1868–1957), who had commanded the Austrian navy during the war, had driven the Rumanians out and become Regent.

Tuesday, June 15, 1920

Budapest, June 7

Within a few hours of arriving in Budapest I encountered the 'White Terror.' The restaurant of my hotel – the famous Hungaria on the Danube bank, once Bela Kun's headquarters, now largely occupied by Entente missions – was raided by well-dressed hooligans belonging to the 'Awakening Hungary' League. Everyone who was or looked like a Jew was seized and beaten. There were a few minutes of confusion, of screams and struggle, and then the incident was over – and forgotten! People sat quietly again at their tables, the waiters resumed their velvet-footed service, the soft purring murmur of a comfortable, elegant dining-room continued as if nothing had happened. British and other Entente officials were present. They too seemed to be equally used to such momentary disturbances.

Emerging into the streets after dinner I found every junction of the streets held by armed police, not singly but in groups. Strong police patrols, with carbines held at the ready, moved slowly along the Corso and other thoroughfares. At various points were stationed squadrons of mounted police, sitting monumentally on their magnificent Hungarian horses. Between the population of all classes and these police there is absolute confidence. Theirs is a peculiar function. It is not to guard the property and lives of citizens against popular disorder, but against a portion of the Hungarian army itself – the Terrorist, criminal special 'detachments' which have for months past made Hungary, both town and country, something like a hell.

As these 'detachments' are tolerated (to put it mildly) and paid by the Government, and one of them furnishes Horthy himself with his favourite bodyguard, it is at first a little surprising to find the police so disposed towards them. Briefly, it is a story of a personal collision between the chiefs of the two forces developing into a static feud. Anyhow, the split, such as it is, is for the good of the town. But the police are few and can do little.

On the Andrassy Street, the Oxford Street of Budapest, a crowd was watching some laughing officers who were extracting a bullet from the plaster wall of a café. A raid like that in the Hungaria had just taken place. Waiters were straightening the overturned tables and chairs. Half a mile further on towards the Town Park I encountered a strong patrol belonging to one of the 'detachments,' soldiers this time, steel-helmeted and with drawn bayonets; sturdy, formidable men, almost indistinguishable save for their patched, untidy uniforms from German troops, and, indeed, closely resembling the notorious Baltic soldiery that I had seen in Berlin during the Kapp *Putsch*.[1] People slipped into the side-streets as they approached. These particular troops, as I learned afterwards, terrorise a whole quarter of the town, not in a political or racial sense, but as mere condottieri, robbing or beating Jew and Gentile alike, and not shrinking from occasional murder. They are only a recent arrival in the town, and bodies have already been taken from the Park Lake showing bayonet wounds.

1. Wolfgang Kapp (1858–1922) staged a monarchist revolt in Berlin, March 1920, defeated by a general strike.

But much more impressive than these daily surface symptoms is the prevailing atmosphere of terror. Men showed a reluctance to meet or talk with a foreign journalist. When they did talk, they spoke of murders, atrocities, mutilations, disappearances, of burying alive, of bodies found in the Danube, of extortions of money under penalty of death, faithfully carried out if the ransom were not forthcoming; but a little attention showed that these graver atrocities were limited in number, perhaps fifty to a hundred cases in all.

Of course the terroristic effect of such atrocities in a civilised land with modern communications, telegraph, telephone, and press is out of all proportion to the actual death roll. The Terror in Hungary no longer requires mass killing. It operates through psychological effect and keeps itself in practice from day to day by the simpler, rather Oriental device of seizing, beating and torturing. 'Marked' men are suddenly seized in their houses or in the streets, carried to one of the hotels or other centres, and there thrashed and tortured. Others are spirited off to prison or the great concentration camp at Hajmasker or minor camps, for there seem to be more than one.

A few months of such a regime would break the strongest nerves, and such has been in fact the calculation. Budapest to-day shows signs of the strain. Respectable people are afraid to venture out of doors after dark. Friends you meet in the street carry the butt end of a loaded rubber baton sticking out of the coat pocket. I have been shown these formidable instruments of defence in a private house that I have visited. In a civilised community reduced to such a state the prevailing atmosphere is inevitably nervous and diseased. Ten months ago when I saw the beginning of the Terror in Budapest I quoted a leading Hungarian Liberal as saying that a man might gladly face a martyr's death, but would shrink from torture or corporal punishment.[1] The remark holds good with manifold greater force to-day, for Terror has an accumulative effect.

1. October 7, 1919

## THE EXPLOITS OF MAX HOELZ

After the Kapp 'Putsch' Voigt set out on an adventurous tour through disturbed Germany. On his way he visited the Communist leader Max Hoelz, who was in power in Falkenstein in the Vogtland, where English and German papers reported a Red Terror and the taking of hostages.

Wednesday, April 14, 1920
*From our Special Correspondent*[1]

Chemnitz, April 4

The Vogtland is a vast land of rolling hills in the south-west corner of Saxony, up against the Czecho-Slovak frontier. Patches of cultivated soil are scattered amongst stretches of dense forest and barren moorland. The rather ugly little manufacturing towns lie embedded in the deep valleys.

It was dusk when the first houses of the little town came into sight. Suddenly a crowd of men gathered in the middle of the road, in front of us, brandishing their rifles. The car stopped, and they thronged around – a wild-looking set, wearing, not the usual red-ribbon, but a broad red band round the right upper arm. They asked what we wanted, but hardly listened to what we said, shouting that we would have to go before the 'Aktionsausschuss' (Executive Committee).

One of them ran in front of the car, showing the way. Another jumped on to the foot-board and stood guard over us. We drove into the 'Schloss,' the residence of the Freiherr von Falkenstein, who had fled as soon as the workmen had begun to take control. It was now the meeting-place of the Executive Committee. A huge red banner was hanging from a pole planted on the square tower.

We were asked where we had come from, where were we going, and what we wanted. To prove that we had come from Gera one of us incautiously showed the permit stamped by the Reuss Government. It was handed back to us with the words 'So you've had dealings with a bourgeois Government, have you?' We repudiated the suggestion and said we had only obtained the permit to pass through Reuss territory without being held up. I asked one of the Committee if Falkenstein was a 'Räterepublik' (Soviet Republic). He said 'No' in a rather mystified manner. I do not believe he knew what a Soviet Republic was. The Committee was driven to the reluctant conclusion that our intentions were honest and not counter-revolutionary. Our

1. F. A. Voigt

voluminous English and American passports, with their heraldic adornments, ornamental lettering, red seals, numerous visés, and punched photographs, made a profound impression. Finally we received permission to spend the night at Falkenstein. We asked to see Max Hoelz. He was away, addressing a public meeting, but he would be back later on in the evening. Perhaps he would see us then.

We drove to the chief hotel in the town. It was rather empty of guests, but it had not been 'communised.' I asked one of the waiters how he liked living under the workers' domination.

'Very bad, very bad,' he answered.

'In what way?'

'People are afraid to come here now – we don't get any visitors at all. As you see, the hotel is nearly empty.'

'But has there been any bloodshed? And have you been interfered with?'

'No, there's been no fighting and no interference, except that the armed workmen occupied the banks and made some of the rich manufacturers pay for the upkeep of the Red Guard. But we don't get any visitors.'

Later on in the evening a messenger from the Executive Committee called at the hotel and informed us that Max Hoelz had arrived and was waiting for us at the Schloss.

Hoelz is a small, lithe, alert, dark-haired, brown-eyed man. He wears a bright red necktie.

Many of the German extremists I have met speak with an arid volubility that is immensely boring. At Gotha I asked one of the workmen's leaders for his version of what had happened there. He went back to Marx, Engels, and Lassalle, described the evolution of German Socialism, the problems of the war, and future hopes and ideals. Amid the irresistible torrent of intensely partisan eloquence the tragic happenings at Gotha were forgotten altogether. After watching for an opportunity I succeeded in slipping in the question, 'What about Gotha?' and my informant suddenly began to tell his personal history – how he was acutely conscious of class-differences as a child, how he had been persecuted at school, how he had been a political fugitive, and how he was acting from ideal motives. While the stream of verbiage poured through his lips his eyebrows remained rigidly and closely knit, his eyes fixed. Whenever he spoke of the Government, of officers, or of militarism he would raise his hands, turn them inwards towards his chest, and curl his fingers spasmodically. He was obsessed by the reality of class-war and eaten up by a class hatred so arid and yet so vehement as to be almost terrifying. This type is common in

Germany, and is, no doubt, common in all countries where political liberty does not exist.

Hoelz was something like this, but not quite. He was rather more human, being adventurous, enterprising, and irresponsible. When he began to speak I observed his brows contract, his hands shake, and his fingers curl. He also spoke with intensity, but was not exceptionally voluble. He answered every question frankly and concisely. Later on I was told that his public speeches were those of the typical political agitator and fanatic, and it may be that he sometimes suspended the working of his alert intelligence and enjoyed the luxury of being borne along unresistingly by the impulse of his own inflammatory eloquence. Before he rose to political fame or public notoriety he had earned a living as lecturer in a moving-picture theatre. It was there, no doubt, that he acquired the art of public speaking. With his keen brown eyes, his alert manner, and his small stature he was certainly a conspicuous figure amongst the slow-witted workmen with their tanned and wrinkled faces, their ponderous fists, their heavy boots, who sat round the table gaping stupidly, or nodding dull approval, or half asleep in the stifling over-heated air of the committee room.

I asked Hoelz what he would do if Government troops appeared in Falkenstein. He said:

'Armed resistance would be quite useless, and we shall not attempt it. But it isn't likely that they'll send a special expedition against a remote place like this.'

'You're a Communist and have got power – why don't you carry out your Communistic principles?'

'Germany is not ripe for Communism. If we were to set up soviets after the Russian model, we would provoke a civil war in which we would be a small minority. We would certainly be destroyed. Besides the country districts would very soon starve any town that went Bolshevik. At the present moment particular party interests must be ignored in face of the militarist reaction that threatens us. Once that is destroyed (and it isn't destroyed yet, by any means) we can return to our party programme – a programme that can only be carried out gradually by political propaganda.'

But it is not his ideas but his deeds that have made Hoelz famous. When the news that Kapp-Lüttwitz had entered Berlin reached Falkenstein, the workers took control in the usual manner. That is to say, the party and trade union leaders met, an executive committee was elected, and an armed workers' Guard was formed. There were no Reichswehr and no Zeitfreiwillige[1] present, so that there was no

1. Volunteers

bloodshed. The Communists were in a big majority. Hoelz was elected President of the Committee. Only members of trade unions and of the revolutionary political parties were admitted into the 'Red Guard,' as it was termed at Falkenstein. The Red Guard policed the town and occupied the banks to prevent the withdrawal of any big deposits. Hoelz then summoned a meeting of employers and factory owners and informed them that they would have to pay for the upkeep of the Red Guard (about 200 strong). The butchers of Falkenstein and the neighbourhood, for example, are organised in a kind of trust and they had to pay a joint sum of 500 marks weekly. Wealthier manu-facturers had to pay more heavily in accordance with their incomes. An armed workman of the Red Guard received 25 marks a day.

In the big prison at Plauen there were a number of political prisoners including Falkenstein Communists, many of whom had been detained without trial for several months (I met one who told me he had been in prison for nine months without knowing why). One day Hoelz and 100 of his guard drove into Plauen in three lorries. He held up the prison warders and liberated all the political prisoners. Then he went to the house of the attorney Dr. Hubert, and demanded all the docu-ments relating to the trials of these men. The attorney surrendered some of the documents, but could not find the others. Hoelz took him back to Falkenstein and told him he would be kept a hostage until the other documents were found. Within two hours the attorney's wife arrived with the missing papers, whereupon he was set free. All the documents were then destroyed.

Some time later news was received that there were corps of Zeit-freiwillige in the neighbouring village of Markneukirchen. Hoelz immediately collected his Red Army, and set out in the three lorries. When he got to Markneukirchen no Zeitfreiwillige were to be seen. They were in hiding, and there was no way of getting at them. Hoelz demanded that all arms in the village should be surrendered. The de-mand was refused, whereupon he went to the local bank and took 100,000 marks, informing the burgomaster that the money would be refunded as soon as the arms were surrendered. Later on I heard that the Chemnitz Executive Council, which is supreme over all the workers' committees in Saxony, ordered Hoelz to pay back the money without delay, and altogether to refrain from harming the cause by such boyish escapades. Meanwhile a price has been set on Hoelz's head by the Plauen police, and it can hardly be long before he is a political fugitive.

(According to the latest telegrams Hoelz is now in full flight for the Bohemian frontier.)

# Lenin's Russia

## AN INTERVIEW WITH LENIN

Tuesday, October 21, 1919
*By our Special Correspondent, W. T. Goode*

The interview with Lenin had been a matter of some difficulty to arrange; not because he is unapproachable – he goes about with as little external trappings or precautions as myself – but because his time is so precious. He, even more than the other Commissaries, is continuously at work. But at last I had secured a free moment and drove from my room, across the city, to one of the gates of the Kremlin. I had taken the precaution at the beginning of my stay to secure a pass that set me free from any possible molestation from officials or police, and this gave me admission to the Kremlin enclosure. Entrance to the Kremlin is naturally guarded; it is the seat of the Executive Government; but the formalities are no more than have to be observed at Buckingham Palace or the House of Commons. A small wooden office beyond the bridge, where a civilian grants passes, and a few soldiers, ordinary Russian soldiers, one of whom receives and verifies the pass, were all there was to be seen at this entrance. It is always being said that Lenin is guarded by Chinese. There were no Chinese here.

I entered, mounted the hill, and drove across to the building where Lenin lives, in the direction of the large platform where formerly stood the Alexander statue, now removed. At the foot of the staircase were two more soldiers, Russian youths, but still no Chinese. I went up by a lift to the top floor, where I found two other young Russian soldiers, but no Chinese, nor in any of the three visits which I paid to the Kremlin did I see any.

I hung up my hat and coat in the ante-chamber, passed through a room in which clerks were at work and entered the room in which the Executive Committee of the Council of People's Commissaries holds its meetings – in other words, the Council Chamber of the Cabinet of the Soviet Republic. I had kept my appointment strictly to time, and my companion passed on (rooms in Russia are always *en suite*) to let Lenin know that I had arrived. I then followed into the room in which Lenin works and waited a minute for his coming. Here let me say that there is no magnificence about this suite of rooms. They are well and solidly furnished; the Council Chamber is admirably arranged for its purpose, but everything is simple, and there is an atmosphere of hard work about everything. Of the meretricious splendour I had heard so much there is not a trace.

I had but the time to make these observations, mentally, when Lenin entered the room. He is a man of middle height, about fifty years old, active, and well proportioned. His features at first sight seem to have a slight Chinese cast, and his hair and pointed beard have a ruddy brown tinge. The head is well domed, and his brow broad and well raised. He has a pleasant expression in talking, and indeed his manner can be described as distinctly prepossessing. He speaks clearly in a well-modulated voice, and throughout the interview he never hesitated or betrayed the slightest confusion. Indeed, the one clearly cut impression he left on me was that here was a clear, cold brain, a man absolutely master of himself and of his subject, expressing himself with a lucidity that was as startling as it was refreshing.

My companion had seated himself on the other side of the table to act as interpreter in case of need; he was not wanted. After a word of introduction I asked what I should speak, French or German. He replied that if I did not object he would prefer to speak English, and that if I would only speak clearly and slowly he would be able to follow everything. I agreed, and he was as good as his word, for only once during the three-quarters of an hour that the meeting lasted did he stumble at a word, and then only for an instant; he had seized my meaning almost immediately.

I ought to state here that the thought of this interview had engaged me from the moment I had entered Russia. There were so many things I wanted to know, scores of questions occurred to me, and to secure the answers I longed to have would have required a discursive talk of hours had I begun my task with this interview. But by leaving it to the last my month's work had brought the answer to many of the questions, and others had been settled by a radiographic interview submitted from Lyons by a combination of American journalists. It behoved me therefore to utilise to the best advantage the time rigidly apportioned to me, wedged in between two important meetings. I had therefore reduced all my curiosity to three questions, to which the authoritative answers could be given only by Lenin himself, the head of the Government of the Soviet Republic. He knew quite well who I was; he did not know what I wanted. There could therefore be no question of preparation so far as he was concerned.

I had spoken of my questions to only one man, the Commissary who accompanied me, and he became very depressed, and gave it as his opinion that Lenin would not answer them. To his unfeigned astonishment, the questions were answered promptly, simply, and decisively, and when the interview was ended my companion naïvely expressed his wonderment.

The guidance of the interview was left to me. I began at once. I wanted to know how far the proposals which Mr. Bullitt[1] took to the Conference at Paris still held good. Lenin replied that they still held good, with such modifications as the changing military situation might indicate. Later he added that in the agreement with Bullitt it had been stated that the changing military position might bring in alterations. Continuing, he said that Bullitt was unable to understand the strength of British and American capitalism, but that if Bullitt were President of the United States peace would soon be made.

Then I took up again the thread by asking what was the attitude of the Soviet Republic to the small nations who had split off the Russian Empire and had proclaimed their independence.

He replied that Finland's independence had been recognised in November 1917; that he (Lenin) had personally handed to Swinhufvud, then head of the Finnish Republic, the paper on which this recognition was officially stated; that the Soviet Republic had announced sometime previously that no soldiers of the Soviet Republic would cross the frontier with arms in their hands; that the Soviet Republic had decided to create a neutral strip or zone between their territory and Esthonia, and would declare this publicly; that it was one of their principles to recognise the independence of all small nations, and that finally they had just recognised the independence of the Bashkir Republic – and, he added, the Bashkirs are a weak and backward people.

For the third time I took up the questioning asking what guarantees could be offered against official propaganda among the Western peoples, if by any chance relations with the Soviet Republic were opened. His reply was that they had declared to Bullitt that they were ready to sign an agreement not to make official propaganda. As a Government they were ready to undertake that no official propaganda should take place. If private persons undertook propaganda they would do it at their own risk and be amenable to the laws of the country in which they acted. Russia has no laws, he said, against propaganda by British people. England has such laws; therefore Russia is the more liberal-minded. They would permit, he said, the British, or French, or American Government to carry on propaganda of their own. He cried out against the Defence of the Realm Act, and as for freedom of the Press in France, he declared that he had just been reading Henry Barbusse's novel

1. An American diplomat who had visited Russia.

*Clarté*, in which were two censored patches. 'They censor novels in free, democratic France!'

I asked if he had any general statement to make, upon which he replied that the most important thing for him to say was that the Soviet system is the best, and that English workers and agricultural labourers would accept it if they knew it. He hoped that after peace the British Government would not prohibit the publication of the Soviet Constitution. That, morally, the Soviet system is even now victorious, and that the proof of the statement is seen in the persecution of Soviet literature in free, democratic countries.

My allotted time had expired, and, knowing that he was needed elsewhere, I rose and thanked him, and, making my way back through Council Chamber and clerks' room to the stair and courtyard, where were the young Russian guards, I picked up my droshky and drove back across Moscow to my room to think over my meeting with Vladimir Ulianoff.


RANSOME MEETS FAMINE ON THE VOLGA

Tuesday, October 11, 1921
*By Arthur Ransome, our Special Correspondent
in the Famine Region*

We went down to the shore of the Volga, down a rough broken street, past booths where you could buy white bread, and, not a hundred yards away, found an old woman cooking horsedung in a broken saucepan. Within sight of the market was a mass of refugees, men, women, and children, with such belongings as they had retained in their flight from starvation, still starving, listlessly waiting for the waggons to move them away to more fortunate districts. Some of them are sheltered from the rain that is coming now, too late, by the roofs of open-sided sheds. Others are sitting hopelessly in the open, not attempting to move, not even begging. I shall never forget the wizened dead face, pale green, of a silently weeping little girl, whose feet were simply bones over which was stretched dry skin that looked like blue-black leather. And she was one of hundreds. A fortnight ago there were twenty thousand waiting beside the quays of Samara. Every day about 1,400 are taken off in waggons. There are, of course, no latrines. The beach was black with excreta until, as an eye-witness (not a Communist) told me, the local Communists arranged a 'Saturdaying' which deserves a place in history, and themselves removed that disgusting ordure, and, for a day or two, lessened the appalling stench that is beginning once more to rise from the beach.

In the morning of the second day we called at one of the sixty 'children's houses' in Samara, so that Ercole could photograph the famine orphans, the children purposely abandoned in the streets, in the state in which they were received. The garden, a plain courtyard with a few trees, was full of children lying in the sun under the wall, staring in silent unchildlike groups, ragged, half-naked, some with nothing whatever but a shirt. All were scratching themselves. Among these children, a man and a woman were walking about, talking quietly to them, and carrying sick children into the house, bringing others out. Ercole had hardly begun to turn the handles of his machine before some of the children saw us, and, some with fright, some with interest, all scrambled to their feet, although many of them fell again, and, too weak to get up, stayed sitting on the ground where they fell. Ercole photographed them as they were. Then he picked four little boys and photographed these alone. Wishing to reward them, he gave them some chocolate before the woman looking after them had time to stop him. 'You must not do it,' she said; 'they are too hungry.' But it was already too late. All of them who had strength to move were on top of each other, fighting for the scraps of chocolate like little animals, with small, weak, animal cries.

That is only one of dozens of such scenes that we witnessed during those two days in Samara. Samara is one place of hundreds. Everywhere people are trying to save the children. Nowhere have they the means that we in other countries have to give what they should be given. And, to the shame of humanity, there are some in Western Europe who have urged that help should not be given.

Outside the goods station is a huge camp of white tents, a military camp of the Red Army, handed over bodily by the army authorities for the use of the refugees. The refugees have over-flowed from the tents and built more tents, and wigwams for themselves out of anything that came handy – rags, branches of trees, pieces of old iron from the railway sidings. Everywhere on the open ground outside the cemetery, whither every day fresh bodies are carried ('Thirty-five this morning,' a man told us, whose little hut commanded the entrance to the cemetery), and along the railway line for half a mile or so, were little camp fires, and people cooking scraps of pumpkin rind, scraps of horse-dung, here and there scraps of bread and bits of cabbage. In all that vast crowd there was not one who did not look actually hungry, and for many mere hunger would be a relief. Among them from tent to tent walked an unshaven young man with a white forage cap, now nearly black, a blue shirt and breeches, and no coat. A mechanic who was carrying the camera tripod for us told me who he was. He was a German, one-time prisoner of war, now a Communist, and 'for all that,' as my man put it, 'a man of God. He has stayed since the beginning. He never leaves them. I don't believe he ever sleeps. Whatever can be got for them he gets it. He has taken and lived through all their diseases. It is owing to that one man that there is such order in this place instead of pandemonium. Thousands owe their very lives to him. If only there were a few more like that.' I wished to speak to that young German, but, just as I was making my way to him through the crowd, a little skeleton of a boy pulled at his sleeve and pointed to a tent behind him. The young man turned aside and disappeared into the tent. As I walked by the tents, even without going into them, the smell of dysentery and sickness turned my stomach like an emetic.

A little crowd was gathered beside a couple of wooden huts in the middle of the camp. I went up there and found that it was a medical station where a couple of doctors and two heroic women lived in the camp itself fighting cholera and typhus. The crowd I had noticed were waiting their turns for vaccination. At first the people had been afraid of it, but already there was no sort of difficulty in persuading them to take at least this precaution, though seemingly nothing will ever teach them to keep clean. The two women brought out a little table covered with a cloth and the usual instruments, and the crowd already forming into a line pressed forward. I called to Ercole and he set up his camera. One of the sisters called out 'Lucky ones to-day; vaccination and having your pictures taken at the same time,' and while the camera worked, those behind urged those in front to be quick in taking their rags off, and to get on so that they too would be in time to come into the picture.

There were old men and women, girls and little ragged children. Shirt after shirt came off, showing ghastly bags of bones, spotted all over with bites and the loathsome scars of disease. And, dreadful as their condition was, almost all showed an interest in the camera, while I could not help reflecting that before the pictures are produced some at least of them will have left the camp and made their last journey into the cemetery over the way, the earth of which, as far as you could see, was raw with new-made graves.

In the siding beyond the camp was a refugee train, a sort of rolling village, inhabited by people who were for the most part in slightly better condition than the peasants flying at random from the famine. These were part of the returning wave of that flood of miserable folk who fled eastwards before the retreating army in 1915 and 1916, and

are now uprooted again and flying westwards again with the whip of
hunger behind them. To understand the full difficulty of Samara's
problem it is necessary to remember the existence of these people who
are now being sent back to the districts or the new States to which they
belong. They have prior right to transport, and, in the present condition of Russian transport, the steady shifting of these people westwards still further lessens the means available for moving the immediate victims of the drought. I walked from one end of the train to
the other. It was made up of cattle trucks, but these trucks were almost
like huts on wheels, for in each one was a definite group of refugees
and a sort of family life. These folks had with them their belongings,
beds, bedding, chests of drawers, rusty sewing machines, rag dolls. I
mention just a few of the things I happened to see. In more than one
of the waggons I found three or four generations of a single family –
an old man and his still more ancient mother struggling back to the
village which they had last seen in flames as it was set on fire by the
retreating army, anxious simply, as they said, 'to die at home,' and with
them a grandson, with his wife (married here) and their children.
Families that had lost all else retained their samovar, the central symbol
of the home, the hearth of these nomads; and I saw people lying on the
platform with samovars boiling away beside them that must have
come from West of Warsaw and travelled to Siberia and back. In the
doorway of one truck I found a little boy, thinner than any child in
England shall ever be, I hope, and in his hand was a wooden cage, and
in the cage a white mouse, fat, sleek, contented, better off than any
other living thing in all that train. There were a man and his wife on
the platform outside. I asked them where they were going. 'To Minsk,'
said the man, 'those of us who live; the children are dying every day.' I
looked back at the little boy, warming his mouse in the sun. The
mouse, at least, would be alive at the journey's end.

## – AND TSAR NEP IN MOSCOW

Tuesday, March 21, 1922
*By our Special Correspondent, Arthur Ransome*
*(who has just returned to this country from a visit to Moscow)*

'Under Tsar Nep everything is allowed.' That was the exultant phrase
I overheard in a conversation on the Kuznetsky Most (formerly the
most famous shopping street in Moscow) between two obvious
specimens of the 'new bourgeoisie.' Tsar Nep is N.E.P., the current

abbreviation for New Economic Policy.[1] No one quite knows what Nep is, not even its promoters sitting up there in the Kremlin, and themselves a little surprised by its certainly astonishing results. But the main point of Nep is seized in the sentence I have quoted, 'Under Tsar Nep everything is allowed.'

Under his rule at any rate has arisen a new Moscow, in a way something of a monstrosity when one thinks of the conditions in the inexorably spreading regions of famine a few hundred miles away, and certainly an extraordinary contrast to the old Moscow of the Communist experiment, with boarded shop windows and rare Soviet shops, some of which were empty and most of which were closed. Nowadays closed shops are comparatively rare. Elisseiev's famous sweet shop has windows stacked with chocolates and cakes. There are any number of fashionable boots and ladies' hats. Huge banners waving across the street proclaim in this one-time Communist city a vast lottery with four milliards in prizes. Cafés are open all over the town, with music, and even the time-honoured gypsies have re-appeared with their bright clothes and unpleasing voices. Characteristic of the new era, I think, were the immense number of notices offering lessons in music, dancing, acting, and the ballet. Characteristic of the transitional stage from the Communistic experiment were the number of shops which described themselves as 'Labour Artels,' (associations of workers sharing labour and responsibility) and as home industries, or announcing in large letters that all was the personal work of the vendors.

The shops, I say, are full. Many of them are full of rubbish. But, at first sight the thing that must astonish the stranger in Moscow is that the food shops are full. Passing from window to window I have seen whole sturgeons, great jars of caviare, monstrous cheeses, even oranges obtained probably through the obliging diplomats of some small nation. (I have heard it said that our own Commercial Mission in Moscow is the only one that does not use its privileges for private money making.) In the old days the food shops used to have cheeses in the windows, but they were wooden cheeses. It was a waste of good cheese to expose it in such a way. Now the cheeses are real. And the reason brings us to the very centre of one of the problems which Tsar Nep is posed with. Money in Moscow decreases in value every hour. Consequently the small trader, the moment he sells something dare not put his money in the till. To-morrow he will be able to buy less with it. Not wasting a moment, he rushes off and buys something else. At all costs he must keep his whole capital in goods and not in the form

1. The New Economic Policy, allowing a fair measure of private enterprise, had been introduced in March 1921. It lasted until 1928.

of money. He buys something. His million passes on to someone else, who in his turn claps his fur hat on his head and, he too, flies off to make a purchase before the fairy gold melts in his hand. Tsar Nep allows everything, but with ceaseless whips he keeps his devotees on the move. Turnover, turnover – that is everything, and the millions whirl round and round like Tibetan prayer wheels devoted to a deity insatiable of active worship. It is perhaps for this reason that the new bourgeoisie are physically quite unlike the old. The old were known for their fatness. The new are lean and athletic in their perpetual hurry to turn paper money into goods.

Under Tsar Nep, society is crystallising again after the plum-pudding stir-up of the Revolution. The spectacle is not edifying. A sort of small aristocracy or *samurai* class consists of a handful of honest revolutionary enthusiasts who try to live on their salaries. But sooner or later these must be swamped in the mass of the new milliardaires. The new bourgeoisie, which has not even the traditions of the old, is without culture of any kind, without moral restraints, recognises no obligations, greedily rakes its money together and grossly spends it, pursuing the coarsest material pleasures with shameless abandon in the midst of the general poverty. There is, however, a sort of vitality in this new blossoming of commercial activities, and perhaps some hope for the future. A young Communist to whom I talked while waiting in one of the offices gravely rebuked me when, in answer to a question, I had expressed disgust at what I had seen of Tsar Nep's more exultant devotees, and said, 'Their gestures are extravagant and ungainly because they have been unable to move for five years. They are naturally yawning and stretching themselves.' He further said, 'You are wrong in thinking that the phenomenon is without seeds of health. It is my business to go through the proposals for new private enterprises, and I can tell you that whereas at first the proposals were almost exclusively for food shops, for antique shops, cosmetic shops, and shops where old secreted stocks could be sold, now every week a larger percentage of the proposals are of a kind that means the making, the production of something. There is promise in that.'

It may be asked, What is left of the revolution? Industrial conscription has gone and unemployment has returned. So far from continuing the nationalisation of factories, the State is getting rid of the responsibility of one factory after another as fast as it can. Even the houses are being handed over to the house committees, who will gradually establish a claim to actual property in them by carrying out repairs. On the face of it, it would seem that everything has gone back to the old state of affairs. That is not so. Something has happened, even if it only is that there is a new bourgeoisie rapidly becoming clearer and clearer in its understanding of the fact that it has everything to lose by any return of the *emigrés*. So far this new bourgeoisie has no very real quarrel with the existing Government. For no one has begun to understand the psychology of the Revolution who has not perceived that the Bolsheviks are not the courtiers of King Canute, who asked their master to turn back the tide. Their aim is not to resist but to understand inevitable processes, not to stay the storm but to ride with it, and to go with complete consciousness whither the storm goes. The storm has brought them to Tsar Nep. Very good. They will not pretend that there was not a moment when they hoped to be brought to something better, but, Tsar Nep being inevitable, they are quite prepared to deck his shapeless bulky person with decrees.

## Mahler Misunderstood

Thursday, May 13, 1920
*From our Special Correspondent*

In 1913 the Hallé's new conductor, Michael Balling, had introduced a Mahler symphony. It was not a great success except with 'Sammy' Langford, *Guardian* music critic, and his appreciation was more for the music than the performance. There was no Mahler in the last pre-war season. In 1920 Willem Mengelberg celebrated his 25 years at Amsterdam and his friendship with Mahler by a festival at which all Mahler's works were performed. Langford wrote long notices of each concert. His introductory sktech shows why:

Amsterdam, Tuesday
In his relation to the modern problem of programme music Mahler occupies a peculiar place. He was born in 1860 in the little village of Kalischt, in Bohemia, and though he left there while still a child, that child remained in him till the end. In his early songs, which were set with orchestral accompaniment to folk-verses from *Des Knaben Wunderhorn*, both the melodies and the instruments were imagined in the terms of the country life he had left. This life remained the light of all his seeing. When he came to write his symphonies he took again the snatches, instrumental or vocal, of these orchestral songs, and made them, in more or less obvious allusion, the key to all his poetic and musical feeling. He never entirely separated the instrumental from the vocal imagination in music. There was no such deliberate resort to the

voice as the crown of everything as in the Choral Symphony of Beethoven. The voice was merely felt as essential to the ideas, and its use was unavoidable. It is a part of Mahler's naïveté that the animals and the angels have their place in his rejoicing. His song turns more and more into the nature of a hymn in which all nature is bound together by love. His Eighth Symphony, for instance, which is choral throughout, is in its first part a symphonic choral setting of the hymn 'Veni Creator Spiritus,' and the second a succession of symbolical passages from the second part of Goethe's *Faust*, where in the turning of the poet's exquisite dactyls things are made to pass before us as in a glass, and the heavenly wisdom is unfolded in a divine ascent which wins the heart into a more serene atmosphere with every turning line.

In this text, which runs in its contemplation through the whole gamut of nature, taking in as much the animal and the natural world as it does the spirit and the intellect of man, we get the best idea of what the symphony of Mahler always had in contemplation. If the technical resources of the art of music were enlarged, it was that this contemplation could be made more simple, more all-embracing, the more direct and the more thorough. It has always been the case that in this kind of expansion the sympathy of the restless and the impatient has been foiled. We had in Manchester during the first year of Mr. Balling's musical direction a symphony by Mahler. The interpretation was casual, and the melody for the most part strained beyond its naïve and easeful expression. The miscalculation might be ever so little, but it was sufficient to remove the composer completely from the general understanding. In that circumstance we had set before us the whole difficulty that lies in the appreciation of such composers as Mahler and Bruckner.

It does not follow even that Mr. Balling's direction of the music was faulty, for the naïve is made of little effect in its working by only a slight admixture of restlessness and scepticism among its interpreters.

There is, then, no solution of such problems as the Mahler question, except by the familiarising process of time. In England it is not at all likely that the problem of Mahler's music will be taken at all seriously during the next few years, though if such a thorough-going disciple as Mengelberg were to introduce even a single work at his English concert engagements, and even a single success was really gained, the public would then approach the composer with a different mind.

# The Atlantic by Air

## Monday, June 16, 1919

THE AIRMEN'S STORY
*From our Correspondent*

Galway, Sunday Night

Captain Alcock and Lieutenant Brown, R.A.F., accomplished the Atlantic flight in unfavourable weather. They landed in Derrygimla Bog, behind the Marconi condenser-house at Clifden, and their approach through the morning mist over the sea was first noticed by an Australian soldier on holiday and a farmer's boy tending cattle near by.

When I saw Captain Alcock some hours after he had landed, he looked as spruce – attired in navy lounge suit and cheerfully smoking a cigarette – as any city man enjoying an hour's leisure.

'Tell you about the flight? Well, we got off very nicely from St. John's in about a forty-mile fresh westerly wind. We got up against that to begin with, but as soon as we got clear of the land we had the wind in our tail, and it remained like that practically all the way over.

'Most of the time we were compelled to fly between clouds and very thick banks of fog. Indeed, the conditions were anything but pleasant for flying. Sleet fell and our radiator shutters got frozen up, while all our petrol gauges were covered over with ice. We kept mounting until we got up to 11,000 feet. We climbed all we could at the outset to try to get out of the clouds, but without avail.

'The weather was very rough and very bumpy and the wind was blowing hard right down to the water. Five hours from land we endeavoured to get out of the clouds and thick fog, but investigated without avail.

'Like myself, the observer got on very well, but he had great difficulty in getting sights, for, as I said before, we were flying most of the time between banks of clouds – indeed, we did not see the water more than six times on the way across. We might as well have been flying over land. The only sights the observer got were through holes in the clouds. We never saw the sky, even, for more than half an hour after the first hour out. For the first hour it was quite clear and pleasant enough for flying.

'When we started to use our transmitter, about half an hour after we left, we found the armature shaft in the dynamo which generates the current fractured for some reason or another, so that our transmitter was useless. Our receiver was working all right. But we got no information at all from any source and we did not exchange a signal with anyone in the outside world. During the entire period of our flight all the wireless that was going on was not for us, and it was merely jamming; therefore we got no help as to direction from any outside source. Our only guide was the stars, and we got occasional sights of the moon. We also managed to get two sights this morning of the sun which was very valuable to us. We got these through the clouds whilst flying at 11,000 feet, just two hours before we landed in Ireland.

'We wanted to get the job over, and we were jolly pleased, I tell you, to see the coast. We first saw the two little islands out in the sea, and then we swung round and landed at the station. Our landing would have been a perfect one, only that we happened to come into the bog. It looked quite all right from the air, but as soon as we touched the ground the machine began to settle down to the axles, and the wheels suddenly stopped, and the machine went down nose first. We were not hurt or shaken, and only a little damage was done to the under-plane of the machine.

'I have done a considerable amount of night flying in the past, and the sense of loneliness that might be supposed to accompany it has long since worn off. Indeed, I do not think that either of us had any thought of what we were flying over, being merely intent on getting the machine across, and the machine behaved perfectly.'

Asked for an opinion as to the future of flying across the Atlantic, Captain Alcock said: 'I think within the next twelve months they will have a cross-Atlantic service – not, of course, on the lines of our trip but with a big flying machine. Of course, it is a costly hobby and may not actually be taken up generally, but there is something in it I have no doubt.'

Captain Alcock showed me a little white mail bag with lead seal unbroken in which he had carried across the Atlantic in a single night eight hundred letters. 'This,' he said, 'is the first Atlantic aerial mail.'

Praising his machine and engine, Captain Alcock said: – 'The engine is a Rolls-Royce, and it ran perfectly all through. We did not lose a spoonful of water on the journey, and no petrol. When I landed I had only two-thirds of the supply exhausted. What was left would have taken us to London easily.

'I believe that the great secret of long-distance flying conditions such as we went through last night is to nurse your engine. I never opened the throttle once. The machine of itself has an ordinary speed of ninety miles an hour. We could have done 115 miles an hour but I never once opened the throttle, and with a following wind we did an average of 120.

'I wore the electrically-heated clothing as an experiment, but I never feel cold flying as the machine is warm enough in itself.'

## COMMENT[1]

The success of Captain Alcock and Lieutenant Brown, while proving, not for the first time, that they are very gallant men, does not, it must be confessed, prove much else. At the present stage of the science of meteorology, each attempt to cross the Atlantic in a heavier-than-air machine, especially in one that cannot take off from the sea, is a gamble in which the pilot and navigator stake their lives on the chance that their own skill and courage and the known capacities of their engines will be greater than the partly unknown, always unmeasured, sum of the weather difficulties will be on that day. It is like diving off a high bridge on a dark night into a river with a good depth of water but much traffic. The diver knows how to dive and swim, and is sure to be all right if he does not dive on to a passing barge. But he may. And so long as he cannot be sure where the barges are, and where the clear water, his dive is a gamble.

As far as can be foreseen, the future of air transport over the Atlantic is not for the aeroplane. It may be used many times for feats of personal daring. But to make the aeroplane safe enough for business use on such sea-routes we should have to have all the cyclones of the Atlantic marked on the chart, and their progress marked in from hour to hour. Then a pilot, with his thirty or forty miles of greater speed than the cyclones, might dodge between them or round them, so far as was permitted by his margin of fuel above the bare requirements of a direct flight. His course would be rather like that of a long-distance airman in war, when he picks his way between the positions, carefully charted on his map, of the enemy's anti-aircraft batteries. So there is no present hope of security against unpredictable bad weather. Nor is there any present hope of the construction of a heavier-than-air machine the occupants of which could, as an ordinary thing, alight like sea-birds on a disturbed Atlantic and rest there indefinitely. Curious as it is, the only practical type of aircraft for the Atlantic crossing is the only one which has not yet made it.[2] The airship will have no need to rush ahead through impossible weather in order to keep itself in the air.

1. Probably by W. P. Crozier.
2. There had already been an American naval crossing by flying boat breaking the flight at the Azores.

# Lord Curzon's Sacrifice

## Saturday, October 25, 1919

A social observer[1] drew my attention to-day to the distressful condition to which Lord Curzon is reduced by changing his position as Lord President to that of Secretary of State for Foreign Affairs. 'It's a big come-down,' he said, 'for Curzon. He drops about forty places. Why, he will go in now with the junior earls. He will go in just in front of Reading. He will be revealed in his nakedness as a new earl. You can't help feeling sorry for him.

'Last week he was sixth in precedence after the Royal Family. Look where he is to-day. It's a tragedy – a sacrifice, and the greater sacrifice because it has happened to George Nathaniel Curzon, whose proud motto is "Let Curzon hold what Curzon held".'

1. Probably Sir George Arthur who, after G. W. E. Russell's time, was the London editor's main recourse in matters of protocol.

# CHAPTER NINE

# The Breathing Space

\*

Looking back, one can see that the period covered by this chapter was just a brief interval between the storms that raged in Europe from 1914 to 1922 and those that blew up as soon as Hitler seized power in Germany. But at the time they seemed years of pretty regular, appreciable progress towards a happier world. The economic mess left behind by the reparation clauses of the Versailles settlement and the network of inter-allied debts were slowly being cleared up. Germany was admitted to the League of Nations; at Locarno the major European Powers underwrote the peace between them; The optimistic spirit of these years found characteristic expression in the simple-minded renunciation of war in the signing of the Kellogg Pact, the first example of public relations diplomacy undertaken in the sight of, and for the benefit of radio and film.

At home, Britain had three general elections, three prime ministers and five governments in half-a-dozen years. Two were Labour governments, but they achieved less than the one pre-war Liberal government in the way of reform. The best remembered event of those years is the General Strike, a revolutionary step taken reluctantly, apologetically, defensively and in vain. The way the country met it and then turned only two years later to friendly and constructive discussions between employers and employed promised as well as the international situation.

In *Guardian* history, the most important event was the retirement of C. P. Scott from the editorship in 1929 and his succession by his son, E. T. Scott. Only slightly less important was the resignation of C. E. Montague which took effect at the end of 1925. Montague continued to write occasional leaders until his death in 1928; C. P. Scott died on New Year's Day, 1932.

# England, their England

## BRADMAN: A PROBLEM EVERLASTINGLY INSOLUBLE

Saturday, July 12, 1930

### THIRD TEST MATCH

#### AUSTRALIA, – First innings

| | |
|---|---:|
| W. M. Woodfull b Hammond | 50 |
| A. Jackson c Larwood b Tate | 1 |
| D. G. Bradman not out | 309[1] |
| A. F. Kippax c Chapman b Tate | 77 |
| S. McCabe not out | 12 |
| b. 1 lb. 8 | 9 |
| Total (for three wickets) | 458 |

To bat: V. Y. Richardson, E. L. a'Beckett, C. V. Grimmett, T. Wall, W. A. Oldfield, and P. M. Hornibrook.

### Fall of the Wickets

| 1 | 2 | 3 | 4 | 5 | 6 | 7 | 8 | 9 | 10 |
|---|---|---|---|---|---|---|---|---|---|
| 2 | 194 | 423 | | | | | | | |

ENGLAND. – A. P. F. Chapman, K. S. Duleepsinhji, Hobbs, Sutcliffe, Tate, Larwood, Duckworth, Hammond, Leyland, Tyldesley (R.), and Geary (G.).[2]

### Umpires, Bestwick and Oates

### By Cricketer[3]

Leeds, Friday

Nature, they say, breaks the mould when she has made a masterpiece. It is not true; nor is it true that history repeats only her humdrum pages. Beauty changes her modes and aspects, but the substance, the

1. Next day, Bradman c Duckworth b Tate 334.

2. In those days English professionals were distinguishable from amateurs by the absence of initials before their names. The practice was not extended to Australians.

3. Neville Cardus

ultimate vision, is the same. Nature is never tired of her good things; every year she repeats the miracle of the spring-time's rapture and the summer's fulfilment. To-day in a game of cricket Nature has lived again in a bygone experience, lived it as though with greater intensity because the genius of it all had once before thrilled her sensibilities.

Four years ago on this very same field of Headingley the Australians began an innings disastrously; they lost the wicket of Bardsley for none, then Macartney came forth and scored a hundred before lunch. To-day Australia lost Jackson with only one run made; then Bradman before lunch made a hundred also. Woodfull, who was Macartney's good companion and audience, was Bradman's. But whereas Macartney gave a chance when he was only two, Bradman sent no catch at all before lunch and was guilty of but a solitary mishit when he was 35 and a high cut flashed yards wide of Chapman at backward point.

At ten minutes to one Bradman attained his hundred, and so joined the immortal company of Victor Trumper and Macartney, the only cricketers who have yet scored centuries in Test matches before lunch. Bradman's bat hammered perpetually; when he ever did stop scoring for a few balls it was as though he had merely run out of nails momentarily. Richard Tyldesley at one o'clock actually bowled a maiden over to Bradman; from internal and external evidence I concluded that it was one of the cleverest bits of bowling he has achieved in his hard-working career. At lunch Australia were 136 for one, and Bradman's innings was arbitrarily compelled for a while to stay its course.

Woodfull had by this time made 29 in two hours. He was as much a man to be noticed in conjunction with Bradman as Kreisler's conscientious accompanist. I can make no better compliment to Bradman – and give no clearer idea of his cricket – than to say that Woodfull of the two men seemed the more vulnerable and fallible. Yet Woodfull was at his stoutest and most watchful. I imagine the English bowlers were trying to get Woodfull out – leaving Bradman to Providence. Not often is an attack reduced to trying to get the stonewaller out while washing its hands of the brilliant player as a problem insoluble, and apparently everlastingly so. Think of it – a brilliant batsman with no edge to his bat and who never takes a risk. In this respect he is different from any other cricketer I have ever known; Macartney, Trumper, and Johnny Tyldesley were always living dangerously on the verge of their resources; Bradman races along on firm feet, with shrewd eyes where he is going. Not once to-day, in spite of all his crashing thunder and brilliance, did he ever pay anything but respect to the really good ball.

At four o'clock Bradman reached 200, after three hours and a half of cricket which for mingled rapidity and security is unparalleled in my experience. But when Bradman achieved his 200 the scoreboard read: Australia 268 for two. Has ever before a Test match batsman made a proportion of runs so handsome as this?

At six o'clock, after slightly under five and a half hours' play, Australia, for the second match in succession, reached the aggregate of 400 for two wickets. Amidst multitudinous cheers Bradman beat the record for the highest innings by any Test-match batsman; it was good that Foster's score had been passed not by a stonewaller hoarding up runs covetously, but by a true son of the game. Bradman arrived at 288 in five hours and a half out of a grand Australian total of 414; no chance to hand had he given and not more than three strokes had he shown which told us that it is human to err. From the last ball of the day Bradman, by a superb drive though the covers, a stroke handsome enough for any batsman who has ever done honour to cricket, hit his forty-second boundary. That was the royal way to finish a day which Australia will not forget as long as the game is played and loved there.

## ROD AND LINE: POACHERS

Friday, September 4, 1925
*By Arthur Ransome*[1]

There was just the beginning of light in the sky and the thick mist over river and meadow was already white. When we came to the Marron Pool nothing was visible more than a few yards away. 'Where are we?' 'You'll find the big stone just before you. The thirty yards below it are the best.' Our voices were low, but in the windless quiet were enough to give warning. Somewhere in the mist below us there was sudden loud splashing. An otter? Then angry low voices. More splashing. Poachers! There was a minute of silence. Then a shrill whistle between the fingers produced a thunderous splash some forty or fifty yards off. Someone had been startled and missed his footing in the river. We moved along the bank to Marron Foot, watching the ground. The poachers, however, had crossed the river and taken to the high wooded bank on the far side, from which they have been known to stone anglers in the water. The pool was useless anyway, and as we walked upstream again, while the light grew and the mist rolled up, we found the tracks in the wet grass showing how the men had come. There could be no fishing in the Marron Pool that dawn.

1. Arthur Ransome's 'Rod and Line' was for several years a regular Friday feature.

Poaching in the Cumberland Derwent is not what it was five years ago, nor what it is to-day in Wales, but the long drought has worn out the watchers, who have to be busy protecting the fish from every kind of disaster, and, after all, watchers are few and poachers know that they must rest sometimes. The poachers had probably seen us fishing the pool at dusk, and, when we went off to brew coffee in the fishing hut and to talk the darkness out of the sky, they must have made sure that place was left to themselves and others on the same bad business, like the heron who, when we disturbed him, went off with loud indignant curses, most unlike the muffled anger of the humans. His attitude towards us was probably like ours towards them. He looked upon us as poachers, creeping quietly along his river to disturb by our crude methods his private, skilful fishing. Most fishermen have a softness for the heron, as they have for the kingfisher and as they have not, usually, for the otter, though 'G.W.M.',[1] of the Derwent, who knows the otter more intimately than most men know their household cats, assures me that the otter is a harmless, not too successful fisherman – fit almost to be a member of an exclusive angling club. The poachers and the heron may have done better than we, but we found the sea-trout at their dourest, hooked one and lost it, rose another, but otherwise, except for the troutlings, might have been fishing an empty river. They were not feeding. That was all, for the river is full of fish.


## THE GOLD RUSH

### Tuesday, September 15, 1925

London, Monday

After an absence of over two years Chaplin himself and his boots and hat and cane came back again to the screen in *The Gold Rush*, a 'dramatic comedy' which was shown in England for the first time to-day.

The *Gold Rush* Chaplin is a man with a tale to tell, not a man with a comic theme, not even a man with a handful of comic themes to blaze in the black and white of the camera's eye. He wants to talk, as men will talk, in disjointed narrative round a camp fire about the trade and adventures of the early gold-seekers in Alaska. And he wants to talk, in particular, about a little tramp whom he calls, for want of any other name, Lonely, but whom he might just as happily call Charlie, as everyone else will.

*The Gold Rush* is rich in nuggets of comic thought, but they are

1. G. W. Muller, a regular contributor to the Country Diary.

scattered, do not lie head to heel in the fullest Chaplin vein. Here is one, with Charlie – how the name creeps in! – eating daintily of a filleted boot; here another, with Charlie alone invisible, in the crowded saloon; there a third, with Charlie kicking a couple of rolls and dinner forks into a grave semblance of a dance. There are other comic nuggets, a whole bowler hat full of them, but the vein does not seem to run as deeply as of old. *A Woman of Paris*, in which Chaplin was all the while behind, not before, the cameras, had in it more pure Chaplin than this film. There was Chaplin then in every figure; now there is Chaplin in Chaplin alone.

The Charlie of *The Gold Rush*, director and actor both, is curiously Latin in his way of thought. A Latin sentiment, not quite the universal sentiment of *The Kid*, has crept into his love story, a Latin exuberance has stolen something of animal joyousness of his body. The cat has smartened up his whiskers and become a Frenchman. The comic mask has sometimes, emotionally, slipped. Perhaps Chaplin has relied too little on himself, too much on the comedy that springs, not from within, but from without. He has packed his plot with episode, rather than stand in the heart of a theme and comedise it with his touch. He has tramped a long way, over great spaces of story, with great crowds of comrades, to find a comedy which was lying beside him in the crook of his cane.

Charlie Chaplin cannot make an insignificant film, even when he spends £200,000 in the process, but his is essentially a miniature art which finds its truest expression in the simple things, reached by the simple steps that children and genius share. When Chaplin is complex he is not true to himself. When we admire his complexities we are not true to him. To acclaim *The Gold Rush* among his finest work would be to confess a misunderstanding of the very qualities that have made Chaplin fine.

C.A.L.[1]

# EISENSTEIN'S *POTEMKIN*

### Saturday, November 16, 1929

Everybody has heard of this film. Few people in England have seen it, and when it came on the screen at the Film Society's show last Sunday the audience found they were watching the most famous of all Soviet films, familiar by hearsay, many of its scenes well known through reproduction of isolated stills, and notorious from frequent bannings.

1. Caroline Lejeune

They had to see the famous scenes, such as the flight down the steps and the piece of bad meat, in relation to the whole, whilst at the same time recognising these scenes and finding others, that they did not know, were equally beautiful and just as effective. And they had to forget that the film was censored if they were to see it for what it was.

*Potemkin* is important, not for being Soviet propaganda, but for being Soviet kinema. While bans exist propaganda is bound to have a distorted significance, but the thing that matters is that Soviet kinema, while being propagandist, contains a use of all the different branches of film-making which is recognised and practised in no other country. Eisenstein works differently from Pudovkin, and the difference is more radical than might appear. Pudovkin, it has been said, has characters, but Eisenstein has events, and his use of kinema in this direction is entirely new. It remains new in *Potemkin*, even though it is five years old. Pudovkin, when he records the end of St. Petersburg, does so with characters. He uses individuals as symbols of the mass, and by the effect of incidents on the individual he shows the trend of events. The way he does it is his own, but it is a method which is not so revolutionary as Eisenstein's.

In *The End of St. Petersburg*, the strike and the revolution are shown by their effect on the peasant from the country who accidentally betrays the people he had hoped to stay with. Technically we see, in watching these films, that the mass is used to light up the central figures, and while we feel that the result is that the central figures are thus able to express the mass, we feel too, I think, that the method is different from and less deserving the word 'great' than Eisenstein's.

It is true that in *Potemkin* there are characters. There is the sailor who is bullied; there are the ringleader of the mutiny and certain identified officers. But they are subservient in interest to the crew as a whole, and this difference becomes clear in the scene on the steps. It is the crowd that Eisenstein uses. The particular shots of one or two individuals – the woman with the pram, the mother of the boy – are only used to bring closer to us the emotions of that mass. They are there to bring the mass closer to us, as a close-up brings out the detail not easily seen in long shots. They may, in fact, be called intellectual close-ups. The crowd itself in Eisenstein is never brought down to the level of intensifying certain parts of it. This is something definitely his own and also something new and something kinematic. It is interesting to know how Eisenstein came to this method. He was twenty-seven when he made this film, which was his second. He came to film-making trained as an engineer and architect. He studied Leonardo da Vinci, and through him came to Freud's book on that painter, and so to psychology. He studied and published works on the Japanese drama. After two years in the Red Army he worked as an artist with one of the theatrical companies at the front, and when he was demobilised worked in the theatre and under Meyerhold. In 1922 he became acquainted with the work of Pavlov, and, as Bryher says in *Film Problems of Soviet Russia*, where all this may be found, he 'practically and theoretically applied this materialistic system to the domain of artistic creation.' It is evident that an engineer and an architect who has studied painting, drama, psychology, and the reflexes will make films, when he turns to them, in the best of new ways – experiment founded on what it sounds pompous to call culture.

R.H.[1]

# IMPERIAL BRUTUS

Friday, September 11, 1925

London, Thursday

He was a nigger and his name was Brutus Jones. For long years he had served on a Pullman car, observing the ways and ambitions of the white man. Then he killed a fellow-nigger in a gamesters' brawl, killed a prison-guard who struck him, and somehow fled away to a West Indian island 'not yet self-determined by white marines.' It was full of bush-niggers, 'black trash' as it seemed to Brutus. He ruled them and robbed them, became their Emperor, and ambled through his palace in the bedizened uniform of a circus attendant. He had the measure of them, and he knew that he could not fool the bush-niggers for ever. He was ready to fly when they were ready to revolt, but they rose before he feared them and hounded him through the forest. Through seven scenes in the night of the hunt the Emperor Jones sweats and faints and plods on in his despair, now cursing, now cajoling the limbs that are too weak for the driving power of his will. He falls into trances, turns every arm of foliage to a figure of fear, is seized by atavistic visions of his ancestors being sold into slavery, prays to his God, the God of the Christian Baptists, and is caught and killed. The exaltation of a throne has passed him by, the agony of its loss is at an end. Imperial Brutus is dead and turned to clay.

It comes off superbly on the stage. The technique of pursuit is a constant factor in the fabrication of absurdity, the man on the run is an abiding pillar of farce. But tragedy and comedy differ not in matter

1. Robert Herring

but in manner. It is only a distinction of emphasis that can decide whether Humpty-Dumpty's collapse is a cause for laughter or a cause for tears. Mr. O'Neill has made his playboy-emperor a tragic hero, and the hunting in the forest creates a tragic spectacle in which every move is raised, as the words of great poetry are raised, to a higher power than is their normal possession. What raises it? There is Mr. O'Neill who invests his negro with all the pathos of a child's cunning, a child's quick penitence, and a child's subjection to invading fears. There is Mr. Paul Robeson, the negro actor, magnificent in physique and vocal range, and yet confining in his ebon breast all the infantile glee and sudden infantile panic of the dark-skinned world. His performance is a fine wrought compound of psychical and mental distress. Rarely does one see an actor so put his mind to the governance of his body that not a muscle may be wasted in the service of his art. Between Mr. O'Neill and Mr. Robeson is Mr. James Light, the American producer. He populates the forest with menaces, and builds the visions that flame up in the darkness round the staggering fugitive. Yet the fantasy is not thrown too violently across the negro's path. There is no rattle-trap ghoulishness employed. The play deserves great acting and discerning production, and receives its merits.

I.B.[1]

# THE END OF THOMAS HARDY

Thursday, January 12, 1928

### HIS DEATH

The death of Mr. Thomas Hardy deprives the art of letters in England of its unquestionable head. He towered over our other writers of fiction like a column, and there was something columnar in the massive grace of his work, in the solid and slowly laid basis of observation and thinking on which it rested, and in a kind of noble plainness that distinguished it. For he was one of the least freakish of writers, one of the least dependent upon any separate ornaments of wit, eloquence, and melody, one of those who have trusted most to right proportion and to the final and total effect of a book upon the reader as distinct from the successive effects of many brilliances achieved by the way. He had been an architect, and more than any other novelist of his time he succeeded in giving to each of his works the strong structural unity of

1. Ivor Brown

fine architecture. The end of a novel of his was always a real climax, as systematically worked up to as the cross on top of a cathedral's dome or the tip of a Chamonix *aiguille*. He would keep a whole book low, as painters say, in tone, denying himself the use of all the easier lures that an expert writer has at his command, and all the time he would be slowly creating in your mind, as by some minute process of molecular change, a state of feeling upon which the climax, with its own tragic quietude, would impinge with a tremendous and unexpected momentum. On almost any page of his greatest novels you will find things beautifully written, but it is usually a beauty that would suffer much by detached quotation – that is, it is highly organic; its perfection is in its position and its relations to the rest. A book like *Tess of the D'Urbervilles* or *Jude the Obscure* invades your spirit like a wonderfully organised and handled army; each separate movement of an advancing column may seem trivial and isolated in itself, but there comes a time when you realise that every avenue of feeling in you has been occupied and all the forces which seemed scattered and slender are combined as by magic to overwhelm you. To no tragic novelist do we surrender more completely at the last. The death of Jude and the death of Giles Winterborne are among the most perfect examples in literature of the poignancy of effect obtainable by the prescient concentration of sustained, unstrained effort on preparation for a tragic close.

In Hardy's later and finer work the gloom of the tragic close came to be embittered more and more by the settled melancholy of his own view of human life as a plaything for casual external forces and for dim, wayward impulses from within. The world, to his maturer scrutiny, appeared to be governed neither by a moral order nor by an immoral one, but by chance drifts of causation so capricious and so unrelated to people's deserts and to the nature and direction of their efforts as to offer a spectacle ranging in its effect from that of ironic whim to that of a savagely mocking malignity. If the fates of men and women were governed by a roulette-table, the result would not be cruel in intention, for the machine would have no intentions, but it would, as often as not, be cruel in effect, and this was the kind of cruelty with which Hardy came to feel that the world was infested. He was one of the most compassionate of all writers; his description of the wounded pheasants bleeding to death in the night after a day's shooting is ineffaceable from the memory; his sympathy seemed even to reach to the lives of the cattle, long dead, whose shoulders had polished the wood of the byres; and behind the matter-of-fact description of Tess at her field-work, after her calamity, you feel a kind of agony of helpless tenderness in the writer for all souls so troubled. This profound kindness of the man was controlled and kept salt and sane in the artist by a strong strain of irony; if no writer had more pity, none could be more incapable of sentimentalism.

## Tuesday, January 17, 1928

### HIS BURIAL

#### By *Alfred Noyes, the Poet Friend of Thomas Hardy*

The burial of Thomas Hardy in Westminster Abbey was in effect a sufficient answer to his own philosophy. It was a strange spectacle touched with something of the bleak irony of a scene from his own *Dynasts*. It would be merely conventional to pretend that his burial was anything but what Thomas Hardy's own family affirmed it to be. And it had something of the effect that might have been produced by the burial of Gibbon in the Holy Sepulchre with Voltaire as one of the pall-bearers. It was the funeral of a man who had been loaded with earthly honours for his exposition of their emptiness and for his affirmation that they never came to those who deserved them. It was the funeral in the central shrine of this country of a man who had renounced all hope both for himself and for the race, a man who in his wish for 1867 had written, 'I could only ask thereof that my worm should be thy worm, love'; and his words were annulled at his own grave-side by words that are more certain of immortality than his own: 'I know that my Redeemer liveth; and though, after my skin, worms destroy this body, yet in my flesh I shall see God.' It was the funeral of a man whose heart had been cut out so that only his ashes should receive the ashes of honour and repose by those of Dickens and Browning. And his own sense of emptiness of these things seemed to chill the whole ceremony. It was – for most of those present – a ritual, a temporal tribute, the best that an essentially pagan intellectualism could offer in an externally Christian country.

Outside the Abbey there was a bleak drizzle which was in harmony with the mental atmosphere. Yet from the point of view of the religion which did him the honour there was something majestic in its utter indifference to his own words and his own philosophy. It was an indifference that would have appealed to Hardy himself. In the very face of all that he had written and of all the Agnostics gathered around him there were uttered once again the sublimest words in the English language: 'I am the resurrection and the life.' The cross was carried before him, and after the Dorset earth was thrown into the grave the sure and certain hope which he had so emphatically repudiated in life was uttered again in ringing tones over his body. It was a ceremony that defied all logic, and illustrated the intellectual and religious confusion of our time as nothing else but the British Constitution itself is capable of doing. Thomas Hardy had drawn a circle around his imagination which shut out almost everything that was assumed in the ceremony, but the faith that had been shut out calmly drew a wider circle which included him and all his doubts and grief.

## 'SITWELLS AND OTHER SILLIES'

Saturday, September 12, 1925

Is it not odd to find that, when G. W. E. Russell[1] is poking a little fun at 'Young Oxford' of the seventies, this is a verse from a poem which he selects for his purpose?

> *Yet all your song*
> *Is – 'Ding, dong,*
> *Summer is dead,*
> *Spring is dead –*
> O, *my heart, and* O, *my head*
> *Go a-singing a silly song*
> *All wrong,*
> *For all is dead.*
> *Ding, dong,*
> *And I am dead!*
> *Dong!'*

Dear me, young Oxford can (and does) do much worse than that nowadays! 'An amazing ditty,' Russell calls it, adding that it is 'dark, and mystic, and transcendental, and unintelligible.' I think of our really 'forward-looking' reviews of the moment, of T. S. Eliot, of Ezra Pound, of the Sitwells and all the other sillies, aspiring or arrived, and I am simply staggered at Russell's complaint. Why the song which he quotes has rhymes, it has metre, it is grammatical, and I should say myself that it is not at all difficult to understand, his poem simply bristles with repressions. It is disciplined all over – obviously he did not know the first thing about really letting himself go, and being a natural son of all the ages (and a good deal of the farmyard).

Well, we have marched a long way since then, and all along our

1. The quotation is from his *Collections and Recollections by One who has kept a Diary*, the original series of *Guardian* Saturday articles which ran throughout 1897 and is still one of the best bedside books.

various paths those cast-off Victorian repressions lie thickly scattered. I wish the excellent 'G.W.E.' could come back and tell us what he thinks about the results of our progress. We have truly 'amazing ditties' which do not rhyme and do not scan and (by this time) do not even shock, for except to their author they convey about as much meaning as the trail of a slug on a cabbage leaf. It is rumoured that young Mr. Poltroon Whiffle's next play will concern itself entirely with two elderly and tipsy captains of industry who are exchanging confidences and quarrelling about the common object of an *affaire de coeur* which would not have been out of place in the Cities of the Plain, with details which even a translator of Petronius would have thought it safer to leave in the original Latin. Every day and in every way we become more and more excellent and unrepressed.

With one extraordinary exception. We have meekly taken over without any modification at all the full burden of Victorian table manners. Satisfying one's hunger is a natural instinct – away with all artificial restrictions on this as on other instincts. You would like to gnaw a cutlet in your fingers? Very well, – gnaw it – obviously it is better to do so than to repress yourself into a nervous breakdown. The soup is good, and you are hungry; your mouth waters. Down with your head, then, and slaver into it as you guzzle. (Come, come, my unrepressed friend – does the mention of slavering into soup affright you? Why, it is not half so disgusting as some aspects of Mr. Joyce's *Ulysses* – and it has the added merit of being over far quicker.)

G.P.[1]


# MARCEL PROUST CONTINUES

## Friday, October 2, 1925

'Ideas transform themselves in us,' observes Marcel Proust in this remarkably good translation of his continuous novel *Remembrance of Things Past*[2]; 'they feed upon rich intellectual reserves which we did not know to have been prepared for them.' The process of feeding goes on, and once again Mr. Scott Moncrieff conveys the impression that Proust's intellectual reserves might with benefit have been supplemented by those of the imagination. For, although in one part of the narrative an evening at the opera occupies no fewer than thirty pages, or approximately nine thousand words, it is merely the result of a logical recounting of actualities and the meditations arising from them

1. Gordon Phillips
2. A review of C. K. Scott Moncrieff's translation of *The Guermantes Way*.

in the mind of the narrator. But this is what Proust's readers have come to expect, for, while in earlier volumes they read an 'exact' study of the growing of consciousness in a rather exotic and not too healthy boyhood and youth, now they have the analysis of an abnormal young man's sensuality as revealed in such spare incidents as his entry into the venerable house of the Guermantes, one of whom becomes his intimate friend. Besides, it all harmonises with the unique method that leads Proust to devote later on dangerously near half a score of pages to a kiss on the girl Albertine's cheek. We do not feel such a description to be disproportionate, however. How could we when, for prelude, the hero is unable to help saying to himself: –

Now at last, I am going to learn the fragrance of the secret rose that blooms in Albertine's cheek, and, since the cycles through which we are able to make things and people pass in the course of our existence are comparatively few, perhaps I ought now to regard mine as nearing its end when, having made to emerge from its remoteness the flowering face that I had chosen from among all others, I shall have brought it into this new plane in which I shall at last acquire a tactual experience of it with my lips.

One feels after this that the same number of pages would be none too many for a description of the hero lifting his tall hat to a lady.

The truth is that a novel by Marcel Proust is not intended for the ordinary fiction reader, who seeks above all things brisk dialogue and action, which are entirely absent from *The Guermantes Way*. The book is simply another page in the literature of psychological art. The style is what Proust's hero would call 'mild'; there is more than a suggestion of effeminacy about his mind – one cannot quite forget that once he confided to us that he 'detested sea-bathing because it took away my breath.' Indeed, the complete visual impression left on the reader is of a table which is spread for him, and which Proust is so fond of describing, with luxurious meats, fruit, a flask of Chianti, and anemones. Those who prefer such a table to good honest bread and cheese on a deal board will approach *The Guermantes Way* as they have approached the earlier parts of what in its way is a triumph in experimental letters – that is, as a feast.

T.M.[1]

1. Thomas Moult

## EPSTEIN

### Saturday, July 20, 1929

London, Friday

The figures on Underground House are now on trial and, as the Scots say, 'tholing their assize.' That they are extremely distasteful on first sight to a considerable number of people of culture and taste is undeniable, much as Rodin's Balzac was to Parisians of that time. Mr. Epstein has at any rate succeeded in making people look at and even think about architectural sculpture, and one cannot easily remember any other architectural sculpture in London that has done that. And his work, however he may shock the complacency of a country that is as poor in sculpture as it is rich in poetry, and has very little to show the stirring of new ideas in art that are moving over Europe, has to be taken seriously, for no one acquainted with the subject will deny that he is a skilled and gifted artist and that his portrait busts, at least, are among the outstanding works of this age. If he chooses to express himself in the arbitrary forms of sculpture he uses, we cannot say that it is because he has not the skill to represent a man as closely as a Madame Tussaud figure does. The groups at Underground House must be accepted as his conception of architectural sculpture, however naughty of him it is to think so. He really must know something about his job.

'Night,' which was the first of the two groups to be free of scaffolding, did not quite rouse the old hostility, although most people frankly did not like it. The subject is a mother figure of a heavy Eastern type with a male figure lying on her lap whom she is stilling to sleep with a gesture of a mighty hand. The shapes are simplified to their bare essentials and carved with a hard, square expressiveness without regard to anything but the sculptural idea. The horizontal line of the recumbent figure repeats with a curved variation the line of the stone course over the doorway; the leg of the male figure, curved at the knee, with its drooping foot is echoed on the other side by the shoulder and head of the female figure. The rhythm of the design runs through all its parts, which fall into three main planes receding towards the top. It is an elemental conception of night, ponderable and remote, making strange calls to our consciousness.

'Day' is harder to accept. A large father figure, with a fierce face, flat and hard and round like the sun at noon, holds and presents a male child standing between his knees, while the child stretches up his arms towards the neck of the father, his face turning upwards in a gesture of reluctance to face his task. The main pattern of the group is made of the two pairs of arms, the small ones within the larger, and the four legs forming the base. It is one of the most inventive Mr. Epstein has evolved. Again the sculptor has sought to express his idea in the starkest, most simplified forms, with a severe squareness of effect. His task was to produce an architectural decoration by carving a projecting part of the actual stone of the building, and this he has done with an appropriate imagination and evocative power adequate for the emphasis of the portal on the face of this sheer, tower-like building with its regiments of windows. But there are points about this group that are difficult to get over, particularly the modelling of the upper part of the child's body, where the chest seems to have been carved away, and the treatment of the arms, while the squareness of the legs changes to a rounded treatment of the body as though the sculptor had two minds about his technique.

But the power to imagine and deliver his idea with its uncanny fire are tremendously there. Learned men tell us there is nothing Assyrian or African about his art and no resemblance to archaic rock-carving; in short they deny the pedigree that many writers would force upon him. But if Epstein has taken his studies of these works so deeply into the body of his art that they cannot be identified, it only increases the suspicion that there is something new as well as something alien to our habits of thought in his sculpture. Before we reject it with abuse we might perhaps take a little time to get used to it. We can't be quite sure right off that he is not saying new things to us that we have to tune our ears to hear. Yes, but do we know that Epstein is bringing new beauty to our generation? Well, it seems to the present writer to be here 'burning bright,' although to many it is still 'in the forests of the night.'

J.B.[1]

The publication of this article and the accompanying pictures of the sculptures led to a brisk controversy in Letters to the Editor – some of which give the impression of having been invited. The following two are typical.

## Wednesday, July 24, 1929

In *Fanny's First Play* I seem to remember that one of the critics is made to say, 'Tell me if it is by a good author, and I will tell you if it is a good play.' For my part, though there is only a small proportion of Mr. Epstein's work that I really 'like,' I long ago accepted him as a great

1. James Bone

sculptor, and where and when we now disagree I am therefore inclined to believe that he is right and that I am wrong – or at any rate 'slow in the uptake.'

But in what might be paradoxically called 'applied sculpture' – that is, where sculpture is or ought to be an integral part of an architectural composition – I have no such diffidence because I have my own clear and considered views, and fearlessly claim the expert's inalienable right to be wrong.

Now the most noticeable and disappointing thing of the great mass of public criticism, mostly hostile, with regard to these figures is that it is entirely unarchitectonic, and takes no account of the ensemble. It attempts to judge them as 'gallery pieces,' or as potential garden ornaments, or even as anatomical studies, portrait groups or 'problem pictures'; that is, by conventions and standards that are utterly irrelevant. It is all so madly beside the point that it is really no more 'criticism' than if we were to point out that acoustics of the Royal Mint are sadly imperfect or that the Albert Hall would never make a decent garage.

Then it seems to me that the public has been scarcely less obtuse in passing its rash judgments on 'Night' and 'Day' as though they were one and indivisible. True, they both seem to me to have an imaginative relation to the underground world that is highly appropriate and that seems to relate them each to each.

But we are surely free to prefer one to the other or even to accept one as appropriate – accept it even as a masterpiece – and yet to reject the other.

For my own part, I thus accept and welcome 'Night' as a focal point of architectural interest at once rousing and satisfying and therefore somewhere in the category of masterpieces, whilst 'Day' has too little obvious relation with its background and surroundings to allow the same pleasurable sensations – at least that is how I justify my preference to myself. Already, however, I suspect that this is a mere rationalisation of the fact that I just happen to prefer the sinuous rhythm of the one to the angular abruptness of the other. I really feel that there are two Mr. Epsteins (probably there are many more), and the one I personally prefer is the one that imagined and wrought the figure of 'Night.'

The other Mr. Epstein alarms me. I feel reproved and a little trivial in the presence of his 'Day' and though that may be very good for me and may indeed be exactly what he intended, I will not pretend that it is an experience that I can enjoy. I think this feeling, consciously or unconsciously, may have been shared by others, but whereas I humbly attribute at least part of my discomfort to my own frailty, these others are, I think, too disposed to 'blame it' all on the sculptor, who has thus succeeded in not only making them (like myself) feel foolish and insecure, but in making them express their feelings all too suitably.

I will say that Mr. Epstein's thunderous technique and the clean, rather 'thin' austerity of Messrs. Adams, Holden, and Pearson's architecture seem to be two opposites rather daringly married. I do not find it a perfect marriage, and had I been doing the match-making I think I should have sought for less tremendous sculpture. But it is certainly not a dull marriage, and, as in all such affairs, we shall be wiser about its wisdom a few years hence.

CLOUGH WILLIAMS-ELLIS

### Thursday, July 25, 1929

It is good of you to give your readers the pictures of the Epstein sculptures. It is always well to know the worst and learn to face it. From a commercial point of view I think the directors, who have been fiercely criticised, have a valid excuse for exhibiting these sculptures, always assuming that their action was not ultra vires under their articles of association. For monuments of so repulsive a character may reasonably be expected to drive the man in the street Underground and thus swell the revenues of the undertaking.

EDWARD A. PARRY

## Another View of England

### ASKING FOR CLASS WAR

The Chief Constable of Liverpool had arranged to swear in groups of British Fascists as special constables. This should have happened on October 5, but was postponed. But the Home Secretary (Joynson-Hicks) said: 'If any organisation or body of men, in Liverpool or elsewhere, is prepared to hand me lists of men to serve, some as special constables or some as drivers of transport, I should be a fool if, on behalf of the Government, I refused them.'

### Tuesday, October 6, 1925

The present Home Secretary is really becoming the gravest of existing menaces to law and order. For many months the rather scrubby little cause of British Communism has had no such public crier to advertise it as he. As a volunteer advertisement agent for 'the Reds' he beats not

merely enthusiastic amateurs in publicity like the Duke of Northumberland, but hardened professionals like Lord Rothermere. At the end of
the Labour party's Liverpool Conference, it seemed as if nothing could
bring Communism back to a state of animation. British Labour had
pounded it within an inch of its life. Every Labour politician of importance had denounced it. You would have thought it had no friend
left in any British party to do it a good turn. But it had. At the nadir
of its fortunes Sir William Joynson-Hicks, the constant and true,
rushed in to give it first aid. Your modern expert in publicity believes
in publicity every time and for all ailments; he would poultice a black
eye with an advertisement and raise the dead with a sky-sign. In that
sturdy faith, or in something curiously like it, our compassionate
Home Secretary instantly opened a dressing-station to tend Communism when it became a casualty at Liverpool. He has gone to
Liverpool himself to take charge of this mission of healing. He was
there yesterday, trumpeting more loudly than the loudest Communist
his belief that Communism has escaped alive from the rough hands
of British Labour, and not only alive but so large and terrific that
Englishmen must sacrifice the character of the English police if they
want to be safe from it.

But many of us are really proud of the high character of our English
police forces. We value the certainty which we have all been able to
feel hitherto that every policeman is out to do his duty fairly between
man and man, and is not a violent party politician got up in official
clothes and armed at the expense of all taxpayers with a truncheon
wherewith to hit any taxpayers whose politics he may dislike. And when
we see an extreme party man like Sir William Joynson-Hicks getting
ready to dilute the police wholesale with bands of partisans picked out
for him by organisers of his own colour, we do what in all such cases
is the fair thing. That is, we imagine all the parts in the situation
reversed and a politician of a different party doing what would most
nearly correspond to what Sir William Joynson-Hicks is doing now.
Imagine a Labour Government in office, a vast and dangerous Labour
dispute apparently approaching, a rather extreme Labour politician at
the Home Office – a politician as much more extreme than Mr. Ramsay
MacDonald as Sir William Joynson-Hicks is than Mr. Baldwin. Then
imagine a wholly Socialist committee, as much a party and class committee as that of 'O.M.S.,'[1] or a Communist organisation as extreme on
the Left as the 'British Fascists' are on the Right – imagine these
bodies approaching Mr. Wheatley or Mr. Gallacher at the Home

---

1. 'Organisation for the Maintenance of Supplies' – in effect a volunteer strike-breaking
force.

Office and asking him to let them draft into the police an organised Socialist or Communist militia to 'protect the community' in case employers should get up a general lock-out or provoke a general strike. Can any of us, whatever his party, honestly doubt what he would think of Mr. Wheatley or Mr. Gallacher if he agreed or, still worse, if he had prompted the request? We should all say he was corrupting the police and preparing a class-war. And, if we go on being honest, we have to own that this exactly is what Sir William Joynson-Hicks is doing.

## 'JIX'S PLAYBOYS OF THE POST-WAR WORLD'[1]

### Thursday, December 17, 1925

The British Fascists – hasn't someone called them Jix's Playboys of the Post-war World? – have a branch in the Manchester area, but it is not a very strong branch, if one may judge from the numbers who turned up in the Memorial Hall, Albert Square, last night. The occasion of the meeting was a visit from Brigadier-General R. B. D. Blakeney, who is the president of the British Fascists. The room for public meetings in the Memorial Hall is not a large one, and it was by no means full. The proceedings had not been long on foot before it became evident that considerably more than half of those present were violently opposed to the Fascists. A strong dash of Stevenson Square[2] soon manifested itself in the mental outlook and vocal capacity of the majority.

The object of General Blakeney's visit was 'to explain to the public the true policy of our movement.' When a vote of thanks was being moved to him at the end of the meeting for having done this, a woman's voice shouted 'But he hasn't done it.' And that was the wisest and truest word spoken at a meeting which, one must admit, was not marked by much intelligence on either hand. It was a meeting which began in disorder and ended in chaos, part of the audience singing the National Anthem and part 'The Red Flag.' Could any conclusion be more lugubrious?

The chairman claimed, amid derisive laughter, that the movement was non-political. 'We have nothing to do with black shirts and that sort of thing,' he said; and, indeed, the British Fascists have no uniform yet sanctioned by 'G.H.Q.' though the literature handed out at the meeting stated that 'commanders will be notified in due course.' In the

1. A report by Howard Spring. 'Jix' was the nickname of Sir William Joynson-Hicks.
2. Manchester's 'Speaker's Corner.'

meantime 'the Fascist salute is made by bringing the right hand across the chest and touching the badge,' which is worn on the left lapel.

General Blakeney complained at the outset that the British Fascists were misunderstood. People said all sorts of things against them – sometimes that they were out against the Communists. The General had apparently overlooked the literature already referred to: 'The British Fascists stand not only for the creation of an anti-Red force . . .'

He then went on to explain nothing whatever about what the Fascists propose to do. He talked of the present economic depression, of the depreciation of the French currency, of the need to emigrate, of the horrors of Bolshevism. We learned that Bolshevism, among other things, was responsible for the recent troubles in Syria. He propounded a theory which one has never heard before; that a group of German-Jew financiers, intent on the destruction of the British Empire and operating from New York, had engineered the Great War, and finding it was not going as they had planned, arranged the Russian Revolution and the financing of Lenin and Trotsky. A later speaker, who was not always intelligible owing to uproar, seemed to suggest that the French Revolution also had originated with German *illuminati*, who aimed at Britain's downfall.

## THE GENERAL STRIKE

### Saturday, May 1, 1926

#### ON THE EVE

*From our Labour Correspondent*[1]

London, Friday

The conference [of the trade union executives] will rank as one of the most remarkable in the history of British Labour. The delegates had been hanging about the Memorial Hall for more than twelve hours. Yet when the negotiators arrived just before midnight they met an audience which crowded the big hall. As Mr. Pugh told his plain tale and Mr. Thomas painted a lurid picture of his hours of pleading, of the miners' reasonableness and the Government's unreasonableness, the conference was deeply stirred. It would probably have declared eagerly for a general strike had it been asked.

1. A. P. Wadsworth

## Monday, May 3, 1926

London, Sunday

Mr. Ernest Bevin announced the general strike (to the conference of executives). He was short and business-like. The miners' case was put by Mr. Herbert Smith in a speech which breathed no defiance, only sadness that things should have come to such a pass. He emphasised, and repeated with emphasis, his offer to the Government that the miners would go all through the Commission's report and accept the outcome of the negotiations, provided they were not asked in advance to say they would accept the wages reductions.

The mood of the conference was best summed up by Mr. MacDonald in one of the most difficult as it was one of the most moving and eloquent speeches of his career. He said little or nothing of the general strike – his opinion of it would probably not bear expression. His words were addressed to the Government and to the wider public outside to compel the Government to reopen negotiations.

But it would be wrong to read into the offers of conciliation the inference that the conference was merely bluffing. As the delegates went away, each with his plan of organisation, one could hear them say: 'Well, we're all in it. We've got to go through with it.'

The Continent will note that the declaration came on May Day, and the hearts of the Communists are already rejoicing. But any such feeling was quite absent from the conference. It had intensity, a curious thrill of adventure, but lacked absolutely any exultation. It was as though an army of martyrs were going out very reluctantly, almost sacrificially, to battle. A placing of the unions' all 'on the altar of our great movement,' Mr. Bevin called it. There can rarely have been in the history of Labour a more revolutionary decision taken with so little hope and so little fervour. The Communists and the theoretical advocates of 'mass action' were left far behind; British Labour entered on a perilous path under the command of a Socialist ex-Prime Minister, a non-Socialist ex-Cabinet Minister, and two 'moderate' trade union leaders, Mr. Pugh and Mr. Bevin. A new chapter must be added to the vagaries of the British political temperament.

## Thursday, May 13, 1926

### THE END OF THE GENERAL STRIKE[1]

London, Wednesday night

*How the War Won the Strike*: The new habit of executive capacity of

1. London Letter paragraphs from the substitute strike issue of the *Guardian*.

the middle classes, and the comradeship which still persists in the minds of both strikers and volunteers, was a big factor in the unparallelled pacific character of this great conflict, which has really been the wonder of the world. Both points worked against the strikers. A generation ago it was all rather different. The average middle class Englishman of twenty years ago, after generations of peace with vast resources of menial labour, could do little except sport with his hands and had not the habit of mind for discipline and adaptability. The Boer War proved it; the Great War cured it. Men learnt that instead of writing letters to the press when things were not done, they could go and do them themselves. The way to get a thing done was to go and do it.

*War Comrades in Conflict*: Many false conceptions died too. It is only men too old to have been in the war who now talk of 'teaching the workmen the lesson they deserve' and 'making them lick it,' and all the ugly, futile old slogans of the stonehenges of the past. The volunteers went on driving 'buses, loading food, and the rest of it, and the strikers went on trying to prevent them, but there was with most of them a sort of understanding that never existed before and they had a common trench language they never had before. How long this thread between them would have lasted in the sharper conflict of another week one cannot surmise, but, happily, the real test never came.

On both sides this was a conflict between men who knew all about arms and bloodshed. Are both sides of these sometime comrades to lose also the industrial peace?

### Friday, May 14, 1926

London, Thursday Night

*The Aftermath*: This has been a shattering day after the great relief of yesterday's calling off of the strike. Even in the middle of the war there were never so many contradictory reports and alarmist statements, nearly all false.

First we heard that the railway companies and the L.C.C. tramways and the London General Omnibus Company were refusing to take the men back in their former status, but only as beginners. It was not till Mr. Baldwin's statement to-night that the story was even questioned. It got general credence and at once affected many volunteers, who made it clear that they would not continue their work if it was not the straightforward settlement that everyone expected. 'We will not take part in a pursuit' was how one of the ex-soldier volunteers put it. The feeling that there were some employers who wanted to turn the general strike surrender into a rout, with lancer work on the disorganised contingents, went completely against the grain of the volunteers who had come out for the national need and not for the cause of any employers.

*Sights of the Strike*: A few of the strange sights of the strike may be set down. An old stage coach with two horses was hired by a city firm to take their clerks to the office. Several men went to business on horseback. A tall man was seen in Holborn on a child's 'scooter.' No bookmakers were visible in the bye-streets.

Some 'buses to-day carried a broom on deck like Van Tromp. On some days all the newspapers selling in Fleet Street came from Sheffield, Leeds and Cardiff. A motorist going fifty miles an hour on the Bedford Road was waved on by a policeman to hurry up a bit (a potato convoy was coming up a side road).

A 'bus with a volunteer driver pulled up at his house in Eaton Square, and the driver and conductor, who had been out all night, went in for breakfast, then remembered that they had a passenger, and the passenger was induced to join them at breakfast.

*Theatres in Strike-Time*: All the plays which had previously shown themselves to be 'good lives' have managed to live on through the last ten days, and some of them report fairly good business.

Mr. Fagan bravely proposed to hold the first night of *The Plough and the Stars,* Mr. O'Casey's new piece, on Wednesday. His courage was rewarded, for the strike was called off at midday, and taxis were about in small numbers by the evening. The usual first-night audience arrived, but their usual unpunctuality was of no account, since some of the scenery had been on strike and could only be got back to work after a delay. Mr. Augustus John, a rare first-nighter, was one of a company which gave Mr. O'Casey a tremendous reception and drew from him a neat little speech.

Evening dress was rare, and it was odd to be at an important theatrical occasion where people sat in the stalls in grey suits, deeply studying country newspapers of whose existence they had scarcely been aware before.

# MOND AND TURNER TALKING JANNOCK

Wednesday, December 21, 1927
*From our Labour Correspondent*[1]

London, Tuesday

The General Council of the Trade Unions Congress[2] decided, after three hours' discussion, this afternoon to accept the invitation of a representative group of employers to join with them in discussions of the problems of British industry. The movement among the employers was begun by Sir Alfred Mond, and the letter of invitation urges in the most general terms the need for co-operation and for discussions 'covering the entire field of industrial reorganisation and industrial relations.'

The debate to-day was spirited and, I am told, on an extremely high level. The minority against acceptance was small.

Opposition to the idea of the conference is already developing. The shipbuilding employers wish that the affairs of their industry should be managed within its scope and are arguing that there is no necessity for co-operation for trades with which shipbuilding has little or nothing in common. The engineering employers, or, at any rate, some of their principal spokesmen, are arguing on the same lines.

On the trade union side the left wing is attacking the conference as a surrender to the employers, the end of militant trade unionism. The view is put in its most extreme form by Mr. A. J. Cook,[3] who declared to-night: –

'I contend it is the gravest decision ever taken by the British trade union movement as well as the most undemocratic one in view of the fact that the General Council had no instructions either from Congress or the affiliated unions, regarding their opinion on the matter. It will do more to create suspicion, distrust, and disruption than anything the trade union movement has ever decided. I am opposed to this conference because the individual employers cannot speak for the whole of the industry and have no power to carry out any proposals agreed upon.'

1. A. P. Wadsworth        2. The chairman was Ben Turner.
3. Miners' Secretary

COMMENT[1]

The invitation was to discuss the broad problems which confront British industry and to see whether there was any common ground for action. To the onlooker this would seem the most elementary common sense, and it would be difficult to explain to the stranger from another planet why any body of workmen or employers should look suspiciously upon such a proposal. There are, of course, a good many reasons. The most fundamental probably is that they have for so long thought of themselves as antagonists that the very notion of co-operation is unfamiliar and distasteful.

The extremists may be irreconcilable, but they are no less certainly a very small minority. More serious is the traditional and often unquestioning assumption of inevitable conflict. To that must be added the very real and natural reluctance of the trade unions to abandon any of their practices or rules which hinder the rapid and effective use of modern scientific methods. These are the rules for which they have fought long and painfully in order to raise or maintain their standards of life. If these rules are to be made more elastic there must be guarantees of another kind to ensure at least as certainly the progressive advance of those standards. The employers, on the other hand, will want to be assured that they will obtain in return a more sympathetic understanding of their difficulties and a more willing disposition to help in overcoming them. Both sides must be ready to sacrifice something – though it may often be no more than prejudice.

## LIFE IN THE CASUAL WARD

Thursday, July 5, 1928
*From a Correspondent*[2]

We left Clitheroe in lovely weather, and, passing through Whalley, struck east for Burnley. About dinner time we felt the need of a drum of tea, and set about looking for one. Chancing to come upon a little country sweet shop, we asked for a tin in which to boil our water. The dear old lady, filled with loving kindness, took down her husband's working tea-can and gave it to us, saying, 'He has no further need of it now.'

1. From a leader by E. T. Scott.
2. Lt.-Col. A. D. Lloyd, dressed as a tramp, had been investigating the casual wards of Lancashire and Yorkshire.

There is nothing more delightful than tea of your own brewing in beautiful surroundings, accompanied by an honest appetite! Passing on through Padiham, we tried for water at a beautiful granite drinking fountain, and found it dry. A mile further on was another fountain in a park wall, also dry. Surely the donors would be grieved to think of weary travellers turning away unrefreshed. The last part of our journey was very hot and tiring over the stone setts of the town.

The porter made a great show of searching our shirts and trousers for vermin, those found guilty being condemned to the stove. This process certainly effects its object with regard to the lice, but it also destroys the stitching and ruins the appearance, unless carried out with scrupulous care. We had a good bath, and were given a cell between us. Clothing bundles outside the door, greatcoats allowed to make up for the poverty of the blanket supply, two being the allowance per man.

The floor of our cell was wood, and it was my turn to sleep on it, while my companion took the wire mattress bed. Our supper of bread, margarine, and tea being finished, we composed ourselves for the night. No sooner had I become drowsy than a stinging bite awoke me to the consciousness that my night shirt was alive with vermin. I tore it off, and lay down again in my greatcoat – alas! they came up into it and I was forced to discard it also. I now lay naked in my blankets, and was devoured from head to foot; so thick were the creatures that there did not seem to be a single inch of my body that was not fully occupied! My mate, chancing to wake up, chid me for imagination, but, on passing his hand down my thigh, changed his tone to one of amazement. At length I could stand it no more, and casting off my blankets, passed the night marooned in a sheet of Agnes Weston's[1] *Ashore and Afloat*, with my feet wrapped in *Tit Bits*.

Breakfast of bread, margarine, and tea was served in a long passage room, and then we were told off to jobs. The little sheds in which some of us were told to saw wood were lined with witty rhymes and drawings:

> *Here I am in a spike to-day,*
> *Where to-morrow I cannot say;*
> *May be in a jail for all I know,*
> *Praise God from whom all blessings flow.*

In another room I saw:

If brotherly love is the mirror in which man sees God's love, well – the casual ward system will drive many to unbelief.

1. Dame Agnes Weston (1840–1918) redoubtable philanthropist, founder of Sailors' Rests.

The doctor stopped with interest at the sight of my disfigured hide, but passed on when I gave him the reason. Receiving our midday meal we departed thankfully.

In common justice I must say that my mate in bed was able to sleep, and a man in the common room told me that he had slept well. It seems that some men, of whom my mate is one, are bug immune. The blanket store, where all blankets and pillows were piled up in the day-time, must be a fine distributing centre for vermin. The inconsistency of the porter's search and the condition of the wood floored cells is striking, to say the least of it.

Our next stage was Blackburn, and our mates all painted a glowing picture of real beds, sheets, and pillows. We took the walk too easily, and arrived after the ward was full – the practice being to admit 34 and to give the remainder tickets for common lodging houses. We found our destination lay in opposite directions, but a piece of twist tobacco, fortunately picked up on the road, soon effected the necessary exchange of tickets.

Of that lodging house I would rather not speak much; it is in the hands of a deputy, it is filled by 11 p.m. Its condition needs the atten-tion of the Inspector of Lodging-houses. But the habitués were kind to us, and that is more than I can say for many of the casual ward porters. Under this system of boarding out casuals the lodging-house keeper provides a bed, the use of his cooking and washing apparatus, and 4d. for supper and breakfast, but I did not discover any provision for a midday meal. We craved for a bit of meat that night, and so pooled our fourpences and had a supper of potatoes and brawn. Unfortun-ately we were faced with a long walk next day with nothing but tea in our stomachs. After five miles exhaustion took hold of me, but a kindly shopkeeper saved the situation with a couple of good scones.

Somehow we managed to creep into Preston, and were much revived by a bowl of hot oatmeal gruel with salt. It flashed into my mind how often I had watched my horse tucking into a bucket of gruel after a long day's hunting. Now I understand his feelings and know that they were good.

Preston is another place of dry ornamental drinking fountains, but its 'spike' is really good. Everything here was clean and in good order – bath, towel, nightshirt, blankets, and cells. I want to advertise the cells, because they gave us the best sleep we had on the roads. They had evidently been pressed for room, and some wise man had hit upon the plan of removing the lower half of the middle wall between each pair of cells, thus making room for an extra bed and allowing a degree of companionship which removed the horror of solitary confinement.

Our mate was a navvy of the old school, and his comments on modern manners, and especially on men with Marcel waved hair, were quite unprintable.

Medical inspection took place in our beds at 8.30 p.m., thereby causing the minimum inconvenience to all concerned. The three chief anxieties in the wayfarer's life are – 1. What will the porter's welcome be? 2. What will the doctor say? 3. Will he get out in the morning?

Called at 5.30 a.m., with ample time for a shave (without a glass) and also a wash before the usual breakfast of bread, margarine, and tea. At eight the labour master took us in hand, my mate to the garden and I to chopping wood. At 9.30 we were released, on application for that favour. The treatment at Preston was both humane and just, the balance being on the side of humanity.

The diet of a casual is a problem that requires a more sympathetic consideration. It is impossible for a man to keep in working condition on the following fare: –

Breakfast: Bread, margarine or dripping, tea or cocoa.

Dinner: Bread and potatoes, with two ounces of cheese (no potatoes if on the tramp).

Supper: Bread and margarine or dripping, with tea, cocoa, soup, or gruel.

Remembering that to beg is to come under the law, is it wonderful that there is a real temptation to throw up the sponge and become an habitual criminal? My own condition at the end of my trek was one of complete exhaustion; bread became impossible to swallow unless soaked in or taken with tea or water.

We left Preston for Bolton and Rochdale.

## Monday, July 9, 1928

### COMMENT: THE CASUAL WARD

Incalculable harm results from treating the casual as if he were a criminal. The final result may be to make him into one. It is no part of the work of a Poor Law authority to shame those who come to it for relief. What alternatives has a man who, whether by his own fault or not, finds himself destitute? Where is he to sleep? He can be arrested for 'sleeping out' or 'loitering with intent.' Where is he to get nourishment? He may happen on charity, but he may be put in gaol for begging, and stealing is even more dangerous. Apart from the Poor Law he has no other choice except to starve, and even attempted suicide is criminal.

## WORKING CLASS CANAILLE[1]

Thursday, December 3, 1925

It is just over twelve months since the Conservative party appealed to the country with a resounding statement of educational policy. Since that time Lord Eustace Percy, who was presumably appointed to carry that policy into effect, has been talking and talking. He has told teachers how to teach, and administrators how to administer, and parents how to bring up their children. He has disposed of social questions which have perplexed generations of less nimble-minded students with bright *obiter dicta* about the fundamental futility of raising the school age. He has dismissed the scholarship system in a few breezy sentences, and has lamented (after scanning, it may be, the countenance of his colleagues at a meeting of the Cabinet) the defects of educational arrangements which bring mediocrity to the top. Teachers and administrators have borne it all philosophically, in the spirit of soldiers who, when whizz-bangs began to come over, murmured wearily, 'Jerry's at it again,' and took to their dug-outs. After all why grumble at the inevitable? Who can loose the bands of Orion, or induce Lord Eustace Percy to think before he speaks? The orator, it seems, is a strong silent man of action. The busy brain, it now appears, was working at high pressure all the time. It was considering how to secure 'a progressive reduction in the size of classes, the improvement, and when necessary the replacement, of insanitary schools, the development of central schools and other forms of education above the elementary stage'[2] and the rest of it. The first-fruits of its lucubrations are contained in Circular 1,371.

Circular 1,371 is likely to be a turning-point in educational policy, though not quite in the sense intended by its author. It is impertinent in form, and deplorable in substance. It is impertinent in form because it announces a revolution in the financial basis upon which the educational system of the country rests without giving those most directly concerned any opportunity of expressing their opinion on the principle of this revolution as distinct from the details of the methods by which it is to be applied. It is, of course, perfectly proper that the merits of the existing 'fifty-fifty' grant system should be considered. It is perfectly reasonable, again, that Lord Eustace Percy should say that he personally is opposed to the present grant system and desires to see it changed. What is highly improper and most unreasonable is that

1. A leader by R. H. Tawney.
2. Promised in the Conservative election manifesto.

he should 'jump the claim' – should pronounce sentence before witnesses have been heard or the trial begun.

What matters most, however, is not the form in which the President's new policy is presented, but its practical results. Those results, if it is carried out, will be quite disastrous. The essence of Lord Eustace Percy's proposal is that the grant to each authority is to be stabilised, its basis being a minimum sum equal to the grant payable for 1924–5, less certain deductions, of which the most important is 30s. for each child, under five years of age on the register. The first effect of this must be, and presumably is intended to be, to shut down at a blow the new developments planned by local authorities, even though those plans may have already been approved by the Board itself. Suppose an authority, desiring to frame its programme upon the most respectable models, has decided to follow the policy outlined in the election manifesto of Lord Eustace Percy's own party, what is its position? It has adopted, as it was pressed last year to do by the Board itself, a scheme for gradually reducing the size of classes. That scheme must now be dropped. It has decided to reconstruct insanitary schools; it must now continue them unimproved. It has put in hand a programme of central schools; it must now scrap it. Continuous progress is in these circumstances quite impossible. Nor is it a matter of trifling importance that the Board, the guardian of the rising generation, should penalise the admission to school of children under five years of age. Lord Eustace Percy, in a statement to the press, referred to 'the strong social tendency of the working-class families to keep very young children at home.' 'The working-class families' will be grateful for his notice. If he will visit a mining village, or a textile town, or the East End of London, and expound his educational policy there, he will probably discover 'social tendencies' of a kind so 'strong' as to surprise him.

There is only one cheering feature about the proposed revolution. It is that it cannot be carried out without legislation. Lord Eustace Percy's calculation is quite obvious. It is that he will buy off the opposition of the large authorities by negotiating with them individually and by promising that they shall be subject to less detailed supervision by the Board in the future than in the past. Let them swim like good little fish into his net, he will promise never to draw it tight. The teachers, he presumably thinks, have been bought off already by the Burnham Scale. There remain only the children, who have no votes, and the parents, who, provided the new financial policy is couched in sufficiently technical language, are not likely to appreciate its true significance. So where the iron hand of Sir Eric Geddes failed the silken glove of Lord Eustace will succeed. The nation will glide gently back into the good old days when there was none of the modern nonsense about giving to the *canaille* of working-class children the opportunities of health and education which ought to be reserved for their betters. The plan is ingenious, but it is unlikely that it will be successful, provided that those who are the trustees for the rising generation stand together. If all who care for education will act at once, and act together, it may not be impossible to persuade the Government that even its own election manifesto was not wholly devoid of meaning.

## THE YOUNG DELINQUENT[1]

Thursday, September 10, 1925

It is a good many years since there was a mild outcry against the extravagance of appointing an official psychologist to the L.C.C.'s Education Department. Professor Burt was the psychologist appointed, and those who read now his remarkable book on the causes and cures of juvenile criminality will realise how fully both the post and the man have justified themselves. The bulk of the case-histories on which the book is based have been obtained under the L.C.C.'s auspices, and they illustrate the great remedial possibilities which lie open to a large local education authority if it approaches this problem in a scientific way.

The treatment of the 'human interest,' while never sensational in the cheap sense, is extremely vivid and arresting. From the first page, on which we are introduced to a 'sobbing little urchin' who at only $7\frac{1}{2}$ years was already 'a thief, a truant, and a murderer,' to the late chapters which discuss complexes, psycho-analysis, and re-education, there are very few dull stretches. One conclusion, which is strongly enforced, is the complexity of most (though not all) delinquent cases; environment, heredity, family circumstances, physical history, mental history, all have their say, and often several says. Another is the absence of any sharp boundary between the delinquent and the non-delinquent. Naughtiness is not crime, but the naughtinesses to which all children are subject have much light thrown on them by the study of these extreme cases. For this reason Professor Burt has a good deal of guidance and suggestion to offer, not only to the teacher and the probation officer, but to normal parents of normal children.

R.C.K.E.

1. A review of Cyril Burt's *The Young Delinquent* by R. C. K. Ensor.

# The Different View from England

## THE BOOTLEGGERS' PARADISE

Monday, August 6, 1923
*From a New York Correspondent*[1]

Prohibition in the Unites States lasted from 1920 to 1933

Rum-running is a romance, and, like all romances, it grows in the telling. Law-abiding people in the United States know it only by hearsay; but there is a basis to the hearsay and the romance is certain. Not only the police records of rum ships captured inside the three-mile limit, not only the evidence of one's nose and eyes in almost any city of the States, but also the visible and unmistakable evidence of the goodly schooners that hang about just off the three-mile line tell the tale. Off Atlantic Highlands, just south of New York City, or off Block Island, just east of Long Island, the rum-running ships from the West Indies are as familiar a sight as coastwise freighters.

Florida, however, is the paradise of the rum-runner. It harbours not only an old-fashioned, hard-drinking, liquor-loving lot of natives, but in winter it is the goal of literally hundreds of thousands of northerners who seek out its resorts with an apparent desire to spend as much money as possible as conspicuously as possible and it has an enormously long-drawn-out low-lying sandy coast-line, cut into sand-pits and inlets, bays and points as if designed by Providence for the protection of bootleggers. There the business thrives.

Let no one doubt the basic facts. Nassau in the Bahamas, a British port, cleared 37,821 gallons of liquor in 1917 and 1,340,443 gallons in 1922. Not for the United States officially, of course, but it is a safe bet that most of it reached the Florida coast or the Atlantic Highlands motor-boats. More than 75 per cent of the clearances in 1922 were to St. Pierre Miquelon, which, as few except stamp collectors know, is a French possession off Newfoundland having an area of 93 square miles and a total population under 4,000. It seems reasonable to suppose that no very considerable part of the $5,402,058 worth of liquor cleared for St. Pierre was consumed by its 3,900 inhabitants, and that the rumours that most of it reached the bootleg trade in the United States are true.

1. The contributor's ledger conceals his name as 'X per J.B.'—Bone, the London editor and friend of every American journalist in London. The fee of £50 for two articles was astronomical by *Guardian* standards. Their relegation to an inside page perhaps reflects the news editor's (W. P. Crozier) firm teetotalism.

Rumour has it also that there is an amiable agreement between Nassau and St. Pierre which makes the adjustment of clearance papers easy; in fact it is said that papers can be purchased in advance, so that the West Indian mariner has no need of making the long journey Newfoundlandwards after he has landed his cargo somewhere off the South Atlantic coast, but can return to his home port with his papers for the round trip in perfect order.

The romance and adventure come mainly in the landing. It is simple enough to sail out from Nassau or Bimini towards the famous three-mile limit, and to sell a cargo over the side to American motor-boats. Yet even here there is the spice of danger. The business is too profitable to be safe. The newspapers are full of stories of bootleg pirates who, armed to the teeth like buccaneers of old, meet the rum ships, take the crews by storm, and, setting them adrift, make off with the precious liquor. It is impossible to prosecute, and the victims are not likely to care to make their woes public. But the sounder half of hearsay has it that most of these reports of rum pirates are concocted to cover 'inside jobs.' Men who will go into the rum-running business are ready to defy the letter of the law in one way, and they are very likely to find the temptation great to stretch it in two directions on the same trip. Crews have often enough played pirates themselves, and when the ship's captain is not a partner of the shipper he may make a lot of money for himself and cover it up by telling a fine tale of attack by pirates. It is notorious that the descriptions of the pirate told by different members of the same crew seldom tally. There was the case, for instance, of a converted submarine chaser, which shipped from Bermuda to Montreal loaded with whiskey. Two weeks later she made her way New Yorkwards up the Narrows and was boarded by American prohibition agents working on a Bermuda tip that the vessel was bootlegging. Not a case or a bottle was to be found. The dapper captain informed the agents that he had been asleep in his berth at eight o'clock the previous morning when he was awakened by a large man with a pistol, who, still holding the pistol in one hand, bound and gagged him with the other. While he was gagged the ship's liquor mysteriously disappeared. Ten or twelve pirates were in the band, the captain said, explaining that he had first mistaken them for prohibition agents. The six burly sailors of the crew all agreed that the ship had been robbed, but none of them had been on at the time or had a sufficient recollection of any of the pirates to describe them.

There are certain rendezvous along the coast, well known to the rum-runners and the bootleggers, and apparently well enough known to the newspapermen, who now and then carry picturesque stories, often enough illustrated with photographs, of the commerce off shore. Most of these rendezvous are off the three-mile line. Some are further at sea. There is Gun Cay, for instance, once a hiding-place for the pirate Blackbeard, and now understood to be a great trading centre. It is a point of volcanic rock thirty-odd miles off the Florida coast, a very convenient point for slow bargaining and comfortable transhipment. Rum ships from the Bahamas can anchor there for days at a time, while the news spreads among the bootlegging fraternity on the Florida coast and the mosquito fleet of motor-boats assembles, 'shops about' from ship to ship, comparing prices and testing the liquor – which is said to be marvellously cut and diluted before it gets into the boot-legging trade – and then makes its adventurous way back across a treacherous bit of sea to the territorial waters of the United States, across shallow sand-bars that prevent pursuit from sea. Then, usually after dark, it proceeds up the inlets or on to the sandy beaches, where the liquor can be 'cached' or transferred to motor-cars which know the roads to safety. And then begin another series of adventures, in which the risk is even greater than at sea and the profits certainly as huge.

## BIG BILL THOMPSON AND THE CHICAGO UNDERWORLD

Monday, April 16, 1928
*From our Own Correspondent*[1]

New York, April 7

The remarkable phenomenon which is Chicago puzzles the rest of the United States almost as much as it does foreign commentators. Some of the things which are happening there have been witnessed in other communities, but never in the same combination or to such high degree. I recently spent some days in that city, in the course of which I talked with a number of the most experienced impartial observers of the local political and social landscape. What follows is a summary of their explanation of what is taking place.

Mayor Thompson is, they say, an intelligent man. He is cynical about the ability of the average voter to distinguish between sense and nonsense. He seems to be justified in his cynicism by the results he has achieved in his two terms in office. He does not believe one word of

1. Bruce Bliven

his own farrago of absurdities about 'King George' and the British threat to Chicago, except that he is generally disturbed about the changes in the history textbooks since he was a boy. Thirty years ago the average American history text was a mass of highly patriotic mis-information. Mayor Thompson studied from such books, has never learned anything about history since, and is distressed when he reads the more accurate, non-Jingoistic history of to-day. Few, however, believe that he is sincere when he attributes this change to British influence. His campaign against the English is useful with the Irish and German voters, of whom there are large numbers in Chicago. When it comes to the Anglo-Saxon Protestants his henchmen whisper darkly, and with great success, that his diatribes against 'King George' do not refer to the King of England at all, but to George, Cardinal Mundelein, the Catholic cardinal who has Chicago in his charge.

Thompson's success is based largely on his skill in making a different appeal to each of the various European groups which make up Chi-cago's polyglot population. He is careful to pick the outstanding Norwegians, Poles, Italians, &c., and give them important sounding but low salaried positions in the municipal administration. In return for this they are supposed to deliver the vote of their colonies to him on election day, and they do.

He is also enormously effective in appealing to the mass of the population in general by the simple arts of the demagogue. Everyone knows how, in his latest campaign, he habitually brought a pair of white rats, in a cage, to political meetings. Naming these for his opponents, he excoriated them 'to their faces' and to the huge delight of the simple-minded citizenry. He wears a vast sombrero which is his trade mark in Chicago, being supposed to typify the generosity, en-thusiasm, and enterprise of the old West. In his present campaign he relies upon the use of songs, especially written for the purpose, and sung with great vigour by his political cohorts. The chief song about himself manages to incorporate the advertising slogan by which he impresses his personality on a careless and inattentive world: 'Big Bill, the Builder.'

> *Who planned our good*
> *And kept on sawing wood?*
> *It's Big Bill . . . the Builder*
> *Who showed them he could*
> *Do all he said he would?*
> *It's Big Bill . . . the Builder*

His partner, State Attorney Robert E. Crowe, also has a song:

> *O when you crow*
> *Just Crow for Bob Crowe,*
> *He's the greatest man I know.*

Governor Small of Illinois, is also one of Thompson's associates. The Governor was recently tried for misusing the State's funds during a previous term as State Treasurer, and ordered by the Supreme Court of Illinois to return £200,000. A few months ago this was adjusted to £130,000, which he had paid back. Governor Small is advertising himself as 'the builder of roads,' which fits in nicely with Mayor Thompson's designation of himself as 'the master builder' – with no apologies to Ibsen, of whom it is improbable that either of these gentlemen has ever heard. Governor Small's song is in part as follows:

> *Highways are happy ways when you go along with Small,*
> *Highways – let's give our praise to the man who built them all.*

A powerful Chicago newspaper, the 'Tribune,' is a fierce opponent of Mayor Thompson. Indeed, most of the newspapers of the city are against him, his only important journalistic supporter being William Randolph Hearst. To offset the antagonism of the press, one song glorifying Mayor Thompson has a special stanza:

> *He's big, real and true*
> *A man clear through and through,*
> *Big Bill . . . the Builder,*
> *We're building with you*
> *Throw away your hammer*
> *And go get yourself a horn;*
> *Don't believe the nonsense*
> *In the papers every morn*
> *America's first, just let our slogan be*
> *Big Bill . . . the Builder*
> *And our libertee.*

The 'America First' campaign also has its special ditty:

> *In song we praise America*
> *First, last, and all the time*
> *United States America,*
> *First, last, and all the time.*

Such antics as these may seem humorous to the outsider, but they are not so regarded by the serious-minded citizens of Chicago, of whom there are a considerable number, even though they are unable to make themselves felt politically. They say that Thompson's buffooneries serve to distract the popular attention while the people are mercilessly exploited by predatory interests. Mayor Thompson, while he never tires of parading as defender of the people's liberties, is notoriously friendly to the big public utility corporations, whether they are seeking higher rates for their services or an extension of their franchise privileges. Thompson was elected on the promise that Chicago would be a 'wide open town,' and there is ample evidence that here is one pre-election promise which has been fulfilled. The city is overrun with gambling-houses, speakeasies (illegal saloons), and houses of prostitution. Bootlegging is a major industry. The chief 'mobs' of bootleggers divide the city among themselves, each having exclusive jurisdiction in its own territory. Most of the murders in the last year or two have been because one group or another has been suspected of violating the terms of this 'gentlemen's agreement.'

How much money bootleggers, gamblers and procurers pay each year to the municipal authorities to be let alone no one knows: but the smallest of several estimates made for me by Chicagoans ran into millions of dollars. The interrelation between the municipal administration and certain elements in the underworld is so open that hardly anyone takes the trouble to deny it.

The Republican primary election this month largely turned upon this question. The Thompson group was opposed by forces headed by United States Senator Deneen. Senator Deneen was, professionally at least, a 'dry,' in opposition to Mayor Thompson, who is openly a 'wet.' [Deneen] was instrumental in seeing that a large number of Federal agents were sent to Chicago to attack the Herculean labour of making it, if not dry, at least less openly moist. One of the first results was that a follower of Senator Deneen himself was murdered by indignant bootleggers to whom he had promised an immunity which they failed to get. A second result was the bombing of Senator Deneen's house, in the course of which, by an extraordinary piece of good luck, no one was injured. Third came the shooting of one of Mayor Thompson's henchmen, a court bailiff, who was killed by a Federal agent in the course of a raid on a speakeasy. The bailiff was presumably resisting the Federal officials, but this unimportant fact is ignored by the Chicagoans, who are outraged that a mere stranger should presume to come to their city and kill a man, a task at which their own virtuosity is admitted. What will come next no one knows, but it is sure to be bizarre and brutal. Those are the characteristics which, so everyone admits, predominate at present in the Chicago scene.

## MUSSOLINI'S ITALY

Mussolini had seized power in October, 1922

Wednesday, July 22, 1925
*From our Own Correspondent*[1]

Rome, Tuesday

Signor Giovanni Amendola, the leader of the Democratic Opposition, left Rome yesterday morning for the climatic station of Montecatini, in Tuscany. This morning he returned to Rome with multiple contusions on the forehead, face, knee, and arms, lacerations of the lips, and with various other injuries reported curable in three weeks, failing complications.[2]

Signor Amendola's one-day holiday was spent as follows. Reaching the principal hotel of Montecatini at three o'clock, at seven he was warned that large bodies of Fascists were concentrating in the neighbourhood. He promptly declared his readiness to depart in the interests of peace, and was advised to repair to a neighbouring building till a motor-car arrived. Before he could do this the Fascists began a siege of the building and broke into the garden.

Eight policemen were the sole defence available. While Signor Amendola and his secretary were seeking refuge in the top storey the Fascists burst in and assaulted the secretary, Signor Donnarumma.

Before they turned their attention to Signor Amendola there was a diversion caused by the arrival of Fascist deputy, Signor Scorza, who harangued the Fascists, persuading them to let Signor Amendola depart in the motor-car. It was now midnight, when Signor Amendola, amid riotous scenes, entered a motor-car with two Fascist guards and departed for Pistoja, followed by a police car.

After half an hour the police motor gave up the pursuit, when almost immediately a group of twenty Fascists appeared in the road, and stopping the car, went for Signor Amendola with clubs and maces, smashing the car windows and inflicting the injuries above recorded.

The car was now allowed to proceed to Pistoja, where the wounds were tended, and Signor Amendola returned to Rome by the night train. One of the Fascist guards also received injuries, the Fascists say, in attempting to defend Signor Amendola.

One seeks vainly for any word of frank regret in the Government press, the nearest approach being a timid suggestion in the 'Popolo

1. Cecil Sprigge
2. In fact Amendola died of his injuries at Cannes on April 6, 1926.

d'Italia' that Fascism had better not forget chivalrous principles even if opponents lose their equanimity. On the other hand the non-Fascist press, even of the least oppositional type, hits out hard. Many papers have been suppressed here to-night for comment on the Amendola affair. The last aggression on Amendola was in December, 1923.

## GANDHI'S RELEASE AND RECOVERY

Saturday, March 15, 1924
*By C. F. Andrews*

Serious and informed English opinion needs to take into account the one patent fact that just as in Egypt it is Zaghlul who now counts and no one else, so in India it is Mahatma Gandhi who counts and the rest are nowhere. Zaghlul came from the peasant class. Mahatma Gandhi became, by an act of religious poverty, a peasant. It is this direct touch with the common folk which has made these national movements in Egypt and India so strong and active. There is no other force in India remotely to compare with that of Mahatma Gandhi. His least word sways the hearts of Mohammedans as well as Hindus. The President of the All-India Christian Conference called him the greatest living 'Indian Christian,' because of his devoted life of love and service. The Parsee priests in their fire temples offer prayers for his long life. He is revered as no Indian in modern times has ever been revered.

Therefore the whole political situation has been lightened by the wise and humane act of his release.[1] There has been an immediate response of the most remarkable kind. From Mahatma Gandhi himself has come a renewed offer of friendship. His words have been echoed by Maulana Muhammad Ali, the leader of Islam in India, and also by Pundit Motilal Nehru, the head of the Swaraj party in the Legislative Assembly. Nationalist papers have vied with one another in praising the Government of India for its kindly deed. There has not been a single discordant note. The opportunity is a great one for a man of imagination to lay hold of and thus to regain something of that earlier friendship between India and Great Britain, which was so deep and true and sincere.

It was difficult for me after leaving England on January 17, to gain any tidings about Mahatma Gandhi's illness. At last, at Aden, the Indian papers brought the welcome news that he had borne the operation well. When the ship reached Bombay a special messenger had been

1. Gandhi had been in prison since 1922.

sent by him from the hospital to welcome me on my arrival and to ask me to come immediately to Poona. There I have been with him, apart from one slight interval, ever since. The privilege of serving him in his present physical weakness is one which I would not have missed for the world.

Words can hardly describe the frailty and weakness of his body after the operation. At one time he looked as if he could hardly recover, and I heard at first hand how anxious the doctors had been. His mind is still as alert and active as ever, almost too active for such a frail and emaciated body. He will give it no rest, and almost from the first day after his release he began to direct from his bedside some of his most devoted followers. The wound, in these circumstances, has healed very slowly indeed; already nearly six weeks have passed and it has not closed yet. The reports sent to England about his having completely recovered his health must be heavily discounted. What I have most feared is that he may be rapidly burning life itself away in the ardour of his indomitable spirit.

The crowd on this occasion has been extraordinarily good, and his very least wish has been observed. But I dread, more than I can say, the time when he is allowed to leave the hospital! It is not unlikely that then the enthusiasm of the masses, who worship him with a blind devotion, will break out in full flood, beyond all control or restraint. I have travelled with him on previous occasions, when the strain of the multitude (even when he was in good health) could hardly be borne. What will it be in his present physical weakness?

The actual news of his release came to him while I was with him one early morning in the hospital. The doctor, Colonel Maddock, who had performed the operation was the first to bring the good tidings. Mahatma Gandhi remained quite calm and collected. 'This is no release to me,' he said, 'but only greater responsibility than ever.' He then said laughingly to the doctor, 'I trust that you will allow me to remain your patient a little longer.' The doctor smiled in turn and said that he would have to obey orders while he was under his charge. A remarkable friendship has grown up between these two men, and the praise given by Mahatma Gandhi for the treatment he has received has been unbounded. The extraordinary outburst of friendly feeling towards Englishmen which spread like a great wave over the country after Mahatma Gandhi's release has been in no slight measure due to the knowledge, which reached to the remotest villages, that Mahatma Gandhi's life had been saved owing to the skill and devotion of Colonel Maddock, the English doctor.

The extremely critical nature of the illness was unknown to me before the time when I heard an account of it from the doctor himself. The trouble was acute appendicitis. It developed so quickly that a few hours' further delay might have proved fatal. The doctor, realising at once, when called in for consultation, the gravity of the case, broke through all the red-tape of prison restrictions and took his patient at once in his own motor-car to the Sassoon Hospital at Poona. Darkness had come on before the operation could be performed. Then, as luck would have it, when the patient was under chloroform, suddenly the electric light fused and they were left in darkness. All that could be found on the spur of the moment was a hurricane lantern. Just as everything was over the light came on again. When one realises all that was at stake, and the amount of good-will and international friendship that depended on the success of that operation, it is not easy to praise too highly the nerve of the doctor. Surely here was Western science at its best, and Mahatma Gandhi, who has all the fervour of an iconoclast against modern civilisation, was deeply impressed. He thanked the doctor and nurses in no measured terms for their tenderness and care. He is fully aware that he owes his life to their skill, and he has gratefully informed the Indian public of the fact. He has used the occasion also for impressing once more the vital point that his opposition is against the bureaucratic system in India, not against Englishmen themselves, whom he counts among his friends.

'Indeed,' he says in his letter, 'we want to regard Englishmen as our friends, and not to misunderstand them by treating them as our enemies. And if we are to-day engaged in a struggle against the British Government, it is against the system for which it stands in India, and not against Englishmen who are administering the system. I know that many of us have failed to understand and always bear in mind this distinction, and in so far as we have failed we have harmed our cause.'

This is a true utterance, generously uttered, and, as I have twice repeated, it has created at once an atmosphere of friendliness in India such as I personally have not known for some years. The Punjab wrongs at Amritsar have at last been forgotten in the outburst of joy over Mahatma Gandhi's deliverance not only from prison but from death. The Mussulmans are not mentioning to-day the Khalifate. They are rejoicing along with Hindus in Mahatma Gandhi's return from the Valley of the Shadow of Death. No other subject is on people's lips, and the papers each day in the vernaculars are eagerly scanned for any fraction of news concerning their leader and friend.

The question may well be asked by those who have followed this narrative whether this is all the news of the political situation in India to-day; whether the Council sessions in Delhi and the Provincial Councils at the different capitals, which are passing their Swaraj resolutions, mean nothing at all. My answer would be that they cannot be compared with the political importance of this one frail, pathetic figure, racked and tormented with pain and suffering, yet bearing each day's burden with a cheerful smile, in the hospital at Poona. For India is vitally, essentially, immeasurably religious; and the influence of one saint who has won the love and devotion of the poor is greater than that of all the rest of the politicians put together. This saint-politician, if I may use the strange hybrid word, has already taken into his own hands the reins of political leadership again. He is ruling India, as no Viceroy can do, from the hospital itself.

## MR. KELLOGG'S SCRAP OF PAPER

Monday, August 27, 1928
*From Our Own Correspondent*[1]

Paris, Sunday
So far Herr Stresemann[2] is the star of this gathering from the world's chief Chancelleries. It is an index of the awful realities of Europe and of the long Franco-German strain that not for sixty-one years has a German Minister made an official visit to Paris, nor has Paris been prepared to offer to a German Minister an official welcome. The last occasion was Bismarck's visit during the Second Empire to the exhibition of 1867. (One cannot, of course, count the corralling of the German peace delegation in the hotel at Versailles as a visit, still less as a welcome.) This more than any other feature strikes the historic imagination of the Paris population. It marks to the people with a stamp of immediate reality the immense change that has already been wrought by Locarno and Geneva; it is taken as a symbol of the opening of a new era.

It is not surprising, then, that vast crowds had spontaneously gathered this afternoon outside the courtyard of the Gare du Nord to await Herr Stresemann's arrival; nor that when he issued from the station he was greeted with a great roar of cheering and the waving of hats. Pale and obviously weak after his illness the great German statesman quietly regarded the crowd, and a smile lit up his face. Perhaps the thought had occurred to him that behind the traditional narrowness of French politicians there is the great and always generous

1. J. G. Hamilton
2. Gustav Stresemann, Foreign Minister from 1923 till his death in 1929.

French people, and the thought may have rekindled hope in this great artisan of reconciliation. Let us pray that this hope may not be too utterly crushed at his meeting to-morrow with M. Poincaré.

The contrast with Mr. Kellogg[1] has proved an utter disappointment. It is his own fault and of his own deliberate will, perhaps due to timidity or, rather more likely, to caution lest by any word or gesture he should injure the chances of his party in the coming Presidential struggle across the Atlantic. From the moment of leaving New York he has imposed an almost absolute rule of silence upon himself. His arrival in Paris was almost furtive. It had been secretly arranged that his train should arrive in Paris an hour before its due time so that he might avoid receptions and publicity. It is true that the Press were invited to meet him yesterday at the American Embassy. At 11 a.m. a mob of some hundred journalists of all countries, some of them writers of European fame, were waiting in the open air under a threatening sky before the Embassy. Suddenly the door opened, and Mr. Kellogg, appearing, addressed a few words to them from the top step. He said little or nothing, and withdrew somewhat precipitately to avoid questions. M. St. Brice, of the *Journal*, cannot refrain from protesting against this rather summary treatment, as well as at the poverty of the few words of 'manna given to the journalists for posterity that to its author may have seemed the more precious as it was parsimonious.'

In the *Echo de Paris*, *Pertinax* gives a blistering portrait-picture, carried almost to the point of discourtesy, of the party lawyer now immortalised by chance, who for his caution, discretion, and gift of silence is, he says, nicknamed in America 'Nervous Nellie.' Journalists' resentment apart, it must be admitted that Mr. Kellogg has not come to Europe in the spirit of an apostle for the great American conception that is now imposing itself on civilised mankind.

## COMMENT: THE SIGNING OF THE PACT[2]

The Pact does not automatically turn the world into a Garden of Eden. It does not even take us automatically out of Bedlam. But it gives statesmanship a new start; it gives mankind a new hope.

The Pact is not a mere act of policy; it is an act of faith. Nobody, therefore, can measure its effect on the imagination of the world. It is here that politicians, always called on to judge what is before them, most easily go wrong. In the eighteenth century the old world of Europe was shaken by a trumpet sound; the phrase 'the Rights of Man.' A cynical observer listening to its ringing echoes might well have said,

1. F. B. Kellogg, Secretary of State 1926-29.    2. A leader by J. L. Hammond.

'Yes, what a delightful and inspiring phrase! What a noble idea! And yet what have the rights of man meant to the great master minds; the men of power who make States or destroy them; who bring happiness or misery, plenty or famine, to the multitude whose ears are flattered by these phrases? What did they mean to Richelieu or Louis the Fourteenth, to Charles the Twelfth or Frederick the Great? What are they going to mean to Talleyrand or Napoleon?' Good common sense, we may say, and yet the man who looks back over the nineteenth century knows how much of its history, good, bad, glorious and terrible, was made by that unsophisticated phrase. Imagination is a force which politicians cannot control, and a phrase has set the imagination of mankind on the march. The Pact has stirred the deepest emotion in man's nature. One of the most moving passages in literature is the speech made to Achilles by Priam, who had come to him, broken with grief, to beg for the body of Hector, a speech describing the cruel lot that the gods spin for wretched man, whether his fortune for the moment is good or ill. Whatever politicians may mean by the Pact, to the masses of men and women it is the symbol of the most passionate of their hopes; the enemies of yesterday speak beside the dead as Greek and Trojan spoke of their longing for escape from that haunting sense of calamity which made the hour of victory so terrible to Achilles. The statesmen who sign are here to-day and gone to-morrow; the next generation may not even know their names. But the Pact that outlaws war, like the message that proclaimed the rights of man, has passed far beyond the horizon of their careful plans into that mysterious world which obeys a power that the Richelieus and Napoleons cannot bind.

Tuesday, August 28, 1928

HOW THE PACT WAS SIGNED
IN THE SIGHT OF THE WORLD

*From Our Own Correspondent*[1]

Paris, Monday

The ceremony of signing the Peace Pact was 'shot,' if that is the right technical 'movie' expression, rather than 'performed' at the Quai d'Orsay this afternoon. One had all the time that curious impression of being in two worlds at once, almost of unreality, that one has in the wings of a theatre. One half of the famous Clock Saloon, the half that will be seen on the films, was all that was dignified and decent, resembling with its row of posing statesmen and heavy, ugly Second Empire

1. J. G. Hamilton

decoration one of those Victorian steel engravings of historic scenes that still adorn the walls of Liberal clubs; the other half was a wild, almost terrifying chaos of wires and cables and instruments of all kinds dominated by huge black-painted projectors on high tripods that reminded one of the original illustrations to Wells's *War of the Worlds*. The sense of being behind the scenes of a theatre was heightened by the bustling feverishness of the kinema stage managers, and, as we were in Paris, where it is the rule in theatres, the presence in his glittering brass helmet and calm indifference, of a pompier (fireman).

Almost at three o'clock to the second the delegates, escorted each in turn by a Swiss Guard armed with a formidable medieval halberd, began to enter.

Suddenly the dim, shaded room, with its heavy curtains and dark hangings and its grave, seated occupants, sprang into a blinding vividness. All that one missed were the three solemn knocks that herald a similar but less startling effect at a theatre. Light, blinding, overwhelming light, poured in through all the windows from vast searchlights hitherto unnoticed on the terrace outside. A more golden, more diffused light streamed from the tripod 'inhabitants of Mars' at the other end of the room. Light in vivid rays from the little spotlights searched, found, and filmed the features of each of the delegates. A high scream of electric arcs rang through one's head, and the pungent ozone of a power station pervaded the atmosphere.

Kinema machines purred, cameras clicked, and then again, suddenly, we were plunged into semi-darkness. A minute spotlight directed from between the chubby legs of a sprawling marble cupid on the mantelpiece picked out the heavy subtle features of M. Briand,[1] the familiar deep voice began to sound through the attentive room. It was a long speech, monotonously recited, and not a very good speech. It was a speech read from a manuscript, a sign that to-day words had to be carefully chosen and weighed before utterance. The great French orator is at his ease and at his best only in improvisations. His performance to-day evidently bored him.

Slowly Herr Stresemann rose from his seat and walked to the little table set in the midst for the signatures. One noticed his face, head, and neck glittering with perspiration, a symptom of physical pain. Herr Stresemann is suffering more than most people know, and has come to Paris accompanied not only by a doctor but by nurses. There was a small flutter of gloved applause. As the German Minister affixed his signature it was observed that the golden fountain-pen of peace

1. Aristide Briand, eleven times Premier, Foreign Minister from 1925 to his death in 1932.

engraved with the olive branch and motto *Si vis pacem para pacem* was not working well. Mr. Kellogg, who followed, had to shake it vigorously – an omen perhaps. The rest dipped it boldly into the Treaty of Versailles ink-pot.

As Herr Stresemann passed after this afternoon's ceremony from the Quai d'Orsay to the German Embassy he was greeted by the enormous crowds deeply massed along the quays and around the Chamber of Deputies with a continuous roar of 'Vive Stresemann,' 'Vive l'Allemagne,' and 'Vive la Paix.' It is hard to resist the feeling that something has changed or is in process of changing when a shout goes up from the throat of a Paris crowd of 'Long live Germany.' But the people are not the politicians, a truism that is always particularly true in France.

All such conferences hitherto have something secret, almost furtive about them. The diplomats and their attendant journalists have met in a sort of intimacy for the making of pacts or the signing of treaties. Ferrero has said that in the soul of diplomats and Foreign Ministers is to be found the last survival of the spirit of Monarchist absolutism. In the attendant journalists there is too often the spirit of the courtier or even the lackey.

This afternoon there were occasional cries of anger from the ranks of the pressmen, who for the most part could see nothing, hear nothing, for the kinema and the broadcasting apparatus had usurped their place. For the first time a diplomatic piece was being played not for a few score journalists but for the eyes and ears of hundreds and millions of ordinary folk throughout the world. To-day's signature marked not merely the abdication of the old diplomacy, always dependent implicitly and avowedly on the *ultima ratio regum*, it symbolised in many ways a coming change of function for the press reporter.

This forenoon Herr Stresemann was closeted for an hour and a half with M. Poincaré. Incredible as it may appear, M. Poincaré can become on occasion personally very charming. His greeting was all that could be desired. Otherwise the interview was a complete set-back. To Herr Stresemann, who urged the evacuation of the Rhineland,[1] he put the question, What have you to offer? As the answer was and could only in effect be Nothing, M. Poincaré made it unmistakably clear that there is no solution but a European settlement linking debts and reparations, and, as the United States is not yet ripe for conference on such a subject, Germany must be content with the status quo.

1. The last Allied troops did not leave the Rhineland until June, 1930. Poincaré had been President of France 1913–20, Premier 1911–13, 1922–24, 1926–29.

# Television—Shadow of Things to Come

Saturday, August 9, 1930

On July 14 Pirandello's *The Man with the Flower in his Mouth* was televised, and on July 28 television by the Baird process was seen, for the first time in any theatre, at the London Coliseum.

My experience with the Pirandello play was unfortunate, for not having a televisor of my own I had to rely on the apparatus at a multiple store. This could only be seen by one person at a time; as there were over a hundred waiting, and as the play lasted thirty minutes, our time before the machine was limited, and I, who was there professionally, as it were, arrived before the screen at the instant of a fade-out. At the Coliseum, however, I saw all there was to see. The screen was about the size of a door, and the image was clear. Whilst it is ridiculous to claim that television is yet 'entertainment,' it is even more foolish to deny the enormous effect it will have on entertainment in the future.

R.H.[1]

1 Robert Herring

# CHAPTER TEN

# The Shadow of Jarrow and Munich, 1932 - 1938

\*

The years from 1932 to 1944 are a distinct period in *Guardian* as well as in world history. They were Hitler's years; they were Crozier's. In April, 1932 Hitler polled 13,000,000 votes in the German presidential election; in May W. P. Crozier became editor of the *Manchester Guardian*. Crozier died in April, 1944; seven weeks later Allied troops landed in Normandy. The Nazi era was ending.

The first six of these years, the subject of this chapter, were the time of Hitler's conquests without war. From a *Guardian* point of view they were the time when Frederick Voigt came into his own. Because he had understood the Germany of the Weimar republic, he was able with authority to tell the truth about Nazi Germany and to foretell with confidence the darkening future. In Britain these were years of mass unemployment, when the people of Jarrow, Tories and Labour alike, united to march to Westminster. They were also years of widespread pacifism, when the Oxford Union resolved 'not to fight for King and Country,' and the Peace Ballot attracted nearly 12,000,000 votes.

## Hitler's Europe

### DELIBERATE FAMINE IN RUSSIA

Saturday, March 25, 1933
*From a Correspondent in Russia*[1]

Living in Moscow and listening always to statements of doctrine and of policy, you forget that Moscow is the centre of a country stretching over a sixth of the world's surface and that the lives of a hundred and sixty millions of people, mostly peasants, are profoundly affected by discussions and resolutions that seem, when you hear them or read of them in the press, as abstract as the proceedings of a provincial debating society. 'We must collectivise agriculture', or 'We must root out

1. Malcolm Muggeridge

kulaks' (the rich peasants). How simple it sounds! How logical. But what is going on in the remote villages, in the small households of the peasants? What does this collectivisation of agriculture mean in practice in the lives of the peasantry? What results has the new 'drive' produced? What truth, if any, is there in the gloomy reports that have been reaching Moscow? That is what I wanted to find out. I set out to discover it in the North Caucasus.

A little market town in the Kuban district of the North Caucasus suggested a military occupation; worse, active war. There were soldiers everywhere – in the railway station, in the streets, everywhere Mongols with leaden faces and slit eyes, others obviously peasants, rough but not brutal; occasional officers, dapper, often Jews; all differing notably from the civilian population in one respect. They were well fed, and the civilian population was obviously starving. I mean starving in its absolute sense; not undernourished, as for instance, most Oriental peasants are undernourished and some unemployed workers in Europe, but having had for weeks next to nothing to eat. Later I found out there had been no bread at all in the place for three months, and such food as there was I saw for myself in the market. The only edible thing there on the lowest European standards was chicken – about five chickens, fifteen roubles each. No one was buying. Where should a peasant get fifteen roubles? For the most part, chickens – the few that remain – are sold in the railway stations to passengers on their way to the mountains in the south for a holiday or for a rest cure in a sanatorium.

The rest of the food offered for sale was revolting and would be thought unfit, in the ordinary way, to be offered to animals. There was sausage at fifteen roubles the kilo, there was black cooked meat which worked out, I calculated, at a rouble for three bites; there were miserable fragments of cheese and some cooked potatoes, half rotten. A crowd wandered backwards and forwards eyeing these things wistfully, too poor to buy. The few who bought gobbled their purchases ravenously then and there.

'How are things with you?' I asked one man. He looked round anxiously to see that no soldiers were about. 'We have nothing, absolutely nothing. They have taken everything away,' he said, and hurried on. This was what I heard again and again. 'We have nothing. They have taken everything away.' It was true. They had nothing. It is also true that everything had been taken away. The famine is an organised one. Some of the food that has been taken away from them – and the peasants know this quite well – is still being exported to foreign countries.

It is impossible adequately to describe the melancholy atmosphere of this little market town; how derelict it was; the sense of hopelessness pervading the place, and this not just because of famine but because the population was, as it were, torn up by the roots. The class war has been waged vigorously in the North Caucasus, and the proletariat, represented by the G.P.U. (State Political Police) and the military, has defeated and utterly routed its enemies amongst the peasantry who tried to hide a little of their produce to feed themselves through the winter. Despite hostile elements, however, the North Caucasus distinguished itself by being 90 per cent collectivised, and then, this year, by fulfilling its grain delivery plan. As a result, this double effort has turned it into something like a wilderness – fields choked with weeds, cattle dead, people starving and dispirited, no horses for ploughing or for transport, not even adequate supplies of seed for the spring sowing. The worst of the class war is that it never stops. First individual kulaks shot and exiled; then groups of peasants; then whole villages. I walked from street to street watching the faces of people, looking at empty shops. Even here a Torgsin shop; good food offered for gold; useful for locating any private hoards that organised extortion had failed to detect.

The little villages round about were even more depressing than the market town. Often they seemed quite deserted. Only smoke coming from some of the chimneys told that they were populated. In one of the larger villages I counted only five people in the street, and there was a soldier riding up and down on – rare sight now in the North Caucasus – a fine horse. It is literally true that whole villages have been exiled. In some cases demobilised soldiers have been moved in to take the places of the exiles; in some cases the houses are just left empty. I saw myself a group of some twenty peasants being marched off under escort. This is so common a sight that it no longer even arouses curiosity. Everywhere I heard that the winter sowing had been miserably done, and that in any case the land was too weed ridden to yield even a moderate crop. Though it was winter in some places weeds still stood taller than wheat and growing thickly. There were no cattle to be seen, and I was assured that, in that part of the North Caucasus at least, there were none at all. They had been killed and eaten or had died of starvation.

Occasionally along the road I met with little groups of peasants with rifles slung over their shoulders; men in fur caps, rough-looking; a kind of armed militia that has also been mobilised for service on the kulak front. I wanted to find out about some future prospects; whether the change from forced grain collections to a more moderately assessed tax in kind was going to make things better; what chances there were even now of retrieving the blunders of the last two years. It is difficult, however, to get people who are starving and who know that, whatever happens, they must go on starving for at least three more months, and probably five, to talk about or take any great interest in the future. To them the question of bread, of how to get enough food to keep just alive to-day and to-morrow, transcends all others. Starving people are not, in a general way, loquacious, particularly when to talk may be to qualify as a kulak and so for exile or worse. I was shown a piece of bread from Stavropol. It was made, I was told, of weeds and straw and a little millet. It seemed inconceivable that anyone could eat such bread; actually it was in the circumstances a rare delicacy.

The peasants in this region had to provide exports to pay for the Five Year Plan; they had to be – to use an expression of Stalin's in a lecture on the peasant question – 'reserves of the proletariat'; and the 'reserves' had to be mobilised, made accessible – that is, collectivised. It is not difficult for the Soviet Government to make collectivisation, in the quantitative sense, an enormous success, so enormous that even the Communist party grew a little anxious and Stalin issued a public warning against 'dizziness from success.' In the event about 60 per cent of the peasantry and 80 per cent of the land were brought into collective farms; Communists with impeccable ideology were installed as directors of them; agronomes were to provide expert advice, tractors to replace horses, elevators to replace barns, and the practice of America combined with the theory of Marxism was to transform agriculture into a kind of gigantic factory staffed by an ardently class conscious proletariat.

As things turned out the Communist directors were sometimes incompetent or corrupt; the agronomes, despite their scientific training, were in many cases a failure in dealing with the actual problems connected with producing food; horses, for lack of fodder, died off much faster than tractors were manufactured, and the tractors were mishandled and broken; the attitude of the peasants varied from actual sabotage and passive resistance to mere apathy, and was generally, to say the least, unhelpful; altogether, in the qualitative sense, collectivisation was a failure. The immediate result was, of course, a falling off in the yield of agriculture as a whole. Last year this falling off became acute. None the less the Government quota had to be collected. To feed the cities and to provide even very much reduced food exports it was necessary for the Government's agents to go over the country and take everything, or nearly everything, that was edible. At the same time, because the policy could not be wrong and therefore individuals, classes, must be at fault, there took place a new outburst of repression, directed this time not only against kulaks but against every kind of peasant suspected of opposing the Government's policy; against a good number of the Communist directors and the unfortunate agronomes. Shebboldaev, party secretary for the North Caucasus, said in a speech delivered at Rostov on November 12:

> At the present moment, when what remains of the kulaks are trying to organise sabotage, every slacker must be deported. That is true justice. You may say that before we exiled individual kulaks, and that now it concerns whole stanitzas (villages) and whole collective farms. If these are enemies they must be treated as kulaks.

It is this 'true justice' that has helped greatly to reduce the North Caucasus to its present condition.

## THE BRUNSWICK REHEARSAL

### Wednesday, March 30, 1932

(There are ugly stories from some of the chief German cities of the way in which the Nazi 'forces' are acting. Our special correspondent[1] has paid a visit of investigation to Brunswick, and in this article describes what he found there.)

Brunswick, Easter Monday

For half a year a Nazi, Herr Klagges, has been Minister of the Interior in the Free State of Brunswick. The Government has only two members – the other is the Minister of Finance, a Nationalist. A Coalition Government of this kind – that is to say, between the Nazis and the other parties of the Right – is not inconceivable as the result of the Prussian elections next month. Whenever the Nazis take office they demand the Ministry of Interior because it gives them control over the police. It was so in Thuringia. It is so in Brunswick, and perhaps it will be so in Prussia.

Their spell of power in Brunswick is a kind of rehearsal and one of very great interest as showing what may happen in Prussia, or later on, throughout Germany. There is political disorder and gangsterdom in Prussia at times, but the police use their truncheons with fair impartiality now. Here in Brunswick, under Herr Klagges, the police have just that slight bias, and the courts just that partisanship, just that

---

1. F. A. Voigt. The day after this message appeared ten reporters were sent by Berlin newspapers to Brunswick. Their stories amply confirmed Voigt's statements.

closing of the eye to one side and that wide-eyed vigilance towards the other; just that reluctance in punishing here and just that alacrity in punishing there which make all the difference between rule and misrule.

Although the Nazis, like the Reichsbanner,[1] are forbidden to wear uniforms in Germany, they go about Brunswick as they do in any other city, in their brown uniforms – a brown shirt, brown riding breeches and leggings. Each one of them cultivates just one irregularity – he goes without a cap, for example, or he wears an ordinary overcoat, and in this way the Nazi in Brunswick is not considered as wearing a uniform by the police or by the courts, so that swarms of young men who would be arrested in Berlin or Munich walk freely about the streets of Brunswick.

The Nazi Storm Troops (called S.A. men) have living quarters which they use as barracks. (One of these quarters is in the richest part of the city.) They also have lorries on which they race along at great speed, their flags (red with a white disc, and on the disc the swastika, their anti-Semitic symbol) fluttering over the bonnet. The sides of the lorries can be clapped down so that the inmates can jump out at a moment's notice.

If there is any real or alleged trouble, the lorry dashes to the spot, the storm troops leap down, blows from cudgels, knives, preservers, knuckle dusters are dealt out right and left, heads are cut open, arms raised in self defence are broken or bruised and crouching backs or shoulders are beaten black and blue. Sometimes shots are fired and knives are drawn. In a few moments all is over – the Nazis scramble back into their lorry and are off. The police arrive to find a man lying dead or several lying unconscious with concussion of the brain, or staggering away clasping an abdominal knife wound or holding a broken head from which the blood drips down on the cobbles. The injured are sometimes Reichsbanner men, sometimes there is a Communist too, and sometimes chance passers by – very rarely are they Nazis.

Never is there any cause for such an assault, never any trouble the police could not have easily dealt with. Usually there has been no trouble at all, but only a pretence of 'comrades in danger' that will serve as an excuse for the assault. The lorry with its load of hooligans can be seen racing along almost any day, and anyone can stand outside the quarters where the 'storm troops' eat, sleep, live, mount guard, draw their pay, or come and go or stand about in the brown uniform that is no uniform.

1. The anti-Nazi para-military organisation, mainly Social Democrat in membership.

Nothing is done to stop the abominations. Those guilty of doing grievous bodily harm or of committing murder can never somehow or other be identified, and the 'storm troops' are left unmolested in their lorries or their barracks.

If the Communists were to do only a fraction of what the Nazis are doing in Brunswick, punishment would be instantaneous and drastic. Uniforms, lorries, and barracks would vanish overnight. And if Herr Klagges – who would, if he were dealing with Communists, surely do his best and his most energetic – were not quite equal to the task, the Central Government would take action, as it did in 1923 when Saxony and Thuringia were invaded by regular troops. But General Groener, the Minister of the Interior and of War in the Reich, has a soft spot in his heart for the Nazis. And so these things are allowed to go on.

I have to-day called on a dozen – only a few amongst very many – of those who have been seriously injured by Nazis in the course of this month. They are all simple working people who have had no quarrel with anyone and have never offered any kind of provocation. Most of the recent assaults have been committed not in Brunswick but in the outlying villages. In one of these, for example, several men and women were going home after a reunion. It was dark, and suddenly a lorry drew up. Whistles shrilled and there were shouts of 'S.A. Drauf!' the Nazi war-cry, meaning 'Storm troops, at them!' and 'Kill the dogs!' and so on. Blows and stabs were dealt out with savage violence. The Nazis carried flashlamps so that they could see but could with difficulty be seen.

An old man who has just told me his story was beaten across the head and then stabbed in the stomach. He was picked up unconscious and bleeding. This happened just over a fortnight ago, on the eve of the Presidential election.[1] He is now recovering, though still pale and weak. His coat and waistcoat show a slit where the knife went through. His cap is stiff with clotted blood. His wife was with him that evening. A light, so she tells me, was flashed into her face. She heard someone shout down from the lorry, 'Don't hit the woman,' but the blows descended upon her too. She raised her arms to protect her face (they still have the bruises) and ran.

In another village there was an altercation between some Nazis and Reichsbanner men over an election placard. There was some rough and tumble, but no one was hurt. Some time afterwards a gang of Nazis arrived in a car – no one knew from where, they all seemed to be

---

1. In which Hindenburg received 18 million votes to Hitler's 11 million and the Communists' 5 million. A second ballot in April gave Hindenburg 19 million to Hitler's 13 and the Communists' 3 million.

strangers. Most of them carried short whips like those used by artillery-men. They broke into a house and searched every room. Finding noth-ing, they searched the bushes outside. Then they raided the public house. One man they caught – he collapsed under the blows.

In village after village I heard similar stories and saw scores of bruises. Since Herr Klagges has been in office – such things were un-known in Brunswick before, even during the Revolution – that is to say, since last September, three persons have been killed and more than a hundred grievously injured in and around the city (which has about 160,000 inhabitants). Those who have had slight knocks and cuts are innumerable. Most of the victims I have spoken to are full of bitterness, and fury. Hardly any have been intimidated, and in most of the villages I passed through Hindenburg had secured an absolute majority.

If the terror, recalling that of the 'Squadristi' in the early days of Fascism, is deliberate policy, meant to break the spirit of the victims as well as their bones, it is a failure. The movement of self-defence against these outrages has become very strong. In the city of Bruns-wick the Reichsbanner – which is made up almost wholly of workmen – can now assemble a thousand disciplined men at a moment's notice. The Reichsbanner is growing rapidly in the villages. Patrols and flying columns are being organised to meet all emergencies. The leaders are having some trouble in restraining their men, for hatred of the Nazis and resentment for the toleration shown them by a partisan Government and bitterness for the falsehoods (accompanied by 'uplift') that are allowed to appear in their newspapers, while the anti-Fascist newspapers are continually being censored or suppressed, are boiling up into a burning and general fury.

But restraint is imperative, for if the Reichsbanner were to retaliate, to storm the Nazi barracks, or hold up the lorries and give the inmates what they have given so many others, the police would develop a tremendous alacrity and long terms of imprisonment or penal servitude would be passed by the courts, and the Reichsbanner, which exists for the defence of the Republic and of the political liberties won in the Revolution, would be totally suppressed as a subversive organisation. Thus the anti-Fascist movement that grows in numbers and efficiency day by day remains on the defensive – for the time being.

Every impartial observer who sees what is happening in Brunswick now is assailed by one importunate question – 'Will it be like this in Prussia, in the Reich? Will a whole nation, one of the greatest and most civilised in the world, be handed over to the brute, the blackguard, and the charlatan?' No one can tell. But Brunswick is an ominous foreshadowing. The answer will surely come before the end of this fateful year 1932.

## THE TERROR IN GERMANY

Tuesday, March 28, 1933
*From a Special Correspondent in Germany*[1]

March 27

There is a widespread belief that Germany has been through a period in which some deplorable but nevertheless natural excesses have been committed – natural in so far as revolutions are habitually accompanied by a certain effervescence that usually leads to disorder and mob violence. Indeed, amongst the supporters of the Hitlerite regime there is a certain pride – pride because the 'revolution' was carried out with so little bloodshed, and the phrase 'unbloodiest revolution in history' has become a favourite catchword.

The German Government by admitting a few and denying the many excesses (while designating the few as perfectly natural, indeed excusable), attempt not only to conceal by far the greater and by far the more terrible part of the truth, but also to make themselves and their so-called 'revolution' appear unique and resplendent by reason of the kindness and the magnanimity of its leaders and the prodigious decency and self-discipline of their followers.

Thus they convert a thing of shame into an object of self-congratulation and boastful pride.

This they are able to do all the more easily because they have the power – there is no press in Germany, and no news that is not all obsequiousness to the will of the dictatorship can be told; no truth can be told by the defeated Opposition, and no falsehood told by the Government can be publicly denied.

This opportunity for spreading untruth and suppressing truth is exploited to the utmost, and with such success that even in Berlin, the scene of countless horrible outrages, there are many persons who will assert with entire good faith that nothing unusual has happened, because they are allowed to see and hear nothing. The untrue assumptions or the downright falsehoods spread by the Government or by its newspapers – for example, that the Communists set fire to the Reichstag (Hitler has in a public speech demanded the public execution of the alleged culprit before he has been tried); that there was a plot to murder Hitler; that the Socialists have asked the French to occupy the Rhineland – all serve the purpose of the Government in so far as they

1. F. A. Voigt

make any excesses committed by its Brown Shirts seem excusable, any repressive action carried out by itself necessary, indeed laudable, while the prostrate opposition is made to appear hateful and contemptible in the eyes of the world.

It is as though Cain, not satisfied with murdering Abel, had blackened his reputation to make his own appear white by comparison, and had forged documents to prove that Abel was really the aggressor, that Cain was compelled to act in sheer self-defence, and that in doing so he had rid mankind of a monster.

The deeds of violence committed in the first period of the Dictatorship were not desultory, they were not mob rule, they were systematic and purposeful. The Opposition (collectively and individually) must not merely be defeated according to normal constitutional procedure, it must be broken up, demoralised, and intimidated by physical force – this, and this alone, is the real intention of the Dictatorship towards that Opposition.

The methods used will be familiar to all acquainted with the history of German reaction ever since the year 1918. They were used in the Ruhr in 1920.[1] They have not changed except in so far as they have been elaborated. They consist essentially in the beating of as many of the Opposition as can be caught, the beatings often taking the most inhuman form. They inflict extreme physical agony and sometimes death, and cause widespread fear – they are meant to cause fear, and to serve as an example and a warning. This, indeed, is their chief purpose, and a whole population can be kept in a state of dread by a dozen such exemplary beatings. The Polish 'pacification of the Ukraine'[2] is a well-known instance of this method – the Brown Terror of the last few weeks is nothing less than the Hitlerite 'pacification' of Republican Germany.

Germany is now in the period of transition between the non-legal Terror (that is to say, the beatings and the non-judicial murders), and the legal Terror (that is to say, imprisonment or death under laws specially enacted so that the Opposition may be kept in a permanent state of fear and demoralisation). The non-legal and the legal Terror are both organic parts of one permanent Terroristic system, the non-legal being a kind of extemporised preliminary to the more ordered legal Terror, which is at least as effective and does not appear so barbaric in the eyes of the world.

1. By the Baltic 'Free Corps' and other extremist groups. Voigt had been arrested and maltreated while investigating this for which the British government received an official apology from Berlin (see *Guardian*, p. 502).

2. This had been the subject of a series of articles by Voigt after a personal investigation.

The extent of the whole truth cannot be estimated. There is nothing but fragmentary news from the country generally, and even in Berlin only a fraction of the atrocities committed by the Brown Shirts can be definitely established. But even that little leaves no doubt at all that the 'Brown Terror' is, both for the number of the victims and for the inhumanity of the methods used, one of the most frightful atrocities of modern times, and in no way comparable with the Red Terror of revolutionary Russia or France, because it is not an instrument used under the compulsion of a struggle for life or death.

The alternative to those two Red Terrors was a White Terror; but to the Brown Terror (which is a variety of the White) there was no alternative Terror, for at no time were the Nazis oppressed or in danger of oppression by their opponents when they were in power as the Nazis are oppressing their opponents now that these are prostrate.

Three instances of the Brown Terror at work must suffice to characterise it in its first non-legal period.[1]

A number of Brown Shirts arrested a Socialist, Mr. ——, early one morning in his own home. He was taken to a 'Brown House' (as Nazi headquarters are called) near by. He was ordered to stand facing a wall with his hands clasped over his head. He was then beaten with riding whips, most of the blows descending on his head and hands. He was then pinioned and taken before a 'court martial.'

On either side of the 'judge' there was a Brown Shirt armed with a pistol. The victim was then cross-examined as to his party, its leaders, where documents could be found, and so on. Whenever his replies were considered unsatisfactory he was beaten. He was told that he had once kicked a Brown Shirt downstairs. When he denied this he was again beaten.

He was then taken to another room where a number of fellow-prisoners were waiting. They had all been beaten, and their faces and heads were bleeding. The faces of some had been beaten almost to a raw pulp. One of them had a smashed eye and another was lying on the floor so injured that he could not rise. A doctor was present administering first-aid. He bandaged Mr. ——'s finger, which had been broken by a blow.

Mr. —— was then taken before the 'court martial' a second time and told that there was nothing against him and that he could go home, though he would be watched, and must never do anything against the new State.

Another Socialist, Mr. ——, was arrested in the street by Brown

1. The names were withheld by Voigt.

Shirts, ordered into a sidecar, a Brown Shirt with a revolver was on the pillion, and taken to the Brown House in the Hedemannstrasse (the most notorious of the Brown Houses in Berlin – innumerable persons have been beaten and tortured there).

He was taken to a room littered with straw. Two other prisoners were there. One of them, apparently a Bulgarian, had been so injured that his condition was critical. Mr. —— was then made to go through some military drill (standing to attention, lying down, getting up, and so on). He was then beaten with a rubber truncheon wound round with wire. He was made to repair the torn uniform of a Brown Shirt and again beaten.

He was taken into another room and questioned. A slip of paper found in his pocket with the names of fellow-Socialists roused great interest. He was asked for the addresses, but when he said he did not know them he was cuffed and punched. A Brown Shirt then struck him across the head with the butt-end of a revolver. The blow dazed him and the blood began to flow from his mouth and nose. He was then taken to a bathroom and told to have a wash. He was then allowed to go. He says that the after-effects of the beating were more painful than the beating itself.

A young workman, a Socialist and a member of the Reichsbanner, was arrested by four Nazis (three of them wore the Brown Uniform). They all had revolvers. He was taken to a room in a public-house near by. When about twenty prisoners had been brought in they were all ordered to go through their military drill and then marched out doing the goose-step. They were ordered into a motor-lorry (a policeman stood by and watched without interfering).

They were driven to the Hedemannstrasse and beaten with whips and rubber truncheons. They were then taken to another room, made to stand facing the wall, and beaten about the head, face, and eyes with whips, truncheons, and chair legs. Some of them fainted and fell to the ground, but were beaten until they got up again.

A Brown Shirt who seemed to be in charge said 'That will do,' and the beatings stopped. They were then ordered to stand to attention and to sing the Horst Wessel song (the Nazi hymn). As they did not know the words they were ordered to sing 'Deutschland Uber Alles.'

Then drill began again. They were made to do the double-knee bend with hands stretched forward, slowly and repeatedly. With their bruised and bleeding heads and faces they looked a strange sight. The Socialist victim heard screams come from a neighbouring room. His coat, shirt, collar, and pullover were soaked with blood. He and his fellow-prisoners were then told to wash and go home.

These three instances of the Brown Terror could be multiplied a thousand-fold. The number of those killed by knife or bullet wounds, or beaten to death, seems to go into hundreds, and of those who have been injured into thousands, while many who have either been murdered or arrested are missing. The number of persons in prisons and concentration camps is variously estimated as between 20,000 and 80,000.

Your correspondent was able to establish one murder and one horrible assault in a certain street in one of Berlin's poorer districts. A workman was beaten by Brown Shirts and then stabbed – the dead body was left lying in the street, and in the same street there was another body, alive, but so beaten that the face was unrecognisable. (The Brown Shirts often smashed the faces of their victims by beating them with their flexible 'steel wands' – this is why so many of the victims have lost their sight.)

In the working-class quarters the inquirer will be told in almost every street that the Nazis murdered So-and-so living at number so-and-so; they have beaten So-and-so living round the corner.

'You could not recognise him when they had finished. He is in an eye hospital now.'

Almost all workmen who were at all prominent in the local organisations of the Socialist or Communist parties, or were known in their district as keen politicians are in danger of their lives. Many are in hiding. They cannot emigrate with their wives and families, having no money even to pay the fare, still less to live abroad.

The German working class is now dominated by an intense mass emotion compounded of fear (a fear that is only too justified) and a controlled fury. A hatred such as never existed before in Germany has been aroused.


## THE JEWS IN GERMANY

Monday, January 22, 1934
*From our Special Correspondent*[1]

This and the following article are an attempt to survey the ten months' anti-Semitic persecution in Germany. Such a survey is bound to be incomplete. Although it is a matter of world-wide knowledge that

1. F. A. Voigt

persecution (and not only of Jews) has been, and still is, going on in Germany, that fact is still officially denied by the German Government and its representatives.

The anti-Semitic laws that have been enacted are, of course, on record, and so are the numerous ordinances and rulings passed against Jews by municipalities, professional associations, clubs, and so on. They, in their totality, are unparalleled in Europe and would alone constitute a persecution of a terrible kind. While not directly killing a single Jew, they make it impossible for thousands of Jews to live, and it is largely they that have caused the epidemic of suicides amongst the German Jewry.

And yet they are only a part of the persecution. The laws that, theoretically, apply to all German citizens, whether Gentile or Jew, in practice give the Gentile every possible advantage and the Jew every disadvantage. They protect the Gentile from the Jew but not the Jew from the Gentile. Thus a Gentile may libel a Jew with impunity, but not a Jew a Gentile – at least, not if the Gentile is a Nazi. Brown Shirts have committed innumerable thefts in Jewish shops – they have habitually asked for cigarettes and other articles at the counter and have received them without payment – while the shopkeeper has had no means of redress. It is easy for a Gentile to recover a debt from a Jew, but very difficult or even impossible for a Jew to recover a debt from a Gentile. In disputes between Jew and Gentile, the law tends very strongly to work against the Jew. Not that justice is never done in Germany (there are some fair-minded judges and magistrates left), but when the plaintiff or defendant is a Jew justice is rarely done or, when done, it is only partial justice. Often it is crude and consciously malignant injustice. The Jew has all the obligations of German citizenship but few of the rights. If, as is proposed, he is deprived of that citizenship, he will still have the obligations (he will, for example, continue to pay taxes) and will have even fewer rights. The fiction put forward by the German Government is that he will have the status of a foreign resident, but as he will be without the protection of any foreign Government he will have no such status.

There can be no complete record of the innumerable acts of violence perpetrated against the Jews under the Dictatorship. The body of un-refuted evidence available is enormous – even if it represented all that had happened the persecution would be one of the most frightful of modern times. But it represents only a small fraction of the whole. We have not, and probably never shall have more than a fragmentary knowledge of the beatings, the murders, the torture, the robbing, the blackmailing, the arrests and imprisonments, not to speak of the humiliations (both public and private) that have been perpetrated by Nazis on the Jews. No systematic inquiry is possible, for a victim of persecution who gives evidence is not only punishable under German law (the evidence being termed 'Greuelpropaganda,' usually translated by 'atrocity mongering') but may be arrested without a warrant and may, without trial, be sent to a 'Brown House' for a beating, or to a concentration camp (a far greater hardship than ordinary imprisonment).

The persecution also varies in severity from district to district. There are Jews – who may be quite open-minded and intelligent – who, although residing in Germany, honestly maintain that 'things are not so bad.' The reason is that in their own district there may be little active persecution, and, as hardly anything appears in the German press, the truth may not have come to their knowledge. In a town like Treves, for example, the cruder excesses have been avoided, although anti-Semitic legislation is operating there as elsewhere. In Baden the persecution of the Jews as well as of the political opponents of the Dictatorship has been relatively mild. In Berlin it has been frightful – in the early days of the persecution hundreds of Jews (and not only German Jews) were physically maltreated. A full account of what happened in Berlin alone would fill several volumes, and it would make such reading as to cause the utmost wonder as to how such dreadful things are possible in the modern world. But Berlin is not the worst – it probably presents a fair average of what has happened to the Jews in Germany. In Hessen the anti-Semitic excesses went on month after month, so that hundreds of Jewish families were compelled to seek refuge in the forests or to leave for other parts – the emigration of the Jews abroad is only part of the total emigration, many having fled from regions of severe persecution to regions of persecution less severe (in Berlin, for example, there are many fugitives from Hessen, Silesia, and elsewhere).[1] The cities of Worms, Brunswick, and Cassel also have an appalling record. In Breslau (the chief Silesian city) and in some of the outlying townships and in some parts of Saxony the persecution has been ferocious. Several townships have expelled their entire Jewish population (the Jews of Neidenberg, in East Prussia, for example, were ordered to leave by the end of 1933).

Many Jews have been victims of double persecution – that is to say, they have been persecuted both as Jews and as political opponents of the Dictatorship. In the concentration camps – that probably hold

1. Adam von Trott, later one of the most honourable victims amongst the opposition to Hitler, was at this time a magistrate in Hessen. He was so stung by this article that he wrote a strong protest to the *Guardian* which he instantly regretted.

about 50,000 prisoners – Jews are often selected for special maltreatment. Thus at Dachau the more repulsive camp duties are assigned to Jews. Several Jews have been murdered at Dachau. One of them is Dr. Spiegel, who became known to the world at large (though not by name) through a photograph that was published in many English and American newspapers and periodicals, showing how he was paraded through the streets of Munich, without shoes, his trousers cut short at the knees, and a placard hanging round his neck with the words 'I shall never complain to the police about the Nazis.' In the concentration camp at Brandenburg Jewish prisoners get no proper rations, but are made to eat the leavings from the meals of the other prisoners from one bowl and without knives or forks. In almost all the concentration camps Jews have to put up with special insults and indignities.

There can be little doubt that the peculiarly malignant character of the persecution of the Jews in Nuremberg, a persecution which is continually being revived, is connected with the incessant agitation of the *Stürmer*, a weekly that specialises in anti-Semitism. (It is edited by the Nazi leader Julius Streicher, who was in charge of the anti-Semitic boycott on April 1.) The *Stürmer* not only incites to ever-renewed persecution but it continually publishes the names of individual Jews, with their addresses, as suitable for victimisation. One of its special features is the 'Pillory' ('Pranger'), in which it publishes the names of Gentile girls who have associated with Jews (whose names are often published as well), demanding that they shall be boycotted by all, thus exposing them to public execration and possibly to violence and economic ruin. The *Stürmer* shows no sign up to date (January) of abandoning its campaign.

The persecution has been organised from top to bottom. Its chief originator and inspirer is, of course, the German Chancellor, Adolf Hitler, and, after him, the other Nazi leaders, and then the professional and academic classes, the students, to some extent the smaller shopkeepers, and, of course, the disciplined Brown Shirts.

Amongst the worst persecutors are doctors, dentists, and other professional men who want the jobs of their Jewish colleagues, and conceal this desire under that enthusiasm for the Nazi cause that makes such a favourable impression of youthful fervour and idealism on visitors to Germany. Jewish professional men are continually being denounced as 'Marxists' (even when they have had nothing to do with politics) to the Brown Shirts or the Secret State Police (now the chief terrorist organisation in Germany) by envious Gentile colleagues. The German professional journals – the *Deutscher Apotheker* and the Berlin *Aertzte Korrespondenz*, for example – continually incite to renewed persecution. Altogether, the persecution is the work of educated Germany. Uneducated persons have, no doubt, been instruments of the persecutors, but uneducated Germany as a whole has had no part in it.

## CHRIST OR HITLER?

Friday, January 3, 1936
*By Dr. Karl Barth*

The new decrees issued by the German Minister of Ecclesiastical Affairs, Herr Kerrl, represent the most formidable attack that has so far been made on the Church by the National Socialist regime. The attack is directed against the very substance of the Evangelical Church, against the Faith itself. It is for the Faith that the struggle is being waged to-day in the deepest and most decisive sense.

The fundamental question is this, Shall the Church obey the Bible and the Gospels, or shall the doctrine of the 'German Christians,' the doctrine that Revelation is to be found in the national life ('Volkstum' – Christ and Hitler), have validity?

The doctrine of the 'German Christians' represents the final product and the most modern synthesis of a long evolution that has proceeded within the realm of religious thought. The currents of the eighteenth century ('Revelation and Reason'), of the nineteenth century ('Christ and Civilisation'), and of the twentieth century ('Christ and Socialism') have been replaced by 'The Gospels and the Nation.' The bearers of this last synthesis are the 'German Christians,' considerable sections of the National Socialist Party, and the 'Ecclesiastical Councils' established by Herr Kerrl.

The whole weakness of Protestantism is revealed in the theory of 'the Gospels and the Nation' as in those that preceded it, the weakness of a Protestantism that has always sought alliances and coalitions with stronger forces. But why have these things become so perilous only to-day? Why are they such a menace to the Church? The explanation is simple. The previous theories were subjects of discussion – opinion was set up against opinion. But the 'German Christians' have turned their theory into a doctrine. The authority of the State, its power, its propaganda, and its coercion support this doctrine. The Church is thereby called upon to make a decision, and, as the decision concerns the Faith itself, the fight now being waged by the Confessional Church is, to a certain extent, a fight that concerns the destiny of the other Churches in the world.

Only now has the synthetic procedure adopted by Protestantism in imitation of Roman Catholicism brought its own revenge. Only now do we see a State and a society take up the offensive against the Church. That State and that society will relent only when the Church is ready to submit unconditionally to the doctrine referred to. But the Church will not submit.

Bound up with the question of doctrine is the other fundamental question – namely: Who is to determine the character of the Church? The Church itself or an alien body? The conviction that it must be the Church itself has not always been as strong as it might have been, even among the German Confessional clergy. And it is precisely the hesitations felt and shown in this respect that have led to much indecision. The lack of inner solidarity in the Confessional Church, with regard to this very question has, during the last two years, led to many useless 'attempts at mediation' and changes in outward attitude. This weakness also made it possible for the Confessional Church to evade decisions whenever National Socialism found decisions inconvenient because there was tension elsewhere.

But now the Confessional Church knows that it can only *suffer* under National Socialism and that faith in Jesus Christ *and* Adolf Hitler is impossible. The servants of the Church have had to go through a long schooling to achieve this knowledge. But that schooling is now complete. The opponent is recognised and so is the path along which the Church will have to go. The uncertainty that prevailed hitherto has been replaced by a determination that will greatly help to overcome future difficulties.

Two statements that have already been significant in the German religious conflict have only now acquired full significance. The decision reached by the Synod of Barmen in 1934 becomes the axis of the whole struggle to-day. This decision must be quoted afresh for its significance cannot be overrated; 'Christ, as Holy Writ bears witness, is the one Word of God, whom we hear, in whom we trust and confide in life and in death.' I insisted that these words be included in the decision of the Synod, and I repeat them when I say 'Back to the Bible!'

To-day I rejoice that I remained steadfast then.

But there are other words occurring in the history of the German religious conflict that now have the greatest actuality. They have acquired immense significance as the guiding principle of the Confessional Church in the present phase of the struggle. This is the decision of the Dahlem Synod of October, 1934, which, in a certain sense, was the logical development of the Barmen Synod. The words are as follows: – 'We submit this, our decision, to the Government of the Reich. We request the Government to take cognisance of the decision and demand recognition that, in matters relating to the Church, to the doctrine and institutions of the Church, the Church alone is called upon to judge and to decide, regardless of the supervisory rights of the State.'

With the attack of the National Socialist regime on the very substance of the Church these decisions of the Confessional Church must become the unalterable guiding principle in all the actions of the Church.

In Germany there is a younger generation of theologians who are ready for the fight. Herr Kerrl will bother them, he will try to paralyse them, he will persecute them but, nevertheless, he will not with his methods and his brown and black hordes win the fight.

The Church will not retreat before these oppressions. The Confessional Church will continue to exist. It will, to the astonishment of all timid and cautious persons, always be present, despite persecution, oppression, and terrorism. Perhaps the Confessional Church has not been consolidated outwardly but inwardly it has been consolidated. We cannot tell as yet what outward forms the Church will be forced to adopt under the pressure of National Socialism, but we do know that the German Confessional Church will certainly be steadfast in all tribulations.

I have said that the struggle of this Church is not a German ecclesiastical struggle. All other Churches can draw their conclusions from this fact. The most decisive help which, for example, the English Church can render the struggling German Church is to recognise that this struggle *has now become an absolute necessity*. As long as English Churchmen are only interested in the struggle of the Confessional Church because it is a struggle against Hitler and against National Socialism no help is possible, for the Confessional Church cannot derive assistance from political emotions. But if the English Church will understand that the cause of the German Confessional Church is the cause of the whole Christian world, then help is indeed possible.

Let us assume that matters come to a head. The English Church need then do no more than declare that 'The Faith of the German Confessional Church is our Faith, also the cause of the Confessional Church is our cause also.' The effect of such a declaration and the help it would give would be great indeed. Such a declaration of solidarity would be the strongest aid that could come to the Confessional Church in its struggle. But it must be a declaration made in community of faith. If this community does not exist, it would be but a pious mumbling for true intercession can only come of a profound community of faith.

Perhaps it will be said that I am trying to inflict 'my' theology on England, just as it is said that I tried to inflict it on the Barmen Synod. But I repeat it is not true, for I speak not of *my* standpoint but of *the* standpoint. If this standpoint is present, then the community of faith is present and messages and declarations of solidarity achieve their highest value.

That this community of faith be attained is my strong hope in consideration of the cause for which the German Confessional Church is fighting. That cause is the cause of all Evangelical Christendom.

## COMMENT[1]

In his book 'Mein Kampf' Hitler again and again asserts the spiritual and temporal supremacy of the 'racial principle.' Here we have the essence of the whole religious conflict, for the 'racial principle' is incompatible with Christianity, seeing that Christianity can admit neither the spiritual supremacy of any secular doctrine nor the supremacy before God of any particular race.

The decrees are a fresh and drastic attempt to achieve the final subjection of the 'Confessional Church' (in which the 'opposition' Protestants are organised). They represent the supreme effort of the modern State to extend not merely a dictatorially administrative but dictatorially doctrinal authority to the religious life of a nation. As Karl Barth points out in his statement, the German Church must fight. While compromise is the essence of politics, it is the privilege – indeed the duty – of the theologian to be absolutely uncompromising in certain ultimate matters. Karl Barth has again and again fought not only the secular foe; he has censured the waverers on the side of the Churches, and some bitter words about his fellow Churchmen have escaped him. But, as his statement shows, he has no doubt at all about the result of the conflict. The 'Confessional Church' insists that while a certain measure of administrative superintendence may be conceded to the State the Church alone has the right to determine its own character. Barth has all along been particularly emphatic in proclaiming this right, and he proclaims it once again. The National Socialist State is equally emphatic on the other side; addressing a deputation of 'Confessional' pastors on November 28, Herr Kerrl declared: 'Gentlemen, it is not the "Confessional Church," but I, who will determine the order

1. From a leader by F. A. Voigt.

of the Church. It is useless to try and convince me that I am on the wrong track. There is only one who can convince me and that is I myself.'

These words show that there can be no compromise. Behind Herr Kerrl is the brute force of the 'Brown and Black hordes' (as Karl Barth calls the S.A. and the S.S.) and the legal and extra-legal coercive measures at the disposal of the 'totalitarian' State. Behind the pastors who faced him there was no temporal power of any kind. To those who were present and who had all this in mind, the scene must have appeared one of the most significant in modern times. And significant not for Germany alone. All Christendom is in a state of crisis and, as Karl Barth points out, the German religious conflict is the concern of the Christian Churches all the world over.

Open persecution has failed once already. It is possible that it will be tried again. If it is, failure, which is certain in any case, will be doubly certain. Here, and here alone, is the 'totalitarian' State faced by something stronger than itself.

## MUSSOLINI'S CONQUEST OF ABYSSINIA

Friday, July 10, 1936
*From a Correspondent*[1]

I recently had the opportunity of talking with a well-educated officer of the Italian army. He is a Fascist by upbringing, but a Fascist who thinks for himself, though his ideas are also those current among many army officers.

What did the army think, I asked, of the war and of the Blackshirt Militia.

'The war,' he replied, 'has been a masterpiece of leadership and, above all, of troop movement. None but Italian soldiers, who are peasants and used to a hard life, could have built the roads on which they advanced or stood the hardships of a country combining a tropical climate with great altitudes. We never had the slightest doubt about victory; only an outsider, with no knowledge of the relative forces, could think otherwise. The English are used to colonial wars, conducted with native troops. They did not realise that in Abyssinia we had on the one side first-class, perfectly organised European troops, and on the other masses of natives, full of warlike spirit, but not to be compared, even from the point of endurance, with our troops, especially

1. The Italian officer is unknown; the interviewer probably Cecil Sprigge.

the Alpini. The question of supply was certainly a difficulty, but it was never decisive. The Italian army made its own roads, but it would have advanced even without roads. It brought its own lorries and tanks with it, but it could have used mules instead and won the war all the same. The quality of the soldier is still a decisive factor in war, and particularly in a colonial war.'

'Then do you think that the Italian soldier has improved under the Fascist regime?'

'Yes, he has. The men are already half-trained on joining their regiment. They need a shorter period of instruction than before; there is a sporting atmosphere in the army which has its utility. Gymnastics and athletic games are the general rule.'

'This is all due to the Fascist regime?'

'As a matter of fact, the modern organisation of the army dates from the Great War and the creation of the shock troops. One might say it began in the last year of the war, when the shock troops were made so much use of, were armed with daggers, and systematically glorified by propaganda leaflets in the trenches. The Fascists came later and reaped the experience of the army.'

'The Blackshirt Militia, I suppose, descends directly from the shock troops and acts as picked storm troops in attack?'

'No, no, per Dio, nothing of the kind. On the contrary.'

'I thought you said something of this sort.'

'A hundred times no. The Militia, from a military point of view, is a dud; everybody knows that. Storm troops indeed! They are police troops, a political police, and the men are ne'er-do-wells whose one idea is not to risk their skin but to let others do the work. It is a military commonplace to say that police troops are of little use in action. Even the Carabinieri, who are beyond praise in their own field of service, proved useless on the Podgora and were withdrawn from the front. The Carabinieri at least knew how to die at their post. But the Militia is only good at looking after its own belly and running away. The army soldiers are young men of twenty, mostly healthy peasants and good fellows, and well-disciplined. Their behaviour is decent and humane. The Blackshirts are a mass of good-for-nothings whose one idea is theft and worse.'

'What use was made of the Militia?'

'The only serious action in which the Militia was employed was at the Uarieu Pass; but their resistance was poor; in fact they fell back from their original position and had to be relieved by Eritrean troops. From that moment on no more was heard of the Militia. It stayed behind in the Tembien, hundreds of miles behind the lines. It couldn't have been otherwise, because the Militia, though better paid and partly commanded by army officers, was morally and physically in pieces. These things are perfectly well known in Italy. When the Duce made his speech in Piazza Venezia announcing the fall of Addis Ababa he tried to exalt the Blackshirts, but his words fell flat. In fact, that was the only passage of the speech that was not applauded.'

'The claque will be organised better next time.'

'Perhaps. But there are 500,000 men in Africa who know how matters stand, and what I am telling you is known in Italy too, not only at the officers' messes but at the street corner. Remember that Costanzo Ciano, speaking in the House in the presence of representatives of the army, said so in so many words: "The war has been won by the troops, above all by the Alpini." The Mussolini family had seen how the wind was blowing and was making the best of it.'

'You are not then an admirer of Mussolini?'

'No. Mussolini is a bluffer. He tries to pass himself off as a great strategist, as a man who won the war, but if it had been left to him we should still be at Makale or the sea. The war had a great military leader in Badoglio, and a great diplomatic fool in Mussolini. This is the pure and simple truth. Mussolini found nothing better to do than to drag fifty-two nations on top of us. And to think that at the same time Japan was eating up Manchuria and Germany occupying the Rhine without any serious opposition. Now the Duce poses as Napoleon. Has not Mussolini bestowed a decoration on himself for having "guided, conducted, and directed" the war? It's an infernal impudence. The army criticised it severely. And then the story of the medals for his sons and son-in-law, altogether, en bloc, without giving any motive except "uncontested merit".'

'Do you think that once the troops are back home Mussolini will try to work up a retrospective legend about the Blackshirts?'

'I don't think so. Military headquarters would prevent him. Baistrocchi might back him up, but not Badoglio. The honour of the army is concerned, as well as questions of preparation for future wars, questions of organisation and tactics. Badoglio is a real general. He cut down the baggage and gave the front place to the Alpini, who travel light and are more independent of supplies. These were his tactics. From the point of view of strategy the war was won chiefly through the manœuvre in the Tembien.

'After this Badoglio gauged exactly the degree of alarm and demoralisation pervading the Abyssinian army, and he risked pushing on almost blindly, reaching Addis Ababa in a few days of forced marches. Graziani, who is an ass, only reached Harar when all the work was done, and you must observe that the southern front allowed the use of lorries and tanks because it is a plain. Nevertheless Baistrocchi and Mussolini are trying to extol Graziani and belittle Badoglio.'

'What do you think of the political situation in Italy?'

'I think Mussolini can't last for ever. His glory is undermined and his demagogic methods are transparent. The Militia will have to be abolished as an organisation unfit for war. As to the army, it does not love Mussolini.'

## CIVIL WAR IN SPAIN

Wednesday, August 12, 1936
*From a Special Correspondent*[1]

Andalusia, August 3

One day about the beginning of July I was walking down the principal street in Malaga. As I passed the Club Mercantil an old gentleman whom I know slightly came to me and in a state of great excitement exclaimed, 'Good news, good news. Within a fortnight Calvo Sotelo [the monarchist leader] will be King of Spain.'

Then on July 12 Calvo Sotelo was taken from his house by night and shot. There is some mystery in this assassination. The usual reason given for it is that it was committed by the Storm Troops or republican police as a reprisal for the murder of one of their officers the day before by Fascists. It is also said that it was done on the orders of those who wished to precipitate a rising of the Right, as they considered that was the only way to a Communist revolution. The one thing that seems certain is that the Government, which was extremely anxious to avoid trouble, had nothing to do with it.

It was decided by the rebel generals to utilise the feeling of indignation which the assassination had caused among their own partisans. The rising, which I am told had been arranged for July 25, therefore broke out on the evening of July 18 in Spain. It had begun on the previous day in Morocco.

What happened in Malaga was this. At five o'clock on the evening of July 18 a company of infantry marched out of the barracks and proceeded, with bands playing, towards the centre of the town. There was already great tension, since the news of the rising in Morocco had become known. As they marched the soldiers were asked where they were going. 'To proclaim a state of war.' This is the legal procedure in

1. Gerald Brenan

such cases, and the soldiers thought that it was by order of the Government. The Governor's office was rung up, and it was learned that no such order had been given. This news quickly spread among the bystanders. The company had reached the Custom offices. Suddenly a workman stepped forward, saluted with the clenched fist, and cried 'Viva la Republica!' The officer in command drew his revolver and shot him. This was the signal. The Storm Troops on the steps of the Custom-house opened fire. Workmen from behind trees and Fascists from windows joined in. The troops tried to storm the Custom-house. But this they failed to do, and after a great deal of firing they were driven into the Calle Larios, the main shopping street of the city, where they were left alone.

Meanwhile the Governor had released the soldiers from their duty to their officers, and they began to stream out of the barracks into the town. They were the less disposed to fight for having been inoculated two days before against typhoid. Some of them approached the pickets of the rebel company. One by one the men slunk away till only one sentry was left. The officers got back to the barracks, where they were taken prisoners. Apart from isolated Fascists, who continued sniping from the roofs – and this did not altogether cease for two days, – the fighting was over. What seems rather odd considering the tens of thousands of rounds let off, less than twenty were killed on that night. On both sides they were bad shots.

At dawn the workmen began to stream out of their quarters of the city. Brandishing revolvers and red flags, singing the 'Internationale,' and making a strange rhythmical sound – 'Uh-uh-uh,' which those who heard it told me was most terrifying, – they marched into the Calle Larios. Selecting particular houses, sometimes those from which snipers fired at them, sometimes those of people particularly hated or known to be concerned in this movement, they began to set fire to them.

It was done methodically. The house was first searched, householders on either side were warned, efforts were made to prevent the fire from spreading. In this way half the houses in the Calle Larios were burnt, about twenty houses in other parts of the town and in the garden suburb to the east of the city some thirty or forty villas. But no churches or convents. These burnings went on all day until about midnight, and then, apart from a small recrudescence, stopped. No one was killed and there was no looting.

A grocer's shop, for example, was broken into: the hams, wines, and liqueurs were piled in the street and set fire to. The workmen, many of whom must have had hungry families at home, watched them burn. I asked one of them why they did not send the food to their union and distribute it. 'No,' he replied, 'Spanish workmen do not steal. They have too much sense of honour.' If one is horrified at the material destruction – and much of it is, of course, perfectly stupid, – one should not forget the provocation.

## REVOLUTIONARY MALAGA

### Wednesday, August 31, 1936
*From a Special Correspondent*[1]

Andalusia, August 24

Life in Malaga goes on calmly enough on the surface. There are, of course, the burned houses and the flags, and one sees fewer well-dressed people than in ordinary times. Only foreigners wear a tie, for ties are now the sign that one is a 'señorito.' The letters U.G.T., C.N.T., U.H.P., F.A.I., and a good many more denoting the various parties are painted on walls, on cars and lorries, on trees, on any surface that will take them. One cannot buy a melon in the market-place that has not got some initials scratched on it. There are also a good many militia about, dressed in their new uniforms of blue cotton overalls with red armlets.

One is no longer aware of the feeling of strain that was so marked all this spring and summer, for the tension has been relaxed by the victory of one party: on the other hand there is a certain inquietude due to the nearness of the front, to the delay in taking Granada, and to the spy mania, which since the discovery of one or two aerials has become very general. Then – a great novelty in Spain – there are no police to be seen; they are the shock troops of the Government, and are all at the front.

The Committee of Public Health and Safety investigates charges of hostility to the regime, provides safe conducts, organises search parties for wanted people, and shoots them. In five days it shot well over a hundred people in Malaga alone. To begin with it shot some thirty prisoners who were kept on a ship in the harbour. Some of these were senior police officers who refused to join the Government; others were prominent people of the Right; one was a marquesa caught using a private transmitting set. They were taken to a cemetery and shot. Then came the people who were dragged out of their houses at night, put in cars, driven off to some quiet road, and killed there. Their only crime as a rule was affiliation to the Ceda, the Right Catholic party, or their

1. Gerald Brenan

having offended some workman or other. Some of these people have been killed with shocking violence. One I saw had his head bashed in; another who had not died at the first volley had had his throat cut; others had their fingers, ears, or noses sliced off, after death, of course; they are cut off to be taken away as trophies.

The men who do this belong to the F.A.I., the anarchist organisation which is so extended in Barcelona and Saragossa and also provides the shock troops and gunmen for the Fascist party, Falange Española. They buy them by giving them work at good wages, with extra payment for assassinations, and as the membership of the Falange is secret they often remain at the same time both Fascists and anarchists.

But there has been a great change in the last few days. The anarchist bands who were dragging harmless people out of their houses after midnight and shooting them have been put down. Some have been shot, and militia patrol the streets and have orders to fire on any cars with armed men in them whom they see about after midnight. No one can be arrested and no house searched without a warrant signed by the Governor. The Committee of Public Safety have advisory powers only.

It seems hardly worth while, in the shambles that Spain is becoming, to deny any stories of atrocities. Yet I would like to say that reports published in the English papers of nuns led about naked in the streets of Malaga are the purest invention; on the contrary, they were taken either to the Town Hall for safety or to their own houses and were treated with perfect respect throughout. Sisters of Charity still go about the streets in their uniforms. Those killed are killed brutally but quickly; the truth by itself, without ornaments, is bad enough.

Yesterday some bombs were dropped in Malaga. A tank of oil and a smaller supply of petrol were set on fire, making a prodigious blaze, but other bombs that fell on a popular quarter killed about forty people and wounded a hundred and fifty, mostly women and children. If Germans had been living all over London during the last war and if the whole of the police and almost every soldier had been at the front I think there might have been some lynchings after air raids.

And, in fact, a mob marched that evening to the prison, took out forty-five prisoners, and shot them. Those who point to atrocities of this sort on the Government side often forget the provocation and the circumstances. When soldiers and police have to go to the front because other soldiers and police have rebelled, who is left to keep order among an enraged population?

# THE GERMANS ARRIVE

Monday, December 14, 1936
*From a Correspondent lately in Spain*

Lisbon, December 4

I made the journey from Seville to Salamanca by motor-car with the war correspondent of a Seville newspaper. This paper, like all the papers published in the territory controlled by Franco, is militarist. My journalist companion was a talkative man: we talked of the avalanche of Germans who have come to Seville – rigid and rubicund, robots who salute with the raised palm of the hand and a dutiful 'Heil, Hitler!'

'The more Germans, the merrier,' said the journalist. 'Germans and Spaniards have always been good friends. During the Great War the true feelings of the ordinary Spaniard were pro-German; only a clique of intellectuals and aged politicians stood up for the Allies, and to-day there are no intellectuals of that type in Spain. They do not dare to come here, and any who do pay for their sins of the past. They have been the enemies of Spain.'

When we reached Salamanca the journalist invited me to lunch in the leading hotel in the venerable Castilian town. The dining-room was full of Germans and Spanish soldiers. General Millan Astray, who had just been appointed head of the Press and Propaganda Department, a physical ruin with only one arm and one eye, went to and fro, greeting the Germans in the hall and the dining-room. He is scarred all over with shot wounds received in the Moroccan war, when he commanded the Foreign Legion. After an hour's waiting the Spanish journalist lost patience and sent for the manager. 'Can we not have anything yet?' he asked.

'I am sorry, sir. We have to serve these German gentlemen; they are very particular and object if they do not get quick service.' We got nothing to eat until, at about 3 p.m., the dining-room had become empty of Germans, and the poor Spaniards who had been waiting began to enter.

'Deutschland über Alles,' 'Giovinezza,' and the Spanish Falangist 'hymn' are given on the wireless. The children whistle the first two in the streets. The Plaza Mayor, the principal square of Salamanca, is full of blond young men who have come to fight. I was told that Madrid is being defended by a Russian army of 30,000 men. 'What do we care?' said a young Falangist. 'Germany is ready to send 60,000 if necessary. The Germans will never allow the Russians to be masters of Spain.'

All the press and propaganda machinery is in the hands of German experts. French and American journalists are being expelled, for no apparent reason except that they are objected to by the Germans. The press agency which sends news to the French papers is German, with German editors and staff. General Mola's chief adviser is a German; they call him Don Walter. A general staff is at work at Salamanca in collaboration with the Spanish military authorities; it is said to be the real author of the new plan for the conquest of Madrid.

Thus we are now witnessing the Germanisation of Spain. It was reported that five thousand Germans had arrived; the truth is that German 'volunteers' have been arriving at Cadiz and Vigo from Germany every week for a month past. It is impossible to give the actual number. Many of them are already fighting on the outskirts of Madrid as legionaries, with their own officers, forming independent units. An approximate calculation made by a Spanish 'Nationalist' put the number of the Germans at 20,000. The Italians are much fewer. Italy is contenting herself with sending her best war material, mobile tanks, and her technicians.

For more than a month past there has been incarcerated in Valladolid a journalist, Aznar, who is accused of having been the author of a violent anti-German campaign during the World War. There is talk of a 'Tcheka' directed by agents of Hitler. A Spaniard, who complained in my presence in the Restaurant Fraile of the excessive number of persons who have been executed in the 'Nationalist' cities, was hotly criticised by a German who was also present. The German gave vent to this opinion: 'Communism needs to be nipped in the bud, and all Spaniards who protest ought to be shot.'

Almost every day groups of Germans march through the Plaza Mayor in Salamanca and down the broad avenues of Seville singing their national anthem and the 'hymn' of the Spanish Foreign Legion. Some of them wear the uniform of the Foreign Legion, but most wear the blue shirt of the Falangists, though without the insignia of that Spanish Fascist group – five arrows and a yoke. Two months ago Moors were to be seen strolling through the streets of Seville. They are disappearing, and their place has been taken by the blond men of the North. In order to conquer Madrid General Franco has been obliged to Germanise his cities, relegating to the background the many Fascist and traditionalist Spanish volunteers who have shown so much enthusiasm until lately. The colonial war which Franco has been carrying on victoriously since July 19 has given place to a modern war, with modern soldiers and a different tactic. Madrid is not to be conquered by columns of infantry nor by light cavalry. Franco's volunteers have disappeared, because neither Franco nor the German and Italian experts consider them sufficiently hardened to fight the powerful Russian army which we are told is defending Madrid.

Until Franco's disaster at the gates of Madrid foreign intervention was limited to the material of war with which the Germans and Italians were ready to experiment on Spanish soil. But since Franco's failure in his attempt to conquer Madrid he has found himself obliged to accept Italy and Germany as advisers and to admit soldiers from those countries. Now no military move is made without the prior approval of Germany and Italy. The destruction of Madrid is the result of the advice of the Germans and Italians, who considered it to be a military necessity to destroy a capital in the power of Communism – a capital, moreover, for which they, unlike the Spaniards, have no love. It is said that Franco had always refused to destroy Madrid, and that it is only in face of German and Italian insistence that he has found himself obliged to take that painful course.

Germany and Italy had arranged to recognise Franco's Government when Madrid had been conquered; but in face of the failure at Madrid and in their eagerness for direct political and military intervention in Spain's internal affairs they precipitated the recognition.[1] This is the explanation that is heard to-day all over Spain. I heard the same explanation in Portugal. The rebels are delighted now with the intervention of Germany and Italy – as saviours, they think; and they make no secret from anyone not even from a foreigner like myself, of the fact that they 'will win the war, because Germany, Spain's natural ally, will fight to the end against Spanish Communism.'

1. Germany and Italy recognised Franco's government on November 18, twelve days after the siege of Madrid had begun and the Spanish government had moved to Valencia.

## MUNICH: PEACE WITHOUT HONOUR

In the spring of 1938 Hitler annexed Austria; by the autumn he was ready to take Czechoslovakia – by war if necessary. It was not. The first two extracts are from messages by M. W. Fodor. The first was sent from Prague after Chamberlain's first visit to Hitler. The second, sent four days later from Warsaw, belongs to the period after Hitler, as usual, had raised his demands. The third, by a member of the London staff, describes Chamberlain's return to London from Munich after his third visit to Hitler and the forced capitulation of Czechoslovakia. A fortnight later Fodor wrote privately to Crozier, 'Prague was the most difficult job I ever went through. It was exactly like a city under siege, and while there we all suffered from a bad attack of claustrophobia.' A month later he told Crozier 'Please do not think of Czecho-Slovakia as the old one – that is gone, though not of her own fault. The present one is a German dependency with Gestapo and other pleasures.'

Thursday, September 22, 1938

### SUICIDE BY ORDER
*From or Central European Correspondent*

Prague, September 21

It is a terrible thing to witness the agony of two countries such as has been your correspondent's fate. Only a few months ago he saw the downfall of Austria, and now in these last days of gloom and desperation in Prague he is witnessing the dismemberment of Czecho-Slovakia. Everything seems to be over now, for under pressure Czecho-Slovakia was obliged at five o'clock this afternoon to accept the demands of France and England.

At two o'clock this morning the French and British Ministers in Prague urged upon President Benes the acceptance of the plan forthwith. They declared that the Anglo-French proposals were to be considered as an entity and must be accepted in their entirety. President Benes, tired and worn out by many nights of unceasing negotiations and discussions in the past ten days, summoned the Inner Council of the Cabinet at 3.30 this morning. Its conference went on until 5.30. After this the Cabinet Council met again and was in session until 8.15.

An hour later the committee of twenty party leaders assembled. They were for acceptance only with qualifications. When at noon this decision became known people in Prague began to be more hopeful.

Then at 2 p.m. the French and British Ministers visited the President and stated that if Czecho-Slovakia rejected the proposals, then she must be held responsible for the results.

Under this tremendous pressure there was nothing left but to accept, and the Cabinet met this afternoon to decide the suicide of Czecho-Slovakia.

Since five o'clock an angry crowd has been marching up and down the main street of Prague shouting: 'Down with Hitler!' 'Chamberlain has sold us!' 'The French have betrayed us!' 'Long live the Army!'

The excitement is enormous in Prague, and a high official told me: 'I am surprised that the French Legation has not yet been demolished.'

## Monday, September 26, 1938

### ESCAPE FROM PRAGUE

Warsaw, September 25

The forty-eight hours which I have spent between Prague and Warsaw were difficult and trying. The drama began at 11.23 on Friday night in Prague, when suddenly the loud-speakers began to announce the mobilisation in Czecho-Slovakia.

When I saw yesterday (Saturday) that telegraphic and telephonic communications were not possible to any part of the world I decided to try to gain the frontier, where communications were not interrupted. The British Legation had already sent warning on Thursday to 700 British subjects. In fact, the British colony succeeded in getting a carriage attached yesterday afternoon to a troop train going towards the Polish frontier. About fifty members of the British colony, with four Americans and three French journalists, accepted this facility.

The train was scheduled for the town of Bohumin, on the Polish frontier. It was so crowded that it was impossible to move away from one's seat, and we sat still from three o'clock in the afternoon to midnight.

In the afternoon Hungary and Poland closed their frontiers. On the train, speeding towards the Polish frontier, we had, of course, no knowledge of this change.

When night came the effect of the mobilisation grew. Everywhere towns had been blacked out, with station lamps covered by darkened shades. On the platforms A.R.P. officials and nurses were busy and brought water and tea as refreshment to the restrooms. In the late evening the atmosphere turned tense. We knew that we were approaching Glatz, the salient where, if war broke out, the Germans would try the so-called 'Moravian nut-cracker' advance. We anxiously watched the horizon for aeroplanes and listened for any bombing, but fortunately nothing was heard, and we knew that the Germans had not started an attack.

At eleven o'clock the frontier station was reached. We expected a Customs examination, but heard instead that trains were no longer crossing the frontier and our train was directed now to Cesky Tesin, and there we were told to try to persuade the Poles to let us cross the bridge. The policeman had not much hope for us because earlier in the day there had been serious shooting between Polish and Czech soldiers on that front and now the bridge was closed. We left the train at Tesin after nine hours of a fatiguing journey during which most of us had neither food nor drink.

With the help of a Czech gendarme the group started the walk towards the bridge, two miles away. It was a pathetic pilgrimage. Amongst the British people were a baby and two small children. The policeman warned us to go very slowly and to obey instantly every halt signal. 'If you hear shooting throw yourself on the ground,' was his final warning. Very soon two shots were fired in the distance. He commanded us to stop, and a long and anxious debate followed. It was a moonless night, and the whispering crowd was waiting in anguish and desperation. Suddenly the baby started to cry. Someone suggested spending the night in an hotel in Czech territory and trying to cross at dawn, but I argued that it was better to try now, because a new shooting incident would close the bridge for two or three days more.

We agreed to send delegates to the Polish side. Our self-appointed leader, a Polish interpreter, and a woman went across to show the Poles that we were a harmless party. They did not return, but suddenly the police told us to continue on our way slowly and carefully. At 3 a.m. the Polish searchlights were turned on us, and we were permitted to cross the bridge. The formalities were short and the reception cordial. As we were in Polish Teschen we could see plenty of manifestos in which patriotic organisations demanded the return of the Teschen district to Poland.

In the early morning we caught a train for Warsaw where we arrived safely at noon.

Saturday, October 1, 1938

RETURN FROM MUNICH
*From our London Staff*

Fleet Street, Friday

No stranger experience can have happened to Mr. Chamberlain during the past month of adventures than his reception back home in London. He drove from Heston to Buckingham Palace, where the crowd clamoured for him, and within five minutes of his arrival he was standing on the balcony of the Palace with the King and Queen and Mrs. Chamberlain.

The cries were all for 'Neville,' and he stood there blinking in the light of a powerful arc-lamp and waving his hand and smiling. For three minutes this demonstration lasted. Another welcome awaited the Premier in Downing Street, which he reached fifteen minutes later. With difficulty his car moved forward from Whitehall to No. 10. Mounted policemen rode fore and aft and a constable kept guard on the running board of the car.

Every window on the three floors of No. 10 and No. 11 was open and filled with faces. The windows of the Foreign Office across the way were equally full – all except one, which was made up with sandbags. Everywhere were people cheering. One of the women there found no other words to express her feelings but these, 'The man who gave me back my son.'

Mr. and Mrs. Chamberlain stood for a few moments on the doorstep acknowledging the greeting. Then Mr. Chamberlain went to a first-floor window and leaned forward happily smiling on the people. 'My good friends,' he said – it took some time to still the clamour so that he might be heard – 'this is the second time in our history that there has come back from Germany "peace with honour." I believe it is peace for our time.'

Crozier did not. That night the *Guardian* wrote:

No one in this country who examines carefully the terms under which Hitler's troops begin their march into Czecho-Slovakia to-day can feel other than unhappy. Certainly the Czechs will hardly appreciate Mr. Chamberlain's phrase that it is 'peace with honour.' If Germany's aim were the economic and financial destruction of Czecho-Slovakia the Munich Agreement goes far to satisfy her. But, it may be urged, while the Czechs may suffer economically, they have the political protection of an international guarantee. What is it worth? Will Britain and France (and Russia, though, of course, Russia was not even mentioned at Munich) come to the aid of an unarmed Czecho-Slovakia when they would not help her in her strength? Politically Czecho-Slovakia is rendered helpless, with all that that means to the balance of forces in Eastern Europe, and Hitler will be able to advance again, when he chooses, with greatly increased power.

## Ill-at-Ease England

### THE PEACEMAKERS

#### Wednesday, February 15, 1933

##### PACIFIST OXFORD

A worse exhibition of newspaper hysteria than that which has followed the so-called 'pacifist' resolution of the Oxford Union Society would be hard to find. 'Foul jokers,' 'sexual indeterminates,' 'posturers,' 'yellow cowards' – these are epithets taken at random from those that have been applied to a body which, as its president says in a letter to us to-day, 'quite fairly represents the views of those undergraduates who are interested in politics.' After this sort of language the mere accusation of Communist corruption (also made) comes almost like a cool draught of level-headed and responsible criticism. What are the facts? The motion, 'that in no circumstances will this House fight for its King and country,' was provocative. When has an undergraduate debating society been anything else? But the real point of the provocation has been ignored, or deliberately obscured, in this newspaper attempt to make the youth of Oxford look as interestingly wicked, as sensationally disloyal as possible. Not a word, in columns of abuse, which even mentions (let alone sympathises with) the obvious meaning of this resolution – youth's deep disgust with the way in which past wars 'for King and country' have been made and in which, they suspect, future wars may be made, disgust at the national hypocrisy which can fling over the timidities and follies of politicians, over base greeds and commercial jealousies and jobbery, the cloak of an emotional symbol they do not deserve. 'For King and country' – there are many, indeed, for whom the phrase still comes trailing its ancient thrill. But the phrase is an abstraction like other abstractions. It may be a noble abstraction; it may be merely, in the words of an eminent Conservative, the last refuge of many scoundrels. But others of us besides the young

'*History repeats itself*' – *a cartoon by Low, April 29, 1960.*

no longer think this abstraction is worthy of the undiscriminating
respect the world once gave it. It has been used as a Moloch to devour
life too often.

### Friday, June 28, 1935

#### THE PEACE BALLOT

In its way this ballot has been the most interesting political experiment of our time. It was not designed to provide new political policies
but to confirm the old – to test, at a time when the League and 'collective security' seemed to be falling into discredit, how far it was the
will of the British people that this country should stand by its pledges.
The answer has now been given with a volume and a clarity that have
astonished the promoters themselves. More people have voted in the
affirmative in this ballot than have voted for any political party at any
ordinary general election. In several constituencies the proportion of
the adult electorate that 'went to the poll' actually exceeded 80 per cent.

So much for the quantitative result. The qualitative result is no less interesting. On some cardinal points of international policy the British people, as tested by this vote, are as nearly unanimous as makes no matter. Ninety-seven per cent of votes were cast for British support of the League. Ninety-four per cent of the 'Yes' and 'No' answers together were in favour of economic measures against an aggressor. Ninety per cent approved of the international prohibition of the private manufacture of arms – as expected, the lowest affirmative vote was cast for the proposal to use military 'sanctions' against an aggressor – a clause on which there were many abstentions.[1] Yet even on this most controversial of the issues it appears that a good majority of the people – 58 per cent of the answers, including abstentions – are in favour of world compulsion on a 'mad-dog' nation to behave itself.

The ballot's achievement can now be put in provisional perspective. It will profoundly strengthen, at home and abroad, the hands of any British Government determined on maintaining the League and the collective system. It will profoundly weaken any Government that is prepared to do neither and that finds excuses in an alleged absence of 'popular support' for its attempt to 'lead the people from behind.' These twelve million votes also provide a shattering and entirely agreeable commentary on the efforts and pretensions of some alleged mass-manufacturers of public opinion. The ballot has had to face a vigorous and partly unscrupulous opposition. A considerable section of the press discovered all kinds of mysterious and inexplicable dangers in the scheme. Its organisers were accused of attempting to make party capital out of it. Eminent Conservatives advised the public to have nothing to do with the paper at the same time (fortunately) that other, not less eminent, Conservatives were advising their constituents to fill it up. The public was informed impartially by various persons that the questions were unnecessary, because everybody approved of them, or alternatively that they were wicked, because far too complex and difficult for the public to answer; the ballot was the work of 'milk-and-water pacifists'; it was also the 'ballot of blood.' To all of this and much more these twelve million votes provide the best, the only answer. The British public made up their minds, and there is no uncertainty about their reply.

1. For 6,784,368; Against 2,351,981; Abstentions 2,364,441.

## HUNGER-MARCHERS IN LONDON

Thursday, October 27, 1932
*From Our London Staff*

Fleet Street, Wednesday
The Lancashire men marchers reached the last stage but one of their long tramp at twilight to-day. With mounted police in front and behind, and flanked by more policemen, the procession came into Brentford. After a good meal provided by the local Labour sympathisers they 'dossed down' on the floor of the schools, obeying with military precision the orders of their leader, a young man named Brownson, who has been in charge of them from the start.

These Lancashire protesters – they call themselves and are generally called 'hunger-marchers' – are nearly all sturdy young men in the twenties. Among them are many cotton operatives, but there are workers in most of the important Lancashire industries – engineers, miners, seamen, general labourers. They carried red banners, some adorned with the hammer and sickle device.

They have reached London in good spirits. This afternoon they were singing scraps of music-hall song, varied with cries of 'Are we downhearted?' About twenty of those who set out have had to give in either from bad feet or other troubles, and these men have been sent home by train. One or two are in hospital.

In a talk to-night the leaders reported that with the exception of two towns all the places on the route have treated them well. At most of the towns where they stayed the night adequate arrangements were made for feeding and 'sleeping' them by the local Labour parties, the I.L.P., and branches of the National Unemployed Workers' Movement. In the case of the Labour parties the helpers, one gathers, have been more 'the rank and file' than the official leaders.

As they went along they collected their quota of signatures for the petition against the means test, which is said to have been signed by about 1,000,000 people altogether. They invariably held an open air meeting in the towns, and have met with little opposition from the crowds. The best test of the feeling towards them is the amount of money collected by the way, and this, they report, has been much more than was expected.

The two places where there was 'trouble' were Birmingham and Stratford-on-Avon, and in both cases apparently it followed from the fact that local voluntary arrangements were not adequate, and the marchers were forced to go to the Poor Law institution for the night. At Birmingham they strenuously objected to the breakfast of bread and margarine offered them at the workhouse, their point being that they were not paupers. Accordingly they marched away breakfastless, with a banner 'We have had no breakfast.'

The worst experience was at Stratford. Here, according to the marchers' story, they demanded from the institution officials a ration of corned beef in addition to the 'pauper fare' provided, and when this was refused they loudly protested, and were thereupon attacked by a large body of police and turned out of the 'cattle shed' in which they had spent the night. In describing this affair the leader said: 'We put up a good fight against great odds.' This was the only clash with the police, and the marchers say that they were praised for their good conduct by most of the police authorities on the route.

### Friday, October 28, 1932

There were minor disturbances at the demonstration the following day. Mounted police charged several times and were pelted with mud and coal. But only 14 arrests were made and only three of the injured were detained in hospital.

Fleet Street, Thursday

It is difficult to recall any demonstration in Hyde Park during recent years that has touched the imagination of the onlookers more than did the march of the unemployed to-day. People accustomed to Labour demonstrations noted with surprise that the crowds which gathered an hour before the processions from the distant outskirts of London were due included an exceptionally large proportion of well-to-do folk, and realised that the convergence of the 2,000 or more hunger-marchers on the capital had certainly given valuable publicity to their cause.

The crowd showed most interest in the men who walked with haver-sacks on their shoulders and boots or other oddments hanging from the haversacks, but its sympathy increased as the local men came by, men in a great many cases of poor physique, with pale, pinched faces and a look of worry in their eyes – young men with the stamp of despair on them and elderly men beside whom the hunger-marchers, chosen for their powers of endurance, looked fresh and vigorous.

It was nearly three o'clock before the head of the main procession passed down Edgware Road and in at the great gates. Behind the line of mounted policemen came the Norwich contingent, headed by a bugle band and carrying a huge wooden Norwich canary on a pole with the red hammer and sickle device at the feet. Far behind it stretched the banners and slogans of Lancashire – Manchester, Liverpool, and Blackpool – and of Birkenhead, of Oxford and Birmingham, banners of the West Country and of the south coast towns. Loud applause greeted the women's contingent.

Seen from the ground the crowd seemed to be enormous. People accustomed to estimating the size of crowds confessed they could not judge the size of this one to within 20,000–50,000 was one guess, 20,000 another. Some of the police escorts reckoned that 10,000 must have marched in the various processions.

## 'LOVE ON THE DOLE'

### Friday, June 30, 1933

We passionately desire this novel to be read; it is the real thing. Mr. Greenwood is a Salford man; while still at school he sold newspapers and (like Harry in his book) worked in a pawnbroker's shop; he has been on the dole. He knows and he can tell. In a first novel he communicates with an ease which makes him, in sheer readability, the superior of most experienced novelists. His ironically happy ending is superb; his use in the manner of a Greek chorus of the terribly – we use the word advisedly – the terribly amusing Mrs. Nattle and her cronies is beautifully judged. Mr. Greenwood can find landscape in Salford for lyrical description, he can discern in Trafford Park a 'Five-year Plan thirty years ahead of the Russian,' he can move us almost unbearably by a hopeless love scene, he is a candid reporter of Salford conversation, a speech less toothsome than the racy Lancashire of, for example, Mr. T. Thompson's remoter districts, slightly flavoured, besides, by Americanese from the talkies. The authenticity is beyond dispute, and squeamish readers must lump its frankness.

'The melancholy hoot of a ship's siren sounded from the Salford Docks' – melancholy and derisive. The Ship Canal offers no escape, and those who are born in Salford stay there. 'He noticed,' at seventeen or so, 'the passing train. The incredible appreciation that he had never been aboard one in his life dawned on him, startlingly.' Yet machines had fascinated Harry Hardcastle, and, refusing the possibility of office work, he had bound himself engineer's apprentice. At 21, since well behaved machines need only boys to tend them, he was a qualified engineer on the dole, a corner boy in love, and the book tells the story of his love for the weaver Helen, and of the love of Sally, his sister, for Larry Meath, whose practical idealism respected the notion that 45s. is a marrying wage. Meath was fatally injured in a police charge during a means test demonstration, and Sally paid for his cremation.

She paid. Sally was lovely, and of the three obscene powers of Salford, pawnbroker, moneylender, bookmaker, it is the bookmaker who is the greatest. We rather doubt if a bookmaker could recruit a man into the police; we don't doubt that the purchase of mistresses is one of the things some bookmakers do with their profits. That is how Sally afforded Larry's cremation and how she made her father and Harry happy with jobs at a 'bus company's.' Fleas have smaller fleas, and we must not forget Mrs. Nattle, who pawned on commission for women too shy to enter the pawnshop, touted for the moneylender, and sold thrippeny nips of whisky; a first-rate portrait of a squalid handmaiden of capitalism.

When early this year we read in *Nobody Starves*, an informing novel, of depressed industry in the States, we felt a twinge of jealousy for England. We, too, had our depressed industrial areas. Here, transcending anticipation, is the novel for which we hoped; we emphasise again its readability.

H.B.[1]

## 'A LONG NIGHT TO THEMSELVES AND A LOAD TO THEIR COUNTRY'

Extracts from articles on areas where unemployment was heaviest and least easily remediable.

### Tuesday, June 12, 1934

#### INDUSTRIAL CUMBERLAND
*From our Special Correspondent*[2]

There is a fine 'gated' road over the fells which is used by tourists passing from Wastwater to Ennerdale Water. On a dry day you will find at each gate a little knot of young men who wait idly for hours in the hope of picking up a penny from a grateful motorist. That is the only contact which a visitor to the Cumbrian Lakes is likely to have with that other Cumberland, which is one of the distressed areas now being visited by a Government commissioner. Like much of the north-

---

1. Harold Brighouse (1882–1958). Walter Greenwood was 30 when *Love on the Dole* was published.
2. David Ayerst

east coast and of South Wales, industrial Cumberland in its decline is an illustration that there are few more rickety foundations on which to build a stable community than iron and coal.

The problem of Cumberland is principally due to the increased efficiency of modern methods of production. Ten years ago there were iron-producing plants at Maryport, Harrington, Distington, and Cleator Moor as well as at Workington; now production is concentrated in this last town. The production of the latest type of furnace is about 100 per cent greater than that of the furnace which it superseded, and this far greater production is achieved with only about 60 per cent of the labour used at the old type of furnace.

In Workington, then, there are pockets of prosperity and pockets of depression. Those men who are working are probably as well off as they have ever been since the war; those who are unemployed exist in increasing misery. Without this rationalisation the industries of West Cumberland could not have survived; because of it the people of West Cumberland cannot survive except at the expense of the public.

Thus Maryport is a town whose people find their main source of income in the rates and taxes. Before the war it was by far the busiest of the Cumberland ports. In 1927 the value of the imports at Maryport was £106,000, in 1928 it was £7,000, in 1929 and 1930 only £1,000. The opening of the new dock at Workington has killed Maryport. It is to-day only a rather picturesque little harbour town with fine views across the Solway Firth and to the Isle of Man. The total population of the town is 10,000. The number of the unemployed has normally been about 2,000 for the last few years. About four out of every seven insured workers in Maryport are unemployed.

But Maryport, desolate though it is, can hardly compare in misery with Cleator Moor. In comparison Maryport gains in two ways – the nearness of Carlisle provides some employment in shops and factories for women workers, and the tradition of the sea has certainly led to a greater vitality and power of resistance to the depressing effects of unemployment. Cleator Moor grew up as an ironstone-mining centre. It was ill-built at a time when ugliness was unconsidered. The men have now no work to do and no prospect of obtaining any.

To the outside observer there would appear to be nothing to keep the unfortunate victims of the economic collapse of Cleator Moor from gladly accepting any opportunity of leaving the district. It is, however, 'home' to its own people, and the many attempts which have been made to transfer workers to other districts have not been particularly successful. The Cleator Moor Labour Exchange area was scheduled as 'depressed' in June, 1928. From that date until June, 1932, 556 men were found work outside the district. By the end of that period 445 of them had returned home.

In this experience Cleator Moor is not exceptional in Cumberland, nor Cumberland among distressed areas. Men may be persuaded to move away if there is work for them to go to, although even then they sometimes find the new surroundings so strange and uncongenial that they will walk back home to unemployment rather than stay away in work. In any case it seems almost impossible to persuade men to stay away once they fall out of employment. A man, for instance, goes to work in Kettering. He loses his job and returns home. 'Where else should I go but home?' he asks. Yet the chances of getting work again in Kettering after a short interval of unemployment are good; back in Cumberland they are negligible. The tragedy of a derelict area like this is that love of home, the English virtue, becomes a vice which must be extinguished if the people are not to perish.

## Saturday, June 16, 1934

### WHAT TO DO?

'The disemployed is a disease, and like a long night to himself, and a load unto his country.' These words of Jeremy Taylor's, written in the seventeenth century, are still true to-day. Protracted unemployment nearly always breeds either bitterness of spirit or apathetic resignation. Sometimes the disease seems to take a worse course and leads to death. Two trade union branches in Cumberland, each with 300 members, drew roughly the same sum each year in funeral benefits. Then in 1932 the works at which the members of one branch were employed closed. That year the union paid out to the branch affected £206 in funeral benefit for the deaths of 19 members or wives of members. The branch whose members were still working drew only £45 in funeral benefit for four deaths. In 1933 the closed works reopened; the works which had been open closed. The first branch fell back to the normal amount in funeral benefits; the second made increased claims to the same extent as the other had done in the previous year. One cannot generalise on so narrow a foundation, but in the town itself it is quoted to prove the truth of the belief that the fretful idleness of unemployment eats away a man's desire and power to live.

For a few weeks an unemployed man has probably plenty of odd jobs to do at home to keep him busy. Later he has exhausted all that can usefully be done at home, and often, in addition, he has had to sell or pawn his tools. It is then that rapid deterioration begins. There is physical deterioration, because after a time the unemployed have to cut down substantially their food bills; there is still more markedly mental deterioration, because the unemployed man has time to spare and nothing to do with it. He has become, as one South Wales miner bitterly put it, merely 'an errand boy to fetch the dole.'

There are some districts – part of the Durham coalfield, for example – which are 'distressed areas' but not 'derelict.' There are others, and these have been the main subject of these articles, which are definitely derelict. Here there is little or no chance of trade reviving in the ordinary way. The Rhondda Valley is a 'depressed area'; Brynmawr is certainly and Merthyr probably a 'derelict' one.

In the merely depressed areas the problem, though difficult enough, is relatively simple. It is to keep unemployed men from becoming unemployable, to keep them fit to take up work when it returns.

In nearly every town and village where there is substantial unemployment there is now some sort of centre or club. They vary enormously in character and utility. In most cases each centre has one strong point, something in which the organiser has a particular interest. It may be boot-repairing, furniture-making, educational work, tailoring, play-producing, or, as in some Tyneside cases, running a fishing boat. It is rare, however, to find a centre which has many different branches strongly developed. This means that each centre appeals only to one or two types of men among the unemployed. Their usual strength in most districts varies between 8 and 10 per cent of the unemployed, and even this does not represent a full-time membership.

Unfortunately we have made no comparable progress with the problem of the derelict areas. Those men who have been unemployed for anything from five to ten years or more have given up any hope of getting back to work; they regard themselves, and with some justice, as just 'a waste product of the economic process.' They have made up their minds that they will have to live without work and that the State will have to keep them. A courageous and gifted handful are finding it possible to combine unemployment with a full life in public and social service, though on a pitifully low standard of living. The majority just drift.

There are certain towns which it is fashionable, though foolish, to laugh at because they are largely populated by retired officers and civil servants. Some of the derelict townships in the mining areas are growing singularly like them. They are becoming poverty-stricken, comfortless Cheltenhams for the unemployed ex-working class.

Can nothing be done to start new industries in these derelict areas? It is plain that industry will not come of its own accord. It will come only as a result of conscious planning, probably by the granting of some kind of protection or subsidy either by the State or by private individuals.

At Brynmawr for some four years there has been working a small furniture factory and a boot factory employing between them about forty people. In Cleveland, more recently, a similar furniture factory on a smaller scale has been established in the village of Boosbeck. They are training boys and young men, who would otherwise never have had a job, to become skilled tradesmen. Neither in Cleveland nor in Brynmawr would a commercial firm have established a factory. Both experiments are a mixture of business and social service.

More has been done in land settlement schemes than in establishing industries. But land settlement in the abstract is of little use. A market is necessary. To some extent there may be a local market to be captured from growers in other parts of England: those who try to save the derelict areas become almost unconsciously local protectionists. They do everything to avoid hurting the local market gardener; the distant grower in Lincolnshire is fair game. But a local market is insufficient. There is need for a canning factory, a bacon factory, a milk-condensing plant, and so on. For these capital is required. Can the Government help with a guarantee or with some other scheme for raising a sum which is too large for the locality to collect, too small to interest the City?

The Government Commissioners who are investigating the derelict areas have had scheme after scheme for the establishment of by-product plants or of secondary, luxury trades submitted to them. Many of these schemes seem to make out a better case for the boon that these industries would be for the derelict areas than for their economic usefulness to the country as a whole. But were all these schemes to mature there would still be a large problem of redundant labour. It is a double problem. The older men, the men over 45, must probably be left as pensioners in their deserted villages; the younger men must be found work elsewhere if they are not to be throughout their life 'like a long night to themselves and a load unto their country.'

# WITH THE JARROW MARCHERS

Tuesday, October 13, 1936
*From our Special Correspondent*[1]

Harrogate, Monday

Harrogate welcomed the Jarrow marchers to-day as cheerfully as if they were a relief column raising a siege. The music of the mouth-organ band might have been that of the bagpipes so surely did it bring the people flocking, and when the two hundred reached the Concert Rooms there were hundreds of folk drawn up on the slopes around to cheer them. The police were in attendance and there was a big banner raised saying, 'Harrogate workers welcome the Jarrow marchers.' At the Drill Hall, the headquarters for the night, the crowd was even denser.

It was the same to-day all along the road from Ripon. The villagers of Ripley and Killinghall rushed to their doors to see the marchers pass; motorists waved as they went by; one shouted, 'How are you sticking it?' and a woman cried, 'Hello, Geordies.' And the 'Geordies' them-selves were in great form, so that every moment I expected the band to change from 'Annie Laurie' and 'Swanee River' to 'Cheer, Boys, Cheer.' Contributions to the 'kitty' fell in as we went; here it was a pound and there it was a penny, the penny specifically being the offer-ing of an ecstatic little girl who ran across the road to meet us as if no one less than Bonnie Prince Charlie was at our head.

There can be no doubt that as a gesture the march is a bounding success. I fell in with it this morning on the Ripon road. Under its two banners ('Jarrow Crusade'), with its harmonicas, its kettledrum, and its four hundred feet, it was going strong. The marchers have with them two doctors, a barber, a group of pressmen, a Labrador dog mascot, and for a great deal of the time so far the Mayor of Jarrow (Alderman J. W. Thompson), who keeps travelling back to Jarrow to maintain touch with his civic duties and then south again to maintain touch with the marchers. It is an example of civic spirit probably without parallel anywhere else in the country.

This is not a hunger-march, but a protest march. The unanimity of the protest that Jarrow is making to the rest of the country is indicated in the fact that the political parties represented on the Jarrow Town Council have agreed to bury the political hatchet to the extent of hold-ing no elections this November. Further, although the town cannot by

1. R. H. Chadwick

law spend a farthing of the ratepayers' money on this demonstration, the labours of its Mayor in despatching about 200,000 letters to other corporations, trade unions, co-operative societies, and similar bodies at the expense of the march fund has raised that fund to £850, and it is hoped to have the round £1,000 before the marchers reach the Marble Arch on October 31.

The more fortunate classes of Jarrow, where not 15 per cent of the employable population is at work, have contributed, but the bulk of the fund has come from the country at large, and more than money. I, for one, had no conception of the cost of organising such a march until I heard about the value of the gifts in kind that ease the drain on the march fund so considerably. Take cigarettes, for instance, and calculate the cost of distributing two twopenny packets per day per man to 200 men. I will not vouch that 'fags' are among the gifts, but it illustrates the point. Any little article costing sixpence means five pounds when distributed to 200 men, and soap, tobacco, and all sorts of things have been given. Before the men set out they all had their boots soled and heeled, and two pairs of socks and two iodine soles were also issued.

With eggs and salmon and such sandwiches as I saw to-day being consumed on the menu it is emphatically not a hunger-march. The men are doing well on it, and only two of them have fallen out for reasons of health in nearly 90 miles of marching. All the time communication is maintained with Jarrow, and if work turns up for a man on the march back he will go to it.

The organisation seems well nigh perfect. It includes a transport wagon – a 'bus bought for £20 and converted – which goes ahead with the sleeping kit, waterproofs for every man worn bandolero fashion, 1s. 6d. pocket-money and two 1½d. stamps a week, medical attention, haircutting (and shaving for the inexpert), cobbling, accommodation at night in drill halls, schools, church institutes, and even town halls, and advance agents in the persons of the Labour agent at Jarrow, Mr. Harry Stoddart, and the Conservative agent, Mr. R. Suddick, who work together in arranging accommodation and getting halls for meetings.

There is no political aspect to this march. It is simply the town of Jarrow saying 'Send us work.' In the ranks of the marchers are Labour men, Liberals, Tories, and one or two Communists, but you cannot tell who's who. It has the Church's blessing; in fact, it took the blessing of the Bishop of Ripon (Dr. Lunt) and a subscription of £5 from him when it set out to-day. It also had the blessing of the Bishop of Jarrow (Dr. Gordon).

With the marchers goes, prominently carried, the Jarrow petition for work, a huge book with about 12,000 signatures, which Miss Ellen Wilkinson, M.P. for Jarrow, is to present at the bar of the House of Commons on November 4. Miss Wilkinson met us outside Killinghall this afternoon and became the only woman in the procession. She had motored from Manchester to-day but had met with petrol trouble and had been delayed. It was interesting to watch motorists who passed us on the road recognise her and lean out of windows as they went by. Like us all she made friends with Paddy, the Labrador dog who accompanied the procession uninvited for five miles from Jarrow before anyone realised that he intended to go all the way. When the marshal's whistle goes he goes too and there is no holding him.

It was interesting, too, to watch men employed on the road rest on their spades to watch men unemployed but also on the road go by. Their eyes spoke their thoughts. Most interesting was the meeting at lunch-time between some of these untravelled men and a real knight of the road who seemed to rejoice in his adventures and who on his way to Ripon told us on our way to Harrogate which were the best casual wards, how bugs make an eightpenny bed unbearable, and what are the duties of a 'tramp major.' One could write columns about it, but we are at Harrogate, and a meeting is to be held at the Winter Gardens with Miss Ellen Wilkinson as one of the speakers. At every stopping-place there is such a meeting so that the world shall know of Jarrow.

## OSWALD MOSLEY'S CIRCUS

Friday, June 8, 1934
*From our London Staff*

Fleet Street, Thursday

Sir Oswald Mosley provided close on 10,000 people in Olympia to-night with an entertainment which Mr. Bertram Mills might at once have envied and deplored. For while Mr. Mills must certainly have envied Sir Oswald the number of his audience and the excitement he and his hecklers provided, he must have deplored the violence with which that excitement was obtained.

For what is described in the talk of the gangsters as 'rough-house work' no meeting in these islands within memory can have shown anything like it.

It is not easy to apportion the blame for the disturbance. For when the anti-Mosleyites – Communists, pacifists, and Left-wing members of the Labour party and the I.L.P. – arrived at Olympia with their placards and pamphlets a couple of hours before the meeting was due to begin it was to encounter massed groups of Blackshirts and a strong force of police, not only on foot but mounted, and it is an odd fact that of all the emblems of authority which drew booing and catcalls from a crowd of British Communists and Left-wingers the mounted policeman seems to be regarded as the most provocative.

For over an hour before the meeting the crowds jostling one another outside Olympia numbered several thousand. There were young men and women in evening dress, there were middle-class family parties with small children, and there was a large gathering of workers in their working clothes.

On the main road forty or fifty policemen frantically tried to move on traffic that would not move. There were catcalls and booing and cheering, and in a scuffle one could catch sight of a yelling demonstrator being dragged off by the police. It was what has so often before, and with much less justice, been described as an 'ugly scene.'

Inside the great hall it was seen that Sir Oswald Mosley had nothing of theatricalism to learn from either Hitler or Mussolini. There was a massed band of Blackshirts, there were flags, the Union Jack, and the black and yellow flag of the British Union of Fascists. There were arc-lamps with a theatrical greyish-blue tinge, and there was an aisle lined with Blackshirts extending from the entrance usually employed by the performing animals at the Royal Military Tournament to a specially contrived platform draped with drugget of a tinned-salmon pink.

And Sir Oswald, in keeping with a nowadays out-of-date theatrical tradition, kept his audience waiting while the band played patriotic marches and other tunes devised for the British Fascists.

Exactly thirty-five minutes after the meeting was due to begin Sir Oswald made his appearance. The lights of the hall flickered, the band dropped into a Low German march of the seventies or thereabouts, the arc-lamps swung round from the platform down the Blackshirted aisle, and there in the foggy distance Sir Oswald appeared – announced by a fanfare and preceded by six men carrying Union Jacks and the British Blackshirt flag. And so the march proceeded to the platform while some people – they did not seem to be many – raised their arms in a Fascist salute and others with less commitment, cheered. Yet above the cheers could be heard the unmistakable sound of booing.

With the arc-lamps swung round on him, Sir Oswald began his speech.

Almost at once a chorus of interrupters began chanting in one of the galleries. Blackshirts began stumbling and leaping over chairs to get at the source of the noise. There was a wild scrummage, women screamed, black-shirted arms rose and fell, blows were dealt, and then above the noise came the chorus chanted by rough voices, 'We want Mosley.'

The arc-lamps swung round from the platform on to the fighters. Sir Oswald stood to attention in the half-darkness, making unintelligible appeals through the amplifiers. In a few minutes there was something like silence again.

For close on two hours the meeting dragged on like that, interruption following interruption and ejection. Now and again a woman would shrill at the top of her voice, a crowd of Blackshirts would hustle round her and, knotting her arms behind her back, bundle her out. The arena was soon full of hooting and whistling and chairs and boots and shoes were flying in the air.

Then came the big scene. Suddenly, as Sir Oswald was speaking during a lull in the interruptions – so placed were the amplifiers that those in the seats reserved for the press could not distinguish his words – a pamphlet fluttered down from the blue gauze-covered roof. Suddenly a voice sounded high up in the girders, 'Down with Fascism!'

Eyes swung upwards and there, balanced one hundred and fifty feet above the crowd, a man was seen clambering across the girders. Then from each side Blackshirts appeared treading the same precarious perch.

Sir Oswald went on speaking, but all eyes were on the climbers. Chaos broke out in the back of the hall. Chairs were cleared away in case the men should fall. The arc-lamps swung round from the platform to show up five or six men threading their way along the girders – a scene that would have thrilled most people in a cinema. Suddenly, as the men seemed to meet in the centre of the girders, the interrupter clambered up above his pursuers and swung along the girders on to a platform high above them. His pursuers followed, straggling on either side, and in a moment all were out of sight.

Sir Oswald still went on speaking until a sudden crash of glass tore the air. Someone had fallen sixty feet at a guess, on to a floor at the side of the hall. At the moment it is not disclosed whether the man was the interrupter or one of his pursuers.

The meeting ended in a mild chaos – not from interrupters but from a general stampede of the audience, who had plainly grown tired of Sir Oswald's two-hour monologue. After ten o'clock it was plainly a struggle between Sir Oswald and the decision of the licensing justices of the borough of Hammersmith. The licensing justices won and Sir Oswald was robbed of his triumphant exit.

# The Sad New World

## BEGGARS IN CARS

Saturday, October 15, 1932

*From our New York Correspondent*[1]

One of the striking phenomena of the depression, although little is heard of it, is the amazing number of homeless people who are now drifting about the United States. Americans have always been a migratory people, but the number of those who are 'on the move' from necessity, not from choice, has increased probably tenfold. In the old days these migrants were practically all men and boys, but to-day there are many thousands of women and children among them. It is by no means an uncommon sight to see on the highway a father, mother, and several small children drifting aimlessly along. The standard history is that they have been dispossessed because unable to pay the rent or to meet the interest payments on the mortgage. They have heard vaguely that things are better in some distant State, and they are going to find out. In the autumn there is a vast migration towards Florida and other States in the warm southern tier, and in the spring the tide turns northward again. There is just enough left of the old pioneer tradition to cause a general slow drift to the West; in the course of a year hundreds of thousands of these destitute travellers get to the Pacific Coast, where they form a desperate problem for the social-work agencies.

Probably only in the United States could one see the phenomenon of beggars in automobiles. Many thousands of these vagrants, and particularly if they are travelling as a family, do so by motor-car. One can buy a dilapidated second-hand Ford for $25 or $50, and every American man is an automobile mechanic. On this country's hard-finished roads cost of operation is surprisingly small, and the money for petrol, tyre repairs, and food is begged along the way. In pleasant weather the tourists camp out in the fields, gipsy fashion; when it storms they can always find some charitable soul in the countryside to take them in, or can apply to the organised charities in the towns.

There are, of course, an enormous number of persons on the highways who lack even the $25 or $50 for a car; and these make their way on foot or 'hitch-hike' – borrow rides from passing motorists. (Many others steal rides on railway goods trains.) Hitch-hiking has become

1. Bruce Bliven

something of a fine art in the United States, there are even books which give instructions on it. One must, for instance, carry no luggage; one must be clean shaven; one must not be sitting by the wayside or even standing still, but walking slowly in the desired direction; one must be reasonably clean and well-dressed. One must never ask for a ride while a car is going up any sort of hill or down a very steep one; one must not ask after sunset, and so on. The standard gesture of application is to stand facing the approaching car and jerk one thumb over the shoulder. Cases are on record where individuals have crossed the United States – 3,000 miles – in this fashion in only nine or ten days by obtaining consecutive 'lifts' from one motorist after another. Nearly all of these persons, of course, are men, although there are a few strong-minded young women who boast of travelling hundreds of miles by this means.

The great majority of the persons now on the road, however, are hardly to be classed as hitch-hikers. Many of them are roughly clad working men who have heard that jobs are to be had in some distant place – and who are almost always disappointed on their arrival. There are many destitute families walking the roads. There is also to-day an American equivalent of the Russian 'wild boys.' Social workers estimate that there are several hundred thousand adolescent boys wandering about the country, most of them the victims of homes broken up through the depression. They are petty thieves or beggars; many of them have got into the hands of tramps who debauch them mentally and physically. If the country were not so preoccupied with other phases of the economic disaster, this one would receive the most serious attention.

The 'Bonus Expeditionary Force,' routed from Washington with such unnecessary violence, contained many families, and most of these are now turned loose on the roads.[1] They came to Washington because they had lost all hope of receiving aid anywhere else; so far from being Radicals they were aggressively patriotic and believed that the war service of the husband and father would certainly cause the Government to look after his family and see that they did not starve. The brutal treatment received at the hands of the troops has simply stunned these people, and they are now wandering the highways, some of them in a condition closely resembling shell-shock. Incidentally, there is an encampment of them in an abandoned reservoir in Central Park, New York, a few yards from the millionaires' homes of Fifth Avenue, and another on the shore of the Hudson River just below the United States' most stately boulevard, Riverside Drive.

In view of President Hoover's charge that the members of the 'Bonus

1. Unemployed ex-Servicemen who had marched to Washington.

Army' were Communists it is perhaps worth while to repeat that so far as can be ascertained the depression has thus far made a Radical of practically nobody. Talk with the homeless man on the street corner and you will usually find that he is still a supporter of the capitalist system and believes in America as 'the land of opportunity.' There is great anger at Mr. Hoover, but if this has any political effect it will be only the election of Mr. Roosevelt, who, while less conservative than the present occupant of the White House, is miles away from being a Radical.

One exception ought to be noted to the statement that the depression has not produced Radicals. There has recently been a remarkable swing towards Communism among the brilliant young writers of the New York intelligentsia. Critics, poets, and novelists who heretofore have ignored economics entirely, in the American post-war tradition, have suddenly taken to a furious reading of Karl Marx and go about writing and speaking the difficult jargon of Moscow. Most of them are not members of the Communist party; but the Machiavellian group uses them skilfully – as 'window dressing,' putting them on 'non-partisan' committees for relief for hungry miners, for propaganda against 'Imperialist war on the U.S.S.R.' and so on. There is, of course, another group of intellectuals, not so spectacular and perhaps on the average a little older, which has amalgamated with the Socialist party; and the quarrel between these two is splitting the literary firmament. They attack each other far more violently than either of them does Republicans and Democrats, who are at the other end of the political spectrum. Whatever their feelings towards the merit of Radical doctrines as such, most thoughtful Americans welcome the new interest in economic and political matters on the part of the young writers. For many years the 'ivory tower' attitude of these men and the general indifference of American youth to public questions have been the subject of adverse comments by European visitors. The college undergraduates still stand aloof in large numbers; but even there the new doctrines are growing, and optimists look forward hopefully to the time when large masses of the students may actually show a definite interest in the activities of the adult world.

# The English in India

Friday, October 2, 1936
*By Rabindranath Tagore*

(Extracts are here given from a letter written by Rabindranath Tagore to a friend in England on the present state of India under British rule.)

You know, and I have never tried to keep it secret from anyone, that of all the Western peoples who have direct dealings with alien races I respect most the British people. Many things have recently happened in our country to wound us to the quick, in the doing of which British agents were concerned, but of which it is forbidden to speak. These have embittered the hearts of our countrymen at large, though the punishment has fallen only on our youths. In spite of it all, I still say that it will not do to isolate such events when coming to our own judgment of the British people. There are other great nations in Europe who exercise dominion over foreign peoples. And we cannot but heave a sigh of relief whenever we recall that it is not they who are our rulers. What I am writing to you now, and the freedom with which our representatives in the Legislatures expatiate on the shortcomings of the Government, would not have been possible under the domination of any other European nation which holds subject races under its autocratic grip. We admire the United States from a distance, because we have no relations with her. But, apart from her inhuman treatment of the Negroes, the instances of rank injustice, perpetrated by her highest courts of law are such as do not fortunately belong to our normal experience in India.

I have seen many great Englishmen. They never hesitate to stand up against wrong, whether done by others or by their own countrymen. These may not be statesmen, for statesmen are not usually to be reckoned as the true representatives of the nation. If the persons wielding political power in England had been able to ignore the silent judgment of the great minds in their country, they might have succeeded in levelling to the dust all the best canons of humanity – as has been done in Germany and Italy, and as might have been done in England if the new-fledged Fascists there had their way. In that case the Andamans[1] would have been fully populated and the key of the speeches in our Legislatures pitched several tones lower – as in the case of Germany and Italy.

1. The Andaman Islands were a penal settlement.

I must admit that my admiration of British character, in so far as that character is reflected in the governing of India, with its penal system, whipping, and solitary cell, does not come to much more than a comparative statement. It is inhuman enough for us, as you must have found from the narrative of Jawaharlal's prison experiences[2] and also from numerous instances of political prisoners, in the prime of their youth, coming out to die after a few years of gaol, miserably broken down in health and spirit. And it is but meagre consolation to us to think that it could even have been worse according to the present standard of civilisation that prevails in a large part of the West.

The chronic want of food and water, the lack of sanitation and medical help, the neglect of means of communication, the poverty of educational provision, the all pervading spirit of depression that I have myself seen to prevail in our villages after over a hundred years of British rule make me despair of its beneficence. It is almost a crime to talk of Soviet Russia in this country, and yet I cannot but refer to the contrast it presents. I must confess to the envy with which my admiration was mixed to see the extraordinary enthusiasm and skill with which the measures for producing food, providing education, fighting against disease were being pushed forward in their vast territories. There is no separating line of mistrust or insulting distinction between Soviet Europe and Soviet Asia. I am only comparing the state of things obtaining there and here as I have actually seen them. And I state my conclusion that what is responsible for our condition in the so-called British Empire is the yawning gulf between its dominant and subjugated sections.

On the other hand, it has to be recognised that there is an inevitableness in the fate that has overtaken Hindu India. We have divided and subdivided ourselves into mincemeat, not fit to live but only to be swallowed. Never up to now has our disjointed society been able to ward off any threatening evil. We are a suicidal race, ourselves keeping wide open for ages, with marvellous ingenuity, gaps that we are forbidden to cross under penalty and cracks that are considered to be too sacred to be repaired because of their antiquity.

2. Nehru's *Autobiography* was published in 1936.

# Arts

## 'STRAVINSKY – QUITE THE CONCERT OF THE YEAR'

### Friday, February 22, 1934

Though the audience was not by any means small for the visit of the most fearlessly original of contemporary composers, there were too many empty seats. The absentees must somehow be identified, collected together, and given a concert all to themselves next season, with a programme made up of 'The Hymn of Praise' and 'The Golden Legend.' Whoever was responsible for this visit of Stravinsky must be warmly congratulated; the great artist brought distinction to the Hallé Concerts, and placed them again, momentarily at least, upon the musical map of the period. To say the truth, Stravinsky treated a Manchester audience gently; he gave us none of his most drastic works – such as the unashamed 'Le Sacre du Printemps.' The Transcriptions for Piano and Violin, played after the interval by the composer and Mr. Dushkin, were mainly enchanting in melody and rhythm – and so simple that Schönberg would probably sing his children to sleep with them. The programme, indeed, revealed Stravinsky as a fine melodist, especially when, in the 'Suite Italienne,' he was composing the lovely tunes of Pergolesi.

The concerto for violin came closer to the Stravinsky of the moment. (He is always casting a skin, and nobody knows what his next work will sound like.) In the concerto we find a remarkable subtilisation of the constituents of music, which are melody, rhythm, and harmony. Here they are reduced to their essences, and so cunningly mingled that each seems a necessary attribute of the other – and, indeed, there should be in true music no domination by any one of these factors. When the admirers of Stravinsky declare of their master that he has gone back to Bach, they do him ill-service by leaving the phrase simply at that. The violin concerto emulates classical models only in so far as it frees music of extraneous poetic significances, and lives in the unburdened movements of its parts qua tonal qualities. The two arias, which make the middle movement of the violin concerto, are pure melody. By pure melody is meant a melody that is not a harmonic or rhythmical offshoot. During the nineteenth century the romantic habit of composers almost destroyed the ear for pure melody. Melody was given the rhythm of the poetry wedded to the music, in song and opera, or else, in symphonic music, it was denied its proper flight by

*Tuesday, November 10, 1959. A drawing by Papas.*

the weight of a harmony which was orchestrally conceived. In 'Lohengrin' there may be a whole bar not written in common time, but nobody save a professor of music has been able at will to put his finger upon it. Such was the effect on the natural movement of melody, and on melody's spontaneous rhythm, of a great dramatic composer's preoccupation with orchestral colour and harmonic suggestion. Stravinsky's melody, in the arias of the violin concerto, is uncommonly beautiful in its flowing shapes and its many refined inflections. So with the gorgeous transcription of 'Les Airs du Rossignol,' where the notes of the violin rise and fall as those of the nightingale itself would rise and fall if the bird were a conscious artist and could organise its throated loveliness into a pattern.

Mr. Dushkin played these airs with a ravishment of tone and phrase which told us he is one of the most melodious violinists of the day, just as in the Capriccio of the concerto he told us he is also the most rhythmical by far. This remarkable movement shows Stravinsky at his finest as a composer of new and fascinating rhythm. Time-signatures seldom express the pulsations of his music; he takes dazzling flights over the bar-line – especially in his 'Les Noces,' where he entirely ignores the old conception of rhythm as an affair of periodic repetition. In a lesser degree we find the same freedom of stress and subtlety of syncopation in the Toccata and Capriccio of the Violin Concerto. There is perhaps a too palpable dexterity; in a short time the mind craves for a richer texture – but no doubt Stravinsky would tell us that this craving was the very thing he is trying to cure in us. He has clarified the general air of music, got rid of a deal of the moonshine, the Wehmut. He has taken the heady wine from the invalid (for obviously music has been an invalid for years – witness Strauss in his old age); he has prescribed an astringent. Not, as I say, that there was anything particularly designed to shake us up in last evening's programme; most of the music is common enough currency nowadays; maybe to-morrow, or the day after, Stravinsky will share the fate of Strauss and Debussy, and be called old-fashioned by the latest young 'bloods,' while the rest of us in our advancing senility cry out 'O for the good old tunes of "Le Sacre".'

The Hallé Orchestra achieved a triumph of score-reading throughout the concert. Stravinsky himself was delighted and astonished at the swiftness of comprehension and attack. Of course the actual playing would have gained in significance and balance of out-of-way tone values had a few additional rehearsals been at the composer's disposal. All in all, it was a memorable and stimulating night, which was full of the sense of culture and independent vision. The charm of Stravinsky's manner won all hearts, his intent and stylish conducting, his perfect bow as he acknowledged applause. And Dushkin's brilliant playing caused quite a stir. These two artists must come to us again. Stravinsky owes it to himself to appear once more at least before a Hallé audience. If he leaves us with only the memory of last night's concert he will go down to posterity, as far as Manchester is concerned, as a maker of beautiful music, of sweet concourse of sounds. He surely would not like that; let him bring 'Le Sacre' with him next time.

N.C.[1]

1. Neville Cardus

## ERNST TOLLER: *DRAW THE FIRES*

### Tuesday, February 12, 1935

Ernst Toller's latest play, *Draw the Fires*, which deals with the revolt of the German navy towards the end of the war, was given its first production outside Germany before a full and enthusiastic house at the Repertory Theatre last night. The play, which opens in the boiler-room of a German battleship in the Battle of Jutland and ends with the triumphant peace demonstration in Kiel dockyard in November, 1918, was running in Berlin when the Nazis came to power. Toller's works, along with those of many of Germany's foremost men of letters, were publicly burned and their author exiled from his country. 'But,' says Toller in a moving passage of his preface to the English edition of his plays, 'even the power of dictators is limited. They can kill the mind for a time, and they can kill it in any one land. But across the border they are impotent; across the border the power of the word can save itself and harbour itself; the word which in the long run is stronger and greater than any dictator, and which will outlast them all. Thus these plays come to be published in the land of Shakespeare and Shelley, the scene of the author's involuntary yet voluntary exile, the land which has become a second home to him.'

*Draw the Fires*, like all Toller's work, is enkindled by his deep conviction that it is not the mission of the dramatist to afford an escape from life nor to depict the inconsiderable adventures of this or that individual, but to seize upon and interpret according to his vision the great movements that for good or evil shake the civilised world to its foundations. A preacher as well as an artist, he has campaigned ceaselessly against what he conceives to be mankind's oppressions – political, industrial, social. As a reformer he disdains the satire of the Shavian method in favour of direct attack. There is little in his work of that balanced presentation of social problems that Galsworthy brought to bear. But the fierce and pure compassion for the suffering of mankind that is the core of his writing puts it on a plane of its own.

Toller has used more than one dramatic style as his vehicle. Sometimes as in *Masses and Man* – the play that 'broke out of him' in the prison fortress of Niederschoenfeld and was put on paper in two days and a half, – he has seen mankind not as individuals but as pawns, cut to pattern, in a tragic game, and has presented his theme in the extreme 'expressionist' manner. Sometimes, as in *Hinkelmann*, that almost unbearably distressing picture of the disruption of body and soul by war, he has concentrated his argument in a single character more or less realistically presented. Here, since history as well as drama is at issue, the realist method is predominant. But it is mingled effectively with the other. The play opens and ends to the rhythmic shovelling of coal and the opening and shutting of furnace doors, while orders are shouted down the speaking-tube to the stokehold. But whereas at Jutland the orders are obeyed with no more than normal stokehold grumbling, in 1918 the fires are drawn. It is the author's purpose to show and account for the change of attitude that intervened. His theme is the budding, the growth, and the final burgeoning among common men under the oppression of slaughter, starvation, and gross abuse of authority and social privilege in the name of patriotism, of the idea that their sufferings are needless if they will but stand together for peace and freedom.

The play is dedicated to the memory of the sailors Kobis and Reichpietsch, who were shot in September, 1917, after the mutiny that began the disintegration of the German fleet; and throughout it till their death they are the chief protagonists. We see them – the one sensitive, volatile, gay, the popular man of the mess, the other quieter and firmer, but both loyal workers for their ship and their fleet – slowly converted to miscreants. Toller stresses the appalling contrast in rations between the officers' mess and the crew's; the needless imposition of tasks upon a fleet boxed up month after month in port; the crass failure of authority to handle dissaffection with any wisdom; the sinister part played by 'counsel for the defence' of the men; and with this selection of facts so ennobles his two stokers that the scene in the condemned cell, after the court martial of 1917, though treated with restraint, has a memorable poignancy, the martyrdom of the two in the minds of their comrades becomes inevitable, and the way is paved for the final and decisive revolt of 1918.

This production has the immense benefit of being directed by the author, and he has made the utmost of the means at his disposal. A specially written musical theme by Hans Eisler that embodies 'Tipperary,' the 'Marsellaise,' and 'Die Wacht am Rhein' adds to the unity of the play. The large cast needed is filled by voluntary help from the Left Theatre group of Manchester. The Repertory Company have brought to it, as the author justly said of them at the end, 'understanding, devotion to art, and power.'

A.S.W.[1]

1. A. S. Wallace

## NOEL COWARD: *TO-NIGHT AT 7.30*
### Wednesday, October 16, 1935

Mr. Noel Coward is a clever satirist, intensely aware of the manners of our time; he has known also how to touch the emotions when he has deserted comment and identified himself with people and with great events, as he did for instance in *Bitter Sweet* and *Cavalcade*. Above all he has been a brilliant writer of comedy, whether in the early *Hay Fever* or the later *Private Lives*. Now, at the Opera House, he presents 'a triple bill,' claiming that the one-act play has qualities which make it worthy of restoration to the theatre. Yet the phrase 'a triple bill' needs amplifying; a triple bill of what? And it is here that disappointment enters. For Mr. Coward's plays are only trifles; there is really no stuff of drama in them. They cannot fail to be amusing or entertaining, because of the author's gift for dialogue and because he and Miss Gertrude Lawrence are wonderfully apt in that dialogue. Would it not be true to say that the plays are written for them, depend upon them, and would be nothing without them? Put anyone else in their parts and the plays would be so thin as to be almost non-existent. What we are seeing, what we are laughing at, is Mr. Coward and Miss Lawrence, as Mr. Coward and Miss Lawrence, presented by Mr. Coward, sometimes we think, almost in a parody of the Coward manner, and it is all very diverting, but it savours too much of a private joke.

*We Were Dancing*, a comedy in two scenes, is the wittiest of the three plays. It is only an episode, but it does contain the drier asides, the sudden descents from the ecstatic to the trivial, which were characteristic of *Private Lives* and which indeed make this play seem a little bit more of that great success. In the devastating rejoinder, the quiet, quick reply, Mr. Coward has no equal. Nor have he and Miss Lawrence any equals in the delivery of this dialogue; the chopped-off utterance, the quick, husky tones; the thing is all of a piece, and in its way quite final and perfect. Against this one must ask if it would be possible for other companies, professional or amateur, to make anything of *We Were Dancing*, and the answer is 'No.'

With *Red Peppers* we find the triple bill finishes on a farcical, even rollicking, note. It is extremely amusing; it is neither more or less than a variety 'turn' by two 'stars.' The Red Peppers are Lily and George, a music-hall pair who, dressed as sailors or as men about town, perform those laborious songs and dances, interspersed with ancient jokes, which we have all seen a thousand times on the variety stage. This is the private joke raised to the highest number; we rightly laugh at the delicious parody which Mr. Coward and Miss Lawrence present, but it is not a play, nor an episode; it is a personal appearance, and as such it is brilliantly successful. Sandwiched between two 'turns' we have a long scene of back-chat in the dressing-room; it is the same inimitable slanging, this time in a rather different idiom and with the accent of a lower class. No one can write it quite like Mr. Coward, no one can speak it in quite the same way, and no one would pay much attention to this *Interlude with Music* if it were performed by a second-rate, unknown company in some little theatre. It is an expression of two brilliant and popular personalities.

The talents for writing words and music, for acting and producing, rarely come together in one person; we must admire the quadruple coincidence in Mr. Coward, regret that his new plays are disappointing in so far as the theatre is to be taken seriously, and remember the cheers of an audience which at the end was undoubtedly enjoying with simple goodwill the unusual spectacle of Mr. Coward and Miss Lawrence capering in sailor suits.

M.C.[1]

## CHAPLIN: *MODERN TIMES*

### Tuesday, July 14, 1936

*Modern Times*, by one of those bewildering dispensations of the film industry, has taken so many months to reach Manchester that nobody would dare to call it 'Charlie Chaplin's new film.' For all we know they may at this very moment be showing one of later date in London, the Isle of Man, Treorchy, or Ardnamurchan. However, here it is at the Gaumont at last, and it is so good that we are compelled to let bygones be bygones.

In *Modern Times* Chaplin proves again what the whole world already acknowledges – that he is the greatest artist of the silent screen as apart from the half-theatrical talking screen, the most eloquent master of mime, and the simplest, most essential, and most touching of comedians. Unless recent impressions have unbalanced the judgment this would certainly appear to be one of his very best films. Not only has Chaplin set to work on new ideas (though they are borrowed from Clair), but he has evolved new comic 'business' and skilfully prepared for revivals of old tricks so that they do not seem mere uninspired repetition. He has restrained the fondness for pathetic effects, which so overbalanced *City Lights*, leaving only a legitimate invitation to

1. Mary Crozier (Mrs. MacManus).

sympathy for the undeliberating, 'take-the-world-as-you-find-it', yet curiously impersonal emblem of humanity which he presents. Watching *Modern Times* one is compelled to marvel again at the miraculous soundness of taste which has led people of so many countries to take Chaplin to their hearts. His reaction to life has a humble, saintly, and therefore triumphant quality.

What Chaplin has borrowed from Clair – it was fitting that he should reborrow from such a disciple – is the idea of satirising mass production and the treadmill of industry, a brief 'Rugby match' with a roast duck, and some hints on the synchronising of film and music. The film opens in a factory of nightmarish efficiency where the 'boss' observes all from his desk by means of television and Charlie is hard at work tightening screws on a moving belt. This is a mine of rich humour, and even when he becomes unhinged in mind the treatment is not distasteful. After that he is thrice in and out of gaol for deliriously funny reasons. His comic adventures are too many to relate, but it may be said that they culminate in a café of 'singing waiters' where, after a wealth of comic 'business' with the tray, he shows his disdain for articulate speech by singing a vividly explicit song in gibberish. There are few feats of virtuosity better than his miming as he rehearses the song and as he performs a short introductory dance. Throughout his facial expressions and bodily gestures make speech and even the delightfully worded sub-titles unnecessary. The writer, having now seen the film three times, declares that they still remain absorbing and full of meaning.

It will no doubt be objected that the sequence of the big machine becomes tedious, and that in construction the film is somewhat ungainly. Such critics are at liberty to count up the faults, if it gives them pleasure, but are certainly pursuing an unfruitful occupation in enumerating these rather than the excellences. The whole film bears the Chaplin stamp, particularly in the exaggerated character of the gesture and the reliance on miming. Paulette Goddard as the *gamin* has taken kindly to his style. She seems fresh and different from all other screen women. In the small parts the acting is all of the same whole. One of the reasons why Chaplin is a great artist is that he is not shackled by the bonds of realism which still limit such diverse imaginative work as literature, the stage, and the screen. He has created his own ideal image of the world, or, rather, of human nature.

R.K.[1]

1. Robert Kemp

# Blenkinsop, a Great Full-Back

## Friday, January 26, 1934

A stranger to Association football watched Sheffield Wednesday play Everton the other day. He was enthusiastic over the tussles between centre forwards and centre half-backs, the fast running and expert centring of the wing forwards, the acrobatic goalkeeping. But at the end of the match he said to his guide, 'The man you said was England's best full-back since the war did not do much, did he?' Admittedly this full-back had not kicked prodigiously, he had not mowed down opponents by mighty charges. The newspaper reports gave him one sentence: he was 'at his best.' The score was Sheffield Wednesday nil (which was not his fault), Everton nil.

Blenkinsop neither by mannerism nor by method compels the spectators' attention. He goes about his work quietly, almost grimly (being a son of Yorkshire) and with an efficiency so mechanical that it is taken for granted. As a man says of his motor-car, 'she's running sweetly to-day,' and drives on, so one says of Blenkinsop, 'he's playing well to-day,' and turns to the forwards. Yet at a first glance, and a second, Blenkinsop seems to be miscast in a great defensive part; he looks too small, a little frail. It is a surprise to find that he is within two inches of six feet, that there is a weight of more than 160 lb. behind his charge. But he is vigorous only when vigour is essential, and even then it is a cultured vigour. Blenkinsop's charge is courteous, almost apologetic. He discovers no peculiar satisfaction in sending his man flat to earth, the sight of which made Hutton – the Aberdonian who defended for Blackburn and whose charge was a very convulsion of nature itself – beam all over his face. Great backs, both of them, Hutton and Blenkinsop represented two utterly different schools. Hutton gave us something of the robust Tudor humours, Blenkinsop gives us the technique of expert swordsmanship – parry, feint, and an occasional thrust.

Blenkinsop plays football as Alekhine plays chess, considering not only the immediate move of his own or of the opposing team, but several moves ahead. His master stroke is something of the checkmate; a slight change of position and the enemy's plan is frustrated; the wing forward racing towards goal is, without physical contact, urged further from it and must either pass or shoot to Blenkinsop's order, which is as much a defensive triumph as violent dispossession, or accept the challenge, which is nearly always to play mouse to the Blenkinsop cat.

This full-back can kick a ball as hard and as far as most, but rarely does so. Generally his passing is the first link in a chain of passing. It all looks exceedingly simple, but that is the way of the really great player.

N.J.N.D.[1]

## The First Belisha Crossings

> Mr. Hore-Belisha, the Minister of Transport, led a coachload of civil servants and reporters round the first 25 miles of London streets to be provided with pedestrian crossings. The *Guardian* called its London Letter paragraph 'Mr. Hore-Belisha's Bravery.'

### Tuesday, July, 10, 1934

Mr. Hore-Belisha dismounted and crossed and recrossed the road in the face of roaring traffic which, as it approached the white lines and the signpost with the large letter 'C', jammed on its brakes and came to a sudden standstill. Other pedestrians then began to make their way between the lines until within a few seconds the traffic on its way to and from Hampstead seemed to have come to a standstill. By the time the party reached Whitechapel pedestrians were making use of the new lines as if they had been in existence all their lives. Women with children in perambulators, pushed their precious cargoes from one pavement to another with smiling faces. Children skipped across them as if they had just found a new playground, and old, crippled men and women near the long stretch of the London Hospital moved across them unhurriedly. [But the motorists' good behaviour did not last, and Belisha Beacons were introduced to supplement the lines. On October 29 the London Letter remarked: 'One's general experience is that at most uncontrolled crossings only the boldest of walkers will risk asserting his rights.']

1. N. J. N. Dixon

# CHAPTER ELEVEN

# 'Times That Try Men's Souls'

*

The war ended one of the two pre-occupations of Crozier's editorship; it intensified the other. The ten years of unemployment came to an end; but outside this country many thought that England, like Denmark and Norway, like the Low Countries, and like France, would become a province of Hitler's Europe. It was no consolation to the *Guardian* that it had foreseen many of the things that happened. Once Churchill had replaced Chamberlain there was no need or time for party politics. But underneath the surface there was, in a phrase that Wadsworth made famous, a silent revolution in progress in the English way of life. The *Guardian* would have welcomed this if it had perceived what was happening for it was indeed in line with its own values. In fact, however, the result of the 1945 election astonished the *Guardian* as much as the country.

The war took most of the young men on the paper off to fight. J. L. Hammond came to Manchester to take a full share in leader-writing, his last and probably his greatest service to the paper. Crozier and Wadsworth carried the main day-to-day burden in Manchester; in London there was still the indomitable James Bone. Evelyn Montague made a fine reputation as a war correspondent until illness overcame him. It was with a largely new team that, after Crozier's death in 1944, Wadsworth began his editorship, though he soon secured the release from the Army of John Pringle, an ex-member of the staff, to become deputy editor.

# From Chamberlain to Churchill

Hitler's lightning conquest of Poland in the autumn of 1939 was followed by the winter of 'the phoney war.' Then on April 8, Hitler invaded Denmark and Norway. British efforts to help Norway failed.

## THE FIRST SHOCK[1]

### Saturday, May 4, 1940

No one who studies the reactions of the British press, let alone those of neutral countries, can doubt the shock that the withdrawal from Mid-Norway has given. We have cut our losses at pretty small cost; that is something to be thankful for. But that is not all. What the ordinary man in this country and in every other sees is that the Allies have failed to protect yet another small country although they made the attempt.

Mr. Chamberlain now defends the lack of foresight by paying tribute to the enemy's cunning; Germany forestalled us by 'long-planned, carefully elaborated treachery against an unsuspecting and almost unarmed people.' But after our experience of Germany since Munich, should not that have been allowed for? He went on in the next sentence to describe how for 'many months' Germany had been massing transports and troops in Baltic ports, and how 'it is evident that some act of aggression was called for.' But because 'it was impossible to tell before-hand where the blow would fall' the British Government dispersed its major expeditionary force.[2]

Mr. Chamberlain complains that the poor victims of aggression 'gave us no warning of an attack, which, indeed, they never suspected.' Did they not? British interference with the Narvik route[3] was confidently forecast and also the certainty of Germany's retaliation. And all this before Mr. Chamberlain told his Tory audience that Hitler had 'missed the bus,' and before General Ironside[4] announced that 'we have actually turned the corner.' What Mr. Chamberlain forgets is that British action in Norwegian waters had been widely canvassed for

1. From a leader by A. P. Wadsworth.
2. Prepared to help Finland in her war against Hitler's ally, Russia, but Finland surrendered in March.
3. The Allies planned to stop the export of Swedish iron to Germany by mining Norwegian coastal waters.
4. Chief of the Imperial General Staff.

more than a week before it took place; the British Government should have known – as it would have known had it even read the English papers – that Germany would counter, and if possible anticipate, the move. Perhaps we shall get more enlightenment when the full story is told next week, but on the face of it Mr. Chamberlain's excuses do not speak well for the Government's prescience. What makes the taste of the whole episode so much more bitter is that it follows so much shallow optimism, not to say boasting from some Ministers. The complacency of the Prime Minister's speech to the Tory conference just before the German invasion was on the same level as his complacency about his pact of friendship with Mussolini and his innocence about his dealings with Hitler. His capacity for self-delusion is a national danger, for it damps the country's awareness of its peril and it almost certainly reflects a complacent handling of our conduct of the war. If Parliament does its duty next week perhaps even Mr. Chamberlain may be brought to understand that we cannot and will not go on in this way.

## 'IN THE NAME OF GOD, GO'

Wednesday, May 8, 1940
*From our Political Correspondent*[1]

Westminster, Tuesday
So far as the debate has gone it has changed nothing in the Parliamentary situation. That is, superficially. One cannot see into the mind of these four hundred Tories. To all appearances it has been just another debate, with the Tories rather more duteously than spontaneously cheering the Prime Minister and resenting criticism of him, the Opposition leaping at every chance of driving a point against the Government home.

And yet there was a difference – a very important difference. To-day's Prime Minister was not the Chamberlain of a few weeks ago; not the Chamberlain whom one heard telling the Tory Central Council that Hitler had missed the bus. The smile, one remembers, that accompanied that announcement to the Tory elect was superb in its self-satisfaction. He was not the cool, assured Chamberlain to-day. One missed the note of confidence in his case and in himself that he has invariably shown. But one can still hear those cheers from the embattled 'Yes men'. [Mr. Chamberlain] spent some time drawing out the

1. H. Boardman

lessons of Norway, and the lessons were those which the Opposition parties have been trying to teach him for months, so that the Labour and Liberal benches rocked with cheers at his discoveries. It was one illustration of Mr. Chamberlain's diminished confidence that he should not have seen the crude dialectical gifts he was making to his opponents; the earlier Chamberlain would have done it much more adroitly.

One lesson of Norway he had discovered was that we had not realised the extent or the imminence of the threat that is impending against us. (Here the Opposition cheered for a full minute, and Mr. Lloyd George with as much vigour as any of them.) We must beware of dispersing our forces, of bickerings and divisions. It was a time for closing our ranks. We should be much better occupied in increasing our war effort. (Again the Opposition struck in with an almost violent cheer.) 'And our production,' interjected a Labour member; and Mr. Chamberlain assented. 'Yes, production in material, 'planes, guns, everything.' We must increase our strength until we were able to deliver our blows where and when we willed. Mr. Chamberlain sat down.

The ironical cheers of the Opposition persisted, and it must be confessed the cheers of the Tories did not seem quite so fervent as when Mr. Chamberlain rose.

Drama touched the debate when Admiral Sir Roger Keyes[1] alleged in effect, if not in words, that Trondheim had been lost to us through faint hearts in Whitehall. He rose in his uniform of an admiral of the fleet, having donned it, as he explained, because he had come down to Westminster to speak for men in the fighting Navy who were very unhappy and who bore not a tittle of responsibility for what had happened at Trondheim. The House was full, the opening of the speech arresting in its implication. Mr. Churchill[2] sat a grave figure through the whole of the admiral's remarks.

The speech fulfilled all the hostile promise of that opening. He could regard the failure before Trondheim as nothing but a shocking story of ineptitude which ought never to have happened. The capture of Trondheim was imperative, vital, and if a few ships had entered the fiord when the Army was ready to co-operate the port could have been taken. Sir Roger made his own suggestions to the Admiralty and even undertook to organise and lead an attack on Trondheim himself, but, as he mournfully confessed, he found that minds were concentrated on

1. (1872–1945), commanded raid on Zeebrugge 1918; became first Director of Combined Operations Command later in 1940.
2. Then First Lord of the Admiralty.

the naval hazards and dangers in the Mediterranean and oblivious of the dangers that the Army ran, without naval co-operation.

It was very pointed how Sir Roger avoided associating Mr. Churchill with his strictures. He referred to Mr. Churchill only in terms of the greatest admiration, but admonished him to steel himself for vigorous action, because he possesses the confidence of the War Cabinet, the country, and the Navy. He ended by reminding Mr. Churchill and the House of Nelson's saying that the boldest measures are always the safest. So far this had been quite the most disturbing speech in the debate.

Sir Roger's speech will probably tell far more against the Government than Mr. Amery's[1] which followed, but Mr. Amery's speech was a sustained and harsh denunciation of the Government for its timidity and ineffectiveness, full of power, and concluding with the savage application to the Government of Cromwell's words to the Long Parliament, 'You have sat too long here for any good you have been doing. Depart, I say. Let us have done with you. In the name of God, go.'

Mr. Amery's philippic was delivered as usual to half-empty benches on his own side, but there was a goodly muster of the Opposition to hear him, including Mr. Lloyd George.

> After a second day's debate Chamberlain got a majority of 81, but 30 Conservatives voted against him and 60 abstained. Two days later the Germans invaded Holland and Belgium, Chamberlain resigned and Churchill became Prime Minister.

## THE TASK BEFORE US[2]

### Tuesday, June 14, 1940

Pitt died with the Austerlitz look on his face, but his heart was undismayed. The British people have had a blow far more severe than the ruin of Pitt's plans on that battlefield in 1805, but their courage will not falter. The French have been driven by the extremities of their distress to open negotiations, and we, like our fathers after Austerlitz,

> *. . . . are left or shall be left alone,*
> *The last that dare to struggle with the foe.*

1. L. C. M. S. Amery (1873–1955), Conservative Cabinet Minister 1922–1929; became Secretary of State for India under Churchill. As a young man he had had a short and adventurous time in the Balkans for the *Guardian*.

2. This leader is most likely by J. L. Hammond.

Yet not the last, for all the States that have been submerged in the flood of invasion are still represented by little armies of brave men, soldiers and symbols of the nation that they were in the past and the nation that they will be once again. But we are not merely the nation that fought after Austerlitz for ten anxious years (our plight was worse after Tilsit in 1807 than after Austerlitz), winning at the last the victory that seemed far beyond our reach. In those days the Britain that fought was the Britain of the two islands. To-day Britain is a great federation of independent peoples, drawing their strength and blood not only from these islands but from France and Holland, combining with the experience of age all the vigour and daring of youth. When Mussolini speaks of us as an old and decadent people, contrasted with the bursting energy of the young people whom he rules, as Mr. Trevelyan says, more drastically than ever Bourbon ruled them, our minds go back to the famous Canadian Division at Vimy Ridge, the Australians in Gallipoli, and the exploits of General Smuts in German Africa. All these peoples are vowed to the liberation of Europe, and none of them will draw back in the hour of catastrophe. That is a firmer coalition than any of those put together by the skill or the subsidies of Pitt and Castlereagh.

We know from the events of the last few months what kind of ordeal we have to face. The full extent of our difficulties and our perils we shall not be able to measure until we know the result of the negotiations between Marshal Pétain and the invaders. But at the best the strength of Germany and Italy, when France is subtracted from the alliance, offers a greater threat to our safety than was ever offered by Napoleon. Huge armies are at their disposal, and Hitler, at any rate, does not mind how much German blood he squanders on land or sea. Their naval force and their air force give them the power to make serious attempts on our shores, and our capacity for handling invasion, in all the difficult and complicated forms that it assumes to-day, will be tried soon and sternly.

We face an enemy or rather two enemies whose combined power on the land and in the air greatly surpasses our own. But our resources are not measured by our own equipment. The United States, it may be assumed, will not be less anxious to help us because we stand alone. The spirit of isolation has lost ground rapidly to a more generous temper. 'Who knows not that there is a mutual bond of amity and brotherhood between man and man over all the world; neither is it the English sea that can sever us from that duty and relation.' What Milton said of the English sea a larger world in the United States is saying to-day of the Atlantic Ocean. Whether that help can be made

*Thursday, January 16, 1969. A Drawing by Abu.*

effective depends on our own power of holding out. Germany has her own weaknesses. Her policy of spreading famine in Europe reacts on her own strength. Her people have made immense sacrifices, expecting early victory. Fox said of the war with Napoleon that the goodwill even of States too small to help was a source of strength to our arms and our policy. To-day every small State has to consider one thing only; how to avert from its own people the storm that has burst over others. As the months wear on, and as the confusion and distress that Hitler creates grow and spread, the dislike and discontent that he inspires may become an element of some importance. But the basis of our faith must be our own resolution. We are now to be tested as a nation. Nobody looking back can think of the last ten years without misgiving and dissatisfaction, for we played a poor part, wanting in spirit, imagination, and sense of duty to Europe. To-day the tone and temper of politics is completely changed. We add the obstinacy of our nature to the resolution with which we have undertaken the struggle for freedom.

We have a Prime Minister whose character has been moulded in a special school. Mr. Churchill has had a unique experience. For six years he has been warning Ministers of our danger in vain. He has lived day and night with this haunting and brooding fear. He has seen the evil force that he dreaded gathering strength in Europe. He has found himself at last called upon to lead the nation when the storm has burst on our shores. This experience seems to many to have affected his character and bearing. In the past he has been known as a brilliant orator, a dashing politician, a man ready for adventure and fond of excitement. To-day he has a depth, a kind of Gladstonian depth, in his speeches that suggests the outlook of a man who is living in spirit with the hopes and tragedies of history. The nation, faced with a summons that demands all its faith and all its courage, is fortunate in finding as its spokesman a man whose great natural gifts discipline has thus raised to a higher and more solemn power.

## The Fall and Rising Again of France

### THE PHONEY WAR: THE PAPERS AND THE CENSOR

Thursday, March 7, 1940

# FRENCH JOKES ON THE PRESS CENSORSHIP

# HOW THE BLANK SPACES WERE FILLED

For the first six months of the war there was a press censorship in France. Papers filled their blank spaces with pictorial comment such as these drawings from the *Oeuvre*, the *Lumière* and the

*Canard Enchainé* which Werth sent the *Guardian*. ('Anastasie' was the censor.) When the censorship was lifted Werth looked through his files to see what had been cut from his own messages. He wrote: 'A lot of the censored copy was extraordinarily harmless, and one could not help chuckling when one saw the following sentence crossed out by a heavy stroke of blue pencil: – "Soldiers on leave often remark that the front is the only place in France where there is perfect freedom of discussion." '

## FROM PARIS TO BORDEAUX

Monday, June 24, 1940
*From our former Paris Correspondent*

I left Paris in the early hours of Tuesday, June 11. It seems months ago. Since then I have dwelt in the two provisional capitals of France – Tours and Bordeaux. I have seen the tragic exodus of the people of Paris. I was at Tours when it was bombed. I have talked to refugees who were machine-gunned on the roads, though I missed that experience myself. It was not apparently practised on anything like the scale used in the case of the fugitives from Belgium.

To one who has lived in Paris and loved Paris and its people for fourteen years it is impossible in a brief article to record the thousand thoughts, emotions, and memories that filled one's mind and heart the moment one had to leave it with the knowledge that the Germans would be there in twenty-four hours or so and that the soul of all one had cherished would be dead, perhaps for many years. To leave there all my possessions, including five thousand books, seemed a trifling loss compared with everything else, and even to leave many old and helpless friends in Paris to a dark and perhaps dreadful future was merely part of the general disaster.

But I shall never forget that last night in Paris. All day thousands of cars had been streaming out of the town, and in the afternoon the main streets were still crowded. It was a hot, sunny day and I decided to go for a last walk along the familiar streets. It was strange. The Boulevard des Italiens looked much the same as usual. The shops were chock full of goods; a cinema was still open. I went into a familiar café. The fat, jovial old waiter thought the Boche would be in Paris within the next forty-eight hours – 'but it doesn't matter – on les aura quand même.' The owner had departed, and had left him in charge. 'I have been a war prisoner in Germany. I know how to deal with the swine,' he said.

But at night it was all different. I drove through deserted streets from the Place de l'Opéra to St. Cloud, where I was joining the party of three cars going to Tours. The only moment of animation was when we passed a crowd of soldiers – tattered, demoralised, ragged-looking, many of them drunk and shouting. There was a red sunset over Paris, and a strange kind of black haze I had never seen before.

When I reached my friend's house at the top of the hill at St. Cloud, with its magnificent panorama of Paris, I said to them when the luggage had been packed: 'Let us go on to the terrace and have another look at Paris.' What happened then was the uncanniest thing in my experience. We looked down and saw nothing – nothing but a black smoke-screen hiding Paris from our view. It was apparently the smoke-screen the Germans had used earlier in the day farther down the Seine to cross the river, and it had drifted eastward over the capital.

I shall not recount in any detail the drive from Paris to Tours. It took fourteen hours instead of the usual three. The first twenty miles were the most difficult of all; the roads were jammed with thousands of army lorries, vans, motor-cars, buses, cycles. It took over an hour to pass through Versailles. Darkness, dimmed head-lights, shouts of the military police, the rumbling of a thousand cars moving in jolts of one or two yards at a time – such was the exodus from Paris. After Rambouillet the driving became a little easier, and we were in the Beauce Plain.

In the villages the people looked with an air of bitter bewilderment at the procession of luggage and mattress-laden cars. At several places the roads were blocked by anti-tank barriers, and in a wood weary looking soldiers with rifles were on the watch for parachutists. At Chartres the cathedral looked strangely serene and alone in its calm beauty in the midst of all this anguish of the French people. Everybody seemed jumpy, nervous, irritable.

And then Tours. It was a kind of comic nightmare. The streets were unbelievably overcrowded, all houses and hotels were packed beyond capacity. Journalists, politicians, and others with familiar faces were sitting about the cafés in the Rue Nationale; little blue tram-cars were rattling across the Loire bridge; but for the luggage-laden cars one might have thought that a Radical congress was in progress. There was talk of Parliament meeting at Tours shortly. One of the hotels had been commandeered for the Senate, another for the Chamber. The Ministry of Information was being established in a ramshackle old building, the former post office.

We spent two days at Tours. On the third day the official people suddenly began to vanish, and by noon everybody had left. However, we stayed on another twenty-four hours. In the 'press room' at the Ministry of Information the job of repapering the walls was left half done. On that last afternoon at Tours we had an air raid; a dozen bombers flew fairly low over the city, and dropped bombs chiefly near the aerodrome. The next morning there was another air raid.

Our journey to Bordeaux was much less eventful. The bulk of the refugee cars had already passed. Bordeaux was all gloom, and there was a slightly panicky atmosphere in the place. It was known that the Government was deliberating 'somewhere in Bordeaux,' and it was said that Mr. Churchill had arrived,[1] but nothing definite was known. The censorship and cable services were scarcely functioning any more. The papers, whether local or the Paris ones now published here (after having for a few days been printed at Tours), were totally uninformative. Even the fall of Paris was announced only by implication. Sitting around the Girondin Column, with its odd horses with frogs' legs and the angel of liberty dancing on top of it, we fed on rumours.

All that was clear was that Reynaud wanted to continue the struggle at least in North Africa, but that those who wanted capitulation were gaining ground. The British in Bordeaux were becoming anxious; for what if the French signed an armistice and the Germans came overnight and occupied this Atlantic port? At the British Consulate there was a stream of anxious inquiries. At last we were told to be ready to leave the next day. We drove to the Pointe de Grave on the mouth of the Gironde to the very spot where the first American troops had landed in 1917. We had a last lunch at the foot of the memorial, and with a heavy heart we left French soil for the British ship anchored at some distance from the shore. Thanks largely to the efficiency of the captain and crew a ship normally holding a hundred and fifty passengers brought comfortably to England no fewer than fifteen hundred.

Once we were attacked by a German bomber while still anchored off the French coast, the next day another bomber was driven off right over our ship and brought down some distance away. Soon after leaving French waters we and another ship were joined by a destroyer. For the last time we looked out on the vanishing shores of France. There was a glorious red and orange and lilac sunset at night. But the light was not on the same side as the French coast, which looked dim and dark. It was on the side of England and America.

---

1. Erroneously. Churchill had been in Tours on June 13. He did not return to France for four years.

## THE FATALISM OF PÉTAIN

Thursday, June 27, 1940
*From our former Paris Correspondent*[1]

London, Wednesday

There seems to be a considerable amount of misconception in this country on the real nature of the French Government.[2] To treat it, as some papers have done, as a 'Right-wing Fascist Government' is misleading. It certainly represents various pro-Fascist tendencies, and the anti-British spirit (which has been quite badly stimulated in France by recent events), but it also represents a point of view peculiar to France of recent years.

In the view of some of the men around Marshal Pétain it is better to keep the French people alive, even through a long period of eclipse, than to run the risk of their extermination. These people liked to take a long view of things, and to play with historical analogies such as the civilising influence exerted in the long run by the conquered Gauls on the Franks, and at the tiny piece of territory around Paris to which at one moment in the fifteenth century the Kingdom of France was temporarily reduced.

This 'decrepit France' idea of Marshal Pétain goes, paradoxically enough, hand in hand with the 'renewal through eclipse' ideas held in certain other quarters, particularly among men of the neo-Socialist school, like M. Déat.

M. Déat took the coming defeat of France for granted for a good long time. After the break-through on the Meuse I heard him remark in the Chamber lobbies, 'Better to make peace on the Somme than on the Seine; on the Seine than on the Loire; on the Loire than on the Garonne,' and the old pro-Munich people now use as their invincible argument, 'If we acted as we did, it was to save you this – which we foresaw.'

As I often pointed out in the past, Munich defeatism was by no means a monopoly of the Right. There were very strong defeatist currents among all the parties, not least among the Radicals and the Socialists. All these Pacifist Left-wing elements are represented in the Pétain Government, and it is therefore erroneous to regard it as a 'Right-wing' Government. It comprises inveterate defeatists of every party.

1. Alexander Werth
2. Pétain had become head of the French government on June 16; the armistice with Germany was signed on the 22nd.

The belief that France 'cannot die' and that she must fight out her own salvation, no matter through how many years of suffering and agony, is deep-rooted in the French mind. One of the most pathetic sights on board the ship on which I sailed from Bordeaux was the fearful internal conflict that went on in the minds of many of the French refugees on board while the ship was still anchored off the French coast. The outcome of this conflict – which manifested itself in some painful family scenes – was that a large number of French passengers decided to disembark and return to Bordeaux, whatever the dangers awaiting them there. Such is that attachment of the French to their native soil, this determination to 'stay together' in France regardless of the calamities through which she was passing.

This feeling of loyalty to the native soil, even defiled by the invader and betrayed by a clique of politicians, is typical of the French character, and it explains in a large measure why so few potential leaders, except some of those in immediate danger of being murdered, have gone abroad. The French people, though they have fled from Paris to Tours and Bordeaux, do not seem on the whole to have made any desperate attempt to go any farther. They are staying in France for better or worse, preparing, perhaps, for passive resistance against the invader.[1]

## PARIS FREED

### Monday, August 28, 1944

The *Guardian* had two accounts by its own men available for that Monday's paper. David Woodward, who had been with Montgomery's 21 Army Group apart from a spell in hospital, sent a story which should have made Saturday's paper if it had not been delayed in transmission. J. R. L. Anderson, who similarly had been with SHAEF (Eisenhower's headquarters) sent a message on Saturday which carried the story on.

### FRIDAY MORNING[2]

Advanced elements of the Second French Armoured Division entered the city last night about ten o'clock, fought their way through the German positions, and reached the headquarters of the French Forces of the Interior,[3] in the Place de l'Hôtel de Ville.

1. De Gaulle had escaped from Bordeaux on June 17 and broadcast from London that night to the French people.
2. By David Woodward          3. The Resistance

With a group of other correspondents I set out for Paris this morning in a jeep, sandwiched between units of the French armour.

First it was a tear across the open countryside, and then the villages grew closer and closer together, blending into a metropolitan whole. At the street corners the people had equipped themselves with boxes of tomatoes, which they handed out as soon as there was the slightest check in the traffic. The more enthusiastic of the people, in fact, threw them at us, but the majority were more careful and made sure they were not wasted by pressing them in our hands. It is a tomato-growing district. Tomatoes were all they had and we could have them, but they wanted to make sure they were not wasted – huge, luscious things, more beautiful than any I have ever tasted.

Across the landscape there was a pillar of towering smoke from burning oil wells. As we went forward for us the most nerve-racking moments were not when an odd shot was heard but when we became involved in those road checks just before the front which are the bane of the lives of all war correspondents. We explained ourselves to a French officer of the division wearing the russet-red forage cap which is its badge and then started off once again. We did not know where we were going or how far we would get, but it was the road to Paris.

On through villages and then into Montrouge, where each of the cross streets was barricaded off with heaps of paving stones and where the trees along the road had been obviously shot through. In the middle of this famous working-class district the women, gathered in the middle of the street, cheered us by. There were very few men around, for there are very few men in Montrouge who are not with the F.F.I. – or who are not in Germany as prisoners of war or as slaves.

We went on through the area of the Porte d'Orléans through streets of closed, shabby shops and groups of very happy people. We got to the Place Denfert-Rochereau with its huge statue of the Lion of Belfort commemorating the bravery of the people of Paris in 1870–71. As we entered the broad street lined with plane trees, undistinguished but as much Paris as anything in the city, we were halted and told that the Germans were dug in in the Luxembourg Gardens down the street.

There were a few shots and lorry loads of F.F.I. in their dirty, worn working clothes went by. As they went they kept their tommy-guns trained on the rooftops. In the middle of the atmosphere of joyousness which overrode the strain, we parked our jeeps on the pavement and started to write what impressions we could give of a moment's glimpse of history. The French surged round us with wine and newspapers. A closed café was hastily opened for us by the patron – a soldier of that army which saved the world in 1914-18 – and we established ourselves at work in mirrored halls amidst piles of tables while the patron and his family fussed about us with more wine and cigars which he had 'acquired' from the Germans.

Outside the long line of French armour went crashing down the street amidst renewed cheers. It was the French Army redeeming Paris, and it was for most of the French soldiers their first sight of Paris since their mobilisation four or five years ago. As the tanks crashed by many of them wrote notes, rolled them up, and threw them into the crowd. I picked one up. It was a message to anyone who found it to tell the parents of the writer who lived in such and such a street that André was safe.

Outside in the street as we worked at our stories our conducting officers and our drivers held court. They were probably the only British troops in the city, and the Parisians, in spite of the wild surge of thankfulness with which they greeted their own men and their cheerfulness for the Americans, were seriously determined that the British Army should have its honours.

A man passed down the street selling copies of the *Figaro*, which had just been produced an hour or so before by French patriots who had seized the plant. It is before me as I write, and from it I summarise an account of the liberation of Paris from within.

The Parisian expected that the relief would be effected by a vast number of Americans in daylight. Instead it was done by a small party of Frenchmen in the first instance. Amongst them was a man who had by the underground movement managed to pass word to his fiancée to meet him at the Place de l'Hôtel de Ville at an appointed time. When his tank clanked into the square his fiancée was waiting.

### FRIDAY NIGHT[1]

Last night (Friday) I watched the French mop up the last organised German resistance in the Senate building at the Luxembourg Palace, but to get there I had to walk all over the area of the left bank of the Seine, dodging down side streets which were not commanded by enemy fire and hastening forward when I found myself alone in a street with no one except the ever-present white-coated doctors and nurses from the nearby hospital in evidence. These medical personnel have been working throughout the fighting, and never seemed to bother about taking cover at all.

At the Seine itself the lead-covered locked-up stalls of the second-

1. By J. R. L. Anderson

hand book-sellers were still there, and across the river was Notre-Dame, untouched save for bullet splashes – about fifty of them – on the principal façade. From it flew the Tricolor masthead high, but on the other side of the square the French colours flew at half-mast from the police barracks and prefecture as a salute to the patriots who had been killed in those badly battered buildings. The inside of Notre-Dame was dark, cool, and completely empty.

I went back to the Luxembourg, having been told by a weary police commissioner that that was now the only German position holding out, the French having taken in succession the École de Mines in the Boulevard St. Michel, the Ecole Militaire at the Invalides, the buildings round the Place de la Concorde, and the Hôtel Majestic – the German military headquarters.

I went by the back streets to the Rue de Vaugirard, in front of the palace, just as a French Sherman with a seventeen-pounder knocked out two German Rénault tanks under the trees and then, coming up to point-blank range, started firing straight into the palace from about ten yards. Whilst this was going on an old woman, one of those black-dressed, white-haired old women of Paris, appeared and began moving through the streets still commanded by the German weapons and picking up likely bits of wooden wreckage and branches of the trees shot down by the guns. This she piled in barrows and took away for firewood.

A few rounds from the Sherman and a white flag appeared from somewhere and French Gardes Mobiles in black helmets and tunics went in to fetch out their prisoners. The Germans came out with their commanding officer last, a tall, thin, middle-aged man wearing the ribbon of the Iron Cross in the button-hole of his tunic. He looked deathly tired, but very spick and span compared with the dusty Frenchmen.

The crowd had let the other prisoners go with boos and cat-calls, but they rushed forward towards this officer and for a few minutes the Gardes Mobiles had to work hard to save his life while he watched, white-faced but rigid, from the front seat of a jeep.

I thought that my adventures for the day were over, but as I made my way home in the dusk fighting quite literally and frighteningly broke out on all sides of me, with tracers coming up and going down four different streets at a cross-road and bullets striking sparks on the pavement as they ricocheted by, with enemy snipers, French patriots' rifles, machine-guns, and twelve-pounders joining in.

From a pile of sand bags alongside the Panthéon I looked down the Rue Soufflet, deserted and with a couple of shops on fire down at the far end nearest the Luxembourg. Splashes of white on the houses caused by bullets and splinters were everywhere. I went on to the Seine past a six-pounder dug in behind a barricade of wrecked German lorries, paving-stones, and furniture which had been firing up the hill from the corner of the Boulevard St. Germain and the Boulevard St. Michel. All the streets leading to the river had been barricaded here, but some of the barricades were already being dismantled.

## SATURDAY[1]

This afternoon General de Gaulle rode at the head of his troops from the Unknown Soldier's tomb at the Arc de Triomphe to the Cathedral of Notre-Dame. With resistance on a big scale at an end last night, the first part of to-day was celebrated with the greatest light-heartedness and enthusiasm.

But while the tail-end of General de Gaulle's procession was passing down the Rue de Rivoli fire was opened on it opposite the Louvre and firing in the Rue de Rivoli and the neighbourhood continued inter-mittently for two hours afterwards as the F.F.I. moved from house-top to house-top rounding up French Fascists who were the cause of the trouble.

There is no clear indication at time of writing that an attempt was made on General de Gaulle's life. If anything of the sort was in any-body's mind, they missed far better chances earlier in the afternoon, when the General himself with his forces, first General Leclerc's armour and then lorryloads of F.F.I., went down the Champs Elysées. Nothing occurred then save that after the trials of four years Paris gave the General the reception of which this steadfast man must always have dreamed during his long exile and his tenacious rebuilding first of French spirit, then of the French Empire, and now of France.

It was upon the hangers-on to the procession, who had added them-selves to it in a free-and-easy way which recalled pre-war France, that fire was opened.

A great outburst of cheering had greeted the arrival of General de Gaulle at the Place de la Concorde, on foot, and accompanied by men of the F.F.I. and the French forces. The crowd were dispersing, happy and gay. Thousands were pressing through the roads leading off from the place.

It was this moment that German snipers and their French Fascist collaborators chose to turn machine-gun fire on the crowd from upper windows and roofs. Many people, like seasoned soldiers, flung them-

1. By J. R. L. Anderson

selves to the ground under the cover of the buildings on either side of the road. Soon people were piled up on top of each other and there was not room for everyone. And so many ran on hoping to get round a safe corner or beyond range.

But – either by prearranged plan or because other snipers, hearing shooting, followed suit – firing broke out in many parts at this hour – four o'clock. Men of the F.F.I. returned the fire of the snipers immediately.

The snipers were in church towers and steeples, at upper windows and on roofs. I turned into the Rue Honoré. This was for some minutes a hot sector. Snipers were shooting along the street from either end, and the F.F.I. were returning the fire both ways from the middle of the street. People turned for shelter into the entrances to apartments, shops, and air-raid shelters. In this part there seemed to be remarkably few casualties, but occasionally amid the shooting Red Cross workers would wheel by a man, woman or child who had been wounded.

Soldiers and men of the F.F.I. were to be seen searching the roofs of tall buildings. A German sniper wearing civilian clothes was caught near the Hôtel de Ville. A woman heard him whistling to another sniper on an adjoining roof. Men of the F.F.I. mounted to the roof and captured him. He wore two pistols, had a hand-grenade in either pocket of his trousers, and had a rifle as well.

The view of the ceremony to-day at the Arc de Triomphe which I had was of that gracious monument standing against the blue sky of a Paris summer draped in a huge French flag which hung from the top nearly to the ground. One had so often hoped to see it like this, and here it was. But too solemn reflections were dissipated instantly by the riotously cheerful crowd. It swarmed over all, including British and American Army transport, which became mobile grand stands, willy nilly, for the Parisians as they drove about the city.

# From Dunkirk to D-Day

## THE MIRACLE OF THE B.E.F.'s RETURN

Saturday, June 1, 1940
*By E. A. Montague*

Fleet Street, Friday

In the grey chill of dawn to-day in a South-eastern port war correspondents watched with incredulous joy the happening of a miracle. By every canon of military science the B.E.F. has been doomed for the last four or five days. Completely out-numbered, out-gunned, out-'planed, all but surrounded, it had seemed certain to be cut off from its last channel of escape. Yet for several hours this morning we saw ship after ship come into harbour and discharge thousands of British soldiers safe and sound on British soil.

We went down to our reception port last night by a train which took more than twice the usual time to cover the distance. The reason was easy to see. Again and again we stopped outside a station while the dim shape of a troop train shot past us northward bound.

When at last we reached the port in the small hours, the chief hotel was packed and every armchair in the lounge held its sleeping soldier or sailor, huddled beneath overcoat or ground sheet. Most of us lay down for a couple of sleepless hours on the floor, and were proud to do it.

As the rising sun was turning the grey clouds to burnished copper the first destroyer of the day slid swiftly into the harbour, its silhouette bristling with the heads of the men who stood packed shoulder to shoulder on its decks. As it slowed down and drifted towards the dock side the soldiers on board shouted cheerful ribaldries to us who stood watching them with a mixture of pride and pity. They at any rate did not regard themselves as the central figures of tragic drama. The gangways were in position in no time – on these ships all ceremony had been waived for the time being – and the unconscious heroes began to clamber upwards to the soil of England.

One watched them with a pride that became almost pain as one cheerful, patient figure succeeded another. They had passed through nights and days of hunger, weariness, and fear, but nearly every man still had his rifle and a clip or two of ammunition: nearly all had brought away their full kit with them – and what an agony its weight must have been at times; most of them had shaved, and quite a number were carrying the extra burden of a Lewis gun or a Bren gun. Their eyes were red with weariness above dark bags of tired skin, but they were still soldiers and still in good heart.

The wonder of their self-discipline became all the greater when one heard their stories. They were of all units and ranks. Some were in the position of the gunners whose battery had been shelled out of existence near Oudenarde, because our overworked fighter 'planes had had no time to deal with the German reconnaissance 'planes. Their battery commander had told them to do the best they could for themselves now that their usefulness had gone, and they had walked thirty miles to Dunkirk, there to take their chance on the Dunkirk beach, which will become as famous in history as the beaches of Gallipoli.

All the stories of the men skirt inarticulately round the beach at Dunkirk. It was, and is, the place to which the isolated but unbroken men came to wait their turn for the ships which came through shell fire and bombing to rescue them. It is a stretch of level sand backed by dunes. The sea in front of it is shallow for some way out, so that ships cannot come close in, and successive sand-banks parallel to the shore catch at the keels of rowing-boats which come in at low tide.

Many of the men have spent two or three or four days on this beach, hiding in hollows scratched in the sand or in communal dug-outs in the dunes from the German 'planes which have scourged them with bomb and machine-gun. Their nights have been sleepless, and they have lived only on biscuits and water. Yet even here discipline holds. Units have been told off to look after 'beach organisation' and to detail men for embarkation whenever one of the gallant destroyers moors beside the jetty.

At other times the various craft, which are risking their lives to rescue the soldiers, cannot come near the shore. When that happens the men must row themselves out in small boats or swim to the waiting ships. I met a Staff officer to-day who had spent the last twelve hours before his embarkation in the sea, continuously in water up to his waist, helping to push off the boats which had grounded on the sand-banks. For a large part of the time he was under fire.

Even when the men have embarked their danger is not over. Every now and then among the men who climb the gangplank into England one sees stretcher-bearers carrying a still form, its face bloodless and remote in some dream of pain, its bandages white and brilliantly stained. It is a man who has been hit by one of the shells from the German shore batteries, or by a bomb from the 'planes which on occasion have pursued the ships to within a few miles of the British coast.

Yet they survive in their tens of thousands and are able to joke and sing as they march ashore.

Their condition is astonishingly good. Perhaps one man in a thousand is shaking with nerves and obviously fit for nothing but hospital. The rest are clearly tired, hungry, and in most cases footsore. They walk stiffly, and some of them obviously find it painful to walk at all.

But there is nothing wrong with them which a few days' rest and good feeding will not put right, and their fighting spirit is quite unweakened. Men who were really exhausted would not be able to talk to reporters; these men can and apparently enjoy doing it, and without being bombastic they make it clear that they are still as good soldiers as ever they were. They are most comforting to see and hear. Their only bitterness is about the lack of R.A.F. 'planes to defend them from the German bombers and that, alas! is no news to us.

The long string of steel-helmeted men passes steadily but swiftly up the gang-plank and away into the station, where they will be put into trains, fed, and dispatched to depots, where they can be reorganised and rested. A few stretcher cases are hoisted out of the ship in slings, the litter of forgotten kit is cleared away into sorting sheds, and in no time the ship is ready to return to Dunkirk.

But long before it is ready another has drawn up alongside, and as often as not the men on the second ship are being unloaded across the decks of the first.

British ships and French and Dutch, warships, drifters, trawlers, yachts, barges, they bring their loads across the hostile Channel and then go back undaunted into the inferno, where Navy and Air Force and Army are fighting furiously to keep open the last loophole of escape for our men. All the selfless courage of two nations is being thrown into the resistance at Dunkirk, and it looks as if it will not be spent in vain.

## READY FOR INVADERS

Thursday, July 18, 1940
*By E. A. Montague*
London, Wednesday

For the last two days I have been travelling through a strange new England, an England stripped and armed for defence against the invader. And yet to a war correspondent it has been hauntingly familiar. Those curiously painted lorries hidden in the orchard, those figures in battle dress lounging under the trees – did I not see them east of Arras last October? The road blocks and strong points outside country towns – it seems only yesterday that I was held up at them by armed peasants outside the villages of Normandy. It was like living in a two-day dream of France.

My tour took me through a big area of that part of Britain which may be threatened by invasion. From the coast to points far away inland I saw evidence that we have not wasted our time.

One cannot describe in any detail what our defences are. They include all the obvious things – pill-boxes, gun-pits, infantry strong points, barbed wire by the hundred miles so it seemed – and certain other things which are not so obvious.

One thing which struck me was the thoroughness with which the construction part of the defence had been carried out. Both the planning and the building have been careful. I saw one battery of howitzers whose crews had dug, fortified, and camouflaged their positions, working day and night. I never saw in France such sound and well-concealed gun-pits.

This battery was some distance back from the coast. It had been given certain most important targets on which to fire in certain circumstances, and was ready to fire on them at a moment's notice at any time of day or night. The crews demonstrated how quickly they could throw off their blankets, man their guns, and go into action. They were keen and confident.

A seaside town was almost deserted by civilians. The sands were empty – empty on a July afternoon. Everything looked normal, apart from the emptiness. It was only when one looked closely that one saw curious alterations in the scene. From a short distance they were invisible. There is nothing wrong with our camouflage.

Driving along the country roads between fields of ripening corn one wondered where the soldiers were. An officer in an innocent-seeming country house told us. The house was the headquarters of a formation whose men were manning trenches and strong points hidden all over the countryside. I thought of France last autumn, and of how difficult it was to realise that two army corps of British troops were hidden in the bare autumn landscape of Artois. In this rich, leafy country concealment is much easier. The troops are there, though one does not see them unless one knows where to look. Army, Navy, and Air Force will be working together when the invasion starts. In a harbour I saw some of the ships which will pounce on the German expeditionary force and harry it as it makes its slow and painful way towards our coast. On an aerodrome ground staffs were working on some of the

Blenheims that have been bombing German barges wherever they began to gather menacingly.

At another aerodrome I talked to young fighter pilots whose most recent job has been to protect our convoys from German bombers. One of them, who talked eagerly about everything connected with his work except the number of his own victims – he has six confirmed victories to his credit – was an Austrian with a famous name. He and his fellows are bubbling with confidence, happy in their machines, and serenely assured that in any fight, whatever the circumstances they will bring down at least three German 'planes to every British one that is lost.

I came back out of this strange new England into familiar London confident that the men who have designed this widely spread interlocking system of defence have taken all the possible forms of invasion into account.

## DAD'S ARMY

### Thursday, August 2, 1940

#### A SONG OF THE L.D.V.[1]
*By Lord Dunsany*

If ever for the L.D.V.
  A badge they should intend,
Give us no star of blazonry,
Of crown or crest, but let it be
  Rather some simple blend
Of traveller's-joy and bryony,
Or such wild blooms as feed the bee
  On hills that we defend.

Allegiance to the Crown our corps
  Have all learned long ago,
But never have we fought before,
  As we are soon to do,
For England's King on his own land,
Where hills of chalk watch wealds of sand
  And hear the thrush's trills.
Give us for badge what some child's hand
  Might gather on those hills.

1, Local Defence Volunteers, the original name of the Home Guard,

## THE LOSS OF THE WESTERN PRINCE

Thursday, December 19, 1940
*From James Bone, London Editor of the 'Manchester Guardian'*
*(who was a passenger in the torpedoed liner)*[1]

A West Coast Port, Wednesday

To-day 140 passengers and crew of the liner *Western Prince*, torpedoed in the Atlantic on Saturday, were landed here from a steamer which came to the rescue. Her name cannot be given at present but it will always be remembered by the rescued so long as they live. Nothing could exceed the skill, resource, and complete hospitality which the captain, his officers, and crew gave to us.

The liner was torpedoed about six o'clock in the dark morning with strong seas running. Just before she plunged we heard two blasts on the whistle. 'That's the old man's last words – "Good-bye to you," ' said a sailor near me in lifeboat No. 3.

Six passengers and eleven of the crew are missing, including Captain John Reed, a Scot of 56, heavily built, deliberate, with the look of a man of strong resolution. It is not thought by his colleagues that he intended to go down with his ship, but that events and his own sense of responsibility to others brought that end about.

Captain Charlton told me that Captain Reed had handed to him his overcoat and had asked to have a lifeboat about later – 'might need it.' Captain Charlton thought that Captain Reed's intention was to try for a boat or a raft at the last. The second officer, Mr. R. F. White, who remained with Captain Reed, was rescued from a raft.

The third man aboard the *Western Prince* was Franks, a steward, who had a personal attachment to the captain. He was seen by one of the last passengers with the purser's key, going down to get the Spitfire Fund raised by the crew to bring it to safety. Another passenger told me that Franks, who was a taciturn man with dark hair and grim humour, said, when pressed to hurry, that he was staying on 'to do a bit of looting.'

All the boats were away within half an hour. There was no rush or shouting. Even the officers gave their orders quietly as the passengers and crew of the liner took their places in the boats.

Three babies were carried aboard without excitement, and the women, who included a mother superior returning with her novice

1. Bone was 68 and recovering from an operation.

after strange experiences in China, took their places with steady step. It was a company that recalled Kipling's story – men from many parts of the Far East and from America, experts in many techniques and trades, a major general with many decorations from the last war, and a colonel who was one of the heroes of Dunkirk, banking advisers and a Treasury lawyer, a shipbuilder, and a Labour candidate (Mr. G. E. G. Catlin, the writer on political science whose wife is Vera Brittain) were among them.

Mr. Howe afterwards, in the rescue ship, said that he had read of passengers fighting for places in a lifeboat, but the crew's difficulty that dark morning was to get passengers into the boats. Everything was orderly and nerves did not react on nerves.

The story of lifeboat No. 3 was much like that of the others. Passengers had prepared, and most of them slept in clothes. When I came on deck the port lifeboats had gone and the starboard were filling. There was a heavy swell, and in the effort to keep off the ship's side oars were broken and the lifeboat's sides were tested. It was a struggle to get away from the ship's sides in the strong swell, but we drew away slowly and rode to about one hundred yards away. We saw a light on the ship and rowed back past the stern, looking out for stragglers in the water. The waves were about twenty feet high, and when we came on another lifeboat it seemed a miniature thing.

All the boats used their sea anchors, which helped in the hard job of keeping their heads to the wind with the heavy oars. Many became sick, including a surprising number of sailors. They lay about, clogging the oarsmen and increasing the congestion at the oars. Suggestions were made in three of the boats, one learned afterwards, to hoist sail. Had that been done they would probably have been lost, away from the area of the rescue ship.

Newfoundlanders did especially good work at the oars, particularly Basil White, a youth whose sturdy pluck put new heart into the weaker men. Mr. R. C. Thompson, head of a Sunderland shipbuilding firm, and Mr. J. Tansey, of the Bank of England, were at the oars all the time, with occasional rests when the sea anchors were out – a remarkable test of strength and endurance. The boats kept company as the only hope of succour. In No. 3 boat there was much congestion, as so many of the 35 occupants were sick. Beside me was imperturbable Mr. Howe, and in front General Macrae, who pulled manfully at an oar the whole time while different men pulled.

A tense moment was when we heard the chief officer saying, not loudly, 'Keep quiet; say nothing; do not show a light.' A ship appeared about twenty yards away on the starboard side of our lifeboat, the tower and part of the deck of the German submarine. She submerged as she passed by, and there was a flash which was thought to mean that photographs of us had been taken. I watched closely the faces of the sailors and firemen, massed in our bows, watching the enemy. I saw no fear in their eyes, but a terrible tension like a white shadow passed over their faces. 'I thought he was going to give us the machine-guns,' said one sailor as he relaxed.

We had been taking in water and the seas broke over the sides, and it was discovered that the after plug at the bottom of the boat was missing, probably jumped out as she struck the water. The first mate did a good job of work down in the bilge, almost flat and wet through, recovering the plug and fixing it in its place. Fast baling in cramped positions in the crowded boat followed.

The boats still hung together, tiny objects in the high waves, whilst squalls of rain and hail passed over us. About six hours had gone – it seemed like six months, – and then Mr. Warburton, a passenger, said in a conversational tone. 'Why, there is a ship; I can see it quite plain.' He pointed without standing up. We had been hoping and praying for that, but there was no shouting. When an officer was hoisted up he could not see anything. The passenger was sure, and soon we could all see a steamer and its smoke. Faster pulling at the oars, but not much progress. Would she pass us? Only now and then could we see the other boats.

We fired five of our nine lights from the patent pistol. It was now barely light, but the orange flares could be seen suspended by the little parachutes after the charge had exploded. Other boats fired their flares, although some counselled prudence. We might need them in the night. It became clear that the ship was approaching, and about one and a half hours later No. 3 boat was under the lee side of the ship. This ship's captain manœuvred cleverly to give us shelter, and oil was thrown over to help us. The sea had increased and we needed all help. Just before we came alongside the sun came out – a grim smile as the boat seemed to huddle itself against the ship's side.

Roderick Henderson, the two-year-old baby, was hoisted in the basket with a lifeline round him in case it capsized. The strong and young scurried up the rope ladders on the ship's side. The elderly and the women climbed up with lifelines round their waists. It took some time, and before we were all up the motor lifeboat was alongside and capsized. I saw men standing on the upturned boat, holding on to ropes, and some of them were in the water. It seemed like a picture in the cinema. I found one's emotional qualities quite dulled and one took everything in a literal way as by instinct until it was all over.

The other boats came up and the empty ones were allowed to drift away. The mother superior came up in the basket, but the novice, Sister Muldoon, the young Irish girl, came up the ladder herself. Afterwards she was wearing the overcoat of Captain Reed, which Captain Charlton had brought on board, but she did not know that. Sir Cecil Carr, the Treasury lawyer, and his wife climbed the ladder skilfully, and Mr. Gick, of the Admiralty, went up and over as in drill. One of the babies was in a case like a dog's basket marked 'Baby, with care.' It came up in the basket, and when Captain Charlton, who had taken a personal interest in its packing, opened the case the infant crowed at him and he said, 'Well, you sweet little thing.' Later, in the rescue ship, the little boy Roderick Henderson was wearing a pair of tiny moccasins which the third officer made from Mistress Henderson's lambskin snow-shoes.

The rescue ship did wonders in succouring the weaker and ill among us. It was blowing up heavily at night and there would have been little chance of the lifeboats riding it out in that sea. The line between wives and widows was a very close one that Saturday.

## MALTESE SPRINGBOARD

Thursday, August 5, 1943
*From E. A. Montague, our Special Correspondent*

With the Eighth Army
in Sicily, August 3

After so much suffering bravely endured – first war, then famine produced by the enemy blockade – the Maltese are exulting in the thought that from their island more than any other single place was launched our attack on the Italians, whom they now hate so bitterly.

For weeks before the invasion of Sicily Malta was packed with troops, and her harbours, even her smallest coves, with shipping. Famous generals with faces known to the whole world went to and fro in her streets. Every Maltese knew – must have known – what was in the wind. But as far as I know not one word leaked out to the enemy. Certainly he made no attempt to bomb the immensely valuable target which Malta presented at that time. Maltese in shops or bars used to look at us quizzically and smile, and sometimes made some obscure knowing remark, but in my experience they never asked questions and never told what they knew or guessed.

To act as a transit camp was the least of Malta's functions. Before and during the first few days of the Sicilian campaign it was the head-quarters from which that campaign was controlled. General Eisenhower, General Alexander, and General Montgomery all worked there with their staffs in rooms hewn out of solid rock, where they worked at unvarnished, wooden tables as simply as if they had been in the field. During the early phase of the invasion the Allied High Command controlled it from Malta by wireless.

It was fighter 'planes from Malta airfields that escorted our assault troops and protected them after their landings until we had airfields working in Sicily. There are even fighting in Sicily troops who have left wives behind them in Malta. No wonder the island feels itself proudly and deeply concerned in the Sicilian campaign.

It was more than a week before the invasion that I came to Malta in a convoy of assault ships which made a slow and tortuous voyage from America. The secret was well kept and none of us knew what our final destination was to be, though many guessed. Our decks were covered with transport ranged wheel to wheel.

On the way we were attacked by enemy bombers with a vigour which earned us the honour of mention in a communiqué: 'Persistent enemy air attacks on one of our convoys.' We were impressed by our own importance when we heard it on the wireless, but mildly surprised. Only two or three times, at long intervals, had we heard the swiftly swelling roar as enemy 'planes swooped down on us out of the sunset and seen the almost leisurely upheaval of smoky water out of the calmly shining sea as a bomb burst below the surface. The fact was that Malta fighters had guarded us from afar, turning back most of the enemy bombers beyond our sight and hearing.

Once in Malta we waited and waited for the mysterious moment. Staff officers with esoteric jobs and complicated titles arrived by the score every day. Ships came in, unloaded men and stores, and slipped away again. We correspondents marked time, forbidden to write, and so idled among the busy thousands.

We wandered among the narrow streets of bombed Valletta, past the wrecked shops and bars with their proudly English names. We endured with what patience we might the dust and the stifling heat and the endless swarms of mosquitoes and sandflies. We bathed every afternoon, and Frank Gillard, of the B.B.C., and I swam long distances in the harbour to keep fit just in case of certain eventualities. In the end they never happened. We stepped ashore on Sicily as prosaically as if we were stepping off a bus.

The day came at last. We had guessed it for two days earlier. Men of the Highland Division in Malta had suddenly put on their divisional badges. That was a gay night in Valletta. The next day we were told what was planned, and that night we lay in bed thinking long of the men in the darkened ships steaming in their hundreds from east and west and south to their places in the silent battle line.

There was thunderous murmur in the sky, swelling and then dying away, and when we ran to windows we saw in the light of the young moon the laden gliders and towing 'planes and big carriers full of parachutists streaming like birds across the sky.

General Alexander was standing on a headland to see them pass on their way from Africa to Sicily, and on another headland was General Eisenhower with some of his staff. As the 'planes went past close inshore and low over the sea General Eisenhower stood at the salute.


## THE BATTLE FOR ORTONA

Wednesday, December 22, 1943
*From C. Ray, our Special Correspondent*[1]

With the Eighth Army
December 20

Canadian tanks and infantry were in the outskirts of Ortona before dusk this evening. Fighting is still going on. The main attack went in from the cross-roads where the coastal road from San Vito joins the Orsogna road: the cross-roads we had taken at half-past three yesterday afternoon. A secondary attack went in up the secondary easterly road, which is little more than a cliff track.

The secondary attack was meant primarily to secure the right flank of the main advance into town, and possibly as something of a diversion. But it seemed that the Germans might expect the centre of our advance to be, as it was, along the main road and be unprepared for a flank attack, and that thus the men taking part in it would be first into town. So I attached myself to it. We went forward in single file, crouching because of mortar fire, along the cliff face. We were within a mile and a half of the town, or thereabouts. A gully separated us from the town, which we could see clearly, apparently little damaged. As we scrambled down into the gully we could hear the crackle of machine-guns from our left. The main attack was under way. Shells still whooshed over and thumped on the far side of the town. We stopped every three or four minutes while our leader, an English company commander, reconnoitred ahead. We leaned against the slope of the

1. Cyril Ray had relieved Montague who was seriously ill.

ground to rest as he did so, the signallers especially being glad to ease the weight of their radio sets from their backs.

In the bottom of the gully we sprinted, doubled up, one at a time across the open cross-roads, then into the safety of a culvert and through a brick factory. There was a minefield here, and a German had been blown up in it.

Out of the gully again and up a sandy bluff. It was hard for the soldiers to scramble up cumbered with their rifles, tommy-guns, and the rest. You shoved at the seat of the man in front of you and he turned to give you a hand up. It was a change to see the next man's face instead of the back of his neck and to exchange wisecracks. All the men were joking.

At the top was a place where the cliff path was open to view from the north, and snipers' bullets were pinging across; first the whip-crack of the rifle, then the bullet. We nipped across smartly, one at a time. You could not feel frightened or hang back when the others were so neat and cheerful about it. Nobody was hurt. (Half an hour later, I learned afterwards, the American correspondent, Lynn Heinzerling of the Associated Press, had a narrow escape here. A bullet went through his coat, blouse, and shirt and left a long ugly weal on his upper arm but did not break the skin.)

We reached the sunken road sweaty and breathless after a scamper across a field. There was still some sniping and now some machine-gunning, but it did us no harm. We were on our first objective without loss and we rested against the bank while the company commander and the sergeant major climbed into an olive grove above to see what lay ahead.

There was a half-wrecked church and some odd scattered out-buildings in the outermost outskirts of Ortona. Immediately below us, to the right, was the harbour. A couple of hundred yards away to our left was a big house, and men of the main attack were bringing out prisoners from it.

Our objective was doubly reached; this meant we had made contact with the other Canadians on our left. What machine-gunning and mortaring we had met – we could hear plenty ahead and to the left on other sectors – had come and was still coming from the church. So we had to climb into the olive grove and split up to take it from the left and right.

That spread us well out, and a battle broke out that we had not ex-pected. It was 'shop-window stuff' in the church. The party on our right was suddenly attacked by Germans charging and throwing hand-grenades. They came not from the church but from holes in the ground and behind straw stacks. To our left were sudden bursts of machine-gun fire heavier than before, and the swish and thud of mortar shells mingled with our own Bren and tommy-gun fire.

We who had been attacked were now on our bellies behind trees and little orchard sheds. Olive leaves were fluttering down cut by bullets. The Germans on our right fell back, but they had done some damage and they knew it. We heard them calling out in English 'Will you give in?' and obscenities from the Canadians.

We were outnumbered, outgunned and had been outsmarted. Our main objective was already behind us and it was not our job to take Ortona. Perhaps we had already done a useful job as a diversion. (We had, as it turned out later.) If we hung on too long for the sake of hanging on one flank might be broken, and with it our contact with the main forces.

The company commander told us to fall back on the sunken road. He himself walked about, upright, conducting the withdrawal, as he had conducted the battle. A messenger went sprinting across the olive grove, bent double, to bring in the men on the right. They brought their wounded, but their dead had to be left sprawling on the slope where the olive grove dipped over the cliff-top.

Back on the road there were stories and water bottles being swopped and the wounded being made comfortable. One corporal was jabbing his clasp-knife into the ground with one hand and ruffling his hair with the other, talking about Jim who had been killed beside him. A sergeant was saying, 'Jeez, they was coming in leaps and bounds, see, in leaps and bounds; so we let 'em have it with grenades, we did, see. They flopped in the grass, just flopped in the grass; all but one guy, and he jumped again before he flopped. Leaps and bounds they was coming.' But there was no end of stories.

It was getting dusk now and it looked as though we were there in the sunken road for the night. So I made to go back. Some of the wounded were cold and nervy so I went down to hurry up the stretcher-bearers and show them the way.[1] As we scrambled down our guns opened up again on the nearer target, an ordered concentration, I suppose, on buildings in the olive grove.

It was when I got back that I learned that the other Canadians were in the outskirts of Ortona. The men in the sunken road would have been more disappointed even than I that they had been beaten to it.

1. Ray was 'mentioned in despatches' for his part in this action. The escorting officer's report recommending this said 'The platoon commander and the sergeant were killed and the company commander asked for a volunteer to take a message ordering the platoon to withdraw. Mr. Ray immediately volunteered to carry out this task, which he achieved successfully, and brought the platoon to safety.'

One corporal had been promising himself loudly the best bed in the town for to-night.

Thursday, December 23, 1943

December 21

A sniper stopped our getting into Ortona by the main road. So we went back to get in from the coast track up which I had gone yesterday with Canadian infantry.

Ortona is shattered, and more of it is tumbling down each hour. The fine face it had presented to us when we saw it yesterday from the cliffs had been the face of roofless and windowless walls. Infantrymen were creeping along the street, hugging the walls, peering round corners. There was sniping here, too.

Civilians were peeping as well from the doors of half-shattered houses. One old man had a gaunt, haughty face like Don Quixote's and the same noble moustachios. But the general aspect of the street could not live up to that fiercely romantic profile; it was dowdy, a little squalid, terribly devastated. It was like half a dozen of the famous old photographs of Mr. Churchill at the Sidney Street siege super-imposed on a 'still' from the Stalingrad film. Yet there were more soldiers than civilians. It is just that one takes soldiers for granted in the foreground of battle, whereas smaller towns than this had emptied themselves of civilians into the hills as the fighting went through.

In this street a platoon of infantry was manœuvring to take a sniper's stronghold from two sides. In a side street an anti-tank gun was firing armour-piercing shells at point-blank range into a house of machine-gunners and mortarmen. Soldiers in ones and twos sidled round corners on secret war-like errands. From side streets rifle bullets pinged across the street.

Not fifty yards from a kicking, roaring anti-tank gun we stood in a dim kitchen hung with onions, garlics, and red peppers, drinking superb Marsala which the local policeman would not stop pouring out. One Canadian soldier drank it in tumblers full and said with cynical satisfaction, 'They will be charging us a quid a bottle for it next week.'

The policeman's womenfolk, old and young, were crying and laughing and kissing our hands. The oldest woman had been wounded in a hand and foot in some previous shelling. She shook with terror at each report of a gun. The house was half-wrecked already, and bricks and plaster fell down at each report. In the next room an old man lay dying of gangrene from a 12-day-old wound. Two women were praying by his bed.

Up in the top gallery of the church a complete artificial leg was leaning against the wall. Some of to-day's sights were as pointlessly lunatic as that. Some were too pointed. At the foot of the church wall lay a dead German soldier; somebody had been through his pockets and all round him against the wall were scattered picture postcards of Hitler – all the same picture of Hitler speaking from a lectern. The soldier must have had a packet of a dozen.

From the belfry we looked down on a town full of dust and din and stealthy bustle. Prisoners were being marched down the street and the machine-gun and anti-tank gun fire seemed to be receding a little. The prisoners looked tired, but young and soldierly. They were men of a parachute division and they had fought hard and cunningly against heavy odds. No town, I fancy, has been so battled for on this side of Italy as Ortona has.

## MONTY

### Wednesday, December 29, 1943

*From C. Ray, our Special Correspondent*

With the Eighth Army
December 26 (Delayed)

General Montgomery's new appointment is regarded by his soldiers here as an earnest that the new campaign will not be long delayed, that it will be the most important in the war, and that it will be consistently successful. It is regarded too by every man in the Eighth Army you speak to as a loss personal to himself.

Italy's Eighth Army is only to a very limited extent the Eighth Army of the Desert – its 78th Division, and its Canadians, for instance, joined it only with the opening of the Sicilian campaign – but every man in it has surrendered to Montgomery's quality of personal leadership and has infinite faith in his wisdom and generalship.

To realise that it is only necessary to drive along a road here behind the Army Commander's car and to see the cheeky, matey way that lorry-borne soldiers being driven the other way wave their hands to him and shout 'Good 'owd Monty' or 'Good luck, Monty.'

It is not the way, perhaps, of other armies and other generals. Montgomery's obvious encouragement of the soldiers' friendliness and his obvious delight in its more informal manifestations, grates on the nerves of some, but it works – and so does what seems to be

Montgomery's main principle of generalship, which, contrary to the ideas of some observers, is extreme caution.

Every soldier in his army knows that he will not go into battle until a way has been made for him by air bombing and by artillery concentrations and until every possible supply has been brought to where it will be needed. Was it Wellington who once said that the secret of his success was 'having an eye, an eye, ma'am to the baggage train'? If so – one has no books here – it is one lesson that Montgomery has learned from a general from whom in personal respects he is curiously dissimilar.

Montgomery will take over the British forces for the next invasion not only with a tradition of consistent success – his name alone must be worth many men, – but with a conception of the interdependency of ground and air forces that has been put into effect nowhere yet but in his campaigns. The Desert Air Forces and the Eighth Army are part of each other. With Britain as our air base for the next campaign, better equipped than any base we have had here, this welding of air and land power may yield astonishing results.

# D-DAY

Friday, June 9, 1944
*From David Woodward, 'Manchester Guardian' War Correspondent*

(Mr. David Woodward was one of the three British war correspondents who were landed in France from the air. He went by glider with a parachute unit. He was wounded, but not seriously, and is now in England.)

Somewhere in England
Thursday

A British parachute unit formed part of the Allied airborne force which was the spearhead of the Second Front. It was landed behind the German lines, seized vital positions, and then linked up with the Allied forces which had landed on the beaches.

I watched the unit go to war at dusk on D–1 (the day before D-Day), parading with everybody, from its brigadier downwards, in blackened faces and wearing the camouflage smocks and rimless steel helmets of the air-borne forces. Each of the black-faced men appeared nearly as broad and as thick as he was tall by reason of the colossal amount of equipment which the parachutist carries with him.

The brigadier and the lieutenant colonel made brief speeches. 'We are history,' said the colonel. There were three cheers, a short prayer, and in the gathering darkness they drove off to the aerodromes with the men in the first lorry singing, incredible as it seems, the notes of the Horst Wessel song at the tops of their voices. The words were not German.

It was nearly dark when they formed up to enter the 'planes, and by torchlight the officers read to their men the messages of good wishes from General Eisenhower and General Montgomery.

Then from this aerodrome and from aerodromes all over the country an armada of troop-carrying 'planes protected by fighters and followed by more troops aboard gliders took the air.

The weather was not ideal for an air-borne operation, but it was nevertheless decided to carry it out. The Germans would be less likely to be on their guard on a night when the weather was unfavourable for an attack.

First came parachutists, whose duty it was to destroy as far as possible the enemy's defences against an air landing. Then came the gliders with the troops to seize various points, and finally more gliders carrying equipment and weapons of all kinds. Out of the entire force of 'planes which took the unit into action only one tug and one glider were shot down.

By the time the glider on board which I was had landed it was very nearly daylight, and the dawn sky was shot with the brilliant yellows, reds, and greens from the explosions caused by the huge forces of Allied bombers covering the sea-borne attack, which was about to begin. A force of Lancasters led by Wing Commander Gibson, V.C., of Möhne Dam fame, put out of action a German battery which otherwise would have made the landing of troops on that beach impossible.

Meanwhile the parachutists had been busy, and the inhabitants of the little French villages near where the landings took place awoke to find themselves free again. In little knots they gathered at windows and at street corners and watched us. They were a little shy and a little reserved for the most part, probably because they remembered Mr. Churchill's statement that feint landings would take place, and they reflected that if what they were watching was a feint then the withdrawal of the British troops would mean that they would be responsible once again for their actions to Himmler and Laval.

These considerations did not affect some of them, however. One elderly Frenchman walked into a cemetery where British wounded were being collected amongst grotesque examples of French funerary art and laid upon the stretcher of one of the most seriously wounded men a huge bunch of red roses – an unwittingly appropriate tribute to the wounded men.

Other paratroops told me that as they marched through a small village which had just been devastated by Allied air bombardment they were cheered by French men and women standing among the still smoking ruins of their homes.

As D-Day went on it was possible for us, studying the maps at the headquarters of the air-borne division, to see the very high degree of successful surprise which the unit had achieved. German officers were captured in their beds in several places, and it became clear that the anti-air-landing precautions were not nearly as thorough as the Germans had been trying to make out for the past two years.

German prisoners proved a very mixed bag. The Reichsdeutsche was usually either a boy in his teens or an elderly veteran of the last war. There were some units of Volksdeutsche who had had German nationality forced upon them after the Hitlerian conquests of Poland and Czechoslovakia, as well as a number of Italians. The generally poor quality of these troops was not unexpected, and it was realised that behind them lay some of the best units of the German Army ready to counter-attack.

As our men prepared to meet these counter-attacks they were continually harried by snipers, who fought with great resolution until they were killed or until their ammunition was exhausted.

Later German tanks and Panzer Grenadiers in armoured lorries began their attack. In theory paratroops, because of their lack of heavy equipment, are considered light-weights for this kind of work, but these men stood up to the Germans just the same. When the fighting was at its most critical a large force of gliders carrying reinforcements flew right into the battle zone and, circling round, landed their cargoes in spite of continued German shelling of the landing zone.

These gliders turned the tide, and next morning it was an easy matter for us to drive in a captured car from the positions held by the air-borne forces to the beachhead formed by the troops from the sea. The countryside looked empty, but it still looked like posters advertising summer holidays in Normandy.

Small bodies of British troops moved along under cover of woods and hedges. Here and there were the discarded parachutes of our troops. Scattered over the ground were the black shapes of our gliders, most of which had been damaged in one way or another in their landings, with wings or tails sticking up at odd angles.

We could see where the beachhead was long before we got there by the clumps of barrage balloons flying over the ships which lay off the shore. Material already landed was being moved forward in ducks or lorries, or concentrated where it would be best hidden from the air. Mine-clearing operations were going on through the streets of a typical small French seaside resort, with occasional actions between our patrols and German snipers. In one corner of the village lay several German miniature tanks, all put out of action.

Down on the narrow beach transport moved over wire netting, shifting the stores, and on huts and tents the usual rash of British military initials had already broken out. Up to their chests in the surf troops were wading ashore from the landing craft. Out in the middle distance were supply ships and destroyers, while the background of the picture was provided by two big battleships slowly, purposefully shelling German positions with their heavy guns.

These guns had already supported the air-borne landings far inland and had badly damaged the local section of the 'Atlantic Wall,' which consisted at this place of medium-sized concrete block-houses and minefields. The Germans had left in such a hurry that they had not removed the mine warnings which they had put up for their own troops so that our work was made simpler by our having the minefields clearly labelled.

A beach dressing station was full of men, British and Germans, mostly lightly wounded. In one corner there I saw a German N.C.O. showing to three British soldiers a set of picture postcards he had bought in Paris representing the principal buildings of the town.

The pilots of the gliders which had done so well the day before were embarking in an infantry landing-craft for England to get more gliders to bring over. Having become a casualty, I travelled with them across the Channel, which in places seemed literally crowded with ships making their way along the swept channels through the German minefields.

The glider pilots landed this morning at one of the ports used to receive men during the evacuation from Dunkirk. One of the glider lieutenants told me he had been brought there at that time. 'The people cheered us then,' he said, 'and now they just watch us go by. Do you suppose the English ever cheer their victories?'

# England in War-Time

## EVACUEES

### Tuesday, August 6, 1940

'They went away. They came back. They are running wild.' That was a comment made in early January on the children evacuated at the beginning of the war. It is fair to say right away that the most serious casualty was the first evacuation scheme itself. The greater part of the appalling disruption of the education and health services has by now been repaired, the many little human hardships have been forgotten. At the same time there are children whose chances in life have been ruined; many of them have been lost to secondary education and the university.

The scheme which was to have kept our children, some of our mothers, and the infirm relatively safe, well educated, and looked after by all the usual social services away from the sharpest dangers of modern war was a failure. How great that failure was can be seen in the January figures: –

| Class | Number originally evacuated | Number returned | Per cent returned |
|---|---|---|---|
| Unaccompanied school children | 734,883 | 351,192 | 43 |
| Accompanied children | 260,276 | 223,381 | 86 |
| Mothers | 166,206 | 145,681 | 88 |

To begin with, these figures show that more than half of the persons who should have been evacuated had refused to be. Why did this happen? An excellent survey by various 'experts' in evacuation problems just published as a report to the Fabian Society gives answers enough.

The first and most obvious cause for failure was that the whole scheme was against nature. So, of course, is bombing. But there was no bombing in the first six months of the war and the greater evil did not exist to make the lesser bearable. Ordinary people without much imagination soon ceased to find any soundness in the reasons for which they were asked to see their families broken up. To these deep natural impulses must be added all the blows to parental or foster-parental pride and wounds to the nature of sensitive children which the inequalities of our social system, the differences between home and home, give relentlessly and unavoidably.

Seeing that this unnatural scheme, though excellent in theory, was certain to be extraordinarily difficult in practice, how did its planners face their tremendous task? Without imagination and without a full and sensible use of the administrative system already in their hands. Criticism of the minds and methods of our Civil Service could have no apter text than the failure of evacuation. As Mrs. Cole remarks, the scheme was unattractively drawn up 'by minds that were military, male, and middle class.' It began life with a lean and haggard look. The Government's publicity was never good enough to turn even for a moment into a fine adventure what most mothers and fathers saw only as a horrible expedient.

Once the movement was under way all kinds of deplorable errors made by the planners became discovered. One thing which would have helped to keep the scheme bearable would have been for the children from one area, from one school, to have gone together to the same district. The transport authorities, however, did not find it possible to send particular groups to particular places. As people were carried into the country haphazard hosts who were prepared, say, to have school children in their houses often found themselves with mothers and young children. Here, to begin with, was a needless kind of irritation.

The Government ought to have enforced liaison between the evacuating and reception authorities. The reception authorities had to grapple with problems the least of which were the whereabouts of the evacuated children's school medical cards and the need for textbooks and paper. If they had expectant mothers or mothers with small children on their hands from several places, which of the several evacuation authorities was responsible for sending more health visitors? The Oxfordshire County Council, for instance, had to look after children from over a hundred evacuating education authorities.

There ought obviously to have been in each evacuation area a body charged to co-operate with the reception authorities after the children had arrived. Planning of this kind was in many places entirely absent. Some – not all – were in the position described by the County Education Secretary of West Suffolk:

It was impossible to make any educational arrangements beforehand for the evacuated children, even of the most tentative nature. This was because no one had any accurate information as to the area from which the children would come, the numbers in which they would arrive, the type of school which they had been attending, and finally, to what village or town they were to go.

We have heard much about the troubles in the reception areas. The Government might have expected and prepared against some of them.

There were verminous children, about which such a hubbub was made. The Ministry of Health might have known before ever a child went away what was going to happen. 'An examination by the Ministry of its own records should have led it to expect an infestation of about 11.3 per cent of the children.'

Two passages from the survey suggest where responsibility for the failure of the scheme lies: –

In reading the circulars issued by the Ministry of Health instructing local authorities how to deal with evacuation problems it is impossible to escape the impression of a Government using the decentralised local government system not as a means of making allowances for local needs and resources, but rather as a method of shirking its own responsibility.

And again: –

Of the departments concerned, the only one which showed sufficient imagination, the Board of Education, was lacking in initiative and allowed itself to be refused any major share of control. The Ministry of Home Security was obsessed by Wellsian visions of destruction and was in any case too busy with other aspects of civil defence; the Ministry of Transport saw the whole business purely as a technical problem; and the Ministry of Health, which was responsible for the scheme, was far too timid to produce any serious policy. Over them all was the control of a parsimonious Treasury.

It is just to admit that not one of the many things the Government left undone would have made a complete success of a scheme which flew in the face of nature – unless heavy bombing which was expected, had begun at once. Even so, had there been efficient planning and proper co-operation between the many local authorities and services the scheme would have been much nearer success than it was. For this wise and energetic guidance was wanted from the Ministries at the centre. It was not there, and the Civil Service missed one more great chance of distinguishing itself.

A.W.J.[1]

1. Walter James

# LONDON UNDERGROUND

Tuesday, November 19, 1940
*From an A.R.P. Correspondent*

London, Monday

Tube 'night life' is beginning to assume a regular form. It is in many ways much different from that of the night life of ordinary London public shelters. Surroundings, though familiar in some ways, are strange in others. There is no noise of bombs and barrage, but there is the traffic of train and passenger. And there is a degree of mobility not possible above ground. Though most of the shelterers stay put, some of the younger are more restless and take trips not only to friends on their own platform but sometimes to friends at other stations.

Patrons of those eighty stations which can give adequate shelter now go fairly regularly to the same stations and to the same places on the platform or in the corridors. Those who have to be at work early choose the platforms where the last train at night is earlier. Queues for admittance form early, but the London Transport Board is lenient and they wind into the bowels of the earth about 3.30. Down below a blanket or a bag is sometimes left to mark a berth while the owner emerges for a spell on other business than keeping a place. Nor is the claim often jumped. Much going and coming is not allowed by the officials. It is especially put down on the part of children or at the rush hours.

The shelterers below are ruled by the stationmanster, who usually is in charge of more than one station, and by his foreman porter, assisted where necessary by the police (women as well as men). In addition there are shelter wardens from the various local authorities to help. The atmosphere is generally a friendly one. Disputes are determined by the station staff, police, or wardens, with the surrounding shelterers as an unofficial jury of comment. Usually from them comes the final word that silences the inevitable back-chat from the rebuked shelterer.

Government is tolerant. Gambling is stopped as soon as it is discovered, and sharks are recommended to take the fresh air. A quiet game of solo, however, is regarded with a friendly eye. Alchohol sometimes finds its way in, especially towards the end of the week when pay envelopes have been distributed. Sometimes it is in a bottle for later absorption. At others it has been preabsorbed. Drunkenness is severely and speedily dealt with, and the general expression of ill-will which it encounters from the vast majority is usually as effective as the methods of the law. The occasional bottle of beer is regarded on the other hand with acquiescence by the police and with envy by the public.

On Saturday nights there is something of an influx of fish and chips, with sweets for the children. There follows a drop in the food sales of the L.P.T.B. and a rise in cases to be dealt with at the first-aid post. Music is allowed and welcomed, provided the musicians stop when the vast majority want to go to sleep, which is about ten, and provided there is no attempt to take a collection. There is singing, with an occasional chorus for 'the ladies only' which takes the place of a comic turn, judging by the subsequent laughter. Favourite tunes vary from station to station.

By eleven most of the shelterers are asleep. The later Tube services are now much reduced for lack of passengers, so there is not much noise from them to wake the sleepers. Maintenance gangs still carry on their work on track and cables and clear the litter which a few careless hands still throw on the track.

## 'COVENTRATED'

### Thursday, November 21, 1940

*From our Special Correspondent*[1]

Coventry, Wednesday

While the Nazis coin a cheap word to describe what they have done here relatives and friends of the civilian dead laid their hopes in a common grave and turned away. The Bishop of Coventry (Dr. Mervyn Haigh) led the mourners to the trenches in which 172 of the bodies were laid. It was perhaps the strangest burial since the Christian service came to the world.

A Roman Catholic ceremony, cold and moving as a Bach fugue; a Free Church prayer, passionate and sincere; and then from the Bishop, 'We commend those whom we love to the mercy and care of God, our Heavenly Father.' 'We commend to Thy hand . . .' 'Give us grace . . .' 'So let us depart in peace . . .' The words came out on the wind and went into the hearts of men. Great clouds were lifting up into the sky from the city, grey and white, urgent, hastening on to meet an untold future, seeming to pause, symbolic above all the trappings of grief.

Men and women had found black to wear even if it were only a veil over fair brown hair or a black raincoat over stained dungarees. A mirror in a bedroom of a broken house caught the light and flashed an

1. Donald Blyth

accusing finger to the sky. The spires of the Cathedral and Holy Trinity looked down, and a factory chimney was smoking.

There were only officials in the cemetery when the coffins were brought in on lorries covered with tarpaulins. Labourers were the pall-bearers. A mechanical excavator was preparing for the next funeral. The clergy wore robing over gum-boots and steel helmets. All of them had come from other duties. The mourners, the majority straight from the work of rescue and repair, came into the cemetery later. Home Guards, A.F.S.[1] men, sailors, soldiers, airmen, St. John Ambulance and Red Cross workers, old women and young boys and girls walked behind the small civic party. They came beneath the immemorial cypress trees and yew, past the craters which bombs had made in the older part of the cemetery.

The Bishop in his brief address said: 'This evil air raid has brought us together in a great bond. In this city we have been better friends and neighbours than we have ever been before. As we stand here, let us vow before God that we will go on being better friends and neighbours for ever, because we have suffered too much together and have stood here together, too.

'Those of you who, with me, believe in the life to come, let us live and face this life in the strength of our faith. Let us go out to try and live unbroken and unembittered, asking the help of God's Holy Spirit to support us and to strengthen us that these dead may be prouder of us when we meet again. I cannot say more. God bless you.'

## 'ENEMY' ALIENS[2]

### Saturday, July 6, 1940

Hitler's conquest of the Low Countries and France was followed by a mass internment of the refugees from Hitler and Mussolini who were living in England.

The Austrians and Germans who until a few weeks ago were still at large have been extremely well sifted; they have passed before tribunal after tribunal, been vouched for by influential Englishmen, and been guilty of no offence. As the Under Secretary of the Home Office has stated in Parliament, no hostile act has been proved in a court of law since the beginning of the war against any 'refugee from Nazi oppression.' These refugees include many men of the highest distinction whose names are known all over the world as scientists, economists, writers,

1. Auxiliary Fire Service.     2. From a leader by A. P. Wadsworth.

trade union leaders, Socialist leaders. The list, if it were published, would be an amazing one. No matter what their record, they have passed from civil life into the control of the War Office, which by some freak of our organisation is responsible for civil as well as military internment. No exceptions have been made. Businesses have been destroyed because the employer has been snatched away. Aged couples have been torn apart. Much of what has been happening is merely the result of bad management, hasty improvisation, and not the persecution for its own sake which it may seem to its victims. But, putting aside the human considerations that at other times might have been paramount, does it not still seem unintelligent and wasteful to deprive ourselves of the aid of these thousands of men and women in our terrific struggle? Are we really so stupid that we cannot distinguish good men from bad men?

## THEIRS NOT TO REASON WHY[1]

### Saturday, August 17, 1940

#### THE INTERNMENT MUDDLE

Fleet Street, Friday

A distinguished anti-Fascist Italian writer visited this office to-day. He has been in prison in Italy because of his politics, and he has been in three British internment camps because of his nationality. He prefers the Italian prison. 'In totalitarian States the rules are well-established and the police are well up in the subject.'

He gave these facts from his experiences. He was interned on June 14, and an order for his release as a man engaged on work of national importance was signed about ten days later. But the order did not reach him because the authorities did not know where they had put him. He was not allowed to send a telegram to his mother until July 6. Then, for the first time, his friends knew where he was. They informed the War Office, and the papers for his release reached his camp a week later.

All his money, and most of his small personal belongings were taken from him on internment. He was given as a receipt, which he showed me, a rough piece of paper on which were written in pencil a number and a figure and a sum of money. When he was released he showed this to his commandant. He was told, 'You could have written this yourself.' Money and belongings have not yet been returned.

---

1. Two London Letter paragraphs.

## LOST AND FOUND

Another Italian with him was on the *Arandora Star*. He had not been told that he was being sent to Canada. Until he saw the ship he thought he was being sent to the Isle of Man. Then he guessed his destination, but still was not told. He denies that there was panic on the ship when it was torpedoed. After the sinking he swam about for an hour and a half, was picked up by a lifeboat, and was landed in Scotland, under guard, from a destroyer. After eight days in hospital as an internee, he was sent to an internment camp.

Meanwhile he had been posted as missing and an order for his release had been signed. He was doing work of national importance, and his case was under consideration when he was put on the *Arandora Star*.

Fifteen days after the sailing, ten days after the order for his release was signed, his friends received a letter from him. They asked the War Office to carry out the order for his release, but were reminded that he was missing. They pointed to the internment camp's address on his letter, and to the date. Authority said, 'But we do not know officially that he is there.' He was not released until a fortnight later.

This man also is so far without the money and other personal things that were taken from him on June 13.

# Changed Direction

## THE BEVERIDGE OVERTURE[1]

### Wednesday, December 2, 1942

The Beveridge 'Plan for Social Security' will stir up more controversy – and raise more hopes – than any project for social change since Mr. Lloyd George's National Health Insurance Bill of 1911. The controversy is inevitable; 'vested interests,' private and bureaucratic, are challenged in a hundred ways. But while many will find room to criticise, it cannot be too urgently pleaded that judgment should not be hasty. Before any of us starts to condemn or to campaign let him be sure he has studied the report as a whole and in its full text. Let him be sure that he has tried to weigh his sectional interest or prejudice against the plan's large purpose. It would be well to remember how time has vindicated Mr. Lloyd George and how misguided the agita-

1. A leader by A. P. Wadsworth.

tions against old-age pensions and health insurance now appear. And those who resist change should also reflect that this is a very different England from that of thirty years ago. It is an England that cannot be frightened by the bogy of State action; it has seen too many ways of life altered to be sensitive to sectional claims if it can be convinced that they stand in the way of the general good. The Beveridge plan is a big and fine thing. It is not only the welding into an administrative unity of our splendid but untidy and wasteful social services, but the charting of a great piece of national reconstruction. If it is carried through by the Government, as in all its essentials it surely must be, it will be the redemption, on a large section of the home front, of the promises of the Atlantic Charter. It will go far towards securing for the British people 'freedom from want' and, completed by a really national health service and by determined attempts to prevent cyclical mass unemployment, it will greatly strengthen our democracy by raising the happiness and wellbeing of 'the common man.'

No one can study the details of the plan – imperfectly presented in the limited space any daily newspaper can devote to it to-day – without gratitude to its author and admiration of his broad grasp and his extraordinary capacity for administrative simplification. One has only to compare it with the numerous sets of proposals that came before the Beveridge Committee (now issued in a separate volume) to appreciate these exceptional qualities. Everyone has talked for years about unifying the social services. Here is the machinery for it carried far beyond previous conceptions into an all-embracing national plan from which no citizen is excluded and which creates for the first time a national minimum. It is not a high level – though vastly better than what is provided at present – but it does bear relation to what the social surveys and the studies of nutrition have taught us about the subsistence minimum. The plan is based, as Sir William Beveridge says, on a diagnosis of want. It provides, therefore, not only against all the various forms of interruption and loss of earning power – unemployment, sickness and accident, old age, widowhood – but it adjusts incomes in periods of earning to family needs. Without children's allowances acute want would still exist among the low-paid workers with large families, and 'in all such cases income will be greater during unemployment or other interruptions of work than during work.' The arguments for children's allowances have nowhere been better stated and the reform has been most ingeniously woven into the social fabric. The omission of payment for the first child (in earning families) makes it financially manageable. The same ingenuity is shown in the treatment of old-age pensions by making pensions conditional on retirement while offering inducement for this to be postponed. There are no more important provisions in the report than these two, which for the first time take account of the two dominating facts about our national future – the decline in the child population and the growing numbers of the elderly.

The attractive features of the plan are innumerable – the extension to the whole population, which carries forward our war ideas of equality and community; the clearing up of sectional anomalies; the abolition of the means test; the emphasis on training and rehabilitation; the special benefits for married women; the administrative concentration; and, above all, the provision of a genuinely national health service covering medical treatment for all. There may be argument against putting so much of the cost on the contributions of employers and workers, but Sir William Beveridge makes out a good case for extending the contributory principle; it has certainly advantages of political expediency. Three proposals touch outside 'vested interests,' those concerning the approved societies, industrial assurance, and workmen's compensation. The arguments of the report are extremely weighty. It needs a surgical operation to fit the present health insurance and workmen's compensation systems into a national scheme of social security. We must do the job thoroughly and be the more determined since present methods are clearly wasteful, costly, and inequitable to the people at large. Sir William Beveridge's detailed examination of industrial assurance (Appendix D) is highly disturbing, and most people who study it carefully will find it hard to resist its conclusion that the country would be better served by a public instead of a private service in this field. The report is now open for discussion and action. It will form a rallying-ground for earnest men and women in all parties. It will rouse keen hopes and expectations not only among the British people here and in the forces but among our allies. The Government and Parliament have an opportunity which they will neglect at their peril and ours. For if we do not get something like the 'Plan for Social Security' into being before the war is over the political consequences will be serious. Instead of victory we shall have suffered defeat.

## THE SOLDIER AND THE ELECTION

Wednesday, July 11, 1945
*From our Rome Correspondent*[1]

'Union Jack,' 'Eighth Army News,' and the weekly 'Crusader,' the three British Service papers here, appointed a Conservative, a Liberal, and a Labour correspondent, who got a third of a page every day, which was headed, 'Election Round-Up,' and there the main speeches and leading articles from all three parties were given in brief. Lately full-length election speeches by Mr. Churchill, Mr. Attlee, and Mr. Ernest Bevin, Mr. Brendan Bracken, Sir Archibald Sinclair, and Lady Violet Bonham Carter have had a page to themselves, and Forces Radio has given a number of election speeches. The Communist party, Common Wealth, and other smaller parties get a look in once or twice a week.

In North-east Italy, in the Eighth Army area, there was much speculation about how the Trieste and Istria chapter would affect the soldiers' vote. Events there somewhat personally affected every serving man, for the whole atmosphere of the town and district during May and June at times demanded especially cool behaviour on the part of Allied troops. It was our first encounter with Communist organisation of civilians, and at first there was real sympathy for the Italians, some of whom were terrified and all of whom were at least familiar to our men, after this eighteen-month Italian campaign. But that was a first impression. Now that Trieste and the territory westwards have been taken over by us, the men notice quickly any tendency we may have to suppress all expressions of Communism, not because many soldiers are Communists but because Communism happens to be the name in this part of the world for co-operation between Italians and Yugoslavs, for reconstruction on a big scale, and for confederation as opposed to nationalism.

One is aware up in the Eighth Army areas of how much interest the serving soldier now takes in European politics. He is a travelled man and usually speaks another language besides his own. Just now he is acquiring a few words of German for the day when the non-fraternisation order is relaxed in Austria. I found British soldiers in the Alto Adige province who were already aware of the Austrian majority problem there. So when the soldier thinks about his vote he no longer only thinks of demobilisation, housing and employment, though these

1. Sylvia Sprigge

still come first, but he wonders how Britain can produce a useful foreign policy in Europe for the pacification of so many warring hungry nationalities and minorities, and the present arrangements tend to seem altogether too military.

I have yet to meet a British soldier in Italy who has not planned to come back here some day on holiday. The Eighth Army has made friends here among the people, and the Northern populations have been a revelation as a hard-working, intelligent, and attractive race. With interest in Italy, and lately in Trieste and Yugoslavia, the Eighth Army soldier will vote with one eye on home and one eye on Europe.

But it is impossible to generalise about the soldier's vote in this area. Mr. Churchill enjoys great popularity with the Eighth Army. His visits at crucial moments have never been forgotten. But the Service man is full of questions about the future, and if European countries really have henceforth to come under one or other security region he would like our security region to have something more positive and interesting to offer than the recurrent talk about 'the Slav peril.' But here he is, speaking himself in his letters to 'Union Jack,' taken at random over the last two weeks: –

From Lieutenant H. S. Beardmore, R.A.S.C., C.M.F., on June 20. 'From the incredible chaos of mud-slinging, recriminations, and criticisms emerges the clear, urgent message of Sir Archibald Sinclair. If speeches can win election, the Liberal party will have their every candidate returned. It was an honest speech, an attractive speech, and it did not float along in a flight of fancy words.'

From A.Q.M.S. N. Bailey, A.C.H.Q., C.M.F., on June 25: 'I am one of many Service men who are convinced that Socialism must be given its rightful place in the future government of our country. But let us not assume that by returning a Labour Government we should thereby install a Good Fairy whose magic wand will cure all our troubles. The present Government has its plans for reconstruction, housing, and the like. They may not be perfect, but we cannot afford to scrap them in favour of untried theories. Let Churchill get on with the job!'

From Rifleman T. W. Clutterbuck, L.I.R., C.M.F., on the same day: 'At the age of 26, having undergone the bombing of London and come into bloody contact with the Germans in North Africa, Sicily, and Italy, I am a Socialist in the Army, one who would stifle British enterprise and freedom. I am a Fifth Columnist in the Eighth Army, waiting my chance to strike at the very heart of my countrymen. That is precisely the meaning of Mr. Churchill's speech on the radio. He has the audacity to tell the people of Britain that their ideas of freedom are, or should be, the Conservative party's "as you were" with no alternative.'

From Major Beck, M.C., Coldstream Guards, c.m.f., on June 21: 'Why has foreign policy not been raised as a major issue at the election? Sir Stafford Cripps has briefly outlined his views that as the European trend is to the Left we can best meet this by Socialist representation. This to me savours rather of the tea-table than the round table. The Liberal policy appears indeterminate, while Mr. Churchill seems content to allow recent actions to be our guide. Personally I feel that the Conservative party has the tried diplomats and is therefore best fitted to mould our international relationships, but then I may so easily be wrong. That is why I ask why the three parties do not clearly state what their foreign policy is to be.'

And so the daily 'What You Think' column goes on with a sincere tribute every few days to the paper itself, because, as one correspondent says, it gives Service men a better chance of deciding which way to vote than people at home get, who only read one paper and one party's policy.

# SILENT REVOLUTION[1]

## Friday, July 27, 1945

Britain has undergone a silent revolution. Few suspected it. Hardly a politician from one end of the country to another had ventured to forecast what has happened at the polls. The people kept their secret. Yet throughout the country, in country no less than in town, they swung to the Left. And when they voted Left they meant it. They had no use for the middle-of-the-road Liberals; they voted Labour and they knew what they were voting for. The Conservative press had seen that they should know the worst; the Prime Minister had tried to scare them in broadcast after broadcast. But their marrows were not frozen; they took the risk. And so here we are for the first time in British history with a clear Labour majority in the House of Commons and the crushing defeat of Conservatism after over twenty-five years of dominance. We enter into a new political world, and though we (and the Labour leaders too) may shiver just a little at the thought of what lies ahead, we enter it with confidence. Many bad things have been made an end of. It is a kind of Progressive opportunity that comes only once in every few generations – in 1832, in 1868, in 1885, in 1906.

1. A leader by A. P. Wadsworth – the title is his.

CHANGED DIRECTION 597

Those were internal revolutions; this is part of a European revolution. The British vote parallels the revulsion of feeling that has occurred throughout Europe against old regimes and old habits of thought. There is encouragement in this, for if our affairs are wisely managed we have a magnificent chance of exerting British leadership in a desperately troubled world. Many of us, perhaps, may have felt in advance a little apprehension at the thought of a Labour victory on the edge of the economic upheaval of demobilisation and with all the great problems of European and Far Eastern resettlement in front of us. Only a Government of archangels could succeed, and it was natural to feel that it might be better from the long-range party view to see the Conservatives back with a clipped majority and the certainty of a crushing defeat in two years' time. But the people has willed it otherwise and the plunge has been taken. A Labour Government will have the responsibility of carrying us through and we must give it all the support and loyalty we can. No Government has ever had a harder task before it in time of peace, but none has ever had a greater opportunity.

First thoughts are inevitably of the Government's defeat and what brought it about. The conclusions are salutary. Uppermost is the lesson that the British people will not be dominated by one man. They admire Mr. Churchill as a great Englishman; they are grateful to the war leader, but they are resentful of the party politician. It is now plain that Mr. Churchill's broadcasts and his attempt to turn the election into a personal plebiscite did him immense harm. As in President Roosevelt's elections the influence of the popular newspapers on political opinion is shown to be far less than their proprietors like to think; they cannot manufacture opinion at their will. But what caused the revulsion of feeling? It can hardly be that Labour has won because of affection for its leader; there is respect perhaps but hardly affection. The overwhelming influence was distrust of the Conservatives. This is not because of what they have done while they were in the Coalition but because of their history before 1940. Munich and the 'phoney war' have been too much to stomach, and even Mr. Churchill has not been able to make people believe that there has been a change of heart. The Conservative record has been enough to wipe out the sentiment for a National Coalition, which again was evidently not as deep as many thought. Reactionary in social and international policy before the war, the Conservative party held out no hope for the future. If reconstruction was to be bold, if the high hopes of full employment and social security were to be fulfilled, it was not the Conservatives who could be entrusted with the task. The soldiers' vote, in particular went against them, but it was only the reflection of the way the mass of the people at home were taking.

There are of course, some things in the election to be regretted. The submergence of the Liberal party is a disappointment. Given Proportional Representation, the party would still have a future, but it is obvious that under the present system its hopes must be slender. The country will part with Mr. Churchill with many regrets. After all, he is the greatest Prime Minister we have known since Gladstone and the greatest national leader since Pitt. But he has been the symbol of an attitude of mind against which the world has turned. The new Labour Government will have new faces and may be in part scratch material. The first thing it will have to forget is the Coalition mind. Its leaders should know how much the Coalition Government, to say nothing of the minority Labour Governments of 1924 and 1929, lost by timidity and shilly-shallying. They will keep the confidence of the country in the degree in which they show themselves to have purpose and conviction and are ready to accept the help of men of goodwill. They must rid themselves of their old inferiority complex, bring in fresh blood, and set out boldly. The country will not be afraid of its first Socialist Government; the Government must not be afraid of the country which has made it.

## THE SLAUGHTER[1]

### Friday, July 27, 1945

For a comparable massacre of Tories one must go back to 1906, when seven Cabinet Ministers (including Mr. Balfour in East Manchester) were voted down together with five of their less exalted colleagues. On that occasion, too, the Tories were confident beforehand that the result would be, at worst, 'nearly a tie, with a very small majority on either side.' Afterwards the *Saturday Review* proclaimed that the 'classes' were 'striking back by the simple expedient of leaving the country.' Instead of going to London for the opening of Parliament they were leaving for the Riviera, Biarritz, Italy, or Japan. This the writer concluded, would bring it home to errant tradesmen that 'it does not pay to drive the upper class out of politics.'

[1]. From a short leader which Wadsworth wrote that night as well as the first leader, 'Silent Revolution.'

# A Talk with Henry Ford

## November 16, 1940; revised April 17, 1947

In 1940 James Bone had long talks with Henry Ford. The original interview was shortened to make room for additional material when it was republished on Ford's death – the version used here.

It was at the time when a building was going up at Dearborn to make Pratt and Whitney engines for war-planes for Britain, but Mr. Ford himself professed still to be against any war work. 'That is the plant,' he said when I raised the point. 'I have got an alibi.' He meant that it was his son's doing.

I had to meet him in the morning at the little 'Martha and Mary' church named after his mother and his wife in the park of Dearborn, where there are old London statues and Revolutionary period inns and shops. I noticed that he got out of his motor-car before it stopped, a tall, spare, active, high-shouldered figure in a grey suit with a Macdonald tartan tie and a hair guard for his watch. He looked at you with a half-serious, half-quizzical expression. He was not taking your questions very seriously, and you were not to take all his replies too seriously.

He had a natural dignity and did not need to stand to it. He had none of the great man's sense of importance; he expected no special deference. 'I'll go up first,' he said, and he ran up the narrow gallery stairs like a youth. 'I wish I could run upstairs like that,' I said at the top. 'Ah, maybe I am just showing off,' said Henry Ford with a grin.

It was a chapel for children from the Ford schools near by with his plan of undenominational service. After the service we walked across the grass to the Clinton Inn, an old Michigan roadside hostelry replanted there and replenished with period furniture and pictures and nothing else. We sat on a horsehair sofa and talked. It was a friendly, homely, disputative talk, probably in some ways much in the vein of talks that have passed on that sofa when it was new. 'Why didn't the English raise their own food?' He had sat next to Churchill at a dinner in London in 1913 and asked him 'Why don't you work the land?' Churchill had said that they could not raise enough food; they had to buy food and make things to sell to other people and that kind of talk. 'I told him they should raise their own food and the next day I bought a farm to prove it.'

He talked of the Boreham farm experiment. From that he passed to his soya bean growing and showed some of the wool – but not the famous Ford suit made from the wool – and spoke of the plastic made from the beans and the cars that were to be made of that light plastic.

About animals, he had doubts of their qualifying for survival. One of these days we would probably get quit of them. The cow's chance was particularly thin but he said nothing about the mechanical cow that he was said to have devised. Constantly he returned to the land and how it could be better used for the good of mankind. On the wall of the gigantic rotunda where the Ford models are shown is the motto that seems to crystallise the great mechanic's code – 'With one foot on land and one on industry America is safe.' One wondered if there was ever another great industrialist who put the land first as Henry Ford did.

One part of his achievement that must interest the social historian, I have thought, was the biological difference he had made to the United States by enlarging the area of marriage selection of rural communities from a buggy ride to a motor-car ride – say, from ten to 150 miles – and so made the melting-pot really melt. Henry Ford, as in everything discussed where there was a side of self-appreciation, brushed that away. It might have made a difference, he admitted, and continued, 'The motor-car is the greatest educator we have got. A man takes his family 500 miles in his car on holiday and they meet some other family from the other side that has come the same distance. They talk together, tell their experiences to one another, and back they go to pass some of it on to their home folk. That is good mixing.' I suggested that the motor-car was preventing the United States from having a peasantry. He said everyone came into town now, perhaps too much.

Of course much of the talk was about the war but nothing that is significant now. War was all wrong; you could get around a table and settle everything. Would Mr. Ford sit round a table with Communists if they had seized his works? He replied that he had never seen a real Communist, although he had seen plenty that called themselves so. He had a respect for the mechanical organisation and ability of the German people. 'War was the best worst thing that could happen,' he ruminated. He said that he liked the English, and when I spoke of the hefty-looking workmen on his assembly lines he replied that the men at Dagenham were every bit as good, healthy, upstanding men – 'all in one model too – English.'

But the English people did not work hard enough. The Americans did not work as hard as they should either. He admitted that he had never been to the Clyde or to Bradford or Birmingham and that he had not seen much of Manchester, but he insisted that he had seen a lot of England.

Speaking of the Ford Peace Ship in the first world war that was 'to get the boys out of the trenches by Christmas,' he said that there were 26 women on board. The ship got to Denmark and the newspaper folk came in, and the discussions on board got worse and everybody talked and talked. The result of it all was, he said, that he got an idea of the forces and the schemers he did not know of behind the war, so he quit. It cost him $400,000, but it was worth it.

It is hard to give an idea of the energy, ingenuity, freshness of mind, naïveté in many ways, originality, native wit, shrewdness, optimism tinted with caustic experience, kindness and flinty hardness, and a strange kind of humbleness ('I am just a tool') in that industrial king. His face in repose had the remote look that we call ascetic, expressive of the rare will-power that can produce periods of complete mental concentration. 'Faith is what we gather from experience' was one of his sayings.

Like many another he had entertained his mind with ideas of having lived before. The thing that really mattered, he said, was what experience we got from a former life and what we gathered in this to pass on to help other people for their next life. It is the sum of what we carry on from one generation to another that makes the essence of experience the thing, he said. As we passed on to lighter themes I asked him if in a future incarnation he would leave old-fashioned things like motor-cars and concentrate on a small aeroplane with, say, a gyroscope. He replied that he did not know anything about that or what he would like in another life. 'The only thing is,' said Henry Ford, 'I should like to be sure of having the same wife.'

'That's the difference between you and me, Mr. Ford,' his interviewer ventured to say, 'I hope that my own wife will have better luck in the next world.' 'There you are, Henry,' said Mrs. Ford, who was sitting near, 'you only think of yourself, but your friend thinks of his wife!' 'It means the same thing,' said Henry Ford, delighted with the turn the talk had taken, and he put out his hand and we shook hands, and the conversation grew in warmth. They had celebrated their golden wedding two years earlier. Ford was 77 when I saw him, and although he could not touch his toes without bending – he tried to do it that day – he could do a crouching exercise at a chair that few men could do at fifty and could dance old-fashioned dances with his wife at family parties.

As I left his home I noticed a bicycle in the hall and that it had no brakes. I asked why it had no brakes. 'Ah, what is the good of a brake going round the garden?' said Henry Ford. 'Just a weight and you don't need it.' 'Then why did I have to take the gravel out of your face, Henry?' asked the doctor. 'Aw – that was the milk girl,' said Henry Ford; 'if I had not fallen off I'd have run her down!' The last words as I left were: 'You're hidebound'; and he added, after a pause, 'Maybe I'm hidebound too.'

## The Art of Music

The first of the 1,698 National Gallery Concerts which gave London, thanks to Dame Myra Hess, uninterrupted first class music throughout the war, was given on Tuesday, October 10, 1939.

There were soldiers, sailors, men of the A.F.S., and women of the A.T.S. among the audience. They cheered Miss Hess when she appeared, and as they listened to her (surely no woman plays Beethoven's 'Appassionata' so well) many did not hide their emotion in the concert-goer's usual tight-lipped way. This indeed was no ordinary concert but a generous civilised gesture in the face of music's great obstacles. War has all but robbed Londoners of music. It seemed a proper and a dramatic thing that this 'musical gesture' should have been made in this temple of another art from which art has fled. [Earlier in the notice the critic remarked that 'some people even improvised seats on the empty picture frames.']

# CHAPTER TWELVE

# A Bleak but Bracing Time

*

There are plenty of similarities between the years after 1918 and those after 1945. The contrasts are, however, more important. In 1918 Lloyd George promised, but did not build 'homes fit for heroes.' Attlee managed to keep a surprising number of his promises. The Fisher Education Act was shelved; the Butler Education Act was carried out – and so on.

In Europe there was appalling chaos after both wars. But, while by 1920 the Soviet revolution had been turned back from Budapest and Warsaw, in 1945 it held the line of the Elbe, and three years later it looked as if the West would have to fight to keep it from the Rhine. 'What matters now is the concerting of Western defence,' a *Guardian* leader remarked, 'It is still the "cold war" and it may possibly not become more. But no one can read the Moscow documents without the deepest apprehension.' (September 18, 1948.) After 1918 those who rose against their new Soviet masters were, most of them, reactionaries; after 1945 they were disillusioned Socialists – but still very much Socialists. After 1918 there was nothing comparable to the peaceful withdrawal of Britain from India.

These were the years of Wadsworth's editorship. He had succeeded Crozier just before D-Day; he died as British troops set out for Suez. For the first six years J. M. Douglas Pringle was deputy editor; for the second Patrick Monkhouse. There was a nucleus of old hands – Harry Boardman in the Parliamentary Gallery, and Neville Cardus at Old Trafford and in the Albert Hall, for instance. There were, as these extracts show, newcomers with the old spirit and the old skills.

## Hangover

### HIROSHIMA: PREFACE TO THE PRESENT

Tuesday, September 3, 1946

Statesmen, archbishops, scientists, and generals have spoken, and been listened to about the atomic bomb, but it is doubtful whether any one of them, at least in America, has struck so arrestingly serious a note as the light-hearted *New Yorker*'s devotion of a whole number to what happened in Hiroshima. It was an inspired editorial decision, justified not only in intent but in performance, for the account by Mr. John Hersey joins at once the highest examples of the reporter's art. He has sought to piece together – a formidable task of research – the experience of six people from the moment the bomb burst above them until well inside the American occupation. He chose two women, a tailor's widow and a clerk in a tin works, two doctors, a German Jesuit, and a Japanese Methodist pastor. We have had from surveys and commissions full statistical reports of the damage done, and they were horrifying enough, but this is the first human story, and it will speak to the conscience more powerfully by touching the heart. It is everybody's reading, a simple primer of the atomic age. Mrs. Naka-mura, the tailor's widow, was cooking some rice for her children; Dr. Fujii was sitting on the steps of his one-man hospital reading the *Asahi*: Mr. Tanimoto, the pastor, was pushing some of his furniture away on a cart to a safer part of the town; and it was into these everyday scenes that the bomb burst with a flash 'whiter than any white she had ever seen,' as Mrs. Nakamura described it, or like 'a sheet of sun,' as Mr. Tanimoto thought. None of them was within three-quarters of a mile of the explosion, and after some suffering all survived. The girl clerk, for instance, after having her leg crushed under her, being dug out and left for two days and two nights under a propped-up roof, was taken through a series of hospitals and at the end of nine months' radiation sickness was discharged – a cripple.

The whole apparatus that a human society builds up to care for its members in trouble broke down in one moment. 'Of 150 doctors in the city 65 were already dead and most of the rest were wounded. Of 1,780 nurses 1,654 were dead or too badly hurt to work.' But if those from whom expert help might have been expected could not be found, ordinary neighbourliness itself was at a loss. Those of Mr. Hersey's six victims who could walk were pursued by pitiful appeals for help as they stumbled along streets all of whose inhabitants were buried beneath their ruined houses. The fires came too quickly behind the blast to make rescue possible:

> He tried at several points to penetrate the ruins, but the flames always stopped him. Under many houses people screamed for help; in general, survivors that day assisted only their relatives or im-mediate neighbours, for they could not comprehend or tolerate a wider circle of misery.

Many who escaped the flames made their way to Asano Park and lay down beneath its trees. There were hundreds there, ghastly in their wounds; there were others whose injuries were hidden but whose help-less retching showed that the atomic poison had them in its grip. They did their best for one another, and in the hours before they died their native grace of manner did not desert them:

> When Father Kleinsorge gave water to some whose faces had been almost blotted out by flash burns, they took their share and then raised themselves a little and bowed to him, in thanks.

Where lies the true greatness of man, we may wonder; in the invention of the bomb itself or in this pitiful observance of the smaller men and women dying in cruel pain from its effects?

And how, when it was all over, did the citizens of Hiroshima regard the atomic bomb? The first thought in the minds of some was of the splendour of their suffering. Mr. Tanimoto wrote in a letter recounting his experiences to an American:

> Next morning I found many men and women dead, whom I gave water last night. But, to my great surprise, I never heard anyone cried in disorder, even though they suffered in great agony. They died in silence, setting their teeth to bear it. All for the country!

There were many stories of how schoolgirls, until smoke choked their breath, had been heard singing the national hymn. A surprising number of Hiroshima's people, Mr. Hersey found, were quite in-different to the ethics of using a bomb; 'it was war and we had to expect it' was one comment. But others felt a hatred for the Americans which nothing, he felt, could possibly erase. One of the two doctors said to him some time afterwards:

> I see they are holding a trial for war criminals in Tokyo just now. I think they ought to try the men who decided to use the bomb and they should hang them all.

It was a thought that could have flown as far as Nuremberg. What the real effects of the bomb were upon the children – those of them who lived – was not easy to estimate; 'on the surface their recollections, months after the disaster, were of an exhilarating adventure.' One hopes that before long all over here, and in the world generally, will have the chance to read these pages. Man has either to abolish war or to accept Hiroshima's fate for his own city in the future. An issue of the *New Yorker* has become an item in his choice and at the same time no small inducement to choose wisely.

# THE BURMA ROAD TO TRAINING COLLEGE

Wednesday, July 30, 1947
*By L. D. Cosgrove*

Edward Broughton is an extremely modest man; according to himself he is also a very lucky man, and I suppose that in some ways he is right. I rather think, however, that other students who are training to be schoolmasters and who have not had his experiences may consider themselves a little luckier. We had been reading *Macbeth* together, and he had obviously enjoyed it, so to start a conversation I asked him how he liked re-reading Shakespeare, as he had probably not had much time for study since leaving school. I now realise that there is probably no other student in England who has read the plays of Shakespeare so often as has Broughton. Overworked and underfed, and in spite of terrible difficulties, he has again and again made his way through the thirteen hundred odd pages, only to turn back to the beginning and to read again.

Broughton's study of Shakespeare began in April, 1942, two months after the fall of Singapore, where he had been taken prisoner. He had been put to work building walls, demolishing walls, doing anything that might be useful to the Japanese, or that might give the Japanese something on which to congratulate themselves. The two months had gone by with nothing to vary the monotony of work and sleep but the daily walk backwards and forwards to the camp. There was never any news; there was nothing to read. One day as he was returning from work along Hokkein Street he noticed an old Chinese candy-seller at his stall. Broughton was not interested in the candy, but he caught a glimpse of what looked like a substantial book. For three days he gazed hungrily upon it, and on the fourth seized an unexpected opportunity to approach the stall. The book proved to be the apparently complete works of William Shakespeare. The candy-seller had been tearing little pieces of the pages in which to wrap his wares, and the front binding was entirely missing; but trade, fortunately, had not been brisk, for though the introduction had disappeared the text of the plays was there for all to read. Shakespeare changed hands for five cents.

Broughton managed to smuggle his treasure into the camp and that night began his course with *Henry VI*. Part I. The Japanese did not encourage reading. He had to keep it hidden in the day-time in his kit bag – he was lucky, he says, that most of his kit had been stolen when he was taken prisoner, so he had plenty of room. For eleven months his book made life bearable, and as he got to know the plays he grew sentimental enough – the phrase is his – to read more rapidly the pages which preceded some passage in praise of England.

In March, 1943, still with his Shakespeare, he was sent to Thailand and set to work on the Kanyu cutting. For three months, half-starved, inhumanly treated, wasted with disease, Broughton was one of those who were forced to help to cut through the solid rock a tunnel one hundred and fifty yards long, forty yards deep, and thirty yards wide. Of the five hundred prisoners in his draft a third had died by the time he himself collapsed and was sent to Chungkai. In those three months Shakespeare remained in his kit. He stayed at Chungkai until March, 1944, and in the intervals between bouts of malaria and building huts he again found time to return to Shakespeare. There were no drugs, no medical equipment, little food, no letters from home; there were only the thirteen hundred tattered pages and the will to read not only of The Boar's Head Tavern, but of Bohemia, Elsinore, Sicily, and Verona, which, after all, are yet in Shakespeare's England. When he left Chungkai he was put to building a camp in Tamuang. Here, again, there was opportunity for reading in the rare hours of respite from work and ill-treatment, but in June, 1944, Broughton and Shakespeare sailed back to Singapore, for transhipment to Japan. He managed once more to take the book with him, but on his way to Japan the ship was sunk by an Allied submarine, and he landed with nothing but the few clothes in which he stood. The course in Shakespeare had been suspended.

He found himself in a village where he had to work for a blacksmith. Until the time of his liberation he was divorced from the outside world. There was no news of any kind except that which he found out from the Japanese themselves; there was no one with whom to talk, and there was nothing whatever to read. Day succeeded day with indescribable monotony. His recollections of what he had read – for as a prisoner he was never able to gain the concentration necessary to memorise – became more and more dim. Two incidents alone stand out in his memory: one of the casual picking up, after many months in Japan, of a piece of paper which proved to be a map showing the Russian line surprisingly near to Berlin and the other the sight of a great flash some twenty miles away, which later he was to learn accompanied the dropping of the atomic bomb on Nagasaki.

He tells me that sometimes when he is reading Shakespeare under far different conditions he momentarily half sees the same words on the large page of that edition which once rested on the stall of a Chinese candy-seller. He has not told me what thoughts passed through his brain as he once sat patiently through a lecture on the teaching of Shakespeare in schools, and then heard a fellow-student argue that it is a crime to read Shakespeare; one should act it or see it acted.

## THE TRIAL AND EXECUTION OF LAVAL

Monday, October 8, 1945
*From our own Correspondent*[1]

Paris, October 7

Pierre Laval has declined to attend any further sittings of his own trial. His lawyers have also withdrawn in protest. The trial is now proceeding without the accused and without defence. Scenes which can only be described as scandalous led to this state of affairs on Saturday afternoon. The Procurator General repeated for the third time all the arguments he had already offered twice – namely Laval was being tried for public acts of which the evidence was the laws promulgated over his signature in *Journal Officiel* ('If I signed them you executed them,' retorted Laval, apostrophising the French magistracy in general) and broadcast speeches the text of which is not disputed.

The Procurator General reasserted that the defence had had all the papers connected with the trial, to which the defending lawyers retorted, 'No, no, it is false.' Laval claimed the right to answer the Procurator; in particular, to state that the charges brought against him at Marseilles were untrue. The Judge denied him this right and reiterated his original question. Meanwhile the assessors were showing themselves angrily impatient. The Judge was obviously losing control of himself, shouting at Laval to be silent when for once he was already silent. Finally he answered his own question.

But the Judge was not to be stopped on the path of self-abasement. 'Do you,' he asked, 'think yourself assured of impunity?' 'No,' said Laval, 'but there is something above us all, above you, above me. It is truth and justice, of which you ought to be the expression.' At this point the assessors began to join in more loudly and words such as 'Provocateur,' 'You'll get your twelve bullets.' 'You'll talk less a fortnight hence,' began to fly. 'The High Court will have the last word,' cried the Judge. 'Do you refuse to reply?' 'I do,' said Laval, who had not up to this moment committed himself to this attitude. 'Reflect,' said the Judge, 'do you refuse to answer my questions?' 'Yes,' said Laval, his dark face darkened with passion. 'Yes, in view of your aggression

1. Darsie Gillie

and of the manner in which you interrogated me. You formulate both question and answer.'

After a long suspension the Court resumed its sitting. As if nothing had happened, the Judge began: 'You have already explained yourself at length on the charges of conspiring against the security of the State (that is, overturning the Republic). We must now pass to the charge of intelligence with the enemy. You may speak on that point.'

Laval replied: 'I have a declaration to make. The insulting manner in which you interrogated me just now and the demonstrations of which I have been the object by several assessors show me that I may be the victim of a judicial crime. I do not wish to be its accomplice. I prefer to be silent.'

Laval was led out and the Judge called for the first witness.

His absence from his own trial has serious consequences. The verdict finally loses most of its authority, more especially as the gravest charges – and those the most difficult to answer – have not yet been dealt with at all by the Court. Laval is a very isolated and bitterly hated man to-day. At the best of times he was respected for his intelligence, but not popular. However, it is not true that, as the Procurator General is so fond of asserting, all Frenchmen have always been opposed to his policy of the 'lesser evil,' and yesterday's events suddenly and quite unnecessarily gave that policy a semblance of moral dignity which at some future date may not be without importance.

## Tuesday, October 16, 1946

Paris, October 15

Pierre Laval was shot to-day at 12.32 after a vain attempt to poison himself had delayed his execution by three hours.

When his advocates told him last night that General de Gaulle would not commute the sentence or the Minister of Justice order a retrial Laval had been composed and cheerful. When this morning at 8.45 M. Mornet, the Procurator General, came to him to inform him that he was to be executed at 9.30 Laval was lying in bed.

Without replying he put his head under the blankets. His advocates thought that he had had a moment of weakness and one of them raised the blanket to ask him to master himself, but he saw at once from Laval's appearance that he must have taken poison. He was already losing consciousness. He had in fact drunk from a small bottle of cyanide of potassium which he still held in his hand, but in his hurry he had not drained the bottle and had not shaken it before drinking.

Immediate medical attention prevented his attempted suicide, and half an hour later Laval was again conscious. A letter by his bedside ran as follows: –

To my advocates – for their information: to my executioners – for their shame.

I refuse to be killed by French bullets. I will not make French soldiers accomplices in a judicial murder. I have chosen my death – the poison of the Romans, which I have carried with me through my long wanderings and which has escaped the searchings of my guards. I wish to be buried with the Tricolour scarf which is round my neck. I die because I loved my country too much. My last thought is for France.

While Laval was being restored to the degree of consciousness required by French law for a man to be executed the firing squad was brought from the Fort of Chatillon, where the execution was originally to have taken place, to the prison at Fresnes. Laval put on one of the white ties which he had worn for years and wrapped the Tricolour scarf round his neck. He asked for and was granted a short respite so that, as he said, he could stand up to the firing squad in a manner befitting an ex-Prime Minister.

Arrived at the place of execution he said to the Procurator General, 'I pity you for the work you have done.' Turning to the soldiers he said, 'I pity you for having to execute this crime. Aim at my heart. Long live France!' At his request his eyes were not bandaged, but he was not allowed to give the order to fire.


# NUREMBERG JUSTICE

## Wednesday, October 16, 1946

There is no reason to suppose that the Germans will ever be convinced that justice was done at Nuremberg, seeing that so many of our own people have declared their uneasiness. We do not doubt that the German leaders were evil and deserved punishment, but we feel that at Nuremberg the victorious Powers appealed to standards of conduct by which they too might stand condemned.

Under the Nuremberg indictment there is not one of the judging Powers, unless it be France, which could not be accused on one or other of the counts. Britain and America share Hiroshima between them. The Russians, even if with the best defensive intentions, opened an aggressive war against Finland in 1939, and were expelled from the League for it. If law is to be respected it must be administered against all, and not by fits and starts. The Briand-Kellogg pact was signed in

1928, and the German Government has been on trial for breaking it, but its breach by Italy in Abyssinia has been passed over. No one of sense would have Italy dragged in at this stage, but her escape illustrates the entirely haphazard character of the law that was upheld at Nuremberg. Further, one would expect from States that have undertaken such great responsibilities before history a profound raising of conduct among themselves. What stultifies the whole Nuremberg process more than anything else is the feeling that if an international wrong were now committed almost anywhere in the world – in the Balkans, say – it would be surprising if the same four Powers could establish the same Court and come to the same agreed conclusions.

## The Europe of Displaced Persons

### THE ITALIAN DOCTOR

Monday, August 20, 1945

The Italian doctor is in charge of the Greek barracks at Feldafing transit camp. The other day he told me his story with a strange half-smile on his face, as though it no longer concerned him, as though long ago he had got to the farther side of all feeling, but felt that his story had an objective, almost entertaining, interest.

'When the Germans first came into Rome, in 1943, after the landing in Sicily, we Jews all hid in various parts of the town and its surroundings, but the Gestapo made no effort to find us, so we all gradually came out of hiding and resumed our work. They were waiting for that. They had a round-up and thousands of us were put into trains and carried off. There were 1,300 in my transport, and I am its sole survivor. We were taken first to the extermination camp of Auschwitz. My wife and child were put into the gas chamber and their bodies burnt. They had peep-holes which they forced us to look through. If you didn't look you were killed. It is strange the desire one has to live – you do all sorts of things that seem impossible afterwards, because of this will to survive. How is it I came through? I don't know. A miracle, and then I was useful because I am a doctor and because I know so many languages.

'Well, I won't tell you any more about Auschwitz – you hear about it all day long from other people. Most of us here have been through that. But there are other things that are interesting. I must tell you about the police dogs – that is very interesting. Wonderful dogs – do you know them? We were working in gangs in Warsaw, and then in July last year the Russian armies were approaching, and our S.S. guards were given orders to march us down across Poland and Germany to Dachau. The S.S. were cunning – they eliminated the weak before-hand. Before we started they assembled us all. "Those who are not fit to walk hold up their hands." I knew it was a trick and I kept still, but the Hungarians who had come recently and who hadn't learned the Nazi ways held up their hands, many of them. There was one Italian with me who held up his hand, too. I shouted to him not to, but he did not heed me. "Right; all of you not fit to walk will come now to the hospital and be moved in lorries along with the sick." The Hun-garians were triumphant. "Ah," they said, "you go on foot and we ride." They went off happy and laughing. A few minutes later we heard "tr-tr-tr-tat-a-tat." Machine-guns. They were killed along with the sick.

'I was going to tell you about the police dogs. That is very interest-ing,' he said, flushing, still with the half-smile that made one somehow, contrary to common sense and all probability, believe that something happier was to come. 'We marched along, and at our sides at intervals were the S.S. guards and between them the police dogs. The guards held their rifles aimed outwards because the Polish partisans had promised to deliver us (they tried it too, but the S.S. were too strong for them). Sometimes we had no food for three days. That was nothing. But the heat was intolerable; we were parched with thirst. It was a day of burning sun. Then suddenly we came to a river. Our guards gave us permission to go in and drink. But the bottom of the river was muddy. The first who went in stirred up the water and it became foul, so those who followed went a little farther. "Jewish swine! Trying to escape!" they shouted, and without warning ordered the dogs to attack. In a moment the dogs had sprung and were tearing the prisoners to pieces. But they were still alive, and the S.S. men ordered their underlings to hold them under the water till they drowned.

'At the end when the Americans were approaching there was a lot of muddle and panic in the German ranks. I believe that orders were given from Berlin that all Jews and political prisoners should be taken off to the Tirol – perhaps to be put in front of the troops so that Americans would not fire on them, perhaps to spread typhus and block the roads, or perhaps to be taken to the extermination camps of Otzted and Mat-hausen. They did not want to kill them at Dachau and Muekldorf (another camp like Dachau) because of leaving traces. But the S.S. guards in Dachau and everywhere else began to think of their own lives. They changed into civilian clothes, tore up their papers, and made off. They only managed to drive off some thousands of us, the Russians on foot, the Jews mostly in trains. We were packed in cattle wagons and shunted about, taking days to go a few miles. At one place the S.S. shouted to us to get down – that we were free. Those who obeyed were shot down. In my transport we were all saved by a sergeant of the Wehrmacht. He had guarded lots of us who worked in an aeroplane factory in Augsburg and had always been good to us. Our transport had got into the Tirol already, but he heard that the Americans were near Tutzing, and he gave orders to the engine-driver to return and at Tutzing we suddenly heard shouts and saw tanks and American flags and we were free.

'We are in paradise here, but we can't realise it. Everybody has complaints, everybody has worries. Everybody is asking how they can begin life again with all their relatives dead, everything gone, only memories still living. The Russians are lucky – they have a country that wants them. But the Jews are not sure.'

FRANCESCA M. WILSON

## OPERATION OASIS

> From all over Europe Jews made their way to the Promised Land. Many were "illegal immigrants", i.e. in excess of the quota fixed by the British government. Those who could be intercepted were sent to camps in Cyprus or even by a singular failure of imagination, to Germany.

Tuesday, September 9, 1947
*From our Special Correspondent*[1]

Hamburg, September 8
The enforced disembarkation this morning of the Jews from the *Ocean Vigour*, the first ship of the convoy of intercepted illegal immigrants, could not be other than an ugly and pathetic scene. Physical force had to be employed against perhaps fifty individuals – not a high proportion of the 1,420 who were disembarked. For the remainder the threat implied or explicit of force was enough; but all maintained that they had come ashore against their will and under compulsion. No one was seriously hurt.

The Press was admitted to Hamburg docks soon after seven this morning. By that time the early stages of 'Operation Oasis' had unfolded. About six o'clock a few sick had been brought ashore to the hospital train. At 6.25 a.m. a brief message had been broadcast in Yiddish, Hebrew, Hungarian, and French, inviting the Jews to dis-

1. John Midgley

embark. Their general situation had been explained to them on the previous afternoon by the Army officer in charge of the ship, who had accompanied them from Haifa. By the time we arrived two coaches of the train which was waiting alongside the quay had been filled, mostly with children.

Little groups were struggling peaceably but unhappily down the gangway. There were as yet few able-bodied men among them. Still, the authorities in charge were hoping that the disembarkation might be peaceably carried out.

No troops had been called in from the shore. The 120 or so troops who had come from Haifa, men of the Sixth Airborne Division in maroon berets and parachutists' jackets, were walking on and off the ship carrying luggage, leading children, and helping old people down the gangway, and everything seemed more harmonious than could reasonably be expected. But the trickle grew thinner after 8.30 and finally dried up.

As they came ashore the Jews after a cursory examination of their luggage, were shepherded on to the train. This consisted of un-furnished coaches such as are used for carrying troops in wartime and could not fairly be described as either comfortable or clean. Arrived on the train the Jews protested that they had not disembarked willingly; the troops had taken them one by one, they said, and they were un-able to resist. They complained that food and accommodation had been poor on the *Ocean Vigour* – many had had no beds but had had to sleep on the floor.

One young fellow said he came originally from Poland. Others refused to say what country they had come from, in what country they were born, from what port they had sailed, or how they came to be on the *Ocean Vigour* at all. There seemed to be a fairly general agreement to give no information. It seemed clear that lacking contact with or instructions from the outside world, they had been advised by the leaders on board ship to say nothing that would reveal the early stages of their journey.

By about nine o'clock five or six hundred people were off the *Ocean Vigour*, but hopes that the remainder would come off quietly were disappearing. Sounds of singing, shouting, and stamping were coming from one of the forward holds. Two correspondents (one British and one American) had been permitted to go aboard represent-ing the press as a whole. The noise they afterwards told me was the singing of a Zionist song, the Hora, and the singers were not disposed to obey orders. About nine o'clock the door leading from the hold was closed.

While I was talking to the women on the train the sound of a disturbance came from the gangway. Doing their best to struggle, two men were being hustled down the gangway. They were pushed, looking angry but unhurt, into the train. After them down the gangway came a soldier carrying a girl in his arms, a woman carried by two soldiers and another soldier carrying a girl. By now a little group of women had gathered by the train protesting, and children began to cry. A man was hustled up to the platform, then he ceased to struggle and climbed quietly into the train.

It was now approaching 9.30. During the few minutes that followed troops assembled on the quay, sixty or eighty military police, and a perhaps larger number of infantry men in denims and respirators, all wearing steel helmets. At 9.30 they went on board. As they ascended the gangway a few young Jews who had been waiting behind the wire on the forward deck ran below. The troops formed a double line leading from the door to the gangway, and others went below. The observers on board later described how the troops cleared first the second and then the third hold by massing at one end and pushing the Jews out in a concerted rush. Truncheons, they said, were used, but not with full force, and were never raised above the head.

After an appeal by a British officer to the occupants in one hold, and after some argument, the children were allowed to go. They fled down the gangway with a number of women and then came the most determined of the resisters.

It was at this time, about 9.45, that one saw signs of frayed tempers among the soldiers. It never proved possible entirely to separate the pacific from the resisters, and it was distressing to see a small girl walking sadly down the gangway alone being pushed from behind by a struggling group until a soldier ran up the gangway and led her away. A young boy followed carrying a market bag and a neatly rolled blanket, looking dignified and small between the two rows of soldiers. Then an elderly woman was gently handed down. A soldier followed with a placid baby resting comfortably in his arms, followed by a woman who might have been the child's mother; then a rapid procession of non-resisters with here and there a soldier carrying a child, helping with luggage, or guiding an elderly woman. Good humour began to return. Soon after tea the first train drove away from the quayside with occupants shouting protests through the wire-covered windows.

## A NEW CHAPTER OF HUMAN MISERY

Wednesday, September 12, 1945
*From our Special Correspondent*[1]

Berlin, September 10

Field Marshal Montgomery to-day presided for the first time over the regular meeting of the Allied Control Council. Little more than half an hour was taken over the agenda, which was mainly concerned with the mass movement of German refugees from the east.

No reliable evidence is available of the number of evicted Germans who are passing through the Russian zone from the eastern frontier, but they probably run into millions, and in their desire to move to the west large numbers of them are coming up against the sealed frontiers of the British and American zones, which already have trouble enough on their hands.

The number of refugees passing through Berlin by train has apparently dropped from 20,000 to 10,000 a day, owing it is stated to a decrease in the flow from the Sudetenland, but any discussion of this tragic problem is unreal until the facts are produced about the extent to which the Poles have been allowed to clear German towns and villages in their forward surge to the Oder and the Neisse, which are expected to mark their new western frontier.

The Potsdam declaration, it will be remembered, called for the humane treatment of expelled German nationals, and in view of the distressing reports laid before the conference of such cities as Breslau and Stettin the countries concerned were urged to postpone further expulsions. No evidence exists that these orders have been observed.

In the Robert Koch Hospital here, which I have visited this morning, there are more than 60 German women who were summarily evicted from a hospital and an orphanage in Danzig last month, and without food and water or even straw to lie on, were dispatched in cattle trucks to Germany. When the train arrived in Berlin they said of 83 persons crammed into two of the trucks 20 were already dead.

A woman recovering from typhoid had, she stated, seen her husband beaten to death by Poles, and she had been driven from her farm near Danzig to work in the fields. Now she has survived the journey to Berlin with two young sons and without money, clothes, or relations, cannot see what the future holds.

Three orphans I saw, aged between eight and twelve, are still

1. J. R. L. Anderson

almost skeletons: none of them weighed more than three stone. Another small boy thrown out of Danzig had a hastily scrawled post-card attached to him stating that his soldier father was long since missing, and that his mother and two sisters had died of hunger.

It is surely not enough to say that the Germans brought these miseries upon themselves. Brutalities and cynicism against which the war was fought are still rife in Europe and we are beginning to witness human suffering that almost surpasses anything inflicted by the Nazis. There is an urgent need for complete information from the Russian zone on these mass expulsions. All the Control Council could do to-day was to refer the subject to its co-ordinating committee for full study.

## WIT AMONG THE RUINS

Thursday, March 25, 1948
By J. M. Douglas Pringle

A cold, white mist climbs slowly off the Alster and settles firmly on the ruins of Hamburg. As night falls one's eye is brought down to the level of the streets, which seem so normal when one cannot see the shattered buildings on either side. They are indeed absurdly animated; a jostling throng of people hurry to and fro as if no bombs had fallen to disturb the complicated mechanism of city life. Like ants in the desert they bustle down streets at the end of which, you already know, there is nothing but a wilderness of bricks. Stranger still not a few of these scurrying ants are theatre-goers, hoping to taste for an hour or two a world of warmth and light and colour and excitement which yet seems more real than their own lives. For Hamburg, which had more houses destroyed in the war than the whole of England, has many theatres, or, to be exact, many places where plays may be seen.

Sometimes they are real theatres, patched up and made habitable; the Hamburg Opera now carries on with the audience, players, orchestra, and all on the stage of its former Opera House. Sometimes they are air-raid shelters or half-ruined halls or even cellars converted with God knows what ingenuity and black-market timber. In a single fortnight recently the citizen of Hamburg could see – though not, of course, on the same night – Il Seraglio and The Magic Flute, Don Pasquale, Tosca, and Peter Grimes, two plays by Schiller, Ibsen's Ghosts, Shaw's Man and Superman and The Doctor's Dilemma, Euripides's The Trojan Women, Mr. Priestley's The Linden Tree, three modern German plays, including the brilliant *Des Teufels General*, and half a dozen operettas, musical comedies and cabarets.

To-night, however, we will go to none of these. We will seek instead one of the little political cabarets which have sprung up in post-war Germany like rosebay-willow herb among the ruins. A few ants turn down a side street which clearly leads to the end of the world, if it leads anywhere at all, and stop opposite a giant crane leaning wearily to one side as if it had long ago despaired of lifting so much rubble. At the foot of a blank wall is a small door and a light; it is the entrance to the 'Bonbonnière.'

These political cabarets are all pretty much the same and are, of course, not new in Germany: a biggish cellar, brightly painted and furnished with simple chairs or stools and little tables, grossly over-crowded and probably dangerous. In one corner a tiny stage, only a few feet across, and below it a piano. Drinks are served, either German beer, which is now more ersatz than anything dreamed by the Nazis, or black-market wine, unnamed, dubious, and expensive. The show's the thing. Here too the form is familiar, though the spirit may vary. The scenes themselves are brief, pointed, and economical: it is a matter of pride to use as few 'props' as possible, and a handkerchief or a false moustache serves for costume.

But the essence is wit, cynical, biting, and, if possible, political. Jokes at the rations, at the occupation forces, the local politicians, at Hitler. They express, as nothing else, the present mood of Germany. Some of these cabarets are outstandingly liberal and outspoken, too much so, indeed for the German audience. Others hint at a nostalgia for the 'good old days,' and one feels that laughter often conceals regret. A few are considered to be 'dangerous.' The audience also varies: they may be young, democratic, and appreciative of every point or well-furred and well-to-do, black-marketers in search of entertainment.

The curtain goes up on a young student crouched on a stool in despair. He is in prison for a black-market offence, and the warder tries to console him. Suddenly his friend arrives, jubilant. He is free! He can go at once! The student and the warder are bewildered until the friend explains that he has just bought the prison for a thousand cigarettes.

A whole scene is built around some toy soldiers – for toy soldiers are forbidden in Germany. Another shows an office for advising former German soldiers in search of a job with one or other of the occupying Powers. The soldier has to read out his 'lebenslauf' or 'curriculum vitæ,' which is then suitably amended for each of the four Powers. His name is wrong for a start – it is Adolf. His education is hopelessly unsuitable. He 'willingly answered the call of his Führer and joined the Army.' Oh, no! 'Though strongly pacifist he was conscripted by the brutal Fascist dictatorship.' And so on, with subtle alterations for Britain, France, Russia, and the United States.

## Britain's Silent Revolution

### OUT IN THE '45

Thursday, August 2, 1945
*From our Political Correspondent*[1]

Westminster, Wednesday

'Which is the way in?' 'Straight on, through there.' The question was asked by Major General Mason-Macfarlane, Mr. Brendan Bracken's vanquisher, and his coach was a policeman, and the place the general was seeking was the Chamber of the House of Commons, and he was only a few paces from it.

It was all of a piece with that to-day. The new-comers were at sea, and there were so many new-comers – 345 – that the old hands were reduced to a wild wonder and uncertainty about their own bearings. An old Labour warrior from Lancashire, who has sat in half a dozen Parliaments, remarked as he pushed his way through the thronged Central Hall towards the Chamber, 'Dear me (he is Welsh), it's like a Labour party conference.' And indeed it was, as will appear. One's ears have grown unduly sensitive. It is from listening so hard for truth, no doubt.

Long before one got into the Press Gallery to-day the dreadful fact was borne in upon one that there was clapping going on in the Chamber. And it would not be the public, for there very few of the public about the place. It must be the Commons their very selves, one decided. So it proved, or rather a large number of those Commoners, Labour Commoners, who to-day alighted for the first time upon the empurpled benches of the former House of Lords.[2]

This was only the first shock. There was now time to look round. One felt more than usually astigmatic. A familiar segment of the old House that used to be on the right had turned up on the left of the Speaker's chair. Mr. Eden, Mr. Lyttelton, Mr. Butler, and the eternal Lord Winterton were on the front Opposition bench, and behind them were Tory faces familiar through the years of close scrutiny. Across the

1. Harry Boardman
2. Because the old House of Commons had been bombed.

floor it was still like home. On the Treasury bench were Mr. Green-
wood, Mr. Dalton, Mr. Alexander, and Sir Stafford Cripps, almost
cheating us into belief that the Coalition was back and the Labour
Ministers were mustered to repel an expected assault from Mr. Aneurin
Bevan, Mr. Silverman, and Ajax from Ipswich, otherwise the giant
Mr. Stokes.

But to lift one's eyes along the rear benches was to encounter a chaos
of anonymous faces; youthful faces, faces expressing all the confidence
of early middle age; a number of women's faces, one almost girlish.
But who were they? There was one handsome bearded face that had
clearly more of the sea about it than Bloomsbury. And there were still
more of them, quite a hundred, standing at the Bar, even standing on
the Bar, a breach of order. They were all hopelessly surplus to the
seating accommodation.

Slowly one recovered some sense of being in touch with reality as out
of the chaos emerged the reassuring countenance of Mr. Gallacher, or
Mr. Ellis Smith, or Mr. Hicks and others of a former Parliamentary
day.

Suddenly there is a yell. You cannot call it anything else. And –
oh dear! – they are clapping again. Mr. Herbert Morrison, Labour's
chief of men until Potsdam restores Mr. Attlee to us, is taking his call,
as it were. And then he sits down between Mr. Greenwood and Mr.
Dalton.

Immediately a wild commotion runs along the Opposition benches.
The Tory members are rising. Hands raised aloft, they are cheering. It
is a cheer so vehement as to be violent. The Labour masses are silent.
And then into one's field of vision looking downward to the floor, is
projected the head with the swell at the temples so indicative of mental
power and the Atlantean shoulders of Mr. Churchill. He has come. He
is not going to sulk in his tent or paint at Westerham – who started that
cock-and-bull story? He is to lead the Opposition. It is a fact of
enormous importance for the future.

As he takes his seat the Tories are still on their feet, cheering themselves almost into apoplexy, until – the amazement of it – the cheers by
some strange process modulate into 'For He's a Jolly Good Fellow.'
The Tories sung it well and in unison. But this, the House of
Commons!

It was plain in an instant that the Labour new blood was ready to
spill itself, metaphorically, in answer to what it took to be a challenge.
Up the new men rose. Fresh from the platform they burst out singing
the 'Red Flag.' All the serried ranks were standing – all save one, the
Ministers on the Treasury bench. Where shall we find decorum if not

here? Two verses of the anthem, each followed by a round of cheers and honour had been satisfied.

'I wondered a moment ago,' said Colonel Clifton Brown later, 'whether I was going to be elected Speaker of the House or director of a musical show.' In this merry English fashion was the curtain rung up on the new Parliament. The members surged out of the Chamber after electing Colonel Clifton Brown speaker. They were as happy as could be, excepting some Tories who certainly looked careworn. One says merry English fashion for in spite of the 'Red Flag' the 390 Labour men had voted for a Tory as Speaker.

Mr. Churchill drew the eyes of all the Labour new-comers when he rose to deliver a few firm sentences in congratulation to the Speaker. He had sat there subdued and grave. Once or twice he spoke to Mr. Eden. That was all. But on his feet he showed the old vigour. He did not get much beyond conventional phrases, but his voice was as strong as ever. The new Labour men should have known the giant when he 'held the heavens suspended.'

One will hazard the assertion that many of the old Labour members found it hard not to cheer in retrospective gratitude. Were they not the men who cheered him in the blackness of 1940 when the Tories were silent?

## BREAD RATIONING[1]

### Friday, June 28, 1946

The decision to ration bread is an historic one for this country. We were near to rationing in the spring of 1918; the plan was ready and the spares in the ration card prepared. We came near to it during the late war, especially when the submarine attacks were at their worst. It is profound irony that it should be in the year of peace and recovery that we have to accept this new hardship. But it is a thing to be taken philosophically and without passion. It stands to reason that no British Government, especially one as anxious to keep popular support as the Labour Government, would needlessly run its head into such fresh difficulties. Nor is it as though we alone were going to be inconvenienced. The United States, flowing with milk and honey and the rest, also is rather short of bread. And from the same causes. Yesterday President Truman was telling American housewives that if they often find it hard to buy a loaf of bread they ought to be pleased, be-

1. From a leader by A. P. Wadsworth.

cause, 'the loaf of bread and the bag of flour they do not buy means that much more for hungry children abroad.' Indeed, if we read some of the accounts of the way the American public has been behaving in the last few weeks we should be glad that the Government is going to even out distribution by rationing. We shall not have bodyguards round bakers' vans to prevent attacks by angry housewives. We shall manage things, we may hope, more decently and fairly.

The essence of the plan is to make our supplies go round until in a few months we get the advantage of the next harvest, which, from all accounts will in general be good.[1] The Government must realise that, besides the unscrupulous political twist which some Conservatives and their papers are giving to the food problem, there is genuine bewilderment among large sections of the people. They understand the grave shortages in Germany and Austria and in India and are ready to help. They are less clear about the shortages in some European countries where black-marketing seems to be a principal industry and where there is at least suspicion that U.N.R.R.A.[2] supplies are being politically manipulated. The facts should be given simply and with candour.

We shall have to see how the scheme works out. But in general the Government must be prepared for a more critical public than that on which Lord Woolton avuncularly bestowed the nation's food as if it were a personal gift. The bedside manner will no longer suffice.


## THE WINTER OF OUR DISCONTENT

Wednesday, December 31, 1947

### LONDON IN 1947

London was obviously picking up. There was plenty of money about; restaurants were managing wonderfully on (and off) the rations. People were wearing evening dress again. Buildings were getting a new lick of paint. Transport was improving. There were even new cabs plying at old rates. And if the capital was still rather austere one could always escape for a week or two to the snows of Switzerland or the Riviera's winter sun.

The great cold, 'the killing frost' that nipped so many roots, began a day or two before the end of January. On the 30th a headline read: 'Thames freezing.' Two days later, when the Royal Family drove by limousine instead of coach to Waterloo to begin their journey to South

1. In fact, bread was rationed until July, 1948.
2. United Nations Relief and Recovery Administration.

Africa, the Mall had two inches of new snow. And on the foggy morning of February 11, when the streets were a misery of dingy, watery snow, the fuel cuts began.

Most offices, restaurants, and public buildings were lighted merely by flickering candles and hurricane lamps. Clerks in overcoats and scarves crouched in the dim light over their books and wrote down figures with trembling hands. Even those offices which had central-heating plants were often without fuel, and it was no better at home. The domestic distribution of coal was upset, and one remembers queueing and pleading at the sidings for half a bag of coal – and being refused. Domestic water systems froze and had to be thawed a dozen times. Leaks grew into bursts and in many a home a ceiling came down.

And yet London found a mad enjoyment in it. Heroic days were here again. It was literally 'a cold war' and it gave opportunities of showing fortitude, resignation, neighbourliness, resourcefulness. It lent itself to self-dramatisation and the wearing of weird costumes, the manifestation of the 'London can take it' spirit. About the enforced idleness of half the country, the loss of production, the shortcomings of a Government that had failed to prepare for a bad winter too few people worried. It was hard to think about anything beyond the personal problems of keeping warm, clean, and adequately fed.

It was mid-March before the cold ended; then came new devastation by flood, which called for a Mansion House fund; and there followed the further trial for some Londoners of a water shortage. The wonderful summer which followed the worst winter in living memory began in mid-May. June was stifling. The refugees in Hampstead withdrew all that they had ever said about the English weather. Almost every event of the season, the race meetings, the cricket matches, regattas, and royal garden parties, took place in a blaze of sunshine. It was as demoralising as the cold had been. Even at Westminster M.P.s, able for the first time in seven years to take tea on the terrace, were insufficiently depressed about the growing economic crisis. On June 28 Eros was restored to Piccadilly Circus (some said that he had been put back facing the wrong way).

It was not until July 25 that the Government found itself in the midst of a crisis. From that moment London has thought more about politics and economics than it has done since 1931. Even at the lightest of social functions the most frivolous of people have been talking earnestly of 'the gap,' 'inflationary pressure,' 'productivity,' 'convertibility,' and 'the sterling area' – words and phrases which until July were hardly heard outside the small circle of experts.

This high seriousness was relieved for a week during the wedding of Elizabeth and Philip. What a pleasant, innocent event that was! It is many a year since one saw Londoners so simply happy. Everybody suddenly became good-tempered and some darker fears were temporarily forgotten. Only the most deeply pessimistic saw this gathering of the last few kings and queens in the world as perhaps the last great royal pageant of history. The royal wedding was, in fact, the beginning of a new age of hope in this country. At that moment some of the most vital production figures began to go upwards.

J.C.B.[1]

## THE PACE OF PRODUCTION[2]

### Saturday, February 28, 1948

The emptying of stocks and the running down of equipment had gone beyond the danger-point when the great frost hit the country. It took many months to overcome the worst of the interruption. A new inquiry just completed shows production still entangled in shortages and industry as a whole working far below capacity. While the pace of production has quickened, the industrial atmosphere has improved, and some of the most damaging gaps have been filled, little real progress has been made towards a solution of the main industrial problems. Demand still exceeds supply so greatly that it tears the productive machinery to pieces. We have not succeeded in transferring enough labour from the less essential occupations to those industries whose low output restricts production throughout the economy.

The output of almost every industry is restricted by scarcity of steel and a long list of other important materials, from iron castings to soda ash, from oils and fats to timber, from silica to salt. Even worse is the shortage of intermediate products or manufactured components, such as yarns and fabrics, dyestuffs and ball-bearings, electrical equipment, and nuts and bolts. Stocks of all these things are either so low that firms cannot plan long runs of production or so high that various resources are tied up for weeks or months. Appalling tales of bottlenecks were eagerly offered by all firms visited. One factory is clogged with engines, representing several months' total production, which cannot be completed for lack of electric motors. Elsewhere a large export order is endangered by lack of nuts and bolts. One engineering shop was brought to a standstill by the inability to replace saw blades.

1. John Beavan
2. By R. H. Fry – the opening section of the annual industrial survey.

Such incidents are widespread and frequent. They interrupt the smooth flow and rhythm of production. They raise costs, reduce output per worker, and break the spirit of managers and workers alike.

This kind of thing has gone on too long to be attributed to temporary shortages. We are obviously trying to produce a volume of manufactured products for which we have no earthly hope of supplying sufficient raw materials and components. The waste of resources caused by this misdirection of effort may well be comparable to the waste incurred before the war by having two million workpeople unemployed.

Labour shortage is still general in the Midlands where many more unskilled workers, both male and female, could be usefully employed. In Lancashire and Yorkshire the textile industries are notoriously short of labour. Iron-foundries are crying out for more men. Almost all over the country skilled workers for particular jobs are scarce. Little progress has been made with the large-scale transfer of man-power from one set of industries to another which has now been recognised as urgent for more than a year. By all accounts, the direction of labour has had hardly any result.

On the other hand, almost every management replied to our questions that labour was now working harder, changing jobs less frequently, and trying more keenly to earn more money. In many places absenteeism is declining. The head of a very large concern said that 'something happened to the minds of the men last autumn'; another important firm reports 'unusual willingness' since October. Many others suggested that the workers themselves have grasped the need of the country more quickly than the local union officials and shop stewards. But it was often added that performance had not really increased except in response to high overtime rates. It seems a fair generalisation that British workpeople have now settled down to their pre-war pace – a little slower here, a little faster there – after the unsettlement of the war and post-war conditions. With a few exceptions, Communist influence is nowhere regarded as a serious factor in the conduct of workers. But a lack of ambition, a desire for leisure rather than for advancement and possessions, was noticed almost universally. That spirit seems to be widespread also among white-collar workers, such as clerks, draughtsmen, and commercial staff. Though people are generally neither tired nor badly fed they seem to believe themselves to be both, and the effect is much the same.

The general productivity of industry – the quantity of output per man – is affected by many other things besides worker effort. The spasmodic flow of production, the difficulty of replacing equipment, and the alarming increase in the proportion of unproductive workers in industry are powerful drawbacks. Another factor is the waste of managerial skill in the struggle with shortages and controls. It must be accepted that personal visits of senior executives to the officials responsible for controls can procure favoured treatment. Scarce materials may be squeezed out of a supplier by personal intervention of the managing director. Bottleneck problems and matters of fuel economy which used to be handled by works managers are constantly coming up to the head of the business. To preserve labour morale he must discuss with the workers points which any foreman could fairly settle. Business men have not enough time left to look after production and selling.

## 'A SPEECH WORTH TEN MILLION TONS'

Thursday, July 8, 1948
*From our Labour Correspondent*[1]

Whitley Bay, Wednesday
Mr. Bevin made a speech to the miners' conference here to-day that ought to be worth 10,000,000 tons of coal. It was one of his great performances. He discussed economics in terms that can be understood at any street corner, and what he said meant simply that if the British people want to eat then everyone in mine and factory has got to work as hard as he can now, and be prepared to go on working hard for a long time.

'We have taken Marshall Aid, for which we are grateful, but we take it in the spirit that we are going to use it wisely,' Mr. Bevin said. 'We are not going to have any debauch, nor yet a night out, we are going on with our austerity because we are determined to hand over to our children a free, independent, up-to-date nation.'

Nations, he said, like people ought to be able to keep themselves. It was not pleasant to try to make a bargain with someone who had a pull over you, even if he did not use it. 'You have a feeling about it,' he added, putting into a simple phrase what a great many people, for all their consciousness of American generosity, do feel about accepting American help. But it is a feeling that can be worked off, and Mr. Bevin insisted that the British people are fully capable of working it off if they try hard enough.

He explained the kind of contracts which the British Government

1. J. R. L. Anderson

nowadays has to make. In the old days, he said, every nation sold goods to every other nation, and the world lived by a system of multilateral trade. But that had broken down, and the Government had to make bargains with individual countries which had the food and raw materials we wanted. These countries did not want our money, but they did want railway engines, saw mills, steel rails, machine tools, and in many cases they wanted our coal. They were sending us food to keep us going while we made the things they wanted. Now we had to keep our side of the bargain and deliver their goods on time. We wanted from Russia large supplies of coarse grain for feeding cattle, to try to increase the meat ration. If the Russians agreed to send us grain by a certain date we would have to undertake to send them the capital goods they wanted within a fixed time.

The Government signed agreements on behalf of the British people just as the Executive of a trade union signed agreements for its members. 'We want the British people to see us through,' he said. Continuing his homely turn of phrase, he added that he saw the British people as 'really one big union' with men and women working, not under the threat of the poor house, but out of a sense of duty to their fellows. 'The conception of Britain as one great union will grow and everybody will obey the rule not by compulsion but as a duty, as proud and honourable members of a club,' he said.

Mr. Bevin made a direct appeal to the miners, 'You have a new employer,' he said, 'but I don't think you ought to regard yourselves as being employed by the Coal Board. It is the public that are your employers, and the board are the managers on behalf of the public. I believe that the British public will be a very fair employer. But if we want, as working people, to have a bigger share in the control of our lives and our industries we have got to have one other very important thing as well. We have got to be willing to take responsibility ourselves in the awkward and unpleasant decisions that have to be taken.'

Sensibly and straightforwardly, Mr. Bevin told the miners not to engage in strikes against the Coal Board because such strikes simply hurt the public, and, in fact, the miners themselves. Could the miners give Britain the coal she needed, he asked. He answered his own question, 'The miners, those great generous souls, will not let us down.'

Mr. Bevin's phrases sometimes look rather empty in print, but they were not made for print. He can do almost anything he likes with a trade union audience; every miner at Whitley Bay to-day probably felt like going straight back to his colliery and hewing hundreds of tons of coal.

# BEVAN AND THE DOCTORS

## A SQUALID POLITICAL CONSPIRACY

Tuesday, February 10, 1948
*From our Parliamentary Correspondent*[1]

Westminster, Monday
Given Mr. Aneurin Bevan's case on the National Health Service Act and the great advantage he had of opening to-day's Commons debate and the rest followed inevitably – a brilliant performance which sent the Labour benches wild with delight. He sat down at the end of it to one of those long, sustained cheers that parties in the House of Commons reserve for an unusual gladiatorial triumph. What could not be foreseen was whether Mr. Bevan was going to play from strength a conciliatory card.

The House was not left in doubt many minutes. Conciliation was decidedly not his line. He had decided to attack the B.M.A. without mercy. He loosed one fierce charge after another at them. According to him they were a small body of raucous-voiced politically poisoned people who as completely misrepresented the medical profession as they had misrepresented the National Health Act. They were engaged in 'a squalid political conspiracy.' They were 'organising sabotage of an Act of Parliament.' They had always been reactionary. They resisted Lloyd George years ago. They had fallen foul of Mr. Ernest Brown and Mr. Willink just as much as they had of him (Mr. Bevan). The Labour benches cheered him furiously again and again as the invective mounted.

Mr. R. A. Butler, who followed him, remarked that Mr. Bevan's speech had done nothing to promote a settlement. That may be so. But whether it is to prove true or the reverse will largely depend on whether Mr. Bevan's obvious tactics succeed – that is, to discredit the B.M.A. in the eyes of the bulk of the doctors. He seems to have risked all on that.[2]

JULY 5

Thursday, May 6, 1948

The National Health Service is saved. That is the upshot of the doctors' second plebiscite. A majority of the profession are still against the terms

1. Harry Boardman
2. In fact, the result of the B.M.A. poll declared the following week showed a six to one majority against Bevan's terms.

of service. But the adverse majority has diminished so markedly since the February vote that the B.M.A. Council has decided to advise the doctors to co-operate. In February only 4,084 doctors said 'Yes,' and only 2,500 of these were general practitioners and their assistants. This time the vote was 12,799 'Yes' and 13,891 'No,' and of the affirmative votes 8,639 came from doctors in general practice. It is generally reckoned that to make a start Mr. Bevan would need not fewer than eight thousand general practitioners in the service; he would be glad of many more. The first vote showed that he could not count on nearly enough. The second suggests that he could get enough to start with, even if the B.M.A. continued to oppose.

In these circumstances the Council of the B.M.A. has chosen wisely in advising the profession to co-operate in the new service. It is a courageous, as well as a prudent, decision.

It is important, first, that people should not expect a magical transformation on July 5; and, secondly, that they should not blame the doctors if at first things fall short of expectation. This is no occasion for triumphing over [the doctors'] change of attitude but rather for profound gratitude that the leaders of a great profession have found it possible to reconcile their sense of what is right with what most people outside the profession believe to be desirable. One must be grateful especially to those who, within and without the ranks of the B.M.A., have striven through what seemed at times almost hopeless estrangements to keep alive the spirit of compromise and co-operation. Blessed are the peacemakers.

# WHY 492 WEST INDIANS CAME TO BRITAIN

Wednesday, June 23, 1948
*From our Special Correspondent*[1]

Tilbury, Tuesday

What were they thinking, these 492 men from Jamaica and Trinidad, as the *Empire Windrush* slid upstream with the flood between the closing shores of Kent and Essex?

Standing by the rail this morning, high above the landing-stage at Tilbury, one of them looked over the unlovely town to the grey-green fields beyond and said, 'If this is England I like it.' A good omen, perhaps. May he and his friends suffer no sharp disappointment.

It was curiously touching to walk along the landing-stage in the grey

1. Iain Hamilton

light of early morning and see against the white walls of the ship row upon row of dark, pensive faces looking down upon England, most of them for the first time. Had they thought England a golden land in a golden age? Some had, with their quaint amalgam of American optimism and African innocence. But these had already been partially disillusioned by Flight Lieutenant J. H. Smythe, a native of Sierra Leone and now a member of the Colonial Office Welfare Department. He travelled with them from the West Indies and towards the end had given them a little homily.

'I could not honestly paint you,' he said to them, 'a very rosy picture of your future in Britain.' That was straightforward. Conditions were not so favourable as they thought. They would see the scars of war wounds that are still bleeding. Were they highly skilled? No – then it would not be easy to find a job.

'On the other hand,' he went on, 'if you are a serious-minded person and prepared to work hard in any vocation, you can make your way. It is left to you to win the respect of all those you come across and do your utmost to succeed in whatever sphere you may be placed.'

Flight Lieutenant Smythe had arranged the immigrants into three groups during the voyage; those who had friends to go to, and some prospect of a job; those, ex-Service men all, who wished to rejoin the Army or the Air Force; and those with neither friends nor prospects.[1]

The Colonial Office sent some welfare people. The Ministry of Labour sent a regional welfare officer and twenty assistants. There was no band, certainly, to greet the immigrants at Tilbury; but it was a welcome and, for officialdom, a warm welcome. The men seemed encouraged by it.

Mr. Isaacs[2] said in the House recently, 'I consider that those who organised the movement of these people to this country did them a disservice in not letting us know.' However, one could discover no evidence of 'organisation.' They had seen the advertisement of the shipping company in their local papers – a thousand berths on the troop decks vacant, £28 each – found the money, and in due time embarked with high hopes.

What manner of men are these the *Empire Windrush* has brought to Britain? This morning, on the decks, one spoke with the following: a builder, a carpenter, an apprentice accountant, a farm worker, a tailor, a welder, a spray-painter, a boxer, a musician, a mechanic, a valet, a calypso singer, and a law student. Or thus they described themselves.

---

1. There were 204 in the first group, 52 in the second, and 236 in the third who were put up in a disused deep air raid shelter.
2. Minister of Labour.

And what has made them leave Jamaica? In most cases, lack of work. They spoke independently, but unanimously, of a blight that has come upon the West Indies since those who served America and Britain during the war returned home. The cost of living is high, wages are low. Many can earn no wages. Some had been unemployed for two years. One of them considered his chances in Britain (he was a builder), and said laconically, 'If I survive – so good; if I don't survive – so good.' Another, lacking this philosophy, said with a bitterness unusual in the company, 'When the situation is desperate you take a chance – you don't wait until you die.'

This man has been idle two years. According to him, a working man in Jamaica, married and with a small family, must earn between £6 and £7 a week in order to live decently. But the average working-class family, where the father is lucky enough to be in work, gets between £4 and £5 a week.

Most of the married men have left their wives and children at home, and hope to send for them later. Only five complete families sailed. Two of the wives are Englishwomen who followed their husbands to Jamaica and now return with them to England. One of them, Mrs. Doreen Zayne, formerly, and soon to be once more, of Blackpool, confessed that she did not care for Jamaica and was glad to be home again. She has two children, a boy and a girl. Her husband hopes to find work in Lancashire.

They are, then, as heterodox a collection of humanity as one might find. Some will be good workers, some bad. Many are 'serious-minded persons' anxious to succeed. No doubt the folk poets will find fit audiences somewhere. So will the complete dance-band which is journeying to Liverpool at this moment. And the boxer, who is going to meet his manager at Birkenhead, will surely find fights in plenty. Not all intend to settle in Britain; a 40-year-old tailor, for example, hopes to stay here for a year, and then go on and make his home in Liberia.

Their arrival has added to the worries of Mr. Isaacs and the trade union leaders. But the more worldly-wise among them are conscious of the deeper problem posed. Britain has welcomed displaced persons and has given employment to Poles who cannot go home. 'This is right,' said one of the immigrants. 'Surely then, there is nothing against our coming, for we are British subjects. If there is – is it because we are coloured?'

## THE SILENT REVOLUTIONARY

This impression by Harry Boardman marked Attlee's resignation of the leadership of the Labour Party.

Thursday, December 8, 1955

An observer in Whitehall on Tuesday afternoon might have seen a man of middle height, wearing a black coat and a black trilby, both of which had seen much service, step from a bus, thrust his hands deep in his overcoat pockets, and set off at a brisk pace towards Westminster. But nobody did observe him. None of the people flowing along the pavement vouchsafed him a glance. Had one man nudged another and said, 'Why: that's Mr. Attlee' (for so it was), the recognition would have counted among the year's remarkable events, and it would certainly have caused Mr. Attlee to sharpen his pace. To be recognised seems positively to pain him. He was safe. There was nothing to distinguish him from the inconspicuous rest. And this was the man who had presided for six years over the first Labour Government to hold power as well as office – the Government that, under his cool leadership, surmounted in its first days the cruel blow that abruptly ended Lend-Lease, and went on to negotiate the American loan; that introduced the national health service; nationalised the basic industries; allowed India, Burma and Ceylon to determine their own future; rose to the Russian menace; joined in defeating the Berlin blockade; introduced conscription for the first time in peace; and took the country into the war in Korea under the United Nations. Much else it did. Questions remain about some of its actions, but it had led a revolution in the social and economic fabric of the country and changed the face of the Commonwealth. And the man who had sustained the chief burden through it all was heading west unregarded with a motley assortment of other pedestrians.

How reconcile this apparently ordinary man with this story of government? And not with this story alone. He has been Leader of the Labour party longer than any of his forerunners. To have kept the saddle through twenty years with a party so unruly and fissiparous in its tendencies, a loose coalition of Radicals, pacifists, moderate Socialists, and Socialist Absolutists – to have done this is itself a very remarkable achievement. As with all party leaders, there have been one or two attempts to unhorse him, but they failed completely. This could not have been done by the negative being of so many people's imagining.

You have only to get close to Mr. Attlee, note the fine balance of the head, and, most of all, regard the strength expressed in the eyes, to realise how far removed he is from mere ordinariness. True, there is no colour, no magnetism, but there is great concentration of purpose, a mind with a razor edge and something of harsh resolution. You would hardly expect it of this apparently withdrawn, reticent man, but ministers he has sacked have been known to tremble at his curt words of dismissal. No capacity for oratory, which has done so much to swell Mr. Bevan's reputation, has ministered to his mastery of the party. The simplest words in the simplest order, and not too many of them, has been his rule. The long speech he has not so much forgone as not needed. Thoughts determine expression, and Mr. Attlee has had the clearest mind in Parliament. It has closed on the essentials of a problem like a spring trap. More than once this faculty for seeing sharply nothing but the relevant and essential has brought him off victorious against Sir Winston himself. He is positive, direct, un-emotional. He is not an intellectual, and the intelligentsia in his party have rather amused him. Has he not himself said they can be trusted to take a wrong view of anything? That was milder than Sir Winston, who is reported to have described them as 'the best educated half-wits in Europe.'

Mr. Attlee has always been your pragmatic Socialist. A Tory in his early manhood, he joined the party as being the only instrument he could see which could sweep away the social inequality and the poverty he had seen at first hand at the Haileybury House Settlement in the East End, where he spent some years. To quote him, 'The rather cynical Conservative had turned into an unashamed enthusiast for the Socialist cause.' That he has remained, and if the enthusiasm has seemed cold it is only because it has been controlled by a strong, piercing intelligence. This Attleean rationalism is strongly needed in the House of Commons. No one else in the Labour party can quite provide it.

## The Arts in Britain

### FIRST HEARING: *PETER GRIMES*

Saturday, June 9, 1945

London, Friday Night

After five years of wandering the Sadlers Wells Opera Company has at last returned to its old home – the first real sign in the London musical world that peace is upon us. Whatever opera was put on for yesterday's opening night, the theatre was bound to fill itself. It was, therefore, something of a gesture, both generous and typical, to give a new British opera the benefit of such an occasion. The opera was *Peter Grimes* by Benjamin Britten.

In the course of three acts there are brawling, malign gossip, seafaring local colour, and no love interest. It is true that a good woman tries to show sympathy and kindness to the outcast (Grimes), but she gets a blow for her pains. Thus the opera is a study of a distempered character, at once the victim and the maker of its evil fate.

If this is accepted as the sole function of the music-drama there can be nothing but admiration for the way Mr. Britten has responded with his imagination and craft. His orchestral score is full of vivid suggestion and action, sometimes rising to a kind of white-hot poetry, resonant of the hates and agonies of the story, and there are outstanding dramatic effects of a purely musical order, especially in connection with the chorus of fisher folk.

If, on the other, hand, it is thought that the first requirement of an opera is that it should be operatic, then *Peter Grimes* must have provoked a great deal of criticism among yesterday's opera-going audience. The fault is largely with the libretto. It is overloaded with scrappy and not always telling incidents, and too much of it is cast in unreal language. Moreover, there is little effective use of that balancing of the dramatic and the lyrical, of progress and pause, that has meant so much in the life of great opera. There are other ways, immediately perceptible but long to describe, in which *Peter Grimes* fails in the important matter of getting itself across. The company, led by Peter Pears as Grimes and by Joan Sutherland as the well-wishing schoolmistress, and conducted by Reginald Goodall, did nearly all that could be done to help the work over its obstacles.

W.MCN.[1]

# FIRST HEARING: *THE MIDSUMMER MARRIAGE*

Friday, January 28, 1955
*By Philip Hope-Wallace*

Michael Tippett's opera, on which (drama and music) he has worked for seven years, reached the stage of the Royal Opera House last night in an air of excitement, not lessened by the confident word-of-mouth prognosis that it would be incomprehensible. The music, if not well

1. William McNaught

organised (any more than the drama), turns out to be warm-blooded, and generous, and often of the greatest beauty. If an opera in the accepted sense of a dramatically cogent entertainment is not achieved, at least here is no dusty answer either. This music is clear and often sweet, without harshness or twisted anger.

No opera composer need break his heart in England. Frankly this is a composition which few impresarios of the kind known in the past would have considered at all, but Covent Garden at least does it proud and is not, in the result, to be faulted for its judgment. This is music to be reckoned with, however harnessed, and its composer must not endure the neglect of a Berlioz.

But opera is a law unto itself. The printed factors, score and libretto, cannot tell half the story. On paper half of Tristan looks a muddle; it is not until one is caught up in the marvel of the music that everything falls into place. In this work the element of the marvellous, as projected by the music, may in fact make poetry of events on the stage which to the eye of a tone-deaf rationalist might look like the junketings of a pack of silly art students before a factory façade on the Great West Road. To others, Barbara Hepworth's 'mock-up' of doors and stairways and great curving balustrades – a temple in wood – may in fact be the perfect imaginative setting for a story which seems a little like *The Magic Flute* – a Puck of Pook's Hill pantheism doing service in place of the masonic mysteries. But mysterious and decidedly without 'chic' it is, and further made difficult to follow as well as to swallow by the very general inaudibility of the words. Statements such as that the sun is rising on Midsummer Morn are easily reinforced by footlights, but there are other and far more recondite statements than that, and if they were not floated on such a tide of fine musical imaginings, the indecisions and misadventures of the two lovers kept apart by self-questionings might grow very tiresome indeed.

If the audience was baffled at times, and perhaps not fully in the picture even at the end, there was still much to enjoy in the allegory, even when it was naïvest.

The second act, if it does not bring illumination, is crisper than the first and offers a long and exciting stretch of ritual dances – the part of the score hitherto given public performance. The last act is the evening of Midsummer Day, and still there are trials and tribulations to be resolved before the lovers can be united – in particular a veiled oracle. Within this visitant (who is, it seems, Truth) there lies the perfect human relationship whither the young lovers are striving. As a last ritual dance breaks forth we are to understand that the perfect synthesis has been achieved, and that Mark and Jenifer will henceforward move to their midsummer wedding, a true marriage.

This high-flown allegory should not be too impatiently rejected, for the music lifts it on to a plane where one is prepared to comprehend it, even as much as Wagner is to be understood, not literally but as argument of sheer feeling. Such at least seems to be the best way to follow it, unless we can presently follow more of the words.

## THE FIRST EDINBURGH FESTIVAL

Saturday, September 6, 1947
*By Neville Cardus*

Frank Harris once said that if Edinburgh were dropped into the Trossachs country we should have another Salzburg. But Edinburgh is as far removed from the baroque, in spirit and external manifestation, as well could be. The 'old town' was hewn from granite; and granite lives have been lived in the twisting declivities of the streets. The 'new town' is a city of Adam mansions and secluded spacious squares. Industry and 'progress' dug a railway in the valley which divides the old town and the castle on the rocks from the new. Smoke trailing like sentences of Carlyle wafts over the handsome gardens which border Princes Street, congested with double-decker trams. Cafés and restaurants close on the Sabbath. Even on weekdays the visitor to the festival from, say, Vienna or Paris might find himself forced back on tea and a sandwich after a performance of *Figaro*, and driven to premature bedtime while his mind craves for conversation until dawn.

None the less the roots have been thrust into the earth. The Edinburgh Festival will I think, continue and burgeon and create sooner or later its own atmosphere and 'Stimmung.' Why indeed drag in Salzburg? – as Whistler said of Velazquez.

On the face of it it is remarkable that Edinburgh should have been chosen to house the first truly international music festival held in Great Britain; for Scotland, not England, is really 'das Land ohne Musik' most days in the year. At any rate, no creative musician has yet emerged from the land. But cultural ties binding Edinburgh and Scotland to Europe were woven long ago. From Edinburgh and Scotland Kant was wakened from his 'dogmatic slumber' by David Hume. Carlyle translated Goethe; and Goethe nourished himself on Walter Scott. Boswell called on Voltaire. Beethoven interested himself for an occasion in Scottish folk-song. Caird, admittedly a dweller amongst

the barbarians of Glasgow (so I seem to remember), beat up mists of
Hegelian metaphysics – mists not unlike the ghostly shroud which, as
I write, conceals the castle on the rock; but not for long. The sun is
once more announcing his opulence. It is royal and day-long sunshine
that so quickly has ripened this festival of the talents of many countries.
Through music Edinburgh picks up again the links of culture forged
by hard thinking, not by the easier sensuous way of music, centuries
since, joining Scotland with the intellectual governance of the world.

From the point of view of musical quality we have certainly been
blessed beyond all reasonable expectations. Some of the concerts have
restored pre-war standards.

Into this challenging air, broad and unbounded, came the Hallé
Orchestra, and made its contribution, definite and characteristic.
Visitors from overseas were incredulous that this was an ensemble of
comparatively brief growth. The playing was entirely free of any
suggestion of provincialism. Barbirolli's achievement in creating this
orchestra has been astonishing – I had nearly said miraculous.

## SIBELIUS AT 83

### Wednesday, December 8, 1948
### *By Stefan Schimanski*

His entry was like his music – sombre and massive and unannounced.
He stood there immobile, as if rooted to the ground, and the expression
on his face was tense and grim. But the moment he advanced the
heaviness vanished and the man stood detached from his background.
His great figure moved lightly; his enormous forehead, with its vertical
frowns rising above each brow, became smooth; his eyes flashed and
sparkled like those of a young man; and his features changed
continually as he relaxed in his chair.

The man who sat there was not the man one sees in his portraits. In
front of the camera he is usually stern and rigid. But in the flesh he is
almost gay, with a childlike contentment in his face, and with a twinkle
in his eyes he prescribed his recipe for happiness. 'Above all,' he told
me, 'you must have a sense of humour. It is the greatest gift a man can
have.' And for the artist he had more advice: forget about politics. His
wife, he would say laughingly, she read the papers and knew what was
going on. 'But I have cut myself off from politics – they do not concern me.' The struggle, one felt, was much more personal, but beyond
the conflict there was the quiet exuberance of a life fulfilled. But there

was also its secret. 'Yes, I too,' he confessed, clutching his chest, 'I too can never speak of my innermost struggles.'

Sibelius had been talking about Mozart ('the greatest musical genius') when he made that comparison, and it is significant. For, like Mozart, his own strength seems to lie in his silence. It must reveal itself – in his music. That is why no one outside his household has ever been allowed into the upstairs study where he is said to compose at night; and why no one, after twenty-three years, has ever penetrated the mystery of the Eighth Symphony. I realised suddenly how foolish it would be to probe the secret and stopped half-way in a sentence. 'No, I'd better not ask you that one,' I said; 'it concerns your music.' Sibelius smiled and said very quietly, 'No, you'd better not ask me that.' Then he turned his face to one side – and his huge ears seemed to grow bigger, as if they were falling on to the jacket of his chalk-striped suit – and he added, 'Tell me; I need not answer you, of course; but I would have liked to know what you wanted to know.' And at this he laughed himself.

The sun streamed through the wide windows, the Lake of Tuusula slept peacefully in the distance, and the cluster of birch trees around the house zealously guarded the master's seclusion. I could not help comparing this Sunday atmosphere with the mood I had encountered only a few days before in the home of Sigrid Undset in Lillehammer. Sibelius grew serious when I pointed this difference out to him. 'She has visions of the past,' he said finally; 'I believe in the future.' And he continued pensively: 'There is a good deal of tragedy in the world – and in art – but I believe everything moves in a spiral. It always goes up. Our period is just a temporary state.'

To underline his faith he quoted a Finnish national poem about man's will to conquer, then suddenly he stopped. 'You know,' he said half-jokingly, half most earnestly, 'I do not like talking about myself. I shall regret it to-morrow.' And so we talked about Oxford (which, 'in moonlight, is just like Venice') and about the Queen's Hall ('It was as if I had been bombed myself when I heard the news') and about Horace and cigars and the difficulty of obtaining them. I told him that Mr. Churchill was still getting his from Havana. 'Ah, yes,' he said with a sigh, 'but then you must be a Churchill to get them.' And this impressive note of humility recurred time and again. 'It is true I have friends among politicians,' Sibelius said, 'but among them I am just like an idiot.'

And there was that other note, that of undivided praise. Shosta-kovitch's last symphony, of which he had the records, was 'invigorat-ing'; Vaughan Williams's Sixth ('especially that last movement') was 'so impressive, so powerful' (and, Sibelius added, 'he is not a young man any more, after all'); contemporary British music, and he mentioned a number of the younger composers, was, 'for these troubled times,' 'surprisingly vigorous'; it was, in fact, 'coming back in a circle to the golden era of Purcell and Byrd.'

And there was one other recurring note, that of old age. 'There will be no more songs,' he told me. 'To write songs you must be young.' And he talked about his youth – how he had started composing at the age of ten; how the law books he was supposed to study turned yellow in the sun because he did not touch them; how his grandmother brought him up and eventually allowed him to devote himself to music; how he composed his Quartet in London ('In such a big place?' I asked. 'There are only two places where you can be at peace and compose,' he replied, 'a big city and a forest – in both you are alone'). And he talked of London and his walks to the East End and how he had enjoyed travelling in the past. The old note had crept in again. I told him of the disappointment felt in Britain at his non-appearance at the Edinburgh Festival. He replied that his doctor had not allowed him to go. But almost immediately he volunteered another explanation. 'I do not want to leave Jarvenpaa. I built this house forty-five years ago. I have not been away for the last ten – not even to Helsinki. My old friends have died one by one. Now I shall stay.' The master had come home to rest among the stark pine trees, the discordant winds, and the mists rising over the dark lakes, which are his music.

## ART FINDS A PLACE IN CHURCH

### Thursday, April 3, 1947
*From our Special Correspondent*

St. Matthew's Church at Northampton has revived a tradition which has been for too long dormant in this country – that of commissioning works of art from the great masters of the day.

In the last four years St. Matthew's has acquired a statue by Henry Moore, a painting by Graham Sutherland, musical works by Benjamin Britten, Michael Tippett, Edmund Rubbra, Lennox Berkeley, and Gerald Finzi, and, not the least original and remarkable, a 'Litany and Anthem for St. Matthew's Day' by W. H. Auden. Each year September 21, St. Matthew's Day, is celebrated by the performance of a newly commissioned work.

St. Matthew's serves a semi-industrial parish of 11,000 people whose incomes and powers of artistic appreciation are repeated in hundreds of suburban parishes in the Midlands. Henry Moore's 'Madonna and Child,' which stands against the north transept wall, was commissioned and presented by the first vicar, Canon J. R. Hussey [father of the present vicar]. It is in blue-brown Horton stone, nearly five feet high, and slightly larger than life size; a work of great dignity and beauty. The parochial church council noted Sir Kenneth Clark's opinion that Moore was the greatest living sculptor. They examined his clay models, debated long and earnestly, and accepted the gift; the diocesan advisory council at Peterborough concurred. The unveiling of the statue provoked a furious local controversy and angry protests were made against the presence of such a 'monstrosity' in a church. These protests did not come from members of the church, nor (in most cases) from members of any Christian body. The church council stood firm, and the outcry subsided. To-day the 'Madonna' is one of the treasures of Northampton, and most parishioners who at first suspended judgment have learned to understand and admire it.

Graham Sutherland's 'Crucifixion,' completed last autumn, faces it across the width of the church from the plain wall of the south transept. About eight feet high and seven and a half feet wide, this splendid painting is far finer than most photographs suggest, and is in harsh contrast to those paintings which ignore the grimness of death in their reverence for the theme of the Crucifixion. Eric Newton[1] has praised it highly:

A lonely figure against a deep and cold blue background suggesting illimitable space, a scaffolding of black lines carrying the rectangular cruciform motive across the whole surface of the canvas, a half abstract indication of darkness and red earth at the base of the cross remove all sense of time and space, and leave one with a complex and rather terrible symbol. Sutherland has dared to stand beside the great men of the Renaissance on their own high ground, and he survives the test.

This 'Crucifixion,' like Moore's 'Madonna,' would never have been painted but for enlightened Church patronage. It was paid for from the vicar's special fund. Its acceptance caused some heartburnings both in the church council and at Peterborough, but to-day some of its former critics are as proud of it as they are of the 'Madonna,' and no other church in England can boast of such a pair of modern masterpieces.

The musical record of this church is no less surprising. For the last four years the patronal festival has been celebrated with the per-

1. Art critic of the *Guardian* 1930–47 and 1956–65.

formance of a new work specially composed by a major musician. In 1943 it was Benjamin Britten's cantata 'Rejoice in the Lamb,' with words from Christopher Smart's long poem; it consists of ten short sections for choir and organ. In the same service a special fanfare for brass instruments by Michael Tippett, was played by members of the band of the Northamptonshire Regiment.

The following September the congregation heard Edmund Rubbra's motet for unaccompanied choir, 'The Revival,' written for the seventeenth-century words by Henry Vaughan. A year later Lennox Berkeley wrote a festival anthem; in 1946 Gerald Finzi provided 'Lo, the full final Sacrifice,' an anthem to words by Richard Crashaw, and Benjamin Britten an organ prelude and fugue on a theme of Vittoria.

The service included devotional readings by Valentine Dyall, the actor, and a special litany for St. Matthew's Day by W. H. Auden. Here are two passages from the litany:

Let us pray especially, therefore, at this time, for all who, like our patron saint, the blessed Apostle and Evangelist Matthew, occupy positions of petty and unpopular authority through whose persons we suffer the impersonal discipline of the state, for all who must inspect and cross-question, for all who issue permits and enforce restrictions. Deliver them from their peculiar temptations, that they may not come to regard the written word or the statistical figure as more real than flesh and blood nor extend an itching palm, nor compensate for some domestic unhappiness by harshness and indifference in their official dealings. And deliver us, as private citizens, from confusing the office with the man so that we hate those who through no fault of their own cause us some inconvenience, from believing that we are the exceptional case who has a right to special treatment and from forgetting that it is our impatience and indolence, our own abuse and terror of freedom, our own injustice that creates the state to be a punishment and a remedy for sin.

And again:

Deliver us, we pray thee, in our pleasure and in our pain, in our hour of elation and our hour of wan hope, from insolence and envy, from pride in our virtue, from fear of public opinion, from the craving to be amusing at all costs, and from the temptation to pray, if we pray at all: 'I thank thee, Lord, that I am an interesting sinner and not as this Pharisee.'

R.G.J.[1]

---

1. R. G. Jessel

## YEATS GOES HOME TO SLIGO

Saturday, September 18, 1948
*From our Special Correspondent*[1]

Sligo, Friday

Here under bare Ben Bulben's mist-shrouded head, five miles outside Sligo, W. B. Yeats was buried in Drumcliffe[2] Churchyard on a wet, Western day, after the long voyage from the South of France. Outside the church stood the ancient cross and the tree-screened ruined Round Tower; inside, lit only by oil lamps, was the tablet recording that his ancestor held the living early in the last century. Every detail, in fact, was exactly as Yeats himself had ordered it when he wrote his own epitaph:

> *Under bare Ben Bulben's Head*
> *In Drumcliff churchyard Yeats is laid*
> *An ancestor was rector there*
> *Long years ago, a church stands near,*
> *By the road an ancient cross.*
> *No marble, no conventional phrase;*
> *On limestone quarried near the spot*
> *By his command these words are cut:*
> > *Cast a cold eye*
> > *On life, on death,*
> > *Horseman, pass by!*

Yeats died in January, 1939, at Cap Martin. Almost his last act was to dictate to his wife some corrections for a poem about Ben Bulben – the whale-headed mountain which was, like so much of County Sligo, almost an obsession with him. In September, 1939, his body was to have been brought from Roquebrune for reburial at Drumcliffe, but the war prevented it. So nine years after, he has had a second funeral in a solemn but not a mournful atmosphere, with every mark of national, municipal, and personal affection.

The coffin, landed from an Irish corvette at Galway in the early morning (to the dismay of local patriots in Sligo), was received at the borough boundary by the Mayor, Alderman Rooney; the Minister for

1. Gerard Fay

2. Fay and Crockford's Clerical Directory prefer the final 'e' for the parish in whose churchyard Yeats is buried; the poet and his publisher spelled it Drumcliff and that spelling is retained in the verse quoted.

External Affairs, Mr. Sean MacBride, stood in the background, and a small 'Who's who' of Ireland's literature, drama, and art clustered round him. Behind the hearse were cars carrying Mrs. Yeats, her son and daughter, Michael and Anne, Mr. Jack B. Yeats, and some close personal friends of the man called by T. S. Eliot 'the greatest poet of our time – certainly the greatest in his language, and, so far as I can judge, in any language.'

The Mayor's welcome was short and pleasingly unpompous. Then behind an un-uniformed town band of wailing Irish pipes and shrouded thudding drums, the procession crawled into Sligo to the Town Hall. Here was the first sign of circumstance, when a military guard of honour filed out to surround the hearse and stand silent with arms reversed and heads bowed while a quiet crowd of townsmen huddled round, curious to see the coffin of the man for whom the tricolours were at half-mast, the shops closed, and the streets lined with policemen.

The coffin remained outside the Town Hall for over an hour, and the crowd stayed round it inspecting the few wreaths and seeking the autographs of the celebrities, Mr. Lennox Robinson, Mr. Micheal MacLiammoir, and many another who had come from Dublin and other parts of Ireland and paid tribute in his own Sligo to their own Yeats. None was more appropriate to the occasion than Mr. MacBride, son of the beautiful Maude Gonne, for whom Yeats wrote so many of his poems early and late, who was a symbol to all Irishmen of their country's struggle for freedom, and who at any time up to 1916 Yeats would so gladly have married.

After this pause the procession formed again, and again the Mayor escorted the hearse to another borough boundary on the road to Drumcliffe. The symbol-seeker might notice that the route lay along Markievicz Road, called after the Sligo girl of whom, when she was Constance Gore-Booth, Yeats wrote the lines beginning, 'When long ago I saw her ride, Under Ben Bulben to the meet.' And so to Drumcliffe, where the crowd pressed into the churchyard close to the grave to hear the unfamiliar Protestant Burial Service conducted by the Bishop of Kilmore, the responses muttered by the few who knew them. Here the dominant figure was Jack B. Yeats, standing tall, bareheaded, and taking in the picture with his artist's eye, which must have seen how the misty rain softened the graveyard scene and how the small birds darted among the trees, deputising for the hawks or eagles which might aptly have appeared for the last moments of his brother's burial.

Surely there was never such a crowd in this quiet country churchyard, and surely there was never such a day in this quiet country town.

There might have been a time when Yeats's funeral would have been a less notable affair – for the good people of Sligo, and of Roman Catholic Ireland as a whole, have not always accepted him without question. It is firmly stated here that there was a time when he was thought to be a magician who could move himself five miles through the air in the winking of an eye; there was a time when his robust, scornful championing of Synge stamped him as an enemy of Ireland's faith; there was even a time when he was called pensioner of the hated British Crown.

But time has veiled these offences as the mists from the Atlantic veiled Ben Bulben to-day, and Ireland has given herself another place of pilgrimage. When Yeats's epitaph is cut in stone and placed on his grave Drumcliffe churchyard will certainly be a place for visitors to see, for whatever may become of Yeats the dramatist, Yeats the poet is clearly a growing force in a world which yearns for poets as wildly as it yearns for the peace they sometimes preach.

## The Cold War

### WHEN LIFE WAS NORMAL IN PRAGUE

Wednesday, July 24, 1946
*By A. J. P. Taylor*

Prague, July
In Czechoslovakia life is normal. This does not seem so surprising if you go from London to Prague by air, travelling more easily and more quickly than from London to Edinburgh. It is incredible and bewildering if you come to Prague overland through the chaos and starvation of any of the surrounding countries.

There are plenty of scars; scars of material destruction, scars from the German Terror, scars from the Communist effervescence of the last twelve months which has only just died down. In fact, most Czechs of liberal mind are still rather dazed to discover that they, and liberty, have survived both conquest by the Germans and liberation by the Russians. For there can be no doubt that liberty has survived.

At any rate, there is not a scrap of Russian interference; there is nothing in the nature of a secret police; there are no restrictions on freedom of movement or of discussion. There is complete religious freedom, a freedom where both Protestant and Roman Catholic leaders take an active part in political life.

There is, too, complete academic freedom. The University of Prague is now the only academic institution of indisputably first rank east of the Rhine. Other English visitors have commented on the Czech desire for cultural contacts with Britain, and culture does not mean here simply literature and the arts. In Moscow, too, everyone listens to Shakespeare and reads Dickens. In Prague they want also our 'political' culture.

The Czech people had, no doubt, a democratic tradition; but the man who preserved that tradition and restored liberty was Dr. Benes. He has obviously had a hard time standing up to the Russians and the Czech Communists; but he has stood up to them successfully. He is that rare thing – a man of principle who is also adroit, even wily, in his tactics. His hand has, of course, been immensely strengthened by having the ideas of Masaryk behind him.

In most European countries liberalism was pulled down by laissez-faire and finally degenerated into 'collaborationism.' Now the competing political philosophies are both totalitarian; they look to the Vatican or the Kremlin. In Czechoslovakia alone it is possible to be a Socialist without being a Marxist; a liberal without believing in capitalism; and religious without being a Roman Catholic.

There is also a more mundane explanation of Czech democracy. Tolerance and liberty flourish with economic prosperity, and the Czech lands never ceased to be prosperous. The Germans murdered over a quarter of a million people in a deliberate campaign to destroy the Czech nation. Therefore they murdered selectively, killing exclusively intellectuals – teachers, administrators, trade union officials, lawyers, writers. The Czech workers had good wages and steady employment; the peasants had high prices and secure markets. Czech industry was little damaged except in the very last weeks of the war, and most of the damage, even the damage to railways and bridges, has been restored. The Republic took over from the Germans a going concern.

The political freedom has, of course, clear limits. It is freedom within the programme drawn up at Kosice before the liberation, freedom on the agreed principles of a nation-State and the nationalisation of industry.

In the Czech lands (Bohemia and Moravia) only four parties are allowed to run candidates and to publish newspapers. All four parties are represented in the Coalition Government, and this gives to the proceedings of Parliament a certain artificiality, or at least dullness. The real debates are within the Council of Ministers (which, having twenty-six members, is itself a debating assembly) and in the party meetings. Parliament records formal decisions and applauds agreements already made. It will face its real test if the Coalition breaks up.

Mr. Gottwald, the Communist Prime Minister, told me that democracy is secure 'so long as the other parties remain progressive,' by which he meant so long as they were willing to co-operate with the Communists. The other parties are likely to remain progressive so long as the Communists remain democratic.

The parties will not differ on the principle of the nation-State. All Czechs dislike the expulsion of the Germans; but all know that it is inevitable. The alternative would be worse; it would be the compulsory turning of Germans into Czechs, a policy only possible (if then) by Nazi methods. All the same, it is a strange historic moment which ends for ever the seven centuries of Czech-German conflict and co-operation in Bohemia.

Nor will the parties differ on the nationalisation of industry. For all practical purposes the controversy between capitalism and Socialism was settled by the Germans. They took over most important industries and ran them for their own purposes. Now it is impossible to 'unscramble' what the Germans have done. Instead the Czechoslovak people have become the residuary legatees of the German oppressors. Socialism has come, as in Great Britain, by legal means though the German occupation was no doubt a very unpleasant way of accelerating it.

In Czechoslovakia, as nowhere else east of the Rhine, there is at present both Socialism and democracy. Many Czechs ask, 'Can we have nationalisation without totalitarian rule?' The answer depends partly on the willingness of the Communists to be satisfied with economic gains without pushing Marxism down everyone's throat. It depends much more on the resolution with which the non-Communist parties defend their liberal morality and philosophy without slipping into a defence of capitalism. And most of all it depends on factors not under Czech control; a satisfactory relation with the Slovaks, a stable European order, and the revival of Czech foreign trade.

# THE DEATH OF JAN MASARYK

Thursday, March 11, 1948

Prague, March 10

Mr. Jan Masaryk, the Czechoslovak Foreign Minister and son of Thomas Masaryk, the founder of the Czechoslovak Republic, was found dead early to-day under the window of his official residence in Prague.

A State funeral, with full military honours, will be held on Saturday.

*From a Special Correspondent lately in Prague*[1]

The manner of Jan Masaryk's death came not only as a profound shock but also as a complete surprise to all who knew him. All his life he had striven to remain faithful to the honoured name and reputation of his great father, whose chief faith was anchored in the conviction that suicide was a cowardly means of escape. If Jan Masaryk finally did choose this way it would be a negation of his whole life's work.

Whether he actually took his own life or whether his death is attributable to other causes may never be known. But the possibility that it was not suicide cannot be dismissed; nor should one forget the comparison with the former Minister of Justice, who was found injured in similar circumstances, but who, according to eye-witness accounts, was assaulted in the streets and then abandoned underneath the window of his flat.

There was certainly nothing in Masaryk's nature to indicate that he contemplated suicide. But ever since the fatal day when he was ordered to withdraw his enthusiastic acceptance of the offer of the Marshall Plan he had been a changed man. He looked older than his 61 years in the last few weeks of his life, his springy step had given way to a sluggish walk, and despondency and weariness characterised his former jovial self. Yet only one day before his end – in what was to be his last personal interview – he did not give the impression of a desperate man. The one wish he then expressed was to attend 'some conference in London soon' and he still thought this a distinct possibility.

But the visitor who saw Masaryk in his official residence could not but be struck by the net that had closed around him. Masaryk was

1. Stefan Schimanski, whose suspicions about Masaryk's suicide are now generally shared.

confined to the Czerninsky Palace, where he had never lived before; he was surrounded by new secretaries who a week previously had not yet been installed; and he was no longer permitted to see visitors alone.

Every statement he had made in the last two weeks was censored; and the appointment of the Czech Diplomatic Service had been taken over by the Communist Minister of the Interior.

Masaryk was a prisoner in every sense of the word; but there was more than one way in which he could have resolved the conflict. And there is reason to believe that, courageous as he was, he would have made a stand in the Czech Parliament which met to-day for the first time since the crisis. He was expected to speak and it is not impossible – so at least those who knew him will believe – that he would have without censorship clarified his position in the light of the many critical messages which he had received from America and England in the last few days and which hurt him deeply.

Masaryk certainly was under no illusion that his country could still be saved for the West. When I saw him on the 16th of last month, a day before the Cabinet crisis broke, he confessed that Czechoslovakia was no longer a bridge between East and West. 'It is now,' he said, with resignation, 'nothing but a bridgehead.'

If Masaryk ever erred in political judgment it was on the occasion of the recent developments in his country. He was convinced the Communists would not come into power for another eight to ten months. 'The end of Czechoslovakia is coming,' he told me, 'but it will take some time.' In the meantime he hoped for intervention from the West, and he even went so far as to confess, in an aside, that he wished 'war would be here already.'

As for himself he was tired of all politics. 'Believe me,' he said, 'I shall be the happiest man in the world the moment I can resign my post and take up a lectureship in Cambridge or America.' As it was he stayed on in the new Government at the express request of President Benes. It was the last visible means to retain a fictitious link with the West, but he knew it could not work.

It was clear that so independent a character and so confirmed a democrat could not remain a puppet in the hands of a dictator for long. But whether he went of his own free will in order to end the farcical puppet show or whether he was made to go before he could use whatever authority and freedom he still possessed to expose the full meaning of Czechoslovakia's 'revolution' will probably remain buried in the tragic situation that was responsible for his death.

# THE SIEGE OF BERLIN

Friday, June 25, 1948

MR. BEVIN'S RETURN

*From our Diplomatic Correspondent*[1]

London, Thursday

Mr. Bevin, who has been on a Channel-cruising holiday in a friend's yacht, returned to Southampton to-day in a motor torpedo-boat which had been sent to fetch him. A car brought him at once from Southampton to London. The present tense situation in Berlin is clearly responsible for this change of plan.

The question which is likely to present itself most urgently and starkly to the Foreign Secretary is how far we are now prepared to go in our determination to remain in Berlin. Are we, for instance, prepared to risk the use of force and the possibility of war? Such an issue, appalling to contemplate though it may be, had certainly been considered at least by the United States before the present crisis came to a head.

The inquiry as to what military contribution France was in a position to make, if need be, to enable the Western Powers to remain in Berlin is proof enough of this. Mr. Bevin's statement, which so much cheered the House of Commons on May 4, that we were in Berlin by right and intended to stay there suggests that we too had gone equally far in consideration of the question. Mr. Bevin may have made this statement after profound consideration of its implications, but it will be surprising if it does not come up again for review by the Government.

There can presumably be no question of our preparing to take extreme measures merely to save our face and vindicate our earlier statements. Nor, though it may be a hard thing to admit, is the fulfilment of our promises to the Germans of the Western sectors the issue which is likely to dominate the thinking of the Government. The most vital question of all seems to be – if we abandon Berlin can we hope to preserve sufficient prestige with the Germans to make Western Germany and the Frankfurt Government a practical possibility? Or shall we have to surrender all Germany to Russian control?

The expulsion of the Western Powers from Berlin – and if we do leave it is too late now to avoid the appearance of expulsion – would not only be a considerable triumph for the Russians and a corresponding loss of face for the Western Powers. It would clearly give to the

1. Richard Scott

German Government the Russians would set up in Berlin – still regarded by almost every German as his capital city, to which he looks as he can to no other German city as the capital of the future unified Germany – a powerful advantage over the Government at Frankfurt in a claim to be the Government of all Germany.

Though it is quite possible, if the Russians continue to isolate the capital from the Western zones, that the Western Powers could maintain at least nominal forces in Berlin by means of air transport, it is obvious that they could not supply by air the 2,000,000 Germans in the Western sectors. It is improbable that the Russians would just leave them to starve, but would assume the provisioning of the whole city, claiming at the same time the control of its administration, which would be purged of non-members of the Socialist Unity party.

The detachments of the three Western powers could then safely be left to stay on, ignored and impotent. If that is indeed the Soviet policy, it is not easy to see how it can be countered by the Western powers without recourse to force.

> Five days later Mark Arnold Forster was able to report from Berlin: 'The sound of aircraft can be heard day and night and the orderly unending procession of Dakotas and Skymasters is visible and audible proof of the Western Allies' determination to do their best. To-day and yesterday the sight has done more to raise the Berliners' morale than the most rousing proclamation could ever do.'

## Tuesday, October 5, 1948

### WINTER BLOCKADE?
### *From our Special Correspondent*[1]

Berlin, October 4

October 2 was the hundredth day of the absolute blockade, by land and water, of Berlin. Three months ago the joint Anglo-American airlift was regarded less as a serious operation than as a generous and spontaneous gesture, capable of heartening the German population but certainly not of supplying them with all the essentials of human existence. Three months ago nobody, save the small band of planners in British and American headquarters, looked more than a few weeks ahead. The supply of over two million people by air was in summer improbable, in winter unthinkable.

The first three months have, thanks to planning initiative and perfect

1. Terence Prittie

technical execution, been successfully bridged. The next three months must still be critical. Berlin is afraid of this coming winter, but Berlin has been afraid of each post-war winter. In every home the chances of the air-lift to carry Berlin into next spring are eagerly debated. What are these chances? For on them depends whether two and a quarter million people can be bullied into submission or whether their late but nevertheless wholehearted espousal of the cause of Western democracy can win them elementary freedom.

What more can be done in Berlin? There is a widely held belief that the domestic fuel problem can be solved by cutting wood. Along Berlin's western boundary stretches the Grünewald with huge reserves of timber. The trees in the city's streets alone can give each household $1\frac{1}{2}$ cwt. of timber – a total around 70,000 tons. Wood is an uneconomic heater, but a big felling programme carried out by labour forces released from coalless industries, may yet have to be considered. Ultimately people must be warmed and emergency schemes for central 'warming-halls' are already in preparation.

Electric power for lighting and cooking is the next problem. During the summer Berliners had four hours' light during the twenty-four. Winter days are inconveniently short and families may have no light whatever after five in the evening. This is a miserable prospect. A few may not even be able to cook a meal for husbands coming home from work. Fortunately 80 per cent of the population cook by gas, but even so many are 'staggering' meals because the gas pressure is so low.

Next to cold, darkness – for candles and oil-lamps are almost unobtainable – is the Berliners' chief dread. Hunger comes a close third. Inevitably the Allies made food supplies the first priority on the air-lift and fulfilled rations requirements before a ton of coal was flown in. The rations are arriving but they are still terribly low. Before the blockade Berliners went out to buy fruit from Werder, vegetables from neighbouring Beelitz, potatoes from as far afield as Mecklenburg and even the Western zones. All that has been stopped and about the only additional source of supply is black market potatoes after the best Eastern German harvest in twenty years. The old, the poor, and the unemployed are striving to do something almost unheard of – live on their rations. Moreover lack of money often makes it impossible to buy all of them.

Berlin has maintained her export trade, and the only transport problem arising is that of heavy machinery from the Siemens and A.E.G. combines. The air-lift is taking no capital goods from Western Berlin or any goods in transit from the Soviet zone and it has no difficulty in moving all exports of manufactured articles. At the moment

90 per cent of the working population is on pay-rolls, although much of their labour is unprofitable.

Public-opinion surveys have shown that confidence in the power of the air-lift to get Berlin through the winter is mounting.

> By the time the air-lift ended twelve months later over a quarter of a million flights had been made.

## THE SIN OF THE SON: U.S. NAVY SEES RED

### Monday, August 8, 1955

> The 1950s were the heyday of the witch-hunt for Un-American activities. Alistair Cooke reported almost every move in the chase. Here is one isolated incident.

#### From Alistair Cooke

New York, August 6

'The case of Eugene Landy' is not yet a classic example of the theory and practice of 'security' in an insecure time; but if the Navy has the courage to hold fast, it may well become one.

Up to yesterday the only people who had ever heard of Eugene W. Landy, aged 21, were the United States Merchant Marine Academy at King's Point, Long Island, where he was the second highest scholar of his year, and a Navy Security Board which sent him on Thursday morning an important personal note. It is said that on Friday, when Landy's class was due to graduate, he alone would be denied the usual privilege (it is, the Navy noted, 'no inherent right') of men graduating from the academy to be sworn in as ensigns in the Naval Reserve.

The Navy had applied to him one of the most delicate security tests and found him wanting. It is one that may be used as a rejection for any position of honour and trust in the armed forces: 'Continuing association with a person or persons who have a past history in the Communist party.'

The sin of Eugene Landy, an otherwise enviable scholar, athlete, personal charmer, a prompt and chronic signer of loyalty oaths, is that he shows a stubborn disinclination to stop 'associating' with his mother. Mrs. Landy is a widow living at a beach town in New Jersey. She is a hand-sewer in a coat factory. Soon after her husband died in 1947 she drifted, as she puts it, into the Communist party. There is evidence that she applied in writing for membership in the C.P. She went to meetings, she has confessed. But she refuses to admit that she was dedicated to the overthrow of the Government of the United

States by force and violence. 'I never intended to bring about a revolution,' this large and comfortable matron remarked yesterday. 'I never found communism to be a conspiracy. Out here in this rural area, it was more a kaffee-klatsch.' (Kaffee-klatsch has passed into the American vernacular as 'coffee-clutch' or 'coffee-break.' It has no dialectical significance whatsoever either in the Communist, Republican, or Prohibition parties.)

These artless words have come before now from cool and plausible spies. They could, of course, also come from a large and lonely hand-sewer who sought out a little friendship in the years of her widowhood. In 1947 or 1948, she's not sure which, her son Eugene, then a rather determined patriot of thirteen, gave her what she calls, 'an ultimatum. He told me to choose between him and the party. I chose him.' She quit the party.

Young Eugene seemed to come through this traumatic episode with puzzling and healthy phlegm. He did well at school. He entered the King's Point Academy, the West Point of the Merchant Marine, four years ago. Yesterday he stood up with the other 95 men of his graduating year, spruce and unrepentant in his white dress uniform. When the moment came to take his oath in the United States Naval Reserve all the men raised their right hands. He was implicitly forbidden to raise his, and it must be said that the news photographers, catching this futile moment, have done as much as anybody to make the ordeal of Eugene Landy become a national affair overnight.

He stands there, a darkly handsome youngster, unscorned by the erect men at his elbow. When the oath is taken, the new ensigns toss their hats into the air. The photographers were ready for that moment, too. The hats peppered the hot air with 95 flying saucers. Landy tucked his hat in the crook of his left arm, while his hand clutched his Bachelor of Science degree, his graduating certificate which details his high honours and allows him the rank and title of a third mate in the maritime service. Indeed, he assumed his duties the same day. Last night he sailed in an oil tanker from Carteret, New Jersey, on a thirty-day voyage to Texas. But not before he had put in an appeal against the Navy's action and made the passing comment: –

'They should have used common sense in evaluating my association with my mother, as they are supposed to do, according to the instructions carried by the naval intelligence men who questioned me. They should have taken the word of the authorities of King's Point, where I have been under close supervision for four years as a student as to my character.'

The Daughters of the American Revolution, the oldest and least revolutionary national society in America, comes into this bizarre story. The D.A.R. holds to the pleasant custom of giving an annual award to the Merchant Academy graduate who is the best naval-science student in his class. This year the winner was Landy. The D.A.R. has no intention of taking it away from him.

By to-day other outsiders were moving in with denunciations and demands that might yet compel the Navy to bow to the opinion of Landy's classmates, in a circulated petition, that he is 'a fine classmate and a loyal American.' One Republican Congressman from New York said the Navy's case was not strong enough to 'warrant his rejection.' The senior senator from New York, Mr. Herbert Lehman, a Democrat, called the Navy's action 'illogical, unjust, and unjustifiable.' He wants, as any senator can surely get, a 'full report' from the Navy. He was joined in this request by Senator Alexander Smith, Republican of New Jersey.

The Navy stayed mum till to-day. It is aware that Mrs. Landy, flying with a mad inconsequence in the face of official wrath, still gets the *Daily Worker*, 'but looks at it only occasionally.' The Navy properly points out, in the words of its officials, that Landy 'is extremely close to his mother.' There is no denying it, and the Navy obviously cannot be too careful about such aberrations. Last night the Secretary of the Navy promised that he would give the case 'a full and impartial review. Mr. Landy will get justice. We are very careful in the Navy. Any complaint gets a full and impartial review.'

## The Thaw that went Away

### HOW MOSCOW BROKE THE NEWS OF STALIN'S DEATH

Saturday, March 7, 1953
*From a Correspondent*[1]

There was a spluttering and an odd, incomprehensible noise issuing from the radio receiver which was tuned in to the Moscow home service. The 0100 hours news bulletin had just been broadcast. It was

1. Victor Zorza. In 1953 Zorza was still on the monitoring staff of the B.B.C., but was already a frequent contributor to the *Guardian*. He had, however, never before visited the office. He arrived at 9.30 and wrote all day.

a repeat of the bulletin that went out at midnight, and that in turn had been a repeat of the evening broadcast.

I waited. The news of Stalin's death had just been released to the outside world by Moscow's foreign services. Now, surely, was the moment for the Russians to be told. But they were not told anything – except perhaps by implication. Solemn orchestral music brimmed out of the loudspeaker, filling the night with an eerie atmosphere of tragedy and sorrow. The Russians who were listening-in at that moment – the broadcast was beamed to Siberia, where it was morning by then – had not been told; but they must have surmised the truth.

As time went on and the customary news bulletins, the early morning broadcast of the physical training instructor, and the talks on political subjects, failed to materialise, the surmise in the minds of the listeners must have turned to a dimly apprehended certainty. There were those, I am sure, who were still hoping against hope. The dread word had not been uttered yet. A crisis perhaps – but surely not death!

At 2.55 the music ceased. For a moment there was stillness in the air, silence in the room – and in the rooms of all the Russians whose sets were tuned to Moscow. Then came the bells. They pealed neither joyfully nor sorrowfully, and yet managed to impart to the waiting minds and straining ears a sense of foreboding something akin to fear – the feeling that overcomes most people at a crisis in life.

At 0300 the bells stopped, suddenly. Again silence. And then the majestic strains of the Soviet national anthem, which replaced the 'Internationale' during the war. The broad melody swept the vast expanses of Russia, of which it is intended to be descriptive. It penetrated into the little huts in the mountain settlements of Central Asia. And far in the North, where the snow and ice never thaw, it was heard by the camp guards who had just come back into the warmth of the guardroom, having been relieved by their comrades on the stroke of three. But the camp inmates – of whom I was once one – probably did not know and, if they knew, were hardly in a condition to care. They had just done a twelve-hour stretch of hard, back-breaking work, some in the forests where they had been felling trees, others in the goldmines of the Soviet Far East.

Five minutes, and the anthem came to a close. Would the ordinary news bulletin now be broadcast? Would it be a repeat of an earlier bulletin? Or would the news, which was by now in all the newspaper offices of the outside world, be told at last to the Russians?

Yuri Levitan, the announcer who during the war brought the Russians the news of victories – but never of defeats – was at the microphone. Slowly, solemnly, with a voice brimming over with emotion, he read:

'The Central Committee of the Communist party, the Council of Ministers and the Praesidium of the Supreme Soviet of the U.S.S.R. announce with deep grief to the party and all workers that on March 5 at 9.50 p.m., Josef Vissarionovich Stalin, Secretary of the Central Committee of the Communist party and Chairman of the Council of Ministers, died after a serious illness. The heart of the collaborator and follower of the genius of Lenin's work, the wise leader and teacher of the Communist party and of the Soviet people, stopped beating.'

The blow was a heavy one, he said. The news would bring pain to the hearts of all men. 'But in these dark days all the peoples of our country are becoming more united in the great brotherly family led by the Communist party, founded and educated by Lenin and Stalin. The Soviet people is united in its confidence and inspired with warm love for the Communist party, knowing that the supreme law governing all activity of the party is to serve the interests of the people.'

The Soviet people, he went on, would follow the guidance of the party, the rightness of whose policy had been demonstrated over and over again. Now, under the party's continued leadership, they would look forward to new successes. They knew, he said, quoting a recent statement of Stalin's without attributing it to the dead leader, that the improvement of the people's material well-being was the party's special concern. They also knew – and here his voice became firm and self-assured – that the defensive powers of the Soviet State were growing in strength, that the party was doing everything to prepare a crushing blow for any possible aggressor.

In foreign policy the party and the Government would strive to consolidate and preserve peace, oppose the preparations for the unleashing of new wars, and work for international collaboration – familiar words, these, coming from Moscow radio. Can there be any more substance in them than on the thousand previous occasions when Soviet spokesmen uttered them?

And then came the first intimate note with another, harder, note superimposed upon it. 'Dear friends and comrades,' Levitan said, 'the great directing and leading force of the Soviet Union in the struggle for the building of Communism is our Communist party. Steel-like unity and a monolithic cohesion of the ranks of the party are the main conditions for strength and power.'

## PICASSO IN TROUBLE

Thursday, March 19, 1953
*From our own Correspondent*[1]

Paris, March 18

'The Secretariat of the French Communist party categorically disapproves the publication in *Les Lettres Françaises* of March 12 of the portrait of the Great Stalin drawn by Comrade Picasso.' This appears on the front page of the *Humanité* under the black headline 'Communication from the Secretariat of the French Communist party.'

M. Picasso's drawing is in the vein of his dove in the sense that the eyes are separated by the nose, with the mouth between the last mentioned organ and the chin. Anatomically there is nothing unusual about it and the draughtsmanship has a fine vigour. But M. Picasso has clearly identified Mr. Stalin with the second rather than the first person of the communist trinity. An idealistic, but bothered young man looks

1. Darsie Gillie

out of the page at the reader and the neck has no modulations whatsoever – a stove-pipe neck. The moustache had once been of more
generous proportions but an india-rubber has reduced it to those of
daily convenience though, perhaps not of majesty. M. Picasso himself
replied to questions of journalists this morning as to how the drawing
had come into existence.

He had not, he said, read the *Humanité*, M. Picasso added:

'When Stalin died Aragon telegraphed to me asking me "to do
something." I am not a writer so I made a drawing. I did what I felt,
for I have never seen Stalin. I did my best to make it a likeness. It
does not seem to have been liked. Last week someone wrote to me
to say so. I did not think any more about it. I get fifty letters a week
and I cannot take them all into account.'

For a long time M. Aragon has been trying to bridge the gulf
between the tastes of French Left-wing intellectuals and those that the
Kremlin has made obligatory.

Last year he contributed to *Les Lettres Françaises* a long series of
articles explaining the virtues of Russian art, both pre and post
revolutionary. The articles were ably argued, but would have been
more convincing without the illustrations. No sensible man, however,
would dispute the thesis that aesthetic views which prevent the production of battle panoramas a hundred yards long like that of the
battle of Borodino at Moscow are undesirable. They might deprive us
of Madame Tussaud's.

To men in the situation of M. Aragon and, indeed, the leaders of the
French Communist party, the harmonisation of respect for M. Picasso
with that for Kremlin truths, has always been difficult. Fortunately
M. Picasso can draw doves. But apart from that he strays. To deny that
he is a great artist is to deprive the party of all the advertising potentials
of his tremendous reputation. But no one could say that to follow his
example would be to please the Kremlin. It has been argued that
abstract art is not bourgeois in practice by M. Picasso, but only when
imitated by lesser men. But what is the good of an artist whom you
cannot imitate?

The incident shows that not even M. Picasso can defy without repri-
mand the order that faces should look like photographs and that all
artistic production should be accessible to the working class and be of
direct utility to the revolution. The incident is much more serious,
however, for M. Aragon than for M. Picasso, since the latter can always
go on selling pictures to the rich bourgeoisie, whereas M. Aragon as
party editor and author of party novels is dependent on party favour.
He seems to be guilty of opportunist toadying to cosmopolitan

intellectuals. No doubt a self-criticism will be needed if he is to keep his job. Otherwise he too will be on the way out of the party with, at the end of the road, a denunciation as 'police agent' and 'traitor.'

M. Aragon can scarcely complain if this happens to him. Until the end of August, 1939, he worked in the closest co-operation with Paul Nizan, a fellow leader-writer of *Ce Soir*. M. Nizan resigned from the party because he could not stomach the Soviet-German pact, went to the front and was killed. When an exhibition of books by authors who died for France was held after the war, M. Aragon swept Paul Nizan's on to the floor and declared that he had always been a traitor and a police spy.

Challenged to justify his words, he has never done so, in the slightest degree. That is the kind of charge he will have to face in the party if he does not tread on the dotted line. Others will not easily forget that he made such a charge himself without a shadow of justification against a former comrade who had died fighting the Germans.

## LEFT SPEAKING TO LEFT

Wednesday, April 28, 1956
*From our Political Correspondent*[1]

While Marshal Bulganin was making a courteous and friendly speech at a luncheon party given by the Speaker at his house yesterday, Mr. Khrushchev interjected – no doubt with gruff humour – 'And I hope next time we come the Labour party will be more friendly.'

Very few of the politicians who were among the Speaker's guests could have failed to discover by midday that the Labour dinner party to Marshal Bulganin and Mr. Khrushchev on the previous night had been less than placid. Moreover it was quite clear when yesterday's luncheon party was breaking up that Mr. Khrushchev was still angered by the affair of the previous night.

Mr. George Brown, the M.P. for Belper, who is Labour's 'shadow' Minister of Supply and had taken a prominent part in the exchanges with Mr. Khrushchev at the previous night's dinner party, approached Mr. Khrushchev at the end of the Speaker's luncheon and, saying that he did not suppose that they would meet again during this visit, offered his hand for a farewell shake. Mr. Khrushchev refused to accept it, with a curt 'Nyet.'

1. Francis Boyd

A number of the guests at the Speaker's luncheon had been present at the famous dinner party. Several other guests had not. They could, however, detect a smell of burning yesterday.

These outside observers of the remains of the fire were the Prime Minister and a number of his colleagues.

They all now know from Mr. Khrushchev's own lips that he will not forget Labour's hospitality for some time. Mr. Brown was snubbed yesterday because during the dinner party on the previous night he had challenged in the vehement and rushing manner which is so familiar to those who attend meetings of the Parliamentary Labour party the account Mr. Khrushchev had been giving of the respective rôles of the Soviet Union and of Britain during the Second World War.

To Mr. Brown on Monday night it appeared that Mr. Khrushchev was claiming that Russia alone beat Germany. This was too much for Mr. Brown's volatile nature, and he exclaimed in a tone which brought Mr. Khrushchev's flow of words to an abrupt halt: 'God forgive you!' An awful pause followed.

Mr. Khrushchev then said to Mr. Brown: 'What did you say?' Another awful pause followed. 'Don't be frightened,' Mr. Khrushchev said. 'Say it again.'

Mr. Brown again said: 'God forgive you!'

There followed a sharp exchange in which Mr. Khrushchev kept to his own analysis of the war situation, and Mr. Brown retorted with anger that British men had been killed in the period of the Second World War when Soviet Russia and Nazi Germany were allies.

This outburst of hostility took place before Mr. Gaitskell, Mr. Bevan, Mr. Sam Watson, and others appealed to the Russians to ease the lot of Social Democrats who are political prisoners behind the Iron Curtain. Yesterday Labour members were wondering whether in all the circumstances this appeal for justice and mercy towards their political comrades in Central and Eastern Europe could have found the Russian visitors at their most receptive.

But evidently some of the leading members of the Labour movement had decided beforehand that it was their duty at the one arranged meeting between the National Executive of the party and the Russians to raise an issue which Social Democrats throughout the world regard as grave – the treatment of their fellow Social Democrats in Communist countries.

There are some Labour members who doubt whether the dinner party was the right occasion for this. There are others who wonder if Mr. Khrushchev would have been less unresponsive to the appeal if tempers had not been stirred beforehand. But there are still others who claim that whatever the outcome, the British Labour party would have betrayed the men and women in prison overseas if the dinner party had been nothing but an exchange of genial toasts with the Russians.


## THE HUNGARIAN FRONTIER

### Monday, October 29, 1956

In October, 1956 the people of Hungary rose against their still Stalinist masters. At first they succeeded. Victor Zorza made his way to the frontier from which he sent this message:


### THE PRIDE OF THE REBELS, AND A QUESTION FOR BRITAIN

*From Victor Zorza*

Nickelsdorf, October 28

The Austrian border guards at Nickelsdorf raised the barrier for a Hungarian rebel leader's car to go through. He had come across to arrange for the passage of medical and food supplies to Hungary. The journalists quickly followed him. We stayed in no-man's land and ran to the Hungarian frontier post.

Could we go on from here? No, we could not. We beseeched the rebel who seemed to be in charge. The other rebels beseeched us.

Finally out of the hubbub a clear Hungarian voice rang out. The man was giving a statement to the world press; a German gave a translation. The Hungarian said that his people wanted to live in peace and friendship with all countries, that they regretted the unfriendliness and hostility of the past.

A girl, the only one in the crowd of rebels, took up the tale. 'To-day is my seventeenth birthday,' she said, a little bashfully, with just a hint of pride in her voice. Seventeen, and she was one of the rebels who were defying the massive might of the Soviet Army. Seventeen, and she had just come from the town of Gjor, sixty or so kilometres from the frontier, where, someone else told us, eighty members of the Security Police had been 'liquidated' by the workers; where, she announced proudly, 'we put up a ladder against the Russian memorial, threw a noose round the Red Star on top of it, and pulled it down.'

She was seventeen, but the Budapest youths who had attacked Russian tanks with their bare hands were younger. Many were now dead. 'What is your estimate of our casualties?' she asked. 'Estimates vary from 200 to – ' Perhaps the journalist who was replying was going to say 10,000, a figure that has been mentioned in some reports. But the girl's question had been purely rhetorical. 'I must tell you that the dead must be counted not in hundreds, but in many, many thousands,' she said. 'What is the feeling of the Hungarian people about the sacrifice they are making?' another journalist asked. 'They believe that by thus drawing the attention of the world to what is happening they will compel the Russians to get out,' she said, and without pausing, asked: 'And what is the feeling of the British people?' We all hesitated. No one was anxious to reply.

Haltingly one of the reporters began to frame an answer. 'First, amazement.' Then a pause. 'Second – admiration.' Then quickly, desperately, as if he wanted to withdraw each word as soon as he had uttered it: 'And a great feeling of guilt.' The girl came back like a flash: 'There is much to be guilty for.'

> There was indeed much to be guilty for. As the Suez War began Russian troops invaded Hungary. Zorza, who had gone on to Budapest, was at that time still a 'stateless person.' He took refuge in the British Embassy. On November 2, Hungary appealed to the United Nations, but was met by a Soviet veto. On November 4, Russian troops reached Budapest.

## Recessional

### THE TRAGEDY OF THE PUNJAB

Friday, October 3, 1947
*By Sir Malcolm Darling*

The tragedy of the Punjab could have been foreseen. 'If you go, we shall kill each other,' said a Sikh peasant to me last December when I was riding across the province. He knew the past – he was 87 – and was terrified of the future. He was not alone in his fear. In greater or lesser degree it was present all along my route from the Indus to the Jumna. In Hoshiarpur, one of the districts most seriously affected, a Sikh officer on leave prophesied civil war, and a young Sikh merchant in the North said, 'Freedom is destruction, and Pakistan is kabaristan – a graveyard.' In that graveyard now lie unnumbered men, women, and children. And three million more are homeless.

How has this happened? The causes are complex and their roots lie deep in the past; but certain factors are clear. The clearest is the religious division between Hindu and Moslem. In March, 1940, the

Moslem League in a meeting at Lahore, adopted Pakistan as their battle-cry and target. Less than a month later the late Sir Sikander Hyat-Khan, then Premier of the Punjab, said to me in conversation that Pakistan was a new idea to the Moslem peasants of the province and it would now run like wildfire through their heads. Till then the communal feeling so prominent in the town rarely found expression in the village, and where, as in the Eastern Punjab, Hindu and Moslem cultivated the land side by side there was often an interchange of civilities at marriage and death. This friendly relationship was still in evidence last autumn, but marked by an underlying tension. In the election earlier in the year the cry of 'Islam in danger' had been raised and, thanks to sustained propaganda, by December the fear of Hindu domination was uppermost in the Moslem mind. 'We don't want to exchange slavery to the English for slavery to the Hindu' was typical of what was said to me in the village. The fear was given a sinister turn by the tales of Moslems massacred in Bihar. The tale of the Hindus massacred in Eastern Bengal was not told.

The fear of Hindu domination was easy to arouse owing to an economic factor. In the Western Punjab the peasant is predominantly Moslem, the trader and money-lender Hindu or Sikh. In the past the exactions of the money-lender had often generated bitter feelings and occasional explosions, but certain Bills passed early in the war had deprived him of his hold. Then came the rationing of grain, sugar, and cloth, and much of the power lost by the Hindu as a money-lender was regained by him as a trader, for the distribution of all necessaries in short supply was automatically placed in his hands, and that too under the control of a department which was notoriously corrupt. All along my route there was 'one universal hiss' against the controls, not from the shopkeepers and their influential clients, who got all they wanted, but from the ordinary peasant, who got far less than his due and was obliged to buy in the black market at exorbitant rates. It is difficult even for a peasant to be philosophic when he sees his last loin-cloth or shirt going to pieces and the cloth merchant with a pile of piece-goods which he will only sell at a fancy price. 'We could not even get a shroud to bury our dead' was the kind of thing being said and sometimes experienced. The shortage of cloth was bad enough, but where, as north of the Jhelum, a succession of poor harvests compelled the purchase of food grains in 'the black' disgust turned to bitterness. And so, when early in March trouble broke out in Amritsar, Lahore, and Mooltan, the Moslems of the North looted the shops and butchered their owners.

Many of the victims were Sikhs, and that brings me to a third factor.

Had Hindu and Moslem alone been concerned the division of the Punjab might have been effected without bloodshed. But the Sikhs also had their claims, and they were as determined to prevent the domination of the Moslem as the Moslems were the domination of the Hindu. Though only about four million in a population of 29,000,000, they are a formidable community with a martial ardour and a pride in their past which makes them unwilling to bow the knee to anyone but themselves and God, and they never forget that it was from them that we conquered the Punjab. No one who knew them could have supposed they would accept peacefully any settlement which cut their small community in two. Yet this was what the new boundary line did, and on August 16 over one and a half million found themselves suddenly cut off from the rest of the community. To the Sikhs this was political suicide, and, inflamed by what they had suffered in the North, they rose in their thousands and butchered.

For that boundary line we were ultimately responsible, and that raises the question: How far are we responsible for what followed? That we had to leave India as soon as we decently could goes without saying, and we might have done that even earlier in the case of the seven provinces with stable Indian Governments. But the Punjab was different. It was not a province to be cut in two like a Gordian knot in traditional Commando fashion.[1] When I was in Lahore last April tension was already extreme and the province a smouldering volcano. Time was clearly needed to let passions cool. Instead we roused them to white heat by the boundary award. Whatever the difficulties we should at least have been true to our hundred-year trust and not handed over millions of helpless peasants, for whose welfare we were responsible, to anarchy and ruin.

## THE FIRST STEP TO APARTHEID

### Saturday, May 29, 1948

The South African elections have gone as badly as they could. Smuts and the United party are out; Malan and the Nationalists are in. The overweighting of the rural constituencies has tilted the scales. The United party has more votes than all the other parties put together (not reckoning the independents); it carried big urban divisions but lost small rustic ones.

The second respect in which the Nationalists' victory is to be regretted is, of course, their attitude towards the Bantu. Dr. Malan may

1. Lord Mountbatten, the last Viceroy of India, had been Chief of Combined Operations.

not find it practicable, once in office, to carry out fully the sweeping measures of segregation and political retrogression which he promised in his election programme. But he will not be able to satisfy his supporters unless he goes some way along this road, and that means restrictions and repression, embitterment and estrangement. The echoes of the Malan policy towards the Bantu will be heard all over Africa. Everywhere from Sierre Leone to Swaziland and Kenya the evolution of relations between black and white is the greatest problem of this century. The spectacle of a clumsy and ill-considered attempt here to thrust the black peoples out from the advance of white civilisation will make it harder everywhere else for those whites who seek to win and to deserve the confidence of the native races. Perhaps one may hope, in the long run, that the segregation policy will be the rope that hangs the Nationalists, or brings them to their senses; that its failure – it cannot be conceived that, in the form put forward in the election campaign, it could succeed – will convince the South African electorate that the policy of Smuts and Hofmeyr is the realistic and practical course. But it may be a costly way of learning.

## KENYA AFTER THE MAU MAU

Wednesday, August 31, 1955
*From Patrick Monkhouse*

Nairobi

The Mau Mau rebellion has failed, but it is not finished. Life in the Kikuyu reserves is no longer precarious. It is not yet normal. Mau Mau forces still in the field may number three or four thousand. They are getting very few fresh recruits; lurking mainly in the forests which flank the Aberdare range and Mount Kenya, they are hard put to it to keep themselves fed. Where two years ago they marched through the reserves fifty or a hundred strong with flags flying and bugles playing, they creep in now by twos and threes after dark to forage, and bury themselves in the bamboo forests before dawn.

Two things especially have contributed to the rapid decline of Mau Mau as a striking force: the strength and growing skill of the military forces concentrated against it and the village policy. The villages may have consequences lasting beyond the emergency.

These villages are the first thing to catch the eye of the returning visitor, particularly if he comes by air. Before, the Kikuyu had no villages. Each family lived in its little group of huts, isolated on its land; and this isolation made them an easy prey for terrorists. Now the bulk of them live in compact villages. A thousand people would make a small village, five thousand a big one; the average would be between two and three thousand. In the more dangerous areas the villages are protected by a ditch and a stockade; in others they rely on their concentration for safety. At dusk the villagers retire to their village, taking all their cattle with them.

The village has two purposes. It protects the loyal against attacks by Mau Mau; and it prevents the fellow-travellers, the 'passive wing' of Mau Mau, from helping members of the gangs with food or shelter. Migration to safety was not for the most part a popular move. Many people were coerced into it. One sees everywhere the old homesteads with their roofs ripped off, to make people go, and incidentally to deny shelter to wandering Mau Mau. Most Kikuyu dislike the cramped dwellings, the social and hygienic discipline to which the life compels them, the constant supervision by detachments of the security forces, tribal police, or home guards, who have a detachment in every village. In the less reliable areas, control is tight even through the day. Parties of twenty or thirty may be seen setting off for their fields shepherded by a tribal policeman or two carrying firearms.

The police, too, have a dual purpose; to protect the workers against possible attacks, now very rare, and to ensure as far as they can that no one, secretly sympathising with Mau Mau, or anxious to reinsure himself or herself against possible changes in the fortunes of war, takes out a parcel of food and deposits it where a Mau Mau forager will find it after dark. This is thought to have been effective in denying supplies to the terrorists, who are driven to take ever greater risks in seeking food in the reserves; it is losing its force just now, as the maize crop is ripening, and foragers can help themselves. In most villages the cattle are stockaded at night, and the food stores are wired round and guarded so that no food can be stolen.

In the Embu district, south of Mount Kenya, a further device is used. The Embu Ditch, which runs along the edge of the forest, is 35 miles long, fifteen or twenty feet wide, and ten to twenty feet deep. The bottom is filled with sharp stakes of bamboo and with trip wires which, if one brushes against them, fire a cartridge to attract attention. Every half-mile along the ditch is a small guard post, from which patrols work to and fro. A skilful and resolute man may at night be able to pass this obstacle, with a great risk of detection. He cannot possibly drive cattle across it, and the Embu people were losing a good many cattle to the gangs before it was built. Another advantage to them is that the ditch keeps away the elephants which used to come out of the forest to raid their crops.

The military force deployed against Mau Mau is massive; eleven battalions of infantry (British and King's African Rifles) with supporting services, and large numbers of tribal police, 'general service' (armed) police, as well as home guards and two Asian 'combat units.' The bombers have gone, unregretted by most. These forces are now expertly and aggressively used. Part of each battalion stays just outside the forest to look out for foragers. The police units have posts in the lower strip of forest, largely cedar and cypress. The forward companies of the infantry battalions are right up in the bamboo forest, where most of the surviving Mau Mau men are.

I was able to visit the headquarters of one such company. It lay on a little bare knoll in the midst of the bamboo, and was reached by a rough track, usable only by a Land-Rover, invaluable here. It was about 8,000 ft. up; the summit ridge of the Aberdares reaches 12,000 ft. The three platoon positions were in the recesses of the bamboo, which grows so thickly that there is barely a yard's passage between its clumps. The troops and their antagonists live in a world of twilight and frequent rain. The platoon commander can see only a few of his men at a time; they bivouac on the ground. Each day patrols, with African trackers, rake through the forest. They search for footmarks, especially crossing the elephant tracks (which the Mau Mau have learned not to follow for any distance), and if a print is found the trackers try to follow it to a hiding-place. There are many disappointments in this fantastic warfare. But the Mau Mau are losing about a hundred men a week.

There is no doubt that the tribesmen find the village life, in its present form, most irksome; the constant supervision, the crowded dwellings laid out in haste and more for security than for comfort or convenience, the occasional petty exactions of home guards abusing their authority. They may react in either of two ways, resentment against the Government, which compels them to live so, or against Mau Mau for making it necessary. The latter reaction seems prevalent at the moment.

They are heartily sick of the emergency and angry with the Mau Mau for prolonging it when there is no chance of winning. They help to kill or capture Mau Mau men who infiltrate into the reserves; there was a strange incident lately when the women of one village sallied out with pangas and chopped to pieces the body of a terrorist leader who had been killed in an ambush or skirmish. (Or was this a precaution against some kind of magic rather than an outburst of resentment?) Yet this feeling might easily turn against the Administration if there is no relaxation of the tight grip in which they are now held; and the idea of village life might be utterly rejected as soon as it was safe to scatter.

This would be a great pity, for the villages, badly planned as many of them are, hold much promise for tribal life if they survive. They will hardly do so on their present scale. They may well do so if they can be decentralised in the near future.

## JEWS AGAINST BRITISH

Wednesday, July 3, 1946

*From our Special Correspondent lately in Palestine*[1]

It is not difficult to imagine the anger, dismay, and, amongst the older generation, sheer bewilderment with which the Jews in Palestine have experienced their first taste of strong British measures against acts of violence. In Palestine violence, although so commonplace now, seems always one step removed from everyday life (which is genial and normal). A bomb explodes, a bridge is wrapped in flames, a soldier is shot in the back, but the ordinary Jew going quietly about his useful work of commerce or agriculture tends to deceive himself that the thing did not happen or, if it did, it was only an isolated case. At night, in his house, he may feel uneasy when a lad of the family comes home, a nephew or son, who is either brooding and silent or else too gay. The older man knows little of the young man's secret life outside of the family circle and asks no questions. Thus has a gulf grown up between old and young in Palestine, though each will cling to the other if faced with a common threat. The older generation is anti-British in a sad sort of way, as though it did not wish to be, but the young are anti-British with a burning zeal. To them, regardless of earlier causes or failures by others, the mandatory Power is the monster that barred the gates of refuge to countless blood-brothers now dead in Europe. They are the children of affliction, reared and nourished on the bitterness of acute bereavement, the loss, which they may not forget, of relations and friends.

This is the emotional background to present-day Jewish terrorism. Capitalised by propagandists, exploited by school teachers, the wounded minds of the young learn to equate their sorrows, quite naturally, with the fight for unrestricted immigration and less naturally, with all the violence of a crude racial nationalism. In this temper and heat have the illegal armies grown. Their development during the years of the war was on similar lines to that of the dual-purpose partisan armies of Eastern Europe. Fighting heroically in the throes of a larger war, the

1 Ann Dearden

spearhead of a nationalist revolutionary movement was also formed. Into this movement both during and since the war all the pride and vigour of Jewish youth has been poured.

It has absorbed all classes. To-day in the common bond of militant enterprise, brilliant young men and women from the Hebrew University and other centres of learning consort with the robust outdoor workers of the agricultural settlements and the harsh primitive, and still illiterate refugees from the European camps. The new young immigrants from Europe have readily flocked to the 'colours.' It has been a hard task for the Jewish community as a whole to adapt some of these tough young people to a well-ordered life, and it was only to be expected that those who were highly trained 'Maquis' in Europe would find in the Jewish illegal military organisations a natural home from home.

> British troops eventually left Palestine in May, 1948. The State of Israel was formed and made good its title in war against the Arab states.

## ISRAEL: THE NATIVE GENERATION

### Friday, November 19, 1948
#### By Arthur Koestler

Tel Aviv, November
Each war and revolution produces its lost generation. Israel's lost generation are the middle-aged, those who came here at a time of their life which still allows them to remember Europe. Not the fleshpots of Europe; for most of them lived in penury. Not the safety of Europe; for they were persecuted. They do not plan or even yearn to go back, for their bridges have been burnt – either by their own free will or by the torches of their persecutors. They know that for them, as for the whole nation, there is no turning back.

Nevertheless they are a lost generation. They finger lovingly their Israeli passports, but they cannot get accustomed to the climate. They are proud of living in Israel's capital, but its provincial atmosphere oppresses them. They hebraise their names, but Hebrew remains an acquired language to them. The children in school take to the Biblical language like ducks to the pond, but the parents speak it haltingly and read it with even greater difficulty; they feel left out.

There also exists a lost generation in a different sense of the word, though the two overlap to some extent. They are the people who have

spent years – sometimes as many as ten – in concentration and displaced persons' camps, and who only survived by becoming condi-
tioned to circumventing the law, for the law for the Jew on the continent of Europe was deportation and death. Few can survive such
pressure without some deformation of character, and a large number of
the immigrants of recent years are psychological problem-cases, some
of them with a marked asocial tendency.

The second main source of immigration, present and future, are the
Sephardic Jews from Syria, Egypt, Iraq, Yemen, and North Africa,
whose economic and physical existence is becoming increasingly precarious. They are Orientals both in character and appearance, and their
colour varies from olive to dark grey; their main language is Arabic.

Already some 25 to 30 per cent of Israel's population are Oriental
Jews; and by virtue both of their higher birth-rate and of increasing
pressure in the neighbouring countries they will, in all probability,
outnumber the European element in the not-too-distant future. This
fact makes the cultural problem of Israel appear in a new light which
as yet few of the political and intellectual leaders of the country are
prepared to face.

In their ensemble these form the lost generation of Israel, a transitory
and amorphous mass which as yet lacks the character of a nation. Only
in the native youth, born and reared in the country, does the first
intimation of the future profile of Israel as a nation begin to outline
itself.

The Palestine-born young Jew is nicknamed 'sabra' after the prickly,
wild-growing, somewhat tasteless fruit of the cactus plant. In physical
appearance he is almost invariably taller than his parents, robustly
built, mostly blond or brown haired, frequently snub-nosed and blue-
eyed. The young male's most striking feature is that he looks entirely
un-Jewish. The girls, on the other hand, seem as yet to remain physically closer to the European Jewish type. On the whole, there can be
little doubt that the race is undergoing some curious biological alteration, probably induced by the abrupt change in climate, diet, and the
mineral balance of the soil. It also seems that the female is slower in
undergoing this transformation, more inert or stable in constitutional
type. The whole phenomenon is a striking confirmation of the theory
that environment has a greater formative influence than heredity and
that what we commonly regard as Jewish characteristics are not racial
features but a product of sustained social pressure and a specific way of
life, a psycho-somatic response to what Professor Toynbee calls 'the
stimulus of penalisations.'

In his mental make-up the average young sabra is fearless to the point of recklessness, bold, extroverted, and little inclined towards, if not openly contemptuous of, intellectual pursuits. The children are particularly good-looking; after puberty, however, their features and voices coarsen and seem never quite to reach the balance of maturity. The typical sabra's face has something unfinished about it: the still undetermined character of a race in transition.

The sabra's outlook on the world is rather provincial and hyperchauvinistic. This could hardly be otherwise in a small and exposed pioneer community which had to defend its physical existence and build its State against almost impossible odds. One cannot create a nation without nationalism.

This, of course, is a temporary phenomenon. In a decade or so, with Israel's position safely established in the Middle East, the cessation of outward pressure will no doubt produce a corresponding change in the mentality of the young generation. But a change in what direction? What kind of a civilisation will Israel's be? Will it be a continuation of Western thought and art and values? Or the superficial veneer of Levantinism? Or will it go back to its ancient roots and develop out of them a modern but specifically Hebrew culture?

For the time being the intellectual leaders of Israel are determined to choose the third alternative. No doubt this 'cultural claustrophilia' is also merely a passing phase. It will vanish with increasing security and self-assurance. What kind of civilisation will take its place one cannot foretell, but one thing seems fairly certain: within a generation or two Israel will have become an entirely 'un-Jewish' country.

## THE END OF THE CHAPTER: SUEZ

Friday, August 10, 1956

The four month crisis started with Egypt's sudden nationalisation of the Suez Canal on July 26. The *Guardian* looked forward when it wrote:

### THE VALUE OF OIL

In Western relations with the Arab world Suez is only a beginning. In the perspective of history, how will Britain's present attitude appear? Shall we not seem to have been blind to what manifestly lies ahead? Some people say that we must resist at Suez because if Colonel Nasser is not stopped other Arab States will nationalise their oil resources and pipelines. Is that not coming anyway? And can it conceivably be stopped

" I wonder why children never want Grandma to depart through the front door but always long to kick her down the back stairs ? "

'*Emotional Nationalism,*' *May 11, 1956*

by military force? Any State has a sovereign right to nationalise industrial concerns and natural resources within its own borders. If Western Governments are far-sighted they will look towards means for a smooth transition. The West may have to pay more for its oil, but the great safeguard is that the Arab States must sell it in order to be prosperous. If people in Western countries refuse in their own minds to accept the prospect, they will be condemned by the under-privileged of the world (Arabs, Asians, Africans, and Latin Americans) as selfish exploiters.

> Before the end of August the *Guardian* was warning its readers of the steps towards war which the British and French Governments seemed to be taking, although of course this was denied. On October 30 Britain and France delivered an ultimatum to Egypt and Israel. Next day air raids on Egypt were carried out, and on November 5 British and French troops landed. Meanwhile Russia had invaded Hungary. (See pp. 661-2.)

## Monday, November 5, 1956

### TO QUELL THE FLAMES[1]

The 'forest fire,' as the Prime Minister calls it, has not been put out. The flames are rising – and not only in the Middle East. They have spread to Eastern Europe. For months or years to come it will be a matter of debate whether Britain's attack on Egypt sparked Russia's attack on Hungary. To say the least, however, it is possible that British aggression tipped the scales in Soviet planning towards violent action. And British defiance of Assembly resolutions has sapped the strength of the United Nations at a most critical moment. Where Britain has rejected the Assembly's wishes, Russia (though her crime may be greater) can follow. For the present Hungary is doomed.

In Egypt the British and French landings are about to begin, or may have begun. Resistance may end immediately, or it may continue for weeks in guerrilla form, sucking in more and more troops. On Israel's borders there is temporary peace, but tension mounts. Syrian troops have been placed in readiness to help Egypt, and Iraqi troops are reported to be moving into Jordan. An explosion on Israel's eastern border seems imminent – and nobody will know who is to blame. There remains a limited hope that the explosion may be averted by strenuous warnings to both sides and by the sheer weight of British intervention in Egypt, as the Prime Minister evidently hopes. But, in the face of growing anger and hostility in the Arab countries, it would be foolish to expect peace to endure. Meanwhile the Suez Canal has been blocked, and the flow of oil from the wells is drying up. Far from restoring peace and stability in the area – as Britain could have done by offering to undertake armed action through the United Nations (the course adopted by the United States over Korea) – the Government has poured petrol on the flames.

How can they be quelled? The first task in Britain is to change the Government. The present Prime Minister and his Cabinet must be removed. Sir Anthony's policy, however sincerely intended, has been hideously miscalculated and utterly immoral. We would strongly urge every man and woman in Britain, who has not already done so, to make his view on British policy known to his member of Parliament. It is best done by telegram or postcard, addressed to the House of Commons, London. It is particularly to be hoped that Conservatives who disagree with the Government – and clearly from our correspondence a number exist – will tell their members.

1. A leader by Alastair Hetherington.

To stop a military assault which has been launched is exceedingly difficult. (It is now clear, however, that on Thursday and Friday the troops and ships were not so far on the way that the Government was unable to halt them, when asked by the United Nations; it simply refused to accede.) The aim of a new Government should be to comply with the United Nations resolutions as quickly as possible. It should state at once that the troops at Suez will be confined to certain limited positions; that they will continue to fight only in self-defence; and that they will hand over to a United Nations force (or accept its orders) as soon as one can be formed. Every possible help should be given to the Secretary-General of the United Nations towards forming an international force, and he should be told that the British and French will withdraw from Suez as soon as is wished.

This is the primary step towards restoring the authority of the United Nations. Much more will have to be done if the flames are to be quelled. The Israeli Government already has said that it will not accept a United Nations force in the Sinai desert. It will have to be put under the strongest pressure to do so; but that is a task for countries other than Britain and France. The main burden must rest with the United States, which has military forces in the Mediterranean available for backing up a United Nations demand. Pressure, equally, will have to be put on Egypt and the Arab States to accept United Nations mediation; but that, too, is a task from which Britain and France have excluded themselves.

For Hungary and Eastern Europe there is tragically little that can be done. Russia can be condemned in the United Nations, but after the past week's events that will mean little.

For Britain the past few days have been the blackest since Munich, and blacker ones may lie immediately ahead. There is a danger that, if policy is not handled better than it has been by the present Government, the fire will grow into a world war. Certainly that is the last thing which Sir Anthony and his Cabinet would want; but they have shown that they cannot be trusted. Warning of the Government's tendency towards militant folly over Suez was given in these columns in August and September (although a number of our readers at that time believed we were badly mistaken). We can only appeal now for a concerted effort, within constitutional . limits, for replacement of the Eden Government.

## Tuesday, November 20, 1956

There was another dimension to the problem. Israel had its own separate grievances against Egypt and fears for her own safety. Its forces attacked Egypt in advance of the British and French action. Was this an independent move or part of a common plan? It was not until November 19 that James Morris who had been in Israel was able to send an uncensored message from Cyprus which confirmed the *Guardian*'s suspicions; and for the first time made the facts known.

### THE ISRAELI ANGLE

Nicosia, November 19

French aircraft flown by French pilots in French uniform played an important, possibly even a decisive, part in the recent Israeli offensive in the Sinai desert. The Israeli censorship has stifled this startling fact, and General Moshe Dayan, the Israeli Chief of Staff, flatly denied it when questioned at a recent press conference. There is, however, no doubt at all that French fighter pilots took part in the battle, and it is suggested that the accuracy of their napalm bombing was one of the most important factors in the rout of the Egyptian Army.

Until a few days ago a line of Mystère jet fighters bearing French markings could be seen tucked away in a corner of Lydda airfield near Tel-Aviv. It is said, however, that French markings were covered on the French Mystères which went into action. One French officer in uniform talked to me very freely about his part in the campaign. He said:

'There was very little opposition except flak. Most of our aircraft came back with a few flak holes in them, but for myself I only saw four MIGs and they ran away.'

This was before the British and French had attacked Egyptian airfields, he said, and he could not understand why the Egyptians had not put up a better fight.

Anybody who has wandered about the Sinai battlefield during the past week or two must have been struck by the vast numbers of Egyptian lorries, tanks, and half-tracks disintegrated by the impact of napalm bombs. More often than not, bombs seem to have struck them smack in the middle, immediately pulverising everything combustible. It is possible that the Israelis themselves have supplies of napalm bombs, but it is said that most of this ghastly accuracy was the work of French flyers.

It is common knowledge that France has been supplying Mystère fighters to Israel beyond the published numbers, and it is possible that some of the French aircraft used in the battle had been technically handed over to the Israelis. Certainly the French pilots whom I met were waiting to be transported home in two French troop-carrying aircraft standing at Lydda airfield, which suggests that they were leaving their Mystères behind. But it is irrefutable that French service pilots took part in the action from the beginning.

It is thus difficult to disbelieve stories that the French Government knew of Israel's plans all along and perhaps even (as some people in Israel have it) provided their inspiration. The British Embassy denies all knowledge, merely suggesting rather wanly that perhaps the French fighters were used only to escort Air France air liners on their journeys to and from Israel (it is true that the air liners were escorted): but probably its staff shares with the censorship department the old philosophy of least said soonest mended.

### COMMENT

Perhaps the collusion was between France and Israel only. If so, were the British not informed in advance? Was the joint Anglo-French ultimatum to Egypt issued while the British were in ignorance of what the French had done? Is it likely that the joint operation to neutralise the Egyptian Air Force and seize the canal would have been launched so swiftly without prior knowledge of the Israeli plans?

## Sheer Gallantry

Monday, August 9, 1948
*From our Athletics Correspondent*

Wembley, Saturday
At three o'clock this afternoon the 41 starters in the Olympic marathon pranced cheerfully before the packed crowd here as they loosened their muscles in the wind-swept sunshine. A few moments later they vanished from our view, led by Choi, of Korea, and for the next two and a half hours were known to us only from bald announcements of the leading positions.

At 10 kilometres, Gailly (Belgium) was leading from a Chinese, a Frenchman, Guinez of Argentina, and two Finns. At twenty kilometres there was no big change except that Cabrora, another Argentinian, and Holden had passed the Finns and lay sixth and seventh. Gailly still led at 30 kilometres, but Cabrora was now fourth, running a nice even race and obviously becoming a danger, whereas Holden had retired owing to a bad blister and Hietanen had vanished.

Five kilometres later, and with less than seven to go, Choi had spurted furiously and fatally into the lead; Gailly had fallen behind Cabrora, and, to the joy of the crowd, Richards of Great Britain was lying fifth, the first we had heard of him since he left the Stadium.

We heard no more news, and as the minutes crept on to 5.30 all eyes were turned to the tunnel leading into the Stadium from under the royal box. And then it happened. A gaunt, tousled, and much-bespattered figure, wearing the faded red vest of Belgium, tottered up the slope on to the track and paused blinking like a prisoner released from some underground dungeon. It was Gailly miraculously restored into the lead; but, alas, the slope up the Olympic Way and that last small cruel rise in the tunnel had brought him to his knees and he turned slowly, oh so slowly, to his right for the last 440 metres of track that lay between him and victory. And this time no man ran to help him as forty years ago they had done to the undoing of Dorando, though it was distressing to watch him in his agony.

Just as Gailly began to move forward a second figure appeared – Cabrora, going very slowly, but actually running with short steady strides and concentrating deeply on his task. Gailly was undone. He probably did not know that Cabrora passed him at once amid tremendous applause. Before they had completed the lap a shout that split the heavens announced the arrival of Richards, still comparatively fresh and spurting hard. Again Gailly could offer no resistance and Richards came home second.

While all three were still on the track a fourth figure emerged, Coleman (South Africa), jaunty and waving his hand to his friends and one realised that poor Gailly, though only 80 yards from the tape by now, might even yet lose the medal for third place. But on and on he tottered like a man who has been dazed in the desert and knows that a few minutes away is water, blessed water. In those last awful seconds he must have been unconscious of everything except that he must carry Belgium's colours to the appointed end even if he fell and died in his track. He had been on those last pitiless 400 metres almost four minutes before, somehow still third, he achieved his goal and collapsed senseless across the line into the awaiting arms. For sheer gallantry there has been nothing in the Games to equal it, and had he fallen before the finish it would have been tragedy unbearable.

L.M.[1]

1. Laurence Montague

# CHAPTER THIRTEEN

# The World We Live In

\*

The world is still run by men to whom Hitler's Europe is part of their personal experience. Middle-aged and old have this in common. But to the men who are coming up it is only hearsay – and so, too, is Stalin's world. Those who can now vote for the first time this year were only two when Stalin died. In the arts, in manners, in morals and in the causes for which men greatly care there have been changes as profound and as rapid as those which divided the England of Charles II from that of Cromwell. But, while man has walked (and motored) on the moon, he is no nearer being able to see that there is enough food for all, or to settling his parochial disputes as events in Ireland show.

In *Guardian* history this chapter coincides with the first fifteen years of Alastair Hetherington's editorship. It has seen the paper printed in London as well as in Manchester, and the editor's home moved south. The extracts in this chapter have been chosen primarily to show the paper's sense of the most important changes taking place in our world. It would be too much to hope that it has got them all right, or that I have made the most appropriate selection. The dust has not had long enough to settle.

## The Mushroom Cloud

### THE HUNDRED-MEGATON BOMB

Tuesday, September 19, 1961
*By John Maddox*

When it was invented in the early fifties the term 'megaton' had an ironic flavour. Among other things its use served to make the point that the explosive power of the weapons now available is greater than anything the classical munitions men could have dreamed of. Yet, as it turns out, the term is almost an indispensable aid to the discussion of the 'hundred megaton' bomb which Mr. Khrushchev has been brandishing about in the last few weeks. There are just too many noughts in the figure of 100,000,000, which indicates the number of tons of conventional explosive that would have to be assembled so as to yield the same power on detonation.

In terms of explosive power the bombs which Mr. Khrushchev has been talking about are as much greater than the Hiroshima bomb as that was greater than the blockbusters used during the last war. Like the four-minute mile, the 100-megaton bomb must seem to some people to represent a significant landmark in an historical trend.

Blast is the main source of physical destruction after atomic explosions and the blast wave from a 100-megaton bomb would inevitably cover a vast area. Pressures of 5 lb. a square inch, which are sufficient to destroy ordinary brick houses, would be found at distances of 17 miles from the point of explosion (one mile from Hiroshima). In other words, ordinary buildings throughout Greater London would be destroyed by a bomb above Westminster. Though human beings survive blast waves well, deaths would be caused by falling masonry and the like.

Perhaps the most dramatic of the consequences of a 100-megaton explosion – especially if this took place high in the atmosphere – would be those of heat radiation. Second degree burns of human skin would be caused within 60 miles of the point of explosion. These same effects would ensure that easily kindled materials such as dry wood and loose paper were set on fire. This implies that both Oxford and Cambridge would be set on fire, and their inhabitants directly burnt by a bomb on London.

Though fortunately there is no experience on this point, it seems probable that the consequences of these fires would be among the most dramatic. Even in the Japanese cities great updraughts of hot air fanned the flames of fires already burning. It has been calculated in the United States that in these circumstances air temperatures of 1,000 degrees (F) might be reached, and that the survival of people in shelters might be impossible if there were no independent air supply.

With heat and blast, radiation is the third member of the trio of physical forces which adds to the disaster of atomic explosions. Under this head, however, are two separate entities. In the first place there is the damaging effect of the nuclear radiation which is given off by the fireball of the explosion just as if it were heat. Then there is the nuclear radiation which comes from radio-activity released by the explosion which is only effective in damaging people's health after it has returned to the ground.

The first of these effects would cause numerous casualties among people in direct sight of the fireball. Radiation sickness of a serious degree would be caused to a distance exceeding three miles from the

*'The last one we tested was a real whopper'* – Papas, *September 1, 1961.*

fireball. The increased size of a 100-megaton bomb pays comparatively small dividends in this respect because of the extent to which nuclear radiations can be absorbed by the atmosphere. The very much smaller Hiroshima bomb produced radiation sickness at a range of one mile.

There are no diminishing returns where the effects of fallout radio-activity are concerned. The amount of radioactive material formed would be so great that even at the end of a day, when some radio-activity would already have disappeared, there would be something like the equivalent of a million tons of radium scattered about. If this material were spread uniformly over the surface of a country the size of England and the land were reinhabited after an interval of a year, there would still be so much radio-activity that every person would get a lethal dose of radiation in about three years.

What would happen to this radio-activity in the event of an ex-plosion in anger cannot be accurately predicted. Possibly the material would be spread out over the surface of the land within a few hours, as happened at Bikini, and possibly the effect of fire storms associated with the explosion would produce some other pattern of fallout. But in any case it would seem wise – and it is certainly conservative – to assume that within an area of 1,000 square miles of the point of explosion people who were unprotected for as long as an hour would die from the effects of fallout radiation.

'What can persuade a soldier against the benefits of such widespread destruction?' The answer here is manifold, but part of it lies in the properties of the smaller weapons, such as those with explosive yields of 10 megatons.

The tenfold increase in explosive power has not led to a tenfold increase in the area over which damage by blast and radiation can be caused. Only where the production of radiant heat is concerned does the larger bomb appear to have a destructive advantage. If one of the objects of an attack were to be the destruction of missile bases, a number of smaller bombs would be preferable to one large one, for by that means the area over which intense blast would work its way would be increased. But if, of course, the object of the attack is the destruction of cities, and of their populations, it may well seem to a potential attacker that the use of very large bombs must have advantages, some of them psychological.

## CUBA - ON THE BRINK OF NUCLEAR WAR

### Saturday, October 27, 1962

A year later the world was faced by a serious threat of nuclear war. Russia was establishing nuclear sites in Cuba. On Friday night Max Freedman reported from Washington.

#### From Max Freedman

Washington, October 26

The officials in their private talks with reporters, gravely say that they are now being called upon to consider the necessity of an invasion of Cuba or the bombing of the nuclear sites or, hideous as the prospect may be, a nuclear attack on Cuba. It is necessary to think even of the ultimate horror of a nuclear attack because there are powerful military arguments which suggest that the defensive power now available to Cuba, as a result of the Russian armament, makes it impossible to wipe out the bases by the method of an invasion or a bombing attack.

Late this evening the Cuban crisis reached its gravest point. Mr. Pierre Salinger, the President's press Secretary, released a statement citing additional evidence that Russia, by methods of camouflage, was working at a rapid pace to achieve a 'full operational capability as soon as possible' in the intermediate range ballistic missile sites. These missiles have a range of 2,200 miles.

It must be reported, on the basis of information provided by senior officials who have worked at President Kennedy's side through the

'*And then I said "To hell with you too"*' – *October 25, 1962.*

long hours of this crisis that the official statement can only be described as 'temperate' in the light of the grim choices now under anxious debate in the highest reaches of the Kennedy Administration.

### COMMENT: WHEN TO BREAK RANKS

People who thought the Cuban crisis was easing – and who sent Stock Exchange prices rising – had better think again. The situation is still full of danger.

Is the United States about to bomb or invade Cuba? This is now the question. Worse, there is even talk of a possible nuclear attack on Cuba. This is reliably reported as under consideration because the authorities in Washington are so troubled by the rapid approach to readiness of the intermediate range bases on the island. It would be madness. There cannot be a shred of justification for the use of nuclear weapons in this situation. It would turn the whole civilised world against the Americans, however much sympathy there may have been for them hitherto in meeting Russian duplicity and provocation. This must surely be apparent to them. We profoundly hope so.

Short of that extreme action, the possibility of an invasion or of 'pinpoint' bombing remains. Both have been under discussion. It seems that preparations for both have been fully made, although no decision to launch either has been taken. A chance survives that U Thant's mediation may be allowed to take its course.

But the words coming out of the State and Defence Departments have an ominous ring. They suggest that if the Russians do not at least stop work on the missile sites with their existing equipment bombing or invasion may begin. If this happens the British Government will have to make up its mind afresh about what it should do. It is one thing for Mr. Macmillan to say that the allies must not waver or break ranks at a time when the United States has done nothing but impose the 'quarantine' on offensive weapons. Certainly America's allies should do their utmost to back her up in this tight corner. But matters will be very different if the United States takes to aggression.

The reason for breaking ranks at that point would not just be that an armed attack on Cuba is unjustified at a time when Cuba is not attacking anybody. The consequences would be great and might be highly dangerous. The Soviet Union has threatened to retaliate with nuclear weapons against an attack on Cuba. Whether it would make good its threat nobody can tell. Possibly the Soviet leaders themselves are not quite sure. It might not come to that. But it is a tremendous risk to run in a cause which, if it came to bombing or invasion, would seem to most of the world to be as much a piece of aggression as the British and French attack at Suez. If it does come to that the British Government should make it clear that it must vote against the United States in the United Nations just as the Americans voted against us at Suez. That is the only course. There are times when ranks must be broken if the cause that unites them is not to become meaningless.

Mercifully the need did not arise. On Sunday, after telephone contact with President Kennedy, Mr. Khrushchev decided to dismantle the sites and ship the missiles back to Russia.

# Reach for the Stars

## THE FIRST MAN IN SPACE[1]

Friday, March 29, 1968
*By Anthony Tucker, our Science Correspondent*

'The road to the planets is open. The flight of Yuri Gagarin has ushered in a new era not only in the development of science, but in the history of all mankind.'

This assessment by Alexander Neseyanov, then president of the U.S.S.R. Academy of Science, is as true now as when it was made on April 12, 1961. Gagarin never flew in space again and his single orbit of 108 minutes is the shortest of all Russian space flights. It remains, and will always remain, the most significant.

In the seven years that have elapsed, a lot of the early enthusiasm has faded and most of the prophecies made in 1961 have slipped – if not fallen. Men were not on the moon within five years, and manned flights to the planets are not yet within sight. But Yuri Gagarin's enthusiasm has never waned, and the stocky, smiling man who won the hearts of Britain and of the world as the most contemporary of all heroes became a centre-pin for the Russian programme.

People tend to remember the smile, the charm, the quick wit. But Gagarin was essentially a serious, dedicated man, whose grasp of astronautics and astro-physics delighted the Royal Society Fellows during an informal lunch three months after his historic space flight.

Perhaps because of their trade, pilots – particularly fighter pilots – tend to be both cynical and flippant. Gagarin was of a very different kind, a man with a sharp mind and unusually developed powers of observation, who learned to fly as a sparetime hobby, and became an amateur ambassador for Russia with powers greater and more successful than the Kremlin could have dreamt.

Recently, having long ago qualified in an industrial college, Gagarin qualified as an engineer and was clearly set to play an important part in the designing and planning of Russian space structures. He has served as controller for manned space flights and, perhaps an important measure of his personality and capability, had been elected a member of the Supreme Soviet.

But none of these commitments and responsibilities seemed to change the man. It was not a matter of growing in stature with success:

1. Gagarin died on March 27, 1968, aged 34.

achievements simply fitted him as neatly as his uniform. Gagarin somehow managed to be both highly unusual and yet impeccably normal.

Perhaps it was unshakable normality that brought him such tumultuous personal acclaim in the West. There is a curious feeling that, having lost Gagarin, we have all lost a very real and very warm friend.

Wednesday, July 12, 1961

'The Major stood erect, uniformed, and smiling in an open Rolls-Royce (with the registered number YG 1). He waved and London waved back.'

## THE FIRST MEN IN THE MOON

Tuesday, July 22, 1969

HOW THEY HEARD THE GOOD NEWS FROM ALASKA
TO FLORIDA

*From Alistair Cooke, Nassau Point (Long Island)*

July 21

Thirty-one hours is a terrible stretch of time to spend continuously with a wife, let alone a network. And the result of it was that to-day is as dead and musty, in the cities anyway, as a Third Avenue saloon the morning after St. Patrick's night.

If all the helpful information necessary to follow the blast-away, the lunar insertion, the powered descent, and the walk around the surface had been fed to us when we needed it, the whole show could have been wrapped up in about fifty exhilarating minutes. It was the other 30 hours and 10 minutes that hurt, requiring, as they did, the desperate corralling of every 'authority' who had ever, it seemed, sailed a ketch, preached a sermon, or owned a pair of binoculars.

We heard from everybody in Europe and America, except Congress and we certainly ought to be grateful for one small mercy.

Beginning in the early morning, we were sitting in Rome with a very learned space scientist who brought the first piercing insight of a myriad. He said the difference between a man and a machine was that the man has initiative, whereas a machine is an automaton.

Whisking now to London, we were glad to have the interviewer's assertion that all explorers are without fear snappily contradicted by Sir Francis Chichester, who said he was scared stiff half the time around the world. Up to Manchester for Sir Bernard [Lovell] and a genuinely informative bit about the progression of lunar orbits.

Out now, 6,000 miles, to – hold it! – Disneyland, in California, where a jolly sports commentator in a check jacket interviewed some of the most cheerful idiots extant. Robert Benchley once said that the vocabulary of dramatic criticism in America had got to the point where a play was either 'swell' or 'lousy.' Yesterday, from the evidence of the microphones pushed into the faces of thousands of onlookers, between Kennedy Airport and Los Angeles, the walk on the moon was either 'fabulous' or 'fantastic.'

There was one thoughtful interlude, from a 20-year-old at Disney-land, who was asked how old he was when the space programme started in 1961. He mused awhile and declined the gambit: 'Gee, like,' he said, 'I was never no good at math.'

Back to New York for Edric Severeid, C.B.S.'s instant philosopher, wondering if we hadn't lost something by discovering that the silvery moon was a bunch of rocks. That led us to Flagstaff, Arizona, and Dr. Newell Trask, of the U.S. Geological Survey, one of those mild, compact American scientists, who told us quietly all sorts of accurate marvels about the lunar module's control problems and modestly shattered the prevailing superstitions (Will the moon dust choke them? Will they sink beyond recall?) about the texture of the surface.

A busy pause now for the powered descent, and, after 4.17.40 secs. p.m. the endless reiteration of 'Golly!,' 'Great show!,' 'Fantastic!.' relieved by the promise that the commentators were speechless. Now out again to Flagstaff, from whose experts it transpires we do not know where they landed. (By noon to-day they were still choosing between three possible sites.)

Then we deserted the excellent simulations from the Grumman Air Base, here, on Long Island, and came to the real thing, a shot, as from the Lumière Bros.' early film, with a bare, off-Broadway set, a perspective of desert, and the white blobs of Armstrong and Aldrin plomping around like little gazelles. This, of course, was the true glory, and only another fourteen hours of it could dim its joy.

In that time, we heard from science fiction men, N.A.S.A. wallahs, the geologists again, and more instant philosophers; and winced through President Nixon's tasteless interlude congratulating the erect astronauts from the tasteful comfort of the White House study.

One science fictioner assured us, minute after soaring minute, that 'This is the Year One. If we don't change our calendars, the historians will. This is Alpha and Omega. This is the Ba Mitzvah. This is the moment of Transition from infancy to adultery – er – to adulthood.' That was worth a replay.

The astronauts continued to bob around on the Sea of Tranquillity while we floundered on the Ocean of Banality.

## Friday, July 25, 1969

### COMMENT: WHAT NEXT?

They are back, these first earthmen to set foot on an alien celestial body, the travellers who, as they stepped down from the fragile ladder of Eagle, initiated day one of a new Genesis. A coldly reasoned argument could never have led to the Apollo programme, but mankind would have been stunted without it. Irrationality and the inspiring sweep of the imagination are the necessities of human progress.

That, more than money or science or engineering, is what space flight is about. But having made one great gesture which has turned an ancient dream into present reality, what does man do next?

The Apollo flights, like the first journeys into the polar regions, have been made entirely without support at their most crucial phases. At every point outside earth orbit a failure could have led to a disaster without hope of rescue. It seems strange that when, in the post-war years, a moon journey was discussed by enthusiasts who were then still regarded as a lunatic fringe, it was always assumed that two or three vehicles would go to the moon simultaneously so that no single failure could lead to the tragic abandonment of men. The Apollo astronauts themselves calculated that their chances of success were about four to one. Should not some priority now be given to rescue techniques, even if this means a reassessment of the entire programme?

If, beyond the great first gesture and beyond adventure, the search is for knowledge of the solar system, then we should next investigate planets like Mercury, Venus, and Jupiter where men can never hope to tread nor even, perhaps, orbit in a spacecraft. There is also a pressing need to establish large manned astronomical observatories out in earth orbit where, above the atmosphere, they can glean secrets from the universe unimaginable on earth. It is in activities such as these that men can learn to master the skills of safe transportation in space.

Russia may, at this moment, be genuinely seeking co-operation in space ventures which, by their very nature, are beneficial and non-competitive. The new challenge is not to put men on Mars but to find a deeper understanding of man and of his mysterious environment. But, with Apollo fulfilled, co-operation in space now represents the greatest challenge and the potentially most fruitful adventure that mankind can undertake.

## A Change of Style

### LOOK BACK IN ANGER

Wednesday, May 9, 1956
*By Philip Hope-Wallace*

The English Stage Company at the Royal Court Theatre last night brought forward a first play by a young man, John Osborne, called *Look Back in Anger*. It is by no means a total success artistically, but it has enough tension, feeling and originality of theme and speech to make the choice understandable, and the evening must have given to anyone who has ever wrestled with the mechanics of play-making an uneasy and yet not wasted jaunt, just as it must have awoken echoes in anyone who has not forgotten the frustrations of youth.

Mr. Osborne's hero, a boor, a self-pitying, self-dramatising intellectual rebel who drives his wife away, takes a mistress and then drops her when, to his surprise, his wife comes crawling back, will not be thought an edifying example of chivalry. But those who have not lost the power to examine themselves will probably find something basic-ally true in the prolix, shapeless study of a futile frustrated wretch, even if they do not get as far as extending much sympathy to him. The brutish Polish husband of *A Streetcar Named Desire* was much less given to windy rhetoric, or at least he remained inarticulate. Tennessee Williams's characters exist and suffer rather than debate their frustrations. But is the dilemma posed here in this ugly, cheerless Bohemia supposed to be typical?

The author and the actors too did not persuade us wholly that they really 'spoke for' a lost, maddened generation. There is the intention to be fair – even to the hated bourgeois parents of the cool and apparently unfeeling wife who is at length brought to heel by a miscarriage. The trouble seems to be in the overstatement of the hero's sense of grievance; like one of Strindberg's woman-haters, he ends in a kind of frenzied preaching in an empty conventicle. Neither we in the audience nor even the other Bohemians on the stage with him are really reacting to his anger. Numbness sets in.

Kenneth Haigh battled bravely with this awkward 'first-play' hero without being able to suggest much more than a spoilt and neurotic bore who badly needed the attention of an analyst. No sooner was sympathy quickened than it ebbed again. Mary Ure as the animal, patient wife, Helena Hughes as a friend, who comes to stay and reign in the sordid attic, and Alan Bates as a cosy young puppy, that third party who sometimes holds a cracking marriage together, were more easily brought to life. Tony Richardson's production and a good set by Alan Tagg help out this strongly felt but rather muddled first drama. But I believe they have got a potential play-wright at last, all the same.

# THE TRIAL OF LADY CHATTERLEY

Thursday, November 3, 1960

## LADY CHATTERLEY ACQUITTED

The jury's verdict on *Lady Chatterley's Lover* is a triumph of common sense – and the more pleasing because it was unexpected.

We shall never know, of course, precisely what the jury thought. They could acquit on either of two grounds – that the book was simply not obscene, or that, even if it was, its literary and other merits nevertheless justified its publication as being for the public good. As ordinary men and women, with their feet well planted on the ground and with the Judge's injunction not to get lost 'in the higher realms of literature, education, sociology, and ethics' in their ears, they would be likely to look at the straightforward question of obscenity. In hearing the defence evidence they may have wondered at the inconsistencies in what the 'experts' said in support of the book (inconsistencies some of which the Judge mentioned in his summing-up). But they may have wondered still more at the prosecution's theme that the book put promiscuity on a pedestal and that it contained only 'padding' between bouts of sexual intercourse. These charges were too exaggerated to survive a reading of the book.

Physical love plays an important part in the book. It is the chief theme – though there is an important secondary theme in the sterility, ugliness, and inhumanity of life in a Midland mining community and in a society devoted to money-making. The theme of physical love calls for detailed description of sexual acts. These are what make the book controversial. But their purpose is an honest one. It is to show the redeeming power of that love and the importance of tenderness. D. H. Lawrence emphasises that where harshness or brutality exist a couple cannot come to a full and harmonious relationship together. Mellors (the gamekeeper) is shown from an early stage as warm and kind, and where he is passionate he is 'wholesome.' That is the key to his influence over Lady Chatterley. To the Judge's question whether there is 'any spark of affection' until late in the book the answer is 'yes.' The compassion of Mellors for the wretchedness of Lady Chatterley is what brings them together at first.

Mellors and Lady Chatterley are nevertheless in an immoral relationship. Here some of the defence witnesses were vulnerable – especially the four Church of England clergy who courageously came forward to

*Abu drew this to illustrate a reader's letter complaining of the Archbishop's opposition to the Divorce Bill – January 22, 1968.*

give evidence. Yet there is a valid answer to the charge of immorality. It is, first, that the Chatterleys' marriage had already withered from within. The wife had sought to hold together her companionship with a husband half paralysed and half mad, but her efforts did not avail. Secondly, she herself is changed by Mellors from frustration and physical decline to being vitally alive. Thirdly, their relationship becomes a dedicated one – and, contrary to the prosecution's view, with a real hope of ultimate and lasting marriage. (That plainly lies behind the concluding letter.) Fourthly, as one of the clergy said, this is a novel and not a tract. Novels deal with life as it is.

Thursday, February 16, 1961

### THE GUARDIAN REBUKED

The Press Council considers that the action of the *Guardian*, the *Observer*, and the *Spectator* in publishing certain four-letter words mentioned in the recent trial of Penguin Books was 'both objectionable and unnecessary.' While disagreeing with the council's judgment, we heed its rebuke.

Two points may be added. First, the question is chiefly one of taste and consequently one on which no judgment can be final. Our view, at the time of the trial, was that a limited use of certain words was relevant. As we stated then, the vulgarity of a word depends on the user, the context, and the manner of its use. D. H. Lawrence, in using the four-letter words in *Lady Chatterley's Lover*, was at least partly trying to restore to them a decent meaning. His use was direct, not furtive or foul-minded.

Secondly, the Press Council did not have the courtesy to tell the *Guardian* (or, so far as we know, the others concerned) that it intended to consider the question. It may hold that there was no need to, since all the evidence is in print. Did it, however, adequately consider the points in our leading article of that time? We cannot know, because the council meets behind closed doors.

# DISESTABLISHMENTARIANISM

Monday, January 7, 1963
*By Norman Shrapnel*

If satire has ever succeeded, which is arguable, it has succeeded by changing things. The current satire cult has bitten home all right, rather in the way that a blunt hatchet might sink into a log of soft wood. Nothing splits. Society absorbs the assault with a minimum of shock, almost without a sound. It changes nothing. Nobody – and this is the crucial point – expects it to change anything.

For satire, in a way that can never have been true in the past, is a part of the social scene it attacks. It is more than 'with it'; it is of it. The hatchet is made of wood too, slightly harder wood sliced from the same trunk. Satire is fashionable: any examination of the cult must start from there. More stimulating than the Madison, intellectually more developed than the producers of sick greetings cards who are its little brothers and sisters, it has woken us all up quite a bit and made us laugh quite a lot. What ought to kill it is the deadly complaisance of its victims. But it is doing too well to despair.

For in one sense it does succeed. Satire is business. It could even, before it is over, become big business. Launched by a group as small as a family circus team, walking a tightrope slung between Cambridge and a precarious staple in the West End, it established itself with acumen and remarkable speed: already the *Beyond the Fringe* pioneers must seem to the newest hatching of satirists, like Old Testament prophets.

There is the Establishment Club, sleeker in every sense than originally envisaged and already having to let out its belt. There is the fortnightly lampoon *Private Eye*, selling briskly and read by many of our best masochists. Most remarkable of all in that it has moved satire into the mass market, and in some respects the most stimulating though by its nature and provenance the most impotent, is the B.B.C. Saturday night show 'That Was the Week That Was,' known to the trade as TW.

The rudest of these media is *Private Eye*. It is also in a way the least pretentious. The last thing it sets out to be is a moral headmaster caning the world for its folly and vice. What it goes in for is a kind of gremlinism, releasing a swarm of mocking imps into the social works. It can be very funny, though it tends to flog its joke techniques over-hard. The favourite is the distributed caption (inappropriate words coming out of the mouths of genuine pictures), which is the magazine equivalent of the rigged tape. This has earned many a laugh and we shall no doubt have every opportunity of seeing how long it can go on doing so.

The best thing about the magazine is the drawings, with their brutal, mock-crude, highly professional line. Professionalism is always good when you can get it. Otherwise its outstanding quality is consistency. It has the absolute impartiality of a judge who hangs everybody who appears before him.

A random parade of its victims would cover the whole social vista from Buckingham Palace to the kitchen sink; there would be gossip columnists, do-gooders, sadistic religious film-makers, Mr. Grimond as well as Lord Home, Mr. Macmillan and the Kennedys, Peter Ustinov, Katherine Whitehorn, John Osborne, the *Guardian*, the Royal Family, and Godfrey Winn. A strange conspiracy of power, one might think, if that was what the Eye was searching out. In fact the moral here, if any moral could be thought to apply, would be that if everybody gets attacked nobody gets hurt.

The TW show is worth staying up late for, or getting home early for, according to your way of life. Sharper cracks on the week's events than any achieved by this team are no doubt regularly made in a thousand bars and bedrooms; but to gear that sort of uninhibited commentary on to the nervy, elaborate, but still primitive and ramshackle machinery of television is a sizeable achievement; while in the dangerously unobtrusive white-hot poker-face of David Frost the domestic screen has undoubtedly found a formidable new thing.

Yet what is remarkable is not that it should be done as well as it is, but that it should have been done at all. The predictable reactions have duly come along and the inevitable reactions to the reactions are now being seen. Having bashed the Government they must also take a knock at Labour, the Liberals, and the B.B.C. itself, to prove their impartiality.

But impartiality, like 'good taste,' is death to satire. It is as though they were being challenged to prove that they believe in nothing at all. And to acquiesce is to acknowledge the fact that contemporary satire is something you lay on, like interior decoration or advertising copy. If there is really going to be a mass audience for it, which must include large groups of collective victims as well as individual ones, there ought surely to be cries of pain and shouts of anger as well as appreciative chuckles. How can it otherwise be regarded as more than a rather rough game?

Whether mass or minority, the contemporary British audience is the surest guarantee that the cult is unlikely to draw much blood. Its mixture of subtlety, vanity, and sheer obtuseness provides an invulnerable defence.

The subtlety comes from the professionals, particularly the politicians. Mr. Macmillan's hooded tolerance which always seems to be saying that the young fellows are doing very nicely, 'almost as good as the Oxford Union in my day,' is reinforced by the fact that he can always parody himself far more effectively than anybody else can do it. As for the vanity and obtuseness, these reinforce each other. A satirist might twist himself in knots with virulent effort and desperately finish up by hanging a 'This means YOU' placard on his victim, only to be rewarded with a detached and indulgent grin.

So what is the poor satirist to do, apart from doing all right with his bank manager? Is he a true satirist at all? The answer, so far as the word is definable, must be yes. He must be getting tired of being told that he doesn't come up to Swift or Dryden, just as Dryden might have been irritated by the complaint that he didn't measure up to some waspish troubadour of earlier days. The contemporary satirist is nearer to the waspish troubadour, though sometimes a bit short on technique. The inspired amateurism on which the cult was so brightly launched still clings to it, with rapidly diminishing returns.

Must satire have moral fervour? Not necessarily, though it does help. One definition in the Shorter Oxford sees it as 'denouncing, exposing, or deriding vice, folly, abuses or evils of any kind'; another,

merely as having the effect 'of making some person or thing ridiculous.'
As for the lampoon, this is seen plainly and without alternative as 'a
virulent or scurrilous satire upon an individual,' which seems to point
straight to the Law Courts.

But here the cult, so far at least, has acquired an artful immunity.
The British, though far from unlitigious, are sensitive about that
Sense of Humour. They may not like being made to look silly in a
magazine or on television as much as they pretend, but they hate being
made to look silly in a witness box.

Perhaps there is too much immunity. Satire hurt most, and cleansed
most, when it was itself most in danger. Nobody wants to see rapiers
flashing again in Lincoln's Inn Fields, or the pillory wheeled out once
more, but if no retaliation is possible the satirists can hardly complain
if their victims respond with broadminded smiles.

Not that they are likely to complain very seriously, as long as the
money rolls in.


## THE DAY OF THE BEATLES

### Wednesday, April 15, 1970
### By Keith Dewhurst

So far as one can tell, and as it seems reasonable to say, there is not
much chance of the Beatles working again as a regularly co-operating
group. Whether they do or not, and whatever happens to them as
individuals, their reputation and critical position is clear: they stand
with Marie Lloyd and Chaplin as the great British popular entertainers
of the century. They are a symbol of social changes that brought
greater opportunities to youth, and yet their music appeals to all ages
and conditions. This made them bigger stars than the Rolling Stones
or Elvis Presley and is, I suspect, the hint that their work will survive
as living art (in the way that Chaplin and Keaton survive) and not just
as period pieces.

Presley, still juddering about in his black leather at the age of 30-odd,
is already a kind of period piece. He has been outdated by electric
rock bands that are more big city, more acid, more sophisticated, and
more disillusioned. The effect of electric rock, the actual sensation
evoked by the amplified sound itself, is that of being alive and at the
edge of to-day's experience: it is living to-day, and not knowing what
to-morrow will bring. Its most intelligent propagandists claim (and
here they align themselves with the *avant garde* tradition in European

high art) that this is the essence of a true artistic experience and that for this reason electric rock is the artistic voice of to-day.

Many people of an older generation dismiss this argument and the music and pop culture that sustain it as mere rubbish, but that is hardly fair. At the very least it is an argument that should make us ask ourselves: 'What is a true artistic experience?' My personal taste would answer that with each passing year Presley, for example, seems less an artistic experience and more a social and historical phenomenon. The moral qualities (that is to say, the sanctification of their particular feelings of rebellion) which the teenagers of the 1950's ascribed to Presley were more in their own situation and yearnings than in his own work.

A particular generation read into the effect of his personality profundities which his material never really possessed. Something of the same has always seemed to me to be true of Bob Dylan (subject his lyrics to a Leavis-type scrutiny and they are full of illogicalities, and incoherent images) and perhaps of the Rolling Stones. The Home Counties suburbs really aren't like Nashville, Tenn., and to perform as though they were is a bit obscurantist; which is not to deny their charisma but simply to question whether it has created such strong artistic images as the Beatles.

The Beatles as personality performers have lived through several changes in pop fashion. The little boys in black leather in Hamburg became the natty showbiz mods who became the flower people who became . . . The music itself is like Chaplin. Although it is rooted in particular times and fashions, it is outside them. It is to do not with decades but with age. It is popular in that it is truly of the people. It is about the common incidents of ordinary lives. Every so often the events of the time, the level of taste and education, and new generations finding themselves, coalesce to give the easy melodics of popular arts the integrity of the high masters. The Beatles represented and took advantage of one such moment.

From many strands of European and American culture they made superb little images. Their songs are about love between two people, about love as the cement of life, about love as the warmth that makes the hard day's night worth while. They are about the people who, like Eleanor Rigby, do not find love and about the way in which childhood places and fantasies stay in the mind. There is both innocence and melancholy about the yellow submarine. Like Chaplin the Beatles are about a time of social change and like him they comment upon it in terms of the value of the past.

Chaplin is about immigrants and the brutal creation of a new kind of life (incidentally that of which electric rock is the voice) in the American cities. His comments upon it are nostalgic. They criticise the New World in terms of the experience of the British proletariat in the Old. It is the same with the Beatles. They criticise a modern world in the emotional terms of the old working-class North of England. It is the old human values of the back-to-back houses that gives their work its dignity. Flower power brought them nothing but confusion. Already the Liverpool they sang about is being ripped down. The world order that created it has changed.

Where are we to go? What are we to do? Will individuals and their love be important any more? This is what the people at the bus stop wonder, when they wonder at all, and it is what the Beatles asked. When they could still work as a group their answers were never statements. They were implicit in shared attitudes, a situation unlike the *avant garde* theory of electric rock in which happiness is a state of being, and rock itself part of the answer. The theoreticians of rock would add that political events in America have changed the scene and given the music a more specific commitment. There is some truth in this, and more perhaps in the idea that like the Beatles at their best an artist is never a man with an answer. An artist is a man with a question.

## What Vietnam Does to a Man

### THE NAKED AND THE DEAD

Tuesday, March 9, 1971
*By Martin Woolacott*

On the Laotian border, Monday
The men of D company were discussing the question of why in hell they had had no beer, or at least soda, for a whole month when I arrived on their hill. They wanted to tell me about those in the rear who were stealing the beer and soda from them, but I wanted to talk about 'the action.' That is 'the action' in which their second platoon lost six killed and eight wounded not so many days ago on another hill, about a mile from where D company is now.

D company's present hill, which is a few miles from the Laos border and inaccessible except by helicopter, is really two knobs with a dip in between. The tall grass has been burnt off, holes dug in the sandy soil, claymore mines laid out down the steep slopes, and a mechanical ambush is set every night on the one trail up the hill. That was the day's big news when I got there: the mechanical ambush had been tripped by a mongoose. Only two of D company's four platoons are now on the hill, but one of them is the second platoon, and eventually I found Private Raymond C. Workman, jun., from Ohio, a short, blond, slightly spotty boy. He told me about 'the action.'

Second platoon, working from another hill, had found a bunker complex. One man was killed when they first found it, but then gunships and artillery worked the area and when the platoon went back the next day they didn't expect any opposition. There was none. They spent an enjoyable afternoon blowing up the bunkers with fragmentation grenades and anti-tank missiles, and they found various weapons, including a North Vietnamese Army (NVA) rocket launcher. 'We was really happy,' Ray Workman said, 'and we was going back to camp carrying all this and they must have got in ambush on us and they were all over the fucking place.'

In the first burst of North Vietnamese fire five men died and the radio handset was smashed to pieces. Ray Workman ticks them off on his fingers: '. . . the dog handler, the ARVN scout, the pointman, the first squad leader, and a rifleman. I ain't going to give you their names because maybe their folks don't know yet.' The second squad leader, running towards the front of the column, was also killed. The rest of the men, wounded and unwounded, hit the ground and started pouring out fire from their M-16s and from the one M-60 machine-gun with them. Workman himself fired more than 25 magazines and threw 13 fragmentation grenades. Then they heard the North Vietnamese shout: 'It's something like la-ri, la-ri, it means let's get the hell out of here.' Because the radio was out, gunships could not 'work' the area effectively.

D company is still bitter about what happened next. There were eight wounded men crying and sobbing on the ground. For reasons still not clear illumination flares were not at once fired to allow a Medivac chopper to get in. The pilot eventually did manage it, setting his helicopter down in the fog and dark, and D company would like to see that pilot get a medal. The five unwounded men and some of the less seriously wounded then retreated to a B-52 bomb crater where they spent the rest of the night.

Private Workman says: 'My best buddies were killed in there. I wish I could tell you my feelings, shit, I wish I could tell you.' His voice begins to break and I suddenly realise he is almost crying. 'You're all together here, you shit together, you sleep together, in that hole, we was all huddled together, trying to keep warm and we was all shivering, we were so scared, we figured if they came back, that was it. I dunno, some of the wounded guys I helped to carry down to the Medivac I'd rather be dead than like that. The shotgun man, oh shit, he was a mess. There ain't no fucking sense in it.'

Private Workman then picks up a piece of newspaper, several weeks old, and begins looking at an ad which says: 'These cold evenings what could be nicer than a beautiful gas log fire in the fireplace.'

## THE U.S. IN ASIA – MAD OR BAD?

Friday, January 29, 1971
*By Ian Wright*

A couple of incidents stick in the mind. The first was 11 months ago aboard the United States aircraft carrier *Constellation*, 83,000 tons, the size of the *Queen Elizabeth*, steaming through the Gulf of Tonkin not 40 miles from the shores of North Vietnam.

Two hours before dawn, half the ship's complement of 5,000 men were out and about and the Phantoms were being brought on deck for the next launching session. Below, the pilots had eaten a hearty American breakfast (fruit juice, cereal, bacon and egg, coffee) and were now getting their briefing.

At that time, 11 months ago, it was not admitted officially that the United States was bombing Laos – or that some days as many as 600 sorties were being flown, a fair proportion of them from the carriers in the Tonkin Gulf. No one mentioned Laos on the *Constellation*. Indeed, out there in that floating city of young Americans with its movies, its snack bars, its duty-free shops – and even its missiles and its bombs – there seemed little conception of the mud and the blood of the war.

This was not, it seemed, because the men were military monsters, if anything they were more thinking, even possibly more compassionate, than their land-based opposite numbers. But the young pilots and the genial, efficient, and unpretentious senior officers who ran the ship were deeply (and by their lights, necessarily) institutionalised. They were technocrats of a high order for whom the war had become the solving of a series of technical problems.

Two weeks later I was in Laos. Almost by chance I came upon a group of refugees, peasants from the Plain of Jars, who had been subjected to American air raids for the best part of five years. (The *Constellation* lost its first pilots over the Plain of Jars in 1964.) Until recently the place they came from had been in an area organised by the Laotian Communists, the Pathet Lao.

It did not take long to realise that these apolitical, conservative villagers had not much cared for the Pathet Lao and their newfangled ways. In their area there had been no military action. They had never seen any North Vietnamese soldiers. And yet they had been bombed night and day, they said.

They told a piteous tale which rang true. Three times their village had been destroyed and for the last 12 months they had lived in caves, going out only in dark clothes or at night to till their fields. American jet planes, said one old man, would even bomb a dog if they saw it moving. On the last occasion their village had been destroyed with phosphorous bombs: 'First the houses and the fruit trees were burned, then the fields and the hillside, and finally even the stream was on fire.'

Perhaps worse, planes had dropped cluster bombs, canisters full of deadly pellet bomblets, each one with hundreds of tiny ball-bearings which when they explode rip human flesh – but do next to no damage to anything else. One woman, struggling against tears, told how her daughter and husband had died.

Had one heard these tales through a Government interpreter on one of those predictable 'guided tours' of North Vietnam or read it on a printed page, it would have been easy to be sceptical. But it seemed to confirm that, at best, American air power was being used extremely stupidly, very callously and, at worst, it was the American Government's intention to blot out society as organised by the Communists on the other side.

Does this amount to genocide and were the men on the *Constellation* war criminals? And what about the men of the National Liberation Front or the North Vietnamese Army who terrorise villages, kill civilians, or launch 122 mm. rockets aimlessly into the centre of Saigon or Hué? Are they war criminals too? Or just freedom fighters?

Genocide, more often than not, is a misused word. It cropped up time and time again at Bertrand Russell's War Crimes Tribunal in Sweden and Denmark in 1967, whose edited proceedings are published under the title *Prevent the crime of silence*.

Misused or not, with Russell dead, Ralph Schoenman no longer with us, and Grosvenor Square once again safe for democracy, it's possible to admit that the Tribunal was a travesty of fair inquiry but to add that it did help rivet attention on the contradictions of American behaviour in Vietnam. In its own way it contributed to the conviction, now held by most reasonable people that the United States must get out of Indo-China – and quickly.

# A Handful Against the World

## CHÉ GUEVARA'S DIARY

Monday, July 22, 1968
*By Richard Gott*

We shall probably never know exactly how Fidel got hold of photocopies of Ché's Bolivian diary. But basically we now have [it] as found in his rucksack, faithfully transcribed in Cuba with the aid of his wife. There can be no doubt that it is genuine.

There can be no doubt either that it constitutes a document of first-rate historical and political importance. Not only does the diary reveal what an astonishing man Guevara was – a gigantic figure by any standard – but it also shows what an amazing amount can be done with very few people and with very little money.

Considering the number of people involved, the impact of the Bolivian Guerrilla was immense. Though it ended in disaster for its participants, can it be doubted that the trial of Debray and the death of Guevara have in fact given a tremendous impetus to the ideas which they sought to propagate? Their example would appear to have crystallised the thought of a whole generation in Europe and the United States. There are few recruits for guerrilla warfare perhaps, but at least there is now a recognisable desire to break with the old political structures and to stop supporting parties with revolutionary slogans which there is no intention of fulfilling. This simple idea, disseminated by a handful of men in Bolivia, is rapidly changing the face of the world.

Guevara once wrote (in his book *Guerrilla Warfare*) that 'a nucleus of thirty to fifty men' should be 'sufficient to initiate the armed struggle in any country of the Americas.' Yet for six months he was forced to operate with a group of half this size, and his diary is full of references to the failure of the Bolivians to provide him with more men. At the end of the very first month of clandestine operations, in November, 1966, he wrote of the need 'to bring the number of Bolivians at least up to twenty,' and he continued to be perturbed by the slowness with which they were recruited from the city. For most of the period of fighting the Cuban contingent seems to have made up about 50 per cent of the guerrilla force.

The blame for the failure to supply sufficient men lies in the first instance with the orthodox Communist Party, which, after initial

*Monday, June 19, 1967. Fidel Castro lights a fuse.*

discussions with Guevara, refused to accept his leadership. Not only did the Communist Hierarchy oppose the guerrilla movement verbally, it also prevented trained cadres who were willing to fight from joining in.

The evidence of the diary indicates that Guevara was far more committed to an independent political line than some of his Bolivian colleagues. He seemed almost relieved when the Communists refused to support him: 'It may help to free me from any political commitments.'

The Bolivians, too, appear to have been somewhat lacking in enthusiasm to continue the fight. In August (1967), when things were beginning to go badly and Guevara had been desperately ill, he lectured his men. He suggested that those who did not wish 'to graduate as revolutionaries and as men' had better abandon the guerrilla, and he noted afterwards that 'all the Cubans and some of the Bolivians proposed continuing to the end.' The following month, two Bolivians deserted, and in the final combat in which Guevara fell wounded on October 8 (1967) he was accompanied by a group reduced to only sixteen men.

There would seem to be some fairly clear lessons to draw from this. Principally one must conclude that although a guerrilla movement can usefully receive assistance from outside, it is a mistake to allow it to be dominated by the foreign element. In an extremely interesting and valuable introduction to the diary, Castro quotes approvingly Ché's enthusiasm for internationalism, and criticises the Bolivian Communist Party for its obscurantist chauvinism. The criticism is reasonable, especially since, as Castro points out, Bolivia was founded by Venezuelans. It should be remembered too that Guevara's group had an international perspective. The uprising in Bolivia was designed to coincide more or less with the formation of similar 'focos' in Peru and Argentina and a recrudescence of the guerrilla movement in Venezuela. But the fact remains that foreigners, whether Americans or Cubans, do not find it easy to understand the very different mechanisms of power which operate in the distinct Latin-American countries.

The diary also throws light on what is in effect a new United States strategy for dealing with Latin-American guerrillas. It has already been used with great success in Guatemala. The Army moves into a potential guerrilla area, befriends the inhabitants, and then withdraws, leaving a few soldiers behind disguised as peasants. This method was described to me in some detail last year by the colonel in charge of the guerrilla zone and Guevara notes on several occasions that the peasants he talked to subsequently turned out to be camouflaged soldiers. As well as informing the Army of the movements of the guerrillas, these soldiers also kept an eye on potentially revolutionary peasants. To those he discovered thus disguised, Guevara gave a stiff lecture on the rules of war, but being almost unwisely humane he let them go. The guerrillas never seem to have been able to bring themselves to imitate the brutality of the Army.

It is partly this naïveté and ingenuousness that gives Guevara's diary its peculiar charm and interest. It is not the diary of a boy scout, but nor is it quite what one would imagine coming from the pen of Mao or Giap. With his disdain for authority, his complete disregard for personal safety, and his championing of other men's causes that he made his own, Guevara seems closer to the lone wolf figure of General Orde Wingate than to other great guerrilla ideologues who have made history in this century.

*September 12, 1968.*

There is a certain lack of ideological toughness about Guevara for which perhaps one should be thankful. Listening to a Budapest criticism, just a month before his death, which described him as a pathetic and irresponsible figure, he unguardedly writes of how he would like to get power 'if only to unmask cowards and lackeys of all kinds and to poke them in the snout with their filthiness.' (My literal translation.) Splendid sentiments, just as his whole revolutionary career was a splendid example of what can be done by one man possessed of a burning desire to change the nature of his environment. But, in spite of their treachery, perhaps the old-fashioned Communists are not wholly wrong when they place the emphasis on organisation – sadly lacking in the Bolivian guerrilla – and for the moment one must unhappily conclude that the United States knows more about anti-guerrilla warfare in Latin-America than the guerrillas know about how to conduct their revolutionary struggle.

# Confrontation

## IN PARIS: MATINEE AT THE ODEON

Friday, May 17, 1968
*From Nesta Roberts*

It was an extraordinary experience this afternoon to squat on a brief-case on the stage at the Odéon from which, a few weeks ago, one had heard Alain Cuny declaiming Claudel, and look out at the glittering semicircle of the auditorium, packed to the eaves with an actively participating audience.

There was a hostile roar when a couple of cameramen crossed the stage. 'The ORTF! Turn them out!' (The ORTF is the French State Radio and Television Service.) 'Comrades,' bellowed the young chair-man, 'it is the team from "Zoom." They gave us a good show on Tuesday.' 'Zoom' is a magazine programme, whose producers had issued an ultimatum to the directors of the ORTF saying that if they were not allowed to broadcast an objective account of the student situation they would sabotage the entire programme.

The team was accepted, and the meeting later declared its solidarity with the trade unionists within the ORTF who had united against official censorship. A student leader confirmed reports that a march will take place to-morrow on the State Radio building.

'Occupy the Maison de la Radio!' cried a voice. There was agree-ment in principle that this would be a good idea, but it was thought that in practice it would not be advisable. 'The flicks (police) are massed near there.' 'Then why not occupy the Senate?' The same objec-tion applied. This, however, was interesting, since it was the first time this week to my knowledge that any of the student body has even mentioned the Senate or the National Assembly.

The leaders of the Left took part in Monday's great march, but they were given no promises. It is reported, indeed, that at one point M. Guy Mollet, leader of the French Socialist Party and a long-service 'professional politician,' was booed. The same source reports that Pierre Mendès-France, seen by the wayside, was cheered. If this is indeed true, it suggests that however faulty the old university system, it has managed to teach something about the critical examination of ideas.

Down at the Ecole des Beaux Arts, in the Rue Napoléon, there was a similar atmosphere. Action committees carried on non-stop discussion in most of the amphitheatres.

*De Gaulle by Papas – March 6, 1963*

In the little Italianate cloister which contains a memorial to the fallen of two wars, half a dozen young men were debating eagerly across the fountain while, as accompaniment, a thrush was shouting its head off.

In all this, there is a kind of order. The atmosphere is something between that of a siege and a picnic, with empty Coke and pop bottles piling up; hard pressed warriors, hacking a length off a roll of bread and spreading it thick with paté; and a night campaigner fast asleep in a corner, three inches of brown skin showing between his shirt and his hard worn jeans. But the stewards are active. There are strict safety rules for the Odéon. At the Sorbonne, it is reported even that a crèche has been set up to allow married students to take part in the discussions.

Virtually all the country's universities are now caught up in the movement. This afternoon students of the Ecole Polytechnique, which is a military establishment, played truant to attend a discussion in the science faculty. Pupils of the lycées, following the lead of older students who threaten to boycott their examinations, are trying to mobilise support for a boycott of the sacred baccalauréat examination. If this comes off the very Tablets of the Law will have been shattered.

The attitude of the workers is somewhat ambivalent. The occupation of various factories is evidence of sympathy with the students. There was a testimony of the reality of this at the Odéon this afternoon, when a worker in the balcony rose to say: 'I used to think students were people who had cars and drank whisky. Now I know they can fight.'

But a trade union speaker in the same session made it pretty clear that having a non-stop joy day is not the way to gain a cause.

Meanwhile, for the students the end of this week must be crucial. They had these few ecstatic days owing to them.

If this exhilarating upsurge of energy is not to trickle away into the sand, the movement must formulate a concrete programme before the Government once more takes up the reins. What has happened during the past week is too valuable to be dissipated.

## IN AMERICA: KING THIS SIDE OF JORDAN

Saturday, April 6, 1968
*By Jonathan Steele*

'He was the first Negro minister whom I have ever heard who can reduce the Negro problem to a spiritual matter and yet inspire the people to seek a solution on this side of the Jordan not in life after death.' So wrote the Negro author Louis Lomax, catching the crucial spark that made Martin Luther King, jun., stand out head and shoulders from his fellow-ministers in the South and step into the ranks of the world's martyrs.

King was above all a man of the Negro South. He knew for himself the deep and hopeless fatigue, the age-long tiredness, that hangs like a dark cloud over the whole communities in the black belts of Georgia, Alabama, and Mississippi. He knew the energy and power that slumbered there, but which only made itself felt in the feet of the few who migrated to the North in the hope of better things, or the voices that turned to the blues and the hymns and the spirituals. King's genius was to waken that energy and send it out into the streets of the South, marching for justice and social change.

To anyone who was ever there when King spoke, the experience was unforgettable. A small man, barely five foot seven, he dominated the pulpit or the podium. In a slow but sonorous voice, the biblical cadences rolled out, and the crowd would sway with them, and punctuate them with the answering calls that are the special feature of Negro churches. 'There comes a time when the cup of endurance runs over' ... 'Amen' from the crowd: ... ' and men are no longer willing to be plunged into an abyss of injustice where they experience the bleakness of corroding despair.' ... 'Yes, Lord.' ... 'For years now we have heard the word "wait". . . . "help him, Jesus," ' ... 'but we are tired of waiting, tired of being humiliated and denied. We have waited for more than three hundred and forty years for our constitutional and God-given rights.' 'Yes, Lord.'

And the church doors would open and the crowd would surge out into the hot and dusty Southern street, and down to the court house in the city hall, with its petitions, its banners and its faith that change at last was on the way.

What a contrast this was to the old-style Southern minister. I remember going with other student workers on the Mississippi summer project in 1964 to a tiny whitewashed, wooden church on the edge of a cotton field on the first Sunday after the 1964 Civil Rights Act was passed, the Act that outlawed segregation in public facilities throughout the country. We thought there must be some reference to this historic milestone in the sermon; but the minister only touched on it once and then merely to dismiss it as a mundane irrelevancy: 'And they can pass Civil Rights Acts from now until kingdom come, but our faith in the Lord is the same.' The small congregation called out 'Amen' as they had done all along, and stumbled out again into the sunshine, and off to their pitiful homes until next Sunday.

King came from a family of ministers himself. He was born in Atlanta, Georgia, on January 15, 1929. His parents were comfortably off, but during his late teens he took a job against his father's wishes in a factory that hired both Negroes and whites. 'Here,' he wrote later, 'I saw economic injustice at first hand, and realised that the poor white was exploited as much as the Negro. Through these early experiences I grew up deeply conscious of the varieties of injustices in our society.'

Thus early in his life King saw, beyond the issue of individual need, the larger problem of group injustice. He was fond of quoting the words, 'A religion that ends with the individual, ends.' And he wrote later in his famous letter from Birmingham City gaol, in answer to eight clergymen – bishops, pastors, and rabbis – who disagreed with his tactics of direct action in the street:

*Well what do you know – it does say something about Race, Colour or Creed'* – Papas, *Agusut 28, 1963.*

'History is the long and tragic story of the fact that privileged groups seldom give up their privileges voluntarily. Individuals may see the moral light and voluntarily give up their unjust posture, but groups are more immoral than individuals.' When he was 15, King went on to Morehouse, a Negro college in Atlanta. There he read Henry Thoreau's 'Essay on Civil Disobedience,' written in 1846 when Thoreau was protesting against American intervention in Mexico. It made a great impression on him, as it had done on Gandhi, and Tolstoy.

Nonviolence as a philosophy and a strategy for social change is often thought of as a late import into American life, brought there by Martin Luther King. But just as violence runs deep in the American system, so too does the tradition of nonviolence. There is a distinctive American tradition which runs back to the Quakers in the seventeenth century. From them it goes to the abolitionists and peace crusaders of the years before the Civil War, the anarchists and pacifists at the beginning of this century, the sit-down strikers of the 1930s and the conscientious objectors of two world wars. King knew this, as he knew his Hegel, Kant, and Gandhi.

King was ordained, did a doctoral degree at Boston University, and then in 1955 became pastor of the Dexter Avenue Baptist Church, an upper-income Negro church in Montgomery, Alabama. It was here that almost by chance he was given the opportunity to put his study of nonviolence into action. For the civil rights movement began by accident.

A Negro seamstress, Mrs. Rosa Parks, was going home one day. She was tired, and sat down in the bus, and when asked to get up for a white man, as any Negro was liable to be, she simply refused. She was arrested. News of the arrest spread and the Negro community was angry. King found himself leading a modest campaign for decent treatment on the buses. After more white provocation and more Negro arrests, including that of King himself, the campaign grew into a mass boycott of the buses with the demand for total desegregation.

The boycott lasted for several months, received world-wide publicity, and ended in victory. King founded the Southern Christian Leadership Conference, to rally his fellow-Negro ministers throughout the South. After that he led march after march in Albany, Georgia, in 1961; the march on Washington, in 1963, and in Birmingham, Alabama, later that summer; Selma to Montgomery in 1965; and the march through Mississippi after James Meredith was shot in 1966. He spent the next few months in the suburbs of Chicago, his first major project in the North. He opposed the war in Vietnam, and the cuts in the poverty programme which it inevitably brought. And later this month he was to have led a march of poor people on Washington.

Death was always near him, and he survived several previous attempts on his life. But he never let this weigh too long on his mind. He had, as he said, to go on. His last sentence to the crowd before he swung out on the first Selma march, in defiance of a court injunction and in the teeth of a hostile police force, was this: 'I would rather die to-day on the highways of Alabama than make a butchery of my own conscience.'

In cold print, that reads histrionically, perhaps. King knew, and has now made others know, that it was a real and conscious choice.

## THE BRUTAL BATTLE OF CHICAGO

Friday, August 30, 1968

*From Alistair Cooke*

Chicago, August 29

Vice-President Hubert Humphrey overwhelmingly won the Democrats' Presidential nomination last night but he, the Convention, and most likely the Democratic Party itself, were wounded beyond recognition by the spectacle, seen by stupefied millions, of a Chicago police force gone berserk in front of the biggest hotel in the world. In 30 years of attending Presidential conventions, I have seen nothing to match the fury and despair of the delegations inside this Chicago amphitheatre, or on the outside, anything like the jumping-jack ferocity of the police corps round the Hilton Hotel.

They began by clubbing and taming peace demonstrators and jeering hippies and ended by roaming the hotel lobby like SS men and roughing up astonished guests, marooned families, and other innocents sitting or walking through the hotel lounges.

By mid-evening, while nominating orators were extolling the saintliness of five candidates (Humphrey, McCarthy, McGovern, a Southern Governor, and a Negro parson), the night air along Michigan Avenue was dense with tear gas, roaring multitudes of youngsters, the smart crack of billy clubs, and the clatter of running feet.

Senator Eugene McCarthy opened up his headquarters in the hotel as an emergency hospital, and he and his daughter moved among the injured comforting them and bathing their wounds. Senator McGovern, the other dove candidate, stood at the window of his fourth floor suite reeling with disbelief and nausea. He turned back from the thing itself to the wider view of it being shown on television.

He telephoned his floor manager, Senator Abe Ribicoff of Connecticut, on the Convention floor. When Ribicoff came to the rostrum to put McGovern's name in nomination, he abandoned his smooth text, stared coolly at Mayor Dalley and the entire Illinois delegation no more than 50 feet away and cried, 'With George McGovern as President we would not have Gestapo tactics in the streets of Chicago.'

Through a tidal wave of boos and derisive cheers, the Illinois delegation stood and lunged their fists at him. Ribicoff, an elegant and handsome man, slowly said: 'How hard it is to accept the truth.' This was too much for the Mayor of Chicago. Dropping his calculated Edward G. Robinson smile, he rose and shouted inaudible horrors at the first man to confess to this Convention that the Democratic Party had been mocked in the name of security to make a gangsters' holiday.

Thereafter, scores of young men employed by a private detective agency locked arms around the Illinois delegation and denied any access to them by other delegates, the press, the television floor reporters, or Convention officials.

Last night they outdid themselves, in their mulish way, and this morning the three television networks and a host of newspapers filed protests with the City of Chicago, the Governor of Illinois, and the National Committee of the Democratic Party.

Even in the clearing haze of the morning after, another crystalline day of late summer, it is almost impossible to describe the progress of the Convention plot; for every parliamentary move on the floor was baffled by the street battles thundering from the television screens in the corridors and soon after by the rage of the delegates who had watched them.

The nominators came in turn and praised their man, but as the word of the battle of Chicago came in even the orators began to salt their bland stuff with acid asides. The television reporters were complaining, in full view of the nation, about these 'thugs' and 'faceless men' at their elbows.

Paul O'Dwyer, the Democratic choice for Senator in New York, walked out and held a caucus of New York, California, and Wisconsin delegates and urged them 'to decline to participate in this mockery.' The purpose of this rebel caucus was declared to be 'to bring to a grinding halt this Convention unless these atrocities are stopped.'

At the end Hubert Humphrey had run up the commanding total of 1,761¾ against McCarthy's 601, McGovern's 146½, with 67½ votes for the Negro parson, 12½ for Senator Kennedy and a sprinkling of oddities, including three votes for the football coach of Alabama State University.

The euphoria of the winners was, I suppose, genuine enough at the moment. But the sight of it on television revealed a gruesome irony. The only unreal place to be last night was in the Convention itself. Fenced in with barbed wire, ringed around with Mayor Daley's tough guys, cut off from the living world of television, the Amphitheatre was a circus in the middle of a plague.

Most of the delegates, it was obvious, had no idea what the grim Ribicoffs and Petersons were talking about. Some personal grudge, no doubt, against Mayor Daley. It was a terrifying demonstration of McLuhanism; the only people who got the whole message were the millions frozen with terror in front of their television screens.

If there is any consolation in all this for the ordinary, agonised citizen it is that Mayor Daley was revealed as an arch bullyboy, the manager and dictator of this Convention inside and out, the last of the city bosses in his dreadful and final hour of glory.

'At least,' said a Chicago police official this morning, 'no one was killed.' No one, that is, except the Democratic Party. Now that the smoke and clatter and weeping have died down, there is only a faint rhythmical sound ruffling the horizon on this beautiful day. It is the sound, North, South, East, and West, of the Republicans counting votes.

## THE PRAGUE SPRING – AND THE
## PROSPECTS FOR HARVEST

Monday, June 10, 1968
*By Geoffrey Taylor*

'I am spending some time in Eastern Europe,' I explained to the man, ' – if you count Czechoslovakia as Eastern Europe.'

'Unfortunately we do,' he said. 'Let us be realistic,' the man said (he was not a Communist). 'We are a Central European country and until the division of Europe is ended we can't walk out of the Warsaw Pact, just like that.'

This seemed prudent. Indeed there were times in Prague when I wished the Czechs' valour would be more discreet than it was, that they would be more careful not to provoke the Red Army intervention which General Yepishev, its political head, was said to be advocating. But they presumably know how far they can go without being trodden on, and the democratic revolution shows no sign of slackening. Novotny and his closest lieutenants have been dismissed from the party. Against Soviet advice a party congress is to be held in September to remove the remaining conservatives from the central committee. The secret police are being purged.

But not all the obstacles to reform can be hastily removed. There is still a lobby of placemen who thrived under the dictatorship, and who fear for their pockets and their power if democratisation is allowed to go on. The highly paid officials in the districts, the privileged party militia in the factories, the trade union bosses, and even some workers, like the coalminers at Ostrava, who have been protected in dying and uncompetitive industries – all these mount an opposition to rapid change, always with strong psychological support from the Soviet Union, East Germany, and Poland.

The figure is quoted of 250,000 men – one million people with their families – who were promoted into bureaucratic posts by the regime. Some of them, mainly local party officials who carried through the collectivisation of the farms, are being intimidated by their former victims. They are discredited men. But unless the new regime can reform the economy as well as the political life of the nation they may again exert an influence among the workers and hence inside the party. Already all talk of a formal opposition has, at least for the time being, been abandoned.

A visitor may puzzle over the contortions by which the party is now condemning its own immediate past, but he will not waste much charity on the regime which governed from 1948 until the end of last year. Czechoslovakia is austere, even drab. Almost everything that raises life above the level of norm fulfilment either, like the beauty of Prague, predates communism, or, like the liveliness of the arts, stems from the intellectual excitement which helped to bring about the revolution in the party. The revolution apart, communism would be hard put to show in what way its 20 years have improved the lot of the people.

This is a generalisation I would not want to make about three other East European countries recently visited. Admittedly Yugoslavia hardly counts in this context; it is alive with innovation and experiment. Bulgaria now manufactures and exports high quality electrical equipment, pharmaceuticals, and opera singers; there could be worse fates for an underdeveloped Balkan province not long delivered from Turkish or indigenous despotism. Hungary, perhaps because one expected the dreariness of hard-line communism, is a pleasant surprise. It has profited by the 1956 revolt, is working its way fairly empirically towards a higher material standard of living (which still counts in Eastern Europe, unfashionable though it may be in the West), and is playing a part in breaking down the barriers dividing Europe.

It is not necessary to allege that the Russians have deliberately milked the Czechoslovak economy. Once Czechoslovakia had fallen within the Soviet economic orbit its fate was decided. Its rôle within Comecon has been to supply the Soviet Union and other Communist countries with the products of the heavy and engineering industries in return for raw materials. But the Soviet requirement has been for unsophisticated, bulky machinery which offered no challenge to Czechoslovak initiative. Industries which were once competitive with those in the West have been allowed to stagnate because the Soviet economy had no call for advanced products.

There is, of course, nothing immoral about making trams, especially if the trams can be sold against the consumer goods which a modern

State needs. But in Czechoslovakia's case they cannot. When they have taken their oil, coal, low-grade ores and wheat from the Comecon countries there is nothing on which the Czechs can spend their huge trading surplus, and this surplus is not transferable into hard currency. Czechoslovakia is therefore in a position of economic stalemate. It cannot improve its standard of living and enter the consumer market without buying from the West. It cannot buy from the West without selling there. It cannot sell there because its industry is, by Western standards, obsolescent. And it cannot bring its industry up to date without capital to spend on Western equipment.

There are Czechs who take an even gloomier view than that. The equipment is not the only thing out of date: so is the mentality. The regime was without incentives. Good work and bad were paid equally, and in any case extra money is no incentive in an economy without goods. This may be unduly pessimistic. The economic reforms of the last few years have gone some way towards restoring both incentives and pride. But the wise man I quoted does not see how Czechoslovakia can break away from Comecon any sooner than from the Warsaw Pact.

The blight of twenty years is obvious in Prague, but more so in the provincial towns and in the forlorn countryside. The guides still extol the beauty of the buildings, but only the prestige buildings have been looked after. Chipped stone and flaking plaster and want of paint symbolise the neglect under which Czechoslovakia has suffered. Budapest also needs a spring clean, but the Hungarian provincial towns and villages, on which some care has been spent, seemed to me to belong to a different order of communism from the war-weariness of Pilsen, Znojmo, Jihlava, and the villages in between.

Yet there is a vigour about life in Prague which Budapest does not enjoy. The walls are covered with the ebullient notices of a young generation freed from censorship. The press is asking questions. The radio has introduced a programme which any ruling class would find intolerable: it takes a subject for the evening, rings up the people it wants to argue with, and broadcasts the conversation live. Mr. Cernik, the Prime Minister, has not escaped the treatment. Nor has the leader of the emasculated Socialist party who was asked before an audience of millions what he had been doing for twenty years. No wonder all those district secretaries, whose image of the working-class is that of the sleeve rolled up, the fist clenched, and the banner flying, think democracy is a lethal virus. On a summer evening, when Wenceslas Square is packed with the bright, handsome, intelligent faces which seem characteristic of the Czechoslovak crowd, one yearns to believe that nothing will stop the revolution. And yet the enthusiasm of May Day, when the

Czechs turned out in hundreds of thousands to applaud Mr. Dubcek, had given way a few weeks later to a more cautious introspection.

Would the old guard come back? Could the economy ever be put right? Was democracy going to be dissipated in a row between Czechs and Slovaks about federalism and wage differentials? 'Fatalism,' I was told. 'It is a thing you must reckon with.' What a disaster if that should be true.

## THE HARVEST SPOILED

### Thursday, August 22, 1968
### By W. L. Webb

Long before Munich, old President Masaryk told a young British journalist that if a little country like his enjoyed liberty for 20 years every now and then 'it could not necessarily hope for more.' This time his people have had barely 30 weeks in which to enjoy a degree of liberty greater than anything that had been known in Central and Eastern Europe since 1948. But if one fights down the sickening, impotent anger that anyone who has witnessed that brief interlude must feel at the news of the past 24 hours, if one looks for any sign of hope in the new darkness that has descended on Czechoslovakia, it is to that unnerving stoicism of Masaryk's that one must turn.

It is a stoicism bred into the Czech people during three and a half centuries of foreign rule by the Habsburgs, by nazism, and by Stalinist communism directed from Moscow. It helped them to learn the diplomatic skills which brought the new State so auspiciously into being at the end of the First World War; it was the backbone of the Good Soldier Schweik himself, a far more real and credible national symbol than John Bull or Marianne, whose talent for looking one way and doggedly going another so maddened the Germans and indeed most of his other neighbours in Europe. More immediately, these were the qualities that brought Czechoslovakia so near to success in its attempt to wriggle out from under the dead hand of neo-Stalinist orthodoxy and get back on to its own road to a valid democratic socialism.

One must date the final break in the closed circuit of total rule from January 5, when Novotny was removed from the secretaryship of the Czechoslovak Communist Party: it was after that that the Czechoslovak press generally began to enjoy a measure of real freedom, as opposed to the freedom at risk which some of the cultural and intellectual journals had been exercising. But the whole point of what we had begun to call the new Czech 'Reformation,' the thing which made its substance so formidable, yet caused its importance to be missed by many people until quite late in the day, was its gradualism. The removal of Novotny was the result of a slow growth of forces, quietly and craftily drawn into alliance over the years, which eventually proved irresistible.

The principal parties in the alliance were Slovak nationalism, the new wave of technocrats and economists who were allowed to organise economic reforms when orthodoxy had run the economy almost into the ground, and the generation of writers and intellectuals who had gone most of the way from adolescent idealism in the late forties to disillusionment but not despair 20 years later. Throughout the sixties these forces grew and slowly, almost reluctantly in the case of some Slovak leaders, began to coalesce.

Slovak nationalism in various forms had always been potentially disruptive of party unity, and the turning point on that particular front came in 1963 with the emergence of Alexander Dubcek as First Secretary of the Slovak Communist Party and as a member of the Czechoslovak Party Praesidium. From then on the Slovaks exerted increasing pressure at the political centre for a measure of autonomy and incidentally but necessarily for a more liberal ordering of things in the nation's life generally.

By 1963 the need for economic reform was painfully clear to the man in the street in Prague and Pilsen, and soon middle-of-the-road men in the higher reaches of the apparat were being forced to acknowledge what Marxism of all codes should have taught them anyway: that economic changes could not be made in a political vacuum – that no technical plan could get Czechoslovakia to work again if the political system still tended to alienate the people instead of enlisting them as individual participants in the ordering of their society.

And, finally, there were the writers, the advance guard of reform in a society which has always respected the word and whose hunger for renewed contact with the main stream of European life and culture caused huge editions of classical and modern literature to be bought up like pop records in the last decade.

Again 1963 was a crucial year. To the fury of Ulbricht's ideologues, Kafka was rehabilitated and then in the summer of 1967 came that congress of the Writers' Union at which the young Czechoslovak playwright, Pavel Kohout, got up and read aloud Solzhenitsyn's open letter describing the tragic fate of Russian literature under the neo-Stalinism which had come to dominate Soviet culture in the years after Khrushchev.

The fury that followed brought the crisis to a head and drew together all the reforming forces that had been working in the earth so well, in a final and successful confrontation. Schweik suddenly stood his ground and outfaced the exhausted oppressors he had so cautiously and patiently worn down.

The canny courage he has shown in the open since then is a more recent and familiar story. It was a particular and infectious kind of courage to watch, rarely posturing or melodramatic, but always human and humorous, not expecting too much but hoping valiantly for the best.

Almost throughout the tense weeks leading up to and including the talks at Cierna and Bratislava the people of Prague seemed to believe that the new force that had grown so steadily and gradually in their society could not be negated, and eventually one came to share their conviction. History, they felt, was moving in that direction; to turn the clock back to 1956 would be an act outside the realm of reason, and in Europe at least there were surely grounds for thinking that reason had begun to order the affairs of nations once more.

Now in spite of all their rational hopes the unreasonable thing has been done, and Czechoslovakia seems to be falling back into the nightmare of unreason, back into the sick world of Kafka's imagination, not Schweik's. The Czechoslovaks' sane and sensible instinct for democracy, which contained also the hope – perhaps the last hope – of a humane and effective kind of socialism, has foundered on the neurotic fear of freedom and nonconformity that shows the dominant force in Eastern Europe to be still essentially and archaically Stalinist.

Less than three weeks ago, feeling the relief in the sane and sunny streets of Prague after Mr. Dubcek had finally broadcast his credible reassurances that he had not retreated, one could scarcely have believed that Soviet tanks would roar along Na Prikope to crush that hope after all. And even now I believe that this solution to the problem of the Communist half of Europe is not credible, does not coincide with the realities of the situation.

This is not 1956, Czechoslovakia is not Hungary nor Poland. It is not credible that Brezhnev and Ulbricht will be able simply to reinstate Novotny and Hendrych and their old colleagues, or that Oldrich Svestka, the editor of 'Rude Pravo,' and the most likely betrayer of the Czech praesidium, will be able to recruit men to run a jackal press of the kind Czechoslovakia has not had for some years now. It is not credible that the Czechoslovak people will return, except under the lash of equally incredibly brutal and Draconian force, to the condition of their lives, not as they were in 1967, but as they were in 1952 and 1953.

Perhaps this is simply the incredulity that the Czechs themselves taught me during my visits to Prague in this year that had seemed so full of promise and recovered sanity, an incredulity that had begun to forget the fact that in Europe there is more than one 'reality.' But if the Czechs can keep their sanity in the shadow of Ulbricht's reality, of Kafka's reality, as Schweik has taught them to, if they can remember what anyone who witnessed it cannot forget, the quality of their courage and stoical patience during the last few months, and what it had managed to achieve, we may yet discover that this is not the end of the affair. Schweik has survived tanks and gauleiters and commissars before. His stoicism and ingenuity should not be underestimated. His grasp of reality is surer than that of his adversaries and he knows what desperate wounds they have inflicted on themselves in wounding him.

He knows, and the world – east and west of Prague – knows whose defeat this is.

## TAKE-OVER AT HORNSEY

Thursday, June 13, 1968
*By Dennis Barker*

'You mustn't expect hundreds of people slopping paint around,' said the charming young lady in the student press office of the taken-over Hornsey College of Art.

'Our projects are nowhere near the final stage. Groups are working on the approaches to the projects, which is a project in itself. Before you can do anything creative you must meditate. Does that sound absurd?'

It did, just a bit. Students of the college have already told their principal he can come into the college as long as he does not use his own office. Now they have set up a system under which the scattered departments can get together and they have originated a huge number of special projects for them to get together about.

There were 26 schemes on the agenda on Sunday night. By Monday morning it had grown to 58. The number is still growing.

The ideas, and their progress, are neatly docketed in a home-made plywood filing system kept by the students. They are broken down into two jargon categories which the students may well have caught off their elders.

First, there are the ones which are 'high-key.' This means big. They include redesigning Oxford Circus Underground, the utilisation of low-cost materials in underdeveloped countries, and conducting feasibility studies into a national football stadium and whether the whole of Hornsey College could move into Alexandra Palace nearby.

Then there are the 'low-key' projects. This means small. Many of them are worthy; like designing toys for handicapped children. Some of them are pointed, like designing a better railway buffet car, re-designing level-crossings, and the provision of modular design lavatories on trains.

Thus do the 900 students justify their claim to be able to run the college for themselves, and thus they give a pointer to what they think art education might be like in the future. 'Of course, this is only an interim system while we negotiate,' said one of the collective voices now speaking for students.

What is really happening to these projects while one group of students sits out on the lawn holding a seminar about the terms of their latest letter to the board of governors?

Where there has been progress on a project it usually turns out that the project is either small or has been started under the regime of the principal (Mr. H. H. Shelton, now incommunicado while local alder-men struggle to put the official line). The toys for handicapped children idea was already in progress. So was the Oxford Circus Underground project. So was work on colour emulsion. So, for that matter, was a project for pneumatic helter-skelter. Of the 58 known projects, work is going on in under half.

But because some of the projects may not achieve practical results, it does not follow there is no genuine creative impulse behind them. 'Industrial design has very strict functional restraints. We were always trying to work towards an optimum solution,' said a disgruntled collective voice. The complaint repeats itself around the college, in the same sort of jargon. The jargon itself must put an intolerable strain on all but the mediocre – even if they cannot see the cause of the strain.

Yesterday students were busy rejecting specialist limitations. Some were rushing round primary schools hearing about their problems (another project). Some were acting as delegates to other students at Exeter and Bath. Others were listening to Mr. Christopher Logue, the poet, on the lawn. A lot were discussing how issues should be discussed.

'Stop me if I am talking jargon,' said a young girl. She was touchingly unaware that she was talking it all the time. 'Oh, damn,' said another girl, 'I've got to run off to see a computer. I am doing a project on computer typesetting and I want to know what a computer looks like.'

Such fey notes are almost bound to incense middle-aged ratepayers.

But in fact the middle-aged should be especially well-equipped to understand the reality of the students' case, even though they may be no more able at present to put it into words than the students themselves.

Students talk about the need for 'interdepartmental cross-fertilisation in the philosophical sense.' By this they mean chat with their intelligent contemporaries. They talk of the need for 'bridge personalities.' By this they mean stimulating human beings who have not looked at life through a specialist keyhole.

Both these points should be comprehensible to people who had their youth before the computer era. 'Things are in an interim stage, and we cannot say definitely where they are moving,' said a collective voice. The impression at Hornsey may well be a significant pointer. It is that the students, knowingly or not, behave as if they believe the specialist is dying of his own tedium and that the versatile man, supposedly extinct, is somehow going to be resurrected.

## THE WAY TO GROSVENOR SQUARE

Friday, October 18, 1968
*By Alan Smith*

Two major demonstrations against the Americans in Vietnam were the climax of the student unrest of 1968. The first in July led to such fierce conflicts between demonstrators and police outside the American Embassy in Grosvenor Square that there was widespread anxiety or anticipation of what might happen on October 27. In the event only the extremists went to Grosvenor Square and the police were able to contain this part of the demonstration with relative ease.

There is no overall conspiracy behind the demonstration on October 27. The militant Left is fragmented into a galaxy of small groups, each of which is deciding where to march on Sunday week, what tactics to use to resist the police, how much violence they are prepared to use.

No one is in a position to predict what will happen – no one has succeeded in master-minding the demonstration, certainly not Tariq Ali and the other members of the Vietnam Solidarity Committee, who are rapidly losing the support of the more militant.

There will be two main centres for the demonstrators. Whitehall, following the 'official' VSC route, and Grosvenor Square, where many Left-wing groups are now determined to make their protest. The leaders of the local groups and branches expect violence; some welcome it.

I attended, unchallenged, a tactical briefing session of 20 leading members of one of London's largest VSC branches. This group considered tactics to be used against tear gas and Mace – the American-developed gas which attacks the eye retinas.

Their planning was based on techniques developed at the earlier Grosvenor Square demonstration. They expected violence from both sides, and assumed throughout that anyone who was arrested would be 'hammered' by the police at the time and afterwards. Those members who were well-known to local police (who are expected to follow local groups in the march) were warned not to go home on Sunday night if they took part in, or were seen near, any violent incidents.

The basic tactics in the crowd is for groups of five or six to march together, people 'who trust each other very well.' This is so that if any one of them is arrested, the others can try to rescue him. Also, a solid core of five in a line of 15 abreast could take the others with them in a window-breaking or Storm-trooping sortie. Do not tell anyone else who you are linking up with, they said, or announce what you plan to do. No heroics, do not get arrested if you can help it – the police will show no mercy.

This hard core group expect about 20,000 people to turn out on the march, with about 70 per cent of 'neutrals' – people who simply wanted to make a protest and who would not start or join in violence. They expect trouble with other Left-wing groups, and the stewards who will be attempting to keep the march moving. They were particularly bitter with the Young Communist groups who, they said, had last time helped the police identify trouble-makers.

They were angry with the VSC executive, which had decided, without the support of many branches, against going to Grosvenor Square, and to have a non-militant demonstration. Liaison between the executive and the branch groups had broken down; several branches would be making their own decisions. It seems certain that there will be, apart from the main Whitehall and Grosvenor Square contingents, many groups which will break away at different times during the afternoon and rampage on the fringes of the march, thus diverting police.

The attitude towards violence was that it was for individuals to decide how far they should go. Some saw the march simply as a protest against American action in Vietnam, others saw it as more than this, a milestone on the path to revolution. There was no direct incitement to violence in this group, but members will be told to carry pins and fireworks to defend themselves against horse charges, and asked to make sure that placards and banners were of stout wood.

The attitude of this revolutionary hard core is that a demonstration is their right, and a step towards revolution their duty. 'Grosvenor Square and the American Embassy must be our target,' said one. 'That is where the enemy is. If the police obstruct us, they become the aggressors too.'

## WHY I'M OFF THE AIR:
## JOHN ARLOTT EXPLAINS

### Friday, April 17, 1970

For personal reasons, I shall not broadcast on the matches of the South African cricket tour of England arranged for 1970. The B.B.C. has accepted my decision with understanding and an undertaking that my standing with them will not be affected by it.

This course of action has not been dictated by mass influences. Apartheid is detestable to me, and I would always oppose it. On the other hand, I am not satisfied that the cricket tour is the aspect of apartheid which should have been selected as the major target for attack. It would have seemed to me more justifiable, more tactically simple, and more effective, to mount a trade embargo or to picket South Africa House. Surely the Nationalist South African Ambassador is a thousand times more guilty of the inhuman crime of apartheid than Graeme Pollock who, throughout the English summer of 1969, played cricket for the International Cavaliers XI with eight or nine West Indians and, before he went home, said: 'What great chaps – there couldn't have been a better bunch to play with.'

Jack Plimsoll, the manager of this touring team, was an intimate friend of mine on the South African tour of England in 1947, before the election of the first – Malan – Nationalist Government, and the introduction of apartheid. Every one of the South African players of my acquaintance has already played with, and against, non-white cricketers. Indeed, only a multi-racial match, played in South Africa before the Vorster (Verwoerd) Government banned such fixtures for ever, provided the expert assessment of Basil D'Oliveira's ability which enabled me to persuade Middleton to give him a contract to play in England. Not all South Africans are pro-apartheid.

Crucially, though, a successful tour would offer comfort and confirmation to a completely evil regime. To my mind, the Cricket Council, acting on behalf of British cricket, has failed fairly to represent those British people – especially cricketers – who genuinely abominate apartheid. The council might have determined – and been granted – terms which would have demonstrated its declared disapproval of apartheid. It did not do so; nor give the slightest indication of a will to do so. To persist with the tour seems to me a social, political, and cricketing error. If I were a supporter of apartheid I would feel the same. It seems to me destined to failure on all levels, with the game of cricket the ultimate and inevitable sufferer. If it should 'succeed' to the extent of being completed, what is the outcome to be – a similarly contentious tour four years hence?

It is my limitation, an advantage, that I can only broadcast as I feel. Commentary on any game demands, in my professional belief, the ingredient of pleasure; it can only be satisfactorily broadcast in terms of shared enjoyment. This series cannot, to my mind, be enjoyable. There are three justifiable reasons for playing cricket – performance, pleasure, and profit – and I do not believe that this tour will produce any of them.

The terms of the B.B.C.'s charter do not permit expression of editorial opinion. It would not be professional or polite to disagree with my fellow commentators on the significance of the tour within the hearing of listeners. It therefore seems to me unfair, on both sides, for me to broadcast about the tour in a manner uncritical of its major issues, while retaining the right to be critical of them in this newspaper.

It is my hope to write and talk about cricket in which the minor issue of a game is not overshadowed by the major issue of principle.

## After the Empire

### A KIKUYU TELLS HIS STORY

Thursday, August 1, 1963
*By Clyde Sanger*

It is sometimes difficult to remember how fast Africa, and particularly Kenya, has changed. Eleven years ago two Old Etonians fought for the votes of 914 people, mostly white farmers and their families, who made up the Aberdares constituency of Kenya. The winner campaigned for early self-government with 'a substantial majority of Europeans' in the Legislature, and with European control to be secured 'for the foreseeable future.' He wanted further Asian immigration 'completely prohibited' and (although he was a lawyer) 'the complete suppression of all seditious and anti-British publications.'

That same month, Josiah Mwangi Kariuki was taking his School Certificate, and a few months later he took two Mau Mau oaths. As a result, he spent seven years in detention camps. Today he is the author of ' "Mau Mau" Detainee', an account of those years. He is also now the hon. member for the Aberdares, and 25,000 farm-workers turned out to vote for him in May. It should be added that the Old Etonians have not emigrated, but are in two of the most important jobs in the new Kenya, and show every sign of enjoying the changes.

Is this a completely happy ending, then, with the transition successfully accomplished? The constitutional and parliamentary changes have been accepted, of course, by the Kinangop farmers and other minorities. But have attitudes altered fundamentally? The fuss this book has caused, even before its publication, suggests otherwise. Seven bookshops which form the biggest chain in East Africa have refused to stock it.

Yet if emotion is stilled and stereotype images of wild-eyed terrorists set aside for a while, this book should be recognised as a powerful force for spreading a more rounded understanding of the emergency. That is, if we accept, as Miss Margery Perham does in the foreword, that it is 'a substantially true account.' Miss Perham explains how, when she first met Mr. Kariuki at Oxford, she quickly felt a liking for this hard-core ex-Mau Mau detainee both because of his modesty and friendliness and because 'more surprisingly he revealed a healing desire for reconciliation with those Europeans and Africans who had ill-treated him.'

The ill-treatment is shaming to read. It is perhaps the more shaming because he is almost casual in describing how, for instance, detainees arriving at Manyani apparently had to run a three-mile gauntlet of 3,000 warders armed with batons to get into the camp, and turns to wryness to explain in detail what contortions are necessary if you want to take your trousers off when you are fettered. But Kariuki was particularly victimised by the warders because he made a practice of smuggling out letters of complaint to British M.Ps and senior Kenya. officials about camp conditions. In one six-month period he says he received 200 strokes, and for another three months was kept on half rations in a cell measuring six feet by four feet.

Yet he seems never to have given way to hatred. He records how at Athi River camp he was beaten unconscious by four Europeans, including an ex-army officer disguised in this book as 'Rochester.' Two years later when they met in another camp, there were no hard feelings and he was soon coaching 'Rochester's' young son in his lines as a nativity play angel. This lack of bitterness is the strongest theme of the book, and seems based on faith that his and the other detainees' sacrifice was a necessary part of the historical process of Kenya's growth from colony to statehood.

This book cannot give a full picture of Kenya's emergency, because Mr. Kariuki was never in the forest. We will have to wait, say, for the memoirs of 'General China' or an inquiry into the root causes of the Lari massacre before light shines on that side. He was arrested at the small Nafluru hotel he was running, presumably because the authorities knew a bit about the little he had done; which was to recruit for the Kenya African Union, take two oaths, warn a number of people that the police were after them, and give a pistol to a would-be forest fighter.

The book is, however, valuable as the first detailed attempt to describe the mental attitude of men who took Mau Mau oaths by one who took two of them, and calls these two 'the only legitimate ones.' The first oath of unity consisted mainly in mixing a few drops of the blood of each oath-taker with some goat's meat which they all then ate. This, the administrator explained, bound them together and to the movement to fight for 'the lands of Kirinyaga which were taken by the Europeans.'

The second, or Batuni, oath, was 'much stronger and taken by all those who were likely to be called on to give active service to the movement. This oath left my mind full of strange and excited feelings. My initiation was now complete and I had become a true Kikuyu with no doubts where I stood in the revolt of my tribe.' He admits some people were forced to take these oaths, and indeed his own first oath-taking came as a surprise to him after he had thought he was setting out on an evening stroll with a friend, and the three initiates with him were 'hit about a little.' He also admits a connection between KAU and oathing, to the extent that he had been picked because he was an active recruiter for KAU. But he claims that widespread stories of oathings which involved menstrual blood or intercourse with animals were 'either fabrications or confined to a minute number of perverted individuals driven crazy by their isolation in the forests.' Both oaths he took contained the recurring phrase 'If I fail . . . may this oath kill me,' but he claims the bond of these oaths removed fear.

If this is the case, the whole British policy of forcing confessions of rehabilitation through hard work, which culminated in the Hola murders, begins to look very foolish if nothing worse. Kariuki ridicules it continuously: the prostitutes whom Moral Re-Armament workers paraded 'to dangle their legs before the detainees to remind them of some of the things they were missing'; the lectures on 'the terrible state of tribal conflict before the arrival of the white man.' Miss Perham in her foreword argues this point, and says the intention behind the policy of pressing prisoners to confess was reformist and not punitive, an attempt to accelerate release by breaking the spell of the oath and passing them 'down the pipeline' to freedom.

Kariuki's indictment of British policy is strong, and raises some ugly questions. For example, how senior were the people who devised the scheme of rehabilitation? After Hola only a few junior heads rolled. And how do the ordinary British, who pride themselves on their decency and tolerance, come by stages to acquiesce and even participate in the brutality of the camps? They are prisoners of the system, some would say. But how far up do we have to go before finding those who controlled the system? Or was it out of control? Kariuki is fair and does not suggest Manyani was a Belsen. Several times he says the good warders balanced the vicious ones, and his perseverance in smuggling out letters of complaint was based on a belief in British justice, which he acknowledges was rarely mocked.

## A LETTER TO MR. SELWYN LLOYD

Friday, February 4, 1966

Dear Mr. Lloyd, – You are leaving this weekend for Rhodesia. You are going there on behalf of Mr. Heath. You will be making your own assessment of the political and economic situation. This is an excellent thing to do: may your journey be profitable.

You will also presumably be considering when and how negotiations with a Rhodesian Government can be resumed. Your leader Mr. Heath holds that the British Government should be ready to talk to Mr. Smith. So long as Mr. Smith and his Ministers 'come back to the constitutional path' then your party's policy is that Britain should treat them as a legitimate Government again.

May I mention some reasons why this view seems unsound? Would you consider these while you are in Rhodesia?

Look first at the kind of society that the Rhodesia Front was creating long before UDI. Events since November 10 have partly covered the evidence but you will find plenty. It was not the kind of society that gave Africans a fair chance and there are 15 Africans to one white in Rhodesia. Here are some of the disabilities.

**Education.** Only one child in 3,000 can hope to complete secondary education at present in Rhodesia – whereas in Zambia the figure is one in 300, in Kenya one in 50, and in Tanzania one in 40. The Government in Rhodesia has deliberately restricted the opportunities for Africans in higher education. The position to-day is much as it would be in Scotland (with a comparable population) if sixth forms there turned out only 60 or 70 pupils a year.

This matters in two ways. It denies Africans the economic opportunities which follow from higher education. It also denies them political equality. To obtain a vote on the 'A' roll – which elects 50 out of the 65 members in the Rhodesian Parliament as at present constituted – a citizen must have full secondary education or large property, or a high salary. Very few Africans at present can hope to qualify.

**Voting rights.** Even on the 'B' roll – which elects 15 of the 65 Members (though there is also a complex form of devalued cross-voting) – income, property, and education still count. When I was in Rhodesia some months ago I tried to obtain figures from the acting Minister of Information about the Government's estimate of the number of Africans then qualified for the 'A' and 'B' rolls. No answer was available. The only official figure that could be given was that 256 Africans were registered on the 'A' roll (against 89,278 Europeans) in May 1964 and 10,466 Africans on the 'B' roll (against 608 Europeans). The number of Africans qualified on the 'B' roll is certainly far higher than the number registered, because there has been a boycott. The fact remains that African representation in Parliament and African voting power are pitifully limited.

**Land and homes.** No African can live with his family or own a house or office in the better parts of Salisbury, Bulawayo, or any other town – however prosperous he may be. The Land Apportionment Act prevents this. The only exception is for domestic servants. Most people with jobs in a town have to live a long way from their work.

**Job reservation.** In theory, there is no distinction between Africans and whites. Any man qualified for a job can have it. In practice, the opportunities for Africans remain somewhat limited. Ask how many African engine drivers there are on the railways in Rhodesia – even on shunting engines. You will, I think, find that there are none.

**Political prisoners.** To-day – as a year ago – more people are being detained without trial or restricted without trial in Rhodesia than in any other country in East or Central Africa. Detention or restriction for up to five years without charge or trial is possible under the Law and Order Maintenance Act. There is no appeal against a detention or restriction order except to the Minister who has made the order. There are more political prisoners in Rhodesia than in Tanzania, Kenya, or Zambia.

**Law enforcement.** On the day I arrived in Salisbury last spring (I mention this because it was said to be an average case), 21 Africans were sentenced to terms of six years or five years in prison for 'malicious

THE GUARDIAN
192 GRAYS INN ROAD LONDON W.C.1
TELEPHONE 01-837 7011 · TELEGRAMS GUARDIAN LONDON · TELEX 22.895
HEAD OFFICE 3 CROSS STREET, MANCHESTER 2 · BLAckfriars 2345 · TELEX 66.300

I'VE STOPPED THE GUARDIAN— NOT ENOUGH WHITE SPACE

RHODESIA HERALD

CENSORED

PRINTED IN LONDON AND MANCHESTER

*March 18, 1968*

injury to property.' The charges arose from an incident at a construction site after a European foreman shot an African labourer in the legs. The African died: but the foreman was not charged. Do look at the newspapers, Mr. Lloyd, on the day you arrive. You will find the court cases revealing.

**The press.** Long before UDI the press was being harassed. The *Daily News* the only daily newspaper with a large African readership was banned in 1964. The *Sunday Mail* was prosecuted under the Official Secrets Act for publishing an analysis of the effects of UDI (the Official Secrets Act being dragged in on the pretext that the newspaper was withholding from the police information about its sources). A political reporter on the staff of the *Rhodesia Herald* was charged. The *Central African Examiner* was prosecuted for publishing a short poem by an American missionary about police dogs. The Rhodesia Tobacco Association was put under great pressure to withdraw its press statement about the possible effects of UDI.

These then are aspects of the society being created by the Rhodesia Front long before UDI. It was and is a society that did not give Africans a fair chance of advancement: it was and is an oppressive society, designed to perpetuate white supremacy.

Examine it for yourself. You will not unfortunately be able to go to Highfields and Harare (the African townships outside Salisbury) and talk to Africans as I did. Your movements will be watched and it would be dangerous for any African to talk freely with you. Nor will it be easy for you to have contact with white opponents of the Rhodesian Front. Mr. Lardner-Burke's warning this week of the action that will be taken against 'fifth columnists' is relevant.

As you know the 1961 Constitution was written with the expectation that it would eventually lead to majority rule (whether in ten or twenty years). But in practice, as worked by the Rhodesian Front, the 1961 Constitution was not leading towards majority rule. That is what lay behind the long negotiations with the Rhodesian Government between 1963 and 1965. Mr. Wilson, like Sir Alec before him, was trying to secure 'unimpeded progress to majority rule.' He also, like Sir Alec, wanted to be sure that any basis proposed for independence was 'acceptable to the people of Rhodesia as a whole.' While Africans were placed under such disabilities, independence under the 1961 constitution stood no chance of being acceptable to Rhodesians as a whole – and stands no chance to-day.

At no time in the past negotiations was there any sign that Mr. Smith and his Ministers intended to allow majority rule in their lifetime – or in this century. Negotiation with them has been tried repeatedly and it has failed. A new start must be made with someone else. – Yours sincerely,                                     A. HETHERINGTON

## THIRTEEN DAYS IN A BIAFRAN GAOL

Thursday, July 20, 1967
*From Walter Schwarz*

Lagos, July 19

Biafra fighting for its life as federal forces advance on two fronts, remembered to disgorge me yesterday from its vast underworld of suspects and detainees. My 13 days as an involuntary observer from below – 11 of them in an Enugu prison cell – ended as alarmingly as they had begun.

At two o'clock in the morning three men with double-barrelled shotguns appeared at my cell door. I was led out and driven away out of town. They were not communicative. To my not altogether joking suggestion that it seemed that I was being driven away to be shot, they replied that they honestly didn't know. They were police officers carrying out an instruction.

The instruction proved benign. In fact I could have not improved on it myself. We drove to Onitsha, the Niger port where I had originally arrived and been arrested and at dawn on Tuesday I was put aboard the ferry to the midwest – and freedom.

I had been led to expect a better reception. 'You must come and see for yourself,' Biafran friends passing through London had insisted.

But luck was against me. Okigbo and Achebe appeared to be out of town. On the other hand, all the officials and top policemen in power during the Ironsi regime which had deported me from Nigeria last year were very much in residence. As for Douglas Ngwube, he was busy coping with the war that, unknown to me, broke out the day I arrived.[1]

I had taken the recognised route across the Niger now that the new bridge is closed – by the sixpenny ferry. I had expected the elaborate security rigmarole – but not its Kafkaesque-Alice-in-Wonderland sequel.

Onitsha police station, where I was made to wait five hours for the superintendent to appear, was my introduction to the underworld of detainees – 'returned' Ibos from all over Nigeria who had failed to prove they were not federal spies, non-Ibo minority groups suspected of dissidence, refugees from the North whose families had not absorbed them.

There was a girl of about 12 whose father had been killed in one of the Northern massacres. Her mother, a Hausa, had stayed behind. Her elder sisters had apparently been locked in the local leprosarium for the enjoyment of the soldiers and if the story be true, were still there.

They told me 'My case' had to be cleared at Enugu. So at two in the morning the superintendent drove me there. During the 70 miles he fell asleep at the wheel twice. He was one of the least likeable people I had met (he confiscated a taxi driver's licence merely for being in his way) but it was in my interest to keep up a lively conversation.

At police headquarters in Enugu I was again a suspect among many. Men, women, boys, and girls spent days and nights propped up on benches and against walls. I found a corner somewhere. Unable to get out, I took to sending plaintive notes to the officers upstairs, explaining

1. Okigbo, the economist; Achebe, the novelist; and Ngwube, an assistant to Col. Ojukwu, the Biafran leader, had suggested the journey to Schwarz.

how precious a journalist's time was. I got a pleasant little interview in the end – but was sent downstairs again to wait.

By a ruse I reached a telephone. None of my Biafran friends were in. In desperation – by now feeling like an outraged British taxpayer – I rang the British Deputy High Commissioner in Enugu. They said they were not surprised and would have warned me not to come to Biafra at such a time. Nowhere is our humbled bulldog more toothless than in Biafra. As a federal relic in a regime Britain does not recognise, the Enugu High Commission is merely tolerated for convenience.

That illicit call was discovered. It caused much gnashing of teeth and may have contributed to my downfall. After a second night waiting, two detectives came up brightly and said: 'All right, get your things together. We are taking you to your High Commissioner.'

Dazed with lack of sleep, I didn't notice the route. We stopped before a flag – but not the British one. Had the idiots taken me to the wrong embassy? The gates of Enugu prison were already opening and we drove in beneath the unfamiliar red and yellow flag of Biafra.

'I suppose I had better sign for the body,' drawled the prison superintendent.

Throughout the night warders came to look at me through the bars, muttering what sounded like sinister Ibo remarks, accompanied by hollow sounding laughter. It sounds silly now, but that night I coldly calculated that if the trigger-happy soldiery of one side didn't shoot me, those of the other certainly would. General Gowon's printed code of conduct to his troops urging restraint in victory had specifically excluded foreign mercenaries.

Things looked much brighter in the morning. The day warders seemed prepared to suspend judgment on me personally, if not my Government. And in daylight, it seemed quite a happy prison. Considering that every one of the 42 other inmates of my block were condemned murderers awaiting their final petitions to Ojukwu, there was a surprising amount of laughter and song, mainly hymns. They talked continually of their 'trouble' and urged me with some success to take mine philosophically.

I quickly learned that no one was impressed when I whined that I had not even been accused of anything let alone tried and wanted only to be back at home with my wife and children. There were 98 people in the prison in precisely the same predicament when I went in, and perhaps twice that number by the time I came out. Unlike me they are still there.

New batches came in almost every day. One day it was border villagers suspected of harbouring enemy soldiers. Another day it was university students suspected of dissidence. Next dubious returnees, minority groups, and suspected profiteers. New arrivals were soundly beaten. I at least was not beaten. I had the unique luxury of a cell to myself – four paces by five – and even a bed. I came to appreciate this one afternoon when the prison burst at the seams and they put a couple of highway robbers in with me for a time.

## PRISON DIET

After starting on African prison diet – cassava meal and watery, peppery soup, eaten by paddling the fingers in it – I graduated to a Eurafrican mixture more to my taste than its British prison equivalent would have been. It was on my cell floor served in dainty flowered china plates. The biggest luxury, shared only with condemned murderers, was weak tea with every meal. I rejected the matching floral teacup in favour of the much bigger prison mug.

I was allowed neither books to read nor exercise. Even washing water was brought to my cell (except the day the warder on duty said: 'I will ask Gowon to fetch your washing water') the mild, kindly superintendent explained that prisons are run on a snakes and ladder system: one had to earn one's privileges. I earned mine assiduously and after five days he said I could have books from the prison library. But his superior, the deputy director of prisons, heard of it and vetoed the books. He was no doubt turned away from lodgings at some early stage by colour conscious London landladies.

What got me out I still do not know. No doubt the humbled bulldog managed a snarl, or at least a whine. I fancy, also, that my wife might have given visiting Biafrans in London quite a rough time. Perhaps one of my friends finally turned up.

# Jerusalem Builded Here?

## THE POOR NORTH

Tuesday, November 13, 1962
*By David Holden*

Unless a man seeks to live in the Lake District, or wants his son to play cricket for Yorkshire, the best advice he can take when embarking on married life is not to raise a family in the North. Not only will his children suffer poorer schooling there that they would get in most places in the South but their chances of physical survival will be less and their hope of ever living in a decent house will be startlingly reduced.

The mortality rate in the 'highland zone' north and west of a line between the Tees and the Exe is 10 to 11 per cent higher than the national average, while in the 'lowland zone' south and east of that line it is from 7 to 11 per cent below. Nine out of ten of the county boroughs with the worst mortality rates are in the North of England – seven of them in Lancashire. In some places in Wales and northern England, it seems, the risk of premature death is 30 to 40 per cent greater than in the healthiest parts of the South.

Smoke and industrial accidents in the towns and a harsher climate in the hills probably account for some of this discrepancy between North and South, but it is likely that, in the urban North at least, the biggest single factor is the lack of decent housing. 'We can't get executives to stay up here,' said a Newcastle man, 'because we can't get houses for them.' A little exaggerated, perhaps: some executives certainly stay – and like it – and the middle-class houses are there all right, but they are generally fewer and poorer than anywhere in the South. In a town like Oldham you must positively search for them in the blackened acres of Victorian slum terracing.

These terraces are typical housing of the urban North, where it is probably a conservative estimate to say that one out of every three or four homes should be classed as unfit for human occupation. Nobody really knows any more precisely. There is no standard definition of an 'unfit' house. There are no recent figures available about the number of houses that have actually been condemned throughout the country, let alone for those that ought to be condemned, but 'in the absence of any better information' the National Housing Institute's spokesman was prepared to suggest to me that between three and five million dwellings out of a total of 14.5 million in England and Wales were in need of demolition or substantial improvement.

At the absolute minimum there are over half a million houses which are unfit for habitation now – and the number is probably growing each year as slum clearance and replacement fails to keep pace with decay. The vast majority of these houses are in the urban North. Indeed, of 50 local authorities listed in 1954 as having a particularly severe slum-clearance problem, all but a handful in Wales and in the Midlands were north of the Trent. Not one was in the South; and in talking to housing officers in southern towns I did not find one who thought his authority had a genuine slum problem. In Luton, for example, the whole slum-clearance programme for the next five years will demolish 750 houses – and there is probably not one of them that would not have to last another 20 years in many a northern borough.

The contrast with a place like Oldham is painful, to the heart and head. Here, out of 42,000 houses, the local planning officer estimates that between 15,000 and 20,000 should be replaced now. In Liverpool there are something like 80,000 unfit homes and 45,000 families on the waiting list for new accommodation – i.e., about the equivalent of the entire towns of Luton and Ipswich put together. In Sheffield, in spite of a large and adventurous building programme, which must be one of the best aesthetically in the country, there are still 42,000 names on the waiting list for houses and some of these, without priority claims, will have to wait 12 years or more on present calculations before their wants are satisfied.

The North is crippled with the burden of the industrial revolution to an extent that the South hardly begins to understand. Virtually the whole social capital of the northern towns, from the antiquated town halls of marble and millstone grit to the grimy schoolhouses among the streets of back-to-backs, is of Victorian origin and desperately in need of renewal. The sheer mental depression that the sight of this decay induces is enough to deter most professional people in the South from ever settling in these towns – and, equally, to encourage the best local boys to get out and stay out as fast as they can. I did not, for example, discover more than half a dozen southern-born officials employed by the four northern local authorities which I questioned in detail about this matter, but in the four southern authorities of Ipswich, Luton, Bristol, and the Isle of Wight, northerners formed a majority of the senior officers – and only a handful of them wanted to go north again. While 80 per cent of Southerners who graduate at Bristol take jobs in the South and only 5 per cent go to the North, 50 per cent of the university's north-country graduates find work in the South and only 40 per cent go north again.

Lists issued by the Medical Practices Committee show that there are nearly twice as many areas in the North of England as in the South (including London) where general practitioners are in short supply, although the population of the two regions is roughly the same. Some evidence of a similar situation in the hospitals is provided by the proportion of doctors from overseas employed by each of the 14 regional hospital groups in England. Of six regions with more overseas doctors than the national average (43 per cent) four are in the North, one is in the Midlands, and only one – East Anglia – is in the South. These figures are supported by the following table that I worked out for myself to show the percentage of overseas doctors employed in hospitals in eight local areas.

|  | *South* |    |  | *North* |    |
|---|---|---|---|---|---|
|  | Ipswich | 28 |  | Oldham | 59 |
|  | Luton | 40 |  | Sunderland | 70 |
|  | Bristol | 34 |  | Sheffield | 51 |
|  | Isle of Wight | 50 |  | Westmorland | 40 |
|  | Average % | 38 |  |  | 55 |

With a few partial and generally rural exceptions, like Westmorland, the North emerges from every statistical comparison that can be made as significantly – sometimes formidably – poorer than the South. But it is not only the social capital that is ageing and impoverished, it is also the industry upon which the nineteenth-century North was built. Most of the traditional industries of the North, especially coalmining, textiles, and shipbuilding, are stagnant or declining, often in absolute as well as relative terms. None can be regarded as a growth industry any more, and they have not been so in peacetime since before the First World War.

There is still plenty of brass in the North – go into a Manchester night club and see it, as brassy as brass can be – but it is no longer as certain or as plentiful as it used to be. And for the jobless boy on the street corner in West Hartlepool or Wigan who has been brought up in a slum terrace and a slum school and may have seen one of his family dying in an inadequate hospital, the only sure road open, if he has any initiative left, is the one that leads south.

## HAROLD WILSON'S DREAM

Wednesday, October 2, 1963
*From John Cole, our Labour Correspondent*

Scarborough, Tuesday
The Labour Party's attempt to marry socialism and science in full view of the electorate was given a superb start to-day by Mr. Harold Wilson, who made the best platform speech of his career.

The annual conference has not previously been a happy hunting ground for Mr. Wilson, who prefers the intimacy of the Commons for his subtler shafts of scorn and wit. But the alchemy of leadership and a shrewd choice of subject to-day combined to produce a 50-minute speech which won him a long, standing ovation.

It also probably did as much as long months of work at Westminster to establish him in the public mind as the kind of man who would make a Prime Minister. But, for the certainty of that, we must await a sharper verdict than the cheers of the committed.

Mr. Wilson's theme was a redefinition of socialism in terms of the scientific revolution, and it drew him on to a fervid denunciation of privilege, poverty, and inefficiency at home, and of underprivilege and poverty abroad. This was a speech on a scale which, for the first time, gave a clear public answer to the question sceptics have asked so often: What makes Mr. Wilson tick? The answer is what it has always been. Labour's new leader showed that he is no more a 'desiccated calculating machine' than was Mr. Gaitskell, and the hard political shell covers a sincere and reforming spirit.

Mr. Frank Cousins was later to describe science as 'a vision with its working clothes on,' and these were precisely the two ways in which Mr. Wilson had chosen to treat it. The vision was there all right – of a Britain enjoying undreamed of living standards and a scale of leisure that now seemed unbelievable. But it was shot through with a Puritan streak which rejected a world consisting mainly of colour television and bigger and better washing machines for sale in European markets while the underprivileged nations starved.

'We should be learning to mass-produce simple tractors and ploughs to increase food production,' said Mr. Wilson, his voice rising to a crescendo of feeling. 'What the world needs is a little 1 or 2 horse-power steam engine that can use local fuel and is able to lift water from that ditch to these fields a few hundred yards away.' It seemed for a moment like bathos, after the space-age talk that had gone before.

But then Mr. Wilson produced a quotation from Swift:

'Who ever could make two ears of corn or two blades of grass to grow upon a spot of ground where only one grew before would deserve better of mankind and do more essential service to his country than the whole race of politicians put together.'

This touched a cord in the delegates who clapped and cheered and suddenly the little steam engine, spluttering usefully beside its far-off ditch, seemed more real than science-fiction.

This was the vision – but what of the working clothes? Mr. Wilson put these in a shop window as well and they, too, were a mixture of gaiety and sobriety. There was no room for Luddites in a Socialist Party, he declared sternly, and added that if Britain tried to opt out of the automated age, it would be left as a stagnant backwater, pitied by the world.

Ten million new jobs would be needed here by the middle seventies and if there had never been a case for socialism before, automation

*January 17, 1968.*

would have created it. Yet Mr. Wilson's was a pragmatic socialism, based on the use of Government contracts to stimulate scientific growth on the principle that State representation should follow State subsidy in industry; yet willing to see joint private and public undertakings; and willing to use competitive State enterprise where the economy needed a jag; a socialism to satisfy both Right and Left, especially in an election year.

There was a message for emigrant scientists, of whom Mr. Wilson said: 'We are not even selling the seed corn; we are giving it away.' The invitation was that they should stay in Britain or consider coming back because the 'Britain that is going to be is going to need you.' As for snobbery and privilege in industry, based on aristocratic connection or inherited wealth, that was as relevant to the society Mr. Wilson wanted as would be the continued purchase of Service commissions by lordly amateurs. 'At a time when even the MCC has abolished the distinction between amateurs and professionals, in science and industry we are content to remain a race of gentlemen in a world of players.'

## SMETHWICK – A WHIFF OF ALABAMA

Tuesday, October 26, 1965

*By Jean Stead*

This was where it all started, a year ago. This was the place where Britain first learned that it had the soul of Alabama. In Smethwick, politics are still equated totally with colour. Black and white live alongside each other in a state of permanent hostility. Anyone wanting to sample the air of the American South needs only to take a ticket to Smethwick and he will get at least a whiff of its authentic smell.

The white housewives of Marshall Street have learned to recognise the face of hate since the general election. They see it daily on the faces of their coloured neighbours. Six months ago, a group of housewives asked the Minister of Housing to lend Government money to buy houses in Marshall Street so that no more could be bought by coloured immigrants. The Minister turned them down sharply, but his rejection was mild compared with that of the immigrant neighbours. 'They've become arrogant,' complained one of the wives this week. 'I don't speak to them because if I did they look at you with a sort of contempt. Because we don't speak to them, they say we operate a colour bar.'

Now that Smethwick council, under some firm pressure, has granted mortgages to immigrant families to buy houses in Marshall Street, the women feel they have only one friend left who understands them.

He is Mr. Don Finney, last year a leading Smethwick councillor and Mr. Peter Griffiths's most ardent and vocal support during the election campaign which so successfully disposed of Mr. Gordon Walker. Mr. Finney lives, appropriately enough, in White Street, a road as genteelly run-down as Marshall Street. He has quietly faded off the council and now devotes all his considerable energies to running the English Rights Association, an extreme version of the Birmingham Immigration Control Association, which he also founded. 'We want to get out of this stinking Commonwealth – it is no good to us,' said Mr. Finney at a meeting of his committee this week. He wants to ship all the immigrants in Smethwick and the rest of the country back to where they came from. The association says that Communist money has been poured into a campaign to fill Britain with coloured immigrants. They do not want harmony between white and coloured, and they dread the emergence of a coffee-coloured Britain. Their aims are the same as those of Sir Oswald Mosley, but they are staunch Conservatives.

Because Mr. Finney is a man of considerable political experience

*May 8, 1968.*

there is no reason to doubt his claim that he will build up his organisation into a powerful force in the country. After all, he got Mr. Griffiths into Parliament. He is writing to every residents' association in the country, has been in correspondence with the London County Tenants' Federation – which has publicised many of the Rachman-landlord stories – and says he is hopeful the federation will become affiliated. 'I am doing for England what Martin Luther King is doing for the Negroes in America. What is wrong in that?' said Mr. Finney.

In a furniture shop at the bottom of White Road is Mr. Ken Bunche, one of his strong supporters who runs a youth club from which coloured children are banned. 'The coloureds will take over Smethwick soon if we let them,' said Mr. Bunche, though the visitor might be inclined to think that anyone who wants the town would be welcome to it, for it is no jewel of urban planning. The Marshall Street housewives have in fact found life more cheerful there since they joined forces to keep out the immigrants. One said it was the first time she had got to know her neighbours, and that it had seemed to bring them together.

Because their children know each other at school, one or two of the white housewives have been drawn willy-nilly into the struggling lives of their immigrant neighbours. One told how an Indian woman had cried on her shoulder for two hours because her daughter had died, and another one had asked her to speak to her husband and tell him she could not stand any more children. Two white wives had sent for an ambulance when a West Indian woman had to go to hospital to have her baby. In almost any other place, these would have been beginnings of lasting neighbourliness. In Smethwick, they were bound to be stillborn – the local racialists are making sure of that.


## NO CHANCE FOR CHOICE

Thursday, August 31, 1967
*By Peter Preston*

If the politicians who debate education cared more about education and less about politics, Bob Mackenzie would be a cause célèbre in his own right. As it is, he has to fight his good fight more or less alone; a few writers and educationists speak up for him, but not enough to sway Fife Education Committee, never mind Edinburgh or Whitehall. Mackenzie's school is under sentence of death, and there's nothing anybody can do about it.

Mackenzie, a grey, mild Highlander, came to Braehead Secondary School in Buckhaven, Fife, ten years ago – headmaster at last after twenty years' teaching, some of it at impeccable Scottish establishments like Kirkcaldy junior secondary, some of it in the wilds of Hampshire at a school run by the 'Order of Woodcraft Chivalry.' The years serving good, orthodox Scottish education taught him what was wrong with the system; the years of Woodcraft Chivalry – 'a bit like A. S. Neill, only less extreme' – showed him what was possible. Right from the start of Mackenzie's reign, Braehead became an extraordinary and important school.

Buckhaven is a dirty old mining town; Braehead is a dirty old school, which gets its intake from the poorest districts and the lower levels of 'primary achievers.' In English terms, it's a secondary modern which isn't modern and is barely secondary – since another school, with new buildings, tends to draw the brighter eleven-plus failures away. In the rigorously academic context of Scottish education, it is a temporary haven for has-beens and the ranks of never-were. Bob Mackenzie's staunchest – Socialist – belief is that all children are equal, all deserve equal care and respect. The Braehead he set about creating is the imperfect, faltering, but determined fulfilment of that belief.

A mere list of activities doesn't truly convey what's different about the school; drama classes, school newspapers, hikes in the remote Highlands, the plan to buy a hunting lodge at Inverlair, the emphasis on individual adventure – all these one might find elsewhere, though desperately infrequently among secondary moderns. What makes Braehead exceptional is the first-class staff Mackenzie has gathered around him (a staff of personalities which wouldn't disgrace the most pioneering of private schools) and the whole slant of the place – free range, committed to child after child, scornful of exams and all the cramming, the blind memorising that goes with them. If Braehead was dourly conventional, you wouldn't expect many shining exam successes from it anyway – the cherished 'O' grades would be few and far between. As it is, Mackenzie gives the kids a choice: if you want to scrabble along the 'O' grade path, we'll accept that and do all we can – if you don't, we'll concentrate on a full education, on studying particular topics in depth, on character forming, on giving you responsibility. The Braehead he's tried to build, in short, is the ideal of the 1944 Education Act: it doesn't treat eleven-plus rejects as predestined failures who might salvage a little exam glory if they're lucky; it loathes but accepts the judgment at eleven and charts a separate path for the throw-outs. Not a path you can test by exam results; not a path you can really test by anything: 'Who counts well-adjusted parents?' After a decade of striving, Mackenzie can produce few tangible examples of his success; but, of their nature, the successes he works for are intangible, unmeasurable.

Now it's all over. Fife is going comprehensive. Braehead, grimy and battered, is the natural school to close and absorb in the gleaming new comprehensive being erected around the caucus of the academic High School. Braehead spirit can't be preserved in the lowest streams of the big educational emporium. Streaming itself would kill it anyway.

Bob Mackenzie believes devoutly in the ideals of comprehensive education. But what, for Buckhaven, does the term mean? The same sparkling buildings, the same school blazers, the same outward prestige, the same theoretical ability for all to compete after the same, unchangeable academic goals. That's a kind of equality. For working-class parents, it's the outward equality which matters; creased trousers, stern discipline, doctor's son and scavenger's son 'ascending together a ladder which leads from heaven to earth.' And never mind if the vast new school, geared to getting the doctor's son into Edinburgh's medical school (150 places, 1,500 applicants), has to stream and push and reject and forget; at least the public show of equality is there, equality to sit for the same exams, compete for the same immutable academic targets.

Of course you can argue with him. His contempt for exams, you say, goes too far. His attitude to the externals of 'school discipline' runs so much counter to British tradition that naturally he stirs distaste at the Scottish Office. Will the new Buckhaven Comprehensive really submerge children so direly? Doesn't he paint pitch black a picture which is really speckled grey? But such argument misses one hard, factual, crucial point. Mackenzie hasn't been offered another headship when Braehead closes – not even a post at the comprehensive. 'I don't know what I'll do. Maybe go back to class teaching at some little school in the Highlands if they'll have me.' The fruit of a decade of experiment, for him, is simple rejection at 57, a blank wall. What huge comprehensive, with a thousand or more children under its roof and no alternative choice for a parent, can afford a headmaster who has novel ideas, who blazes his own trails?

Duane at Risinghill showed it starkly; Mackenzie underlines the lesson. Big comprehensives can experiment in technical sense, with language laboratories, closed circuit television, all the paraphernalia. But can they afford to cut across established notions of academic excellence or discipline, can they experiment with the children themselves? The answer, as Braehead demonstrates, is drearily predictable. The new system we're building, because it insists on size, complete entry from set catchment areas, inevitably involves consensus education. There is no chance to go out on a limb, to change directions. Comprehensive education means the disintegration of Bob Mackenzie's individual work; well, that's perhaps inescapable and open to debate. But comprehensive education, too, seems to leave him without a school to toil for, without horizons to explore.[1] And that is a damning indictment which must give every educationalist pause.

1. But he is now a headmaster in Aberdeen.

# Ulster's Red Hands

August, 1969 was the decisive month in Ulster. On Tuesday the 12th there was serious rioting in Londonderry. Harold Jackson and John Cunningham had been covering the Protestant Apprentice Boys' March. They described how that night 'In one of the small terraced houses in the heart of Bogside, a hasty council-of-war was held by Catholic leaders crowded into the sitting-room. One of the men, who earlier had been trying to keep the peace while the march was taking place, said despairingly: "We tried our best, we really wanted peace, but the people of Derry wouldn't have it. It has been their decision and now it means war".' It did.

## TERROR IN THE FALLS

### Saturday, August 16, 1969

Belfast, Friday

The cartographers can start redrawing the map of Belfast right now. Conway Street can be rubbed out and so can Norfolk Street. Even eight hours after the first shock it is hard to believe it can happen in Britain in 1969. These two whole streets – 63 houses in Conway Street, 27 in Norfolk Street – have been totally destroyed. Not one house in either can ever be lived in.

This morning a few of the shocked survivors picked over what they could find of their possessions and tried to talk of Thursday night. One young mother started, burst into tears, and could only repeat time and again 'How could they? How could they?'

This is not an impartial account for a simple reason – the Catholics who were petrol-bombed out of their homes will willingly tell their story; the Protestants who are alleged to have wreaked this primitive vengeance meet the reporter with obscenities and sticks. The authorities, who are also implicated, will say nothing at all.

The two streets lie in the Falls Road area, at the point where the fiercest fighting took place last night. To-day the roadway is blackened and scorched, heaps of bricks lie strewn across the carriageway, and the odd wisp of smoke still rises. A young man from Norfolk Street, who gives his name, but would rather it wasn't used, tells what happened.

The police, he says, came down at about 10 p.m., when crowds of both religions had started to gather, to tell the Catholics that the 'B'

Specials would control the Protestants. The Catholics in turn said they
would only defend themselves; if the Protestants made no move there
would be no trouble.

'About half an hour afterwards two armoured cars came down
Cupar Street, after the Protestants had got there, and drove right at the
barricades and wrecked them. Then the Protestants got through – they
and the police were fighting hand-in-hand. A Protestant man with the
peelers went along banging all the shutters in. Then the armoured car
opened up and some bloke was hit on the corner, by the butcher's.'

The families started streaming out of their houses as the trouble grew
and clustered in the area of Divis Street. Miss Bernadette Hyndman
said that the 'B' Specials constantly fired towards the Catholic families,
making them retreat from their houses. Her mother and two brothers
were among them but her father had a heart attack and had to be rushed
to the Royal Hospital. As the police drove the families back, she said,
the Protestants from Second Street and Third Street moved in behind
them.

They then started methodically burning each house in turn. Certainly
it is inconceivable that the work could have been casually achieved. I
walked along as far as was safe – the Protestants were busy building a
huge barricade at the end of the road and were extremely hostile – and
could see that each house had been totally gutted. Many had no roof,
none had any trace of furniture or fittings left inside. Even the cookers
had been wrecked and the gas meters broken open. In No. 44 Conway
Street, water from a broken mains pipe gushed down into what had
once been the kitchen.

Mr. Joseph Butler was in his house with his two sons and left to see
that his mother-in-law was safe. When he returned his house was destroyed and his sons had had to escape over the back wall. He then
saw the Protestants going into houses already burned and systematically
smashing everything that remained. At No. 30 Conway Street a semi-
invalid woman of 95 had to be rescued by her daughter-in-law of 75.

Throughout the night, the Catholics say, there were Protestant
snipers firing at them from the ruins of the Catholic pub in Ashmore
Street and from the wreckage of the mill which runs along one side of
Conway Street. One lad from a family of seven, says his parents are
on holiday in Southampton. They have no idea that their home is no
more. Meanwhile, their children are in a rest centre.

Another youth says that he has been busy breaking open the gas
meters in houses where they are still intact. 'The Prods are going to
come down again to-night to get the cash and we'll get charged for it.
We might as well make sure we keep the money.'

And on the corner of Falls Road and Divis Street, as a lorry laden with furniture drives off, cursing men roll huge metal drums into place as a barricade. They start throwing paving stones on top with a mind-shattering clatter. They shout and bang unnecessarily loudly while they work, venting their rage on mute metal and stone. 'The bastards, the bastards,' shouts one impotently at the Protestants gathering at the far end of his wrecked street.

A woman grips my arm gently. 'We had a Protestant to tea yesterday. She came to tea with us.' Behind us lie 90 gutted houses where there will be no more tea parties.

## FEAR IN SHANKILL

Monday, April 26, 1971
*By Elizabeth Dunn*

For the past three years Mrs. Anne Crawford has put her two sons to bed leaving the next day's clothes ready and all her important documents – the car papers, the insurance – tied together in a special bag. In an emergency she can dress the children in minutes, pick up the bag and abandon the house: 'I just want to feel that even if we lose the house we'll still have something.' The drill comes as automatically as switching off the lights or putting out the cat. The Crawfords live in Belfast's Protestant Shankill area barely a hundred yards from the Peace Line ('the Berlin Wall') separating Shankill from the Catholic Falls Road.

The neat little terrace house is five minutes' walk away from the Royal Victoria Hospital in Falls Road. For some time after the Troubles started, Mrs. Crawford and her mother-in-law (a frequent visitor to the clinic) continued to walk to the hospital: 'We made a mistake once,' said Mrs. Crawford. 'Billy's mother said to me: "Come on, we'll cut up here. Up Norfolk Street." We went half way up and there was a woman come out of a house; she had a labrador *that* size. She looks at us and she knows who we are – they can always tell like we can always tell Catholics. It's something you feel. I said: "I'm not going any farther." And Billy's mother said "Come on. We can get through."

'This woman came out of her front door and she crossed the road. She went into the house; then she came out and went into the next one. She stood in the doorway with the door open and the dog barking and growling. That finished me. I said: "I'm not going through there for anything." ' To-day the Protestant women catch a bus into the town centre, then another bus out again to the stop outside the hospital.

But the Troubles have produced a situation which, even during peaceful interludes, is more than just inconvenient. Like the airport hares which have learned to live with the clatter of aeroplanes bouncing on and off their runways, Belfast children have learned to live through the fighting with chilling calm, acting out their own religious war games in the same way as English children still fight the Second World War. A toyshop in the Shankill Road stocked up with plastic replicas of British army rifles and was sold out well before Christmas: 'They're going round with these rifles,' said one prominent figure in the Protestant community. 'And they're not shooting Japs and Jerries. They're shooting the people who have burned their Orange Halls and their own homes.'

'You can't expect our children to be tolerant,' said Mrs. Crawford.

Again, like the airport hares which (Belfast men contend) can forecast the runway on which an aircraft will land in time to get out of the way, the children are learning to judge the proximity of explosions and gunfire in spite of the city's misleading acoustics. In 1969 they were not used to it.

'When the Troubles started,' said Mrs. Crawford, 'Bill, my older boy, said: "Will they come to our house mum?' and I told him: "No, they'd never get up Conway Street." (Lower Conway Street was an isolated patch of Catholicism in the Shankill.) Bill was so broke down I had to arrange for my brother-in-law to take him and his brother and my husband's mother away to the caravan out of the way. I was ringing up every day to say we were all right, you know.

'You're going to bed at night, trying to lead a normal life and then: Boom. They seem too close to us. The next thing we knew they were coming up Conway Street burning all the houses.'

Living under such pressure has affected Mrs. Crawford more severely than she might like to admit. She has developed a nervous skin rash which comes up as large brown smudges on her arms and legs. So far the doctors have been unable to isolate its physical cause or find a cure.

The pattern of domestic routine has changed in the years since the Troubles started: 'Before you could go out and leave the children and you'd know they'd be all right. You could get your shopping done. Now you never know what sort of bother you might run into. We were coming back from the caravan one Sunday afternoon quite early, 3.30 or so. We thought we'd get back before anything started. But they were firing rubber bullets on the Road. In the Shankill you hardly have to do anything but the army lifts you or starts shooting the rubber bullets. In the Falls they have to start firing before anyone touches them.

'If my husband goes out,' said Mrs. Crawford, 'I ask him what time he'll be back, talking to him as he was a child. He'll say: "Maybe ten or so." Ten comes and I'm in and out of the front door, in and out, even if he's just a bit late coming home from work. I always think: "He's been lifted or something's happened on the Road".'

## HOW THE GUERRILLA WAR BEGAN

Friday, June 23, 1972
*By Simon Winchester*

Towards the end of October, 1970, when there were only about 8,000 British soldiers in Northern Ireland, the then Commander of Land Forces, General Farrar-Hockley, announced that given another few weeks of this peace 'he would begin to run down his force levels in the province.' A week later a tough, diminutive falsetto-voiced Republican from the Ardoyne called Tony Doherty – or 'Dutch' to his mates – ran down Kerrera Street, just by his home, and lobbed a small fizzing parcel out on to the Crumlin Road.

His action was to be the first offensive deed in the Provisional IRA's 'struggle for freedom' – the shaky and uncertain entry of the Provisionals into the world of the Stern Gang, EOKA, the Palestine Liberation Front and Irgun Zvei Leumi.

For what Doherty threw that night – October 31 – was a nail bomb, a one-pound stick of gelignite, looking for all the world like marzipan but wrapped around with six-inch nails and bound in black insulating tape. At 1 a.m. on that Saturday the little bundle hit the ground just beside a party of eight Royal Marines. All of us thought it was just another gas canister. The rioters in Ardoyne had thrown any number of them that night – and so no one moved with undignified haste.

But seconds later there was a huge unforgettable bang and every man in that Marine patrol fell screaming to the ground. From the blackness down the street came cheers and chants of glee. 'Up the Republic,' they yelled. 'That'll teach youse bastards!'

Such then was the putative beginning of the Provisionals' campaign. For another three months after it started there was a heaven-sent quiet in Belfast and what had happened in Ardoyne seemed in retrospect to have been a trial run. Under men whose names have since become legendary – Patrick Leo Martin, Kevin Hannaway, Frankie Card, Billie McKee, Sean McNally, and Billie Kelly – the 800 or so prospective Provos were taken back again to Donegal or Wicklow to train and organise for the coming push. For three months, until late

January, 1971, the only bad trouble in the city was the riots which the Fianna (youth movement), left at home, were more than happy to arrange.

In the months leading up to October, 1970, such military operations as the Provisionals carried out – and in those days the phrases were grander than the reality – were essentially defensive. Indeed, of course, the whole essence of the movement's formation back in November, 1969, was based on the need to defend the nationalist areas of Belfast and Londonderry against the Protestants and RUC who, as the Republicans saw things, were bent on teaching the Catholics a stiff lesson.

In the days that followed the formation of the Provisional movement and in the weeks leading up to Christmas, 1969, there were perhaps as few as 30 activists who saw the need for a militant Republican movement and who had thus split away from the Marxist 'political' Official IRA men who had in some eyes let the Catholics in Belfast down so badly in the August riots, just past. Sean MacStiofain, the man who led these 30 away, was reportedly not worried by the smallness of his band. His knowledge of Irregular army tactics convinced him then that he could mount an effective defence campaign – and later on, perhaps, even an offensive war – with as few as 100 dedicated volunteers.

And let there be no doubt about this: while MacStiofain's short-term aim was clearly to defend the Catholic areas, he and Leo Martin had clearly fixed in their minds the old idea of the forced unification of Ireland; to bring about a 32-county republic was, right from the early days, one of their principal goals.

But for the first few months, as they trained, collected money, guns, and explosives under the unseeing eyes of the British Army, the main purpose was the defence. And many of their early operations bear this out.

There was, for instance, the time on June 27, 1970, when Billy Kelly and Billy McKee – the latter against orders – bedded down in the churchyard of St. Matthew's RC Church on the Newtownards Road to protect the Catholics in the Short Strand from the Protestant mobs who were rioting on their doorsteps. Kelly and McKee fired any number of shots that night – the first occasion since the split in which IRA men actually went into battle with their guns. And a bloody battle it was, with four Protestants killed and all, probably, with Provisional bullets.

Then only six days later there was the Lower Falls curfew.

The cordoning and searching of a Catholic area of the city, acutely sensitised by the East Belfast shootings of the previous weekends, is still reckoned to be one of the worst errors which the army and

Ministry of Defence have ever perpetrated in Ireland. At the time the Ministry of Defence was staffed by the new men of the Tory Government elected only in the previous month, and one can perhaps ascribe the error to their unfamiliarity with the Northern crisis.

But in any case, the soldiers moved in to raid a house – 24 Balkan Street – on the evening of July 3. There was some stoning as they pulled out with a few guns and the army decided, as had already been planned, to impress the locals with a show of force. More soldiers were brought in, vast quantities of gas was fired, and the stones changed to nail bombs and, later, to bullets.

More and more troops poured in from every quarter of the city – there were Black Watch, Lifeguards, Devon and Dorsets, KOSBs – and yet the trouble got worse and worse until finally, at 10 pm, Lieutenant-General Sir Ian Freeland, the man who had been put out to grass in what was then a peaceful Northern Ireland, ordered the area to be curfewed.

The announcement was made in sepulchral god-like tones from a hovering helicopter and from 10 pm for a day and a half a square mile of the Catholic heartland was firmly under the thumb of the British Army. Anyone who broke the curfew – and there were nearly 100, including a *Sunday Times* reporter – were roughly arrested and dumped into three-tonners for the ride to the cells.

One hundred and six guns were found and 20,000 rounds of ammunition. Four people, including a Polish postman with the memorably non-Irish name of Zbigniew Ugilik, were killed. Charges against the soldiers of looting and smashing of the terrace houses were never to be forgotten and although such IRA men as were involved were all Officials, recruitment to the militant branch, as the Provisionals were by then being recognised, turned from a trickle to a deluge.

Six months before MacStiofain had started with 30 men; by May he had 200. By the time of the East Belfast defensive operation he had 100 more and, after the Lower Falls fiasco, he had well over 1,000 with more coming in by the hour. He could confidently organise, British Army-style, three battalions in Belfast alone, and, in each of these, as many as a dozen companies.

Dutch Doherty, who started it all, belonged to C Company of the third battalion; the first IRA man to be killed while on active service during an offensive operation was a member of F Company; he was James Saunders, a staff officer, and he was just 19. He was killed on the night on which war was openly declared – three months after Dutch threw his nail bomb, the night of February 6, 1971.

That night the first British solider was shot dead by a Provisional sniper. He was Gunner Robert Curtis, a Geordie 20 years old; he was shot and killed in the New Lodge Road in the north of the city during a brief but vicious gunfight. Three of his colleagues were also hurt that night, one of them critically. All the men came from 94 Locating Regiment, RA – a crack BAOR missile unit – and it was a sign of the importance which the Ministry of Defence was now reluctantly having to attach to Ulster that they had to withdraw critically placed units from scanning Russia to patrol Belfast.

Since that February night MacStiofain's ugly obscene, but brilliantly planned and organised military campaign has unrolled its way.

## The World of Willy Brandt

### Wednesday, May 5, 1971

The *Guardian* gave a dinner on its 150th birthday. The principal guests were the Prime Minister, Edward Heath, and the German Chancellor, Willy Brandt. They had these things in common with each other and their host – a conviction that Federal Germany must live in peace with its Soviet neighbours, a belief that Britain has a role to play in Europe, and pleasure that the way to both was opening. Terry Coleman called his interview with the Chancellor 'The Chain of Generations.'

The furnishings in the Chancellor's office in Bonn, the clock, and the pictures on the walls, are still those chosen by Adenauer. In 1969 Willy Brandt has not changed them. The only piece of his own seems to be a bust of Abraham Lincoln, whom he admires.

Why Lincoln? 'Well,' said the Chancellor, 'the way he went from a very modest . . .'

From a log cabin?

Like yourself?

'Well . . .'

'Yes.'

As a boy in the North German town of Lübeck he was very poor. He remembers that at the end of the great inflation, in 1923, when he was about nine years old, they were asked at school to collect the old worthless notes and were paid a few coppers for them as wastepaper.

'Well I remember we collected some bundles. Ten billion marks would make one pfennig in the new currency. Out of this 10 billion we would be able to buy a little piece of liquorice.'

And how many pieces of liquorice did he make? He answers this with a great big roaring laugh. 'In this operation only one.'

At first he wanted to be a ship's captain, but in the seaport of Lübeck that was as usual an ambition as wanting to be an engine-driver. As it happened, his first earning apart from the liquorice money, came from journalism, for pieces for the local paper for five or seven marks. He did one piece on fishing which was not a success. The fisherman's union protested that he did not know what he was writing about. He says he would now. He still goes fishing.

As a young boy he became an active Socialist at a time when that was a dangerous occupation in Germany. When the Nazis came to power the Social Democratic Party sent him to Norway, and except for a time when he worked as a journalist in the Spanish Civil War and a time with the Socialist underground in prewar Berlin, he spent the years of Hitler's Reich and all the war years in exile in Scandinavia first with the Norwegian Resistance and then in Sweden.

He did not adopt the name Willy Brandt until he became an active Socialist. It was his political name. After the war he kept it because it was the name under which he had made his reputation. As a boy he never knew his father and was given his mother's surname of Frahm and the Christian name of Ernest. As governing mayor of West Berlin, as leader of the Social Democrats, and even as Chancellor, he has had to endure a lot of mud-slinging from his political opponents who have attempted to make a party issue out of his origins. Letters still occasionally arrive for him insultingly addressed to Herr Herbert Frahm, Bundeskanzler.

He is a man extraordinarily diffident about his inner life. In his writings there are hints and no more than hints, that he may now be a religious man. This, in a man who in his early life was politically anti-clerical is interesting, but when you ask him he says he does not believe in mixing religion and politics as some other parties do in Germany and elsewhere. But party-religion aside, does he derive any inner strength . . .? 'Well of course, to the degree that one knows about the limits of what one can do oneself . . . It marks a barrier against . . .' I did not understand the German words he used here when he could not express the nuances of his meaning in English but I think he meant that he saw religion as something that kept a man from hubris.

He is a strong European convinced that a united Europe is unthinkable without Britain, and saying that this demands of Britain that she shall renounce the insularity of her past greatness.

But is not this a real insularity? Whatever one thinks, is not Britain an island?

It is still an island, he says, but he is often surprised by English usages. He remembers a meeting in London some years ago when

Hugh Gaitskell introduced him. 'He greeted me as "our friend from overseas." This is, of course, quite natural. But for someone who had just crossed that little channel it was rather strange.'

But was not it much easier for, say, a boy from Bonn to feel himself a European than for an English boy from, say, Salisbury? The boy from Bonn was near Belgium, Holland and France, and he saw trains at the station going to Vienna, Rome, and Naples. The boy from Salisbury saw trains going to London.

He said that a boy from Bonn was not the same a as boy from Berlin or Lübeck, who was much more remote, but still a boy from Lübeck would understand that the seas connected, and did not only divide.

Herr Brandt has often been scathing about Prussia. Did not he once say that it was a place where life offered so little that the people became enthusiastic about death? He replied that one might sometimes rightly ask if Prussia was not an army which founded a state and not the other way round as it normally is done. But on the other hand, Prussia had a purpose, and a hard-working tradition; parts of old Prussia were not rich but still Prussia became an important state. It grew to power through hunger.

Would Herr Brandt think it outrageous if I went back to 1870 and to Ludwig II, King of Bavaria, friend of Wagner, and builder of lots of castles, without whose consent the German Empire could probably not have existed in the form it did because if in that year he had declined to join other German states it also might have declined? If he had declined and there had been no German Empire, would it have been better for the history of Europe?

Herr Brandt was inclined to believe that Bismarck's contacts in Munich were so good that Ludwig had no choice.

But even so would it have been better? – 'No. No. It would have been better for the history of Europe if liberalism had shown greater strength and greater courage after Bismarck had formed the Reich, but I do not believe that the preservation of all, not only the large but also the small, German states would have brought greater stability. There was already such a drive for national unity.'

Then we came to German responsibility for the Third Reich. Herr Brandt rejects Vansittartism, a theory named after a former official in the British Foreign Office, which asserts that Germans are somehow naturally evil. The Chancellor says this is nonsense. But he does take on himself and he does seem to expect other Germans to bear, an enormous responsibility for the crimes of the Third Reich.

Early in the interview I had asked him about the time in Warsaw last December when in the old Jewish ghetto he walked up to the stone commemorating 100,000 Jews murdered there by the Nazis, stood with his head bowed, and then fell on his knees.

What was in his mind as he knelt?

He said: 'The gesture should stand for itself. It was not planned. It happened. And I'm not ashamed of it.'

Then, later in the interview, he repeated the idea of collective responsibility.

Was not this being a bit hard on himself? Was not it time this was forgotten?

He said that the responsibility was one that had to be accepted even by opponents of nazism.

Why?

'Because one was not strong enough or able enough to make it impossible for Hitler to come to power.'

But he had done all he could?

'I still belonged to a political movement which failed and one has also to take the consequences of failure.'

To this day?

'This is not a guilt, but this is a reason to take responsibility. But even apart from that, even if you take the young generation which was brought up during those years, even those who entered life after the war, no generation can jump out of the chain of generations. If one is – wants to live – within the family of nations, then one has to accept history. And to become an equal member of the group one must not run away from the past, but try to overcome it by one's actions, not just leaving the thing. But this, of course, does not exclude that one takes a self-confident position and also asks others not to be hypocritical about things and not to put on a new generation's shoulders what that generation should not bear.'

# The Guardian Then and Now

\*

When I joined the *Guardian* in Manchester twenty-one years ago, there were no telephones either in the editorial 'corridor' or in the reporters' room. This was not because the *Guardian* scorned modern machinery: at that time its technical director was developing the most advanced form of facsimile transmission in the world. It was because the people who edited the paper cared about other virtues: rational thought, good writing, and the peace to concentrate. The atmosphere of the office was that of a senior common room: collegiate, thoughtful, friendly, and at once both intensely serious and cheerfully irreverent.

The *Guardian* and the world have changed a great deal since then. The *Guardian* to-day has twice as many pages as in 1950, twice as many reporters, and a telephone for almost every ear. It tries, nevertheless, to be thoughtful and literate. It remembers that there is much wrong in the world which ought to be put right. And in keeping with advice from A. P. Wadsworth it tries to avoid taking itself too seriously.

*Alastair Hetherington* on the paper's 150th anniversary, May 5, 1971.

# Biographical Index of
# Contributors

*

The dates in italic are those between which most of their work for the *Guardian* was done. Only one italic date, the date of the extract, is given for those who were not members of the staff or regular contributors. Contributors for whom further information is given in *Guardian, Biography of a Newspaper* are distinguished by an asterisk. Those included in the *Dictionary of National Biography* are indicated by DNB. Some extracts are identified only on indirect evidence. This is indicated by a square bracket round the page number of the extract concerned.

Abu (b. 1928), *1964-1970*: 553, 691, 702, 704, 729, 738, 740
Anderson,* J. R. L. (b. 1911), *1944-1967*: 561, 563, 616, 626
Anderson,* Matthew (1894-1969), *1918-1926*: 408
Andrews, C. F. (1871-1940), *1924*: 473
Appleton, Rev. Richard (b. *c.* 1804), *1843*: 82
Arlott, John (b. 1914), *from 1969*: 723
Arnold,* W. T. (1852-1904), *1879-1898*, DNB: 171, [176]
Arthur, Sir George (1860-1946) *1919*: [433]
'Artifex' *see* Green, Peter
Atkins,* J. B. (1871-1954), *1896-1905*: 211
Ayerst, David (b. 1904), *1929-1934*: 522

Barker,* Dennis (b. 1929), *from 1963*: 719
Barth,* Karl (1886-1968) *1936*: 498
Beavan,* John (b. 1910), *1946-1955*: 622
Belloc,* Hilaire (1870-1953), *1905*: DNB: 259
Bliven,* Bruce (b. 1889), *1925-1947*: 468, 532
Blyth,* Donald (1909-1959), *1936-1948*: 588
Boardman,* H. (1886-1958), *1919-1958*: 334, 549, 619, 628, 632
Bone,* James (1872-1962), *1902-1945*: 448, 570, 599
Boyd,* D. F. (b. 1895), *1920-1936*: 402
Boyd, Francis (b. 1910), *from 1934*: 659
Brenan, Gerald (b. 1894), *1936*: 505, 507
Brighouse, Harold (1882-1958), Dramatic critic and reviewer, *1913-1949*: 521
Brotherton,* Edward (1814-1866), *1864*: DNB: 142
Brown,* Ivor (b. 1891), London dramatic critic, *1919-1935*: 441

Cameron, Miss B. R.: *1901*: 220
Cardus,* Sir Neville (b. 1889), *from 1917*: 435, 537, 636
Chadwick,* R. H. (b. 1889), *1926-1954*: 527
Clark H. F. (1894-1917), *1913-1914*: 336
Clarke,* Sir Basil (1879-1947), *1904-1910*: 272

Cole, John (b. 1927), *from 1956*: 736
Coleman, Terry (b. 1931), *from 1961*: 751
Cooke,* Alistair, K.B.E. (b. 1908), *from 1945*: 652, 686, 711
Cosgrove, L. D. (1899-1961), *1947*: 606
Crozier,* Mary (Mrs. MacManus (b. 1908), *1931-1966*: 542
Crozier,* W. P. (1879-1944), *1903-1944*: DNB: 337, 432

Darling, Sir Malcolm (1880-1969), *1947*: I.C.S. 1904-1946: 662
Dearden, Ann (b. 1907), *1944-1947*: 668
Dell,* Robert (1865-1940), *1912-1918*; *1929-1939*: 326
Dewhurst, Keith (b. 1921), *from 1965*: 695
Dickinson,* Goldsworthy Lowes (1862-1932), *1913*: DNB: 308, 309, 311
Dixon,* N. J. N. (1897-1972), *1919-1963*; chief sub-editor; Regular writer on Association Football: 545
Dodd,* Francis (1874-1949) *1905-1914*: DNB: 248, 545
Drummond,* Hon. R. C. (1850-1921) *1897-1921*: 251
Drysdale,* James (1866-1924), *1889-1924*: 305, 328
Dunn, Elizabeth (b. 1943), *from 1971*: 746
Dunsany, Lord (1878-1957) *1940*: DNB: 569

Eliot, T. S. (1888-1965) *1916*: 377
Emanuel,* F. L. (1865-1948) *1887-1914*: 262
Ensor, R. C. K. (later Sir Robert) (1877-1958), *1902-1904* and subsequently a reviewer and contributor: DNB: 465
Evans,* Sir Arthur (1851-1941), *1877-1882*, many later contributions: DNB: 185

Fay,* Gerard (1913-1968), *1939-1967*; the last 'London Editor' of the *Guardian*: 642
Fodor,* M. W. *1919-1940*: subsequently *Washington Post*: 512
Freedman,* Max (b. 1914), *1953-1963*: 681

# General Index

*